Readings in
INDUSTRIAL ORGANIZATION AND PUBLIC POLICY

THE SERIES OF REPUBLISHED ARTICLES ON ECONOMICS

Volume VIII

Selection Committee for This Volume

RICHARD B. HEFLEBOWER

GEORGE W. STOCKING

The participation of the American Economic Association in the presentation of this series consists in the appointment of a committee to determine the subjects of the volumes and of special committees to select the articles for each volume

READINGS IN

Industrial Organization and Public Policy

Selected by a Committee of

THE AMERICAN ECONOMIC ASSOCIATION

1958

Published for the Association by

RICHARD D. IRWIN, INC.

HOMEWOOD, ILLINOIS

First Printing, September, 1958

Library of Congress Catalogue Card No. 58–11852

PRINTED IN THE UNITED STATES OF AMERICA

Preface

This volume has two purposes: to provide for nonspecialists a convenient compilation of the more important articles in the field of industrial organization and public policy that have appeared since *Readings in the Social Control of Industry* was published in 1942, and to provide a book of readings useful in teaching graduate courses in this field.

The field of industrial organization and public policy has neither a well-defined content nor precise boundaries. This became apparent to the editors when they began discussing the articles to be included in the volume. It became more evident as they received suggestions from economists teaching graduate courses in this area. Lacking a coherent and unified content, this volume may not fit a particular graduate course as precisely as have other collections sponsored by the Association.

The lack of unity in the articles selected reflects the variation in content of the graduate courses. Some courses emphasize the organization and characteristics of industrial markets in general and of some markets in particular. Others are designed to show the relationship between industrial markets and price theory and to modify and extend that theory in the light of the facts of industrial organization. Still others are concerned primarily with public policy issues, with little attention given to an analysis of market organization or to price theory.

Reflecting somewhat this divergence of emphasis, the editors have classified the materials of this volume in five categories. They found it easier to establish the categories than to classify the articles. Nevertheless they believe that a grouping of articles by subject matter, imperfect though it may be, makes for a more orderly presentation of the materials than would a chance or arbitrary distribution. The categories selected are: The Structure of Industries and Markets; Case Studies in Industrial Structure and Behavior; Generalizations about Market Behavior; Industrial Organization and Economic Theory; and Competition, Monopoly, and Public Policy.

This outline indicates how far the current conception of industrial organization and public policy differs from that of *Readings in the Social Control of Industry*. The latter volume was concerned almost exclusively with policy issues. Several of the articles dealt with the governmental problem of regulating prices, a topic omitted entirely from the present volume. Differences in the subject matter of the two volumes reflect differences in the content of graduate courses twenty years ago and today. Graduate courses are now concerned largely with the characteristics of markets of few sellers and the policy problems growing out of them. Policy problems are conceived as problems of antitrust rather than problems of government regulation. But as antitrust problems they are concerned with an industry's organization and economic performance rather than with traditional legal concepts of antitrust administration.

In determining the content of this volume the editors have received helpful suggestions from a number of specialists in the field. These were first asked to submit a list of articles which in their judgment should be included. The editors meanwhile had drawn up their own list. While numerous articles received the votes of two or more consultants, numerous other articles received only a single listing. This reflects both the diversity of emphasis in the content of graduate courses mentioned earlier and differences of judgment on the relative merits of articles. With the numerous suggestions before them the editors, relying on their own judgment where there was no agreement among consultants, drew up a tentative list for inclusion. This list, together with several specific titles which the editors were considering but on which they had not definitely decided, was submitted to consultants for comments and suggestions. The consultants' comments helped to narrow further the choice of articles. In the end the editors had to rely almost entirely on their own judgment in selecting articles representing a quarter or more of the pages reproduced here.

In selecting or rejecting articles the editors established certain rules of eligibility. They decided against including sections of books, proceedings of conferences, and governmental hearings. A journal article that had been published in another book of readings was not automatically excluded. Articles representing a digest or survey of the literature, such as might appear in a professional law or business journal, were rated low by the editors. Preference was given to articles based on important research and on articles developing significant viewpoints on analytical or policy issues. Articles presented at professional meetings and subject to review and criticism by formal discussants provided a perplexing problem, for in some instances the discussant's comments were quite as significant as the original papers. Space limitations made it impossible to publish all of them. Recognizing that no one will be pleased with all our decisions, the editors have in some instances included such discussions but more frequently have not.

Some who glance at the table of contents may be surprised that no article is included which makes use of "game theory" or "organization theory" in analyzing the conduct of firms in markets where sellers are few. No economist consulted by the editors incorporates these topics in graduate courses in industrial organization and public policy. This practice may change. But with only limited space available, the editors decided to include only articles which reflect the more clearly neo-classical orientation.

While the editors are grateful for the help of the consultants, they accept responsibility for the final selections made. They also gratefully acknowledge the painstaking work of Mrs. Elizabeth R. Post, a member of the economics department at Vanderbilt, and Hans G. Mueller, graduate assistant, in compiling the bibliography.

RICHARD B. HEFLEBOWER
GEORGE W. STOCKING

Contents

I. THE STRUCTURE OF INDUSTRIES AND MARKETS

II. CASE STUDIES IN INDUSTRIAL STRUCTURE AND BEHAVIOR

III. BUSINESS PRACTICES AND MARKET BEHAVIOR

I. THE STRUCTURE OF INDUSTRIES AND MARKETS

1

The Measurement of Industrial Concentration*

By M. A. ADELMAN†

It is a resounding phrase, "the concentration of economic power," more often spoken than explained. By welding into a single expression the concepts both of a certain size structure and of a certain relation among the various parts of the structure, it suggests that instantaneous and transparent connection between cause and effect which is all too rare in the imperfect science of economics. Yet it appears also to have a certain poetic ambiguity. For one possible meaning of "economic power" is simply size—a corporation owning, say, $100 million of assets has, by definition, twice as much "economic power" as one owning $50 million. A second meaning is power over competitors or customers, power to insulate the firm against competition—in short, monopoly.

Now the equating—by definition—of size with monopoly has oratorical advantages but may have analytical disadvantages. Our purpose is to explore concentration in the structural sense only, without regard to its behavior consequences; this paper is a study in the anatomy rather than the physiology of American industry. Over the past twenty-odd years, considerable information has accumulated in this field, but knowledge is still considered unsatisfactory.[1]

A study of size structure is fairly distinct from a study of oligopoly in

---

* *The Review of Economics and Statistics*, Vol. XXXIII (1951), pp. 269–96. Reprinted by courtesy of the publisher and the author.

This article is a revision, considerably enlarged, of sections of a report submitted by the author last year to the Business Advisory Council of the Department of Commerce. (The Council is an unofficial body, with no government status or budget.) Before any intensive research began, the Council granted the author full advance permission to publish any or all of the results as he saw fit, with the understanding that the Council was not necessarily in agreement with all of it or any of it. For this complete research freedom, my hearty thanks are due to the Council, and particularly to Blackwell Smith. Acknowledgment is also due to Murray F. Foss, Seymour E. Harris, Richard B. Heflebower, A. D. H. Kaplan, John Lintner, Herbert C. Morse, and George J. Stigler, for helpful comments; and to John A. Menge, for skillful and devoted assistance. But none of those mentioned bear any responsibility for any error.

† Massachusetts Institute of Technology.

[1] *Report of the Joint Committee on the Economic Report*, February 1949, p. 91.

various markets, which is outside our province.[2] For the phenomenon of few sellers is conceptually different from the phenomenon of "big business": a small market may be occupied by a small number of small producers. This is not only a matter of arithmetic; a glance at Europe reveals business concerns generally smaller than in America, but markets smaller still, so that fewness is no less prevalent.[3] Our object, however, is not to measure the connection of fewness with size, but to measure size as such—the place of the big business units in the economy.

In parts I and II, some conceptual problems of measurement are discussed. Part III presents estimates of concentration in several important dimensions for the post–World War II period. Parts IV–VI test the hypothesis that concentration has increased during certain periods. Use is made of both primary and secondary sources, so that the article is in part a critical summary of the work of others, and in part an additional contribution, designed to undergo in time the same critical process.

I

Concentration among business firms, like concentration of income or wealth among individuals or households, is fundamentally a measure of inequality of distribution. The usual practice in measuring inequality is to arrange the units in order of increasing size, and to express inequality in terms of percentages: thus the highest x per cent of all the units hold y per cent of, say, the total income of all the units. The comparison is most often made in terms of the familiar Lorenz curve, where percentages in terms of the possessing units are the horizontal axis, and percentages of the dimension possessed are the vertical. Obviously, a diagonal line from (0,0) to (100,100) expresses perfect equality, since at every point on the line the percentages are equal. The Lorenz curve is not only a simple and graphic presentation of the data; the ratio of the area between the diagonal and the curve to the whole area serves as a coefficient of inequality.[4]

The Lorenz concept of inequality is fundamental, yet this brief description should indicate its serious limits for our special purpose. For example, if an industry consisted of 1,000 firms, each with 0.1 per cent of the assets, it would show no more perfect equality than one containing two firms, each with one half. Tools of measurement should be adapted to the purpose of the inquiry, and it is obvious that our interest in the phenomena of big business and industrial concentration is not confined to the primary focus of great inequality of distribution; it is concerned

[2] William Fellner, *Competition Among the Few* (New York, 1949), pp. 17–24.

[3] The point is vigorously made for local American markets by Jesse W. Markham, "The Effectiveness of the Antitrust Laws: Comment," *American Economic Review*, XL (1950), pp. 167–69.

[4] The most usable form of the Gini coefficient which the author has found is described in Horst Mendershausen, *Changes in Income Distribution during the Great Depression* (New York, 1946), Appendix C-2.

also with small absolute numbers. What we are really trying to describe are the very small number of very large firms, and their place in the economy.

The 200-odd concerns which are the largest employers are roughly one two-hundredth of one per cent of all business firms. In the presence of so extreme a degree of inequality, percentage distribution figures have very little meaning. The number of decimals becomes a serious matter, and the extent of rounding may lead to very great discrepancies among versions based on the same statistics.[5] These arithmetical difficulties reflect a deeper problem. It is no simple matter to decide how many units there are in the population, i.e., what constitutes a business firm.[6] (By comparison, the definition of a household is fairly simple.)[7] Large changes in classification of firms can be made, and large differences generated in the number of possessing units, with only negligible differences in the total amount possessed. Where so many of the units are peripheral and exert no market influence, percentages become even more ambiguous, and inter-temporal comparisons virtually impossible. In recessions, the total number of business firms shrinks greatly; contrariwise during revival and inflation.[8] Therefore, if the number and holdings of the largest units remained constant, the decline in the total number of units would cause the largest units to become a relatively much larger fraction of all units. Hence Lorenz-type measurements would show a spurious de-concentration during recession, and an equally spurious increased concentration during revivals.

One expedient is to assume that the total number of firms is constant throughout a time period, and equal to the earlier or later total, whichever is smaller. The effect is to disregard firms entering and leaving the periphery of the business population. The procedure has much to recommend it, and has been used in two recent studies.[9] But by assuming the base population to be constant, one assumes in effect that a constant small number of firms is a constant percentage. For example, if the business population is four million firms in the earlier year of comparison, and three million firms in the later year, and the comparison is made of the holdings of the largest (say) 0.1 per cent in the later year, this amounts to comparing the share of the largest 3,000 firms in both years.

---

[5] Edwin B. George, "How Big is Big Business," *Dun's Review,* March, 1939, presents an amusing example.

[6] See Betty C. Churchill, "Revised Estimates of the Business Population 1929–48," *Survey of Current Business,* June, 1949.

[7] *Cf.* Mendershausen, *op. cit.,* pp. 3–4; and the periodic *Surveys of Consumer Finances.*

[8] *Cf.* Churchill, *op. cit.*; and the *Survey of Current Business,* May, 1949, p. 3.

[9] John Lintner and J. Keith Butters, "Effect of Mergers on Industrial Concentration," *Review of Economics and Statistics,* XXXII (1950), pp. 46–47; G. Warren Nutter, *A Quantitative Study of the Extent of Enterprise Monopoly in the United States* (unpublished Ph.D. thesis, University of Chicago, 1949), pp. 43–46.

Thus comparisons of a partition value, with the base population held constant, come to the same thing as comparisons of a small absolute number. A Lorenz or Gini measure would give something more than this: the distribution among the three million. But it would not be free of ambiguity. Suppose the Gini coefficient to decrease because of greater equality of distribution among the lowest 99.9 per cent of all business firms; but suppose also that within the topmost group the largest 1,000 firms gained at the expense of the other 2,000. One would hesitate to describe this as de-concentration in any meaningful sense. There is no practical way of avoiding this ambiguity, as long as our real interest is in the tiny uppermost portion of the Lorenz curve, except the inelegant procedure of making separate calculations for that group. Even here, the grouping would be essentially arbitrary, for there is no way of demonstrating that the top 0.1 per cent was any better or worse a partition than the top 0.05 per cent or the top 0.15 per cent. In a word, there is no objective reason for taking the largest 1,500 rather than the largest 4,500, or vice versa. These are wide margins. So far, then, there is a fundamental unclarity about just how small is the number of very large firms that we wish to study, whether in some particular industry or in the whole economy.

Industry Concentration

Measures of concentration for the whole economy are less popular than measures for particular industries. The well-known "concentration ratio" for manufacturing industries is obtained by dividing total sales (or other dimension of size) of the largest four sellers by total sales of the whole group. The number four was chosen because the Census may not disclose data for any smaller number of firms. The ratio is used for two rather different purposes, however. One is to measure the share of the largest four sellers of a particular product in a particular market, i.e. the extent of oligopoly.[10] (And oligopoly, as we have seen, has no necessary relation to size.) The imprecision of the market concept—Marshall's "industry"—is well known and needs none of the fatuous over-elaboration from which Stigler[11] and Fellner[12] have rescued us.

The second purpose, which is ours, is to measure the relative size of the largest units, regardless of the degree of oligopoly. The two- or three-digit "industries" of the Standard Industrial Classification, which we shall use, are even more imprecise than the product groupings of the TNEC Monograph 27; but even if we made the ridiculously extreme assumption that firms within the same industry had no relations among themselves, i.e., that the two-digit industry was a purely random group-

[10] Thorp, Crowder, *et al., The Structure of Industry* (TNEC Monograph 27, Washington, 1941), Part V.

[11] George J. Stigler, *The Theory of Price* (New York, 1946), pp. 280–83.

[12] Fellner, *op. cit.*, pp. 50–54.

ing, it would still have a statistical usefulness. Industries would be a set of samples to be tested for concentration, and the mean result would be statistically much more reliable than a single estimate based on the whole population. It would indicate whether a change in concentration was characteristic of industry in general, or whether it had affected only certain segments; it would supply the measure of dispersion without which a mean is of very limited use. Actually, the usefulness of industry groupings is vastly greater than this. For even the most extreme opponents of the industry concept would need to admit that industries were rational subgroups into which to divide the population for enumeration; otherwise, they would need to repudiate nearly every statistical series now in use.

A Suggestion for Measuring Concentration

The industry concentration ratio, and all the others based on small numbers, suffers from the arbitrary element in the choice of numbers, and also wastes all the available information about the structure of the group itself. There is certainly a difference in structure between two industries, each with a concentration ratio of (say) 0.50, but with the largest firm in one industry having 15 per cent of total output, and the largest firm in the second industry having 40 per cent.

Now if we knew that firms A,B,C, etc., had respectively 20, 15, 10, etc., of the industry total, we can call x the number of firms, arranged from highest to lowest, and y the cumulative total. Then, as x equals 1, 2, 3, etc., y equals 20, 35, 45, etc. (An example is the column of cumulative percentages in Table 4.) The curve described is concave downward. It starts from the origin, when x and y are zero; it approaches 100 per cent, and equals it at some finite and sometimes very small value of x. The slope is always positive but always decreasing. A very simple form would be $y = 1 - e^{-cx}$, where e is the Naperian constant.[13] This equation meets all our conditions, except that y can only equal unity, or 100 per cent, as x becomes indefinitely large. This seems to be of very little importance, since y can be made to approach unity so closely that the difference is negligible.

The principal virtue of fitting such a curve would be not the curve itself but the possibility of summarizing it in a single number. Professor John Lintner has suggested the use of the second derivative, which would express the rate of falling off; perhaps an even more intriguing possibility is the use of the exponent c as the coefficient of concentration. In either case, all the information is used, the derivative or coefficient can be calculated regardless of the size of the topmost group, and

---

[13] If $y = 1 - e^{-cx}$, the first derivative is $\frac{dy}{dx} = ce^{-cx}$, and the second derivative is $\frac{d^2y}{dx^2} = -c^2e^{-cx}$.

comparisons can be made even when the groups being compared are of unequal size.

Preliminary trials indicate that the equation $y = 1 - e^{-cx}$ is not sufficiently flexible; at Massachusetts Institute of Technology, Professor Robert Solow and Mr. William C. Hollinger have experimented with logarithmic transformations. One can only hope that much work will be done in this area, for much is needed.

II

Thus far, we have discussed measures of distribution, and avoided the question of what is being distributed. There are four principal dimensions of size: employees, sales, income generated, and assets.

Principal Dimensions of Size

Employees. If one wishes to analyze the social and political aspects of industrial concentration, the distribution of employees is probably the most relevant single measure. Quite aside from this, number of employees is the only way of measuring changes in size (not concentration) over some time period. Monetary measurements are deficient not only because of price changes, for which allowance could be made, but because the significance of a given amount of output or assets is very different according to the general productive powers of society. If output per capita has, say, doubled over some time period, a firm which produces twice as much at the end as at the beginning can scarcely be said to have doubled in size. In society, man is still the measure of all things. The ultimate scarce factor, as we learned during World War II and will doubtless learn again, is labor.

Sales. Sales provide the most easily available measure of size, but the weakest, in that they disregard the extent of vertical integration. Thus, two firms may each make ten per cent of an industry's sales; but if one merely purchases all the components, adds "a lick and a promise," and re-sells, it is obviously much smaller than the other, which undertakes all or much of the whole productive process. (Vertical integration is not relevant to concentration in the sense of the number of sellers in a market.)

Income Generated. The best single measure of economic size is income originating in the firm or industry, a concept almost identical with that of the Census "value added by manufacture."[14] Unfortunately, it is

[14] Value added is the total spread or margin between purchases (of raw materials, fuel, containers, and power) and sales. A. D. H. Kaplan has pointed out to me that the *1947 Census of Manufactures*, for the first time, excludes excise taxes, when they can be identified, from value added. Net national income also excludes indirect taxes; net national product includes them; both exclude depreciation. See the *Survey of Current Business, National Income Supplement*, July, 1947, p. 10(D) and Table 4.

rarely available by firms, although it could easily be calculated if corporate annual reports showed either (1) total purchases from other firms or (2) total wages and other income elements as well as profits. It would be even better to have both items and be able to cross-check. Corporate practice has improved in this respect, and it is to be hoped that despite the opposition of the public relations experts,[15] such statistics will become available for a sufficient number of firms to permit some useful computations.

Assets. Assets reflect the depth of productive activity in the firm in a manner analogous to income originating. If size is considered as the present result of forces operating in the past, assets are a better measure of size than income originating. Indeed, any real discrepancy between assets and income (aside from a statistical discrepancy which was due to imperfect data) would be not a difference in estimates of the same variable, but the difference between assets—the past absorption of resources—and production—the current addition to resources. A very familiar example of this approach is the comparison of corporate profit with corporate assets or net worth—the rate of return. The ratio of total income originating to total assets would be a kind of index of productivity. Unfortunately, the data are too rough to permit such a computation; in this article, assets and income originating are assumed to be proportional.

But although assets are thus an important measurement of business size and concentration, their use presents certain difficulties. Assets are the result of accumulation over time. If prices have changed to an appreciable degree, comparisons among firms or groups of firms are impaired by variations in the time pattern of accumulation. The problem of estimating the valuation of income and assets during a period of rising prices has been exhaustively discussed.[16] Little more can be said here, except to point out the obvious: the longer the time period over which the assets have been accumulated, the greater the uncertainty about their valuation on a common basis. This uncertainty is widened still further by the variations in accounting and valuation methods among corporations; again, the longer the time period, the greater the room for error.

An Example of Asset Concentration

Since assets are used so frequently as a dimension of size and concentration, it is doubly useful to explore certain problems which their use involves by examining a recent and widely quoted report by the Federal

[15] For a typical argument see Don Knowlton, "Annual Reports as Public Relations Tools," *Journal of Accountancy*, November, 1947; this may be profitably compared with an article in the same issue by J. M. Galanis, "The Security Analyst on Financial Statements."

[16] Much the best discussion is by Alexander, Bronfenbrenner, and Fabricant, in *Five Monographs on Business Income*, published by the Study Group on Business Income of the American Institute of Accountants (New York, 1950).

Trade Commission.[17] Table 1, which is based on that report, shows the percentage of the various types of assets held by manufacturing corporations whose total assets in the first quarter of 1947 were over $100 million. The report used the category "net capital assets" as the best measure of size and concentration and applied it to 26 industries, despite the fact that this measure accounts for only one third of all assets. Some explanation is obviously necessary for this omission of two thirds of the information.

The omission of cash and cash equivalent (government securities) is not explained, except by a quotation from Gardiner C. Means[18] which

TABLE 1

SHARE OF ASSETS HELD BY CERTAIN LARGE CORPORATIONS, FIRST QUARTER OF 1947

Type of Asset	Amount Held by All Manufacturing Enterprises* (*$ Billion*)	Per Cent Held by Corporations with Assets Exceeding $100 Million
1. Cash and government securities	19.5	39.8
2. Accounts and notes receivable (net)	13.1	31.8
3. Inventories	28.6	35.6
4. Miscellaneous current assets	1.5	17.8
5. Total current assets (1+2+3+4)	62.6	35.7
6. Net capital assets	34.9	46.1
7. Total tangible assets (3+6)	63.5	41.4
8. Other assets (including deferred charges)	7.8	47.8
9. Total assets (5+6+8)	105.4	40.0

* Includes unincorporated enterprises.

Source: Federal Trade Commission, *Report on the Concentration of Productive Facilities, 1947* (Washington, 1949), p. 16.

Note: Detail does not always add to total because of rounding.

explains that the "ideal" figure *for comparison with national wealth* would be that of tangible assets, i.e., capital assets plus inventories. But since the comparison here is being made, not with national wealth but with the assets of other business concerns, the omission of cash is a serious mistake. Economic theory and business practice both emphasize the importance of liquidity to the business firm. Cash is not only an important asset; it involves no valuation problems. At any given moment, a dollar is worth the same in anybody's bank.

The omission of receivables is explained only by an extremely brief reference to their "highly variable" nature.[19] What this probably means

[17] Federal Trade Commission, *Report on the Concentration of Productive Facilities, 1947* (Washington, 1949).

[18] *Ibid.*, pp. 6–7.

[19] *Ibid.*, p. 6.

is that short-term payables and receivables can be increased together by almost the same amount, leaving the net position (in some sense) of the firm little changed. But borrowing on short term to acquire the means of accumulating receivables is no different in principle from borrowing on long term in order to acquire durable assets; and a certain normal amount of receivables is therefore a normal part of assets. If it is likely that both receivables and payables are temporarily inflated and will soon decline, one would welcome an attempt at adjustment, but there is no reason simply to disregard them. In point of fact, there has been no such decline in receivables since the first quarter of 1947, and this was obvious in 1949, when the report appeared.

The exclusion of inventories—part of the "ideal" figure—from the measure of concentration is the strangest part of the whole procedure. It is explained as follows:

> According to reports of the Senate Small Business Committee, numerous small firms experienced great difficulty during that year [1947] in obtaining adequate inventories of raw materials. If inventories were thus relatively shorter in small than in large firms—as there is every reason to believe was the case—the inclusion of inventories in the measure would have the effect of overstating the degree of economic concentration.[20]

Setting aside the question of the reliability of the evidence, our concern is with the logic of the procedure. A glance at Table 1 will show that the over-$100 million group held 35.6 per cent of inventories. According to the report, this was an abnormally *high* percentage. In a more representative year, that is, it would be lower. Suppose we were to disregard this qualification for the moment, and add inventories to net capital assets to obtain net tangible assets—the "ideal" figure—as a measure of concentration. Then the percentage held by the largest corporations would be not 46.1 per cent but 41.4. But in a normal year, according to the report, the largest corporations would have held a *smaller* proportion of inventories than 35.6 per cent and therefore a *smaller* proportion of total tangible assets than 41.1 per cent. The FTC explanation can therefore be paraphrased as follows: to have used the estimate of 41.1 per cent would have resulted in an overestimate of the degree of concentration; *therefore,* we are using an estimate of 46.1!

The report states that "capital assets consist of land, buildings, and equipment, which are physical, tangible, items."[21] "Capital assets" are no such thing. They are the record of money outlays on land, buildings, and equipment, over a fairly long period of time. The actual current value of the physical assets varies according to the time pattern over which they have been accumulated; and matters are made still more uncertain by adjustment for depreciation according to simple formulas whose chief virtue is convenience, and which vary among firms. In a

[20] *Ibid.*, p. 7.

[21] *Ibid.*, p. 6.

TABLE 2A

LARGE FIRMS' SHARE OF TOTAL EMPLOYMENT, BY INDUSTRY, 1948

Industry	All Firms		Firms Employing 10,000 or More		
	Number* (*Thousands*)	Employment* (*Thousands*)	Number†	Employment† (*Thousands*)	Per Cent of Total Employment‡
All Industries	3,966.8	36,450	260	8,282	22.7
Mining	34.4	898	3	50	5.5
Construction	312.4	2,053	2	26	1.3
Manufacturing	329.3	15,839	163	4,873	30.8
Food and kindred products	36.1	1,464	17	463	31.6
Textile and textile products	43.5	2,566	11	183	7.1
Leather and leather products	6.7	423	4	80	18.8
Lumber and lumber products	84.4	1,146	0	...	0
Paper and allied products	4.2	462	3	57	12.4
Printing and publishing	45.5	733	1	11	1.5
Chemicals and allied products§	10.4	814	15	347	42.6
Petroleum and coal	1.3	354	15	418¶	...
Rubber products	1.5	298	5	267	89.7
Stone, clay, and glass products	12.5	520	7	113	21.7
Metals and metal products	58.6	6,519	80	2,867	44.0
Primary metals	6.3	1,296	21	876	67.6
Fabricated metals	18.0	1,004	5	116	11.6
Machinery, except electrical	19.1	1,536	14	342	22.3
Electrical machinery	4.9	1,012	6	413	40.8
Transportation equipment	6.7	1,397	30	1,069	76.5
Professional instruments, etc.	3.6	223	4	51	22.8
Other Manufacturing ‖	24.5	592	5	69	11.6
Public utilities	186.5	4,123	54	2,268	55.0
Communication and other public utilities except transportation	n.a.	n.a.	11	882	n.a.
Transportation	n.a.	n.a.	43	1,386	n.a.
Wholesale trade	201.4	1,985	2	29	1.4
Retail trade	1,704.2	7,016	26	840	12.0
General merchandise	78.8	1,423	21	649	45.6
Food and liquors	492.8	1,275	5	191	15.0
Finance, insurance, and real estate	345.8	1,749	6	141	8.1
Service industries	852.8	2,788	4	55	2.0

* March 31, 1948.
† December 31, 1948.
‡ Percentages were calculated before rounding employment figures.
n.a. = Not available.
§ Includes Eastman Kodak and Celanese Corp.
¶ Includes employment other than refining and foreign employment.
‖ Includes tobacco and the Armstrong Cork Co. (classified under "Textiles" by the Department of Commerce), in addition to other miscellaneous manufactures.

Sources: *All firms* from Murray F. Foss and Betty C. Churchill, "The Size Distribution of the Postwar Business Population," *Survey of Current Business*, May, 1950.

For firms with 10,000 or more employees, the following master lists were consulted: (a) Department of Commerce, *1000 Largest Manufacturing Corporations by Industry Groups* (1948); (b) Securities and Exchange Commission, *Survey of American Listed Corporations* (1948); (c) Federal Trade Commission, *Report . . . on the Concentration of Productive Facilities*, 1947; (d) *Poor's Annual Register of Executives* (1948); and (e) An unpublished table available by courtesy of A. D. H. Kaplan, presenting the 100 largest industrial corporations in 1948, by asset size.

The following procedures were used:

1. *Mining, construction, and manufacturing.* All firms which appeared in either (a), (c), or (e) were checked in *Moody's* for their 1948 employment figures. Firms for which no 1948 figures were given were checked in *Poor's*. Source (b) was utilized by comparing sales, assets, and similar figures listed in this source with the sales, assets, etc., of those firms already examined which had barely attained the 10,000 employee level. The firms thus selected on this basis from (b) were then checked as before in *Moody's* and *Poor's*. Source (d) was used only as a check to discover

word: the percentage of net capital assets is the best measure of concentration if and only if one wishes to maximize the probable error of the estimate.

III

Tables 2–4 present estimates of postwar concentration in three important dimensions: employees, assets, and research personnel. The small topmost group includes in each case all firms which surpassed a given size in the particular dimension. The absolute numbers of the groups are not too greatly different—260 in Table 2A and 273 in Table 3A. In view of the interest, which has become traditional, in the top 200 firms, calculations for them are also presented, but in brief.

Employment and Asset Measures

Tables 2A and 2B need little comment. The percentage figures for particular industries are often of ambiguous meaning because the large firms have employees outside the industry of their principal activity, as well as employees abroad. The most important cases are petroleum, chemicals, rubber products, and metals. Moreover, the percentages of Tables 2A and 2B are somewhat inflated because December 1948 employment was higher than March 1948. The largest 200 employers account for one fifth (19.8 per cent) of all employees in private nonagricultural establishments, and for one eighth (12.4 per cent) of the total civilian labor force (Table 2B).

Tables 3A and 3B are concerned only with corporations. It will be observed that of the nearly four million business firms in existence by the end of 1947, less than one tenth took the corporate form. This underlines in dramatic fashion the warning given above about the peripheral nature of most business firms, and the unreliability of percentages of the

---

whether or not any obvious cases had been overlooked which might have 10,000 or more employees as given by *Moody's* or *Poor's*.

2. *Trade, service* (includes motion picture producers and distributors), *finance, and public utilities except transportation* listings were obtained from (b), (d), and (e). The process of listing firms and deriving their employment data was, with one exception, exactly analogous to the process employed in obtaining the listings in mining, construction, and manufacturing. The exception is that in several categories, such as "public utilities except railroads," and "finance," *Poor's* listings were small enough to permit a complete cross-check on employment data between *Moody's* and *Poor's*.

3. "Public utilities-transportation" was taken directly from an unpublished table by Murray F. Foss, of the Department of Commerce, listing total employment figures for all railroads and similar carriers within different size classes, on the basis of number of employees per company. To this was added employment in airlines and local transit systems and similar carriers, obtained by procedures similar to those outlined above.

4. One problem still remained. There were some firms which met the criteria of assets, sales, etc., but for which no 1948 employment figures were available in *Moody's* or *Poor's*. In the list of 260 firms employing 10,000 or more employees, such data were not available for 26 firms, of whom 14 also belong among the 200 largest. There were, however, previous employment figures, from 1940 to 1947, available for 13 of the 26 firms (and 8 of the 14). Estimates were then made from these figures, on the basis of the trend of employment for the industry, through 1948. This still left 13 firms in the largest 260 (and 6 firms in the largest 200) for which additional estimates were needed. This was done by ranking, on the basis of assets, sales, etc., these "unknown" firms relative to the firms in the same industry class for which employment figures were available. From their relative positions in these rankings, employment figures were then interpolated. Errors in estimates of this sort are inevitable, but only 14 of the first 200 were involved in any estimating procedure, and for only 6 of these were there no employment data at all. Assuming, therefore, as much as a 50 per cent under- or over-estimation for the whole group we would not find the over-all employment figures altered by more than ½ to ¾ of 1 per cent. Similar results hold for the largest 260 employers. Most of the estimates were for the class "manufacturing-textile products," and here the error may run as high as 7 to 10 per cent.

total number of firms. Table 3B embodies certain adjustments of Table 3A which were possible only for very broad industrial classes. The purpose of the adjustments is to correct for some known inaccuracies, which tend to understate the degree of concentration, and which are explained in detail below.

But although the figures for individual industries are not satisfactory, they suffice to show that concentration is not only great but is itself highly "concentrated." Within the over-$100 million group, public utility corporations account for nearly half the total assets, and a single firm—the Bell Telephone System—accounts for one tenth. Among manufacturing industries, four industries—steel, automobiles, chemicals, and oil—account for nearly two thirds of the assets of the over-$100 million group. No more serious error could be made than to suppose the giants of American industry spread out evenly over its length and breadth.

TABLE 2B

SHARE OF EMPLOYMENT OF LARGEST EMPLOYERS, DECEMBER 1948

	Number Employed (*Millions*)	Per Cent Employed by Largest 260 Employers	Per Cent Employed by Largest 200 Employers
1. Total labor force	62.8	13.2	12.1
2. Civilian labor force*	61.4	13.5	12.4
3. Civilians gainfully employed†	59.5	13.9	12.8
4. Private employment‡	53.8	15.4	13.4
5. Nonagricultural employment§	52.1	15.9	14.6
6. Employees in nonagricultural establishments¶	45.3	18.3	16.8
7. Employees, nongovernment‡ ‖	38.5	21.5	19.8

* Excludes military.
† Excludes unemployed.
‡ Excludes government employment.
§ Includes nonagricultural self-employed and government employment.
¶ Excludes nonagricultural self-employed but includes government employment.
‖ Excludes all self-employed, but includes non-profit organizations and employees rendering professional services, in addition to employees of business concerns.
Source: Table 2A and *Survey of Current Business.*

An estimate of total wealth held by the largest 200 corporations is desirable in order to compare over-all concentration in this dimension with concentration in employment (the "top 200" are not the same in each case). Our best estimate is that the largest 273 corporations hold 46.3 per cent of total corporate assets. In order to eliminate the lowest 73, an estimate of their holdings must be made. Let us for the moment make the arbitrary assumption that each of these 73 has just $100 million in assets. In that case, the group would account for $7.3 billion, which is just 3 per cent of total corporate assets, and the holding of the top 200 would be 43.3 per cent (46.3 less 3.0). If we suppose that the average holding is not $100 million but $200 million, the lowest 73 would account for $14.6 billion, or 6 per cent of total corporate assets, and the holdings of the top 200 would be 40.3 per cent.

Table 3A reveals that, of the over-$100 million group, there are eleven industrial groups, comprising 43 corporations, which average less than $200 million. It seems likely that in order to eliminate not 43 but 73

TABLE 3A

ASSETS OF LARGEST CORPORATIONS BY INDUSTRY, 1947*

	NUMBER OF RETURNS WITH BALANCE SHEETS		TOTAL ASSETS (*Millions*)		
INDUSTRY GROUPS	Total (1)	Total with Assets Exceeding $100 Million (2)	Entire Group (3)	Corporations with Assets Exceeding $100 Million (4)	Col. 4 as Per Cent of Col. 3 (5)
All industrial groups (except finance)	364,996	287†	236,782	101,556	42.9
Total mining and quarrying	7,280	6	7,186	1,082	15.1
Total manufacturing	105,390	133	111,356	45,082	40.5
Food and kindred products	10,042	14	9,742	2,767	28.4
Beverages	3,048	2	2,855	340	11.9
Tobacco	222	4	2,164	1,591	73.5
Cotton manufactures	932	0	2,330	0	0.0
Textiles, other	4,861	4	4,267	593	13.8
Apparel	13,099	0	2,653	0	0.0
Leather	2,935	1	1,341	109	8.1
Rubber	602	4	1,931	1,233	63.9
Lumber and timber	3,329	1	2,121	191	9.0
Furniture	5,640	0	1,767	0	0.0
Paper and allied products	2,444	3	3,992	545	13.7
Printing and publishing	11,000	2	4,095	308	7.5
Chemicals	7,013	17	10,120	4,347	43.0
Petroleum and coal	519	28	15,517	14,360	92.6
Stone, clay and glass	3,870	2	2,814	288	10.2
Iron and steel	8,487	16	12,616	5,862	46.5
Nonferrous metals	4,083	5	3,535	1,667	47.2
Electric machinery	2,830	5	5,559	2,599	52.8
Machinery except electric and transportation	8,336	9	9,378	1,944	20.7
Autos and equipment	1,090	7	6,528	4,535	69.5
Transportation equipment	1,013	8	2,857	1,183	41.4
Other manufacturing	6,374	1	2,062	284	13.3
Manufacturing not allocable	3,621	0	1,112	0	0.0
Total public utilities	20,376	125	68,037	50,179	73.8
Public utilities—transportation	15,072	57	34,905	25,915	74.2
Public utilities—communication	2,778	15†	11,084	9,597	86.6
Other public utilities	2,526	53	22,048	14,667	66.5
Total trade	163,300	17	38,122	4,125	10.8
Total service	39,896	5	6,517	800	12.3
Construction	18,398	0	3,419	0	0.0
Total agriculture, etc.	6,153	1	1,757	289	16.4
Nature of business not allocable	4,203	0	390	0	0

* Nonfinancial corporations.

† "Public utilities—communication" contains largely members of the Bell Telephone System which should be counted as one firm. The total at the head of column (2) then becomes 273.

Sources: Treasury Department, Press Service No. S-2449, *Statistics of Income* for 1947, Part 2, and unpublished data from the Bureau of Internal Revenue.

TABLE 3B

Share of Assets Held by Largest Corporations, End of 1947*

Industrial Group (1)	Corporations with Assets Exceeding $100 Million: Number (2)	Total Assets (*$ Billion*) (3)	Total Assets, All Corporations (*$ Billion*) (4)	Col. 3 as Per Cent of col. 4 (5)
	A. Unadjusted			
Total manufacturing	133	45.1	111.4	40.5
Public utilities: communications	15	9.6	11.1	86.6
All other	139	46.9	114.3	41.0
Total	287	101.6	236.8	42.9
	B. Adjusted			
Total manufacturing	132	50.2	114.7	43.8
Public utilities: communications	3	10.2	11.1	92.0
All other	138	52.2	117.5	44.4
Total	273	112.6	243.3	46.3

* Nonfinancial corporations.

Sources: Unadjusted data from Table 3A.

Adjusted data: Manufacturing, see Table 11 below.

"All other," adjusted by the factors developed for manufacturing.

Communications: Federal Communication Commission, *Statistics of the Communications Industry, 1947* (Washington, 1948). The three corporations are the Western Union Telegraph Co., General Telephone Co., and the American Telephone and Telegraph Co. (Bell System). The last-named includes the Western Electric Co., which manufactures telephone equipment, and the total assets of all operating Bell System subsidiaries, although some of them are only partly owned by A.T.&T. The most important is the Southern New England Telephone Co., only 26.7 per cent of whose stock is so held. It was impossible to make any estimates for International Telephone & Telegraph Co., and it was excluded from the table; its U.S. assets seem below $100 million.

firms we would need to go well over the $200 million mark, and raise the average for the whole group to about $200 million.[22] This would mean that the share of the top 200 was 40.3 per cent.

So much for the corporate universe. How large a part is it of the whole economy? The best comparison would be between the tangible wealth of the corporate universe and the total national wealth. However, this is impossible. Estimates of national wealth are still in a relatively undeveloped stage; before the work of Kuznets and the National Bureau of Economic Research,[23] they were hardly respectable. Moreover, although paper claims could be stricken from both sides of the comparison, the item of land presents serious analytic difficulties.

A simpler method is to assume that assets are proportional to income originating. In 1947, 58.8 per cent of total *private income* originated in corporate enterprise,[24] and we therefore assume that this represented a like share of total income-yielding wealth. In choosing this figure, we

[22] Since there would be 30 corporations with assets over $200 million to be eliminated, their higher average assets would be expected to balance their slight numerical disadvantage.

[23] Simon Kuznets, *National Products Since 1869* (New York, 1946), pp. 185 ff.; National Bureau of Economic Research, *Studies in Income and Wealth*, Vol. XIII (New York, 1950).

[24] *Survey of Current Business*, July, 1950, p. 14.

place consumer and government assets outside the universe in which corporate assets belong. Considerations of space forbid a defense of these two exclusions.

If, therefore, 58.8 per cent of national income-producing wealth is held by corporations, and the largest 200 of these possess 40.3 per cent of the corporate holdings, then the "top 200" hold 23.7 per cent of the total. In language less precise but more accurate, we can say that the "top 200" hold between a fifth and a fourth of income-producing national wealth.

According to Table 2B, the largest 200 employers account for 15.4 per cent of the total nongovernment labor force. Thus concentration in the dimension of asset ownership is about 60 per cent higher than in the dimension of employment; that is, employment among the top 200 is about 60 per cent more capital-intensive than employment in the economy as a whole.

Research Personnel

At the end of 1945, according to the National Research Council, there were 2,443 industrial research laboratories employing 133,515 persons, of whom 54,321 were professional scientists or engineers. The Council estimated, however, that total personnel were underestimated by about 5,000 because of the failure of some large corporations to answer their questionnaire. Thus, under the assumption that unreported personnel were divided between professional and unprofessional in about the same proportions as reported, it is possible to say, in round numbers, that there were 138,000 employees, of whom 56,000 were professionals.

Table 4 shows the professional personnel of the largest 75 corporation laboratories, which account for nearly half the total. Close to one third of all professional personnel are employed by a score of the largest firms. It is clear that most of the organized industrial research is carried on by a very tiny fraction of all business firms, or even of all corporations. Moreover, the picture would not be greatly changed if the noncorporate research laboratories, governmental and nongovernmental, were included, for they employed only 4,300 scientists and engineers, fewer than the two largest corporate laboratories employed.

A word of caution is needed in interpreting Table 4. The year 1945 was obviously abnormal; specifically, it is not believed that normal research employment in the aviation companies, marked with an asterisk in the table, is as high as indicated by the 1945 data. Unhappily, 1951 and later years may prove to be equally abnormal.

IV

The outbreak of the Korean War, and the transition of this country to a more or less permanent state of semi-mobilization, have given a renewed and very practical interest to the question: What happened to the

TABLE 4

NUMBER OF PROFESSIONAL SCIENTISTS AND ENGINEERS EMPLOYED IN LARGEST INDUSTRIAL RESEARCH LABORATORIES, 1945

Corporation	Corporations	Professional Personnel	Cumulative Number	Cumulative Per Cent
Bell Telephone System	1	3,976	3,976	7.06
E. I. duPont de Nemours and Co.	2	1,669	5,645	10.03
Radio Corp. of America	3	1,146	6,791	12.06
General Electric Co.	4	1,071	7,862	13.96
General Motors Corp.	5	1,057	8,919	15.84
Bendix Aviation Corp.*	6	1,020	9,939	17.65
American Cyanamid Co.	7	800	10,739	19.07
United Aircraft Corp.*	8	739	11,478	20.39
Shell Union Oil Corp.	9	699	12,177	21.63
Dow Chemical Co.	10	665	12,842	22.81
Standard Oil Co. (N.J.)	11	641	13,483	23.95
Monsanto Chemical Co.	12	623	14,106	25.06
B. F. Goodrich Co.	13	562	14,668	26.05
Socony-Vacuum Oil Co., Inc.	14	483	15,151	26.91
Union Carbide and Carbon Co.	15	438	15,589	27.69
Chrysler Corp.	16	408	15,997	28.41
Hercules Powder Co.	17	383	16,380	29.09
International Harvester Co.	18	379	16,759	29.77
United States Steel Corp.	19	378	17,137	30.44
The Texas Co.	20	358	17,495	31.07
The Sperry Corp.*	21	357	17,852	31.71
Lockheed Aircraft Corp.*	22	331	18,183	32.30
Standard Oil Co. (Ind.)	23	289	18,472	32.81
Philco Corp.	24	280	18,752	33.31
Eastman Kodak Co.	25	256	19,008	33.76
Pittsburgh Plate Glass Co.	26	255	19,263	34.21
Phillips Petroleum Co.	27	238	19,501	34.64
Standard Oil Co. (Calif.)	28	232	19,733	35.05
Interchemical Corp.	29	227	19,960	35.45
The Procter and Gamble Co.	30	226	20,186	35.85
Sylvania Electric Products, Inc.	31	218	20,404	36.24
Gulf Oil Corp.	32	213	20,617	36.62
General Aniline and Film Corp.	33	205	20,822	36.98
Westinghouse Electric and Mfg. Co.	34	204	21,026	37.35
Remington Rand, Inc.	35	203	21,229	37.71
Goodyear Tire and Rubber Co.	36	192	21,421	38.05
Consolidated Vultee Aircraft Corp.*	37	191	21,612	38.39
The Sherwin-Williams Co.	38	188	21,800	38.72
Armour and Co.	39	178	21,978	39.04
International Tel. and Tel. Corp. (Federal Telecommunication Labs. Inc.)	40	177	22,155	39.35
Merck and Co., Inc.	41	171	22,326	39.66
Curtiss-Wright Corp.	42	165	22,491	39.95
Johnson and Johnson	43	159	22,650	40.23
Swift and Co.	44	155	22,805	40.51
National Lead Co.	45	154	22,959	40.78
The Atlantic Refining Co.	46	152	23,111	41.05
Ford Motor Co.	47	148	23,259	41.31
Ethyl Corp.	48	147	23,406	41.57
Thomas A. Edison, Inc.	49	143	23,549	41.83

(*Continued*)

TABLE 4 (*Continued*)

Corporation	Corpora-tions	Professional Personnel	Cumulative Number	Cumulative Per Cent
Lilly & Co.	50	143	23,692	42.08
General Foods Corp.	51	138	23,830	42.33
Aluminum Co. of America	52	137	23,967	42.57
Continental Can Co., Inc.	53	137	24,104	42.81
Celanese Corp. of America	54	127	24,231	43.04
Reeves-Ely Laboratories, Inc. (Claude Neon, Inc.)	55	127	24,358	43.26
Owens-Corning Fiberglass Corp.	56	125	24,483	43.49
E. R. Squibb & Sons	57	125	24,608	43.71
Vick Chemical Co.	58	124	24,732	43.93
Armstrong Cork Co.	59	121	24,853	44.14
Electric Auto-Lite Co.	60	121	24,974	44.36
Sun Oil Co.	61	120	25,094	44.57
Sinclair Oil Corp.	62	115	25,209	44.78
Stromberg-Carlson Co.	63	115	25,324	44.98
Upjohn Co.	64	112	25,436	45.18
Reynolds Metal Co.	65	111	25,547	45.38
Union Oil Co. of Calif.	66	110	25,657	45.57
Continental Oil Co.	67	110	25,767	45.77
American Can Co.	68	110	25,877	45.96
Corning Glass Works	69	108	25,985	46.15
Wyeth, Inc. (American Home Products Corp.)	70	104	26,089	46.34
Western Union Telegraph Co.	71	102	26,191	46.52
Parke, Davis & Co.	72	100	26,291	46.70
Johns-Manville Corp.	73	100	26,391	46.88
Sterling Drugs, Inc.	74	99	26,490	47.05
United Shoe Machinery Corp.	75	95	26,585	47.22
Total—all corporate laboratories	2,443	. . .	56,300	100.00

* Aircraft production. These companies are believed to have carried an abnormally large number of research employees in the year covered by the table.

Source: Compiled from National Research Council, *Industrial Research Laboratories in the United States* (1946). The 1951 directory appeared too late for tabulation and inclusion here.

pattern of concentration during World War II? On December 7, 1950, the Attorney General of the United States submitted a report to the President and Congress on the subject of "dangers to a competitive enterprise economy which are inherent in mobilization for defense."[25] Two themes are apparent: one, the need to prevent collusive understandings under cover of industry defense planning; the other, the need for special favors to smaller business concerns in order to avert the possibility of increased concentration. The Attorney General makes the not unreasonable assumption that what happened during the last period of mobilization will probably happen during this one. On the basis of information supplied by the Federal Trade Commission, the report starts with the statement that "during the last war the long standing tendency toward economic concentration was accelerated."[26] Since increased concentration

[25] Letter of Transmittal attached to the *Report of the Attorney General of the United States Prepared Pursuant to Section 708(e) of the Defense Act of 1950.*

[26] *Ibid.*, p. 4.

is regarded as undesirable, it is considered necessary to counteract it even if this means that the Government will have to pay higher prices for defense supplies[27] or accept non-combat items of less reliable quality.[28]

The wisdom of these or any other policies is beyond the scope of this article. Our concern is simply with the factual hypothesis: economic concentration in manufacturing increased during the period of the last war. Is this consistent with the available evidence, which may be itemized as follows:

1. For the years 1941 and 1942, J. L. McConnell has adjusted corporate rates of return for officers' compensation included in profits. Profits

TABLE 5

EFFECT OF TAXES ON CORPORATE PROFITS, BY SIZE GROUPS, 1942

TOTAL ASSETS CLASS (*$ Thousand*)	ADJUSTED RATE OF RETURN (in per cent of net worth)	
	Before Taxes	After Taxes
Under 50	19.5	13.5
50–99	20.0	12.9
100–249	22.4	12.7
250–499	23.8	10.9
500–999	26.0	10.6
1,000–4,999	26.7	10.4
5,000–9,999	26.3	10.3
10,000–49,999	24.7	9.8
50,000–99,999	20.9	8.8
100,000 and over	13.8	6.9

Source: Joseph L. McConnell, "1942 Corporate Profits by Size of Firm, " *Survey of Current Business*, January, 1946.

before taxes for those years show little relation to size, except for a slight droop at both extremes, and a slight tendency to a maximum in the $5 million to $10 million group. However, when data are given separately by industry groups, even this regularity disappears.[29] Profits *after* taxes, however, show a definite inverse relation with size. As Table 5 shows,

[27] *Ibid.*, p. 39.

[28] *Ibid.*, p. 36. The more euphemistic and also ambiguous original is that "efforts are being made to encourage the use of commercial or off-the-shelf items instead of technical military specifications wherever the rigors of actual military specifications do not otherwise require."

[29] Joseph L. McConnell, "Corporate Earnings by Size of Firm," *Survey of Current Business*, May, 1945; "1942 Corporate Profits by Size of Firm," *ibid.*, January 1946. McConnell's methods are not beyond dispute, and my personal belief is that they tend to overstate the profits of the smaller size groups, although not sufficiently to change the relation evident in Table 5. But Sidney S. Alexander, who used an entirely independent method, reaches the same conclusion for profits before taxes in 1937. See "The Effect of Size of Manufacturing Corporation on the Distribution of the Rate of Return," *Review of Economics and Statistics*, XXXI (1949), pp. 233–35.

profits after taxes as a percentage of net worth were almost twice as high for the lowest as for the highest size group. Thus, for the war year 1942, one would expect smaller corporations, *ceteris paribus*, to be growing faster from retained earnings than larger, and concentration to be on the decrease.

2. The Office of Price Administration compiled profits and assets of 2,500 corporations, arranged by size classes, for the years 1939–44, which are summarized in Table 6. They show a rough inverse relation between

TABLE 6

GROWTH IN ASSETS AND NET WORTH OF 2,500 CORPORATIONS, 1939–44

	NUMBER OF COMPANIES				INDEX NUMBERS (1936–1939 = 100)							
					NET WORTH				TOTAL ASSETS			
1939 ASSET SIZE (*$ Million*)	Durable Mfrs.	Non-durable Mfrs.	Non-mfg.*	All Companies	Durable Mfrs.	Non-durable Mfrs.	Non-mfg.*	All Companies	Durable Mfrs.	Non-durable Mfrs.	Non-mfg.*	All Companies
Under 1.0	272	425	30	727	163	132	104	143	261	149	133	182
1.0–2.4	215	249	67	531	162	128	123	141	276	143	150	197
2.5–4.9	145	173	71	389	150	124	117	132	240	138	132	175
5.0–9.9	127	119	69	315	154	126	122	136	233	140	139	177
10.0–19.9	77	99	51	227	143	128	124	132	226	140	135	169
20.0–49.9	64	69	30	163	136	126	122	129	209	135	123	163
50.0–99.9	18	33	16	67	129	127	113	124	209	139	133	157
100.0–199.9	13	22	9	44	114	114	109	113	124	126	109	122
200.0–499.9	12	10	4	26	126	116	130	123	161	139	129	147
500 and over	3	7	1	11	119	120	113	119	139	122	107	128
Total	946	1,206	348	2,500	129	121	119	124	177	132	125	147

* Construction, mining, trade, services, and transportation (excluding railroads).
Source: Office of Temporary Controls (OPA), *War Profits Study No. 16* (Washington, 1947), Tables 23, 27.

prewar size and subsequent growth of assets and net worth. In every case, the largest size classes grew more slowly than did the whole group.

3. A larger OPA sample, confined to manufacturing, was subsequently published by the FTC (Table 7). The same relation is apparent for most but not all industry groups. The "$10 million and over" group grew more than the whole industry in 4 cases, grew less in 15 cases, and data were unavailable in 3 cases.

4. The Federal Reserve Board, in collaboration with the Robert Morris Associates, made a survey of business finance for the years 1940–44. They also found, as Table 8 shows, an inverse relationship between size and both profitability and rate of increase in assets.[30] It must be borne in

[30] See the following articles in the *Federal Reserve Bulletin:* 1945, F. C. Dirks, "Wartime Earnings of Small Business" and "Wartime Financing of Manufacturing and Trade Concerns"; Doris P. Warner, "Financial Developments in Manufacturing and Trade in 1944"; 1946, Albert R. Koch and Eleanor J. Stockwell, "The Postwar Financial Position of Business."

TABLE 7

Assets in 1945 of 22 Manufacturing Industries as Per Cent of Assets in 1941, by Asset-Size Groups

Industry	Asset-Size Group ($ Million)				Total, All Asset Sizes
	0.25–1	1–5	5–10	10 and over	
Food	131	116	125	114	116
Beverages	139	142	141	135	139
Tobacco	204	142	*	145	145
Textiles, except cotton	121	118	111	114	115
Cotton	120	114	113	118	116
Apparel	122	105	136	...	115
Leather	113	108	115	...	112
Rubber	147	152	127	137	137
Lumber	107	112	100	103	104
Furniture	111	111	108	109	110
Paper	116	116	120	109	112
Printing and publishing	116	113	145	†	125
Chemicals	126	128	117	117	119
Petroleum and coal	111	106	105	115	114
Stone, clay, and glass	116	105	93	114	110
Iron and steel	124	119	120	97	104
Nonferrous metals	131	126	155	103	115
Electrical machinery	147	175	178	136	141
Machinery except electrical	131	125	132	124	125
Automobiles and equipment	181	197	173	118	121
Transportation equipment	138	160	92	121	121
Other manufacturing	135	124	156	126	130
Number of companies	2,223	1,284	279	321	4,107

* Two companies of this group included in $1–5 million group.
† Not shown to avoid possible disclosure of individual company information.
Source: Federal Trade Commission, *Report on Wartime Profits and Costs for Manufacturing Corporations* (Washington, 1947), pp. 3, 19.

mind that the FRB–Morris Associates sample is very imperfect, as the first article in the series clearly explains. However, a later unpublished check of the estimates against the *Statistics of Income* showed a closer agreement than was expected by the careful authors of the study.[31]

5. The growth of assets of the 200 largest manufacturing corporations has been compared with that of 800 other corporations of medium to large size. For the period 1939–46, the former group increased its assets by 41 per cent, the latter by 102 per cent.[32] However, the value of this comparison for our purposes is somewhat weakened by the fact that the 800 "other corporations," although chosen to be a "reasonably" good sample by industry and size, may yet be biased in some unknown way; the method of selection is not explained in detail.

6. Data on the increase of stockholders' investment after 1940 in twenty-three selected manufacturing industries, as given in Table 9, show

[31] An unpublished comparison was examined by courtesy of Dr. Susan S. Burr and her staff at the Board of Governors of the Federal Revenue System.

[32] K. Celeste Stokes, "Financial Trends of Large Manufacturing Corporations," *Survey of Current Business*, November, 1947.

TABLE 8

PERCENTAGE INCREASE OF ASSETS OF MANUFACTURING AND TRADE GROUPS, BY ASSET-SIZE GROUPS

PERCENTAGE INCREASE OF ASSETS DURING:	ASSET SIZE, END OF 1941 ($ Thousand)				
	Under 250	250–1,000	1,000–5,000	5,000–10,000	10,000 and over
	A. Manufacturing—War Industries				
1940–43	201	242	222	188	146
1943–44	123	106	103	94	100
1940–44*	247	256	229	177	146
	B. Manufacturing—Other Industries				
1940–43	163	139	126	129	128
1943–44	115	105	106	105	105
1940–44*	187	146	134	135	134
	C. Wholesale Trade				
				5,000 and over	
1940–43	134	122	131	131	
1943–44	106	105	105	102	
1940–44*	142	128	138	134	
	D. Retail Trade				
1940–43	118	135	140	134	
1943–44	110	106	107	106	
1940–44*	130	143	150	142	

* Product of the two preceding lines, each based on a different sample.

Sources: F. C. Dirks, "Wartime Financing of Manufacturing and Trade Concerns," *Federal Reserve Bulletin,* April 1945, pp. 1–18; Doris P. Warner, "Financial Developments in Manufacturing and Trade in 1944," *Federal Reserve Bulletin,* December 1945, pp. 1–6.

that in 19 out of 23 industries, the percentage increase in the stockholders' equity was greater for the smaller companies than for the top four in the industry. For the year 1947 (nearest to the war's end), the median increase among the big four was 42 per cent; for the others, 54 per cent.

It is scarcely necessary, in a professional journal, to point out that all of the foregoing six items are imperfect and subject to varying margins of error. But the data all point in the same direction; the whole is greater than the sum of the separate items,[33] and indicates a slight de-concentration during the wartime period. The only way to escape this conclusion is to assume a substantial wartime merger movement or wartime bankruptcies involving a considerable fraction of corporate assets. But mergers and bankruptcies were very few and the assets involved were insignificant.

This is clearly incompatible with the sweeping statement upon which the Attorney General's report is based. We turn therefore to the source of that statement. The report was required under section 708(e) of the Defense Production Act of 1950, which states that the appropriate research may be done by the Federal Trade Commission. The Commission

[33] Cf. Morris R. Cohen and Ernest Nagel, *An Introduction to Logic and Scientific Method* (New York, 1935), pp. 282–84, 335, 349.

TABLE 9

PERCENTAGE GROWTH OF STOCKHOLDERS' EQUITIES, LARGEST AND OTHER MANUFACTURING CORPORATIONS, 1940–49

Industry	Stockholders' Investment,* as Per Cent of 1940		
	1947	1948	1949
Dairy products			
4 largest companies	142	155	168
15 other companies	192	205	218
Bakery products (bread)			
4 largest companies	81	86	92
17 other companies	147	159	173
Biscuits and crackers			
4 largest companies	107	117	130
2 other companies	278	234	185
Cigarettes			
4 largest companies	130	143	158
4 other companies	162	167	179
Cigars			
4 largest companies	108	114	120
5 other companies	135	135	128
Wool carpets and rugs			
4 largest companies	130	148	161
9 other companies	137	158	177
Linoleum and felt base			
2 largest companies	135	154	173
3 other companies	127	143	151
Paper and allied products			
4 largest companies	147	171	206
100 other companies	177	202	213
Industrial chemicals			
4 largest companies	140	160	175
24 other companies	154	171	194
Rayon			
4 largest companies	138	160	192
3 other companies	132	145	49†
Soap, cleaning and polishing preparations			
4 largest companies	149	170	182
4 other companies	202	210	196
Petroleum refining			
4 largest companies	137	154	169
36 other companies	141	165	188
Tires and inner tubes			
4 largest companies	173	187	199
12 other companies	354	385	395
Flat glass, glassware (pressed and blown)			
4 largest companies	142	157	172
7 other companies	103	103	105
Abrasives, asbestos, and misc. nonmetallic mineral products			
4 largest companies	172	196	216
12 other companies	166	193	214
Blast furnaces, steel works, rolling mills			
4 largest companies	114	128	145
30 other companies	126	143	159
Primary smelting and refining nonferrous metals			
4 largest companies	120	128	133
15 other companies	125	135	143

TABLE 9 (*Continued*)

Industry	Stockholders' Investment,* as Per Cent of 1940		
	1947	1948	1949
Engines and turbines			
4 largest companies	196	226	258
11 other companies	246	276	302
Tin cans and other tinware			
4 largest companies	116	125	133
2 other companies	132	143	156
Office and store machines and devices			
4 largest companies	149	174	200
11 other companies	138	158	172
Electrical machinery, equipment and supplies			
4 largest companies	153	175	198
61 other companies	191	215	232
Motor vehicles			
4 largest companies	144	166	196
14 other companies	188	207	219
Motor vehicle equipment			
4 largest companies	195	228	264
37 other companies	219	245	268

* Adjusted to exclude accelerated amortization on wartime facilities.
† Erratic decrease not explained.
Source: Computed from Federal Trade Commission, *Rates of Return for 529 Identical Companies in 25 Selected Manufacturing Industries, 1940, 1947–49* (Washington, 1950).

relied upon a single source for its statement of greater concentration during the last war: a Senate document[34] which, unlike the data cited up to now, was not incidentally but explicitly a study of wartime changes in the pattern of concentration. A careful examination of this report (hereafter called the SWPC report) is therefore of methodological and practical importance.

The SWPC report appeared in January 1946, when items (1), (2), and (4) above had been published or their contents known to interested economists. There is no reference to these three items, nor any reason given for not accepting them. The FTC report to the Attorney General mentioned none of the six.

The conclusions of the SWPC report rest on two propositions, which may be examined in turn.

1. The report estimates that the 250 largest manufacturing corporations held 66.5 per cent of total usable manufacturing facilities in 1945, including government-owned plants which they had an option to purchase if they so wished. In 1939, the identical corporations held 65.4 per cent of total usable manufacturing facilities. As proof of increased concentration, this statement rests on (*a*) a logical fallacy, and (*b*) an unacceptable estimate.

[34] *Economic Concentration and World War II*, Report of the Smaller War Plants Corporation, 79th Congress, 2d Sess., Senate Committee Print No. 6. The following remarks are partly adapted from the writer's "Effective Competition and the Anti-trust Laws," *Harvard Law Review*, September, 1948.

a. "These 250 largest manufacturing corporations are, for the most part, the traditional giants of American industry. *But they include also a few corporations which have risen to positions of dominance during the war.*"[35] The error in this kind of reasoning is easily seen by observing that *all* corporations existing today own 100 per cent of the assets. These identical corporations owned a much smaller share than 100 per cent in previous years—many did not even exist. The increase to 100 per cent is scarcely a proof of greater concentration. Had the 250 largest in 1939 increased their share of the assets by 1945, or had the 250 largest in 1945 held a larger share than the 250 largest in 1939, that would be another matter. The report avoids these two comparisons, and makes one which has no bearing on changes in the degree of concentration.

b. "The report offers the estimate that *about $20,000,000,000 of the $26,000,000,000 wartime plant is usable for the production of peacetime products,* either immediately or after only minor reconversion. . . . This is simply an estimate of the portion of new facilities which are readily adaptable from a physical point of view."[36] Many products were needed in wartime in amounts far in excess of peacetime demand even under high employment. The estimate of the report is not the most probable value of usable facilities but the maximum value. A striking example is the aircraft industry, no less than 87 per cent of whose war-installed facilities were considered "usable"; for manufacturing facilities as a whole, the comparable figure was only 77 per cent.[37]

Accordingly, the corresponding estimate of the SWPC report that $11.5 billion, or two-thirds of the $17.2 billion of federally financed facilities held by the largest 250, would be usable,[38] must be drastically scaled down. In fact, the Civilian Production Administration had *already* estimated that only about one third of federally financed plants would be "readily usable in peacetime."[39] The SWPC report did not mention this. The two estimates may be consistent, since they do not refer to the same thing. But only the CPA figure is economically relevant.

Therefore, if we make the appropriate adjustment, the largest 250 manufacturing corporations in 1945 had $5.75 billion less in assets which they could take up at the war's end than the SWPC report estimated. If they took up *all* of it, their share of the total would then be barely over 60 per cent—an actual decline of about 5 per cent since 1939. This does not support the hypothesis of greater concentration.

2. "Small business was shoved into the background. Small firms (those with less than 500 employees) accounted for 52 per cent of total manu-

---

[35] *Ibid.*, p. 40. Italics supplied.

[36] *Ibid.*, p. 39. Italics in original.

[37] Calculated from *ibid.*, Table D–1, p. 343.

[38] *Ibid.*, pp. 38, 40.

[39] Civilian Production Administration, *War-Created Manufacturing Plant Federally Financed, 1940–1944* (November 15, 1945), p. 3.

facturing employment in 1939. In 1944 this figure had fallen to 32 per cent."[40] But in fact as the small firms prospered, a sizable number of them "graduated" out of the less-than-500 class; and a little reflection will show that the *more prosperous* the condition of small manufacturers, the *smaller* the number and share of those remaining and the "worse" the statistical picture. Again and again, for each industrial group, the SWPC report rings all the changes on this elementary fallacy. One might as well argue as follows: in 1935–36, a large percentage of all families received annual incomes of $750 or less; today hardly any do; it was impossible to keep body and soul together on so little; *therefore*, this unfortunate class has been wiped out by the ravages of poverty. What the data indicate is an increase in average size. But they are compatible either with increasing or decreasing concentration, and therefore prove nothing one way or the other.

The authors of the SWPC report had the opportunity to make a real contribution in a field important both in peace and war. Unfortunately, their data are simply irrelevant. There is no use crying over spilled milk; but there is every reason to urge that public policy be made on the basis of fact rather than warmed-over fiction.

V

Let us now consider the trend of concentration over the period 1909–47. The year 1931 was a noteworthy one in the statistical study of concentration. First, the *Statistics of Income* began to present balance-sheet data classified by industry and size; second, there appeared an article by Gardiner C. Means which may be said to have inaugurated the systematic study of concentration, and to which every student of the subject must be indebted.[41] For the first time, the topmost group of corporations was identified and placed in context. These findings were embodied in the better known book by Berle and Means,[42] published the next year, and elaborated some years later in a study of the National Resources Committee.[43] The estimates precipitated a long controversy, often acrimonious yet often fruitful, which has been summed up with a light but masterful touch by Edwin B. George.[44]

Our chief concern at this point is with the trend of concentration rather than the level. References to increasing concentration are ex-

[40] SWPC report, *op. cit.*, p. 24.

[41] Gardiner C. Means, "The Large Corporation in American Economic Life," *American Economic Review*, XXI (1931), pp. 10–42.

[42] A. A. Berle and Gardiner C. Means, *The Modern Corporation and Private Property* (New York, 1932).

[43] National Resources Committee, *The Structure of the American Economy*, Vol. I (Washington, 1939), particularly Appendices 10 and 11.

[44] Edwin B. George, "How Big is Big Business," *Dun's Review*, March, 1939; "Is Big Business Getting Bigger," *ibid.*, May, 1939; "How Did Big Business Get Big?" *ibid.*, September, 1939.

tremely frequent. But nobody, to our knowledge, has stated the hypothesis with so much clarity as Berle and Means:[45]

> Within "the corporate system" there exists a centripetal attraction which draws wealth together into aggregations of constantly increasing size. . . . *The trend is apparent, and no limit is as yet in sight.* Were it possible to say that circumstances had established the concentration, but that there was no basis to form an opinion as to whether the process would continue, the whole problem might be simplified. But this is not the case.
>
> Just what does this rapid growth of the big companies promise for the future? Let us project the trend of the growth of . . . the twenty years 1909 to 1929, then 70 per cent of all corporate activity would be carried on by two hundred corporations by 1950. If the more rapid rates of growth from 1924 to 1929 were maintained for the next twenty years, 85 per cent of corporate wealth would be held by two hundred huge units. It would take only forty years at the 1909–1929 rate or only thirty years at the 1924–1929 rates for all corporate activity and practically all industrial activity to be absorbed by two hundred giant companies. . . . Whether the future will see any such complete absorption of economic activity into a few great enterprises it is not possible to predict. . . . The trend of the recent past indicates, however, that the great corporation, already of tremendous importance today, will become increasingly important in the future.

The Berle-Means projection was based on their estimate that the assets of the largest 200 were increasing during 1909–29 at the rate of 6.83 per cent annually, while all nonfinancial corporations were growing at the rate of 3.72 per cent per year. Thus the top 200 were increasing relatively by 2.03 per cent per year. During 1909–24, the relative increase had been 1.66 per cent per year; during 1924–29 it had been 3.14 per cent.[46]

Increased concentration during the 1924–29 period may be regarded as proved, i.e., the estimated change in the share of the top 200 seems to be greater than the reasonable limits of the dispersion around it. The real difficulty has been with the fifteen-year period 1909–24, and it has been best stated by George:[47]

> The growth of both contestants was in fact understated because of the absorption of water. Which of them suffered from that fact the most? . . . Until that surrealist equation is solved there is no precise answer to the basic question of who grew faster, and how much.
>
> Disputes touching the amount of water in 1909 capitalization and 1924 gross assets tend to throw us away from a measurement of finite bodies and toward one that could well bear the title *A Few Speculative Thoughts on the Effect of Assumed Leverages on Unknown Weights*. . . .
>
> We have little here but material for broad impressions. This is Dr. Means' own view of the matter, and he does not regard this particular stretch of his findings as other than reasonably indicative of an unequal rate of growth.

There the matter rests. For what they are worth, the 1909–24 figures do show increasing concentration; we are not dealing with the kind of

[45] Berle and Means, *op. cit.*, pp. 40–41. Italics supplied.

[46] These are all compound rates.

[47] Edwin B. George, "Is Big Business Getting Bigger?" *op. cit.*, pp. 36 and 56.

irrelevancies reviewed in Section IV above. But the data seem far too weak to support much in the way of inference.

This is not the case, however, with Means' later work for the National Resources Committee, which was based on unpublished income-tax data. For the years 1929–33, as Table 10 shows, there was a very appreciable

TABLE 10

ASSETS OF LARGE CORPORATIONS AS PER CENT OF TOTAL ASSETS* OF RESPECTIVE GROUPS, 1929 AND 1933

Large Corporations	1929	1933
200 Large nonfinancial corporations	47.9	54.8
75 Large manufacturing corporations	36.2	40.2
85 Large transportation and other public utility corporations	79.0	86.1
25 Large "other" corporations	10.9	14.8

* Excluding nongovernment securities.

Source: National Resources Committee, *The Structure of the American Economy*, Vol. I (Washington, 1939), Appendix 11, Tables IV, V.

increase in concentration, both with respect to the top 200 as a whole and also its three main subgroups. The objection may, of course, be made that 1929–33 is not a "representative" period, as—thank heaven—it could not be. But this point really comprises two very distinct ones: (1) a statistical peculiarity of assets during periods of rapidly changing prices, and (2) an assumption or prediction about future economic fluctuations. These may be considered in turn.

(1) The top 200 had and have a disproportionately large share of the capital assets. Thus, while they held 47.9 per cent of total assets (less nongovernment securities) in 1929, they held 58.0 per cent of capital assets. Now capital assets consist of the historical cost of durable plant and equipment, while inventories consist of the current cost of nondurable assets. Given a period sufficient to turn over the capital assets, the latter come to reflect price movements. But after a short period of rapidly falling (rising) prices, there is bound to be the appearance of an increase (decrease) in the relative holdings of corporations that possess more durable assets. Hence the share of the top 200 in total assets less taxable investments is overstated as of 1933. A rough calculation suggests that from one third to one half of the 1929–33 increase in concentration is a statistical mirage.

(2) But the rest of the increase is well established. Not only are the underlying data of high quality, but it also is well known that larger corporations make larger profits (or smaller losses) during an economic holocaust like 1929–33.[48] There is no question, therefore, that concentra-

[48] W. L. Crum, *Corporate Size and Earning Power* (Cambridge, Mass., 1939), especially Appendix Table B.

tion must have increased during 1929–33, and that it may be expected to increase during any deep depression.

The Trend of Concentration 1931–1947

An attempt to plot the trend of concentration for later years runs into certain difficulties. One is the treatment of public utilities. During both the 1909–24 and the 1924–29 periods, this branch of the economy was notable both for rapid growth and rapid concentration. For example, of the 150 corporations included among the top 200 in both 1919 and 1928, the railroad group showed an increase in assets of 24 per cent, the industrials of 58 per cent, and the utilities of 194 per cent. For the hectic years 1924–28, the annual rates of growth were, respectively, 2.3 per cent, 6.0 per cent, and 15.9 per cent.[49] By 1930, according to a somewhat sketchy estimate, the three largest utility systems controlled about half the industry, and another ten controlled three fifths of the remainder.[50] In 1932, according to a better estimate, the operating companies controlled by the eight largest holding company systems generated 73 per cent of all privately produced electric power.[51] In 1933, the largest 40 public utility corporations controlled over 80 per cent of the industry's assets.[52]

Under the Public Utility Holding Company Act of 1935, public utility holding companies had divested themselves of $16 billion of assets up to June 30, 1950.[53] This sum is over 70 per cent of the total assets owned by all electric and gas utilities in 1947.[53a] Moreover, of the 41 electric and gas utilities which were among the 200 largest corporations in 1935, an incomplete count shows that at least 15, which accounted for well over half the assets, have been dissolved.[54] Ought this massive de-concentration to be included in any measurement of trend? This depends fundamentally on the context into which one wants to put the study. It would be necessary to include the utilities if our subject were the relation of concentration to both economic and political forces. Since our subject excludes the latter, it seems more appropriate to exclude public utilities.

Moreover, there is general acceptance of the dichotomy between the competitive area of the economy, and the legal ("natural") monopolies. Of our 200 largest companies (whether by employment, assets, or research effort), about 150 are in the competitive area, and of these all but a score are in manufacturing. Hence an estimate of the trend of concen-

[49] Berle and Means, *op. cit.*, p. 34.

[50] Charles S. Tippetts and Shaw Livermore, *Business Organization and Control* (New York, 1932), p. 509.

[51] Securities and Exchange Commission, *Tenth Annual Report* (Washington, 1945), p. 85.

[52] National Resources Committee, *op. cit.*, p. 291, Table V–D.

[53] Securities and Exchange Commission, *Fifteenth Annual Report* (Washington, 1950), pp. 62–63.

[53a] *Cf.* Table 3A.

[54] National Resources Committee, *op. cit.*, pp. 275–76, and SEC, *op. cit.*, pp. 96–119.

tration in manufacturing goes nearly all the way in meeting our need for estimates of concentration in this area. Moreover, should it turn out that concentration in manufacturing has been either stationary or declining, it becomes apparent that concentration for the economy as a whole must have decreased inasmuch as it has done so in the area of legal monopoly.

In 1931, according to *Statistics of Income*, there were 139 manufacturing corporations with assets of over $50 million, and they accounted for 46.5 per cent of the assets of all manufacturing corporations. But this must overestimate the number of corporations in the "over-$50 million" class, and it must underestimate their assets. For in some cases two or more subsidiaries of a large company made out separate tax returns, which caused that enterprise to be counted twice. Furthermore, there must have been separately incorporated subsidiaries which owned less than $50 million in assets, and these assets were therefore excluded from the total for the 139 largest.[55]

For 1947, as for no previous year, we are fortunate in having a reliable test of consolidation, and a means of correction. The Quarterly Industrial Financial Report Series, prepared jointly by the FTC and the SEC (hereafter called the FTC-SEC data), gives income and balance-sheet statements for all manufacturing corporations classified as to size, and these data are on a completely consolidated basis. (The data for the largest corporations rest not on sample estimates but on a complete count.) In Table 11 the FTC-SEC data for the end of 1947 are compared with those of the Bureau of Internal Revenue. At the end of 1947, according to FTC-SEC, manufacturing corporations with assets of over $100 million held a little more than 43 per cent of the assets of all manufacturing corporations. The agreement with the Treasury statistics is extremely close, and some congratulations are in order for the inter-departmental group of government statisticians who devised and launched the series. Line 7 of Table 11 shows the Treasury data as adjusted for consolidation.[56] Are there more or less in the top 1947 group than in the top 1931 group?

This question is not too difficult to answer. The Department of Commerce has compiled a list of *The 1000 Largest Manufacturing Corporations* as of the end of 1946.[57] At that time, there were, on a consolidated

[55] For the years 1935–41 inclusive, the privilege of filing consolidated returns was withdrawn from nearly all corporations except common carriers. Hence the corporate *Statistics of Income* for those years are not comparable with earlier or later years. But there was always some separate filing before 1935, and has been since 1941, because the tax advantage may be overborne by other considerations.

[56] It would be preferable to adjust on the basis of total assets net of marketable securities, but the data are not available separately for the "over-$100 million" group. Our adjustment has the effect of removing marketable securities, calculating the adjusted percentages net of the type of asset, and then applying the percentages to all assets including marketable securities. This inflates the amounts but does not affect the ratios.

[57] Mimeographed, 1948.

basis, 113 manufacturing firms with assets of $100 million or over.[58] During the next year, some must have crossed the line, but how many? From the end of 1946 to the end of 1947, according to the Treasury, the assets of all manufacturing corporations increased by 11.2 per cent.[59] On the assumption that the corporations in the neighborhood of $100 million increased about as fast as manufacturing in general, it follows that a corporation with $86.5 million or more in assets in 1946 would be over the

TABLE 11

ESTIMATED ASSET HOLDINGS OF 139 LARGEST MANUFACTURING CORPORATIONS, END OF 1947

(*All money figures in $ million*)

	Inventories	Net Capital Assets	Total Tangible Assets	Total Assets Less Non-gov't Securities	Total Assets
1. All manufacturing corporations*	27,634	33,351	60,985	100,654	111,356
2. All manufacturing corporations with assets exceeding $100 million*	8,977	16,057	25,034	n.a.	45,082
3. Line (2) as per cent of line (1)	*32.4*	*48.2*	*44.3*	n.a.	*40.5*
4. All manufacturing corporations†	26,473	32,321	58,794	96,901	97,564
5. All manufacturing corporations with assets exceeding $100 million†	10,175	16,093	26,268	42,070	42,197
6. Line (5) as per cent of line (4)	*38.1*	*49.8*	*44.7*	*43.5*	*43.2*
7. Line (2), adjusted by line (6) (1.066)	...	...	...	n.a.	48,200
8. 7 additional manufacturing corporations					700
9. Line (7) plus line (8)					48,900
10. Line (9), adjusted for wartime amortization‡					50,910
11. Line (1), adjusted for wartime amortization‡					114,694
12. Line (10) as per cent of line (11)					*44.4*
13. Line (12), adjusted for abnormal inventories§					*45.1*

* Bureau of Internal Revenue.
† Federal Trade Commission—Securities Exchange Commission.
‡ See Table 12, Part A.
§ See Table 12, Part B.
Sources: *Statistics of Income*, 1947; *Quarterly Industrial Financial Report Series*, Fourth Quarter, 1947.

$100 million mark in 1947. There were 19 such corporations on the Commerce list. Hence it is probable that the over-$100 million class included 132 corporations (113 plus 19) at the end of 1947. To reach a total of 139, we need to add 7 more. In Table 11 the arbitrary assumption is made that each of the 7 are just barely under the $100-million mark, and should in the aggregate be credited with $0.7 billion of assets in all. This is of course an overestimate, but a very slight one.

Two other adjustments are shown in detail in Table 12. The one for wartime accelerated amortization needs no comment. The other corrects

[58] Following the example of the FTC, we have added to the Commerce list two large firms whose assets were not made public.

[59] *Statistics of Income* for the respective years.

for the abnormal type of asset structure discussed earlier (Section II). As Table 12 shows, the item of inventories was about 14 per cent of total assets in 1931, but nearly 25 per cent of total assets in 1947. It is obvious that because of the sharp price decline during 1929–31, inventories were abnormally low in the earlier year; and that because of the even sharper rise in prices through 1947, inventories were abnormally high in the later one. Since the largest corporations hold a smaller share of inventories than of total assets, this rise in the price level and in the value of inven-

TABLE 12

EXPLANATION OF AMORTIZATION AND INVENTORY ADJUSTMENTS

A. Adjustment for Wartime Accelerated Amortization
(*All money figures in $ thousand*)

1. Total manufacturing, accelerated amortization, 1944	740,721
2. Total manufacturing investment thus amortized (line [1] × 5)	3,703,605
3. Regular depreciation rate, 1944, in per cent	3.59
4. Undepreciated per cent of (2) (100–[3 × line (3)])	89.22
5. Undepreciated portion of (2), end of 1947 (line [4] × line [2])	3,338,000
6. Per cent of amortization in 1944 claimed by all corporations with assets exceeding $100 million	60.3
7. Line (6) × line (5)	2,010,000

B. Abnormal Inventories, 1947
(*All money figures in $ billion*)

1. Year	1929	1931	1941	1947	
2. Ratio of inventories to total assets	17.95	14.3	23.5	24.8	
3. Factor, 14.3 ÷ 24.8					0.577
4. Total 1947 manufacturing inventories, adjusted ($26.5 × 0.577)					15.2
5. Total 1947 manufacturing assets, adjusted ($97.6 less $11.3)					86.3
6. Inventories of the largest corporations, adjusted ($10.2 × 0.577)					5.9
7. Assets of the largest corporations, adjusted ($42.2 – $4.3)					37.9
8. Line (7) as per cent of line (5)					43.9
9. Adjustment factor, line (8) ÷ 43.2*					1.016

* For the source of this figure, see Table 11, line (6).
Sources: *Statistics of Income* for the respective years.

tories is a statistical distortion tending to understate concentration. Some upward adjustment is necessary in estimating concentration in 1947. Of course, were we to follow the suggestion of the FTC study discussed in Section II above, we would be compelled to make a *downward* adjustment.

As an approximation to a "normal" year, it is helpful to examine the ratio of inventories to other assets for other years of high peacetime employment, as given by *Statistics of Income*. The results are inconclusive.

For 1941, the ratio of inventories to total assets was 23.5 per cent, almost as high as 1947. But 1941 must also have been abnormal because of the defense boom and the shortage of materials apparent throughout. Hence the nearest year of high peacetime employment is 1929, when inventories were 17.95 per cent of total assets. However, to adjust both 1931 and 1947 would involve greater uncertainties than to adjust either year so as to make it comparable with the other. Hence we have abandoned the attempt to estimate a normal ratio and have put 1947 on a 1931 basis; if inventories are adjusted accordingly (in effect, if the 1931 weights are substituted for the 1947), the share of the largest 139 corporations rises from 44.4 to 45.1 per cent. If we assume that the consolidation adjustment for 1931 (1.066) was the same as for 1947, then our best estimate is as follows:

In 1931, the largest 139 manufacturing corporations held 49.6 per cent of the assets of all manufacturing corporations. In 1947, the largest 139 held 45.0 per cent. (The unadjusted percentages would be 46.5 and 40.5, respectively.) This comparison covers sixteen years, but they were no ordinary years. As Means wrote at the halfway mark in 1939:

> An analysis of the economic structure . . . is greatly aided by the depression. The rapid drop in national production . . . and the very considerable recovery since that time, give the economic analyst what is almost equivalent to a laboratory experiment on the basis of which structural characteristics may be observed . . . just as a high wind brings out the structural difference not evident on a windless day between the tree that bends to the wind and that which stands unbending.[60]

These words are even more true today than in 1939, for since then we have had a strong wind blowing in the other direction: full and often overfull employment. As Table 13 shows, even seemingly slight tendencies toward greater concentration would cumulate to formidable proportions within 16 years. Had the relative rate of growth estimated by Berle and Means for 1924–29 continued during this time, the unadjusted asset holdings of the largest 139 manufacturing corporations would in 1947 have been over $85 billion, about three fourths of all manufacturing corporate assets. Even at the relatively low rate of growth for 1909–24, they would by 1947 have held well over 60 per cent of those assets. The rate of growth indicated over the entire period 1909–29 would have resulted in a figure between 60 and 70 per cent. Instead, the data show a *reduction* of nearly 10 per cent in the share held by the largest 139.

That there seems actually to be a decline in concentration sounds more impressive than it should. Too many "bugs" remain in the statistics, and three further adjustments, at least, would be needed: (1) There were write-downs of assets during the 1930's, which were presumably more important among the large corporations. (2) There has been a long-term

[60] National Resources Committee, *op. cit.*, p. 4.

drift toward incorporation of an increasing fraction of business activity. But during World War II, a substantial number of smaller corporations became partnerships or proprietorships in order to avoid the excess profits tax; and not all had reverted to corporate status by 1947. Neither of these adjustments would be large; moreover, they would be in opposite directions, and the resultant would be smaller than either. (3) Possibly most important are the changes in industry classification since 1931, which might have involved large firms. However, our universe of manufacturing corporations is an extremely large one; and the reader has probably been struck by the minor percentage effects of large absolute adjustments. But let us waive any claims to precision, and summarize this long and arid inquiry:

TABLE 13

Hypothetical and Actual Share of Assets of 139 Largest Manufacturing Corporations, 1931 and 1947

	Billions of Dollars		Per Cent of Assets of All Mfg. Corporations	
	Unadjusted	Adjusted*	Unadjusted	Adjusted*
Total assets, end of 1931	29.6	31.6	46.5	49.6
Hypothetical total assets, end of 1947, assuming rate of growth relative to all manufacturing corporations, in per cent per annum:				
1 per cent	62.3	66.5	54.4	58.0
2 per cent	73.2	78.0	63.9	68.1
3 per cent	85.6	91.3	74.6	79.5
4 per cent	98.7	105.2	86.2	91.9
Actual total assets, end of 1947	45.1†	50.9*	40.5†	45.1*

* Adjustments were made as follows: Line 1, for consolidation; lines 2 to 6, for consolidation, accelerated amortization, abnormal inventory holdings, and for the 7 additional corporations.

† Includes 7 corporations added to the over-100 group as shown by *Statistics of Income*.

If there has been any strong and continuing tendency since 1931 to greater concentration in manufacturing, it must be detectable in the corporate balance sheet statistics for that period. These statistics do not show it. Therefore the tendency probably does not exist.

If we suppose that the same economic forces were at work before the 1930's as since then, these findings cast doubt on the Means estimates (outside of public utilities) for 1909–24. The two are not necessarily incompatible, since they refer to different periods. But those who, unlike Means, have confidently extrapolated the 1909–29 tendencies forward, thereby implying that the two periods were substantially similar, are now in the embarrassing position of having to extrapolate figures back, and discovering that there has been no increase in concentration since 1909. But the safer procedure is simply to stick to the facts.

VI

Concentration in Manufacturing, 1901–47

Toward the end of 1949, the student of concentration was blessed with two sets of data which could together be used to compare concentration over nearly half a century. One was a set of concentration ratios from the 1947 *Census of Manufactures;* the other was G. Warren Nutter's patient archeological reconstruction of the period just after the turn of the

TABLE 14

MEASUREMENT OF CONCENTRATION IN MANUFACTURING INDUSTRIES, 1901 AND 1947

	AROUND 1901*			1947		
	VALUE ADDED (*$ Million*)					
MAJOR INDUSTRY GROUP (1947 Census Classification)	Industries with Concentration Ratio over 50 Per Cent (1)	Total Industry Group (2)	Col. 1 as Per Cent of Col. 2 (3)	Per Cent of Value of Product† (4)	Per Cent of Value Added‡ (5)	Weighted Average (by Value Added) of Columns 4 and 5§ (6)
Foods	276.6	709.9	39.1	22.0	0.0	18.8
Tobacco manufactures	85.3	170.8	49.9	87.7	....	77.7
Textile mill products	143.9	710.6	20.3	5.3	100.0	9.0
Apparel and related products	....	....	...	4.4	....	2.2
Lumber and products (except furniture)	2.6	534.8	0.5	2.0	....	2.0
Furniture and fixtures	....	....	...	8.0	....	8.1
Paper and allied products	66.3	93.4	71.0	1.3	....	1.6
Printing and publishing	2.7	284.4	1.0	0.0	....	0.0
Chemical and allied products	47.8	196.7	24.3	30.3	....	33.7
Petroleum and coal products	21.1	45.1	46.8	12.3	....	13.6
Rubber products	39.6	39.6	100.0	64.9	....	59.9
Leather and products	49.0	186.7	26.3	0.0	....	0.0
Stone, clay, and glass	25.9	194.6	13.3	44.2	....	43.9
Primary metal industries	161.5	221.9	45.7	44.3	7.0	21.0
Steel works and rolling mills	336.1	427.8	78.8	44.7	....	....
Fabricated metal products	....	....	...	11.5	....	8.4
Machinery except electrical	200.0	482.7	41.4	20.2	0.0	18.5
Electrical machinery	....	....	...	65.3	0.0	53.2
Transportation equipment	103.3	180.8	57.3	51.3	100.0	84.2
Instruments and related products	....	....	...	45.8	....	45.0
Miscellaneous manufactures	2.8	102.2	2.7	21.0	....	21.2
Total all industries	1,505.5	4,579.5	32.9	21.9	48.0	24.0

* 319 industries.

† Per cent of *total value of product* of industry group accounted for by individual industries with concentration ratio over 50 per cent (440 industries).

‡ Per cent of *total value added by manufacture* by industry group accounted for by individual industries with concentration ratio over 50 per cent (12 industries).

§ Column 6 substitutes a set of weights by value added for the system of weights by value-of-product which is given in Column 4. Hence Column 6 differs from Column 4 even when it is not necessary to average in the results of Column 5.

Sources: Cols. 1–3, G. Warren Nutter, *A Quantitative Study of the Extent of Enterprise Monopoly in the United States, 1899–1939* (Unpublished Ph.D. thesis, University of Chicago, 1949).

Cols. 4–6, Letter from Charles Sawyer, Secretary of Commerce, to Emanuel Celler, Chairman of Sub-Committee on Study of Monopoly Power, Washington, December 1, 1949, Table V appended; and *Census of Manufactures, 1947.*

century.[61] Nutter's contribution is one of the most important in recent years.

As Table 14 indicates, around 1901 nearly one third of the value added by manufacture was produced in industries where the concentration ratio was 50 or more. Since then, there has been both further concentration and de-concentration. But the net result was that by 1947, only about one fourth of the value added was so produced.

As usual, one must caution against hasty conclusions. In the first place, the skill of the investigator can only ameliorate his very faulty materials. Many of Nutter's sources are sketchy and unreliable, although they seem about as likely to be wrong in one direction as another. There seems no reason to impute any systematic bias to them; nevertheless, the standard error is inescapably large.

Secondly, the concentration ratio itself has certain serious limitations, discussed in part earlier. The 50 per cent dividing line is, after all, an arbitrary one. Appreciable changes can occur in the extent of concentration without changing this ratio. For example, the share of the largest four might increase from just over 50 per cent to nearly 100 per cent, or from nearly zero to 49.9 per cent, without changing the ratio. However, this is just where the industry-by-industry measurement of concentration is the most useful, in that it breaks up the whole class into many subgroups. It is highly unlikely that there could be many such shifts which carefully respected the 50 per cent line. With more than 350 observations, one would expect such sampling fluctuations—for that is essentially what they are—to become quite small. Table 15 presents a fre-

TABLE 15

FREQUENCY DISTRIBUTION OF CONCENTRATION RATIOS OVER 50 PER CENT IN ALL INDUSTRIES

Concentration Ratio	Number of Industries	Value Added (*$ Billion*)	Per Cent of Total Value Added in All Industries	Cumulative Per Cent
90–100	11	1.34	1.80	1.80
80–89.9	20	1.17	1.58	3.38
70–79.9	30	4.23	5.68	9.06
60–69.9	35	3.65	4.90	13.96
50–59.9	54	7.49	10.05	24.01
Total over 50	150	17.88	24.01	

Sources: Letter from Charles Sawyer, Secretary of Commerce, to Emanuel Celler, Chairman of Sub-Committee on Study of Monopoly Power, Washington, December 1, 1949, Table V appended; and *Census of Manufactures, 1947*.

[61] Nutter, *op. cit.* Incidentally, his purpose, as the title indicates, was to measure the extent of *monopoly* rather than concentration, and his conclusion was that during 1899–1939 there was a slight increase in monopoly over the whole economy. Outside of manufacturing, there were no systematic data available, and he was compelled to separate sheep from goats in somewhat arbitrary fashion. Those who would reject such methods out of hand are urged to devise better ones.

quency distribution of the concentration ratios in 1947. There is obviously no bunching at the highest levels, but an irregular decline from the 50–59.9 class upward.

But other defects of Table 14 cannot be so clearly tested and dismissed. An increase in concentration via greater vertical integration might not be fully reflected in the concentration ratio.[62] The available evidence points to no increase in vertical integration by manufacturing establishments; in the absence of any other evidence, this would indicate no increase in concentration by firms; but the matter cannot be regarded as

TABLE 16

INCREASE IN NUMBER OF MANUFACTURING ESTABLISHMENTS, 1899–1947

Year	Number of Establishments (*Thousands*)	Percentage Increase
1899	204.8	
1904	213.4	
1914*	268.4	
1899–1914:		30
1914†	173.6	
1939	173.8	
1947, adj.‡	233.9	
1914–1947:		32
1899–1947:		64

* Old basis, i.e., counting all establishments selling at least $500 of product.

† New basis, i.e., counting all establishments selling at least $5,000 of product.

‡ According to the *Census of Manufactures, 1947*, Vol. 1, General Summary, p. 4–5, sec. 8, "Change in Scope Between 1939 and 1947," it appears that the changes in classification brought about a gain of about 23,000 establishments, and a loss of about 15,400, i.e., a net gain of about 7,600. This has been lowered to 7,000, to make allowance for the general growth of establishments since 1939, and subtracted from the 1947 total of establishments to obtain an approximation to the total that would have been obtained on a 1939 basis.

Sources: *Census of Manufactures*, respective years.

settled. Finally, there can be significant differences in structure which any concentration ratio fails to reflect and which the exponent c, discussed in Section I above, was designed to measure. Not even a rough adjustment can be made on this score; it is certainly a subject for later investigation.

Both c and the concentration ratio measure concentration by the share

[62] Suppose the economy to consist of two industries, the first producing semifinished goods which it sold to the second. One of the big four in the second might buy up (a) one of the big four in the first, resulting in a spurious decrease in the concentration ratio; (b) a firm not among the big four, resulting in a spurious increase in the concentration ratio. The mathematical theory, and the extent to which such distortions are overcome through value-added weighting, remain to be worked out. Were the concentration ratios themselves computed on the basis of value added, there would be no such problem, since value added reflects the degree of vertical integration.

of the small absolute number of the largest firms. But, the number of firms increased considerably during the half-century under study. A given *number* of firms became a progressively smaller *per cent* of all firms, and if the share of the smaller per cent in the later years was no less than that of the larger per cent in the earlier years then concentration in some meaningful sense would have increased. In other words, for comparisons over such long time periods, we need some indicator of Lorenz concentration, faulty as it is. Unfortunately, the basic figure for any such computation, the number of firms in manufacturing, does not exist. Let us, however, make shift with such data as we have on the number of manufacturing establishments, as summed up in Table 16, and assume that the number of manufacturing firms has also increased by about 64 per cent. Now the 1901 data are divided into 319 industries and 1,276 firms among the "big four"; the 1947 data have 452 industries and 1,708 firms, an increase of 43 per cent, or much less than the increase in the total number of firms. Thus the number of the largest firms has declined, relatively speaking, to 87 (143 ÷ 164) per cent of the 1901 level. But value added in industries where they hold at least half has declined more, to 76 per cent,[63] indicating a decline of Lorenz-type concentration of between 10 and 20 per cent.[64]

All the available evidence suggests that the number of firms has increased by less than 64 per cent, and therefore that the decline in Lorenz-type concentration is greater than just estimated. First, we have used the 1899 figure for number of establishments, rather than trying to interpolate for the 1901 figure, which would be larger. Second, if it is true that the average number of establishments per firm is larger today than at the turn of the century, as is generally believed, then the increase of manufacturing firms must have been less than the increase of establishments. Third, the years after World War II contained a cyclical peak in the number of firms. It is impossible that all of the new ones will survive. If we were able to make allowance for the normal shrinkage, the increase in the number of firms since 1939 (and 1899) would be much less. Our inability to make any precise estimate of the total number of firms is, as was indicated in Section I, the fundamental defect in Lorenz measurement.

Tables 14 to 16 appear to show a substantial decrease of concentration

[63] This amounts to the convention that the growth of the economy has been coterminous with the addition of new industries, which is of course not the case. However, the validity of the method is not affected by using this fiction.

[64] In an earlier draft, an error was committed which may also tempt some reader. The concentration ratio for the earlier years was multiplied by two factors: (1) the increase in the number of industries, and (2) the decline in average size of firm as the number of industries was increased. Such a procedure is valid in estimating the height of the curve controlled by an exponent of the type of c for any given year—it deals with a movement along the curve. The procedure cannot be used in order to decide how much the whole curve ought to be shifted to make some kind of allowance for the increased number of firms.

in manufacturing since around 1901. But in view of the roughness of the early data and the crudity of some estimates, it seems best to state conclusions as follows: The odds are better than even that there has actually been *some* decline in concentration. It is a good bet that there has at least been no actual increase; and the odds do seem high against any substantial increase.

The Trend of Concentration and the Role of Mergers

The historian and the statistician use very different methods; fundamentally they have the same task. Confronted with scattered pieces of evidence, each of them a more or less imperfect sample of the population concerning which information is desired, each attempts to draw up such hypotheses about the population—whether of events in time, or a distribution in space—as will not conflict with the data and may even enable one to predict what later pieces of evidence will look like. This article has been an attempt to explore a segment of American economic history since 1900 by way of the available statistical record, and that record is not plentiful. We have dipped into it at irregular intervals, and found no continuing growth in concentration, but rather a surprising stability. It is clear that among nonmanufacturing industries, the railroads underwent both gigantic growth and great concentration before 1900; but they have not changed much with respect to concentration (and a few other things) since then. In the field of public utilities, Wall Street gave in the 1920's and SEC took away in the 1940's. As for the field of distribution, the rise of chain stores and mail-order houses since 1900 probably contributed to some increased concentration, although this can easily be exaggerated: most of the large distribution firms are department stores, and most of them are of a venerable age. Since 1929, as Table 17 shows, the chain stores and mail-order houses have not increased their share of the retail market. The field of financial and nonfinancial services is almost entirely unilluminated. This is not a very impressive body of evidence.

Thus the field of manufacturing acquires a pivotal importance: because it is large and a decisive trend in it would determine the trend for the economy; because it is the locus of such a disproportionate share of innovation and change; and because, not wholly without reason, we treat it as a sample of the whole economy. The following would seem to be a plausible sketch of developments there. In the nineteenth century, particularly after the Civil War, there was a pronounced increase in the scale of manufacturing establishments and of firms, owing both to new technical developments which made larger-scale production profitable, and perhaps even more to the rise of the railroad systems, the possibilities of nationwide distribution, and the hope of controlling the wider markets. Whatever the reasons, there occurred during the 1870's and 1880's not only growth of existing and new firms to larger size, but a great many mergers. The public reaction to "the trusts" was of course the Sherman Act.

Another wave of mergers came in the period of 1897–1903. Whether they were relatively more or less important than those of earlier years will perhaps never be known; but they were of extraordinary size. While the resulting increase in concentration cannot be measured, there is no question of the effect.[65] There is a compilation by the Census Bureau[66] of 185 "combinations" formed up to June 30, 1900. The time period is thus very restricted: U.S. Steel, the greatest of all mergers, is excluded, and others as well. But the definition of a "combination" is also very narrow:

TABLE 17

SALES OF CHAIN STORES AND MAIL-ORDER HOUSES COMPARED WITH RETAIL SALES, 1929–50

Year	All Retail Sales (*$ Million*) (1)	Sales of Chain Stores and Mail-Order Houses (*$ Million*) (2)	Col. 2 as Per Cent of Col. 1 (3)
1929	48,459	10,412	21.49
1933	24,517	6,618	26.99
1935	32,791	8,040	24.52
1936	38,338	8,960	23.37
1937	42,150	9,426	22.36
1938	38,053	8,872	23.31
1939	42,042	9,570	22.76
1940	46,388	10,382	22.38
1941	55,490	12,434	22.41
1942	57,639	14,064	24.40
1943	63,721	14,441	22.66
1944	69,573	15,523	22.31
1945	76,644	16,352	21.34
1946	100,787	21,158	20.99
1947	118,908	25,334	21.31
1948	130,042	27,804	21.38
1949	128,184	27,192	21.21
1950	140,249	29,077	20.73

Source: *Survey of Current Business*, various issues, 1943–51.

two or more previously independent firms united by a charter obtained especially for that purpose, thus excluding purchases, exchanges of stock, and holding companies. Yet even this sadly truncated list accounted for 8.4 per cent of all manufacturing employment in 1900. I doubt whether any such list, drawn up for any recent periods, would contain any occupants. Nothing like this wave of mergers has ever been seen again.

The last important wave of mergers was in 1924–29, hardly comparable to the earlier one, but still of substantial importance.[67] The Great De-

[65] J. Keith Butters, John Lintner, and William L. Cary, *Effects of Taxation: Corporate Mergers* (Boston, 1951), chap. x.

[66] *Twelfth Census of the United States, 1900*, Vol. VII, Part 1, pp. lxxv–xci. The number of combinations formed prior to 1897 was 65; to 1897, 7; to 1898, 20; to 1899, 79; to 1900 (through June), 13.

[67] Means, *op. cit.*, and Lintner and Butters, "The Effect of Mergers . . . ," *op. cit.*

pression promoted further concentration, but the recovery and the wartime boom apparently worked in the opposite direction.

After World War II there was another merger movement. The average annual number of mergers in 1946–47, as compiled by the Federal Trade Commission, was about one third as high as in 1929, and was exceeded by 10 out of the 13 years, 1919–31. Moreover, there were more firms in existence during the 1940's so that the rate of merger would need to be adjusted even further down. But of course the small *number* of mergers means very little. In the absence of data concerning the amount of assets absorbed, and by whom, it would not be proper to cite the low rate of mergers as proof that merger activity was not affecting concentration. The Commission, however, for reasons not explained in its report, interpreted the low rate of mergers as evidence that the mergers were actually "increasing concentration" and "strengthening the position of big business."[68] Its report concluded:

> . . . If nothing is done to check the growth in concentration either the giant corporations will ultimately take over the country, or the government will be impelled to step in and impose some form of direct regulation. . . . Crucial in that fight must be some effective means of preventing giant corporations from steadily increasing their power at the expense of small business. Therein lies the real significance of the proposed amendment to the Clayton Act, for without it the rise in economic concentration cannot be checked nor can the opportunity for a resurgence of effective competition be preserved.[69]

The painstaking work of Lintner and Butters has shown that the 1940–47 merger movement had little or no effect on concentration.[70] The reader would do well to consult their article, and the later book, but the main conclusions can be summarized here. (1) Mergers of giants with giants, so prominent in the earlier merger movements, were unknown. (2) For all manufacturing and mining companies, the smaller the companies, the more important were mergers as a source of growth. (3) Among the 1,000 largest manufacturing firms, the lower 500 (assets \$7 million to \$18 million) grew more proportionately by mergers than the upper half, i.e., there was some slight de-concentration through merger. (4) For the whole field of manufacturing and mining, the Gini coefficient (population assumed constant) increased through merger from .809 to .816, i.e., less than one per cent in eight years.[71]

So much for the negligible effects of mergers on the pattern of con-

---

[68] Federal Trade Commission, *The Merger Movement: A Summary Report* (Washington, 1948), p. 25. See also the *Report of the Federal Trade Commission on the Present Trend of Corporate Mergers and Acquisitions* (1947).

[69] FTC, *The Merger Movement: A Summary Report*, p. 28.

[70] Lintner and Butters, "The Effect of Mergers . . . ," *op. cit.*

[71] Messrs. Blair and Houghton replied to Lintner and Butters, *Review of Economics and Statistics*, XXXIII (1951), pp. 63–67. They conceded all but the second point, and their attempt to defend even this one led to fresh errors. See the rejoinder by Lintner and Butters, *ibid.*, pp. 67–71.

centration. But whatever these effects, they were swamped, and submerged by other forms of growth. A generous estimate is that not over $5 billion was involved in all manufacturing and mining mergers during 1940–47.[72] But during this period, according to a source which is biased downward, the total assets of all corporations in these fields increased from $67.8 billion to $118.6 billion;[73] the increase was over ten times the amount involved in mergers. As we saw earlier, no growth of concentration is visible either in 1931–47, or in 1939–47.

The statement of the Federal Trade Commission is in part a policy judgment, with whose wisdom we are not here concerned.[74] It is also a statement of fact, and as such it is doubly wrong: there has been no increase in concentration, and mergers have not been important enough to be of any effect, one way or the other.

VII

The most obvious conclusion is also the most depressing one: how little we know of our industrial structure and its evolution. At the beginning of this paper, we deliberately renounced all the more difficult problems of economic behavior and aimed only at description. Yet even the simplest problem could not be approached without all manner of approximations and expedients which quickly dissolved any hope of precision. Not only are the most important basic data not available; we have scarcely even begun to decide what questions we want answered.

Need for Further Research

Work is needed in three directions: (1) The meaning of concentration and the development of indices of the degree of concentration. Earlier we indicated one type of curve which could be developed for this purpose, but the surface has scarcely been scratched. (2) The historical development of concentration and de-concentration in specific industries. This should not only be of considerable intrinsic interest but should contribute to our better understanding of the techniques of measurement and the economic determinants of concentration. (3) Measurement of the place of the very largest corporations in the economy. Thanks to the National Bureau of Economic Research and its collaborators, we now have good estimates of manpower and of income originating, by broad industrial groups, back to at least 1870.[75] It should be possible to dig out

[72] Lintner and Butters, "The Effect of Mergers . . . ," *op. cit.*

[73] *Statistics of Income.* During 1935–41 inclusive, balance sheets were filed on an unconsolidated basis, resulting in duplication and overstatement of the total of assets. The 1947 data, however, are largely consolidated. Thus the increase from 1940 to 1947 is less than actually occurred.

[74] It would take the author too far afield to indicate why he favored the recent amendment to the Clayton Act: not because of but despite such arguments as those of the FTC.

[75] Simon Kuznets, *National Product Since 1869* (New York, 1946); *Studies in Income and Wealth,* Vol. II (New York, 1949).

the employment and the value added or income generated by the hundred or so largest corporations starting about 1900 or perhaps even earlier, and to prepare decade estimates. Some of the work of identifying the largest concerns during the earlier decades has already been done by the Brookings Institute. The number of firms for which data were available would, of course, increase irregularly through time, but this is just where a measure of the type of *c* discussed above, would be most useful, since it is independent of the number of firms.

Public Policy

This article may be summarized in three statements. (1) The American economy is highly concentrated. (2) Concentration is highly uneven. (3) The extent of concentration shows no tendency to grow, and it may possibly be declining. Any tendency either way, if it does exist, must be at the pace of a glacial drift.

What are the implications for public policy? Strictly speaking, none. No deployment of facts, no analysis of them, however correct, can ever yield an imperative for action until those facts have been compared with some kind of standard or norm of desirability. For example, we might reason as follows:

1. The American economy is highly concentrated.
2. (*a*) It *ought to be* much less concentrated.
   (*b*) It *ought to be* much more concentrated.
3. It gives few or no signs of becoming either more or less concentrated.
4. *Therefore,* measures should be taken to
   (*a*) promote de-concentration;
   (*b*) promote concentration.

Given the opposing premises in (2), the opposing conclusions flow with equal validity. Of course, statements of the type of (2) can themselves be decomposed further into statements of the relation between concentration and some kinds of desirable and undesirable behavior, such as the relation between concentration and monopoly, however defined. This would take us very far from our present subject. But clearly the results presented in this paper do not imply that public policy ought to be modified or, in particular, that antitrust policy should be changed. There is no escape from the pain of choice.

But although a given set of facts is compatible with more than one policy conclusion, this does not make it compatible with *any* conclusion, i.e., the facts are not simply irrelevant. Stated somewhat differently: our conclusions, if correct, should mean something for the atmosphere in which policy is formed. References to "the growth in economic concentration," or statements that "during the past 16 years [1932–48] big business has been getting bigger and little business littler," or that "the forces of concentration [are] growing stronger by the hour," or that "concentration of industry is increasing so fast that no half-measures can stop it," and many others of like tenor—these must now be dismissed as unfounded. Concentration may be a problem, but for better or worse it is not threatening to engulf the economy. The moral, therefore, is simply that there is time to stop, look, and take thought. This may detract from the color and excitement of our public life, but it may also contribute to better results.

Uses of Ideology

It is unfortunately the case that much of the discussion and research in the field of big business and concentration is marked by emotion, and the procedure is often to choose one's side and be stuck with its story. There may be political repercussions from a research study, and the research worker who is interested in these results may hear the devil quoting Shakespeare to his purpose:

> Get thee glass eyes,
> And, like a scurvy politician, seem
> To see the things thou dost not.

Nothing can be done about this; and nothing should be. That a man speaks with emotion, even prejudice, does not mean that he may not be speaking correctly. It is not who says it that counts but what he is saying. Nor is this all. The urge to convince others of the truth of one's "vision," as Joseph Schumpeter reminded the American Economic Association just a year before his death, "induces fact finding and analysis and these tend to destroy whatever will not stand their tests. . . . And so—though we proceed slowly because of our ideologies, we might not proceed at all without them."[76]

[76] Joseph A. Schumpeter, "Science and Ideology," *American Economic Review*, March, 1949, p. 359.

2

Economies of Scale, Concentration, and the Condition of Entry in Twenty Manufacturing Industries*

By JOE S. BAIN†

Ever since the merger movement of the late nineteenth century, American economists have been recurrently interested in the extent to which large size is necessary for business efficiency. Was the merger movement necessary; was the rule of reason economically justifiable; can this or that concentrated industry be atomized without loss of efficiency? These continue to be important questions to students of recent industrial history and contemporary antitrust policy. In the last three decades, with the notion that plant or firm size is related to efficiency formalized in long-run average-cost or scale curves, there has been much speculation and some inquiry concerning the shapes and positions of those scale curves in various industries and the placement of existing plants and firms on them.

To the economist qua economist, a knowledge for its own sake of the scale curves in particular industries is obviously unimportant. Only idle curiosity could justify his learning without further purpose how many barrels of cement a plant should produce to attain the lowest unit production cost, or how many passenger cars an automobile firm should make to minimize its production costs. But inferences which can be drawn from such knowledge may be important in several ways.

First, the proportion of the total output of its industry which a plant or a firm must supply in order to be reasonably efficient will determine the extent to which concentration in that industry is favored by the pursuit of minimized production costs. In any industry, the minimal scales of plant and of firm which are required for lowest production costs—*when these scales are expressed as percentages of the total scale or capacity of the industry* and are taken together with the shapes of the scale curves

* *The American Economic Review*, Vol. XLIV (1954), pp. 15–39. Reprinted by courtesy of the publisher and the author.

† University of California.

at smaller capacities—determine the degree of concentration by plants and firms needed for reasonable efficiency in the industry.

Second, the same relation of productive efficiency to the proportion of the market supplied by a plant or firm in any industry will have a profound effect on *potential competition*, or on the disposition of new firms to enter the industry. If a plant or firm needs to supply only a negligible fraction of industry output to be reasonably efficient, economies of scale provide no deterrent to entry other than those of absolute capital requirements. If, however, a plant or firm must add significantly to industry output in order to be efficient, and will be relatively inefficient if it adds little, entry at efficient scale would lower industry selling prices or induce unfavorable reactions by established firms, whereas entry at much smaller scales would give the entrant a significant cost disadvantage. In this situation established firms can probably raise prices some amount above the competitive level without attracting entry. In general, the "condition of entry"—measured by the extent to which established firms can raise price above a competitive level without inducing further entry—becomes "more difficult" as the ratio of the output of the optimal firm to industry output increases.[1]

Third, the amount of money required for investment in an efficient plant or firm—as determined by size—will affect the availability of the capital necessary for new entry. When the supplies of both equity and loan capital in the range needed for a unit investment are either absolutely limited or positively related to the interest rate, the number of dollars required to establish an efficient plant or firm will clearly affect the condition of entry to an industry.[2]

Finally, a comparison of the scales of existing plants and firms in any industry with the most efficient scales will indicate whether plants and firms are of efficient size, or whether or not the existing pattern of concentration is consistent with reasonable efficiency. Have plant and firm concentration proceeded too far, farther than necessary, just far enough, or not far enough—from the standpoint of productive efficiency? A knowledge of scale curves is prerequisite to an answer.

Although information on the relation of efficiency to scale thus has some importance, relatively little has been done to develop this knowledge through empirical research; economists have relied mainly upon *a priori* speculations and qualitative generalizations of the broadest sort. A popular American view is that economies of large-scale plant do exist—and that the efficiency of plants as large as are built may be conceded—

[1] See J. S. Bain, "Conditions of Entry and the Emergence of Monopoly," *Monopoly and Competition and Their Regulation*, E. H. Chamberlin, ed. (London, 1954), for a development of this theory.

[2] But the absolute capital requirement for efficiency need not, as we move from one industry to another, be systematically related to the proportion of industry output needed for efficiency.

but that further economies of large multiplant firms do not exist, or if they do, are strictly pecuniary in character and hence not to be sought or justified as a matter of social policy.[3] At the extreme it is argued that increasing the size of the firm beyond that of an efficient plant does not normally lower costs at all, so that the scale curve is approximately horizontal for some distance beyond this point. The dominant British view, expressed by such writers as Steindl, Florence, and E. A. G. Robinson, gives more credence to the alleged economies of large-scale firms. Both schools rely upon qualitative and substantially untested generalizations about productive and commercial techniques which supposedly determine the response of production costs to variations in the scale of plant or firm. Yet in spite of the extremely sketchy nature of this sort of knowledge, it is common to presume, for instance, that there are numerous examples of each of two sorts of oligopolistic industries—those where scale economies encourage a high concentration, and those where such economies do not but something else does.[4]

Direct empirical investigation has not added much to our knowledge of scale curves. The principal studies employing accounting cost data are found in TNEC Monograph No. 13, and in later work by J. M. Blair,[5] of the Federal Trade Commission. Unfortunately the industries studied have been so few, the periods of time reviewed so remote and brief, and the use and interpretation of the statistical data in most instances so open to question that no reliable generalization regarding scale curves can be drawn from this body of material. There is more available in the way of profit-rate data for firms of various sizes, but here the unsupported assumptions which are normally necessary to argue from higher profits to lower costs are so numerous as to vitiate any attempt to infer scale curves from profit rates. Somewhat more satisfactory information has been developed, for a very few industries only, through "engineering" estimates of the scale curve for plant or firm. But in general our information is such that we are ill-prepared to say much about actual scale curves and their implications.

I. SCOPE OF THE PRESENT STUDY

In the course of a recent general study of condition of entry to American manufacturing industries,[6] it has been possible to develop some fur-

[3] See, *e.g.*, TNEC Monograph No. 13, *Relative Efficiency of Large, Medium-sized, and Small Business*, pp. 95–139.

It may be noted that the income-distribution effects of strictly pecuniary economies may not be inconsequential in many settings.

[4] See, *e.g.*, Fellner's "Case 1-a," "Case 1-b," and "Case 2" oligopolies, in his *Competition Among the Few* (New York, 1949), pp. 44 ff.

[5] See *e.g.*, "Technology and Size," *American Economic Review Proceedings*, Vol. XXXVIII (May, 1948), pp. 121–52, and "Relation between Size and Efficiency in Business," *Review of Economics and Statistics*, Vol. XXIV (Aug., 1942), pp. 125–35.

[6] I wish to acknowledge the generous assistance provided for this study since 1951 by the Merrill Foundation for the Advancement of Financial Knowledge,

ther data on economies of scale therein. The portion of this information presented here concerns, for each of twenty selected manufacturing industries: (1) the relationship of the output capacity of a plant of lowest-cost size to the output capacity of the industry, together with the shape of the plant scale curve at smaller sizes; (2) the relationship of the capacity of a firm of lowest-cost size to industry capacity, and the firm scale curve at smaller capacities; and (3) the absolute amount of money capital required to establish an optimal plant and an optimal firm as of the current decade.

These data have been developed almost entirely from managerial or "engineering" estimates supplied by certain firms in the industries involved; precisely, they reflect estimates of scale economies and capital requirements which were prepared, in response to detailed prearranged questioning, either by or at the direction of high-level executives in these firms. The general procedure for securing such data included: (1) a lengthy preliminary survey of each of the twenty industries, based on available monographs, documents, and other published and unpublished secondary materials; (2) the subsequent preparation for each industry of a separate, special, and rather lengthy series of questions designed to elicit certain information having bearing on the condition of entry; (3) securing, after explaining the project involved and assuring confidentiality of replies, an advance offer of cooperation in answering these questions from executives in a large number of firms; (4) actual submission of the questions, followed (except in those cases where cooperation was subsequently withdrawn) by obtaining answers, in writing or orally or both. The method used thus involved neither shot-gun dissemination of an all-purpose questionnaire nor postprandial armchair quizzes, but rather a more or less hand-tooled questionnaire procedure in the case of each of twenty industries.

The questions submitted relative to scale economies in each industry were designed in general to elicit information concerning the minimal plant size requisite for lowest unit costs and the shape of the plant scale curve at smaller sizes, the same information for the firm, and the capital required to establish a plant and a firm of most efficient size. Direct and (with exceptions to be noted below) explicit answers to these questions were normally secured. In many cases, there was abundant evidence in the length and documentation of replies of a careful estimating procedure; in some, figures submitted were frankly characterized as unsubstantiated armchair guesses, though in most of these the respondents were very well qualified to guess. By and large, the writer is inclined to feel,

through a grant made to the Research Group on the Monopoly Problem at Harvard University, directed by Dean E. S. Mason. Acknowledgment is also due for the assistance in preceding years of the Bureau of Business and Economic Research, University of California, Berkeley, where essential initial background studies were undertaken.

on the basis of checks against other sources and of comparisons of different and independent replies to the same questions, that this is generally a fairly reliable body of data, in which the bulk of individual industry estimates are likely to be fairly accurate. The data have the advantage, so far as they are reliable, of reflecting "engineering" estimates in the sense that they represent expert *ex ante* predictions of the net relations of cost to scale, rather than an *ex post* comparison of gross cost results at different achieved outputs. Thus they refer in general directly to scale curves as understood in economic theory.[7]

The twenty manufacturing industries studied may be designated as those producing cigarettes, soap, distilled liquor, shoes, canned fruits and vegetables, meat products, passenger automobiles, fountain pens, typewriters, flour, rubber tires and tubes, refined petroleum products, farm machinery, tractors,[8] steel, copper, cement, gypsum products, rayon, and metal containers. The sample was obviously not drawn at random. It was selected to obtain a maximum possible diversity of industry types consistent with the availability of data, but the fact that data have been more frequently developed for large and for highly concentrated industries than for others has resulted in some systematic differences between the sample and the whole population of manufacturing industries.

The following characteristics of the sample deserve brief note: First, it features large industries, with fifteen of the twenty having value products above a half billion in 1947. Whereas it includes only a little over 4 per cent of the total number (452) of manufacturing industries in 1947, it accounts for about 20 per cent of the value product of all manufacture in 1947.[9] Second, it contains a substantially larger proportion of moderately and highly concentrated manufacturing industries than the total population. Nine industries of the sample had 75 per cent or more of value product controlled by four firms, three had 50 to 75 per cent so controlled, eight had from 25 to 50 per cent, and none less than 25 per

[7] The general time reference of all estimates is the period 1950 to 1952. From two to five such estimates were received in each of the twenty industries in question. Other sources of data which were available for some industries—such as comparisons of accounting costs or the personal estimates of authors of industry studies —have been deliberately neglected here in order to give a more uniform consistency to the data presented. The only other data presented here, and these largely for expository purposes, are plant and firm concentration data prepared from the *1947 Census of Manufactures*. Since the engineering estimates which supply the bulk of our data were generally secured under guarantees of secrecy as to source, no acknowledgments or references to source can be supplied.

[8] For present purposes only we follow the Census in the dubious experiment of segregating tractors from other farm machinery.

[9] The total population of industries described, as well as all data on value products and on concentration by firms, is derived (except as otherwise noted) from the *1947 Census of Manufactures*, and in particular from a special analysis of concentration prepared from this Census and published as an appendix in *Hearings, Subcommittee on Study of Monopoly Power, Committee on Judiciary, H. R., 81st Cong., Serial 14, Part 2-B.*

cent controlled by four firms.[10] In the total population of manufacturing industries, the corresponding numbers in the four concentration classes were 47, 103, 164, and 138. This bias must be recognized in interpreting findings.

Otherwise, the sample is fairly representative. Eight industries are classed as making consumer goods, eight producer goods, and four goods bought by both producer and consumers. The outputs of eight are nondurable in use, whereas twelve are durable or semidurable. As to type of technique or process, five industries may be classified as engaged in processing farm products and four minerals, three as chemical industries, five as manufacturing or assembling mechanical devices, and three as in miscellaneous fabrication.[11]

II. OPTIMAL PLANT SIZE AND PLANT CONCENTRATION

Our first question concerns the shape and position of the plant scale curve (relating unit costs of production to the size of the individual factory or plant) in each of the twenty industries, and the apparent consequences of economies of large plants for entry and for seller concentration. We are interested initially in the scale curve reflecting the relation of production cost to the output or capacity of the plant *when the latter are expressed as percentages of the total output or rated capacity supplying the market to be supplied by the plant.* When output or capacity is expressed in these percentage terms, what is the lowest-cost or "optimal" size of plant and what is the shape of the plant scale curve at smaller sizes?

An initial clue to the potential importance of economies of large plants is supplied by certain data on plant size assembled in the 1947 *Census of Manufactures.* This Census shows for each of many industries the number of plants in each of several size-classes (size being measured by number of employees), and also the proportion of Census industry employment and of total industry "value added" accounted for by each size-class of plants. From these data[12] certain inferences can be drawn about the sizes of existing plants. For exploratory purposes here I have tried to

---

[10] In three of the twenty cases, value added rather than value product figures were used by the Census in calculating concentration. For automobiles, registration rather than Census figures are followed in describing concentration, in both the sample and the total population, because of deficiencies in Census data.

[11] One further characteristic of the sample may be noted—Census industries have been selected which correspond fairly well to "theoretical" industries, or for which industry concentration as computed tends to reflect closely the relevant theoretical concentration of corresponding or component theoretical industries. This matter is discussed at length in J. S. Bain, "Relation of Profit Rate to Industry Concentration," *Quarterly Journal of Economics*, Vol. LXV (August, 1951), pp. 297–304.

[12] The data were previously used by the Federal Trade Commission for its study *The Divergence between Plant and Company Concentration, 1947.* The staff of the Commission has kindly made available its tabulated calculations on plant concentration as based on the Census data.

develop from them some upper-limit estimates of the plant sizes requisite for greatest efficiency in the sample industries, by computing first the average size of plants in the largest size-class in each industry (expressed here as the percentage supplied per plant of the total value added of the Census industry), and second the maximum possible average size (similarly expressed) of the largest four plants in the industry.[13] If we neglect such obvious limitations as those of using value-added data, these estimates may be considered maximum percentages of the national industry outputs requisite for efficiency, on the grounds that in nearly every case we refer to the average size of a few of the largest plants actually built, and that the firms operating them were not restricted from building them to optimal scale. That is, they are generally multiplant firms which could bring a single plant to optimal scale before adding another, if indeed they did not in some cases duplicate optimal technical units on a single location.

The results of these estimating procedures are as follows: Eighteen industries were examined (automobiles and copper being eliminated because of gross deficiencies in Census data); for the eighteen the number of plants in the largest size-class lay between 3 and 15 in all but three cases; in those three it was large enough to make our estimates quite hazardous. The average share of Census industry value added supplied by plants in the largest size-class ranged from 20.1 per cent (typewriters) to 0.7 per cent (shoes), with a median at 3.8 per cent. The maximum possible average share of the largest four plants ranged from 19.1 per cent (cigarettes) to 1.7 per cent (shoes), with a median at 7.9 per cent.

The character of the data is more fully revealed in the frequency distributions in Table 1. The first frequency column therein (f_1) classifies industries according to the market-share interval within which the average size of plants in the largest size-class of plants falls, market share being measured by the percentage of the Census industry value-added supplied by a plant. The second frequency column (f_2) shows the same information when the plant size referred to in each industry is the maximum possible average market share of the largest four plants.

These findings, showing that in from seven to twelve of the 18 Census industries (depending on the method of estimate) the value added of the largest plants amounted to over 5 per cent apiece of total industry value added and that in from two to seven cases the figure was over 10 per cent apiece, suggest an importance for economies of large-scale plant which is substantial in some of these industries and small in others. But a detailed interpretation of the findings is not justified for several reasons. First, value added in a single year is a rather unsatisfactory measure of

[13] The latter figure is derived in general by attributing to all but the first four plants in the largest size class the minimum possible market share (*i.e.*, for each the mean share of plants in the second size class) and by dividing the remainder of the total market share in the largest size class among the first four plants.

"scale" as that term is ordinarily understood. Second, the largest plants as identified by the Census may have resulted from building multiples of optimal technical units on single locations, and if so, the figures presented may overestimate optimal scales. Third, the data in question express the output of the plant as a percentage of the total national value added within the Census industry, whereas in fact the theoretical industry or separate market which a plant supplies may be somewhat smaller.[14] In these cases—where a Census industry is in fact made up of several

TABLE 1

CLASSIFICATION OF EIGHTEEN CENSUS INDUSTRIES ACCORDING TO PERCENTAGES OF INDUSTRY VALUES-ADDED SUPPLIED BY THE LARGEST PLANTS, 1947[a]

PERCENTAGE OF CENSUS INDUSTRY VALUE ADDED SUPPLIED BY THE AVERAGE OF THE LARGEST PLANTS	NUMBER OF INDUSTRIES WITH THE LARGEST PLANT SIZE IN THE SPECIFIED PERCENTAGE INTERVAL	
	When "Largest Plant Size" Refers to Average Size of Plants in Largest Size Class of Plants (f_1)	When "Largest Plant Size" Refers to the Maximum Possible Average Size of the Largest 4 Plants in Industry (f_2)
0– 2.4	6	2
2.5– 4.9	5	4
5.0– 7.4	2	3
7.5– 9.9	3	2
10.0–14.9	1	3
15.0–24.9[b]	1	4
Total	18	18

[a] From *1947 Census of Manufactures*. The composition of sample is described in the text.
[b] The highest value in this class was 20.1 per cent.

theoretical industries corresponding to distinct regional markets or product lines—the "percentage-of-industry-output" derived from Census data for large plants is very likely to be below the theoretically relevant figure,[15] and revisions are in order. We thus turn at once to direct engineering estimates of optimal plant sizes.

Table 2 reviews the engineering estimates of the optimal scales of plants for twenty industry groups. In each case, the plant size referred to is the minimal physical production capacity of plant required for lowest production costs, this capacity being expressed as a percentage of total national capacity within the Census industry. In each case also the costs referred to are total production costs, including costs of outshipment where the latter are strategic to the determination of optimal plant scale.

Table 3 summarizes the data of Table 2 by classifying industries ac-

[14] It may also conceivably be larger, as in the case where imports are omitted from Census data or where the Census industry is too narrowly defined, but these contingencies are not realized in any important degree in this sample.

[15] It will be if the plant specializes as to area or product line.

cording to the market-share interval in which the mean estimated size of an optimal plant falls, when size is measured as a percentage of the national industry capacity. These "engineering" data seem generally more satisfactory than those previously developed from Census figures. They reflect rational calculations rather than historical happenstance, and designed plant capacities rather than transient additions to value of output,

TABLE 2

PROPORTIONS OF NATIONAL INDUSTRY CAPACITY CONTAINED IN SINGLE PLANTS OF MOST EFFICIENT SCALE, FOR 20 INDUSTRIES, PER ENGINEERING ESTIMATES CIRCA 1951

Industry	Percentage of National Industry Capacity Contained in One Plant of Minimal Efficient Scale	Industry	Percentage of National Industry Capacity Contained in One Plant of Minimal Efficient Scale
Flour milling	1/10 to 1/2	Rubber tires and tubes[g]	3
Shoes[a]	1/7 to 1/2	Rayon[h]	4 to 6
Canned fruits and vegetables	1/4 to 1/2	Soap[i]	4 to 6
Cement	4/5 to 1	Farm machines, ex tractors[j]	4 to 6
Distilled liquors[b]	1 1/4 to 1 3/4	Cigarettes	5 to 6
Petroleum refining[c]	1 3/4	Automobiles[k]	5 to 10
Steel[d]	1 to 2 1/2	Fountain pens[l]	5 to 10
Metal containers	1/2 to 3	Copper[m]	10
Meat packing:[e]		Tractors	10 to 15
Fresh	1/50 to 1/5		
Diversified	2 to 2 1/2		
Gypsum products[f]	2 1/2 to 3	Typewriters	10 to 30

[a] Refers to shoes other than rubber.
[b] Capacity refers to total excluding brandy. Costs refer explicitly to 4-year whiskey, packaged but ex tax.
[c] Optimal balanced integration of successive processes assumed. Outshipment largely by water assumed; optimal scale may be smaller with scattered market and land shipment.
[d] Refers to fully integrated operation producing flat rolled products.
[e] Percentages are of total nonfarm slaughter; diversified operation includes curing, processing, etc.
[f] Combined plasterboard and plaster production assumed.
[g] Purchase of materials at a constant price assumed; production of a wide variety of sizes assumed.
[h] Refers to plant producing both yarn and fiber.
[i] Includes household detergents.
[j] Refers primarily to complex farm machines.
[k] Plant includes integrated facilities for production of components as economical. Final assembly alone—1 to 3 per cent.
[l] Includes conventional pens and ballpoints.
[m] Assumes electrolytic refining.

although they still reflect percentages of the national capacities of Census industries.

It appears from them that in nine of the twenty industries an optimal plant would account for a quite small fraction of national capacity (under 2½ per cent), whereas in five others the fraction would run above 7½ per cent. In general, the industries with slight economies of scale of plant are engaged in processing of agricultural or mineral materials, whereas greater plant economies are frequently encountered in industries making mechanical devices. The engineering estimates of the importance of economies of large plant present an over-all picture for these industries not greatly different from that derived by calculating average plant sizes in the largest plant-size intervals (column f_1 of Table 1), but they clearly ascribe less importance to such economies than the estimates of the maximum possible average sizes of the largest four plants in each of these industries (column f_2 of Table 1).

Before we interpret these findings, however, two further matters must be discussed: the shapes of the plant scale curves at capacities short of the estimated optima, and the revisions in the estimates of optima which are needed if the division of Census industries into separate regions or product lines is recognized.

As to the shapes of plant cost curves at capacities short of the estimated optima, relatively fragmentary information has been received. In four industries the plant scale curve appears to be horizontal back to the smallest size considered, or ¼ per cent of national industry output; these are flour, shoes, canned fruits and vegetables, and "fresh" meat packing. In ten cases—steel, metal containers, diversified meat packing, gypsum products, farm machinery, automobiles, fountain pens, copper, tractors, and typewriters—quantitative estimates of the shapes of the plant cost curves are not available, although in some cases (*e.g.*, diversified meat packing and metal containers) it is suggested that substantially smaller than optimal plants would entail only slightly higher costs, whereas in some others (*e.g.*, typewriters, automobiles, and tractors) a distinct rise in costs is suggested at half the optimal plant scale. For the seven remaining industries, the estimated relation of production cost to plant scale is shown in Table 4, where costs of 100 represent the lowest attainable costs.

TABLE 3

Classification of Twenty Industries According to Percentages of National Industry Capacities Contained in Single Plants of Most Efficient Scale (from Table 2)

Percentage of National Industry Capacity Contained in a Plant of Optimal Scale	Number of Industries with Optimal Scale Plant (Per Mean Estimate) in the Specified Percentage Interval (f_3)
0– 2.4	9
2.5– 4.9	2
5.0– 7.4	4
7.5– 9.9	2
10.0–14.9	2
15.0–24.9	1
Total	20

A mixed picture again emerges. In some cases (liquor and cigarettes, for example) the rise of production costs at suboptimal scales is evidently quite small; in others (soap, petroleum refining, tires and tubes) it is moderate but by no means negligible; in some—*e.g.*, rayon and cement—the rise is great.[16] One might hazard the guess that in from a half to two-thirds of all the industries sampled the upturn of the plant scale curve at suboptimal scales is such as to discourage very much smaller operations unless there are forces counterbalancing production cost disadvantages. In the other one-third to a half of cases, a wide variety of plant sizes might prosper indefinitely in only slightly imperfect markets.

The findings of Tables 2 and 3 however—reflecting as they do the percentages of national Census industry capacities supplied by single plants—can hardly be taken at face value so long as the suspicion remains that many Census industries may be broken into several separate and largely noncompeting regional or product submarkets and that a plant may specialize in only one such submarket. In these cases the relevant

TABLE 4

RELATION OF PRODUCTION COST TO PLANT SCALE IN SEVEN INDUSTRIES

	Percentages of National Industry Capacity in One Plant					
	5%	2½%	1%	½%	¼%	
Cement	100	100	100	115	130	Relative costs of production
Distilled liquor	100	100	100.5	101	102	
Petroleum refining	100	100	102	104	107	
Tires and tubes	100	100.3	103	104	105.5	
Rayon	100	107	125	Very high		
Soap	100	103	105	Above 105		
Cigarettes	100	101	102	Above 102		

measure of plant size must be the proportion of the capacity supplying a submarket which is provided by an optimal plant, and this proportion will be larger than the proportion of national capacity provided by the same plant.

In eleven of the twenty cases listed in Table 2, a revision of plant-size figures is in order because of the apparent division of the national market into distinct submarkets, coupled with plant specialization among them. In seven of these cases—flour, cement, petroleum refining, steel, metal containers, meat packing, and gypsum products—the important segmentation of markets is geographical in character; national markets are broken into regions, and a single plant will mainly supply only one region. In the other four cases—shoes, canned fruits and vegetables, automobiles, and fountain pens—markets are divided to a significant extent among distinct product lines. In all cases, the relevant measure of plant size is

[16] It will be noted that the industries with the highest degrees of plant concentration are generally those on which it has been most difficult to secure quantitative estimates of the shape of the scale curve. In general, our information on plant scales seems sketchier and perhaps less reliable at this end of the sample.

the percentage it may account for of the total capacity supplying any submarket it may supply.

The industries in which market segmentation is important are predominantly those for which the percentages of national industry capacities represented by single plants are quite small. The data for nine of the first ten industries in Table 2 require revision because of market segmentation, and only two for which revision is required lie in the range of high plant concentration nationally. Where technology does not give some importance to plant economies in industries of our sample, geography and product specialization (by plants) apparently do. Correspondingly, revised plant-size data showing percentages of individual submarket capacities will differ markedly from those in Tables 2 and 3.

To make the revision mentioned, the optimal plant capacity for each of the eleven industries involved has been restated first as a percentage of the capacity supplying the largest submarket identified, and second as a percentage of capacity supplying the smallest of the major submarkets identified. For example, four major regional markets were identified in the petroleum refining industry. The proportion of national capacity supplied by a single optimal refinery had been estimated at 1¾ per cent (Table 2); the corresponding percentages for the largest and smallest of the four major regional markets were 3⅓ per cent and 11½ per cent. In the fountain pen industry the proportion of aggregate national capacity supplied by an optimal plant was estimated at from 5 to 10 per cent. Dividing the market into high-price or gift pens and low-price pens including ballpoints (and recognizing differences in techniques for producing the two lines) the corresponding percentages become 25 to 33⅓ per cent and 10 to 12½ per cent.

When these revisions have been made for the eleven industries, and the results combined with the unrevised data for the remaining nine, we are prepared to present two frequency distributions parallel to that in Table 3 above. They classify industries according to the percentage of market capacity provided by an optimal plant, in the first case (column f_4 of Table 5) when the capacities of optimal plants in the eleven revised industries are expressed as percentages of the total capacities supplying the largest submarkets in their industries, and in the second (column f_5) when optimal capacities in the eleven industries are expressed as percentages of the total capacities supplying the smallest major submarkets identified. The last column in Table 5 repeats column f_3 from Table 3 for purposes of comparison.

Subjective judgments have inescapably influenced the content of columns f_4 and f_5, particularly in the identification of regions, the decision as to what is a "major" region or product line, and the decision as to whether market segmentation is significant, but we have tried to follow available information and industry practice systematically. If there is a bias, it is in the direction of defining areas and product lines quite broadly, of considering only a few dominant areas for analysis, and of recognizing segmentation only if there is strong evidence supporting the recognition.

Interpreting Table 5 with appropriate reference to the earlier discussion of the shapes of plant scale curves, we may emphasize the following conclusions about the importance of economies of large-scale plants within the industries of our sample. First, if the reference is to the largest submarkets of industries with segmented markets (plus the national markets of those with unsegmented markets), then in nine of the twenty cases an optimal plant would supply less than 5 per cent of its market,

TABLE 5

CLASSIFICATION OF TWENTY INDUSTRIES[a] BY PERCENTAGES OF INDIVIDUAL MARKET CAPACITIES CONTAINED IN A SINGLE PLANT OF MOST EFFICIENT SCALE

Percentage of Individual Market Capacity Contained in a Plant of Optimal Scale	Number of Industries with Optimal Plant Scale in the Specified Percentage Interval		
	Where Percentage Is That of the Total Capacity Supplying the Largest Recognized Submarket (f_4)	Where Percentage Is That of the Total Capacity Supplying the Smallest Recognized Submarket (f_5)	Where Percentage Is That of the Total Capacity Supplying the National Market (f_3 from Table 3)
0– 2.4	4	2	9
2.5– 4.9	5	2	2
5.0– 7.4	5	4	4
7.5– 9.9	0	1	2
10.0–14.9	5	3	2
15.0–19.9	0	2	0
20.0–24.9	1	2	1
25.0–29.9	0	2	0
30.0–34.9	0	1	0
35.0–40.0	0	1	0
Total	20	20	20

[a] The meat packing industry is considered for purposes of this table as only involving so-called *fresh* meat packing.

and in five additional cases less than 7½ per cent. If this is true and if, further, the plant-scale curve is usually fairly flat for a moderate range of suboptimal scales, then in many of these fourteen cases the scale requirements for an optimal plant should not provide a serious deterrent to entry. A firm constructing one reasonably efficient plant should not ordinarily induce serious repercussions from established firms in its market.

On the other hand in six cases—gypsum products, automobiles, typewriters, fountain pens, tractors, and copper—the proportion of the total capacity supplying either the national market or the largest submarket which is provided by a single optimal plant runs from 10 to 25 per cent. Precise data are largely lacking on the shapes of scale curves in these industries, but if they are much inclined upward at suboptimal scales (as is suggested qualitatively in several cases) then the economies of large plant should provide a very significant deterrent to entry to the markets in question. Further, a substantial degree of oligopolistic concentration by firms might easily be justified by the pursuit of plant economies alone. The substantial diversity of situations among industries of moderate to high concentration deserves considerable emphasis.

The picture changes markedly if our attention shifts in the case of the eleven segmented industries from the largest to the smallest major submarkets. Now we find that in eleven of the twenty cases (rather than six) the proportion of the relevant market capacity supplied by an optimal plant exceeds 10 per cent, and in six cases it exceeds 20 per cent. Plant economies sufficient to impede entry very seriously are potentially present in half or more of the cases, and high plant and firm concentration is encouraged by technology. The importance of plant economies thus potentially bulks large indeed in the smaller regional submarkets and the smaller product lines, whereas it is evidently less in the major submarkets and frequently so in the industries with relatively unsegmented national markets.

III. OPTIMAL FIRM SIZE AND FIRM CONCENTRATION

The extent to which further economies of large scale are realized if firms grow beyond the size of a single optimal plant has been a subject of controversy among economists. If a distinction is drawn between "production cost" and other advantages of scale—so that sales promotion, price-raising, and similar advantages of big firms are properly distinguished from cost-savings in production and distribution—there is no general agreement among economists as to whether or to what extent the multiplant firm is more economical.[17] It thus may come as no surprise that business executives questioned on the same matter with regard to our sample of industries evidenced a similar diversity of mind. Very distinct differences of opinion relative to the existence or importance of economies of multiplant firms were frequently encountered in the same industry, and in a pattern not satisfactorily explicable in general by the hypothesis that the individual would claim maximum economies for his own size of firm. Any findings presented here on estimates of economies of large-scale firm should thus be viewed as extremely tentative.

Whatever the ostensible importance of economies of the multiplant firm, exploitation of them will not *necessarily* require the multiplant firm to control a larger proportion of any submarket than is needed for one optimal plant. In those instances where national markets are segmented regionally or by product lines, the multiplant firm *may* realize its econ-

[17] This disagreement is, as noted above, complicated further by difference of opinion as to whether the disputed economies are real or strictly pecuniary in character.

omies while operating only one plant in each submarket. Then concentration by firms in individual submarkets is not further encouraged and entry is not further impeded[18] by economies of the multiplant firm. An optimal cement plant may supply about 1 per cent of national capacity, or percentages of regional capacity ranging very roughly from 5 to 30 per cent in eleven regional submarkets. The fact that a multiplant cement firm could secure lower costs than a single-plant firm by operating one optimal plant in each of the eleven regions—thus accounting for 11 per cent of national capacity—would not imply that it need have a higher proportion of capacity in any one region than a single-plant firm of optimal size. Except for an increase in absolute capital requirements, the assumed economies of the multiplant firm would not encourage regional market concentration or impede entry.

Suppose on the other hand that there are economies of multiplant firms which are to be realized through operating two or more optimal-size plants either in a single submarket or in a single unsegmented national market. This will evidently encourage a concentration by firms in the relevant submarket or national market greater than that encouraged by plant economies alone, and will further impede entry. If a single plant of most efficient size would supply 5 per cent of the relatively unsegmented national cigarette market, whereas a single firm operating three such plants could lower costs of production and distribution perceptibly, economies of the multiplant firm would favor greater effective concentration and provide further deterrents to entry to the cigarette industry.

Findings relative to the economies of multiplant firms, together with certain related data, are presented in Table 6. The second column therein repeats the estimates of percentages of national Census industry capacities required for optimal plants, from Table 2. The third column indicates the estimated extent of economies of multiplant firms (*i.e.*, firms of sizes beyond those of single optimal plants), costs of distribution but not of sales promotion being included. The fourth column indicates the percentages of national industry capacities required for firms with lowest production plus distribution costs, while the final column shows the average percentage per firm of the national market supplied by the first four firms in 1947. The last provides a measure of actual concentration by firms. The estimates in question are entirely those of executives queried in connection with the investigation underlying this study.

The data presented in Table 6 shed light on two questions: (1) to what extent do the economies of the multiplant firm tend to enhance concentration and impede entry, and (2) to what extent is the existing concentration by firms greater than required for exploitation of economies of large plants and of large firms?

Concerning the first question a varied picture appears. In eight indus-

[18] Except for the increase of absolute capital requirements.

tries (Group 2 in Table 6) no definite estimate could be obtained of the extent, if any, of economies of the multiplant firm. This is in spite of the fact that in most of these industries the degree of concentration by firms substantially exceeds that requisite for exploitation of estimated economies of the large plant. In six industries (Group 1 in Table 6) it was

TABLE 6

THE EXTENT OF ESTIMATED ECONOMIES OF MULTIPLANT FIRMS IN 20 MANUFACTURING INDUSTRIES

Industry	Percentage of National Industry Capacity Contained in One Optimal Plant	Estimated Extent of Multiplant Economies (As a Percentage of Total Cost)	Percentage of National Industry Capacity Contained in One Optimal Firm	Average Percentage Share of the National Market of First 4 Firms in 1947[a]
Group 1:				
Canned fruits and vegetables	¼ to ½	None	—	6.6
Petroleum refining	1¾	None	—	9.3
Meat packing:[b]				
Fresh	⅒ to ⅕	None	—	—
Diversified	2 to 2½	None	—	10.3[c]
Fountain pens	5 to 10	None	—	14.4
Copper	10	None	—	23.1[d]
Typewriters	10 to 30	None	—	19.9
Group 2:				
Flour	⅒ to ½	No estimate	—	7.3
Distilled liquor	1¼ to 1¾	No estimate	—	18.7
Metal containers	½ to 3	No estimate	—	19.5
Tires and tubes	3	No estimate	—	19.2
Rayon	4 to 6	No estimate	—	19.6
Farm machines, ex tractors	4 to 6	No estimate	—	9.0
Automobiles	5 to 10	No estimate	—	22.5[e]
Tractors	10 to 15	No estimate	—	16.8
Group 3:				
Shoes	⅐ to ½	Small, or 2 to 4	½ to 2½	7.0
Cement	⅘ to 1	Small, or 2 to 3	2 to 10	7.4
Steel	1 to 2½	2 to 5	2 to 20	11.2[c]
Gypsum products	2½ to 3	Small	27 to 33	21.2
Soap	4 to 6	½ to 1	8 to 15	19.8
Cigarettes	5 to 6	Slight	15 to 20	22.6

[a] Market shares are average percentages of 1947 national values of shipments unless otherwise indicated.
[b] Plant percentages refer to total of nonfarm slaughter, firm percentages to wholesale fresh meat packing only.
[c] Expresses average percentage of total value added rather than value of shipments.
[d] Expresses average percentage of electrolytic plus other national copper refining capacity, 1947.
[e] Expresses approximate average percentage of total 1951 passenger car registrations.

the consensus that economies of the scale of firm beyond the size of a single optimal plant were either negligible or totally absent. In these cases estimated cost savings of the multiplant firm cannot justify concentration beyond that required by plant economies alone (either in submarkets or in unsegmented national markets) nor can they make entry any more difficult than it is already made by plant economies. With respect to the first four industries in the group, a multiplant firm with plants in several regions or product lines would, according to the estimates received, realize no net cost savings by virtue of this aspect of its organization. In the second three industries in this group, however, economies of the large plant alone are sufficient to support a high degree of concentration by firms and to impede entry.

In the remaining six industries (Group 3 in Table 6) perceptible economies were attributed to the multiplant firm. The extent of these economies is in no case huge, being characterized as slight or small in three cases and as in the two to five per cent range in the remaining three. Nevertheless, two or three percentage points on total cost can be significant in any industry if the ratio of operating profits to sales is not beyond five or ten per cent and if product differentiation and other market imperfections are not dominant. What further tendency toward concentration and what further impediment to entry would the existence of these economies imply?

The optimal multiplant firm as estimated in Group 3 of Table 6 includes two or three optimal plants in the soap industry, three or four in the cigarette industry, four or five in the shoe industry, and about ten in the gypsum products industry. Estimates for the steel and cement industries run all the way from one or two to ten plants per optimal firm, and the range of disagreement among authorities is wide. Applying these estimates, the proportion of national industry capacity needed for best efficiency in a multiplant firm is raised; but is the proportion of the capacity supplying any particular regional or product submarket also raised? It will not be if the efficient multiplant firm includes only one optimal plant per submarket, and it will be if it includes two or more per submarket or if the national market is unsegmented.

In Group 3 in Table 6 no more than one optimal plant per region is attributed to the optimal firm in cement or in steel, and the proportion of any regional market which need be supplied for efficiency is thus not increased by the incidence of economies of the multiplant firms. In the remaining four cases the conclusion is different. Soap and cigarettes have relatively unsegmented national markets, and the proportion of the market required for best efficiency is doubled, trebled, or quadrupled by the emergence of economies of the multiplant firm. In shoes the assumed specialization to a single product line of the four or five plants needed for efficiency raises the requisite firm concentration by product lines by corresponding multiples. In the gypsum industry it was evidently assumed that an optimal firm would operate several plants in each of one or more major regions. In all of the last four cases, therefore, economies of the multiplant firm encourage greater effective concentration by firms and impede entry. But in these cases (possibly excepting shoes) the economies of the large firm were characterized as slight, so that the effects just listed may be weak.

With respect to the effect of the economies of multiplant firms on concentration and on entry, these conclusions appear. In eight of twenty industries in our sample, no estimate was obtained of the extent of these economies. In two-thirds of the remaining cases, economies of the multiplant firm were held either to be absent, or to take such a form that exploitation of them would not require higher proportions of market control by the firm in any submarket. In one-third of the remaining cases, some encouragement to higher concentration by firms in submarkets was provided, but it was a small encouragement in view of the generally slight economies attributed to the large firm. Economies of the large-scale firm apparently do not represent a major force encouraging concentration or deterring entry in this sample of industries. The data on which this guess rests, however, are far from adequate.

Our second question concerns the extent to which the existing degree of concentration by firms within industries is justified by the estimated economies of large plants and firms. This is a rather complicated question, and may be broken down into three subquestions: (1) Is the existing concentration by firms for national Census industries justified by the economies of single large-scale plants? (2) If not, is the existing concentration by firms nevertheless consistent with no higher concentration within individual submarkets than is required by a single efficient plant —*i.e.*, need there be more than one optimal plant per large firm in any one submarket? (3) In any case, to what extent is the multiplant character of large firms apparently justified by the economies of such firms?

A first approximation to answers to these questions may be made by taking the concentration figure in Column 5 of Table 6 as a simple and crude measure of national industry concentration by firms.[19] On the basis of this measure, the answer to the first subquestion is simple and unsurprising—concentration by firms is in every case but one greater than required by single-plant economies, and in more than half of the cases very substantially greater. Generally it is only within some of the industries with very important economies of large plant—*e.g.*, fountain pens, copper, typewriters, autos, tractors, farm machines—that concentration by firms has not been much greater than required by single-plant economies. Even in these cases it may be two or three times as great as thus required. In the other cases concentration by firms tends to be a substantial or large multiple of that required by single-plant economies. Remembering that we are dealing in general in this sample with the more concentrated industries, it might be said in summary that nearly all of the industries tended to become moderately or highly concentrated (by firms) whether economies of the single plant were important or not.

The second subquestion is whether the existing degree of concentra-

[19] The average share of national industry output per firm for the first four firms obviously is smaller than the market share for the first firm, larger than that for the fourth firm, etc.

tion by firms is consistent or inconsistent with the existence of a single optimal plant per firm in each recognized submarket. In seven of the nine cases where the national market has been considered substantially unsegmented—copper, typewriters, liquor, tires and tubes, rayon, farm machines, tractors, soap, and cigarettes—the degree of concentration by firms within a single market is greater than required by such plant economies, although in all but two of the seven cases (liquor and tires and tubes) it is greater by at most a multiple of three or four. This last is found probably in part because economies of the large plant seem very important in most of these industries.

In eight of the remaining eleven cases—canned goods, petroleum refining, meat packing, fountain pens, metal containers, cement, steel, and gypsum products—the degree of national concentration by firms is not grossly inconsistent with the larger firms on the average having but a single optimal plant per submarket in each of several submarkets. (*This is certainly not to deny that the largest single firms may have more than this and probably do; we refer only to the average of the largest four firms.*)

In the last three cases—flour, automobiles, and shoes—the degree of concentration by firms exceeds by a multiple of two or three that required for each of the four largest firms on the average to have an optimal plant in each submarket. In general, our showing is that in ten of twenty industries the existing degree of concentration by firms, as measured by the average size of the largest four firms, is significantly greater than required for these firms to have only one optimal plant per submarket; in the other ten cases concentration is at least roughly consistent with such a condition.

The third subquestion concerns the extent to which the existing degree of concentration by firms is justified by the exploitation of economies of multiplant firms. We will go no further with this question here than a comparison of the fourth and fifth columns of Table 6 will take us. In Group 1 in that table, the alleged absence of any economies of multiplant firm implies that there is no justification in terms of costs for the excess of concentration by firms over that required for single efficient plants, although in one case (typewriters) the existence of an excess is uncertain, and in four others (all but copper) it is not necessarily accompanied by accentuated concentration in individual submarkets. Here, therefore, the lack of an evident cost justification for multiplant firms raises not so much the issue of concentration in separate markets as the issue of the other advantages and disadvantages of a diversified firm operating in each of several related submarkets.

In Group 2 no estimates of multiplant economies are available; we need say no more than that in five of eight cases (excluding metal containers, farm machines, and tractors) there is a concentration by firms much greater than that required for efficient plants in each submarket, and that this requires evaluation from a cost standpoint. In only one of the industries in Group 3 (shoes) does the degree of concentration by firms seem to have clearly exceeded that required for economies of production and distribution by the large firm.

In the sample as a whole the existing degree of concentration by multiplant firms lacks a clear cost justification in perhaps thirteen of twenty cases, although in seven of these we have a simple lack of any definite estimates. In two more cases the multiplant phenomenon is not very important. Further information is needed on this matter, particularly with reference to cases in which multiplant firm organization has increased effective concentration in individual submarkets or in unsegmented national markets.

IV. ABSOLUTE CAPITAL REQUIREMENTS AND ENTRY

The effect of scale economies on the condition of entry so far emphasized is transmitted through their influence on the share of market output which an efficient plant or firm will supply. This impact is important, but it is not proportional to the importance of scale economies measured in such terms as the absolute number of employees or the absolute size of investment required for an optimal plant or firm. This is because the proportion of a market supplied by an optimal plant or firm (which determines the degree of oligopolistic interdependence between the potential entrant and established firms) depends not only on the absolute size of the plant or firm but also on the size of the market. Thus an investment of over $200 million dollars might add only one per cent to national steel capacity, whereas an investment of $6 million might add five or ten per cent to the capacity for producing fountain pens. In addition to the effect of scale economies on entry via the proportion of the market an efficient entrant will supply, there is a distinct and not closely correlated effect via the absolute size of the efficient plant or firm, or, to choose a popular measure, via the total money investment needed to establish such a plant or firm.

To determine the importance of scale economies in establishing sufficient capital requirements to impede entry seriously, we have queried the same sources on the investment requisite for the most efficient plant or firm in the twenty industries sampled. The findings relative to capital requirements for the large plant are fairly comprehensive, and are summarized in Table 7. Column 2 of this table shows the estimated percentage of national industry capacity provided by one efficient plant, and Column 3 the total investment required to establish such a plant (ordinarily including working capital) as of about 1951. The industries are grouped according to the importance of scale economies from the previously emphasized percentage standpoint. The first category of industries are those in which a single efficient plant will supply no more than 5 per cent of the largest submarket or unsegmented national market; the sec-

TABLE 7

ESTIMATED ABSOLUTE CAPITAL REQUIREMENTS FOR PLANTS OF ESTIMATED MOST EFFICIENT SCALE, CIRCA 1951, FOR 20 INDUSTRIES

Industry	Percentage of National Industry Capacity Provided by One Efficient Plant (from Table 2)	Total Capital Required for One Efficient Plant[a]
Category 1:		
Flour milling	1/10 to 1/2	\$700,000 to \$3,500,000
Shoes	1/7 to 1/2	\$500,000 to \$2,000,000
Canned fruits and vegetables	1/4 to 1/2	\$2,500,000 to \$3,000,000
Cement	4/5 to 1	\$20,000,000 to \$25,000,000
Distilled liquor	1¼ to 1¾	\$30,000,000 to \$42,000,000
Petroleum refining	1¾	\$193,000,000 ex transport facilities \$225,000,000–\$250,000,000 with transport facilities
Meat packing[b]	1/50 to 1/5	Very small
	2 to 2½	\$10,000,000 to \$20,000,000
Tires and tubes	3	\$25,000,000 to \$30,000,000
Category 2:		
Steel[c]	1 to 2½	\$265,000,000 to \$665,000,000[d]
Metal containers[e]	½ to 3	\$5,000,000 to \$20,000,000
Rayon	4 to 6	\$50,000,000 to \$75,000,000[e] \$90,000,000 to \$135,000,000[f]
Soap	4 to 6	\$13,000,000 to \$20,000,000[g]
Farm machines ex tractors	4 to 6	No estimate
Cigarettes	5 to 6	\$125,000,000 to \$150,000,000
Category 3:		
Gypsum products[h]	2½ to 3	\$5,000,000 to \$6,000,000
Automobiles	5 to 10	\$250,000,000 to \$500,000,000
Fountain pens	5 to 10	Around \$6,000,000
Copper	10	No estimate
Tractors	10 to 15	Around \$125,000,000
Typewriters	10 to 30	No estimate

[a] These estimates generally exclude anticipated "shakedown losses" of new entrants, which in some cases may be large and prolonged.
[b] The two rows of estimates refer alternatively to fresh and diversified meat packing.
[c] Percentage of an efficient plant in the largest regional market may exceed 5 per cent.
[d] Excludes any investment in ore or coal.
[e] Acetate rayon.
[f] Viscose rayon.
[g] Excludes working capital.
[h] Percentage of an efficient plant in the largest regional market may exceed 10 per cent.

ond includes those where the corresponding percentage is 5 to 10 per cent; the third includes those where the percentage is above 10 per cent. We may thus observe the extent to which the "percentage effect" of scale economies is of the same order as their "absolute capital requirement effect."

The findings in Table 7 speak fairly clearly for themselves, but a few comments may be in order. First, there is no evident correlation of the absolute capital requirements for an efficient plant with the percentage of market output supplied by it. The size of the market is an erratic variable forestalling such a correlation. Second, absolute capital requirements for an efficient plant in all the manufacturing industries examined are large enough to restrict seriously the ranks of potential entrants; even 500,000 dollars, the smallest amount listed, will not be forthcoming from savings out of salary or from the winnings in a poker game.

Third, the absolute capital requirements in some cases reinforce but in other cases weaken the "percentage effect" on entry of economies of scale of plant. For each of the eight industries in Category 1 in Table 7, for example, the percentage of market output supplied by a single plant seems small enough to provide no serious deterrent to entry. In three of these cases—flour milling, shoes, and canned goods[20]—the absolute capital requirements are also so small that entry may not be seriously restrained thereby. But in four others, capital requirements ranging from 10 to 42 million dollars per plant provide a greater deterrent, and in one (petroleum refining) they impose a truly formidable barrier.

In the six industries of Category 2, where the "percentage effect" on entry of economies of scale of plant is moderate, it is strongly reinforced in four cases (possibly excepting metal containers, and farm machines, for which there is no estimate) by absolute capital requirements. The effect is very much increased in both the steel and cigarette industries. In the six industries of Category 3, where the "percentage effect" appears quite important, it is strongly reinforced in the cases of automobiles and tractors by absolute capital requirements, but in the fountain pen and gypsum industries capital requirements are relatively small. Thus a generally mixed picture regarding the dual effects of economies of large plant emerges.

The extent to which economies of multiplant firms as already noted increase the capital requirements for efficiency may be readily ascertained by comparing the findings of Table 6 with those of Table 7. Since the existence of such economies was denied in six industries, not estimated in eight others, and held to be slight in at least half the remaining six, detailed comment on this matter does not seem justified.

V. CONCLUSIONS

When the answer provided by empirical investigation to an initial inquiry concerning the values of certain economic data is that the values are highly irregular and variegated, and when the answer is therefore found only in a great array of numbers, any brief summarization of the findings may be difficult to make and misleading if attempted. Since this situation is encountered with respect to each of the major questions posed at the beginning of this paper, no comprehensive summary of findings will be attempted here. Certain salient conclusions may be restated

---

[20] As well as in fresh meat packing.

briefly, however, in each case with the proviso that they may have general validity only so far as the sample of industries selected is generally representative of moderately to highly concentrated manufacturing industries in the United States.

Regarding the importance of economies of large plants, the percentage of a market supplied by one efficient plant in some cases is and in some cases is not sufficient to account for high firm concentration or to impede entry. Where it is, these economies might easily propagate high concentration and serious impediments to entry; the number of cases where it is sufficient increases as we refer to the smaller regional or product submarkets in various industries. A significant corollary of these findings is that the following popular horseback observations are apparently *not true:* that economies of scale of plant are never or almost never important in encouraging oligopoly or impeding entry, and that such economies always or almost always are important in these ways. The picture is not extreme in either direction and not simple.

The economies of large plants frequently erect formidable barriers to entry in the shape of absolute capital requirements. Moderately to very high barriers of this sort were found in all but four or five of the industries studied. The height of such barriers is not clearly correlated with percentage of the market supplied by a single plant, so that a relatively independent influence on entry is discovered.

The economies of large multiplant firms are left in doubt by this investigation. In half the cases in which definite estimates were received, such economies were felt to be negligible or absent, whereas in most of the remainder of cases they seemed slight or small. Perhaps the frequently expressed suspicion that such economies generally are unimportant after all is supported, and perhaps we are justified in saying that we have had difficulty in accumulating convincing support for the proposition that in many industries production or distribution economies of large firms seriously encourage concentration or discourage entry.

Our reference here has of course been strictly to the effect of the size of the plant or firm on the cost of production and distribution, and thereby on entry and on concentration. Needless to say, parallel studies of other factors bearing on entry, including the effects of scale on price and on sales promotion, are required for a full evaluation of the entry problem.

3

Monopoly and Oligopoly by Merger*

By GEORGE J. STIGLER[†]

The growth of individual firms to great size through merger with rivals is an outstanding development of modern economic history. As late as 1890, Marshall could view the life history of the firm as a silhouette of that of man in an age of high infant mortality: the firm began as a small venture; if it survived the early years, it straggled along or grew at a rate governed by the entrepreneur's ability—occasionally reaching large size if his ability was extraordinary or his children's abilities great—but eventually it languished into obscurity and then into oblivion.[1] The whole process usually took place, one infers, in one or two generations. I have no reason to question the realism of this picture in the age of noncorporate enterprise; and there are reasons for not wholly abandoning it even today. An anthropomorphic theory of the growth of the firm, however, scarcely fits our modern giants. There are no large American companies that have not grown somewhat by merger, and probably very few that have grown much by the alternative method of internal expansion.[2]

The present paper seeks to summarize some of the major episodes in the development of the merger movement, with special reference to the question of monopoly. The discussion is restricted to so-called "horizontal" combinations, which are quantitatively much the most important form of merger.[3]

---

* *The American Economic Review*, Vol. XL (Proceedings of the American Economic Association, 1950), pp. 23–34. Reprinted by courtesy of the publisher and the author.

† Columbia University.

[1] *Principles of Economics* (8th ed.; London, 1920), Bk. IV, chaps. xi, xii.

[2] Unless otherwise indicated, size of the firm is to be measured relative to the size of the industry.

[3] In 1937, 85.7 per cent of the manufacturing establishments belonging to "central offices" (i.e., multiple-plant firms) were engaged in "uniform" activities. Of course many of these plants were constructed by the parent concern, and there are other deficiencies in the data, but it is probable that horizontal mergers are more important than all other forms of interplant relationship combined (see TNEC Monograph No. 27, *The Structure of Industry*, p. 164).

I. SOME GENERAL THEORETICAL CONSIDERATIONS

We wish to examine the conditions under which it is profitable for competing firms to merge for monopoly. It is expedient to begin with four unpromising assumptions, all of which will be relaxed or defended subsequently: (1) long-run average and marginal cost of production are equal for firms of all relevant sizes;[4] (2) entry of new firms is free, although not necessarily inexpensive; (3) the demand for the output of the industry is stable; (4) the specialized resources ("fixed factors") employed in the industry are indestructible.

Under these conditions, will mergers for monopoly occur? The tempting offhand reply is in the negative, because under these conditions there can be no monopoly profits in the long run; the first two conditions are sufficient to insure this. This offhand reply, however, is to the question:

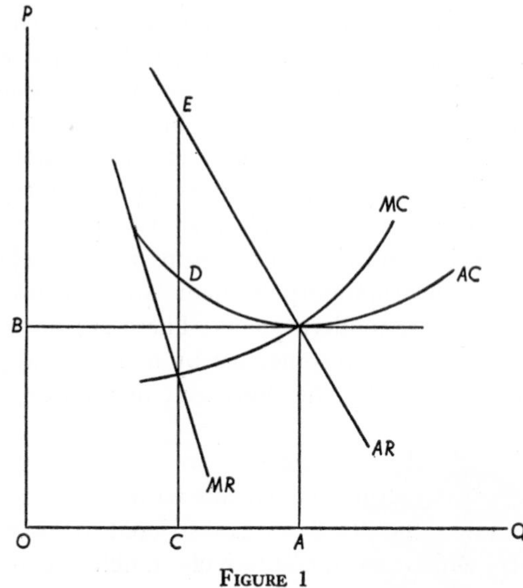

FIGURE 1

will mergers for monopoly exist? It is not an answer to our question: will mergers for monopoly occur? They may occur.

The argument that monopolies may be profitable even under these unfavorable conditions will be developed with a partial geometrical illustration. Consider an industry meeting the four conditions listed above and consisting of numerous identical firms which are in long-run competitive

[4] This assumption will be discussed below, but perhaps a remark is called for on the indeterminacy of the output of the firm under competition when its long-run average cost curve is horizontal. The simplest way to eliminate the indeterminacy is to sacrifice the perfection of competition (but nothing else) by having each firm have a demand curve with an elasticity of (say) −100.

equilibrium. Each firm will have the short-run cost curves displayed in Figure 1, and it will be operating at output *OA*, price *OB*, and making no profits. All the firms are now merged into a monopoly, and each plant (= former firm) now has a pro rata share of aggregate demand, *AR*, with corresponding marginal revenue, *MR*. Accordingly it operates at output *OC* and makes profits of *OC* times *DE*. Entry of new firms therefore takes place, and the pro rata demand curve of each plant in the merger now shifts to the left, price falls, and profits diminish.[5] Eventually the number of rivals will grow until the merger is reduced to the long-run equilibrium level of permanent loss, since neither the merger nor the new rivals can withdraw from the industry.

The simple but important conclusion to be drawn from this argument is that a merger for monopoly may be profitable, in the sense that the present value of the monopoly profits and (so to speak) monopoly losses is positive. If the entry of new firms is not too rapid, the merger may make monopoly profits for a considerable period; and, even though thereafter the losses are permanent, their discounted value need not be so large as to wipe out the initial gains. The essence of the explanation of mergers under these conditions therefore lies in the time required to achieve long-run equilibrium; and this essence lingers in the more general case.

If we relax our assumptions "2," "3," and "4," the prospects of net gain from merger for monopoly are increased in frequently encountered circumstances. If the specialized resources of the merger are not indestructible, investment can be withdrawn from the industry so that, after the initial period of gain and a subsequent period of loss, the long-run equilibrium will be attained, with the merger receiving a competitive rate of return on its investment in the industry.[6] If the industry's demand is growing, the amount of resources the merger must withdraw will be reduced; and, if the demand is growing sufficiently rapidly, no investment need be withdrawn: the merger can maintain its absolute size but decline in relative size.[7] If the entry of new firms and the expansion of rivals can be hindered or prevented, of course the monopoly profits will accrue for a longer period. If the rate of entry is a function of price and profits, the merger can reduce or retard entry by a lower price pol-

---

[5] The explicit analysis can be carried through by a conventional application of the dominant-firm analysis; that is, by constructing the demand curve for the monopoly by subtracting from the aggregate quantity demanded at each price the amount that the new firms (acting competitively) will sell (see my *Theory of Price* [New York, 1946], p. 227).

[6] The period of loss arises because in general it requires less time to increase than to withdraw investment.

[7] This assumes (with what validity I do not know) that the rate of entry of new firms will not be increased by the existence of the merger; but see the last point in the paragraph.

icy; in effect it buys a longer period of monopoly at the price of a lower rate of monopoly profits.

Let us consider now the mechanics of mergers for monopoly. (We defer the question of why mergers occur when they do.) If there are relatively few firms in the industry, the major difficulty in forming a merger is that it is more profitable to be outside a merger than to be a participant. The outsider sells at the same price but at the much larger output at which marginal cost equals price. Hence the promoter of a merger is likely to receive much encouragement from each firm—almost every encouragement, in fact, except participation. In order to overcome this difficulty, it will often be necessary to make the participation of each firm contingent on that of other firms and execute the merger in a single act. We know too little of the theory of coalitions to be able to predict the percentage of the industry that will be merged, but of course it must be fairly high if it is to have any purpose.

If there are relatively many firms in the industry, no one firm plays an important role in the formation of the merger; and it is possible for the merger to expand in a more gradual process and acquire firms on less exacting terms. In fact, several firms may enter upon programs of growth by merger.

Let us return to our first two assumptions. Our first assumption—that there are neither economies nor diseconomies of scale—will please few beside Euler. Two widely accepted, and somewhat inconsistent, beliefs clash with this assumption: (1) mergers are effected to obtain the economies of large-scale production and (2) the diseconomies of scale are the chief bulwark of competition. Both these beliefs will be discussed below; here we shall enter briefly into discussion of the validity of the assumption of constant returns to scale.

The comparative private costs of firms of various sizes can be measured in only one way: by ascertaining whether firms of the various sizes are able to survive in the industry. Survival is the only test of a firm's ability to cope with all the problems: buying inputs, soothing laborers, finding customers, introducing new products and techniques, coping with fluctuations, evading regulations, etc. A cross-sectional study of the costs of inputs per unit of output in a given period measures only one facet of the firm's efficiency and yields no conclusion on efficiency in the large.[8] Conversely, if a firm of a given size survives, we may infer that its costs are equal to those of other sizes of firm, being neither less (or firms of this size would grow in number relative to the industry) nor

[8] As commonly conducted, statistical comparisons of costs or rates of return are not even conclusive on the "static" problem. They demand arbitrary asset valuations to avoid the tautological result that differences in costs measure returns on differences in capital values; and they usually cover too short a period to avoid the regression problem (on which, see M. Friedman and S. Kuznets, *Incomes from Independent Professional Practice* [New York, 1945], chap. vii).

more (or firms of this size would decline in number relative to the industry).

A combination of this argument and casual observation suggests that the economies of scale are unimportant over a wide range of sizes in most American industries, for we commonly find both small and large firms persisting. We shall recur to this matter, but two observations should be made now. The first is that our analysis of mergers still holds if there are minor economies or diseconomies of scale, but fails if they are large. With large diseconomies, mergers are unprofitable; with large economies, monopoly or oligopoly is inevitable, and there will not be many rivals to merge. The second point is that the equality of private costs carries no implication that social costs of firms of different sizes are equal.[9]

Free entry—our second assumption—may be defined as the condition that long-run costs of new firms if they enter the industry will be equal to those of firms already in the industry. This does not mean, as many infer, that a new firm can enter and immediately be as profitable as an established firm. We do not begrudge the new firm a decent interval in which to build its factory; we should be equally willing to concede a period during which production is put on a smooth-running schedule, trade connections are developed, labor is recruited and trained, and the like. These costs of building up a going business are legitimate investment expenses, and, unless historical changes take place in the market, they must be equal for both established and new firms.[10]

With this understanding, free entry seems a valid characterization of most American industries. One may concede this and still argue that, because of the large capital requirements necessary to establish a new company of minimum efficient size, free entry is often difficult, and firms in industries with (absolutely) large capital requirements have a sheltered position. I have as little basis for my skepticism of this argument as its many adherents have given for supporting it.

This brief discussion leaves many questions about mergers unanswered. We shall attempt to answer some of them—and in the process discover new questions—by an examination of the merger movement in America. We shall find it useful to divide this history into two periods, in which monopoly and oligopoly, respectively, were the primary goals.

[9] A comparison of the social costs of firms of different sizes would require, for example, the elimination of differences in private costs arising out of differences in "bargaining power" in purchasing inputs. It is tempting to argue that if the large firm is not more efficient than the small firm in private terms, it is less efficient in social terms (for then its monopolistic advantages are eliminated). I am inclined to yield to the temptation, although small firms have some private advantages (chain-store taxes) and large firms have private disadvantages (maintaining good public relations).

[10] On this view, the infant-industry argument for tariffs is mistaken (at least when external economies do not enter).

II. MERGER FOR MONOPOLY

The era of merger for monopoly ended in this country roughly in 1904, when the *Northern Securities* decision made it clear that this avenue to monopoly was also closed by the antitrust laws. The transition was abrupt in a historical sense. It is revealed by the fact that the United States Steel Corporation, which had quietly picked up in 1902–4 a few steel firms overlooked in the haste of organization, felt it necessary to obtain permission from President Theodore Roosevelt to acquire the Tennessee Coal and Iron Company in 1907.[11]

When and why did the merger movement begin? Sporadic mergers, often founded on marriage, are no doubt as ancient as man; probably for long they were occasional and relatively small in scale, and they were offset by the divestitures necessary to endow sons in a more fertile age. In this country mergers for monopoly began on a large scale only in the eighties, they reached a minor peak at the beginning of the nineties, and they attained their pinnacle at the end of the century.[12]

Our theory is that mergers for monopoly are profitable under easy assumptions that were surely fulfilled in many industries well before the mergers occurred. The only persuasive reason I have found for their late occurrence is the development of the modern corporation and the modern capital market. In a regime of individual proprietorships and partnerships, the capital requirements were a major obstacle to buying up the firms in an industry, and unlimited liability was a major obstacle to the formation of partnerships.

General incorporation laws antedate the Civil War,[13] but the powers of these early corporations were severely limited. They could not hold stock in other corporations; they could not merge with another corporation; limits were placed on their capitalization; often they could not do business outside the state of incorporation; exchange of capital assets for

---

[11] Union Steel (1902), Troy Steel Products (1903), and Clairton Steel (1904) together had twice the ingot capacity of Tennessee Coal and Iron. On the last merger, see the hearings of the Stanley Committee, *Hearings before the Committee [of the House] on Investigation of United States Steel Corporation* (Washington, 1911), Parts 1–6.

[12] The number of combinations with capitalization of 1 million dollars or more, as compiled by Luther Conant, varied as follows:

Year	Number	Year	Number	Year	Number
1887	8	1892	10	1897	4
1888	3	1893	6	1898	20
1889	12	1894	2	1899	87
1890	13	1895	6	1900	42
1891	17	1896	5		

(Eliot Jones, *The Trust Problem in the United States* [New York, 1921], p. 39). There was an earlier era of railroad consolidations (see, e.g., George P. Baker, *The Formation of the New England Railroad Systems* [Cambridge, 1937], especially chap. xi).

[13] See G. H. Evans, *Business Incorporations in the United States, 1800–1943* (New York, 1948).

stock required the unanimous consent of the stockholders; etc. Only in the eighties did New Jersey initiate the competition among states for corporations, which in twenty years eliminated almost every restriction on mergers.[14] In this same period the New York Stock Exchange developed into an effective market for industrial securities. These institutional changes seem to be the proximate causes for the development of the merger movement in the last two decades of the nineteenth century.

Almost invariably the leading firms joined together simultaneously, as our theory leads us to expect.[15] The combinations frequently attained high percentages of national output but seldom became strict monopolies. The contemporary estimates of their shares of the market are rough, and little attention was paid by the estimators to the shares of the firm in particular geographical and product markets. With these provisos, we may note that the mean share of the market controlled by the mergers studied by the Industrial Commission was 71 per cent.[16] In the ninety-two large mergers studied by Moody, the distribution by share of market was similar: seventy-eight controlled 50 per cent or more of the output of the industry; fifty-seven controlled 60 per cent or more; and twenty-six controlled 80 per cent or more.[17] Even in Dewing's fourteen industries in which the mergers failed, the mean percentage was 54.[18]

Almost invariably the share of the merger in the market declined substantially as time went on. Sometimes the entry of new firms was successfully prevented or delayed by ruthless warfare (National Cash Register), patents (Eastman, United Shoe Machinery), or coercion of suppliers or buyers (American Tobacco). These instances are not numerous, however, and such tactics were successful chiefly in small industries; in steel, sugar refining, agricultural implements, leather, rubber, distilleries, cans, etc., the dominant company lost ground relative to the industry.[19]

Why was merger preferred to collusion? Part of the answer lies in the

---

[14] See E. Q. Keasbey, "New Jersey and the Great Corporations," *Harvard Law Review*, 1899–1900, pp. 198–212, 264–78; W. C. Noyes, *A Treatise on the Law of Intercorporate Relations* (Boston, 1902), and, especially, R. C. Larcom, *The Delaware Corporation* (Baltimore, 1937).

[15] The most prominent exception, Standard Oil, is in one sense no exception. It is more an instance of involuntary merger, and its history seems to me one of the relatively few cases appropriately analyzed in analogy to warfare.

[16] The distribution was:

Per Cent	*Companies*
25– 50	1
50– 75	11
75–100	10

(United States Industrial Commission, *Report*, Vol. XIII, *passim.*)

[17] John Moody, *The Truth about the Trusts* (New York, 1904), p. 487.

[18] A. S. Dewing, *Corporate Promotions and Reorganizations* (Cambridge, 1914), p. 526.

[19] For some instances see my *Five Lectures on Economic Problems* (London, 1949), Lecture 5.

prima facie illegality of collusion after 1890. This point should not be pressed, however. The effectiveness of the Sherman Law in dealing with conspiracies was not clear until 1899, when the *Addyston Pipe* case was decided;[20] and there was a contemporaneous wave of amalgamations in England, where conspiracies were unenforcible but not actionable.[21] Mention should also be made of the conflicting tendencies of the greater durability of mergers and the ability to avoid diseconomies of scale through collusion. I am inclined to place considerable weight upon one other advantage of merger: it permitted a capitalization of prospective monopoly profits and a distribution of a portion of these capitalized profits to the professional promoter. The merger enabled a Morgan or a Moore to enter a new and lucrative industry: the production of monopolies.

It is sobering to reflect on the attitudes of professional economists of the period toward the merger movement. Economists as wise as Taussig, as incisive as Fisher, as fond of competition as Clark and Fetter, insisted upon discussing the movement largely or exclusively in terms of industrial evolution and the economies of scale. They found no difficulty in treating the unregulated corporation as a natural phenomenon, nor were they bothered that the economies of scale should spring forth suddenly and simultaneously in an enormous variety of industries—and yet pass over the minor firms that characteristically persisted and indeed flourished in these industries. One must regretfully record that in this period Ida Tarbell and Henry Demarest Lloyd did more than the American Economic Association to foster the policy of competition.

III. MERGER FOR OLIGOPOLY

One great change has taken place in the merger movement since the *Northern Securities* decision: the share of the industry merged into one firm has fallen sharply. In the early period, as we have seen, the leading firm seldom merged less than 50 per cent of the industry's output; in the later period the percentage has hardly ever risen this high. The new goal of mergers is oligopoly.

The change has been most striking in the industries which were merged for monopoly at the beginning of the century. The merger firm has declined continuously and substantially relative to the industry in almost every case. The dominant firm did not embark on a new program of merger to regain its monopolistic position, however; the new mergers were undertaken by firms of the second class. The industry was transformed from near-monopoly to oligopoly. Cement, cans, petroleum, automobiles, agricultural implements, and glass are examples. We may il-

[20] See W. H. Taft, *The Anti-Trust Act and the Supreme Court,* and J. D. Clark, *The Federal Trust Policy.*

[21] J. H. Clapham, *An Economic History of Modern Britain* (Cambridge, 1938), Vol. III, chap. iv.

lustrate the development by the steel industry (Table 1): United States Steel's share of ingot production dropped sharply, but the company absorbed only two small rivals (Columbia Steel, 1930; Geneva plant, 1945), and the chief mergers have been Bethlehem and Republic. Even if one lumps together the (say) four largest firms in the industry, in general there has been a decline in the concentration of production.[22]

The merger movement has also reached the many-firm industries in the later period. We may measure mergers between 1919 and 1937 in a

TABLE 1

MERGERS BY LEADING STEEL FIRMS MEASURED BY PERCENTAGE OF INDUSTRY INGOT CAPACITY

		Per Cent of Industry's Capacity			Per Cent of Industry's Capacity Acquired by Merger	
Company	Initial Year	Initial Year	1908	1948	Initial Year–1908	1908–48
U.S. Steel	1892	14.49	50.14	33.14	33.75	1.00
Bethlehem	1892	3.29	0.56	14.64	....	12.66
Republic	1896	2.08	1.46	9.13	1.08	7.23
Jones and Laughlin	1898	4.59	4.17	5.03	0.18	2.05
National	1920	....	....	4.30	....	0.90
Youngstown Sheet	1908	....	1.76	4.25	....	2.01
Inland	1904	0.50	0.59	3.61	....	....
American Rolling	1901	0.07	0.15	3.57	0.05	2.28
Sharon	1904	0.28	0.26	1.67	....	1.34
Colorado	1901	0.96	2.93	1.54	....	0.19
Wheeling	1901	0.73	0.56	1.50	....	1.41
Crucible	1898	0.71	1.01	1.33	1.06	1.49

Source: Compiled from directories of iron and steel works. The data presented by United States Steel Corporation indicate a much larger control in the first decade, presumably because the industry's capacity was overstated in the directories (see TNEC, *Hearings*, Part 26, pp. 13, 852).

rough fashion by comparing the number of manufacturing establishments belonging to central offices at the two dates (Table 2); it appears that the food industry was the chief center of merger activity, although the paper and printing and iron and steel industries also saw much merger activity. National Dairy is perhaps the most striking example of merger in the food industries—it acquired 331 firms in the decade ending in 1933[23]—but Borden, General Foods, General Mills, and the bakery chains also date from this period.[24] In general, such mergers led to local oligopoly in the primary products (fluid milk, bread, etc.) and to national oligopoly in lesser products such as cheese.

[22] See my *Five Lectures, op. cit.*, pp. 63 ff.

[23] Federal Trade Commission, *Agricultural Income Inquiry* (Washington, 1938), Vol. I, p. 237.

[24] There was also much merging in fuel and ice; City Ice and Fuel is perhaps the largest merger, but several others, such as American Ice and Atlantic Company, were very active.

The Sherman Law seems to have been the fundamental cause for the shift from merger for monopoly to merger for oligopoly. Sometimes its workings were obvious, as when Standard Oil was dismembered and when the leading baking mergers were prevented from combining.[25] More often, however, its workings have been more subtle: the ghost of Senator Sherman is an ex officio member of the board of directors of every large company. This explanation for the new direction of mergers is vulnerable to the criticisms that it is simple and obvious, but no plausible alternative explanation is available.[26]

It is my impression—based chiefly upon the more modest issuance of

TABLE 2

MANUFACTURING ESTABLISHMENTS IN CENTRAL OFFICES, 1919 AND 1937

Industry	1919	1937
Food and kindred products	4,544	8,529
Textiles and their products	2,832	2,703
Iron and steel and their products	1,602	2,420
Lumber and its remanufactures	2,829	2,390
Leather and its finished products	495	503
Paper and printing	918	1,865
Liquors and beverages	268	738
Chemicals and allied products	2,409	2,800
Stone, clay, and glass products	1,100	1,325
Metal and metal products other than iron and steel	445	530
Tobacco manufactures	533	124
Vehicles for land transportation	287	390
Miscellaneous industries	1,362	1,382
Total	19,624	25,665

Source: 1919 data from W. L. Thorp, *The Integration of Industrial Operations* (Washington, 1924), p. 113; 1937 data, which are only roughly comparable, from TNEC Monograph No. 27, *The Structure of Industry*, p. 211.

securities of mergers and the apparent ease of entry into the new merging industries—that the mergers for oligopoly in the later period have been less effective in restraining or postponing competition than the earlier mergers for monopoly. This is not to argue, however, that they left competition as they found it; indeed, the one important weakness in the Sherman Act as it is sometimes interpreted is the belief that oligopoly affords a satisfactory form of organization of our economy. This belief is apparently held, as it was certainly fostered, by one of the greatest of contemporary judges, Learned Hand, the author of the famous dictum that control by one firm of 64 per cent of an industry may not be mo-

[25] *Agricultural Income Inquiry*, *op. cit.*, p. 308.

[26] It is suggestive that mergers for monopoly continued to be typical in England in the twenties (see Patrick Fitzgerald, *Industrial Combination in England* [London, 1927]).

nopoly and that 33 per cent surely is not.[27] It is true, no doubt, that oligopoly is a weaker form of monopolization than the single firm, but it is not so weak a form that it can be left to its own devices. If this view—which is almost universally held by modern economists—is correct, then our chief task in the field of antitrust policy is to demonstrate beyond judicial doubt the social undesirability of permitting oligopoly by merger (or by other methods) in large American industries.

IV. CONCLUSIONS

The foregoing survey of the merger movement raises a set of interrelated questions; they concern the economies of scale, the capital market, and the entry of firms into an industry.

The broad sweep of our discussion would suggest that the private diseconomies of large-scale production are only an occasional and minor barrier to merger for monopoly. The chief barriers to monopoly, in addition to the Sherman Act, have been the capital requirements of mergers and the tendency of rivals to grow in number and size.

To find in an imperfect capital market a bulwark of competition seems paradoxical, but the paradox is not deep. Until recent times the personal distribution of wealth set a limit upon the size of firms, and modern economic societies have been sufficiently egalitarian to make personal monopolization of large industries impossible. The corporation and the securities markets have severed the connection between personal wealth and industrial size and thus weakened the institutional basis of competitive enterprise.

The diseconomies of scale offer a weak supplement to the limitations once provided by personal wealth. Properly interpreted, conventional theory does not contradict this tentative finding. We customarily find in entrepreneurship the limitation to the size of firm, and we find the chief tasks of the entrepreneur arising out of uncertainty. Much, although of course not all, uncertainty stems from the competitive behavior of rivals, so that entrepreneurship may well be subject to increasing returns to relative size as well as to decreasing returns to absolute size, with no clear verdict for either force over a wide range of sizes.

We are thus led to "new entry" as the chief defense of competition—a most unseemly reversion to the ruling economic theory of 1900. It is now popular to deprecate the importance of new entry because few firms can accumulate the capital necessary to produce efficiently in the great industries. To the extent that the criticism rests on the alleged economies of scale, I have argued that it is mistaken; to the extent that it rests on imperfections of the capital market it runs contrary to (but is not necessarily inconsistent with) the argument we have advanced that the cap-

---

27 ". . . it is doubtful whether sixty or sixty-four per cent would be enough [to constitute monopoly]; and certainly thirty-three per cent is not" (*United States* v. *Aluminum Co. of America*, 148 F. [2d] 424).

ital market has been improving—in certain directions, at least—too much! Yet there is support for the skeptics of easy entry in the fact that the mergers for monopoly have frequently been very profitable.

Such inconclusive conclusions are not too troublesome. This paper is designed to be only an introduction to the merger problem. To this end, it is sufficient if I emphasize again the significance of the movement. To the theorist it offers a stimulating challenge: the merger movement does not fit too well into the received categories of stable competition and irresistible monopoly. To the student of social policy it offers the promising hypothesis: it is possible to change the trend of industrial organization by the lackadaisical enforcement of an antitrust law. And to the student of social sciences it offers the supremely optimistic—and pessimistic—suggestion: when economists agree that a movement is inevitable, it is not.

II. CASE STUDIES IN INDUSTRIAL STRUCTURE AND BEHAVIOR

4

An Alternative Approach to the Concept of Workable Competition*

By JESSE W. MARKHAM†

I

Economists, recognizing the shortcomings of the theory of perfect competition in framing public policy for oligopolistic markets, recently have endeavored to define a more realistic standard of economic performance—workable or effective competition.[1] Since the concept owes its creation to a public policy need and not to the logic of abstract theory, it can, at best, be divorced only in part from value judgments. To the unswerving socialist, nothing short of complete government ownership and control of all economic activity may make for a workable society. To him, no economy is workably competitive if it is privately competitive. Yet a proponent of unlimited free enterprise would probably view any economy not subject to governmental intervention as workably competitive. Thorough-going antitrust sympathizers may reject any definition of workable competition that falls noticeably short of pure competition. On the other hand, economists who subscribe to the Schumpeterian theory of creative destruction may willingly accept, in fact, insist upon the acceptance of, far less. Nor is it quite clear that the degree of competition clamored for by constituents of each school of thought is always compatible with the economic framework of the society they hope to create or maintain. Those who insist that workable competition falls little short of perfect competition, in their efforts to preserve a free enterprise economy, may be unwittingly leading us toward stringent state controls. For, it is difficult to visualize the maintenance of atomized industries by any means other than strong police power. On the other hand, passive acceptance of a high degree of con-

* *The American Economic Review,* Vol. XL (1950), pp. 349–61. Reprinted by courtesy of the publisher and the author.

The paper has profited considerably from criticisms made by Professors George W. Stocking and Roland McKean of the Vanderbilt University economics department.

† Princeton University.

[1] The term "workable competition" was first used by J. M. Clark in his article "Toward a Concept of Workable Competition," *American Economic Review,* Vol. XXX (June, 1940), pp. 241–56.

centration in many industries on the theory that other entrepreneurs with other products will destroy it through a natural evolutionary process may be an invitation to industrial fascism.

That the term "workable competition" defies precise definition, even in the presence of agreed upon standards of workability in some political or moral sense, becomes evident when one attempts to define the "industry" to which the concept is to be applied. Concentration ratios are often employed to indicate the degree of monopoly which exists in a particular industry, but concentration ratios in themselves might be quite meaningless unless they relate to a well-defined market. For example, E. I. du Pont de Nemours and Co., Inc. is the sole producer of a particular synthetic yarn known as nylon; but du Pont accounts for only about 10 per cent of total *synthetic* yarn production and accounts for only an infinitesimally small percentage of total domestic yarn production of all kinds. Obviously, therefore, any measure of du Pont's monopoly power in the textile industry is dependent upon whether one has in mind the domestic nylon market, the synthetic yarn market, or simply the yarn market.

Most definitions of workable competition have been patterned largely after the traditional definition of perfect competition. That is to say, the definitions consist of listing a set of conditions the fulfillment of which determines whether or not a specific industry is to be judged as workably competitive. By and large, none of these definitions presents insuperable difficulties so long as their application is limited to near-perfectly competitive industries and well-defined market areas; i.e., although few would argue that the American cotton textile industry has traditionally fulfilled all the conditions of perfect competition, it is unlikely that any would argue that competition in cotton textiles has not been effective or workable. Most of our industries, however, are not so highly competitive that they differ but little from purely competitive industries nor are market boundaries in our economy always clearly delineated. When applied to monopolistically competitive and oligopolistic markets, the weaknesses of most definitions of workable competition begin to appear. Yet, these are the market areas with which public policy is largely concerned. This paper purports (1) to set forth the actual conditions that exist in a fairly typical oligopolistic industry—the rayon yarn producing industry; (2) to demonstrate the difficulties that arise when an attempt is made to determine the workable competitiveness of an industry by applying to it a specific set of conditions; and (3) to suggest an alternative approach to the problem of defining workable competition that may possibly be more useful for purposes of public policy.

II

Apart from the fact that the author has made a rather extended study of the industry, the rayon yarn industry offers itself as a particularly good candidate upon which the various definitions of workable competition may be tested. Since the industry is composed of a limited number of producers, it falls far short of fulfilling one of the most essential conditions of pure competition. On the other hand, market practices in the industry have never precipitated an antitrust case.[2] Hence, at the outset, there is no basis for *a priori* judgment or public policy bias. In addition to these features, however, the industry poses many of the debatable questions that would necessarily arise in the process of determining whether or not an industry is workably competitive. The significant characteristics of the domestic rayon yarn industry are as follows:[3]

1. Rayon is produced in the United States under the viscose, acetate and the cupramonium processes.[4] All basic patent rights to these processes have become public property. The American Viscose Corporation monopolized the industry until 1920, at which time its American rights to the Cross and Bevans and Topham patents expired. Since 1920, approximately twenty new firms have entered into rayon production under one of the three processes listed above. A number of small firms did not survive the 1930–1933 depression. Concentration ratios have declined rapidly since 1920. Currently, the largest producer accounts for 33 per cent of total domestic output and the four largest producers account for about 75 per cent.

2. The rayon industry is an oligopoly nominally consisting of fourteen firms. If cognizance is taken of inter-company affiliations, however, the actual number of financially independent producers is eleven. The chief limitation to the number of firms is an economic one: The long-run cost curve for the firm, at least to the extent it is indicated by available plant cost curves and other data, places the rayon industry among the natural oligopolies. Economies of scale obtained through rapid expansion of capacity by entrenched firms have made it increasingly difficult for new firms to enter the industry since 1930 in spite of the gradual dissemination of technical "know how" and the expiration of several special patents that occurred over the past twenty years. However, two

---

[2] The Federal Trade Commission investigated charges against the ten largest viscose yarn producers (1934–37) that they conspired to fix prices between October, 1931 and May, 1932. Charges were made by a large textile fabricator. The Federal Trade Commission issued a cease and desist order in 1937 but mentioned no specific price-fixing practices. *Viscose Co., et al.;* Docket No. 2161; *Summary of Decisions of the Federal Trade Commission.*

[3] These characteristics have been taken from a larger study by the author entitled *Price and Output Behavior in the Domestic Rayon Industry.* The original study was presented as a Ph.D. thesis at Harvard University, September, 1948. It is currently being revised for publication. Although, for purposes of this paper, the features of the rayon industry could as well be hypothetical as real, documentation of them may be found in the thesis deposited in the Harvard University Library.

[4] Although there are important chemical differences among yarns produced under the three processes, rayon yarn will be treated as a homogeneous commodity in this paper.

new rayon producers, Beunit Mills, Inc., and the United Rayon Corporation, have entered the field since the War and were planning to have plants in operation before the end of 1949.

3. The industry has been characterized by a very rapid rate of expansion of production facilities,[5] but only during the period between 1920 and 1930 was any of this increase due to the entrance of new firms. A sharp secular decline in price (12.8 per cent per year) and rate of return on investment (100 per cent 1915–19 to 6.9 per cent 1930–38) has accompanied the rising trend in investment and output. Therefore, *trends* in prices, profits and investment are consistent with those which would have been expected under highly competitive conditions.

4. The rayon price series indicates a high degree of short-run stability relative to rayon sales and to natural fiber yarn prices. Prices often remain unchanged for from one to two years. However, over the course of several business cycles rayon price has moved in almost perfect consonance with silk and cotton yarn prices. Both synthetic and natural fiber yarn producers view the yarn market as highly competitive. There are several logical explanations for the short-run stability of rayon price: (1) The prices for all variable cost factors (wages, chemicals, wood pulp, etc.) are extremely stable. (2) All rayon producers are large corporations; it is generally conceded that this form of business organization transmits price changes to the market much more sluggishly than do small-owner controlled corporations and proprietorships. (3) Rayon producers seem to feel that a stable yarn price stimulates long-run demand; it eliminates possible inventory losses and the necessity of hedging by textile fabricators. (4) Few producers initiate price changes independently; most producers usually wait for a large producer to initiate a price change (see 5, below).

5. The price relationship among rayon producers has varied somewhat with respect to particular phases of the business cycle, but there is fairly conclusive evidence of price leadership. The largest rayon producer has been the first to announce a list price change in all but a few instances; the two largest producers have accounted for 90 per cent of all list-price revisions since 1926. However, in periods of severe depression such as 1930–32 and, to a less extent, 1934 and 1938, many list-price changes merely took *de jure* recognition of *de facto* market prices. There is tremendous pressure upon producers, particularly smaller producers, to maintain close to maximum capacity output for cost considerations. Short-run plant cost curves have a steep negative slope that continues all the way to installed capacity output. The smaller the plant, the steeper the slope over the range of 75 per cent to 100 per cent of installed capacity. Thus, when the rayon market becomes severely de-

[5] Many statistics textbooks use the rayon production series to illustrate the applicability of the Gompertz curve. See F. C. Mills, *Statistical Methods* (rev. ed.; New York, 1938), pp. 671–75.

pressed, small producers will shade prices in order to maintain a high rate of output rather than abide by list prices and commit financial suicide. Also, extremely tight rayon markets have occasionally given rise to premiums above list price of varying magnitudes and, since the War, there has been some variation in quoted prices among producers for the first time in the history of the industry. Market conditions intermediate to an acute yarn shortage and a severe depression, however, appear to be characterized by close agreement between list price and net realized price and by identical quoted prices for all producers.

6. Similar to the price series, the rayon output series is highly stable in the short-run relative to the deliveries series. Generally, irregular and seasonal fluctuations in demand are absorbed by inventory fluctuations. Several factors account for the reluctance on the part of rayon producers to curtail output to meet temporary market disequilibria: (1) Rayon is produced by a continuous process; plant shut-downs are costly and several weeks are usually required to get plants back up to top operational efficiency. (2) As indicated above, total unit costs increase rapidly as output is contracted below capacity. This is true when all variable factors may be adjusted to the new production schedule; the increase in unit costs is aggravated in the immediate short-run that would probably include seasonal and irregular fluctuations in demand for which complete adjustment of variable factors is seldom if ever made.

7. By way of an appraisal of the above points, the arbitrary power that rayon producers may exercise over their price is extremely limited if we concede that producers attempt to maximize profits. In no case has output curtailment in the industry proceeded by as much as 25 per cent of installed capacity without an accompanying price reduction. A confluence of several economic forces accounts for this price breaking point: (1) Large firms have reasons for suspecting off-list selling when only 75 per cent of installed capacity operations is necessary to fill orders at existing list prices. (2) Total unit costs (under conditions of stable factor costs) are considerably higher when firms operate at 75 per cent of installed capacity than when they operate at 100 per cent. (3) The prices of the competitive natural fibers have probably been noticeably reduced by the time textile fabricators are demanding only 75 per cent of capacity rayon output; hence, it behooves the nominal price-leader or some other firm to reduce rayon prices in order to regain part of its market lost to natural fibers and thereby maintain a higher level of output.

8. Although rayon producers do not seem to be willing to engage in much price competition when the market is "normal," they vigorously compete among themselves in other ways. The rate of technological innovation in the rayon industry has been almost unbelievably high. For example, output per man-hour increased about tenfold between 1925 and 1938. Also, numerous acid recovery systems have been devised to cut costs. In their efforts to produce at a cost lower than their rivals, rayon

producers have engaged in vigorous competition. Further, rayon producers have aggressively explored and exploited the long-run demand possibilities for their product. The quality of rayon has been steadily improved or altered so that it could reach new fabric markets. In 1920 rayon was, at best, a cheap silk substitute. Today rayon is used in the production of all kinds of wearing apparel and household and industrial fabrics.

9. The domestic rayon yarn industry has received a considerable amount of tariff protection.[6] Since the passage of the Tariff Act of 1930, domestic producers have been relatively free from foreign competition. Under the recent Geneva Trade Agreement, however, import duties on rayon yarn were reduced by 50 per cent on January 1, 1948. Although it is too early to tell what the long-run effects of tariff reduction upon the domestic yarn market will be, rayon imports increased considerably in 1948.

Obviously, these are not all of the characteristics of the domestic rayon yarn industry that must be determined before a final verdict can be rendered upon the workable competitiveness of the industry. However, for illustrative purposes, they serve as a tolerably good testing ground for the applicability of some of the more familiar definitions of workable or effective competition. They at least serve our purpose sufficiently well to bring into sharp relief the extent to which one must engage in making value judgments in any such process.

III

There have been several serious attempts made to define the term "workable competition." In no case, however, has an author set forth conditions so completely devoid of value judgments or so all-embracing that he feels free to acclaim the universal applicability of his definition. Professor J. M. Clark, the creator of the term, places much emphasis upon rivalry among selling units and the "free option of the buyer to buy from a rival seller or sellers of what we think of as 'the same' product."[7] Professor Clark concedes, however, that the "specific character of competition in any given case depends on a surprisingly large number of conditions—so many, in fact, that the number of mathematically possible combinations runs into the hundreds of thousands—and suggests the possibility that every industry may be in some significant respect different from every other, or from itself at some other stage of development."[8]

---

[6] When discussing the workable competitiveness of the domestic rayon yarn market in this paper, the tariff policy will be accepted as a datum. Public policy can always be directed toward making any domestic market more or less competitive than it now is by eliminating tariffs, subsidizing imports, imposing higher tariff walls, etc.

[7] John M. Clark, *op. cit.*, p. 243.

[8] *Ibid.*

On a number of counts, the domestic rayon industry would be workably competitive under Professor Clark's definition. He himself would probably place the rayon industry under the following caption in his classification of competition scheme:[9]

II. Modified, intermediate or hybrid competition.
  A. Standard Products, few producers. The most important cases involve formally free entry, but no exit without loss.
    3. Quoted prices, sloping individual demand curves.
      b. Demand schedules indefinite (limited freight absorption).

There is room for little doubt about the existence of rivalry among the producers of rayon. In depressed markets rivalry has taken the form of price cutting and price shading. Even during normal market periods when the price leader's list price seems to have prevailed in the industry there has been intense rivalry among producers in the form of cost cutting and quality competition. Except possibly for the brief interval between October, 1931, and May, 1932, when the price-fixing conspiracy was alleged, it can be fairly concluded that rayon purchasers have had a real option before them as to their source of supply. At times when all producers rigidly adhered to the price leader's quoted price, the buyer's option was limited to quality and grading differences among producers. However, to the extent buyers regard rayon, nylon, silk, cotton and wool yarns as "the same" commodity, they have always had, in addition to the above, a real price option. Hence, on most counts the rayon yarn industry would qualify as workably competitive under Professor Clark's definition. At least, any disagreement with this conclusion would evolve from a different interpretation of such terms as "rivalry," "option," and "the same" commodity.

To Professor Stigler, "An industry is workably competitive when (1) there are a considerable number of firms selling closely related products in each important market area, (2) these firms are not in collusion, and (3) the long-run average cost curve for a new firm is not materially higher than that for an established firm."[10] The workable competitiveness of the rayon industry under Professor Stigler's difinition would depend upon the interpretation given to the term "closely related products." If all textile yarns are in some sense to be considered as closely related, and the competition among them in specific market areas indicates that they should be so considered, the rayon industry (as a small segment of the total yarn market) would be considered as highly competitive under the above definition. If, however, the product of one rayon producer be considered as closely related only to other rayon, other features of the definition come into play and the conclusion is not so evident. The workable competitiveness of the rayon industry would then depend upon how

[9] John M. Clark, *op. cit.*, p. 245.

[10] George J. Stigler, "Extent and Bases of Monopoly," *American Economic Review*, Vol. XXXII, Suppl. (June, 1942), pp. 2–3.

Professor Stigler would answer the following questions: Do fourteen producers constitute "a considerable number of firms"? Do sporadic price shading and price cutting so invalidate the normal acceptance of price leadership that it could be fairly concluded that rayon producers neither tacitly nor explicitly avoid price competition? Unless both of these questions could be answered in the affirmative there would be some doubts as to the amount of price competition that has characterized the domestic rayon industry. Even under the more restrictive interpretation of the term "closely related products" the industry would be considered workably competitive in periods when the rate of sales is extremely high or low relative to installed capacity. But in instances where all firms have operated somewhere between 80 per cent and 95 per cent of installed capacity and have passively adhered to the price leader's price, the industry may not qualify as workably competitive because of the second provision of Stigler's definition.[11]

Corwin Edwards has also defined workable competition in terms of the structural characteristics in a particular market. They are as follows:[12]

1. There must be an appreciable number of sources of supply and an appreciable number of potential customers for substantially the same product or service. Suppliers and customers do not need to be so numerous that each trader is entirely without individual influence, but their number must be great enough that persons on the other side of the market may readily turn away from any particular trader and may find a variety of other alternatives.
2. No trader must be so powerful as to be able to coerce his rivals, nor so large that the remaining traders lack the capacity to take over at least a substantial portion of his trade.
3. Traders must be responsive to incentives of profit and loss: that is, they must not be so large, so diversified, so devoted to political rather than commercial purposes, so subsidized, or otherwise so unconcerned with results in a particular market, that their policies are not affected by ordinary commercial incentives arising out of that market.
4. Matters of commercial policy must be decided by each trader separately without agreement with his rivals.
5. New traders must have opportunity to enter the market without handicap other than that which is automatically created by the fact that others are already well established there.
6. Access by traders on one side of the market to those on the other side of the market must be unimpaired except by obstacles not deliberately introduced, such as distance or ignorance of the available alternatives.
7. There must be no substantial preferential status within the market for any important trader or group of traders on the basis of law, politics, or commercial alliances.

The structural characteristics of the rayon market since 1932 would seem to fulfill the requirements of workable competition by this inter-

---

[11] This would depend upon whether Professor Stigler considers the temporary acceptance of a price leader's price as a "tacit avoidance of price competition for fear of retaliation of close rivals." See his footnote, *op. cit.*, p. 3.

[12] Corwin Edwards, *Maintaining Competition* (New York, 1949), pp. 9–10.

pretation even under the more rigid definition of an industry. Professor Edwards states that there must be an appreciable number of sources of supply, but neither suppliers nor customers need to be so numerous that each trader is entirely without individual influence. There must, however, be no agreement among rivals with respect to commercial policy. It would appear, therefore, the oligopolistic markets are ruled out under the above set of conditions only when individual firms act in concert to an extent that implies either an agreement or the possession of coercive power by a large producer. The off-list selling by individual rayon producers in periods marked by a noticeable decline in demand, the differential premiums for quick delivery when yarn shortages appear, and the quoted price differentials among producers since the War would probably constitute sufficient evidence that rayon price is not a result of a collusive agreement. Although American Viscose has generally led the industry in effecting list price changes, on several occasions the admitted purpose of the price revision was to bring list price more in line with the *de facto* price. Also, several other producers have occasionally taken the initiative in revising price schedules.

These features of rayon price behavior would seem to be compatible with the structural characteristics required of a particular competitive market as set forth above. There is evidence that each firm considers the effect his actions will have upon his rival's behavior, but there is a sufficient amount of independent pricing over the period of a business cycle to give buyers a variety of options among sellers. When this type of price behavior appears in a market, fourteen producers probably constitute an "appreciable number of sources of supply." It is not likely that Professor Edwards would have considered the industry to be workably competitive during the 'twenties. From 1920 to 1930 the American Viscose Corporation was sufficiently large relative to its rivals to exert a substantial amount of coercive power. Also, and this logically follows, the remaining producers did not collectively control enough productive capacity to be able to take over a substantial portion of the trade that usually went to the American Viscose Corporation.

Although it is *possible* to classify the domestic rayon industry among the workably competitive industries by an application of any one of the above definitions, it should be reiterated that results obtained from the application of each involves a value judgment. Hence, it is unlikely that any prescribed set of market characteristics would either obtain the approval of all economists or could uniquely determine the workable competitiveness of any given industry. Those who reject any set of conditions that falls noticeably short of the classicists' ideal of perfect competition would find few workably competitive markets. Those who place much reliance upon the dynamics of creative destruction would find many more. In the absence of known consequences of an active pursuit of either of the foregoing implied policies toward industrial markets, it is perhaps just as well that policy making has never been left to either of these two groups to the complete exclusion of the other. Even within each group that harbors no ideological conflict it is most unlikely that all would ascribe to any single set of market conditions universal applicability. In any case, the workable competitiveness of a particular industry is open to debate only after the structural characteristics of its market and the dynamic forces that have shaped them have been appraised.

IV

A relatively small number of large producers (hence, fairly high concentration ratios), short-run price stability, and the acceptance of a price leader appear to be the most obvious differences between the rayon market and the competitive market of the classicists. In an industrialized society in which perfect competition cannot be expected, are those differences sufficiently inimical to the public welfare to conclude that competition in the domestic rayon industry is "unworkable"? An answer to this question involves an appraisal of these differences against the background of the dynamic aspects of the rayon industry and an examination of the changes that an enlightened public policy would envisage in order to eliminate them.

Although concentration ratios have been high in the rayon industry, rapidly declining prices and profit rates, the gradual decline in the relative position of the largest and four largest producers, and the increase in the number of rayon producing firms over the past twenty-eight years are consistent with that which would be expected under conditions of competition. In 1920 the American Viscose Company was a highly profitable (156.83 per cent return on total investment!), patent-protected monopoly which sold 150 denier rayon for $4.50 per pound. By 1940 there were fifteen rayon yarn producers, the average annual rate of return for the industry was about 7 per cent, and the price of rayon yarn had declined to $0.53 per pound. Over the twenty-year period the quality of rayon was greatly improved and domestic output increased from 10.1 million pounds to 380.1 million pounds per year. Currently, American Viscose accounts for only 33 per cent of total domestic output and the four largest firms, for about 75 per cent. Two new firms have recently entered the industry. Hence, with respect to the number of firms, the degree of concentration of productive capacity, and the secular behavior of prices, profits and output, competitive forces seem to be accomplishing automatically what would presumably be the objectives of an enlightened public policy. Profits and prices are declining while output is increasing; the number of firms is increasing and the degree of concentration is decreasing.

Both the short-run stability and the price leadership which characterize rayon price behavior stem from the oligopolistic features of the rayon market. It has been previously pointed out, however, that there have been a number of significant departures from the general price leadership pattern. Several downward price revisions admittedly have merely taken *de jure* recognition of *de facto* prices. Also, although rayon prices are more stable than natural fiber prices, there is much interdependence among all textile prices. Any appreciable change in silk or cotton prices has immediate effects in the rayon market. Since natural fiber prices are usually accepted as being highly competitive, it should follow that closely related commodity prices geared to them take on some of their competitive aspects. In any case, the only obvious way to eliminate practices born of oligopolistic rationality is to eliminate the foundations of the oligopoly market, i.e., increase the number of independent producers in the industry. Hence, the crucial question becomes whether or not public policy could be directed toward reducing the market control of the larger producers more effectively than it is already being accomplished by competitive market forces. A final decision as to whether the rayon industry is workably competitive or not is contingent upon how this question is answered.

Economies of scale in rayon production have been referred to elsewere in this paper. That the largest *plants* currently producing rayon are the most efficient plants can be established beyond any reasonable doubt. It can be fairly safely concluded, therefore, that nothing could be gained at present by placing a limitation upon the size of rayon plants. Short-run price flexibility, if obtained by this method, is hardly worth the social costs involved. But the twenty-eight rayon plants are controlled by fourteen firms. Could anything be gained by limiting each firm to one plant? An answer to this question hangs largely upon the interpretation of all the available evidence. Estimates made by construction engineers and the financial statements of individual firms indicate that economies of scale are obtained by increasing the size of the firm. Nor is there any evidence that any single firm in the rayon industry has expanded beyond the point where further economies are impossible. Therefore, to farm out all plants to an independent producer would, assuming that buyers could be found, entail some duplication in overhead (research, physical and chemical testing laboratories, management, sales offices, etc.) and thereby raise costs. On the other hand, it is quite likely that an increase in the number of rayon producers from fourteen to twenty-eight (again assuming that buyers for all plants could be found) would eliminate some short-run price inflexibility and make price-leadership more difficult. However, strong competition from other yarns already limits the amount of control the price leader may exercise over rayon price. Also, since rayon producers have maintained a high level of output in the short run because of cost considerations, they have rendered inadmissible a number of arguments against short-run price inflexibility; there is no resultant unemployment to attribute to the "administered" rayon price. Hence, at the present stage of development of the domestic rayon industry, it would probably be unwise to place legal limitations upon the size of the firm, particularly since the number of firms is still increasing. The expected gains to be derived from such a policy do not clearly offset the expected losses.

V

In concluding that the rayon industry is workably competitive, the author lays no claim to having found a more workable definition of workable competition. Indeed, he would be among the first to admit that others might easily have arrived at totally different conclusions. It might, however, not be amiss to state, by way of summary, the guiding principles employed in concluding that the domestic rayon industry falls within the workably competitive segment of the American economy.

One of the obvious shortcomings of those definitions of workable competition which set forth a necessary set of conditions is that they neglect the dynamic forces that shape an industry's development. It is difficult to visualize a set of static conditions that would not include some mention of the number of firms. Yet, no one would expect to find "a fairly large number" of firms in an industry one or two years after a single firm's patent rights to a production process had expired. Should such an industry be judged *a priori* unworkably competitive because it does not meet with a stated number of conditions? If changes in the structural characteristics of an industry over time are to be admitted to the concept, a stated set of conditions is not only inapplicable to all industries at once but also loses its applicability to the same industry at different stages of development. Further, one might well ask whether it is ever worthwhile to conclude that a particular industry is not workably competitive by a static definition if there are no visible means whereby public policy might be directed toward making the industry more competitive. To apply rigorously a stated set of conditions might put us in the extremely embarrassing position of having caught a host of criminals before we have devised an appropriate penal or reform system.

A possible alternative approach to the concept of workable competition may be one which shifts the emphasis from a set of specific structural characteristics to an appraisal of a particular industry's over-all performance against the background of possible remedial action. Definitions of workable competition shaped along these lines might accept as a first approximation some such principle as the following: An industry may be judged to be workably competitive when, after the structural characteristics of its market and the dynamic forces that shaped them have been thoroughly examined, there is no clearly indicated change that can be effected through public policy measures that would result in greater social gains than social losses. Tautological through this type of definition might be, it at least avoids the pitfall of listing specific market conditions that can have very limited general applicability. Also, it would ascribe paramount importance to that which should be uppermost in the minds of those who formulate public policy—the possibility of prescribing appropriate remedial action. For, unless the concept of workable competition is to be an instrument of public policy, there is little reason for differentiating between workable and pure competition. But to frame definitions for public policy purposes without taking cognizance of the different structural features among industries and within the same industry at specific stages of development, and without recognizing at the outset the political and economic limitations placed upon policy-making authorities, would be to ignore the primary purpose of such definitions, i.e., to indicate wherein an industry does not operate in the public's interest and what appropriate remedial action is possible. It seems hardly necessary to point out, however, that definitions of workable competition which follow the above suggested pattern, like all others, will not be divorced from value judgments.

5

The Decline of Monopoly in the Metal Container Industry*

By JAMES W. McKIE†

I

The Clayton Antitrust Act is now over forty years old, and economists are still uncertain about its role in antitrust policy. Most would doubtless agree on the need for some instrument that is more flexible than the Sherman Act. That Act cannot be applied until monopoly control is well established, and one purpose of the Clayton Act has always been to prevent monopoly by arresting it in an incipient stage. Its success in this respect has been mixed; many persons have pointed out of late that a policy of prohibiting competitive practices that could eventually result in monopoly may be leading us toward *per se* rules of business conduct that are impossibly confining. But the Clayton Act has also been used against business practices in markets that already have a monopolistic structure. Sometimes this has been done merely to provide a bill of particulars in cases tried chiefly under the Sherman Act; but sometimes it has been done in an attempt to weaken monopoly through an attack on its manifestations. Doubts have also centered on the wisdom of this latter policy, on the ground that it does very little good to prohibit a market practice if the underlying monopoly power which makes it oppressive remains untouched.

The American Can case of 1950 illustrates in almost unexpected circumstances the force that the indirect and peripheral approach of the Clayton Act may have to make competition more effective. This was a case in which a specific market practice was the key to market power. The practice had nothing to do with the creation of market power, since it supervened upon a monopolistic structure that was already there; but it played a decisive part in the maintenance of market control after the foundations of monopoly had been undermined.

A cursory examination of the structure of the metal container industry just before the antitrust suit began in 1948 might well have made any-

* *The American Economic Review*, Vol. XLV (Proceedings of the American Economic Association, 1955), pp. 499–508. Reprinted by courtesy of the publisher and the author.

† Vanderbilt University.

one skeptical of the success of a policy which did not involve fundamental structural reorganization. The industry was highly concentrated, and still is: the two leading firms, American Can Company and Continental Can Company, together accounted for nearly 80 per cent of total sales, and American alone had over 45 per cent.[1] There were in addition a number of small sellers—no one of them more than one-eighth as large as American—which occupied sheltered and specialized positions or else appeared to subsist on a margin of tolerance. The major companies manufacture a product-mix of containers for different purposes, but differentiation within each product line was and is insignificant. Cross-elasticities of demand between metal cans and substitute containers are very small. The prices of the two leaders, as well as their other market policies, have long been substantially identical. Prices for given products in given sales regions were set by one of the large firms, the other following; a policy of universal freight equalization eliminated the uncertainties of geographical differentiation; and prices exhibited the characteristic rigidity that we have come to associate with tacit oligopolistic collusion.

Tacit collusion in circumstances like these might be expected to result in the maximization of joint profits. However, the maximization of joint profits is always subject to limitations in any oligopoly structure, and in some instances the limitations are so severe that the principle loses its explanatory value. Economists have long preferred an eclectic approach to this problem. No universal solvent has yet been found that will exempt us from a detailed examination of the structure of particular oligopolistic markets and their history, as a prerequisite to explaining their behavior. The limitations upon monopoly power are often hidden from immediate view. A detailed analysis of the metal container industry reveals a number of them.

II

There is time for only a brief summary here. The first thing to be noted is that the limited-duopoly structure in the can industry is a relatively recent development. Twenty years ago any industrial economist would have classed the industry with those dominated by a single firm. American Can was organized originally as a trust controlling virtually the entire capacity of the industry. It suffered the fate of many of the trusts organized at the turn of the century: the umbrella it held over the industry encouraged the growth of competition, and within a dozen years its share of the market had fallen to 50 per cent. It was about this time, in 1916, that American was first charged with monopoly under the Sherman Act. Professor Hession in his able study of the food container industry (*Competition in the Metal Food Container Industry, 1916–1946*

[1] *United States of America* v. *American Can Company*, Civil Action No. 26345-H. In the United States District Court for the Northern District of California, Southern Division. Exhibits UU and 3124 (Stipulation on Statistics, March 31, 1949).

[Brooklyn, 1948]) calls American Can "the trust that wasn't busted." The court refrained from dissolving it principally because of the rapid decline in its market share, and the judge expressed the hope that the growth of rivals would soon restore competition in the industry.

Competition was not quickly restored. American possessed nothing approaching pure monopoly after 1916, but it remained the dominant firm. Its market share ceased to fall, and its capacity remained for a time enormously greater than its rivals'. American's prices determined the prices for the whole industry. It maintained its lead by rapid development and expansion from within. Nevertheless, its power to control the industry was considerably weaker in 1948 than it was in 1916.

This slow metamorphosis was due partly to developments within the industry, partly to the impact of the antitrust laws. The structure of the industry altered gradually as Continental Can began to challenge American's leadership. In 1916, Continental was a small cloud on American's horizon, hardly distinguishable from a number of other small rivals. Throughout the following decades, Continental grew rapidly with a bold program of acquisition and merger as well as by rapid expansion from within. By 1939, it was half as large as American; by 1950 it was three-fourths as large. Its growth eventually put it in a position that rivalled American's. Prior to the middle thirties, American was the only metal container manufacturer with an important research program and was practically solely responsible for the progress and development that had occurred up to that time. Moreover, it was the only manufacturer up to then that was fully able to realize certain other advantages of scale. These are not production economies, but are achieved through the interlocking of separate plants so that the extreme uncertainties of demand for food containers in any one area are diffused along a chain of production sites. The ability of American to offer certainty of supply, together with its facilities for research and customer service, made it the only acceptable source of supply to many buyers of cans, including most of the large and stable ones, until a second large seller appeared.

By the end of the thirties, American was at last confronted with a powerful, efficient, and progressive rival in practically every geographical region and every product, including many in which American had earlier enjoyed a monopoly. It took time for Continental to break into the geographical strongholds of American and to build up an effective and experienced research staff, but in the end the supremacy of American was undermined.

Conditions were more stringent for the smaller firms. No other was able to achieve anything like the growth of Continental; in fact, several of those which had begun to grow to substantial size were acquired by Continental. A few producers of food cans managed to build up integrated regional organizations, securing at least part of the advantages of size, and compensated for their inferior research and service facilities by charging somewhat lower prices. Two firms even succeeded in entering the industry and establishing themselves in the food can market. All of these smaller producers were potential bases for expanded competition; that this potential was not fully realized was due to certain market practices of the larger firms which held the smaller ones in check.

A significant change was forced by the tightening of the law against price discrimination after 1936. The Robinson-Patman Act affected two markets: tin plate and tin cans. Tin plate accounts for 60 per cent of metal container costs. In the days of the Steel Trust and the Can Trust the tin plate market was almost a classic bilateral monopoly. The monopolies on both sides lost their near-exclusive control, but the "leading bargain" between U.S. Steel and American Can continued to determine the price of tin plate. In this market it appeared that monopoly power was offset by monopoly power. The benefits of this countervailing power, however, were mixed. Improvement and development in the tin plate industry, for instance, have been rapid and considerable, and there is no doubt that the large buyers, especially American, have pressed the steel producers closer to the maximum attainable rate of progress—both in product improvement and cost reduction—than would have been the case if buyers had been small and impotent. On the other hand, the price benefits of countervailing power filtered down to consumers very slowly; it requires a substantial degree of competition in subsequent markets before countervailing power in a prior market amounts to anything more than a division of spoils. One result of American's dominant position as a buyer of tin plate in the early years was that the tin plate producers favored it with secret rebates and systematic price discrimination. After a second buyer of substantial size had entered the market a new dimension of strategy emerged, and price reductions negotiated between individual buyers and sellers became more difficult to confine to the largest buyers. Nevertheless, systematic discrimination continued in various forms up to the passage of the Robinson-Patman Act, at which time American actually capitalized its claims to discriminatory treatment and liquidated them by accepting substantial lump-sum settlements from United States Steel and other suppliers. After 1937, countervailing power was exercised in behalf of all buyers of tin plate. This benefited the ultimate buyers of cans only insofar as there were limits to the exercise of monopoly power in the can market.

The buyers of cans were themselves not entirely helpless, though none had anything like the bargaining power that American had in the tin plate market. Even in the days when there was only one large can manufacturer, the big canning companies had the option of manufacturing for themselves. Backward integration is not extremely difficult for a large user, and it would have taken only a slight widening of the profit margin on cans to make it economical. Potential entry from the buying side limited monopoly power on the selling side. At first the result was systematic, secret discrimination in favor of the buyers who could offer this threat. After a second seller grew to large size, the bargaining position of the large buyers was strengthened, since they could play one off against the other. The Robinson-Patman Act obliged the major can companies to abandon secret discrimination. It was replaced, not by uniform prices to all buyers, but by an open schedule of volume discounts, which eventually came to be based on total purchases of all kinds of containers from the supplier. The discounts were greater for large-volume purchasers than any concession that the smaller can companies could easily offer, and there is no doubt that these discounts worked to their disadvantage. On the other hand, the continuous alteration and reshaping of the discount structure did afford a means of limited price competition between the two leaders; and the large buyers had at least the potential power to enforce this competition between them.

III

Though the monopoly power once possessed by the dominant firm had been markedly eroded by 1950, the effect of the underlying structural changes on competition remained more potential than actual. The reason was that the leading firm followed several policies which concentrated its remaining market power in the most effective way, and its large rival did likewise. There were three important instruments of commercial dominance. The first was the volume discounts just mentioned. The second was the practice of selling under long-term requirements contracts. It is fair to say that neither of these could have had a powerful enough effect to justify action under the antitrust laws, though they did tend to reinforce each other. The contracts were written for specific containers for use at specific plants. Smaller can companies occasionally succeeded in becoming secondary suppliers of large buyers, but it was the usual practice for a buyer to concentrate all his purchases on a single source of supply. There were some buyers whose purchases considerably exceeded the volume necessary to get the highest discount that was offered, but most of these also had long-term requirements contracts with a single supplier or, less frequently, split their purchases between American and Continental. The amount of business that the smaller can companies were eligible to compete for at any given time was thus restricted. Volume discounts were partly responsible, but the superiority of the two large sellers in research and customer service may have been equally important in determining the result.

The third instrument of control was the practice of tying the lease of can closing machinery to the sale of cans. (This was not done through an explicit tying clause, but by arranging the expiration dates of separate contracts so that no canner would be able to retain American's machinery to close competitors' cans. There were minor exceptions.) This requires a word of explanation. If the manufacture of closing machinery had been perfectly competitive, the larger can companies would have gained no net advantage by this practice. But American's can machinery has long been recognized as the best and most complete in the industry, and its progressiveness in this field is beyond dispute. Continental began late, but was overtaking American rapidly in the late thirties. Both large firms followed the same policy. Rentals on closing machinery, which also covered servicing by the manufacturer, were set below actual cost, to induce buyers to lease machines. Most can buyers were allowed to retain the machinery only as long as they purchased the cans to be closed on it from the same firm. The moderate advantage which the major sellers possessed in closing machinery was thus extended forward and magnified in the can market. The relation between supplier and customer became harder to break. (Closing machinery is generally unimportant for nonfood cans, and both major companies faced much more vigorous competition from independents in this field.) In markets for food cans, the smaller manufacturers were forced to imitate the leasing practices of the majors; but since they had to buy somewhat inferior closing machines on the open market and lease them at below-cost rentals, they reaped no comparable advantage. (One or two of the smaller companies also entered the manufacture of closing machinery, without much success until recently.) A side effect of the practice was that no canner would buy machinery in preference to renting it, and independent machinery manufacturers faced an uneconomically thin market.

IV

The government might have attempted a major Sherman Act case, with wholesale dissolution and structural reorganization of the industry as the objective. But this would have been risky, since the specific charge of monopolization had been tried in an earlier case and the judge had refused the suggested remedy of dissolution. Instead, the government attacked the practice of tie-in sales directly under Section 3 of the Clayton Act, retaining a Sherman Act charge to scoop in the requirements contracts if possible and to provide for equitable relief. There is some evidence that the Antitrust Division was not entirely satisfied with the form that its case eventually took in consequence, but it won the case nevertheless. The court decided that American had violated both the Clayton Act and the Sherman Act.[2] In addition to a number of minor matters, which need not concern us here, the 1950 decree altered market practice in the metal container industry in three ways. (Continental accepted the same judgment in a consent decree.)

1. The major firms were prohibited from offering any annual cumulative volume discounts.

[2] 87 F. Supp. 18 (1949). A simultaneous case against Continental was not brought to trial, Continental having agreed in advance to accept any judgment entered against American, short of divestiture.

2. Requirements contracts were limited to one year. American Can had presented convincing evidence that requirements contracts are necessary to protect food canners, in view of the great uncertainty of crop yields and timing, and that canners preferred them to fixed-quantity contracts; hence the court did not prohibit them altogether. The court also ordered that separate contracts be written for individual plants when the customer had more than one cannery. The buyer could still place all his contracts with a single seller if he chose, but smaller can manufacturers would find it easier to bid at least for the business of a single plant of a multiplant buyer.

3. The tie between machine leasing and the sale of cans was broken. The major companies were permanently enjoined from conditioning the lease of machines on the sale of cans, by any subterfuge. In addition, they were ordered to sell their existing closing machines at bargain prices to anyone who wanted to buy them, giving priority to existing lessees. This order applied to all machines to be built in the future as well, for a period of ten years. The can companies were required to make all technological information and know-how available to buyers, to set up schools to train service men employed by the canneries, and to license closing machinery patents without royalty. The court recognized that there were certain advantages to integration between machinery manufacture and can manufacture, since can manufacture and can closing involve much the same technology, and so it did not order divestiture. The can companies were required to lease to everyone any machine that they were then leasing to anyone. Moreover, rentals had to be fully compensatory, including a fair profit, after the end of 1953. (Continental has asked for a postponement. Fully compensatory rentals on its diminished stock of equipment would be prohibitive, it claims, since overhead has not been proportionally reduced.) No more could below-cost rentals be used as an inducement to lease.

V

This decree knocked out practically all the remaining props of market control. The decree has been in effect now for over three years. Some of its consequences have been striking. One instance is the sale of closing machines, which has greatly exceeded everyone's expectations. The can manufacturers had claimed that customers would be reluctant to buy them—that customers would prefer to lease instead and pay the supplier the appropriate fee for bearing the risk of obsolescence and the task of servicing and maintenance. If this reluctance ever existed it was quickly overcome. The bargain prices the court set on the machines existing in 1950 made it uneconomical not to buy them, and in addition American and Continental, in wholehearted compliance with the letter and the spirit of the decree, have made vigorous efforts to sell both old and newly manufactured machines. By the middle of 1954 both American and

Continental had sold over 75 per cent of the closing machines they were leasing in 1950. While the lease market may revive in the future, can buyers are no longer heavily dependent on their can suppliers for closing machinery, and there is no way now for the machinery supplier to apply commercial leverage to the can market. After the transition period is over, the independent manufacturers of machinery will be able to market closing machines directly to the canning industry, and they have already responded to this broadening of their opportunities.

A second result has been an extensive breakdown of exclusive supplier-customer relations. While fruit and vegetable canneries have largely continued their requirements contracts, the large packers operating several canneries have begun to allocate them to different suppliers. Other canners have begun to split requirements within the plant, closing cans from several suppliers indiscriminately on the machines of several manufacturers. There has been an enormous growth in open-order purchasing at the expense of contract purchasing. Small firms are now better able to detach fragments of business which used to be held firmly by the large can suppliers. They can enter large-volume markets either by carrying off supply contracts for individual canneries in a chain or by becoming secondary sources of supply within the plant. The vertical partitions in the market which formerly made the ties between particular buyers and sellers very strong have been demolished, and competitive forces, wherever they originate, can sweep across it largely unimpeded. The market position of smaller manufacturers has been greatly strengthened.

It is interesting to note that these changes in the can market have been accompanied by some instability in the tin plate market. At least part of this instability has been transmitted backward from the can market. Prices have become more flexible; open-order purchasing has grown in volume; the leadership of the leading bargain between U.S. Steel and American Can has weakened further. The tin plate suppliers still feel the weight of the large buyers' bargaining power, but this is more likely now to work to the benefit of ultimate consumers of cans.

It is possible of course to expect too much of the decree. The gross structure of the industry has not changed very much and probably will not change much in the immediate future. Doubtless the effects of a decree of dissolution, if American had been convicted of illegal acquisition and maintenance of monopoly, would have been more spectacular. Several firms could have been fashioned out of either of the leaders without an appreciable loss of efficiency, and the market would in time have enforced a high degree of competition among the fragments. However, such a monopoly charge could not have been sustained. We must decide whether we have any better ground now than the court did in 1916 for expecting workable competition in the future.

American and Continental together would still be able to dominate the industry in the short run if they maintained effective collusion in every dimension of the market. But instead the two large firms are in a state of intense rivalry. The challenger is staging a vigorous drive on the markets of the leader. A number of large accounts previously held by American have now been split. Technological rivalry is unrestrained. While open price warfare has been avoided, except in a few local instances, there is protracted maneuvering in an atmosphere of great uncertainty when the time for quoting new prices and renewing contracts comes round every year. American's price leadership is now merely barometric, and it cannot count on being followed by Continental or by any other seller.

The smaller firms, aided by a strong growth trend in the industry, have been establishing themselves on a more secure footing and have also been edging into the markets of both the leaders. In several instances recently the price structure of the majors has had to be adapted to the independent competitive tactics of a smaller firm aggressively reaching for a larger share. Although the oligopoly structure remains, enough has been said to show that the competitive pattern is in a state of flux.

No outsiders have entered can manufacture in the last three years, but the threat of entry from the buying side has been intensified. Large buyers can no longer be pacified with volume discounts. During the past year the very largest consumer of packers cans began to manufacture part of its own requirements, and another large buyer, located in one of American's few remaining monopoly territories, has announced plans to manufacture all its own containers. The effect of these events is incalculable. Both of the large sellers are constrained as never before by the threat of backward integration, and the restraints exercised on profit margins in cans work to the benefit of all buyers.

American itself has no monopoly weapons left in its hands. Any firm which relies on size and the momentum of past achievements alone to protect it against competition is likely to find its position deteriorating with alarming speed. What American can do is to take advantage of the moderate superiorities it evidently has in efficiency and research. It can maintain its leading position by reducing costs and continuing its rapid rate of product development, passing along the benefits to consumers. Its large rival will push it, or perhaps lead it, in this respect. Its smaller rivals will offer a stronger competitive challenge as time goes on. And its large customers will never be more than a few years behind in potential efficiency if they should decide to produce their own supplies. A forecast of workable competition appears to be justified. Thus it seems that the Antitrust Division, in choosing to make a limited attack on market practices—however much it may later have doubted its own wisdom—made a good decision after all.

6

The Tobacco Case of 1946*

By WILLIAM H. NICHOLLS[†]

"If the law supposes that," said Mr. Bumble, ". . . the law is a ass, a idiot."

—Charles Dickens, *Oliver Twist*

The ways of the law are devious and unpredictable. Since the law is (in Tennyson's words) a "wilderness of single instances," it is dangerous to assume that future court decisions will always be fully consistent with those of even the recent past. Yet, being neither prophet nor crystal-gazer, I must credit the courts with a logical consistency which I know they do not possess. I can therefore discuss even the probable economic consequences of the *Tobacco* case only upon the basis of two dubious assumptions: (1) that the courts really said what I believe them to have said in the *Tobacco* decision; and (2) that they will carry to their logical conclusion the legal implications of that decision. Having satisfied my conscience by this urgent prefatory *caveat,* I can more honestly turn to the difficult task at hand.

THE SIGNIFICANCE OF THE TOBACCO DECISIONS

It is the task of the law of monopoly to distinguish between business practices which are in the public interest and those which are not. In carrying out this difficult problem of evaluation, the courts have had to devise and apply tests capable of differentiating between approved and disapproved practices. As elsewhere in the law, the law of monopoly has reflected the perennial conflict between certainty and change. Two tests of monopoly have become traditional: (1) On the question of conspiracy, does the evidence show that competitors actually agreed? (2) On the question of monopolization, was there overt predatory action to exclude competition? These two tests had the advantages of certainty—they could be applied with sufficient consistency to assure equality of treatment before the law; and they were sufficiently concrete to indicate the practices which must be avoided to escape condemnation under the law.

* *The American Economic Review,* Vol. XXXIX (Proceedings of the American Economic Association, 1949), pp. 284–96. Reprinted by courtesy of the publisher and the author.

I am indebted to my colleague, George W. Stocking, for his helpful but sometimes dissenting criticisms of the original manuscript of this paper.

† Vanderbilt University.

Unfortunately, however, these tests have become increasingly inadequate as the structure and practices of American industry have taken new and more subtle forms. Thus, the need for change—for adapting the law to a new industrial environment—has become more and more apparent.

In the *Tobacco* case,[1] at the necessary cost of new uncertainties, the courts finally met this need for change in two ways. First, the Court of Appeals brought wholly tacit, nonaggressive oligopoly fully within the reach of the conspiracy provisions of the Sherman Act. Prior law already had made clear that—in the absence of "formal agreement"—an unlawful conspiracy can be inferred from "concert of action," "unity of purpose," or "a common design." Furthermore, in the *Tobacco* case, there was plentiful and undisputed evidence that the three defendant dominant firms had behaved identically with regard to prices, terms of sale, and general business practices. Nevertheless, the case was probably unique in that there was not a whit of evidence that a common plan had even been contemplated or proposed.[2] The government's evidence was admittedly *wholly* circumstantial. The fact of identity of behavior was offered as the basis for inferring both the existence and the elements of the alleged common plan and the defendants' knowledge of that plan. Each was alleged to have acted similarly with the knowledge that the others would so act, to their mutual self-interest. Thus, the *Tobacco* case brought the basic assumption of modern oligopoly theory squarely before the courts. In finding in the facts a reasonable basis for the jury's inference of unlawful conspiracy, the Court of Appeals accepted the practical implications of that assumption; namely, that a few dominant firms will, perhaps independently and purely as a matter of self-interest, evolve nonaggressive patterns of behavior. Thus, attention was shifted from form to probable results. Upon final appeal, the Supreme Court refused to review this part of the lower court's findings.

Second, in the *Tobacco* case, the existence of power to exclude competition, not the abuse of that power, became the new test of illegal monopolization. Thus, the recent *Aluminum* doctrine[3] was approved and was extended to conspiratorial oligopoly. Accepting without review the judgments below that a conspiracy had been established, the Supreme Court held that neither the exertion of power to exclude nor the actual exclusion of competitors is necessary to the crime of monopolization.

---

[1] *American Tobacco Co., et al.*, v. *U.S.*, 147 F. 2d 93 (1944); 328 U.S. 781 (1946).

[2] In this regard, it therefore differed from the *Interstate Circuit* case (306 U.S. 208, 1939), upon which the government relied. There it was held (at 226) that the finding of an agreement among distributors, while supported by the evidence, was not necessary: "It was enough that, knowing the concerted action was contemplated and invited, the distributors . . . participated in it." In that case, however, unanimity of action would have served only as evidence of adherence to a common plan, the proposal of which was supported by direct evidence.

[3] *U.S.* v. *Aluminum Co.*, 148 F. 2d. 416 (1945), the Circuit Court serving as the final court of appeal.

Existence of the power and intent to exclude will suffice. Since the Court was willing to infer intent from the concerted action of the conspirators, the power to exclude—as shown by the degree of market control of the combination—was made the crucial issue. Thus, attention was shifted from monopolization as an *action* to monopoly as a *condition*. The Supreme Court explicitly limited the precedential significance of this decision to cases in which conspiracy is an essential ingredient. Nevertheless, so broad was the lower court's application of the law of conspiracy to the facts that, if it were generally followed, the behavior of few oligopolies could probably escape condemnation as "conspiratorial."

It should be obvious that the *Tobacco* decisions of 1946 must be given a prominent place in the historical development of the case law of the antitrust acts. And, if my interpretation of their legal implications is correct, the *Tobacco* decisions have gone far to close the wide gap between the legal and economic concepts of monopoly, which became so apparent to economists during the thirties.[4] In accepting detailed similarity of behavior among a few dominant firms as a reasonable basis for inferring illegal conspiracy, the courts have finally brought the law of conspiracy into harmony with the economics of oligopoly. Furthermore, the legal and economic concepts of monopoly (including conspiratorial group monopoly) have been brought closer together. Thus, Rostow is correct in finding, on the basis of the *Aluminum* and *Tobacco* cases, that "market control is now a far more important theme in Sherman Act cases than handicaps on an individual's power to do business. The old preoccupation of judges with evidence of business tactics they regarded as ruthless, predatory and immoral has all but disappeared. . . . We are close to the point of regarding as illegal the kind of economic power which the economist regards as monopolistic."[5] That the *Aluminum* and *Tobacco* decisions have revitalized the Sherman Act, especially Section 2, seems beyond serious doubt. Furthermore, economists can rejoice that the precepts of modern economic analysis have so quickly found their way into the case law of monopoly.

Unlike lawyers of the Antitrust Division, however, economists cannot be satisfied simply by the scoreboard of cases won by the government. Although some important legal "twilight zones" remain, the widespread application of the new tests of monopoly to oligopolistic industries should lead to a high proportion of government victories from now on. It is clear, however, that without remedial action, these legal victories will be of relatively little economic or social consequences. And, if

---

[4] Cf. E. S. Mason, "Monopoly in Law and Economics," *Yale Law Journal*, Vol. 47 (1937–38), pp. 34–49.

[5] Eugene V. Rostow, "The New Sherman Act: A Positive Instrument of Progress," *University of Chicago Law Review*, Vol. 14 (1946–47), pp. 574–75 *et seq.* For a more cautious appraisal of these two cases, cf. Edward H. Levi, "The Antitrust Laws and Monopoly," *ibid.*, pp. 172–81.

remedial action is taken, it is by no means certain that the economic consequences will always be in the public interest.

THE PROSPECTS OF GOVERNMENT "VICTORY"

With regard to the *Tobacco* decision, counsel for Reynolds Tobacco Company argued that:

> . . . the significance of these convictions extends far beyond the immediate consequences to petitioners and the tobacco industry. . . . For, *if these convictions be lawful, the pattern of prosecution is applicable—with the result of almost certain and repeated conviction—to every other executive and corporation in a mass production industry* . . . in which, as a matter of common knowledge, economic forces have produced identities or close similarities in manufacturing, packaging, pricing, advertising, marketing and even raw material acquisition.[6]

The present writer is willing to accept this appraisal as being at least within the realm of possibility. Given the widespread pattern of domination-by-a-few in modern American industry, counsel for Liggett and Myers was also probably correct in arguing that "the common practices of the tobacco industry are in many instances usual features of business life today, and in all instances practices which businessmen guided by . . . self-interest, acting reasonably and in the absence of agreement, might adopt."[7] In view of this fact, the conviction of the major tobacco companies suggests at least a presumption in favor of the view that the Antitrust Division's ability to find and prosecute monopolies successfully is now largely limited only by the extent of its own resources in bringing cases to trial.

Nevertheless, we must recognize that at least two important questions are as yet unanswered. First, what types of similarity of behavior among oligopolistic competitors will the courts hold to be insufficient to sustain an inference of illegal conspiracy? In the *Tobacco* case, the circumstantial evidence supporting such an inference was very strong—considerably stronger than the evidence which could be marshaled against many other oligopolistic industries. However, the extent to which the courts are willing to go in finding illegal conspiracy among oligopolists will depend at least as much upon their judgment and preconceptions as upon the facts of any specific case before them. The conspiracy doctrine of the *Tobacco* case certainly permits them to go about as far as they like in this direction. Second, what is the legal status of a single dominant firm of intermediate size (say, controlling 50–65 per cent of an industry), such as was involved in the *Steel* and *Harvester* cases? Until the courts explicitly apply recent doctrine to a situation of this sort, the law will continue to treat loose "conspiracies" more severely than (within

---

[6] In the Supreme Court of the U.S., October Term, 1944, No. 840, *Reynolds* v. *U.S.*, Petition for Writ of Certiorari, p. 14. Italics added.

[7] In the U.S. Circuit Court of Appeals, 6th Circ., No. 9138, *Liggett and Myers* v. *U.S.*, Brief on Behalf of Appellants, p. 234.

certain limits) such a single dominant firm with an equal or greater degree of market control.[8]

Despite these remaining "twilight zones," the conclusion is apparent: in antitrust action against oligopolistic industries, the prospects of government victory are now relatively bright.

"VICTORY" WITHOUT REMEDIAL ACTION

It is the writer's belief that, in the *Tobacco* case, the courts reached a conclusion which—in the main—economic analysis would support. Nevertheless, the fact remains that the court in effect condemned the natural, normal, and intelligent consequences of an oligopolistic market structure. The difficult question of appropriate remedial action was therefore placed in bold relief. As a criminal prosecution, the *Tobacco* case provided no remedial action. Thus far, therefore, the government's victory has been (apart from a quarter-million dollars of fines) almost an empty one.

Given the present structure of the industry, until now left untouched by the government, the writer must admit a feeling of some sympathy for the arguments of counsel for the tobacco companies. Thus, counsel claimed that, even if guilty, they were "entirely without guide as to how they may lawfully avoid the creation of evidence of future Sherman Act violations against themselves, unless they cease business altogether." For example, must Reynolds refrain from "percentage buying" of leaf? And if it does, and its competitors do likewise, "will it or they not then be accused of manipulating prices, allocating tobaccos, and discriminating against growers through intermittent buying . . . ?"

---

[8] Reynolds' counsel posed essentially this same problem in the following argument, even though (written prior to the final *Aluminum* decision) it was based upon a false premise. Since it was not denied that "exclusionary action is essential to monopolizing by a single person or entity":

"It should *a fortiori* be held essential in a case involving a number of separate entities severally engaged in competition (albeit imperfect) with each other. Otherwise, the whole notion of group monopolizing becomes illusory. Without concerted action to exclude others from the field, there is no justification for analogizing the position of the several entities to that of a single trading unit seeking sole, or practically exclusive, trading privileges. Nor is there any warrant for aggregating their power in order to show control over the field. For, until action to exclude is taken, the power of none is employed to fence in the field in the interest of the group. On the contrary, the power of each is being employed in competition with the others and constitutes a disruptive or centrifugal force. And an unexecuted intent to exclude someone else at some indefinite time and by some undetermined means does not serve to fuse that power and make of it a centripetal force." (In the Supreme Court of the U.S., October Term, 1945, *Reynolds* v. *U.S.*, Brief for Petitioners, pp. 47–48.)

The extent to which the *Aluminum* doctrine is applicable to single dominant firms in other industries is obscured by the fact that Alcoa's percentage control was very large (90 per cent). In the *Aluminum* opinion, Judge Hand himself expressed doubt that a single firm controlling 60–64 per cent of a market was a monopoly; he was certain that 33 per cent was not. Significantly International Harvester's market position had been 64 per cent.

Or "must Reynolds desist from charging for its product the price charged for a competitive product, and must Reynolds, by prosecution or otherwise, attempt to prevent a competitor from selling at Reynolds' price?"[9] Or again:

> What are the specific policies and practices we must abandon, modify, or adopt in order to conduct our business according to law? . . . Presumably, the appellants were convicted of agreement, not of the particular operations alleged to constitute agreement. Yet, on the Government's theory, continuation by more than one of the appellants of the operations alleged is evidence of a further Sherman Act agreement. . . . If this is so, how is Liggett & Myers to carry on? Must it start all over again with new management, with a new system? Is everything the appellants do illegal, or evidence of illegality, if done by more than one of them?[10]

Since neither the prosecution nor the courts provided an answer, the major tobacco companies have themselves done so; namely, to follow essentially the same cigarette price policies since the trial that they followed before. The evidence upon which the *Tobacco* decision was based extended only through July, 1940. Effective July 1, 1940, the three major cigarette companies had increased their list prices by identical amounts from $6.25 to $6.53 per thousand cigarettes to take account of an increase in the federal cigarette tax from $3.00 to $3.25 per thousand. As a result, their net realized price after discounts to wholesalers (10 and 2 per cent) and federal tax was virtually unchanged (dropping from $2.512 to $2.509 per thousand). Although the price history of the industry since 1940 has been dominated by price controls, the recent behavior of cigarette prices is of considerable interest. On December 27, 1941, American raised the list price of Lucky Strikes from $6.53 to $7.10. This represented the first time since the period of virtual list price identity began in 1923 that American had attempted to lead upward in a price change although it had twice led downward in 1933. Reynolds and Liggett and Myers refused to follow, however. Whether their failure to do so was the result of their unwillingness to recognize American as the price leader is impossible to determine because of two other important factors in the picture at that time. First, the three companies had just filed an appeal to the unfavorable district-court verdict which had been largely based upon identity of price behavior. Second, Price Administrator Henderson immediately asked American to rescind its increase pending investigation of the increased costs by which the increase was allegedly justified. When American refused unless formally ordered to do so, the OPA on December 30 froze all cigarette prices at their Decem-

[9] In the Supreme Court of the U.S., October Term, 1944, No. 840, *Reynolds* v. *U.S.*, Petition for Writ of Certiorari, pp. 12–13. Cf. *ibid.*, *Liggett and Myers* v. *U.S.*, pp. 5, 26.

[10] In the Circuit Court of Appeals, 6th Circ., Brief on Behalf of Liggett and Myers, *op. cit.*, p. 27.

ber 26 levels, although it permitted the list prices of the economy brands to be raised from $5.05 to $5.15.[11]

Although the price ceilings on the economy brands were gradually raised, OPA did not permit any increase in the prices of the standard brands (except one to compensate for the increase of $0.25 in the federal tax on November 2, 1942) until April, 1946. As a consequence, the net price to the major companies, after discounts and federal tax, remained virtually constant at $2.51 from January, 1937, to April, 1946. During this same period, with rapidly rising manufacturing costs, the three companies' net incomes as a percentage of their net worths (after deducting book value of good will) fell from 15–20 per cent to 9–11 per cent. On April 26, 1946, OPA raised the price ceilings on standard and economy brands to $7.09 and $6.10, respectively.

On July 1, 1946, existing price controls expired and the new act of July 25 exempted tobacco products. On July 30, Liggett and Myers announced a price increase of $0.22 per thousand on Chesterfields, but rescinded it retroactively a week later when other manufacturers refused to follow.[12] Thus, in its first attempt since the dissolution to lead in a price change, Liggett and Myers was unsuccessful. That the other companies did not follow may have reflected their unwillingness to concede a position of price leadership to Liggett and Myers. On the other hand, fear of adverse public opinion in the turbulent days of mid-1946 may have been a factor. On October 7, however, American raised the price of Lucky Strikes from $7.09 to $7.38. Liggett and Myers' Chesterfield followed upward by an identical amount within a day or two. Finally, on October 11, after most other manufacturers had also followed American's lead, Reynolds increased the price of Camels to $7.35, three cents per thousand below the other major brands. This minute price differential was sufficiently unique to attract considerable notice in the press. With this minor exception, all standard brands were apparently raised to an identical higher list price.[13]

On July 28, 1948, American again led in a price increase from $7.38 to $7.78. All of the other major companies followed within twenty-four hours, the prices of Camel and Philip Morris being raised to $7.75 and $7.79, respectively. It is believed that Chesterfields were raised to $7.78. Up to the present time, however, the writer has not been able to obtain

---

[11] *Business Week,* January 3, 1942, p. 8; 7 *Federal Register* 1322.

[12] *Wall Street Journal,* July 31, 1946, p. 14; *ibid.,* August 6, 1946, p. 4.

[13] These price data are from the *Wall Street Journal* (October 8, 1946, p. 14; October 9, 1946, p. 4; October 12, 1946, p. 2), which reported that the following other brands were all raised to $7.38: Pall Mall and Tareyton (American); Old Gold (Lorillard); Philip Morris (Philip Morris), increased the same day as Lucky Strike; and Rameses (Stephano Bros.). Marvel (Stephano), a leading economy brand, was also increased from $6.10 to $6.40. The price changes on Brown & Williamson brands (Raleigh, Kool, Wings) were not listed.

the exact list prices of the other major brands (including Chesterfield), but he is certain that they were raised by almost identical amounts.[14] Insofar as price differences among the standard brands do now exist, it is obvious that they are of no practical importance, being too small to be reflected in different retail prices. Furthermore, there have been no changes in the customary discounts to wholesalers. Hence, even though very minor price differences may have resulted from the *Tobacco* decision, they are significant only as a means of attempting to avoid the absolute price identity there condemned. In fact, with the minor exceptions noted, the list prices, terms of trade, and timing of price changes are probably more nearly identical today—if one considers all of the standard brands—than prior to 1940.[15]

This limited evidence supports the view that, if there was illegal conspiracy before 1940, there is still illegal conspiracy today. Furthermore, if the economic power of the three major companies combined constituted illegal monopolization before 1940, it does so *a fortiori* at the present time. Between 1939 and 1947, during which domestic cigarette sales nearly doubled, the three defendant companies expanded their share of the domestic cigarette market from 68 to more than 85 per cent. Thus, they appear to be fast approaching their position of 1931, when they sold 91 per cent of the nation's cigarettes. Meanwhile, the economy brands' share of the domestic market has dropped from 14 to about 1 per cent in the face of high consumer incomes, high manufacturing costs, and a narrowing price differential below the standard brands. As a consequence, the smaller companies which grew rapidly on economy brands during the thirties have lost much ground since 1939, their standard brands (if any) failing to share sufficiently in the shift to a higher-priced product to compensate for their declining low-priced market. Apart from Philip Morris (which has not quite held its own despite its purchase of Axton-Fisher in 1944), all companies other than the Big Three have suffered moderate to severe losses of market position since 1939. Within the Big Three, Liggett and Myers' share dropped slightly while American's jumped from 22.7 to 36.1 per cent, and Reynolds' from 23.7 to 28.8 per cent. Not since 1931 have one or two com-

---

[14] These price data are from the *Wall Street Journal* (July 30, 1948, p. 12; July 31, 1948, p. 2) and the *New York Times* (July 29, 1948, p. 23; July 30, 1948, p. 11). The prices of the two principal economy brands, Marvel and Wings, remained unchanged at $6.40 and $6.38. Attempts to verify all of these data by visits to three Chicago wholesalers were unsuccessful. All were reluctant to give exact price information. One frankly stated that the current asset value of his presence on the manufacturers' "direct lists" was at least $5,000 and expressed fear that, if the divulgence of such confidential information were traced to him, he might be removed from their "direct lists." He therefore refused to talk.

[15] Thus, during the thirties, the list prices of Pall Mall, Tareyton, Philip Morris, and Raleigh frequently differed both in level and timing of price changes from the three major brands. These differences now appear to have almost wholly disappeared.

panies been so dominant.[16] The two recent price changes suggest that American—now that it has again clearly established itself as the nation's largest cigarette manufacturer—has displaced Reynolds as the recognized price leader of the industry. It is even possible that Reynolds has voluntarily abdicated its traditional position as price leader in order that it can be certain to avoid the absolute price identity so recently condemned.

Despite the absence of any fundamental changes in their historical pattern of similar price behavior and despite their recrudescent degree of market control, the three convicted tobacco companies nevertheless appear to have followed a more moderate price policy since 1946 than that of earlier years. Net prices to the major manufacturers are now only about 33 per cent above 1939 and the Big Three's rates of profits are currently running at about 13–16 per cent (1948) as compared with 14–18 per cent in 1939 and 17–22 per cent in 1931. (Meanwhile, Lorillard's rate of profits has increased slightly to 10 per cent [1948] and Philip Morris' has fallen from 25.2 per cent in 1939 to 8.6 per cent in 1947.) This more moderate price policy is probably in part due to the Big Three's desire to fend off the existing and potential competition which they found so unexpectedly strong in the thirties. Apparently such price policies—in conjunction with the continued powerful differential advantage of their highly advertised brands—promise to maintain or increase the Big Three's market control where the more grasping price policies of the past failed to do so. Undoubtedly, present cigarette prices also still reflect to some extent the long period of controlled prices. Finally, because of the legal doubts which it cast upon the whole fabric of traditional cigarette price policies, recent antitrust action should probably receive part of the credit for these more moderate prices. If so, however, until effective remedial action is taken, the Antitrust Division's

[16] The following table summarizes the relevant data by companies:

Company	*Cigarette Sales (Billions)*			*% Total Tax-Paid Cigarette Production*		
	1931	*1939*	*1947*	*1931*	*1939*	*1947*
American	46.1	41.1	121.6	39.4	22.7	36.1
Reynolds	33.3	42.8	94.7	28.4	23.7	28.1
Liggett and Myers	26.6	39.0	69.0	22.7	21.6	20.5
Philip Morris	0.4	12.6	23.0	0.3	7.0	6.8
Lorillard	8.2	10.2	14.6	7.0	5.7	4.3
Brown & Williamson	0.3	19.1	11.0	0.2	10.6	3.3
Stephano	0.1	6.0	1.2	0.1	3.3	0.4
Axton-Fisher	0.8	4.3	—	0.7	2.4	—
Larus	0.3	2.3	?	0.2	1.3	?
Miscellaneous	1.0	3.3	1.7	1.0	1.7	0.5
Total tax-paid production	117.1	180.7	336.8	100.0	100.0	100.0
Big Three	106.0	122.9	285.3	90.5	68.0	84.7
Economy brands	0.4	25.6	2.7	0.0	14.2	0.9

The 1931 and 1939 data are compiled or computed from *Record on Appeal*, Exhibits No. 638, 702, 677, 428, 293, 437, 1268, 1265, 1266. The 1947 data (domestic sales only) are estimated from *Business Week*, January 17, 1948, p. 42.

victory at best may have brought somewhat lower cigarette prices (at least in the short run) at the cost of that increasing concentration of economic power which it so much abhors. With this possible exception, the current history of the tobacco industry suggests that the widespread conviction of oligopolistic industries, though now legally possible, will produce only relatively unimportant economic consequences unless accompanied by measures to change the underlying industrial structure which makes the condemned behavior almost inevitable. Thus the difficult problem of evaluation and prescription in the public interest still remains.

THE PROBLEM OF REMEDIAL ACTION

The Antitrust Division has certainly not been unaware of the need for remedial action in the tobacco industry. In response to warnings from the Department of Justice following the 1946 decision, the convicted companies claim to have made changes in their policies which eliminate the possibility of further violations of the antitrust laws. That the Antitrust Division has not yet been convinced is indicated by the fact that, during the last year, it has held several conferences with the three companies to consider the terms of a proposed consent decree.[17] I am extremely skeptical, however, about the efficacy of any consent decree which falls short of dissolution. And even with the bargaining strength which its recent successful criminal action gives the Division, we can hardly expect the companies to agree to dissolution in such an out-of-court settlement. Yet in the civil suit recently instituted against the four major meat packers, the Division reveals that it considers dissolution the appropriate remedy for oligopoly. In this suit, patterned in detail after the *Tobacco* decision, the Division seeks dissolution of the four principal firms into fourteen companies.[18] Why, then, has not the Antitrust Division brought a civil suit seeking dissolution of the major tobacco companies?

I suspect that the principal reason, apart from the need for economizing resources, is that the Division recognizes the difficulties involved in formulating a dissolution plan for the tobacco industry. Each of the three

[17] R. J. Reynolds Tobacco Co., Prospectus on an Issue of Debentures, September 29, 1948, pp. 27–28.

[18] In the Dist. Ct. of the U.S., Northern Dist. of Ill., Eastern Division, *U.S.* v. *Armour, Swift, Cudahy, and Wilson*, Civil Action No. 48C 1351, September 15, 1948. The complaint alleges that, as a continuing offense since 1893, the four defendants have (1) refrained from competition among themselves by market sharing (constant percentages) in the purchase of livestock and the sale of meats, and by identical cost-figuring, prices, and terms of trade for both livestock and meats; (2) restrained competition by independents through the formulation of policies which the latter were urged to follow; and (3) excluded competitors by purchase or by resisting expansion of independents. As relief, the government asks (1) that each defendant be enjoined from following each of the practices complained of and (2) that Swift and Armour each be dissolved into five companies, and Cudahy and Wilson each be dissolved into two companies.

companies has three to four cigarette manufacturing plants which could be made into separate firms. Furthermore, it is almost certain that the principal economies of scale, beyond those of the individual plant, are those of advertising and market control; hence are private rather than social. Nevertheless, there are at least two important barriers to dissolution. First, each of the three firms has concentrated wholly (Reynolds) or largely (85 per cent or more) upon a single brand of cigarettes. Since a single brand of cigarettes could hardly be divided among several successor companies, the present major brands would probably have to be abolished. The original Tobacco Trust, having a multiplicity of brands, did not present this difficulty to those responsible for developing the details of its dissolution. Second, the paramount importance of advertising and sales effort in the industry cannot be overlooked. As Jones once pointed out, the dissolution of the Tobacco Trust "led to a duplication of selling organization and an increased overhead expense; and the result was a general *increase* in selling costs." Between 1910 and 1913, the selling costs of the successor cigarette companies increased by 85 per cent, and the advertising expenditures more than doubled, in comparison with those of the Trust.[19] True, the dissolution ushered in a decade of innovation and price competition which was strongly in the public interest. Thereafter, however, the industry settled down into a pattern of non-price competition which it is doubtful that even a second dissolution could fully avoid. In other words, the cigarette industry is of such a nature that competition, at best, must continue to have important imperfections. Nonetheless, despite such difficult problems as these, a workable plan of dissolution could probably be devised upon the basis of a careful study of the structure of the tobacco industry.

Whether or not dissolution is resorted to, however, supplementary techniques should not be ignored. Although lying outside of the limits of antitrust action, two other measures deserve consideration as means of encouraging competition in the tobacco industry. First, a sharply progressive tax might be imposed upon the individual firm's total expenditures for advertising. Ideally, the tax should apply only to advertising expenditures greater than those already being made by firms of intermediate size, thereby permitting small firms to expand their advertising outlays somewhat but forcing the largest firms to curtail theirs considerably. Such a tax should go far toward eliminating the overwhelming advantage which large-scale advertising gives to giant firms, both in holding their market position against existing small firms and in limiting the entry of new firms. If clear limits were established on the extent of advertising, resort to price competition should also be encouraged. The great practical obstacles to this proposal are obvious. First, since such a tax might have to apply to all industries nondiscriminately, it would be

---

[19] Eliot Jones, *The Trust Problem in the United States* (1922), pp. 40–44.

difficult to make due legislative allowances for important differences between industries in the absolute and relative levels of advertising costs. Second, insofar as large firms lost business as a result of the lower advertising expenditures caused by the tax, a question of constitutionality under the "due process" clause might be invoked. Third, one could hardly expect the press and radio to support such a tax with enthusiasm or complete objectivity. Nevertheless, this proposal does center attention upon one of the key problems involved in introducing a modicum of competition into industries—such as tobacco, liquor, drugs, cosmetics, etc.—which rely heavily upon advertising.

A second measure for encouraging competition in the tobacco industry would be the sharp reduction or elimination of the federal and state cigarette taxes. These taxes have now reached so high a proportion of the final retail price as to make price competition among cigarette manufacturers almost prohibitive. Thus, at the present time, in a state levying a three-cent-per-package cigarette tax in addition to the federal tax of seven cents, a manufacturer would have to cut his final net price by about 15 per cent to lower the retail price by 5–6 per cent (or one cent a package). Since distributing margins are very small, the elimination of the cigarette tax would bring these two percentages very close together and make price competition among manufacturers much more attractive. Valuable though cigarette (and liquor) taxes may be as a lucrative source of governmental revenues, that they strongly foster monopolistic price policies has been almost wholly overlooked. It is true that, in the short run, the elimination of such taxes might simply increase the monopoly profits of the major firms. But the long-run result would probably be strong encouragement of entry and price competition, especially if combined with the advertising tax previously mentioned. If cigarette taxes are not eliminated, however, at least they should be based upon value rather than quantity of product. The present flat tax per thousand cigarettes is inexcusably burdensome upon the economy brands, which are the only real element of price competition in the industry. While a graduated tax, based upon two or more price classes, has been frequently proposed, it has never met with Congressional favor.[20] Far better than such a graduated tax would be a straight ad valorem tax which would encourage a full continuum of possible prices, thereby helping to undermine the present pattern of virtual price identity for both standard brands and economy brands.

In spite of its apparent reticence to dissolve the major cigarette companies, the Antitrust Division may be expected to use dissolution pro-

[20] See, for example, Senate Committee on Finance (73d Cong., 2d sess.), *Hearing on Reduction of Tax on Cigarettes*, 1934. In December, 1948, the House Select Committee on Small Business recommended to Congress "a graduated ad valorem rate of tax" on cigarettes. *Report of House Select Committee on Small Business, Problems of Small Business Resulting from Monopolistic and Unfair Trade Practices* (80th Cong., 2d sess.), pp. 10–11 and 26.

ceedings much more frequently in the future than it has previously done. Unfortunately, drastic though it may be, dissolution appears to be the only really effective remedy for oligopoly which lies within the limits of antitrust action per se. If the current suit against the meat packers is indicative, the Division may even be launching an unprecedented drive toward atomization of American industry. The economic consequences of such remedial action, if generally executed,[21] would certainly be far-reaching. Whether they would always be in the public interest as well is less easy to foresee. The danger is that the well-known antibigness bias of the Antitrust Division will lead to an overzealous disregard for economies of scale and other basic economic realities in at least some of its dissolution proposals.

CONCLUSION

The *Tobacco* case is clearly a legal milestone in the social control of oligopoly. By permitting the inference of illegal conspiracy from detailed similarity of behavior and by shifting attention from the abuse of power to its mere existence (as indicated by degree of market control), the courts have at last brought oligopolistic industries within reach of successful prosecution under the antitrust laws. This is all to the good. The economic consequences will depend, however, upon whether government victories are accompanied by appropriate remedial action. If they are not, such victories will be nearly futile. On the other hand, if remedial action is taken, the Antitrust Division must assume a new and heavy responsibility to restrain the narrowly punitive spirit to which its antibigness bias so easily leads; and to prescribe remedies solely with a view to their contribution to the public interest, broadly conceived and based upon thoroughgoing economic analysis. Although the courts now may have largely abandoned the "rule of reason," the Antitrust Division —in deciding what industries to prosecute and in preparing appropriate corrective measures—must develop a "standard of reasonableness" of its own if the public interest is to be properly served. Finally, it must be recognized that other legislative reforms—though lying outside the bounds of antitrust action—can do much to supplement or complement the antitrust laws in attaining the goal of a more competitive economy.

The *Tobacco* case is indeed a legal milestone. Whether it will be an economic milestone—or millstone—will depend upon the judiciousness with which its doctrines are applied. Certainly, the law and economics alike should combine their best efforts in meeting the new challenge which the *Tobacco* decision has so forcefully laid down.

---

[21]Even if the Division should meet with success in the courts, however, widespread dissolution proceedings (because of their drastic nature) would be not unlikely to lead to countermanding legislation by Congress.

7

The Cellophane Case and the New Competition*

By GEORGE W. STOCKING and WILLARD F. MUELLER[†]

On December 13, 1947 the Department of Justice instituted civil proceedings against E. I. du Pont de Nemours & Company, charging du Pont with having monopolized, attempted to monopolize, and conspired to monopolize the manufacture and sale of cellophane and cellulose caps and bands in the United States in violation of section 2 of the Sherman Act. Almost precisely six years later Paul Leahy, Chief Judge of the United States District Court for the District of Delaware, rendered a decision in the matter.[1] He pointed out that the charge against du Pont of having monopolized cellophane involved two questions: "1. does du Pont possess monopoly powers; and 2., if so has it achieved such powers by 'monopolizing' within the meaning of the Act and under *United States* v. *Aluminum Company of America* [?]" He concluded that "unless the first is decided against defendant, the second is not reached."[2] Judge Leahy did not need to reach the second question for he found the defendant not guilty. In doing so he concluded that "[f]acts, in large part uncontested, demonstrate du Pont cellophane is sold under such intense competitive conditions acquisition of market control or monopoly power is a practical impossibility."[3] In reaching this conclusion Judge Leahy reviewed at length evidence introduced by the defendant to show that du Pont behaved like a competitor, not like a monopolist. The court found that du Pont conducted research to improve manufacturing efficiency, to reduce cost of production, and to improve the quality and develop new types of cellophane. It promoted the development and use of

* *The American Economic Review,* Vol. XLV (1955), pp. 29–63. Reprinted by courtesy of the publisher and the authors.

† Vanderbilt University and the University of Wisconsin, respectively.

[1] *United States* v. *E. I. du Pont de Nemours & Co.*, 118 F. Supp. 41 (D. Del. 1953). This study is based largely on the testimony and exhibits in this case, but it does not consider cellulose caps and bands. Du Pont discontinued making caps before the government filed its complaint, and the district court, as with cellophane, found no monopolizing of bands. The Supreme Court has indicated that it will review this decision. References to the government's exhibits will be designated as GX, to the defendant's exhibits as DX, and to the transcript of testimony as T.

[2] 118 F. Supp. at 54.

[3] *Ibid.*, pp. 197–98.

packaging machinery that could handle both cellophane and other flexible wrapping materials. In doing so it not only helped to increase cellophane sales but stimulated improvement in rival flexible wrapping materials. It supplied customers with technical services to help them solve problems created by the use of cellophane. It developed over fifty types of cellophane tailored to meet the special wrapping needs of particular products. It studied the buying habits of the public. It conducted market studies to determine the effect on sales of packaging a product in cellophane. It promoted sales by educating potential cellophane users to the sales appeal of a transparent wrapping material. It reduced prices to get into new and broader markets. The court found that in response to price and quality changes buyers at times shifted from cellophane to competing products and back again. The court concluded that "[t]he record reflects not the dead hand of monopoly but rapidly declining prices, expanding production, intense competition stimulated by creative research, the development of new products and uses and other benefits of a free economy."[4]

This conclusion, based as it is on 7,500 pages of testimony and 7,000 exhibits, cannot easily be dismissed. Many economists relying on the logic of the "new competition" will find in it support for their theories. One has already pronounced Judge Leahy's opinion a victory for our profession.

Such an optimistic conclusion so lightly reached by an economist and such high praise so extravagantly given by a judge warrant, first, a brief statement of the criteria by which economists can determine the existence of monopoly and, second, an application of the relevant criteria to du Pont's cellophane operations in an effort to answer the question, has du Pont had monopoly power in making and selling cellophane?

Detecting monopoly is simpler than measuring it.[5] While economists recognize that few if any industrial markets are free entirely from the influence of monopoly, by studying the structure and behavior of markets they can generally isolate characteristics which taken together will permit them to classify markets as effectively competitive or noncompetitive. In trying to classify du Pont's market for cellophane, we shall rely primarily on three criteria: (1) What role has business strategy played in du Pont's production and sales policies? (2) Is cellophane sufficiently differentiated from rival products to have a distinct market, or is its market that of all flexible wrapping materials? (3) Do the trend and level of its earnings reflect monopoly power or competition?[6]

---

[4] *Ibid.*, p. 233.

[5] Fritz Machlup is probably correct in concluding that "so many different elements enter into what is called a monopolistic position and so complex are their combined effects that a measurement of 'the' degree of monopoly is even conceptually impossible." *The Political Economy of Monopoly* (Baltimore, 1952), p. 527.

[6] Clair Wilcox uses the following criteria in classifying markets in his TNEC study, *Competition and Monopoly in American Industry* (1940): (1) the number

I. BUSINESS STRATEGY AS EVIDENCE OF MONOPOLY

Economists have said a good deal about the role which strategy plays among oligopolists jockeying for market position. They have said less about the significance of business strategy as a basis for classifying an industry as monopolistic or workably competitive. We believe it is an important criterion. Purely competitive markets do not generally confront buyers and sellers in the business world. Frequently sellers are few, products are differentiated, knowledge is imperfect, obstacles to the movement of factors exist. Business firms from time to time make deliberate adjustments in both their price and production policies; they resort to strategy to improve their lot. Strategy may be directed to other than price and production policies. Business executives are constantly alert for any business advantage that will make their market position more secure or isolate them from the impact of competitive forces. They seek control of the sources of the best raw materials and the richest natural resources. They try to improve their products and processes or to discover and develop new and better ones. They try to protect their accumulated know-how as business secrets or, where they can, to obtain patents that legalize monopoly.

Economists recognize these practices as manifestations of business rivalry, as aspects of the sort of competition that characterizes modern industrial markets. Business rivalry is itself a symptom of the absence of pure competition. Farmers who, lacking government aid, sell in competitive markets do not regard each other as business rivals but as neighbors. But even when businessmen forego active price competition, they generally do not abandon all rivalry. Correctly, economists have concluded that this rivalry may protect the public interest. It leads to technological innovation and to economic progress. Although economists recognize that business strategy may lead to monopoly, some economists believe that in a dynamic capitalistic society monopoly is inevitably short-lived. It is continually being undermined by the rivalry of other firms. The better product, the better process of today gives way to the better product, the better process of tomorrow. Only the imperfections and mortal-

of producers and the extent of industrial concentration, (2) uniformity of price quotations, (3) degree of price flexibility, (4) volume of production and extent of utilization of capacity, (5) rate of profit, and (6) rate of business mortality. Alone no one of these is a satisfactory index, and together they may be misleading unless perchance there is a consistency among the several indexes. We place considerable emphasis on two factors not included in Wilcox's list, business strategy and product differentiation, and we consider only incidentally if at all most of the factors on which Wilcox relied. Applying Wilcox's criteria to our conception of the cellophane market, we find that producers are few, concentration is high, profits are high, turnover of producing units is low, business mortality is low. These criteria suggest monopoly power. On the other hand, cellophane prices have been flexible and surplus capacity has been negligible. These characteristics suggest competition. Whether or not the factors we have chosen are adequate to answer the question we have raised we leave to the reader.

ity of monopoly make it tolerable. Businessmen striving for monopoly promote the public welfare by failing to achieve their goal. Where they achieve it, either by independent business strategy or by collusive action, the public interest may not be served.

With these principles in mind, let us examine du Pont's strategy in developing the cellophane business in the United States. In doing this we do not mean to suggest that its strategy was immoral or unlawful. As Knauth has so well said:

> The contracts and arrangements which businessmen make from day to day seem to them wise, prudent, sound, and inherent in the nature of modern business. When their practices receive legislative interpretation and are denounced as monopolistic, they are puzzled. What has hitherto been deemed eminently proper and ethical now subjects them to unexpected criticism and opprobrium.[7]

No opprobrium is intended in this analysis.

Du Pont became acquainted with cellophane through its production of artificial silk. In 1920 it had entered into a contract with the Comptoir des Textiles Artificiels, a French corporation, which through its affiliates was then an important manufacturer of rayon in France, Switzerland, Belgium, and Italy, for the joint operation of an American rayon company using the viscose process. The viscose solution for making rayon was practically identical with that used in making cellophane.[8] The Comptoir had made about 970,000 pounds of cellophane in 1922, nearly 40 per cent of which it sold in the American market as a transparent wrapping material. Aware of the affinity of rayon and cellophane processes and impressed by the prospects of large cellophane sales in the American market, du Pont in 1923 signed an option contract with Arena Trading Corporation,[9] a Delaware corporation which was acting for itself and its associates, including La Cellophane, Société Anonyme, the Comptoir's affiliate which made cellophane. Under the option Arena provided du Pont with all relevant economic and technical information to enable it to decide within four months whether it wished to make and sell cellophane in North and Central America through a corporation jointly owned by it and La Cellophane. If du Pont decided affirmatively, Arena agreed to transfer to the new corporation its technical knowledge, patent rights, trade marks, and good will and the exclusive right to make and sell cellophane in the North and Central American markets. This arrangement apparently contemplated the new corporation's becoming the sole producer of cellophane in these markets. At that time only the French Comptoir through its affiliates made cellophane any place in the world.

On June 9, 1923 du Pont entered into an organizational agreement

---

[7] Oswald Knauth, *Managerial Enterprise* (New York, 1948), p. 11.

[8] Report of Dr. Fin Sparre, head of du Pont's development department, April 14, 1923, GX 392, pp. 5431–32.

[9] Agreement of January 6, 1923, GX 1458, pp. 5999–6008.

providing for the transfer to the new company, Du Pont Cellophane Company, Inc., of "an unqualified, unrestricted and exclusive right to use all and every process now owned" by Arena "or which may hereafter be acquired by it . . . in connection with the manufacture of cellophane."[10]

Before entering into this agreement du Pont had made an intensive study of the market possibilities of cellophane and of its production problems and decided that Arena could not deliver all the protection from competition that it had promised. About the patents du Pont's development department had said: "[T]he patent protection at present is exceedingly inadequate not to say worthless, and the future patent protection is problematical because it is based on applications for patents, the issuance of which may not be determined for a matter of two years or more."[11] The development department had concluded that it was "by no means certain that the American Cellophane Company could *maintain* a monopoly on the strength of either present or prospective patents."[12] Du Pont accordingly insisted on a provision in the organizational agreement that should the patent protection prove inadequate, Arena was to forfeit ten thousand shares of common stock in the new company.[13]

Du Pont apparently recognized that La Cellophane's trade secrets promised a protection from competition that the patents did not, and that as the first domestic producer of a differentiated if not unique product[14] it could for some time at any rate anticipate monopoly revenue in making and selling cellophane. It calculated that with an investment of $2,000,000, at current domestic prices for imported cellophane it could earn $631,832, an annual rate of 31.6 per cent.[15] This it regarded as sufficiently attractive to justify the venture.

Du Pont the Sole Domestic Producer

Du Pont became the sole domestic producer of cellophane and thereby a monopolist in its sale. The Department of Justice contended that it was an unlawful monopolist from the outset,[16] but the district court decided

[10] GX 1001, p. 992. The agreement specifically excluded processes which might subsequently be acquired by Arena from third parties, but it gave du Pont an option to purchase such rights for the North and Central American markets. Although Arena did not guarantee the validity of the patents to be licensed (*ibid.*, p. 989), it specifically promised to give the new company "the exclusive right to manufacture cellophane in North and Central America to be used for any purpose whatsoever." *Ibid.*, p. 993. Arena and Du Pont Cellophane signed their license agreement December 26, 1923. GX 1002, pp. 998–1001.

[11] GX 392, p. 5433.

[12] *Ibid.*, p. 5434. Emphasis supplied.

[13] GX 1001, pp. 989–90.

[14] Du Pont's development department concluded that glassine, sheet gelatin, and tin foil, cellophane's closest rival products, offered no serious competition because of price or quality differences. GX 392, pp. 5437–38.

[15] *Ibid.*, p. 5451.

[16] Brief for the United States of America, pp. 150–56, *United States* v. *E. I. du Pont de Nemours & Co.*, 118 F. Supp. 41 (D. Del. 1953).

otherwise. Whether lawful or not, du Pont was a monopolist in producing cellophane, and it anticipated and in fact earned monopoly profits from the outset.

This is a characteristic of any successful innovation. As Knight has pointed out:

> There is . . . no clear distinction in practice between profit and monopoly gain. . . . New products . . . must also yield enough temporary monopoly revenue to make such activities attractive.[17]

But as Knight has also pointed out, we must distinguish between justifiable monopoly revenue—returns to the innovator—and what Knight calls monopoly gains. Monopoly gains according to Knight are monopoly revenues that are "too large or last too long." What is too long or too large Knight does not say, but he clearly implies that the procedure by which they are made large and perpetuated may convert justifiable monopoly revenue into socially unjustifiable monopoly gains.

Having achieved at the outset a monopoly in producing and selling cellophane in the American market, du Pont took steps to protect its position.

One of its first strategic moves was to obtain an increase in the tariff. This became urgent in 1925, when Société Industrielle de la Cellulose (SIDAC) completed a cellophane plant in Belgium and began exporting cellophane to the American market at cut-rate prices. Du Pont first considered a patent infringement suit against Birn & Wachenheim, SIDAC's American distributors, but fearful that it would lose such a suit decided against it and in favor of a try for higher duties.[18] Its first step in getting the tariff raised was to request the United States Commissioner of Customs to reclassify cellophane as a "cellulose compound" instead of as a "gelatin compound." When the Commissioner refused, du Pont appealed to the United States Customs Court. Its appeal was successful; the court ordered a reclassification and on February 24, 1929 the duty increased from 25 to 60 per cent ad valorem.[19] Apparently this was enough to pre-

---

[17] F. H. Knight, "An Appraisal of Economic Change—Discussion," Proceedings of the American Economic Association, *American Economic Review,* Vol. XLIV (May, 1954), p. 65.

[18] About the suit Dr. Sparre of du Pont wrote W. C. Spruance, du Pont vice president, on August 3, 1925: "My belief is that it would cost a whole lot of money and that we would lose in the end, that is if the other side would be willing to fight." GX 1069, p. 1153. About du Pont's effort to get higher duties on cellophane, L. A. Yerkes, president of Du Pont Cellophane, had written Spruance on July 25: "In order that you shall be entirely familiar with the Cellophane status, I want to let you know that we are endeavoring to have the duty on Cellophane raised from 25% to 45%, and Curie, Lane and Wallace are of the opinion that we have a fair chance of getting this through." GX 1068, p. 1142.

[19] The district court appropriately characterized du Pont's protest against what du Pont regarded as an improper classification of cellophane as "the normal act of a business concern engaged in active competition with importers of foreign products." 118 F. Supp. at 167. The court also recognized that the tariff readjustment eventually shut out foreign competition. *Ibid.*, p. 221.

vent price cutting by importers. At any rate du Pont's quarterly competitive report for the second quarter of 1929 stated:

> The present tariff rate (.40 per pound) as fixed by the United States Customs Court, has increased the cost of importing Transparent Cellulose Sheeting to such an extent that the competitors are adhering more rigidly to their published price list. Their selling policy in the past has been to obtain preference with the manufacturer by offering special price concessions.[20]

Du Pont won the field so completely from imported cellophane that its cellophane sales for 1929 represented 91.6 per cent of the total business in the United States,[21] whereas importers had had 21 per cent in 1927 and 24 per cent in 1928.[22] The Tariff Act of 1930 fixed the duty on imported cellophane at 45 per cent ad valorem,[23] and cellophane imports were never again significant. In no year between 1930 and 1947 did they amount to 1 per cent of cellophane consumption in the United States.[24]

Division of World Markets

La Cellophane's plan to develop the American market through a single company jointly owned by it and a domestic firm was not unique. Before transferring to Du Pont Cellophane Company, Inc., its rights to the American market, La Cellophane had made a similar agreement with Kalle & Company (hereinafter Kalle) covering the German market. Ultimately Kalle obtained exclusive rights to La Cellophane's process and patents for the manufacture and sale of cellophane in Germany, Austria, Hungary, Czechoslovakia, Yugoslavia, Poland, Russia, Romania, China, Denmark, Sweden, Norway, and Finland.[25]

Although La Cellophane had agreed to furnish du Pont with such technological information and patent rights as it might later acquire from its other licensees, du Pont sought to fortify its market position through a direct agreement with Kalle.[26] On May 7, 1929 both parties agreed to exchange free of charge except for patent fees all patent rights and tech-

---

[20] GX 432, p. 5690.

[21] Du Pont Cellophane's quarterly competitive report, fourth quarter 1929, GX 434, p. 5714.

[22] *Ibid.*, first quarter 1929, GX 431, p. 5677.

[23] 19 U.S.C.A. sec. 1001, par. 31(c). In 1951 the tariff was reduced to 22½ per cent ad valorem. *United States* v. *E. I. du Pont de Nemours & Co.*, 118 F. Supp. 41, 167 (D. Del. 1953).

[24] GX 182A, p. 515A; GX 182, p. 515.

[25] Letter of October 30, 1929 from C. M. Albright, Du Pont Cellophane vice president, to the Buffalo office, GX 1091, p. 1195.

[26] As early as September, 1925, J. E. Crane, du Pont's European manager, had written H. G. Haskell, du Pont vice president, of talks with Dr. Duttenhofer of Kalle & Company on the desirability of cooperation between du Pont and Kalle. Crane wrote: "Dr. Duttenhofer stated that as we were to cooperate in other matters it would be a pity to compete in artificial silk and cellophane." GX 1393, p. 1800.

nical data covering cellophane that they then had or might later get.[27] This agreement did not specifically recognize a division of markets, but on October 30, 1929, C. M. Albright, Du Pont Cellophane vice president, listed for the Buffalo office the countries to which Kalle had exclusive rights. About the agreement Albright wrote: "The agreement, for obvious reasons, does not include the territorial limits, and it is suggested that this letter be attached to the copy of agreement for our future guidance."[28] By the summer of 1930 du Pont had patents on its moistureproof cellophane in the United States and possessions, Belgium, France, and Italy and had applications pending in Great Britain, Canada, Japan, the European countries in Kalle's exclusive territory, and eight South American countries.[29] Du Pont assigned its moistureproof patent rights in the countries in Kalle's territory to Kalle or gave it implied licenses under which Kalle took out patents in its own name.[30]

Five years later du Pont entered a technical exchange and license agreement with British Cellophane Limited (hereinafter BCL), a La Cellophane licensee, which specifically delineated the territories within which each party would operate.[31] Under this agreement du Pont was to assign its British patents on moistureproof cellophane to BCL. Du Pont also assigned its French patents on moistureproof cellophane to La Cellophane[32] and its Canadian patents to Canadian Industries Limited.[33]

Meanwhile all the world's leading cellophane producers except du Pont had tried to establish an international cartel to assign territories and fix quotas among themselves. Du Pont representatives attended the first day of the cartel conferences in Paris February 11–12, 1930 as "guests and observers" but did not sign the "official report" (agreement).[34] The

[27] GX 1087, pp. 1183–86. Perhaps another reason for du Pont's wishing to deal directly with Kalle is that on April 1, 1929 Du Pont Cellophane became du Pont's wholly owned subsidiary by an exchange of stock. Du Pont organized a new corporation, also named Du Pont Cellophane Co., Inc., La Cellophane to sit on its board as long as du Pont considered this in the new company's best interest. The 1923 agreements remained in force. Agreement of March 18, 1929 between du Pont and La Cellophane, GX 1003, p. 1005. On July 1, 1936, du Pont dissolved Du Pont Cellophane Co., Inc., and replaced it with a cellophane division in its rayon department. Memorandum dated February 17, 1944, on the history of du Pont cellophane, prepared in du Pont's cellophane division, GX 1, p. 8.

[28] GX 1091, p. 1195.

[29] Memorandum dated August 26, 1930, from Du Pont Cellophane's cellophane department to W. S. Carpenter, Jr., chairman of its board of directors, GX 2469, p. 3164.

[30] Du Pont Cellophane memorandum dated March 17, 1933, GX 1098, p. 1205; letter to Kalle dated March 20, 1933, GX 1099, p. 1206; memorandum dated April 27, 1934, Review of the du Pont–Kalle Relations, prepared by du Pont's patent service, GX 1102, pp. 1210–12.

[31] Agreement of May 3, 1935, GX 1109, pp. 1229–34.

[32] GX 1102, pp. 1210–12.

[33] Letter dated February 12, 1942, transmitting patent assignments, GX 1187, pp. 1409–26.

[34] GX 1414, pp. 1841–44.

district court found that they were not authorized to make commitments for du Pont and made none. Nevertheless the agreement recognized the North American market as belonging to du Pont and Sylvania.[35] It did not cover moistureproof or photographic cellophane. SIDAC and La Cellophane agreed to study the possibility of pooling their patents but with the understanding that this would not apply to du Pont patents.[36]

In 1934 du Pont relied on the 1930 cartel agreement in asserting its right to the West Indies as against BCL, to which La Cellophane had granted a license and with which du Pont was then negotiating its technical agreement. In a December 13, 1934 letter to La Cellophane[37] du Pont referred to the minutes of the February 11–12, 1930 meetings of cellophane producers and quoted La Cellophane's letter of April 1, 1932[38] describing the cartel's division of the world and containing the phrases, "Cuba being situated north of the Panama Canal, belonging thus to your territory." By May 21, 1935 the du Pont–BCL agreement[39] had been signed and du Pont and La Cellophane had agreed that du Pont's territory included the West Indies except the possessions of European powers.[40]

The cartel's course was not an easy one. World depression and the pressure of totalitarian governments for foreign exchange turned members' eyes toward South American markets, and even with agreements and quotas South American prices were unstable. Du Pont's sales there under its 1930 agreement with La Cellophane (discussed in the following subsection) were particularly disturbing to cartel members.[41] On Sep-

[35] Sylvania Industrial Corporation's entry into the American market is described in the following subsection.

[36] The court was not impressed by the "official report" of the cartel agreement. It stated: "Failure to prove any effect from it, this cartel aspect of the case raises a straight issue of fact. Du Pont did not make such an agreement." 118 F. Supp. at 221. Moreover, the court found that the actual conduct of the producers implicated in the agreement was inconsistent with the existence of a cartel. In the court's inimitable language, "Intricate theories of a conspiratorial network is cast aside." *Loc. cit.*

[37] GX 1034, pp. 1064–65.

[38] GX 1022, p. 1044.

[39] Agreement of May 3, 1935, GX 1109, pp. 1229–34.

[40] Memorandum dated May 21, 1935, "to be attached to original contract between E. I. du Pont de Nemours & Co. and Arena Trading Corporation of June 9, 1923," GX 1040, pp. 1075–76.

[41] Du Pont's 1930 agreement with La Cellophane gave du Pont half of whatever rights La Cellophane got in South America and Japan. Early in 1932 du Pont wrote La Cellophane that "we have made our prices in South America on plain Cellophane to correspond with yours" (letter dated January 29, 1932, GX 1112, p. 1248), and it tried to find out what quotas for South America La Cellophane and the other producers had agreed on; but it became dissatisfied with the operation of the agreement and on June 2, 1932 informed La Cellophane that henceforth du Pont would "consider ourselves free to pursue our own policy of sales in South America, Japan and China." GX 1023, p. 1045. La Cellophane did not take this declaration of independence too seriously and continued to point out that du Pont sold more than La Cellophane did in South America and Japan. On December 27, 1934 du Pont, al-

tember 6, 1938 La Cellophane wrote du Pont that "it is apparently impossible to bring about a price accord for South America in our Convention."[42] The second world war weakened still further agreements to divide markets. Du Pont's agreements with Kalle and BCL were to run twenty years, subject to renewal, but in 1940 du Pont disavowed all formal territorial limitations, not only with these companies but with Canadian Industries Limited and La Cellophane as well, "in the light of legal developments in this country."[43]

SIDAC Competes with La Cellophane and with du Pont

Although La Cellophane had promised du Pont a monopoly in making and selling cellophane in the United States, it could not fulfill the promise. As du Pont feared, neither its patents nor its know-how was sufficient to protect it from competition. In 1925 two former employees of La Cellophane, using La Cellophane's trade secrets, helped establish SIDAC, which began to sell in the rich American market.[44] It made its first sales through Birn & Wachenheim, who had handled La Cellophane's business in the United States before the organization of Du Pont Cellophane. In 1929 SIDAC established an American subsidiary, the Sylvania Industrial Corporation of America, and quit exporting cellophane to the United States.[45] By this time it had subsidiaries in England and Italy and competed in La Cellophane's export markets. La Cellophane sued SIDAC for patent infringement and in settlement accepted a stock interest in SIDAC; thus indirectly it became through Sylvania du Pont's competitor in the American market, in violation of its 1923 agreements with du Pont.

Negotiations over this matter were prolonged. Du Pont conceived its problem to be how to "accept reparations and at the same time protect its future position without contravening American statutes."[46] In lieu of reparations La Cellophane lifted the 1923 restriction limiting du Pont to the North and Central American markets. La Cellophane granted it equal rights with itself in Japan and South America.[47] La Cellophane also agreed to keep technical information, patents, and other data which it received from du Pont from going directly or indirectly to SIDAC or Sylvania.

though reiterating its stand taken in 1932, expressed willingness to exchange figures on its sales in those markets for La Cellophane's and those "of the other members." GX 1037, p. 1070.

[42] GX 1445, p. 1920.

[43] Identical letters dated October 17, 1940, GX 1273, p. 1602, GX 1274, p. 1603, GX 1275, p. 1604, GX 1276, p. 1605.

[44] Memorandum dated February 17, 1944 on the history of du Pont cellophane, prepared in du Pont's cellophane division, GX 1, p. 12.

[45] Du Pont Cellophane's quarterly competitive report, third quarter 1929, GX 433, p. 5702.

[46] Memorandum of a November 14, 1929 discussion by du Pont officials, GX 1410, p. 1831.

[47] Letter dated March 6, 1930 from du Pont to La Cellophane, GX 1013, pp. 1027–29; excerpt from minutes of May 8, 1930 meeting of du Pont's board of directors, GX 1015, p. 1031.

Du Pont Seeks Patent Protection

When du Pont obtained its option to participate jointly with La Cellophane in developing the American market, it had not investigated the validity of La Cellophane's patent claims. The terms of the option had been "predicated on the practical absence of serious competition on the part of other manufacturers either in this country or other countries."[48] Shortly after its organization Du Pont Cellophane launched a research program designed to strengthen its market position by improving cellophane. One of its chief defects was its permeability to moisture. Du Pont promptly attacked this problem and by 1927 had developed a moistureproofing process and had applied for patents. Its basic patent covering moistureproof cellophane, Church and Prindle patent No. 1,737,187 issued in 1929, was a product patent broad in scope and extensive in claims.[49] J. E. Hatt, general manager of Du Pont Cellophane's cellophane department, in summarizing du Pont's moistureproof cellophane patent situation in 1930 recognized its vulnerability and indicated that du Pont had taken steps to bulwark it. He described patent applications that du Pont had filed and quoted patent counsel's opinion that they promised "important and substantial additional protection."[50] Between 1930 and 1934 Du Pont Cellophane authorized a research project further to bolster its patent position. In reporting on the success of this project in 1934 President Yerkes said:

> This work was undertaken as a defensive program in connection with protecting broadly by patents the field of moistureproofing agents other than waxes which was the only class of material disclosed in our original Cellophane moistureproofing patents.
>
> The investigations on this subject did, in fact, lead to the discovery of a number of classes of materials which could serve equally well for moistureproofiing agents. . . . Each of these classes has been made the subject of a patent. . . . Altogether, 13 patent applications are being written as a result of the work done under this project, all in view of strengthening our Moistureproof Cellophane patent situation.[51]

---

[48] Report dated April 14, 1923 by Dr. Fin Sparre, director of du Pont's development department, GX 392, p. 5455. See also pp. 5453–56.

[49] A problem arising during the second world war when the government needed more moistureproof laminated products than du Pont could supply directly, reflects the breadth of the patent claims. Hines of du Pont posed the problem in this way: "What is the best procedure to give the Government these laminated products necessary to win the war and, having decided on that, what can be done to preserve du Pont's position in a postwar economy?" Recognizing that the government's interest might best be served by allowing converters to make them, du Pont feared that the converters might "at the end of the war, be possessed of a great deal of information with respect to the preparation of moistureproofing compositions and the technique of moistureproofing film with them and would be disposed to continue in such a business on a peace-time basis to the detriment of the Company's interests." Memorandum dated January 26, 1942 from du Pont's patent service to du Pont's cellophane research section, GX 2497, pp. 3255–57.

[50] Memorandum of August 26, 1930, GX 2469, p. 3160.

[51] December 1933 report to Du Pont Cellophane's board of directors, January 22, 1934, GX 488, p. 6478. Du Pont spent $19,503 on this research project. This compares

These steps proved adequate to forestall other domestic competition[52] and to bring Sylvania Industrial Corporation to terms when it invaded the American market.

Sylvania Reaches Accord with du Pont

Sylvania completed its Virginia plant for making cellophane in 1930. Apparently its early experimental research to develop a moistureproof cellophane rested, as did du Pont's, on the use of a nitrocellulose base to which gum, wax, and plasticizer were added. When du Pont's Church and Prindle patent covering moistureproof cellophane was issued, du Pont advised Sylvania informally of its claims and Sylvania after considering them "felt obliged to discard the work they had done up to that time, and approach the subject from a new angle."[53] Their new angle substituted a vinyl resin base for the nitrocellulose base. Du Pont, regarding this as an infringement, advised Dr. Wallach, Sylvania's president, that "we would be obliged to enforce our patent"[54] and eventually filed an infringement suit against Sylvania.[55] In the antitrust proceedings against du Pont the government contended that the "entire infringement suit was nothing more than a harassing action designed to coerce Sylvania into entering a highly restrictive agreement."[56] The district court in finding for du Pont rejected this contention.[57] Since the court has

with an expenditure of only between $5,000 and $10,000 authorized in October 1924 to hire a single chemist to develop the original moistureproofing process. DX 393 and DX 394. Total expenditures for "technical activities expenses," which included all types of technical work designed to improve cellophane production and processes, came to only $32,048 during 1925 and 1926. DX 387.

[52] Du Pont's strong patent position may not have been wholly responsible for the reluctance of other domestic companies to produce cellophane. Apparently Union Carbide & Carbon Corporation in the 1930's considered entering the cellophane field. It purchased rights to a process for making a transparent wrapping material similar to cellophane. Lammot du Pont in a letter of December 2, 1931 to L. A. Yerkes, president of Du Pont Cellophane, stated that in the course of an hour's conversation on this topic with Messrs. Jesse Ricks and Barrett of Union Carbide & Carbon "[t]hey assured me repeatedly they did not wish to rush into anything, most of all a competitive situation with du Pont. Their whole tone was most agreeable. . . . In the course of the conversation, various efforts at co-operation between Carbide and du Pont were referred to, and in every case assurances of their desire to work together, given." GX 4381, p. 4300.

[53] Memorandum dated February 18, 1931 from J. E. Hatt, Du Pont Cellophane's general manager, to its executive committee, GX 2482, p. 3204.

[54] *Loc. cit.*

[55] The bill of complaint in *Du Pont Cellophane Company* v. *Sylvania Industrial Corporation* appears in the record of the Cellophane case as GX 2479, pp. 3183–90, and Sylvania's answer as GX 2480, pp. 3191–99.

[56] Statement to the court by J. L. Minicus, counsel for the government, T. 2472.

[57] Judge Leahy said: "Neither party dictated the terms of the license agreement by which the suit was settled." 118 F. Supp. at 151. He based this finding on testimony by L. A. Yerkes, president of Du Pont Cellophane. Although Judge Leahy had said that if he found that du Pont did not possess monopoly power it would be unnecessary for him to pass on whether it had monopolized cellophane under section 2 of the Sherman Act and the principles of *United States* v. *Aluminum Co. of America*, 148 F. 2d 416 (2d Cir. 1945), he nevertheless made a decision on

spoken, we do not express judgment on this issue. But we wish to review briefly evidence that throws some light on du Pont's strategy.

The record indicates that (1) du Pont in negotiating for reparations following SIDAC's entry into the American market considered and rejected a proposal that it grant Sylvania a license which would restrict its output; (2) after warning Sylvania that it would defend its patents and learning that Sylvania challenged their validity, du Pont postponed action while entrenching its patent position;[58] (3) although professing confidence in its ability to establish its patents' validity, du Pont offered to settle the issue by granting a license limiting Sylvania's production of moistureproof cellophane to 10 per cent of the companies' combined output;[59] (4) on Sylvania's rejecting this offer du Pont formally notified Sylvania that it was infringing du Pont's moistureproofing patents and asked that it cease;[60] (5) upon its refusal to desist du Pont formally inaugurated infringement proceedings; and (6) before the proceedings were carried to completion du Pont and Sylvania settled the suit by a patent exchange and licensing agreement.[61]

Both parties no doubt thought that they stood to gain by a settlement. If Sylvania lost the suit, it would be forced to stop producing moistureproof cellophane or to produce it on such terms as du Pont might offer. If it won, anyone with adequate resources could produce cellophane, and selling cellophane would become a competitive enterprise. After a discussion with Sylvania's general counsel du Pont's patent attorney summed up Sylvania's plight as follows:

> During the conference Mr. Menken stated that in his opinion the case should be settled. He said that they were very fearful of what the result would be to their company in the event they succeeded in having the claims of the patents

that charge also. He ruled that du Pont's licensing and technology exchange agreements with La Cellophane did not unreasonably restrain trade and that their territorial limitations were ancillary to the acquisition of trade secrets. 118 F. Supp. at 219. He ruled that the circumstances under which du Pont acquired its patents failed to show that the "acquisitions affected its ability to exclude competition" (*ibid.*, p. 212), and that du Pont placed only "lawful and reasonable limitations on use" in its licenses (*ibid.*, p. 211). In any event, he ruled, du Pont had a lawful monopoly in its moistureproof cellophane patent. He said: "Evidence does not disclose combining of competing or independent process patents or efforts to control unpatented products" (*ibid.*, p. 214).

[58] A running memorandum of developments in the du Pont–Sylvania patent controversy between July 9, 1931 and April 6, 1933, in the du Pont files, contains the following statement: "At Board meeting on 8/21/31 . . . [i]t was felt by Mr. Pritchard [du Pont's patent counsel] that actual suit against Sylvania should not be instituted until we have these claims issued in form of actual patents. . . . L.A.Y. [Yerkes, Du Pont Cellophane's president] still felt it would be desirable for us to have Sylvania under a license agreement if possible." GX 2478, p. 3181.

[59] *Loc. cit.* On August 27, 1931 Yerkes wrote to Dr. Wallach confirming an oral offer made on or about July 9, 1931. A memorandum dated July 13, 1931 outlines the terms of the offer. GX 2483, p. 3206.

[60] GX 2478, p. 3181. The memorandum refers to a letter dated 11/19/31 which lists the patents du Pont claimed to be infringed.

[61] Agreement dated April 26, 1933, GX 2487, pp. 3212–33.

which are involved in the litigation held invalid. He seemed to realize the old adage that the defendent can never win. . . . If the Du Pont Cellophane Company succeeds and the patents are held to be infringed, Sylvania Industrial Corporation will be under injunction and will be obliged to stop manufacturing moistureproof wrapping tissue. On the other hand, if they succeed in having the broad claims of the patents held invalid they will throw the art open, as far as the broad claims are concerned, to anyone and therefore will have additional competition. Sylvania . . . has plenty of ready cash but are hesitant about enlarging their plant facilities pending the litigation since, if successful, they will only invite further competition.[62]

With neither side ready to test the validity of du Pont's patents, the parties compromised. The compromise constituted no threat to du Pont's dominant market position.

Under the settlement reached April 26, 1933, Du Pont Cellophane granted Sylvania a nonexclusive license (made exclusive in 1938) of du Pont's five basic patents on moistureproof cellophane and agreed to license to it any patents within their scope which du Pont might get before October 16, 1948. Sylvania agreed to grant similar rights to Du Pont Cellophane under any patents which it might get. Sylvania agreed to pay du Pont a royalty of 2 per cent of its net cellophane sales for the use of du Pont's basic patents and an additional 2 per cent if Sylvania accepted licenses under future du Pont patents representing departures from the five basic patents. But the settlement went further than a mere cross-licensing of present and future patents. It provided that Sylvania's production be restricted to a fixed percentage of total moistureproof cellophane sales, beginning with 20 per cent in 1933 and increasing by 1 per cent until it reached 29 per cent in 1942. Should Sylvania exceed its share in a given year, it agreed to pay a penalty royalty of 20 cents a pound or 30 per cent of its net cellophane sales, whichever was higher. If du Pont used any of Sylvania's patents, it agreed to a similar penalty for exceeding its basic quota. But it never used them.

Until June, 1951 du Pont and Sylvania were the only producers of cellophane in the American market.[63] Between 1933 and 1945 (when they contracted for smaller royalties and abandoned penalites for exceeding their quotas), with Sylvania's output geared to du Pont's, du Pont could determine how much cellophane should come on the market. Actually the penalty provision of the agreement never operated and its deletion from the 1945 agreement produced no marked effect on Sylvania's production. The court found that "[i]ts policies as to expansion in no way changed following the termination of the 1933 agreement in 1945."[64] Although their shares varied from time to time, du Pont supplied

---

[62] Letter dated August 4, 1932 from W. S. Pritchard to B. M. May, GX 2811, pp. 6073–74.

[63] In June, 1951 Olin Industries, Inc., began the production of cellophane at Pisgah Forest, North Carolina. Testimony of Fred Olsen, Olin vice president, T. 6829.

[64] 118 F. Supp. at 157.

about 76 per cent and Sylvania 24 per cent of the market from 1933 to 1950.[65] But gearing Sylvania's production to du Pont's must have lessened Sylvania's incentive to independent, vigorous rivalry, price or nonprice, and the record indicates that until January 1, 1947 Sylvania's quoted prices were generally identical with du Pont's.[66]

Conclusion

Du Pont's moves and countermoves to protect its domestic market were the strategy of a producer operating in a monopolistic, not a competitive, market. Its agreements with foreign producers to license patents and exchange technical data, its domestic patent program, its effort to get higher tariffs, its restrictive market agreement with Sylvania, all reflect du Pont's effort to preserve what it apparently regarded as a monopoly market. That du Pont and Sylvania (whose production was geared to du Pont's and whose quoted prices were generally identical with du Pont's) together monopolized the market for cellophane seems scarcely debatable. That du Pont acted as though in its monopoly of cellophane it had a valuable property right which it sought to exploit is equally clear. But was du Pont mistaken? Were available substitutes so similar that du Pont's monopoly of cellophane was in reality a mirage or a phantasy? Is there in fact no distinct market for cellophane, but only a larger market for flexible wrapping materials with producers so numerous that none can make monopoly profits? Let us turn to that question.

II. CELLOPHANE—A DIFFERENTIATED PRODUCT?

For several years du Pont was the sole domestic producer of cellophane and for a quarter of a century Sylvania and du Pont were the only producers. But buyers of flexible wrapping material need not rely solely on these two suppliers. Several hundred rivals produced flexible wrapping materials, in many uses substitutes for cellophane. May not these

---

[65] Data on production, 1933 to 1950, table in *United States* v. *E. I. du Pont de Nemours & Co.*, 118 F. Supp. 41, 116 (D. Del. 1953). In the five years following the expiration of the 1933 agreement Sylvania's percentage of total domestic production was only 1 per cent higher than its percentage in the five years preceding the expiration of the agreement. American Viscose Corporation acquired Sylvania in 1946.

[66] Du Pont and Sylvania not only quoted identical prices for their most important cellophane types, but their price changes almost always became effective on the same date. GX 549, pp. 7128–66. During the postwar period of short supplies and after the government had instituted its suit against du Pont, differences in Sylvania's and du Pont's prices appeared. DX 591, p. 1128. Judge Leahy was impressed not by the identity of quoted prices but by the fact that Sylvania at times made discounts from its list prices which du Pont did not match. In speaking of du Pont–Sylvania competition he declared that Sylvania "has continued to expand to the full extent of its financial resources" (118 F. Supp. at 212); and that although du Pont was superior in the services rendered to customers, in technology, in price, and in the development of special types of films, competition between the two companies has "flourished" (*loc. cit.*).

have converted a monopolistic market into one of workable competition? Let us examine briefly the relevant theory and then the facts.

Price Theory and Product Differentiation

Although others have made important contributions to an understanding of the significance of interproduct competition, Chamberlin, the pioneer, offers a good starting point for this discussion. Chamberlin has recognized that "[a]s long as the substitutes are to any degree imperfect, he [the seller] still has a monopoly of his own product and control over its price within the limits imposed upon any monopolist—those of the demand."[67] But Chamberlin also recognized that rival products, where entry is free and differentiation not marked, could eliminate excess profits even in the "monopolized" field. Expressing his findings diagrammatically, he concluded that the sloping demand curve facing the producer of a differentiated product may become tangent to the cost curve somewhere above lowest average cost. Chamberlin regarded this as a "sort of ideal" solution. As he put it, "With fewer establishments, larger scales of production, and lower prices it would always be true that buyers would be willing to pay more than it would cost to give them a greater diversity of product; and conversely, with more producers and smaller scales of production, the higher prices they would pay would be more than such gains were worth."[68]

Chamberlin's conclusion that the entry of producers of substitute products will eliminate monopoly profits is based upon two important assumptions: (1) his uniformity assumption—"both demand and cost curves for all the 'products' are uniform throughout the group";[69] and (2) his symmetry assumption[70]—"any adjustment of price or of 'product' by a single producer spreads its influence over so many of his competitors that the impact felt by any one is negligible and does not lead him to any readjustment of his own situation."[71]

If cost and demand curves are not uniform, of if the "group" of firms producing the substitute products is sufficiently small to introduce the

---

[67] E. H. Chamberlin, *The Theory of Monopolistic Competition* (5th ed., Cambridge, Mass., 1947), p. 67.

[68] *Ibid.*, p. 94. This assumes, of course, that buyers know what they get and get what they want in buying a differentiated product. This is a dubious assumption. Years ago a well-known pharmaceutical company by its advertising endeavored to create a widespread fear of halitosis. "Not even your best friends will tell you." Having created a fear of halitosis, it provided a product to dissipate it, thereby rendering the buyer a service for which he was willing to pay.

[69] *Ibid.*, p. 82. To simplify his exposition Chamberlin first assumes uniformity in cost and demand curves. Later he abandons this assumption in the interest of reality. In abandoning it he reaches the conclusion indicated in the text: where sufficiently effective substitutes are not offered in the market, monopoly profits result.

[70] G. J. Stigler so describes this assumption. *Five Lectures on Economic Problems* (London, 1949), p. 17.

[71] Chamberlin, *op. cit.*, p. 83.

oligopoly problem, we may expect a divergence from the above solution. As for the uniformity assumption, Chamberlin says: "[I]n so far as substitutes of such a degree of effectiveness may not be produced, the conclusions are different—demand curves will lie to the right of the point of tangency with cost curves, and profits will be correspondingly higher. This is the explanation of *all* monopoly profits, of whatever sort."[72] Thus, unless effective substitutes exist, Chamberlin argues that monopoly profits may be "scattered throughout the group."[73] If Chamberlin's symmetry assumption is not fulfilled, an oligopoly solution may be expected.[74] In either case monopoly profits result.

In applying Chamberlin's theory to the flexible packaging materials market and to cellophane's position in it, the empirical issue revolves about (1) the degree of effectiveness of substitutes and (2) the number of rival firms. If substitutes are not effective enough to eliminate monopoly profits, it is not necessary to consider the oligopoly problem.

Clark's analysis[75] leads to similar conclusions, viz., that competition among substitutes may eliminate monopoly profits; but Clark goes further than Chamberlin in finding these results salutary. According to Clark the high cross elasticity of demand tends to flatten the monopolist's demand curve. Moreover, the monopolist's fear of potential competition may lead him to behave as though potential competition had become a reality. These two restraining forces, rival substitute products and potential competition, may yield cost-price relationships similar to those of pure competition. They may make imperfect competition workable.

An increasing number of economists have come to believe this. Robertson develops the idea somewhat further. In reviewing the significance of interproduct and interindustry competition he concludes that we really

---

[72] *Ibid.*, p. 111. Emphasis in original. This statement of the problem seems to make it similar to if not identical with the conventional, neoclassical conception of monopoly. Richard T. Ely for example pointed out: "The use of substitutes is consistent with monopoly, and we nearly always have them. For almost anything we can think of, there is some sort of a substitute more or less perfect, and the use of substitutes furnishes one of the limits to the power of the monopolist. In the consideration of monopoly we have to ask, what are the substitutes, and how effective are they?" *Monopolies and Trusts* (New York, 1912), pp. 35–36.

[73] Chamberlin, *op. cit.*, p. 113. By the "group" Chamberlin apparently means firms making products which although differentiated are designed for the same use, e.g., toothpaste manufacturers. In his "Monopolistic Competition Revisited," *Economica*, Nov., 1951, N.S. XVIII, 352, 353, he abandons the group concept, arguing that "competition is always a matter of substitutes, and . . . substitutes are always a matter of degree." In abandoning the group concept he does not abandon the conclusion that where substitutes are similar enough and entry is free, monopoly profits will disappear and the demand curve will be tangent to the cost curve at some point above minimum cost. But he also recognizes that the "isolated" monopolist, in spite of close substitutes, may find the demand for his own product strong enough to yield him "profits in excess of the minimum."

[74] *Monopolistic Competition*, p. 102.

[75] J. M. Clark, "Toward a Concept of Workable Competition," *American Economic Review*, Vol. XXX (June, 1940), pp. 241–56.

need not worry about monopoly for "there is probably not much of it." There is not much of it because the "old-fashioned apparatus of competition works in new ways to save us."[76]

Moreover, this new apparatus of competition once more makes relevant a theory of competition based on large numbers.

> To assess the competitive situation of a firm we must still resort to counting numbers. We cannot do away with the group, for the group exists in the real world. Yet counting only those firms which are within the "industry" tells us very little. We must do our counting by taking categories of uses for the output of an industry, considering what products of other industries directly compete within these categories.[77]

Since a monopolist's product may serve in a great variety of uses, a monopolist may find it "profitable to forego monopoly control in one use in order to push the commodity into many uses."[78] Thus monopoly serves the public by serving itself and in doing so loses its power over the market.

What Robertson has discovered for the economists, businessmen had already professed. David Lilienthal, writing about the "new competition," said:

> I am not saying that active competition between the producers of the same product is of no present consequence. It certainly is. My point is that under present-day conditions it is often the least significant form. The competition between alternative materials, or ways of satisfying human needs and desires, has become a new dimension of competition.[79]

It was on such principles that Judge Leahy relied in reaching his conclusions in the Cellophane case.

This calls for a more careful consideration of the uniqueness of cellophane, of du Pont's pricing policies in selling it, and of the rate of earnings realized in doing so. If cellophane is sufficiently differentiated from other flexible wrapping materials, its demand curve may "lie to the right of the point of tangency with its cost curve" and its producer may receive monopoly profits in making and selling it. If cellophane is a less highly differentiated product within Chamberlin's conception of the term and if entry to the manufacture of rival wrapping materials is not blocked, the maker of cellophane will be faced by a sloping demand curve; but the curve will be tangent to the cost curve at some point above lowest average cost, and the seller will not make a monopoly profit. If the differentiation is so slight and potential competition so imminent as to bring it within Clark's concept of the term, the seller's long-

---

[76] R. M. Robertson, "On the Changing Apparatus of Competition," *American Economic Review*, Vol. XLIV (Proceedings of the American Economic Association, May, 1954), p. 61.

[77] *Ibid.*, pp. 53–54.

[78] *Ibid.*, p. 57.

[79] D. E. Lilienthal, *Big Business: A New Era* (New York, 1953), p. 60.

run demand curve will be close to the horizontal (his control over price will be slight) and prices will be close to lowest average cost. If the cellophane market conforms to Robertson's model, cellophane's differentiation will be too slight to count, monopoly profit will not exist, and its price will be competitive. To which of these models does the market for cellophane conform?

The Market for Cellophane

As a first step in answering this question we will examine briefly the flexible packaging materials market. The district court in determining whether du Pont monopolized the market for cellophane concluded that "the relevant market for determining the extent of du Pont's market control is the market for flexible packaging materials."[80] In this broad market the court found several hundred firms selling a variety of differentiated products for an even wider variety of uses. They sold either directly to packagers or to converters who prepared packaging materials for special uses. The court found that in 1949 du Pont cellophane accounted for only 17.9 per cent of the total square yardage of domestic output and imports of flexible packaging materials.[81] (Apparently this did not include kraft paper.) Such a small percentage scarcely demonstrates that du Pont had monopolized the *flexible packaging materials* market. Nor had it. But in passing judgment on the validity of the court's view that there is a single market for flexible packaging materials it may be helpful to classify the major contemporary materials according to their special qualities and major uses.

Cellophane is a thin, transparent, nonfibrous film of regenerated cellulose. It comes in two major types: plain and moistureproof. Moistureproof cellophane far outsells plain. In 1950 plain cellophane sales totalled $12,005,737; moistureproof cellophane sales, $116,660,209.[82] Because moistureproof cellophane sales are over nine times those of plain, our analysis will give primary consideration to moistureproof. Moistureproof cellophane is highly transparent, tears readily but has high bursting strength, is highly impervious to moisture and gases, and is resistant to grease and oils. Heat sealable, printable, and adapted to use on wrapping machines, it makes an excellent packaging material for both display and protection of commodities.

Other flexible wrapping materials fall into four major categories: (1) opaque nonmoistureproof wrapping *paper* designed primarily for convenience and protection in handling packages; (2) moistureproof *films* of varying degrees of transparency designed primarily either to protect, or to display and protect, the products they encompass; (3) non-

[80] 118 F. Supp. at 60.

[81] *Ibid.*, p. 111.

[82] Table showing comparison of du Pont and Sylvania plain and moistureproof cellophane sales, 1924–1950, 118 F. Supp. at 123.

moistureproof transparent *films* designed primarily to display and to some extent protect, but which obviously do a poor protecting job where exclusion or retention of moisture is important; and (4) moistureproof *materials* other than films of varying degrees of transparency (foils and paper products) designed to protect and display.

Kraft paper is the leading opaque nonmoistureproof wrapping paper. For general wrapping it has no equal. It is cheap, strong, and pliable and gives adequate protection. On a tonnage basis it easily tops all other packaging materials in total sales. But it is neither designed for nor adapted to the special uses for which cellophane was created and, as one market expert has put it, "in the true sense" does not compete with cellophane. More accurately, we think, cellophane does not compete with it. On a cost basis it cannot compete. At less than one cent per thousand square inches, kraft paper sells for less than cellophane's manufacturing cost.

The leading moistureproof *films* which might compete with cellophane include polyethylene, Saran, and Pliofilm. Relatively these are newcomers in the packaging field. In some qualities they match or even excel cellophane. But we have it on the authority of du Pont market analysts that these films have offered little or no competition to cellophane in its major markets. According to du Pont's 1948 market analysis, prepared by its experts for company use in making decisions, although Saran was "superior in moisture protection, no significant commercial uses" had developed for it "due principally to its high price" and "no substantial cost reduction" was in sight.[83] In 1949 a thousand square inches of 100-gauge Saran #517 sold for about 2½ times as much as the same amount of moistureproof cellophane (see Table 1). Du Pont experts found polyethylene lacking in transparency, "too limp to operate satisfactorily on wrapping machines, . . . difficult to heat seal, print and glue," with "poor surface slip and high static, and . . . permeable to volatile oils and flavorings."[84] Pliofilm, an older rival first marketed in the mid-thirties, has a rubber base and is particularly well adapted to packaging foods preserved in liquids, a relatively narrow market. Despite its superiority in this use, its high cost (in 1949 a thousand square inches of 120-gauge Pliofilm N2 sold for about 1⅔ times as much as moistureproof cellophane) made it "an active competitor of Cellophane only in those fringe uses bordering markets that need greater moistureproof protection than Cellophane provides."[85] In 1939 Pliofilm sales were only 2 per cent of cellophane sales; by 1949 they had increased to only 4.4 per cent.[86]

---

[83] DX 595, p. 1156.

[84] *Ibid.*, pp. 1155–56. The court said of polyethylene: "Many of these deficiencies could be corrected through research, and were." 118 F. Supp. at 81.

[85] DX 595, p. 1153. In 1950 Goodyear developed a type satisfactory for fresh meats. 118 F. Supp. at 81.

[86] GX 531, p. 7101; GX 81, p. 309; DX 596, p. 1173.

Cellulose acetate, a nonmoistureproof transparent *film,* is an old cellophane rival. First appearing in 1931, by 1939 its sales were only 3 per cent of cellophane's. Ten years later they were only 3.7 per cent.[87] Its chief quality disadvantage is that it is not moistureproof. It compares in

TABLE 1

COMPARISON OF AVERAGE WHOLESALE PRICES OF CELLOPHANE WITH PRICES OF OTHER FLEXIBLE PACKAGING MATERIALS IN 1949

Packaging Material	Price per 1,000 Sq. In. (Cents)	Per Cent of Cellophane Prices		Price per Lb. (Cents)	Per Cent of Cellophane Prices	
		Moistureproof	Plain		Moistureproof	Plain
Saran 100 gauge #517	6.1	265.2	290.5	99.0	207.1	221.0
Cellulose Acetate .00088″	3.3	143.5	157.1	82.0	171.5	183.0
Polyethylene .002″—18″ flat width	5.4	234.8	257.1	81.0	169.4	180.8
Pliofilm 120 gauge N2	3.8	165.2	181.0	80.8	169.0	180.4
Aluminum Foil .00035″	1.8	78.3	85.7	52.2	109.2	165.2
Moistureproof Cellophane 300 MST-51	2.3	100.0	109.5	47.8	100.0	106.7
Plain Cellophane 300 PT	2.1	91.3	100.0	44.8	93.7	100.0
Vegetable Parchment 27#	1.4	60.9	66.7	22.3	46.7	49.8
Bleached Glassine 25#	1.0	43.4	47.6	17.8	37.2	39.7
Bleached Greaseproof 25#	.9	39.1	42.9	15.8	33.1	35.3
Plain Waxed Sulphite 25# self-sealing	1.1	47.8	52.4	15.2	31.8	33.9
Plain Waxed Sulphite 25# coated opaque	.7	30.4	33.3	11.9	24.9	26.6

Source: Prices per thousand square inches and per pound, *United States* v. *E. I. du Pont de Nemours & Company*, 118 F. Supp. 41, 83 (D. Del. 1953). Robert Heller & Associates, management consultants, conducted the price survey for du Pont on which DX 995, the original source of these data, is based. G. W. Bricker, who personally supervised the survey, testified that "each of these materials is a principal standard material of that type." T. 4497. In selecting a particular grade Bricker relied on the advice of the Bureau of Labor Statistics, American Pulp and Paper Association economists, and the individual companies from which he got his data.

quality with plain cellophane, but its 57 per cent higher price in 1949 placed it at a serious competitive disadvantage.

About these several films du Pont in its 1948 market analysis concluded:

> The principal markets for non-viscose films have been competitive with Cellophane only to a very minor degree up to this time. Some are used very little or not at all in the packaging field—others are employed principally for

[87] Comparison of total du Pont and United States production of cellophane and imports of selected flexible packaging materials, 1925–1949, DX 981, p. 1.

specialty uses where Cellophane is not well adapted—none have been successfully introduced into any of Cellophane's main markets due to their inherent shortcomings.[88]

On the superiority of cellophane as compared with other films for most of cellophane's uses, the experts apparently agreed. Olin Industries, Inc., later to become the third domestic cellophane producer, after investigation reported: "According to du Pont, Cellophane is considered the only all purpose film, and any product to be *truly competitive* with Cellophane must have the following attributes: (1) low cost, (2) transparency, (3) operate with a high efficiency on mechanical equipment, (4) print well both as to speed and appearance."[89] Olin concluded:

> There are no films currently marketed which are potentially competitive to any substantial degree in Cellophane's major markets when measured by the above attributes necessary for wide usage. Other transparent films will find their place for those low volume uses which can absorb the additional cost of the film and which necessitate certain physical properties not possessed by Cellophane.[90]

Consumer decisions confirmed the judgment of the experts. In 1949 converters used roughly fourteen times as much cellophane as all other packaging films.[91]

Apparently cellophane has no effective rival in another segment of the flexible packaging material market, the outer wrapping of packaged cigarettes. Clear as plate glass, flexible, easily ripped open, moistureproof, it displays and protects with such perfection that except when they can't get it cigarette makers use no other overwrap.[92] The court recognized this, noting however that makers of Pliofilm, glassine, and aluminum foil keep trying to break into this market. They have not succeeded.

The court to the contrary notwithstanding, the market in which cellophane meets the "competition" of other wrappers is narrower than the market for all flexible packaging materials. Cellophane dominates the market for cigarette overwraps, it does not compete with kraft paper for general wrapping, and in its more specialized markets the nonviscose films do not compete with cellophane except in fringe uses.

Food Packaging

In 1949, 80 per cent of du Pont's cellophane sales were for packaging food products; here cellophane encounters its most vigorous rivalry,

[88] DX 595, p. 1147.

[89] Report on "the evidence in support of entry by Olin Industries into the Cellophane business, based on the purchase of patent license and 'know-how' from du Pont," December 15, 1948, GX 566, p. 7575.

[90] *Loc. cit.*

[91] DX 985. This is a market analysis prepared for du Pont by Robert Heller & Associates.

[92] A shortage of cellophane in the mid-forties forced some cigarette makers to use other materials. Brown and Williamson Tobacco Company once experimented with selling Kools and Raleigh cigarettes in a one-piece foil package. 118 F. Supp. at 108.

"competing" with vegetable parchment, greaseproof paper, glassine, wax paper, and aluminum foil. Each of these wrapping materials is a differentiated bundle of qualities, competing in a wide variety of uses. Users attach a different importance to the several qualities. Many value transparency highly, a quality in which cellophane is outstanding. Some, however, regard transparency as a disadvantage. All are likely to rate moisture protection as important, but wax paper, aluminum foil, and some types of glassine are about as good as cellophane in this. Food packagers in selecting wrapping material no doubt consider carefully the unique combination of qualities represented by each of these materials. They resell the product they wrap and they are cost-conscious. Presumably they try to select the material that, quality considered, will give the greatest value. In determining values they must consider consumer response to the several materials. In any event, some buyers of packaging materials changed from one kind to another in trying to get their money's worth. Some candy makers and some bread bakers, for example, operating on narrow margins, in the mid-thirties switched from cellophane to a less costly wrapper when their other production costs mounted. The court concluded from the evidence that "shifts of business between du Pont cellophane and other flexible packaging materials have been frequent, continuing and contested."[93] In no one of the more important uses for packaging foods did cellophane in 1949 supply as much as 50 per cent of the total quantity (in square inches) of wrapping materials used (see Table 2).[94] Only in the packaging of fresh produce did cellophane sales top the list. Its percentage of total sales varied from 6.8 per cent for packaging bakery products to 47.2 per cent for fresh produce. Like du Pont's percentage of total sales of all flexible wrapping materials, these specific figures scarcely demonstrate that du Pont has monopolized the sale of flexible packaging material to food packagers.

Such facts apparently led the court to conclude that du Pont, although selling about 76 per cent of the cellophane and together with Sylvania—whose production was geared to du Pont's—selling all of it, had not monopolized the market for *all* flexible wrapping materials. No one is likely to quarrel with this finding. But in an economic sense a firm may have a monopoly of a differentiated product, that is, it may behave like a monopolist and enjoy the fruits of monopoly in selling it, even though it meets the rivalry of substitutes. That is the economic issue here. Is

[93] *Ibid.*, p. 91.

[94] Table 2 is based on evidence which the court reproduced in the opinion. In less important uses not included in the court's tabulation cellophane accounted for the following percentages of total quantities of the selected flexible wrapping materials used: dry beverages, 6.4 per cent; breakfast cereals, 12.6 per cent; dry fruits and vegetables, 63.7 per cent; frozen dairy products, 1.1 per cent; flour, meal, and dry baking mixes, .5 per cent; nuts, 77.3 per cent; paste goods, 97.4 per cent; paper products, 38 per cent; and textile products, 62.3 per cent. DX 984.

cellophane so highly differentiated that du Pont in selling it can follow an independent pricing policy, that is, is the cross elasticity of demand for cellophane so low that du Pont, while pricing it independently, can enjoy a monopoly profit in its sale? Let us examine this issue.

When du Pont first marketed cellophane, it apparently thought cellophane had unique qualities and it adopted a strategy designed to prevent competition from any other producer, in short, to protect its monopoly.[95] It also priced cellophane from the outset to yield monopoly revenue. Its long-run aim in selling cellophane was apparently that of any monopolist, viz., to maximize revenues. But the maximization of revenues over time even by a monopolist may call for a farsighted and vigorous policy in

TABLE 2

COMPARISON BY PERCENTAGES OF TOTAL QUANTITY OF SELECTED FLEXIBLE PACKAGING MATERIALS, CLASSIFIED BY END USES*

Type of Material	Bakery Products	Candy	Snacks	Meat and Poultry	Crackers and Biscuits	Fresh Produce	Frozen Food Excluding Dairy Products
Cellophane	6.8	24.4	31.9	34.9	26.6	47.2	33.6
Foil	.2	32.5	.8	.1	.2	.1	.7
Glassine	4.4	21.4	62.8	2.7	10.0	.1	2.1
Papers	88.6	21.6	4.4	57.5	63.2	45.6	60.3
Films	.0	.1	.1	4.8	.0	7.0	3.3
Total	100.0	100.0	100.0	100.0	100.0	100.0	100.0

* Based on 1949 sales (in millions of square inches) of nineteen major converters "representing a substantial segment" of the converting industry, *United States* v. *E. I. du Pont de Nemours & Company*, 118 F. Supp. 41, 113 (D. Del. 1953). G. W. Bricker of Robert Heller and Associates, management consultants employed by du Pont, testified that the above data covered two-thirds of du Pont's and Sylvania's cellophane. T. 4474.

exploiting a product. Monopolists, although they can restrict output and charge relatively high prices, may not find it profitable to do so. Du Pont argued and the court concluded that the test of monopoly is the power to exclude competition and the power to raise prices. A more logical test is the power to exclude competition and the power to *control* prices. That a monopolist may find it profitable to lower prices, increase sales, and reduce costs, even though the public benefits, does not necessarily mean, as Robertson suggests, that he has relinquished monopoly power. To use monopoly power rationally is not to forego it.

President Yerkes of the Du Pont Cellophane Company, Inc., concluded as early as 1924 that to maximize earnings du Pont should reduce cellophane prices. On this issue he said:

95 If cellophane had encountered the effective competition of rival wrapping materials, du Pont would have had nothing to gain by impeding entry. That is to say, if cellophane were merely one of many substitutable products among which effective competition prevails, the price of each would be driven down to a competitive (cost-remunerative) level and it should be a matter of indifference to du Pont whether this results from rival products or from new producers of cellophane.

I am in favor of lowering the price. . . . [I] think it will undoubtedly increase sales and widen distribution. . . . Our price I think is too high based purely on manufacturing cost and too high in comparison with other wrapping papers on the market, and while we cannot approach the price of glassine or other oil papers, if we make a substantial reduction we will in some cases get somewhere near there.[96]

Walter S. Carpenter, Jr., chairman of du Pont's board of directors, expressed a similar idea when he testified in the Cellophane case:

. . . the purpose of reducing our price and also improving our quality was to broaden our market. . . . As a general philosophy I was always in favor of the reduction of the price as we were able to do so by the reduced costs, and I think that I consistently urged that on the management.[97]

The Yerkes-Carpenter philosophy apparently prevailed. The price of cellophane, which averaged $2.508 a pound in 1924, was reduced in every year until 1936, when it averaged 41.3 cents a pound. With minor interruptions the decline continued until cellophane sold for an average price of 38 cents a pound in 1940. Inflation accompanying the Second World War reversed the trend. With few exceptions cellophane prices moved upward until 1950, when they averaged 49 cents a pound.[98] But despite the reductions moistureproof cellophane (300 MST-51, the principal type) sold at from two to seven times the price of 25# bleached glassine and from two to four and a half times the price of 30# waxed paper, its most important rivals.[99]

Du Pont's Independent Pricing Policy

On its face du Pont's pricing policy was consistent with that of a monopolist. Other evidence supports this conclusion. Had cellophane's major rival wrapping materials competed with it effectively (*i.e.*, had the cross elasticity of demand between cellophane and other wrappers been high), the prices of such wrapping materials would have moved concurrently to prevent, as Chamberlin says, "incursions by one seller, through a price cut, upon the markets of others."[100] In fact, however, while du Pont was "broadening its market" by reducing cellophane prices, the prices of other wrappers did not follow a similar pattern. Bleached glassine prices were constant from 1924 until 1933 and again from 1934 to 1938. They rose in 1939 and again in 1940. Waxed paper prices fluctuated between .5 cent and .52 cent per thousand square inches from 1933 through 1939 and in 1940 increased to .62 cent. Vegetable parch-

---

[96] Memorandum of some remarks made at a meeting of the board of directors, Du Pont Cellophane Company, Inc., December 11, 1924, DX 337, p. 643.

[97] T. 6278–79.

[98] Table of annual average prices from 1924 to 1950, *United States* v. *E. I. du Pont de Nemours & Co.*, 118 F. Supp. 41, 82 (D. Del. 1953).

[99] Defendant's Brief on the Facts and the Law, Appendix A (graph based on prices per 1,000 sq. in.), *United States* v. *E. I. du Pont de Nemours & Co.*, 118 F. Supp. 41 (D. Del. 1953).

[100] Chamberlin, *Monopolistic Competition*, p. 90.

ment prices declined from 1.3 cents to 1.0 cent per thousand square inches between 1924 and 1928 and thereafter fluctuated between .95 cent and 1.05 cents. Bleached greaseproof prices rose from .45 cent per thousand square inches in 1933 to about .55 cent in 1940.[101] But du Pont's cellulose acetate film dropped in price from 59.3 cents a pound in 1935 to 53.6 cents in 1940,[102] and aluminum foil prices dropped from 2.45 cents to 1.65 cents per thousand square inches between 1928 and 1940. The prices of these rival products and of cellophane followed the same trend, but cellophane and cellulose acetate film sold for substantially more than aluminum foil; and it seems likely that the cross elasticity of demand between the cellulose films and aluminum foil is even less than between them and the other products compared.

Under inflation wrapping material prices have increased since 1940, but not similarly. Average cellophane prices increased by about 20 per cent between 1940 and 1949, but the prices of most other wrappers increased more rapidly: vegetable parchment, about 40 per cent; bleached glassine, 40 per cent; cellulose acetate, 50 per cent; waxed paper, 75 per cent; and bleached greaseproof, 80 per cent. The only two wrappers to increase less in price than cellophane were Pliofilm, 13 per cent, and aluminum foil, 9 per cent.[103] These price patterns indicate that cellophane continued to decrease in price relative to most other wrapping materials.

The above facts demonstrating cellophane's independence of other wrapping material prices strongly suggest that du Pont was not selling cellophane in an effectively competitive market. Either cellophane's rival products were not close enough substitutes to feel the effect of cellophane price decreases (*i.e.*, the cross elasticity of demand between cellophane and these products was low) or they were already selling at cost and could not prevent cellophane's invasion of their markets. In either event they did not constitute sufficiently close substitutes to insure effective competition.

Although du Pont lowered its cellophane prices from time to time as it re-examined its demand and cost functions, at no time did it compete with its most popular rivals on a price basis. As H. O. Ladd, director of du Pont's trade analysis division, put it:

> The main competitive materials . . . against which Cellophane competes are waxed paper, glassine, greaseproof and vegetable parchment paper, all of which are lower in price than Cellophane. We do not meet this price competition. Rather, we compete with these materials on the basis of establishing the value of our own as a factor in better packaging and cheaper distribution costs and classify as our logical markets those fields where the properties of Cellophane in relationship to its price can do a better job for the user.[104]

[101] DX 994-A. These price comparisons, like those for 1949 in Table 1, rest on data collected for du Pont by Robert Heller & Associates and are based on the prices of one principal standard material of each type named.

[102] GX 490, p. 6507; GX 495, p. 6665.

[103] DX 994-A.

[104] GX 589, p. 7530.

But while du Pont resorted to aggressive selling, emphasizing the superiority of its product and extending its services,[105] the evidence does not indicate that at any time it carried quality competition so far as to equalize average cost and selling price. Price differences no doubt reflected at the margin the customers' evaluation of differences in quality, but the record does not indicate that they reflected differences in cost. If they had, with as many firms as are selling flexible wrapping materials, monopoly profits would have disappeared and the market would have become effectively competitive. Let us turn then to du Pont's earning record.

III. HAS DU PONT EARNED MONOPOLY PROFITS?

As du Pont reduced cellophane prices, output and sales expanded rapidly. In 1924 du Pont produced only 361,000 pounds of cellophane and sold $1,307,000 worth. A decade later it produced 39,358,000 pounds and sold $18,818,000 worth. In 1940 when cellophane sold at 38 cents a pound, its all-time low, du Pont produced 81,677,000 pounds and sold $31,049,000 worth.[106] Such increases in output and sales had called for a continuous expansion in investment. In 1925 du Pont's fixed and working capital in producing cellophane was $2,122,000. In 1934 it was $24,008,000 and a decade later $41,133,000 (see Table 3).

Du Pont's production and pricing policies paid off. In 1925 it earned, before taxes (operating earnings),[107] $779,000 on its cellophane operating

---

[105] Du Pont showed great ingenuity and aggression in developing new uses for cellophane and expanding old ones. R. R. Smith, assistant director of sales of du Pont's film department, testified that in 1934, when white bread regularly sold for 10 cents a loaf and its profit margin was small, he and other salesmen actually created the specialty breads industry—new varieties of bread which could be sold at a price large enough to cover the higher cost of wrapping them in cellophane. T. 5704–5. In 1936 Smith studied the sales methods of door-to-door bakery salesmen and du Pont made a sales training film "which had nothing to do with packaging" (T. 5721) but showed the way to higher profits even when using cellophane. "The promotion was extremely successful." T. 5705. In 1951 du Pont had about 45 per cent of the variety bread-wrapping business. T. 5721.

[106] See comparisons of du Pont and Sylvania production and sales, 1924–1950, *United States* v. *E. I. du Pont de Nemours & Co.*, 118 F. Supp. at 116, 123 (D. Del. 1953).

[107] Du Pont computes operating earnings for each operating division by deducting all of the expenses directly related to its operations from its sales. Among these expenses are production, selling, administration, and research expenditures conducted within and for the particular division. Du Pont calculates its rate of operating earnings on the basis of its working and fixed investment allocated to its cellophane operations.

Net cellophane earnings are calculated by allowing for federal income taxes, capital stock tax, franchise, state income, and foreign taxes, "B" bonus, and fundamental research by the chemicals department. Federal income and other taxes constituted the great bulk of these deductions: 90 per cent as early as 1935 (GX 490, p. 6506) and during the Second World War practically all, when the company was paying large excess profits taxes. Consequently, cellophane operating earnings may be thought of as primarily representing earnings on total cellophane investment before taxes, and cellophane net earnings as earnings after taxes.

The problem of empirically determining profit rates is subject to many pitfalls. However, the procedure used by du Pont to determine cellophane earnings is sub-investment. In 1934 it earned $6,000,000 and in 1940, $12,000,000. Although its annual rate of earnings before taxes declined somewhat from a high of 62.4 per cent in 1928, in only two years between 1923 and 1950 inclusive did the rate fall below 20 per cent (see Table 3).

Du Pont's cellophane pricing policy is consistent with the economists' assumption that a rational monopolist aims to maximize profits. This did not always call for a price reduction. In 1947 du Pont earned only 19.1 per cent before taxes and only 11.2 per cent after taxes on its cellophane investment[108]—the postwar low. Raising the average price of cellophane from 41.9 cents a pound in 1947 to 46 cents a pound in 1948 paid off. By May, 1948 du Pont's operative earnings had increased to 31 per cent. At that time its division manager announced that "if operative earnings of 31 per cent is [*sic*] considered inadequate, then an upward revision in prices will be necessary to improve the return."[109] He suggested a schedule of prices which would increase operative earnings to about 40 per cent.[110] This was not put into effect until August, 1948. Operative earnings for 1948 averaged only 27.2 per cent; but by 1949 they had increased to 35.2 per cent and by 1950 to 45.3 per cent. Operative earnings after taxes yielded 20 per cent on du Pont's investment in 1950.

Du Pont's pricing policy in the postwar inflation is also consistent with the theory of monopolistic behavior, but the record indicates that profit maximization was not the sole factor affecting price decisions. The divi-

---

ject to fewer criticisms than are usually encountered in profit estimates. It is true that earnings may be understated somewhat because of expenditures not directly related to cellophane manufacture and sale as noted above. On the other hand, some might argue that actual earnings are overstated in some years and understated in others because operating investment is necessarily based in part on historical rather than replacement costs. This error is reduced by the fact that du Pont has increased its capacity periodically by substantial amounts, so that of its historical costs a substantial portion is always recent history. However, some of the most frequent and important shortcomings of profit estimates are not involved in our calculations; operating investment does not include assets capitalized in expectation of excess profits, nor has overcapacity broadened the investment base. Probably the most convincing argument as to the credibility of these earnings is that du Pont has no reason to delude itself as to what it is earning in making cellophane. The investment base which du Pont uses to calculate its rates of operating and net earnings is its estimate of the actual total investment involved in its cellophane operations. Such an investment base is considerably larger than that used by the Federal Trade Commission in its study, *Rates of Return (after Taxes) for 516 Identical Companies in 25 Selected Manufacturing Industries, 1940, 1947–52* (Washington, D.C., 1954), which uses stockholders' investment as its base. If this base were used in calculating rates of cellophane earnings they would undoubtedly be greater for all years. For example, in 1935, the year before Du Pont Cellophane was consolidated with du Pont, the latter's equity in Du Pont Cellophane was only $9,696,000. GX 490, p. 6504. If this were used as a base upon which to calculate du Pont's rate of earnings in that year, instead of that actually used in Table 3, its rate of operating earnings would be about 60 per cent instead of 24.6 per cent.

108 One reason for the relatively low earnings in 1947 was du Pont's inability to put its new capacity at Clinton, Iowa into production as early as predicted. DX 372.

109 GX 591, p. 7539.

110 *Ibid.*, p. 7540.

TABLE 3

Du Pont's Operating Investment, Operating Earnings, and Net Earnings on Cellophane, 1925–1950*

Year	Operating Investment (000)	Operating Earnings (000)	Rate of Operating Earnings (per cent)	Net Earnings (000)	Rate of Net Earnings (per cent)
1924	$ 2,000				
1925	2,122[b]	$ 779[a]	36.7[b]	$ 650[b]	30.6[a]
1926	2,482	1,447	58.3	1,191[c]	48.0
1927	2,464	1,104	44.8	906[d]	36.8
1928	2,559	1,597	62.4	1,318[e]	51.5
1929	5,099[a]	2,845[f]	55.8[f]	2,645[f]	51.9
1930	11,178	4,460[g]	39.9[g]	4,273[g]	38.2
1931	18,163	5,431[h]	29.9[h]	5,196[h]	28.6
1932	21,600	3,888[i]	18.0[i]	3,882[i]	17.9
1933	23,277	4,958[j]	21.3[j]	4,800[j]	20.6
1934	24,008	5,978[l]	24.9[k]	4,325[l]	18.0
1935	24,598	6,051[k]	24.6[k]	4,934[k]	20.1
1936	26,262[m]	7,642[m]	29.1[m]	6,119[a]	23.3[m]
1937	27,284[o]	6,876	25.2[n]	5,293	19.4[n]
1938	30,655[a]	8,430[p]	27.5	6,867	22.4
1939	31,837	11,833	36.8	9,137	28.7
1940	33,737	12,179	36.1	6,882	20.4
1941	40,995	16,234	39.6	6,231	15.2
1942	43,482	11,566[q]	26.6	3,652	8.4
1943	42,449	14,263	33.6	3,821	9.0
1944	41,133	13,903	33.8	3,990	9.7
1945	40,431	13,868	34.3	5,620	13.9
1946	41,495	12,241[r]	29.5	6,929	16.7
1947	53,424	10,204	19.1	5,983	11.2
1948	64,800[s]	17,600[s]	27.2	n.a.	n.a.
1949	n.a.	n.a.	35.2[t]	n.a.	n.a.
1950	67,532	30,592[t]	45.3[t]	13,506	20.0[t]
	Average Rate of Return........		34.4		24.2

* For definition of operating investment, operating earnings, and net earnings see footnote 107. Before 1937, investment and earnings figures include cellulose caps and bands, cellulose acetate, and adhesives, for some years. On the whole this inclusion decreases the rate of return figures for cellophane slightly, since some of these items were actually sold at a loss at times. The net effect is insignificant, however, since they represent such a small proportion of total earnings and investment—less than 5 per cent in 1935. GX 490, p. 6507.

[a] Derived from relevant columns
[b] 1925–1928, GX 483, pp. 6409, 6410
[c] GX 481, p. 6375
[d] GX 482, p. 6396
[e] GX 483, p. 6418
[f] GX 484, pp. 6431, 6433
[g] GX 485, pp. 6441, 6443
[h] GX 486, pp. 6453, 6455
[i] GX 487, pp. 6464, 6466
[j] GX 488, pp. 6479, 6481
[k] GX 490, p. 6503
[l] GX 489, p. 6493
[m] GX 384, p. 969
[n] 1937–1947, GX 591, p. 7539
[o] GX 492, p. 6571
[p] 1938–1941, GX 495-A, p. 6716
[q] 1942–1945, GX 499, p. 6839
[r] 1946–1947, GX 501, p. 690
[s] GX 577, p. 7323
[t] GX 573 (I), p. 8. Exhibit impounded by court, cited in government's Proposed Findings of Fact, p. 48, and Brief for the United States, pp. 144, 145, *United States* v. *E. I. du Pont de Nemours & Company*, 118 F. Supp. 41 (D.Del. 1953).

Sources: The exhibits referred to are annual profit and loss statements of Du Pont Cellophane Company or the cellophane division of E. I. du Pont de Nemours & Company.

sion manager in suggesting price increases called attention to other relevant factors:

2. What effect, if any, will a price increase have on our case when it is heard before the Federal Judge? I have not covered this with our Legal Department but in view of the position they took last July and August, prior to

the October increase, I am inclined to think they should be brought in for a discussion on this matter.

3. The du Pont Company may get some undesirable publicity from the press. A price increase on Cellophane could be looked upon as added fuel to the present recent spurt in the inflationary spiral and add to the present pressure for an increase in wages. This question is currently a live one at several of our Cellophane plants. Probably it would be in order to discuss this with Mr. Brayman.[111]

After considering these questions du Pont executives decided on the price increase.[112]

Cellophane's earnings record offers persuasive if not convincing evidence that du Pont has had monopoly power in selling cellophane. A comparison of du Pont's earnings from cellophane with its earnings from rayon lends force to this conclusion.[113] Despite the dissimilarity of the end products, several factors justify the comparison. Cellophane and rayon stem from the same basic raw materials. Both are radical innovations. Both were initially manufactured under noncompetitive conditions and both enjoyed substantial tariff protection. The same business management produced both products. The French Comptoir shared in the management of both Du Pont Cellophane and Du Pont Rayon until 1929. Yerkes, president of Du Pont Cellophane, was also president of Du Pont Rayon. Presumably du Pont in controlling business policy for both companies was actuated by similar business motives.[114] Both products have had several reasonably close substitutes. The production and consumption of both increased phenomenally.[115] Cellophane and rayon have been

---

[111] *Loc. cit.* Mr. Brayman was the director of du Pont's public relations department.

[112] In considering the probable effect of a price increase on cellophane earnings, the division manager stated the matter as follows: "Can we sell the capacity output of our plants? . . . The District Managers are divided in their opinion. . . . However, the majority of the District Managers, the Director and Assistant Director of Sales are of the opinion, barring a recession, the tonnage can be sold." *Ibid.*, p. 7539. Although this reasoning is consistent with that of a monopolist interested in maximizing profits, Judge Leahy cited it as evidence that du Pont did not have the power to raise prices arbitrarily. *United States* v. *E. I. du Pont de Nemours & Co.*, 118 F. Supp. 41, 179 (D. Del. 1953).

[113] Data are not available to compare du Pont's earnings from cellophane with the earnings of producers of other wrapping materials. These are without exception diversified firms producing a variety of products. However, the record discloses that in every year from 1935 through 1942 du Pont failed to cover costs in selling cellulose acetate film, which it sold in competition with two other concerns (GX 490 through GX 497).

[114] The district court found: "Same individuals were the principal du Pont executives in du Pont Rayon Co. and du Pont Cellophane Co. Same policies of improving quality, lowering cost of production, and reducing unit price to gain greater volume of sales were followed as to both companies"; and that du Pont's "price policy for rayon was the same as for cellophane." 118 F. Supp. at 86.

[115] United States consumption of rayon increased by about 320,000,000 pounds between 1920 and 1938. Jesse W. Markham, *Competition in the Rayon Industry* (Cambridge, Mass., 1952), p. 230. Cellophane consumption grew by about 80,000,000 pounds between 1924 and 1938. DX 600, p. 1216.

similarly characterized by rapidly developing technology, rapid reduction in costs, and rapid decline in prices.[116] The chief difference in the manufacture and sale of the two products significant to the course of profits apparently lies in the structure of the rayon and cellophane industries. Although rayon manufacture began in this country as a monopoly, rival firms came into the industry promptly. American Viscose

TABLE 4

Investment of Principal Companies in Rayon, Investment of Du Pont in Rayon, Investment of Du Pont in Cellophane, and Annual Rate of Return Before Taxes on These Investments, 1920–1938

Year	Total Rayon Investment of Principal Rayon Companies (millions of dollars)	Du Pont's Rayon Investment	Du Pont's Cellophane Investment	Average Rate of Return of Principal Rayon Companies (per cent)	Du Pont's Rate of Return on Rayon Investment (per cent)	Du Pont's Rate of Return on Cellophane Investment (per cent)
1920	$ 40.7			64.2		
1921	51.2	$ 2.9		42.0	(−2.1)	
1922	66.0	4.0		50.1	34.1	
1923	89.1	6.3		43.2	38.9	
1924	110.6	8.9		26.7	27.9	
1925	141.7	14.0	$ 2.1	30.6	34.2	36.7
1926	159.3	20.2	2.5	20.1	15.2	58.3
1927	166.7	24.4	2.7	25.8	27.0	44.8
1928	199.1	29.6	2.6	24.5	26.6	62.4
1929	228.0	38.4	5.1	18.1	19.0	55.8
1930	244.6	41.1	11.2	5.0	(−0.9)	39.9
1931	234.5	37.0	18.2	3.4	4.5	29.9
1932	223.2	33.5	21.6	1.5	1.2	18.0
1933	238.3	32.4	23.3	12.2	12.7	21.3
1934	249.9	38.7	24.0	6.9	8.6	24.9
1935	255.4	46.0	24.6	6.7	5.3	24.6
1936	267.0	50.0	26.3	11.5	11.0	29.1
1937	281.3	54.6	27.3	12.1	13.1	25.2
1938	296.6	61.7	30.7	2.5	4.2	27.5
Average Rate of Return..................				21.4	15.6	35.6

Sources: Rayon investment and earnings, Federal Trade Commission, *Investments, Profits, and Rates of Return for Selected Industries* (a special report prepared for the Temporary National Economic Committee, 76th Cong., 3d Sess.), 1941, pp. 17988, 17990, 17998. Cellophane investment and earnings based on Table 3. Comparable data on total rayon investment and earnings are not available beyond 1938.

Corporation began as the sole domestic producer of rayon shortly before the First World War and du Pont followed in 1920. By 1930 these concerns had eighteen rivals. As late as 1949 fifteen firms occupied the field. Although the four largest firms in recent years have usually accounted for about 70 per cent of the total output and although most of the firms have generally followed a price leader, Markham from his painstaking

[116] Rayon prices dropped from $6.00 a pound on February 1, 1920 to $0.51 a pound on July 29, 1938. Federal Trade Commission, *Investments, Profits, and Rates of Return for Selected Industries* (a special report prepared for the Temporary National Economic Committee, 76th Cong., 3d Sess.), 1941, p. 17985. Cellophane prices dropped from $2.51 in 1924 to $0.42 in 1938. DX 336, p. 642.

and exhaustive study concludes that freedom of entry and the pressure of substitute products have made the rayon industry workably or effectively competitive.[117] The course of both du Pont's and the industry's rate of earnings supports this conclusion (see Table 4). Federal Trade Commission data reveal that in 1920, when du Pont first produced rayon, American Viscose Corporation, until then the country's sole producer, realized 64.2 per cent on its investment.[118] Although du Pont showed a loss in 1921, its rate of earnings rose to 38.9 per cent by 1923. Thereafter its rate of earnings and those of the industry declined until by 1929 they had fallen to 19.0 and 18.1 per cent, respectively. When six more firms entered the industry in 1930,[119] average industry earnings fell to 5.0 per cent and du Pont suffered a loss of 0.9 per cent. During the following eight years du Pont averaged only 7.5 per cent on its rayon investment, and the industry as a whole put in a similar performance.

In striking contrast, du Pont with only a single rival in producing cellophane (and that rival's output closely geared to du Pont's) earned less than 20 per cent on its cellophane investment in only one depression year. From the beginning of the depression in 1929 through the succeeding recovery and the 1938 recession du Pont averaged 29.6 per cent before taxes on its cellophane investment. On its rayon investment it averaged only 6.3 per cent.

IV. CONCLUSIONS

Apparently the cellophane market does not conform to the Chamberlinian model in which substitutes are so close that no producer may long enjoy monopoly returns—a "sort of ideal" equilibrium adjustment with the demand curve tangent to the cost curve at some point above lowest average cost. It does not conform to Clark's model of workable competition wherein rival products and potential competition reduce the slope of the demand curve, or to Robertson's model wherein substitutes are so close as to result in a competitive price. Rather, cellophane is so differentiated from other flexible wrapping materials that its cross elasticity of demand gives du Pont significant and continuing monopoly power.

Du Pont has used its power with foresight and wisdom. It has apparently recognized that it could increase its earnings by decreasing its costs and prices, by educating its potential customers to the benefits of wrapping their products in cellophane, by improving machinery for packaging, by helping converters and packagers solve their technical problems. It has built a better mousetrap and taught people how to use it.

---

117 Markham, *op. cit.*, pp. 181, 206, 208.

118 Federal Trade Commission, *op. cit. supra* note 116, p. 17644. In this report the Commission's method of estimating rates of earnings on the basis of total investment is apparently similar to du Pont's method of calculating its operating earnings for its various divisions. See note 107 *supra*.

119 Markham, *op. cit.*, p. 47.

But du Pont has not surrendered its monopoly power. Its strategy, cellophane's distinctive qualities, and the course of its prices and earnings indicate this. Du Pont's strategy was designed to protect a monopoly in the sale of a product it regarded as unique, and its pricing policies reflected the judgment of its executives on how best to maximize earnings. We think its earnings illustrate Knight's distinction between justifiable profits to the innovator and unjustifiable monopoly gains. They have been "too large" and have lasted "too long."

III. BUSINESS PRACTICES AND MARKET BEHAVIOR

8

Basing Point Pricing and Public Policy*

By CARL KAYSEN[†]

I

The Supreme Court's reaffirmation (by a 4–4 tie vote without written opinion) of the Federal Trade Commission's decision in the Rigid Steel Conduit Case finally settled the legal status of basing point pricing systems.[1] The earlier Cement Case[2] had defined any agreement to use basing point pricing as unlawful, and put a wide construction on what was evidence of an agreement. In the Conduit Case the Federal Trade Commission ruled that the concurrent use of basing point pricing by numerous competitors was sufficient evidence of unlawful conspiracy. Further, it held that individual use of the system by a single firm in the knowledge that it was being used by competitors was likewise illegal. The Circuit Court, in upholding the Commission, asserted that the legal question presented by that case was identical with that presented by the Cement Case. Under no circumstances, therefore, could basing point price systems be free of the vice of unlawful conspiracy, which make them "unfair methods of competition" under the Federal Trade Commission Act.

This decision will probably give further impetus to the discussion of legislation to make basing point pricing legal by amending the Clayton and Federal Trade Commission Acts. The discussion was initiated in the Eightieth Congress by the Republicans through the medium of a subcommittee of the Senate Committee on Interstate Commerce, under the

* *The Quarterly Journal of Economics*, Vol. XLIII (1949), pp. 289–314. Reprinted by courtesy of the Harvard University Press and the author.

The material in this paper was first presented to an informal discussion group on antitrust policy consisting of Prof. M. A. Adelman of M. I. T. and Professors S. S. Alexander, R. R. Bowie, D. F. Cavers, L. Gordon and Dean E. S. Mason, all of Harvard. I am much obliged to them for valuable suggestions and corrections. They are not, of course, either individually or collectively responsible for the argument here presented or the errors it may contain.

† Harvard University.

[1] The FTC decision is given in *Rigid Steel Conduit Association*, 38 F.T.C. 534 (1944). The decision was upheld on appeal by the 7th Circuit Court of Appeals, *Triangle Conduit and Cable Co.* v. *Federal Trade Commission*, 168 F. 2d 175 (1948). The high court decision is recorded in *Clayton Mark & Co.* v. *Federal Trade Commission*, 336 U.S. 956 (1949).

[2] *FTC* v. *Cement Institute, et al.*, 333 U.S. 683 (1948).

chairmanship of Senator Capehart of Indiana (Rep.). It is being continued in the present (Eighty-first) Congress; and a bill was introduced to effect such amendments (S.236) by Senator Johnson of Colorado (Dem.) early in January.

The need for dispassionate examination of basing point pricing and the possible alternatives to it in terms of public policy is clear. The present essay is an attempt to do so, by no means the first in this knotty field.[3]

Before examining the tests by which public policy in this field should be measured, let us summarize briefly the characteristics of markets in which the basing point pricing system is used, and the chief features of the system in operation. The characteristics which follow are typical, but not every industry operating under the system will possess them all.[4] The product sold is essentially standardized, so that the output of one producer at a given consuming point is a perfect substitute for the output of another producer at that point. Therefore, in an equilibrium situation, the prices charged by two producers at any given point must be the same. The product also is low in value per unit weight, so that for shipments over all but very short distances, the transportation cost forms a substantial fraction of the delivered price. Thus spatial differentiation of the product, delivered to the consumer, forms an essential element of the system. Shipments do, in fact, take place over fairly long distances. This can arise either from economies of scale which make local producers serving local markets uneconomical, or from strong locational factors which lead to the concentration of production in a few areas, or both. The cement industry furnishes an example of the operation of the first reason; the maple flooring industry (located in the region of timber stands in Michigan and Wisconsin), of the second; and the steel industry, the classic example of basing point pricing, of the combination. The efficient scale of operations is large, capital investment in an economical plant is fairly great per unit of output, and the ratio of marginal cost to average cost is low for all rates of operation below "full capacity." The

---

[3] Some of the recent articles have been: Frank A. Fetter, "Exit Basing Point Pricing," and Corwin D. Edwards, "Basing Point Decisions and Business Practices," both in *American Economic Review*, December, 1948; J. M. Clark, "Law and Economics of Basing Points," *American Economic Review*, March, 1949; and Edwin B. George, "The Law and Economics of Basing Points" (3 articles), *Dun's Review*, September, October, and November, 1948. A book on the subject was published in April, 1949: Fritz Machlup, *The Basing Point System* (Philadelphia: Blakiston, 1949).

[4] In general, factual material on the operation of the basing point system is not too abundant, and nearly all that is available bears on only two industries of the many in which the system was used—steel and cement. All the factual material referred to in this paper is drawn from the experience of one or another of these industries. This experience is described in various places. See especially: A. R. Burns, *The Decline of Competition*, chap. vi, "Price Discrimination"; *TNEC Hearings*, Parts 19, 20 and 27; TNEC Monographs 42, *The Basing Point Problem*, and 41, *Price Discrimination in Steel;* and the Supreme Court opinion on the Cement Case, 333 U.S. 683, which provides a good brief summary of the operation of basing point pricing in the cement industry.

rate of operation of the plants in the industry is frequently below full capacity, often because there are large cyclical fluctuations in demand for the product. Production equipment employed is specialized and long-lived, and thus exit from the market, either by product substitution or by allowing plant to "die" through non-replacement, is a difficult and protracted process. The market demand for the product is generally inelastic at and below prices which correspond to output considerably less than the full capacity of the industry. Finally, the market contains few enough sellers so that oligopolistic calculation plays an important role in the actions of firms in the market. This is clear enough in the steel industry. The large number of firms in the cement industry seems to contradict this statement, but shipments of cement rarely move more than 200 or 300 miles, and in any local market the number of competing firms is very small, fewer than 10 in most areas. The combination of small numbers and spatial differentiation makes these industries classic examples of monopolistic competition.

The mechanics of basing point pricing are well known, and need not be rehearsed here. Certain features of the operation of the system, however, deserve the emphasis of repetition. Its outstanding feature is the creation of a fixed, well-defined price structure, with delivered prices of all sellers identical to all consumers at each specific location. The effective operation of this system requires basing points and base prices publicly known (in the trade), and uniquely defined freight costs from every basing point to every possible consuming point. This last requirement is usually fulfilled by the use of a common compilation of freight rates in the form of a freight book by all firms in the industry. In practice, the system usually operates on the basis of all-rail freight in the calculation of delivered prices, although it could conceivably forego this restriction. Since rail freight costs must be paid, rail freight is used almost to the exclusion of water and truck transport.[5] Lastly, there is always a significant amount of market interpenetration, defined as occurring when mills sell to customers located where mill prices plus freight costs from other mills which could handle their orders are lower than from the selling mill. This market interpenetration usually involves freight absorption (when there is a multiple basing point system) and always involves selling costs in excess of what would be spent without market interpenetration. The end result of market interpenetration is a complex structure of geographical price discrimination, determined by the locational pattern of mills and consumers, and the actual degree of market interpenetration.

---

[5] In steel, consumers were allowed to take delivery in their own trucks on payment of 35 per cent of rail transportation costs. See *TNEC Hearings*, Part 27, pp. 14182 ff. See also Part 20, pp. 10830–45, and correspondence on pp. 11005–6 for the reaction of the Steel Corporation to attempts of a consumer to take delivery in his own barge at a point not the point of consumption.

So much for the circumstances and consequences of basing point pricing. In order to examine this pricing practice from the point of view of public policy recommendations, it is necessary to formulate both a set of alternative situations which are feasible of attainment through governmental action, and a set of standards by which the desirability of the alternatives can be tested. There are four models which cover fairly well the essential features of the wide range of geographic pricing practices:

(1) *Single Basing Point Model.* The use of a single basing point; or a single major basing point and subsidiary basing points with base price differentials over the primary base of the same order of magnitude as the costs of shipment between them. Basing point quotations are strictly adhered to; all freight computations are made on an all-rail basis.

(2) *Universal Freight Equalization Model.* Every producing mill is a basing point. There is no f.o.b. mill selling, and standardized all-rail freights are used in calculating delivered prices. In this model, the relationship of the base prices of the several producers can range from rigid price leadership, in which differentials among the various mills always remain the same, to complete independence in setting base prices.

(3) *Uniform F.O.B. Mill Price Model.* Each seller maintains an announced mill price which is the same to all buyers (at any given time). The buyer takes possession at the mill, and chooses the method of delivery and pays the freight. Here again, the model does not specify the relationship between the mill prices of the various sellers.

(4) *F.O.B. Mill Selling with Price Discrimination Model.* The sellers maintain no announced prices, but deal with each customer as best they can. As in (3), customers can choose the method of transportation and pay the freight. When base prices are independently determined, model (2), universal freight equalization (if modified by allowing the customer the election of delivery method), amounts substantially to model (4).

These models differ only in the specification of pricing practices; it is assumed throughout that the basic features of the industries using basing point pricing remain unchanged, except insofar as the change in pricing practice in itself reacts on the structure of the industry and changes it. This is, of course, the assumption appropriate to an examination of the effects of possible changes in pricing formulae on the functioning of industrial markets. It is assumed further that this range of pricing practices represents possibilities which could be achieved in practice by government action, an assumption for which there is some justification. The first model was more or less exemplified in the operation of Pittsburgh Plus pricing in the steel industry until the U.S. Steel Corporation abandoned it under pressure from the Federal Trade Commission in 1924. A stage between the first and second was represented by the recent history of the steel and cement industries, until the Cement Institute decision.

The third model is what would seem to be the only legal method of pricing in the present state of the law. Given a change in the interpretation of the Robinson-Patman Act shown in recent Court decisions,[6] or its outright repeal, the fourth model might be taken as a rough prediction of how industry pricing practices could respond to the law on basing point pricing as laid down in the Cement and Rigid Steel Conduit Cases.

The proposed standards for evaluating the alternative pricing practices are likewise four in number.

(1) What is the effect of the pricing system on the level and rigidity of prices? This involves the effects of the pricing system on the flexibility of margins, the ease with which downward adjustments in margins can occur, and the effects of pricing practices on the level of costs.

(2) Do the pricing practices facilitate or retard the adjustment of capacity to demand in the long run? This question has two aspects—the problem of aggregate adjustment, and the problem of the regional and local balance between capacity and demand. The second aspect shades over into the problem of the influence of pricing practices on the general locational structure of industry.

(3) What effect does the pricing system have on cyclical fluctuations in prices and output? Since the basic characteristics of the industries in question guarantee that their capacity cannot be adapted to cyclical fluctuations in demand, this question really asks how well or how badly the pricing system functions in helping the industry to achieve the appropriate minimum average rate of return over the cycle.

(4) How does the pricing system affect the organization of the industry? To what extent are the number of producers, the scale of production, and the relative viability of large scale and "independent" producers in the competitive struggle affected by pricing practices?

The application of these four tests to the four models will give each model a set of "marks"; a comparison of these marks should give some guidance on the desirable aims of government action.

II

In considering the relation between pricing formulae and the magnitude and flexibility of margins, the basic oligopolistic character of the markets under consideration must again be stressed. In a situation of unused capacity and inelastic demand, what prevents "cutthroat competition" from driving price down to marginal cost? It is oligopolistic rationality—the realization by each seller that his cuts will be followed by his rivals, and that therefore he has little to gain by cutting, and much to lose by initiating a process of reducing margins. The importance of pricing

[6] Such as *United States* v. *New York Great Atlantic and Pacific Tea Company*, CCA 7th, 1949; and *Standard Oil Company* v. *Federal Trade Commission*, CCA 7th, 1949. On this whole matter see the stimulating discussion by M. A. Adelman, "Integration and Antitrust Policy," to be published in the *Harvard Law Review*, October, 1949, and his article "The A & P Case: A Study in Applied Economic Theory," *Quarterly Journal of Economics*, May, 1949.

formulae in this situation lies in the extent to which they make it easy for each member of the group to follow what every other member of the group is doing. For example (in addition to the important role it has in making possible an intelligent comparison of the offers of various sellers by buyers in a market with an extremely complex product structure) the "extra list" in steel serves a vital function in reducing the dimensionality of the price structure, and thus making it feasible for the rival sellers to compare each others' price quotations. And it is significant that the extra list is explicitly agreed upon among the various producers.[7] In an oligopolistic market, especially one such as steel in which sales are frequently made on contracts for large quantities running over periods of time, it is almost inconceivable that price reductions would be made if they had to be made uniformly to all comers at one fell swoop. Rather some kind of piecemeal reduction, involving various kinds of price discrimination, is to be expected; and, in fact, seems to be the rule. Any reduction of quoted prices is usually preceded by a period of "price shading," during which "secret" concessions are made to customers, concessions which differ widely as between customers.[8] In this process of discriminatory price reduction, various asymmetries in the market undoubtedly play an important role: large customers get better prices than small ones; smaller producers, or financially weak producers, may be the first to offer concessions; producers located in relatively disadvantageous positions may be prompted to strive, through concessions, for more business in local areas where mill nets are high; and so forth.

To the extent that a pricing system formalizes quotations, and publicizes (in the trade) the "proper" prices at which transactions should be made, it discourages the processes by which prices are reduced. Judged on this ground, the single basing point system is undoubtedly the worst offender among our four models. The only "proper" channel for price change is controlled entirely by the single producer who sets base prices. He is formally the price leader for the industry, and knows that any base price changes he makes are changes in the industry's prices, not only in his own. Moreover, the fact that under this system, the basing point producer can penetrate into any market without suffering lowered mill nets might well make for greater caution on the part of other producers in making secret concessions. A universal freight equalization system may in fact function as a rigid system of price leadership, and be just as effective in narrowing the amplitude of price adjustments as a single basing point system. But the very fact that many producers

---

[7] See *TNEC Hearings,* Part 19, pp. 10557–80, testimony of Benjamin Fairless and other United States Steel executives, and pp. 10621–35, testimony of Eugene G. Grace, president of Bethlehem Steel Company.

[8] See TNEC Monograph 41, *Price Discrimination in Steel,* for evidence of discrimination between large and small purchasers of steel in a period of slack demand. Also, see Table 1 below for an indication of the range of price concessions in steel.

can, at least potentially, set base prices independently, and the further fact that limits to market interpenetration, and thus to "punitive" invasions of markets, are set by the costs of freight absorption, probably make such a system more flexible in its operation than the single basing point system.

It seems doubtful that uniform f.o.b. mill pricing would produce any better results from the point of view of price flexibility than a universal freight equalization system, and it might even produce somewhat inferior ones. The uniform, published mill price of each producer would certainly make each seller's price policy highly visible to his rivals. Each seller would fix his attention on the market area of his rival, rather than on his delivered prices, as he would under any basing point scheme; but the rival's price behavior would be revealed just as clearly. Moreover, although each seller would be free to fix his own mill price (provided he wanted to exercise such freedom in an oligopolistic market) any change in price he made would have to be uniform to all customers. This enforcement of uniformity, added to the "visibility" of his behavior to rival oligopolists, would do much to discourage any producer from initiating a price change. Finally, uniform f.o.b. mill selling would end market interpenetration. Market interpenetration in the context of a rigidly operating basing point system with strong price leadership, has no competitive virtues. However, in a situation characterized by the possibility of discriminatory price shading, market interpenetration, which spreads the rivalry among sellers over a large area of the market, instead of concentrating it along the fringes where the market areas of rival sellers meet, undoubtedly increases the speed of price changes and probably their magnitude also.

The foregoing argument shows that the fourth model, f.o.b. mill selling with price discrimination allowed, would be the one in which the pricing method would offer the least assistance to rival sellers in behaving "rationally" in accordance with the oligopolistic character of the market, and would discourage the formation of a fixed pattern of price leadership. The question arises as to whether such a situation would not lead to "too much competition," with prices cut to marginal costs whenever unused capacity existed, and even efficient firms driven into bankruptcy.[9] No categorical answer can be given to this question. It is the author's opinion that the danger is unlikely, for although the abolition of formula pricing would make it more difficult for firms to abide by the oligopolistic calculations which militate against price reduction, it would not eliminate such calculations entirely. The fundamental oligopolistic character of the market appears to be a sufficient brake on really destructive competition.

Thus, in terms of the four models of pricing systems, the greatest gain

---

[9] See Professor Clark's article, *op. cit.*

in the flexibility of margins is promised by a change from a single basing point system, or a multiple basing point system with fairly rigid price leadership, to f.o.b. mill pricing with discrimination. A change to uniform f.o.b. mill pricing seems to offer little along these lines; a little more may be expected from independent base pricing in a multiple basing point system; i.e., the elimination of price leadership.

In practice, in recent years basing point pricing systems have been of the multiple basing point variety, with fairly strong price leadership. The increase in flexibility of margins which can be expected from changes in the direction of more independence in pricing depend on the rigidity with which the systems have operated in the past. Some light is thrown on this point in a study by the Bureau of Labor Statistics of the prices actually paid for steel products by a large sample of consumers over the period 1939–42. Some of the results of this study are given in summary form in Table 1. This tabulation suggests that there is still room for a substantial increase in the magnitude of price reductions in periods of low output. In the second quarter of 1939, when output ran about half of rated ingot capacity, average price concessions ranged from 8 per cent in sheets to only 3 per cent in structural shapes. These averages concealed wide variations as between customers, some of whom paid prices as much as 25 per cent under published prices. But these were only a small proportion. A year later, with output at 72 per cent of rated ingot capacity, the spread of concessions was much reduced, even though average prices increased but little. Thus, in hot rolled sheets—the product for which concessions were greatest—a quarter of the sales were made at concessions of 15 to 25 per cent on the published price in 1939. By the following year, the number of sales at prices 15 per cent or more under the published price had fallen to fewer than 5 per cent of the total. All in all, the figures of Table 1 speak well for the efficacy of the basing point system as a method of price leadership in the steel industry.

The level of prices depends on the level of costs, as well as on the seller's margin. To the extent that different pricing systems affect differently the level of costs, the choice between them may influence the level of prices. Any pricing system which allows market interpenetration adds the cost of freight absorption to the other costs of the mill; it is the mill net yield and not the delivered price less the calculated freight which is the "price" from the point of view of the seller. This cost is present in three of the four models; only with uniform f.o.b. mill selling is market interpenetration ruled out entirely. Some notion of the magnitude of the cost of freight absorption can be gained from a study of steel shipments made for the TNEC.[10] The study covered the month of February, 1939,

[10] See *TNEC Hearings*, Part 27, appendix, pp. 14331–14428. The study was based on a sample of steel shipments of all major producers in the month of February, 1939. The sample covered shipments aggregating some 600,000 tons, or about 25 per cent of the total shipments of steel during the month. February, 1939 was a period of slack operations, about 50 to 55 per cent of rated ingot capacity.

a period of slack demand in which it is likely that market interpenetration was extensive. Freight absorption in this month ranged from about 3 to 5 per cent of the delivered price for various products. This is a small cost; nor is it certain that it is all reflected in price. In an oligopolistic market, part of it may be absorbed by sellers through a reduction in profits.

TABLE 1

ACTUAL PRICES COMPARED WITH PUBLISHED PRICES*

Product and Year (Second Quarter Figures)†	Operating Rate (Per Cent Ingot Capacity)	Per Cent of Number of Sales Made at Actual Prices which Were Given Percentages of Published Delivered Price‡							Average Ratio of Actual to Published Delivered Price‡
		75 to 80	80 to 85	85 to 90	90 to 95	95 to 98	98 to 101	Over 101	
Hot Rolled Sheets									
1939	51	5.2	20.4	12.4	19.7	19.7	11.0	11.6	92
1940	72	1.5	2.9	7.1	60.0	4.3	24.2	..	94
1942	98	..	..	..	0.4	1.2	96.0	2.4	101
Cold Rolled Sheets									
1939	51	..	..	28.6	28.5	7.1	32.2	3.6	95
1940	72	..	2.1	..	74.6	4.2	19.1	..	95
1942	98	..	..	..	..	3.2	93.6	3.2	101
Hot Rolled Strip									
1939	51	16.2	12.9	9.6	9.6	22.6	17.2	12.9	92
1940	72	..	2.0	..	59.3	8.1	26.6	2.0	95
1942	98	..	..	..	1.7	..	98.3	..	100
Plates, Universal and Sheared									
1939	51	..	3.0	6.0	9.0	12.6	61.0	8.4	97
1940	72	..	0.9	2.5	8.8	12.5	70.2	5.1	98
1942	98	..	..	..	..	..	85.0	15.0	103
Structural Shapes									
1939	51	..	1.0	8.2	16.5	10.4	61.8	2.1	97
1940	72	..	1.0	1.6	15.8	13.5	67.0	1.3	98
1942	98	..	..	..	..	..	96.6	3.4	101

* The data presented in this table come from a study made by the Bureau of Labor Statistics in 1943 entitled *Consumers' Prices of Steel Products*. The study was prepared for the use of the Office of Price Administration and the War Production Board. It was reprinted in *Iron Age*, April 25, 1946, under the title "Labor Dept. Examines Consumers' Prices of Steel Products." The study was based on an examination of data furnished by 629 companies consuming steel products, widely distributed by region and industry. The sample included only carload lot purchasers, and excluded distributors, warehousers, and subsidiaries of steel-producing companies. The companies in the sample accounted for 15 per cent of steel consumption in 1940. For each company, price information was obtained only on products purchased more or less regularly (monthly, if possible) in carload lots (except for alloys) between 1939 and 1942, and for which customer specifications remained constant over the period. The very largest consumers (e.g., the major automobile producers) are excluded from the sample, and therefore the actual extent of concessions is probably understated somewhat. The study presents data for the third quarter, 1939 and the second and fourth quarters, 1941 as well as for the three quarters shown in Table 1. In addition to the products for which prices are shown there, the study gives figures for cold rolled strip, merchant bars, and cold finished strip. The original tabulations are made in items of class intervals of one per cent (ratio of actual price to delivered price) which are here consolidated for brevity. Note that in every case the largest concession is included. The selection of time periods and products given in Table 1 is, in the author's opinion, a sufficiently representative one to yield a fair picture of the results of the whole study. Neither for the other products or for other time periods does the pattern of actual prices relative to quoted prices and the utilization of capacity appear significantly different from that here presented.

† The percentages given are for the second quarters of each of the years 1939, 1940 and 1942.

‡ The published delivered price was built up for each sale from the appropriate published base price, the freight from the applicable basing point, and the published extras. The published delivered prices entering into the comparisons of actual and published prices are those of April, 1942. But these differed if at all from published prices in the various quarters only by very small amounts; since extras remained constant for the period, the greatest change in base prices was a few per cent, and freight rates increased about 6 per cent in March, 1942. The error introduced by the use of 1942 prices runs in the direction of exaggerating the magnitude of the concessions in the second quarters of 1939 and 1940: the size of this error is very small.

A rigid basing point system with price leadership eliminates price competition and channels rivalry into selling efforts. Since products sold under basing point pricing are characteristically standardized, the cost of selling effort is largely remuneration of salesmen. Such selling costs will be present to some extent under any pricing system in which market interpenetration exists and customers must choose between the products of rival sellers offered at the same delivered price. This will obviously be the case under any form of basing point system. Under f.o.b. mill selling with price discrimination, there will be occasions on which a seller offers to meet rather than shade a rival's price, and relies on a combination of selling efforts and customer loyalty to swing the buyer's decision. Under uniform f.o.b. mill selling, pure selling costs would theoretically disappear, if mills were widely separated and the freight rate structure such that boundaries between mills were lines rather than regions. In fact, neither of these conditions is met. In many cases rival mills are located close to each other so that there are numerous consuming locations at which prices from two sellers would be the same.[11] Moreover, the existence of "blanket rates" covering long-distance shipments to and from large areas would produce overlapping market areas under f.o.b. mill pricing even if rival sellers were not located side by side. In any case, the total cost of the sales force cannot be considered as an "unnecessary" selling cost attributable to the existence of non-price competition. The salesmen perform certain necessary functions in the distribution process; at a minimum, order taking, and where the product is complex, as in steel, the transmission to buyers of information on specifications and the suitability of the many grades and types of product for various uses. To the extent that salesmen's pure "selling" functions are performed jointly with these other duties, no extra cost of selling exists. All in all, it is doubtful that changes in pricing practices will produce significant changes in selling costs through lessening the importance of non-price relative to price competition.

The possibility of cost saving on the freight bill through the use of cheaper means of transport under other than basing point pricing, will be discussed below in considering the relation of pricing practices to location and utilization of capacity.

Finally, the influence of flexibility of margins itself on costs should not be neglected. The existence of fairly strong downward pressure on margins in periods of unused capacity, which would be expected under some pricing arrangements, would be a strong stimulus to energetic efforts at cost reduction by management. The use of the most efficient known pro-

[11] See, for example, the map of counties in Western Pennsylvania and Eastern Ohio, showing towns in the market areas of various steel sheet mills under an f.o.b. mill selling system with an assumed level of mill prices; *TNEC Hearings*, Part 27, appendix, p. 13832. This map was prepared by the United States Steel Corporation.

duction techniques is not, in practice, something that occurs automatically. Every change in methods is painful (and even costly) in a large organization, and the existence of a fairly stable profit margin per unit tends to favor let-well-enough-alone policies. This aspect of the relation of prices to costs will probably be more important, in the long run, than the (at least conceptually) more easily measured differences in freight absorption and selling costs contingent on the use of differing pricing practices. It is another important argument in favor of giving high marks to the fourth model, or pricing practices resembling it.

III

The second standard for the evaluation of alternative pricing systems is the relation between the pricing system and the adaptation of capacity to demand in the long run. There is no general theoretical rule on the responses of an oligopolistic group of suppliers to long-run changes in demand. The persistence over time of high margins (which formula pricing facilitates) would indicate some restriction of supply in comparison with what would happen in an otherwise similar competitive market. This is not a very helpful criterion in practice, however, and something more concrete is needed. The impact of the pricing system on the adjustment of supply depends on the direction of change in demand over time; in particular, the case of an increase in demand over the long run must be treated separately from the case of stationary or declining demand.

If demand is stable in the long run and excess capacity (the existence of which is postulated as characteristic) is present only during cyclical troughs, capacity may be considered as adjusted to the long-run level of demand. The problem of cyclical adjustment which remains in this case will be treated in the following section. The situation in which excess capacity exists at cyclical peaks as well as during troughs with the long-run level of demand stable is similar to one in which the long-run level of demand is declining, in that the appropriate adjustment requires the elimination of some producing units. Whatever adjustment takes place must be brought about by losses which are large enough and continuous enough to drive firms into bankruptcy, or at least to threaten them with it. It is true, of course, that bankruptcies may not be sufficient to bring about an immediate adjustment of capacity to demand, since they can result in the reorganization of old firms, or the creation of new firms in which the equipment of the original firm is valued at less than its reproduction cost. These successor firms may survive for a while; but the necessity of replacing old equipment will finally confront them with the same problems which caused their predecessors to fail. Again, the process of bankruptcy and reorganization might well be repeated in a new cycle, or even several new cycles. It must be assumed, however, that eventually old equipment will wear out, and potential investors and entrepreneurs will learn something from the previous history of the industry, and thus reductions in capacity will ultimately occur.

In a situation in which a reduction in productive facilities is required, it is clear that a working basing point system interferes with the proper adjustment. In the first place, to the extent that it functions as a device for maintaining high margins, the whole process of failure is slowed down. Moreover, a basing point system entails market interpenetration, which means that existing markets are shared among many producing points. The nearer a mill approaches failure, the greater would be its incentive to attempt to cut into any market, no matter how distant, in which sales promised some mill net return over marginal cost. Thus the impact of a decline in demand, which in general will be greater in some areas than in others, will not be concentrated on the mills located in the areas of most rapid decline, but spread out more or less evenly over all producers. This will further slow down the process of failure, as compared with what would happen if the mills in areas of more rapidly falling demand sold only in their home markets. The spreading of the impact over all producers also means that differences in financial strength have relatively more, and differences in productive efficiency and location, relatively less influence in determining which firms will leave the industry than they would under a pricing arrangement which did not permit market interpenetration.

The hindrances to appropriate adaptation of output discussed above, except for the first—maintenance of high margins—arise out of market interpenetration, and their importance is measured by the extent of it. Market interpenetration is a feature of three of the four models; only under uniform f.o.b. mill pricing would it be absent. The extent of market interpenetration depends, in the other three models, more on the geographical pattern of demand, costs, and freight rates, than on the specific pricing practices in which the models differ. There is one exception to this, however; market interpenetration probably is greatest, other things being equal, under a single basing point system, in respect of the relations between the base mill (or mills) and all other mills. Thus in the special circumstances in which the home market of the base mill is the region of the greatest decline in demand, the single basing point system would lead to a slower reduction of capacity than a universal freight equalization or discriminatory f.o.b. mill system of pricing.

Demand may be rising in the long run (instead of falling or remaining stationary) and the appropriate adjustment of supply to demand will require additions to productive facilities. In this situation, excess capacity may be present at cyclical peaks as well as during troughs, because of a certain rate of building in anticipation of increasing demand, or it may exist only during cyclical lows. In either event, the effect of the pricing system on the expansion of capacity will depend on the geographic pattern of the change in demand. If it is fairly uniform from market area to market area, the existence of market interpenetration will not alter the local incidence of the stimulus to new investment. The only significant difference between the alternative pricing systems then which would affect the rate of investment would be the difference in profit margins expected under them. The higher margins expected under the more rigid formula pricing arrangements might then act to stimulate a more rapid increase in capacity than would be made with more flexible and competitive pricing systems.[12] This additional stimulus, however, might be cancelled in large part, or even overbalanced by the greater pressure on the individual firm under more competitive pricing systems.

If, as is more likely, the growth of demand is geographically uneven, market interpenetration becomes more important. This is most clearly seen in a situation in which the expansion of demand takes place entirely in new regions, not near existing mills, while demand in old regions remains stable or even declines. Under uniform f.o.b. mill pricing, a new mill would be constructed in the region of new demand whenever entrepreneurs and investors foresaw enough demand in the region to maintain an economically sized unit in operation at an average output rate which would yield a sufficient profit. Under the other three pricing systems, characterized by market interpenetration, the entrepreneurs in the new region would have to anticipate penetration of their market by sellers in the old regions. Nor could they expect to retaliate by penetrating markets in the old regions to the same extent, since these regions would be crowded with suppliers, and their long standing relationships with local customers would be a further barrier to new sellers. Thus the building of a new plant in the new region would wait for a higher level of demand under pricing systems characterized by market interpenetration than under a uniform f.o.b. mill system. The same kind of forces would be at work, although with diminished strength, in a situation in which there were large differences in the rates of change in demand among several regions without differences in the direction of the change. Thus the use of any pricing system which permits market interpenetration will lead to a slower rate of increase of capacity in response to a given rate of growth of demand unevenly distributed among regions, than would take place under uniform f.o.b. mill pricing.

This lag in the regional adjustment of capacity to demand is not undesirable. In many situations it may provide a closer approximation to an "ideal" utilization of resources than would a more prompt increase of capacity. The general economic rule for the substitution of new for old (but still useful) capital equipment is that such replacement is desirable only when average costs with the new equipment are less than marginal cost with the old. Under the conditions analyzed above, with demand in-

[12] This argument is essentially similar to Professor Schumpeter's arguments in favor of monopoly. See *Capitalism, Socialism and Democracy*, chap. viii.

creasing rapidly in a new region, but remaining stable in an old region where there is excess capacity, it is economic to supply the new region from the old plants as long as the marginal cost of production in the old plants plus transportation to the new region is less than the average cost of production would be for a new plant in the new region. Under uniform f.o.b. mill pricing, as argued above, new plant would be built in the new regions while there was still unused capacity in the old regions. Since marginal costs are characteristically much below average costs at outputs below capacity in the industries under consideration, this can mean that the new plants represent uneconomic additions to capital. With market interpenetration, the addition of new capacity will wait until much more of the old capacity is utilized. The reasons for not anticipating a general lowering of prices to the level of marginal costs under f.o.b. mill pricing when unused capacity exists such as would bring the new areas within the market areas of the old mills have been examined above.

The appropriate adaptation of capacity to demand implies an economical geographic distribution of capacity, given the pattern of demand, as well as a suitable aggregate volume of productive facilities. Therefore, the possible impact of alternative pricing systems on the location of producers must be examined. And, since the location of producers of products which are further fabricated may affect in turn the location of the fabricators, an examination of their location must also be included. In general, the location of producers depends on the relations between the locations of raw materials, labor supplies, markets, and transportation costs. For a pricing system to influence the location of producers, it must work through one of these factors. In cement, the location of the consumers is fixed independently of the location of producers; and of the two major raw materials, coal and limestone, the more important limestone is nearly ubiquitous. In these circumstances the use of one rather than another pricing system would have no locational influence on producers, and could not, in the nature of the case, have any on consumers.

In steel, there is a more complex situation. Producers of steel are heavily raw-material oriented; they locate in points where the assembly costs of coal, ore and subsidiary raw materials are low; but markets are not without locational pull.[13] Markets consist in fabricators of steel; many of these in turn locate with reference to the source of their major raw material. To the extent that a pricing system makes the geographical pattern of steel prices different from the "real cost" pattern, consumers will locate in accordance with the geographic price structure rather than with the underlying real cost structure. The location of consumers may in turn influence the location of expansion in steel production, which further reacts on consumers, and so on. Thus, a cumulative process of distortion of locational patterns can occur. This process is not infinite, since

[13] See W. Capron and W. Isard, "The Future Locational Pattern of Iron and Steel Production in the U.S.," *Journal of Political Economy*, April, 1949.

the fabricators have to consider the costs of reaching out to their own markets which increase as they all concentrate at one point. This process is best exemplified under single basing point pricing. Under this system, locations at the basing point are superior to locations at non-basing point mills for the fabricators, other things being equal. Therefore, fabricators tend to concentrate near the basing point, and mills there tend to grow relative to mills at non-basing point locations. This is true even though the basing point ceases to be the lowest cost production point, as it may well have been at one time. Thus, under Pittsburgh Plus, the rate of expansion of steel production in Chicago and Birmingham relative to Pittsburgh[14] was probably slowed down substantially.[15]

The locational pull of base mills operates only relative to non-base mills. Under universal freight equalization, or any other system in which each mill is in effect a base, it would disappear. Nor is there any difference between uniform f.o.b. mill pricing and the other two pricing models in this respect: market interpenetration in itself has no localizing effects.

The alternative pricing systems here discussed may have a further impact on location through their effect on transportation costs. Basing point systems, both single and multiple, in which prices are calculated on the basis of all-rail freight discourage the use of other methods of transportation by the consumer. This means that in steel, for example, a potentially advantageous site connected to a supplier by water will not have its transportation advantages considered by a fabricator who is choosing a plant location, since he cannot reap the savings arising from this location. The same is not true, of course, of the steel producer. To the extent that his customers will accept shipment by water, he will ship by water and increase his mill net yield by the difference between rail and water freights, and thus he may consider the advantages of waterside location.

In addition to its possible indirect effects on location of production, the discrimination against cheaper forms of transport embodied in basing point pricing—models (1) and (2)—operates directly to distort the allocation of resources employed in transportation. Any alternative pricing system which gives the customer the option on the method of delivery, without taxing particular modes of transport, will thus result in a more economical utilization of transportation resources. No indication of the magnitude of these economies can be given because of the lack of basic statistical data.

It is important to note that whatever advantages of efficiency in geo-

---

[14] See A. R. Burns, *The Decline of Competition*, pp. 340–45, esp. Figure 48.

[15] The further effect of basing point pricing on the location of fabricators of steel producing goods to which fabrication-in-transit (f.i.t.) freight rates apply are not considered here. This is a problem more germane to a discussion of freight rates than to a general survey of basing point pricing.

graphical allocation of resources the foregoing analysis indicates will result from the use of one rather than another pricing system, will apply only to plants as yet unbuilt. Thus the benefits of a change would be spread out over a long future period. On the other hand, some existing plants might become unprofitable as a consequence of a change from one to another pricing system, but little can be said in general terms about the magnitude of this transition problem.

IV

The two remaining standards for grading alternative pricing arrangements are the effects of the pricing arrangements on cyclical fluctuations in output, and on the organization of industries using them. There is less to be said under these heads than under the two preceding, not because they are intrinsically less important, but rather because the questions raised under them are less amenable to general analytical answers than those previously discussed.

The essence of the cyclical problem in industries of the sort under discussion lies in the cyclical unadaptability of capacity to demand in the short run on the one hand, and the high income elasticity and low price elasticity of demand for their products on the other. This means that a capacity just sufficient to meet the minimum level of demand at the cyclical trough would fall far short of producing what was required (at constant prices) in a boom. Further, the increase in prices and profits caused by the impact of sharply rising demand on limited capacity would not lead to an increase in capacity within the short period. Conversely, capacity sufficient to meet boom-time peaks in demand implies the existence of much unused capacity during times of slack business, since price cuts would not greatly increase demand. The problem then is, how shall the costs of providing the peak load capacity be met.

Ideally, a two-part price system would answer the problem—marginal cost pricing for output, with any deficits separately financed from tax revenues, and the amount of plant decided by a central authority on the basis of the usual welfare criteria.[16] A fairly close approximation to this ideal method in practice could be achieved as follows. In any industry under consideration, private firms would own and operate enough plant to produce for periods of slack demand. Additional plant would be owned by the government, and turned over without fee to the private firms for operation during periods of peak demand. Marginal cost pricing would be prescribed. The amount of government plant, and the amount to be brought into production at any time would be determined by the prescription of some average normal profit rule for the private firms. While such a scheme might be practicable from an economic point of view, it would involve substantial administrative problems, and also, probably cannot be considered practicable politically.

[16] See H. Hotelling, "The General Welfare in Relation to Taxation and to Railway and Public Utility Rates," *Econometrica,* July, 1938.

Within the framework of purely private operation of industry, two general approaches to the problem of paying for the appropriate level of capacity over the cycle are possible. The first, represented by Professor Machlup in his recent book,[17] is that the proper pricing rule requires marginal cost pricing at all times; in other words, pure competitive pricing. Under this rule, capacity would be determined at a level such that the returns during periods of high demand would cover the deficits incurred in periods of slack demand and provide for normal profits. Prices would fluctuate quite widely over the business cycle, since at any output level below full capacity, marginal cost would be much below average cost, while in the neighborhood of capacity, marginal cost would rise very sharply over a short range of output.

While this price policy—if it were followed—might be desirable in certain industries using basing point pricing, it is doubtful that it is suitable for steel and other basic industries producing investment goods. The demand for such products varies greatly over the business cycle. In general, demand for these products is price inelastic; this is especially true in periods of low and falling income, when investment is unresponsive to current cost changes in the face of poor expectations. An exception to the general rule may occur during the course of a recovery, especially after the most obvious and profitable investment opportunities have been exploited. At that time, a sharp rise in the price of investment goods might well react unfavorably on the volume of investment, and so shorten the recovery. Thus a steel industry which had capacity substantially short of that needed to meet peak demand in terms of a fixed price level (say, the average level over the cycle) might be an agent in cutting down the total level of investment and income over the cycle. This, in turn, would lead to further losses in the steel industry, and thus to further shrinkage in capacity. Even if the initial situation were one in which capacity was larger than needed to meet peak demands, rather than the reverse, it is not certain that a flexible price policy would lead to a desirable adjustment. If capacity could change only by fairly large steps—equivalent to the output produced by a single firm—the first reaction to the initial situation could lead to a position of undercapacity, and further adjustments would again lead away from equilibrium instead of toward it. In general terms, it may be stated that a flexible price policy in an industry of the kind under consideration will lead to an equilibrium in capacity only if the cyclical fluctuations in aggregate income are independent of the price fluctuations in the products of the industry. Where it is unlikely that this is the case, as in steel, which is needed for many investment goods and has no effective substitutes over a wide range of uses, it is clear that there is no strong prima facie case for a cyclically flexible price policy.

The other approach to the question of cyclical price flexibility is that

---

[17] *Op. cit.*, chap. 6, esp. pp. 210–11.

which involves a fairly great degree of stability, with prices substantially above marginal costs in periods of low output, and perhaps below marginal costs at the highest peaks of demand. There is no single, definite pricing rule which characterizes this view; it includes the range from the advocacy of strict full cost pricing, to the broad proposition that it is undesirable to allow prices to fall all the way to marginal costs during slumps in demand. Something near the first view is typically the view of businessmen in the industries under consideration; many economists, of whom J. M. Clark is one, have expressed the second.[18] Acceptance of the general proposition that complete flexibility in the sense discussed above is not desirable, leaves unanswered the question of how much inflexibility is necessary, and what arrangements will produce it. Industry advocates of basing point pricing advance this system as a necessary barrier to undesirable price flexibility. The validity of this contention turns on the factual issues of profitability and the adequacy of investment. It is difficult to examine these factual issues in detail, because the necessary information is lacking. Nevertheless, in the important case of the steel industry, the level of profits (even during the thirties) and of investment do not suggest that the multiple basing point system just barely succeeded in maintaining the necessary capacity. The analytical argument stated above in connection with the discussion of the level of margins and prices applies here too; given the fundamentally oligopolistic character of the markets in question, the danger of extreme price competition which would drive prices down to marginal costs in periods of slack demand seems small. The recognition by each of the rival sellers in the market of the relations between his price policy and those of the others should suffice to restrain the downward movements of prices in cyclical troughs before they reach danger levels. This presumes that the differences in costs among the firms are not so great that a price which seems reasonable, or even high, to one seller, will be such as to drive another into liquidation. In such a situation, some redistribution of capacity among the firms in the market seems to be indicated. This possibility raises broad problems of public policy on the conflict between considerations of efficiency in performance and considerations of numbers of competitors and other aspects of market structure in the application of anti-monopoly policy which cannot be pursued here.[19] Nonetheless, the assertion that any increase in cyclical price flexibility over that

---

[18] For an expression of the business view, see the now famous letter of John Treanor of the Cement Institute, cited in Machlup, *op. cit.*, p. 41 n. in which the cement industry is characterized as one which "above all cannot . . . stand free competition." It is clear from the context that price competition is meant. For an expression of Clark's views see the article in *American Economic Review, op. cit.*, and "Basing Point Methods of Quoting Prices," *Canadian Journal of Economics and Political Science*, November, 1938.

[19] See E. S. Mason, "The Current Status of the Monopoly Problem," to be published in *Harvard Law Review*, August, 1949, for a discussion of this conflict.

achieved under basing point pricing would lead to an undesirable extension of concentration requires more proof than has yet been offered.

This discussion of the relation between alternative pricing systems and the adjustment of capacity to cyclical fluctuations in demand can best be summarized by saying that there is little evidence to show that one model is preferable to another on this ground. While a pricing arrangement which led to complete price flexibility—defined as prices always equal to marginal costs at the going output rate—might have undesirable repercussions on the level of capacity in the industry, there is little to show that any of the four alternative pricing systems here examined would lead to such an extreme degree of flexibility. Aside from this, whatever advantages arise from those models which encourage more flexible pricing have already been discussed above in the section on price levels.

The last test is the effect of alternative pricing practices on the organization of industries using them. It is appropriate to examine under this head an argument made repeatedly by businessmen defending the basing point system: namely, that under it, market interpenetration allows larger scale production than would an f.o.b. mill pricing system.[20] This argument is advanced with an earnestness and frequency that betokens firm belief in it by its proponents. Yet it is clear that a given group of plants will have, together, the same number of customers and the same amount of demand (assuming a given level of prices) under one pricing system as under another. Differences in the allocation of these customers among the several mills, arising from the presence or absence of market interpenetration, will not affect the average output of the mills. Thus the choice of pricing system will not in itself make either for a greater average utilization of capacity at a given scale of production or a larger average scale of production. Nor, as was argued above, is it likely that a rigid basing point system will lead to a *lower* price level than uniform f.o.b. mill pricing—thus, perhaps, stimulating a greater expansion of demand, and allowing larger-scale production. A lowering of the price level could be expected from a system which allows market interpenetration but does not have the rigid price leadership of the basing point system, but this is hardly what the argument under consideration is advanced to defend. Perhaps the business belief derives its earnestness from the individual entrepreneur's experience of the necessity of market interpenetration to his firm in periods of slack demand: he sees it as a means of getting more orders and thus increasing his production rate. Failing to appreciate the relations of his efforts in this direction to those of other entrepreneurs, he generalizes his experience to the whole industry.

The single basing point system, and the multiple basing point system

[20] See for example Vol. III of *TNEC Papers* published by the United States Steel Corporation, *The Basing Point System*, especially the discussion of "local monopolies" which would arise under f.o.b. mill pricing.

with strong price leadership may well promote the growth of smaller rivals relative to the larger price leader. These rivals are likely to be the first to shade prices if any shading is done, while the leader adheres to the formula; thus they can be more aggressive in reaching out for customers. Against this, for the single basing point system, must be put the opportunity the price leader has for penetration into the market of any other seller without reduction in mill net. The leader may use this opportunity in such a fashion as to discourage efforts at too fast growth by smaller rivals.[21] Under the multiple basing point system, the cost of freight absorption sets limits to the ability of the leader to penetrate other sellers' markets, and thus his ability to use penetration as a punitive measure. The steel industry offers an example of the decline of the price leader's share of the market which was continuous over the whole history of the firm. U.S. Steel's share of the market for steel measured in terms of ingot production declined from 66 per cent in 1901 to 33 per cent in 1938.[22] This decline went on under both Pittsburgh Plus and multiple basing point pricing, suggesting that whatever opportunities for punitive retaliation were open to the Steel Corporation under Pittsburgh Plus were not effectively utilized.

Under uniform f.o.b. mill pricing, while price leadership could continue to function, secret price cutting would not be possible, and therefore, the leader and the followers would be similarly placed in this respect. Thus large firms might maintain their relative dominance better under uniform f.o.b. than under basing point pricing. Under f.o.b. mill pricing with discrimination, a firm pattern of price leadership would not develop; a dominant producer might or might not compete aggressively against smaller rivals, and thus might or might not maintain his share of the market. This would also be true under universal freight equalization with independent base price determination.

The fact that a change in the relative shares of the market over time which lessens the dominance of the largest producer is facilitated by basing point pricing (with price leadership) is not in itself necessarily desirable. To the extent that this change results from a kind of competition in which the level of prices and margins is little affected, whatever gains are made in terms of transferring production to more efficient units are retained by these firms, and the change produces no general benefits. If a market in which the same number of firms share more rather than less equally is considered preferable on grounds of the undesirability of "bigness" as such, even though the change has no effect on their behavior, then the kind of change the basing point system promotes is desirable. It often happens that the firm with the largest share of the mar-

[21] Professor Machlup, *op. cit.*, makes much of this point. See especially chap. 5, pp. 151–68. In fact, he makes somewhat too much of it, in the author's opinion.

[22] *TNEC Hearings*, Part 26, appendix, p. 13853.

ket is a long-established producer with less favorable plant sites and a greater proportion of old equipment than some of his smaller rivals. Then the kind of competition promoted by the fourth model pricing system or some similar arrangement is likely not only to cause a change in the relative shares of dominant and smaller firms in the market, similar to that favored by basing point pricing, but also to result in lower costs and prices.

A multiplant firm may find it possible to practice geographic price discrimination even under uniform f.o.b. mill pricing by what might be called "internal freight absorption." It could do this by shipping goods from a distant plant and billing the customer from a nearby one, or by making the actual transfer of the product from one plant to another. Another variation of this practice would be possible where output was produced in several stages; but all the final stages of production could be carried on at one location, while finishing was done elsewhere and the final product marketed from the finishing points. In either case a multiplant producer could sell in a certain local market area with much less investment than required of a single plant producer: in the first case by operating only a small plant in the area and using excess capacity elsewhere to augment the supplies of the local plant; in the second, by operating only a finishing plant (or even a warehouse) locally, while the major part of the production took place in other areas. Such practices, by permitting larger producers to penetrate the markets of smaller ones more easily than the smaller can retaliate, might decrease the ability of local producers to survive. Under present law, however, these practices could be restrained. Either the Robinson-Patman Act, forbidding price discrimination not justified by cost differences which tend to injure competition; section 5 of the Federal Trade Commission Act, which forbids unfair methods of competition, as found by the Commission and upheld by the courts; or even, in some situations, section 2 of the Sherman Act, which makes monopolization or attempted monopolization of a market illegal, could be invoked against a large firm which used such devices to the detriment of local producers. With any pricing system which permitted market interpenetration, the local producer would be placed under no special disabilities in competing with his larger multiplant rivals. He could choose to retaliate against penetration of his market, and would have only those handicaps imposed on him by his smaller size and limited financial resources.

All in all, uniform f.o.b. mill prices appear to be no more, and possibly somewhat less, favorable to the existence and activity of independent competitors in the market than the other pricing models considered. Whatever virtues are possessed in this respect by basing point systems with price leadership are present in a stronger form in systems which allow market interpenetration but do not encourage price leadership. None of the systems offers any savings from changes in the scale of production, save as the lowering of price levels under model (4) or variants of it might stimulate a greater rate of growth of demand.

V

The results of all four tests taken together indicate that basing point pricing with price leadership (that has been characteristic of it) rates fairly low. In the form of a single basing point system, it receives low marks on all the tests. A universal freight equalization system with price leadership rates somewhat better in respect to the adaptation of capacity to demand in the long run, including its effects on location, and perhaps in respect to the level and flexibility of price and to the viability of independent competitors too. A change from basing point pricing to uniform f.o.b. mill pricing would not be a great improvement, judged by the foregoing tests. In respect to price flexibility and the size of margins, uniform f.o.b. mill pricing would be little better than the basing point system. As far as it affected the ability of small producers to compete successfully against large ones, it might even be a little worse. Only in two respects does uniform f.o.b. mill pricing show clear advantages over basing point pricing: it would function much more effectively in facilitating the reduction of capacity in the face of a long-run decline in demand, and it would eliminate the wastes incident to the uneconomical use of transportation arising from the discouraging of road and water transport, as well as that arising from cross hauling. The situation of secularly declining demand is hardly typical for the American economy, and therefore the importance of the first advantage is not great.

On the other hand, a change from the basing point system to some pricing system which, while allowing market interpenetration, made difficult the formation of a rigid pattern of price leadership and still allowed customer choice of means of transport, could be expected to lead to fairly substantial improvements from a social point of view in the performance of the industries concerned. Most important would be the increased scope of price competition, with its effects in lowering costs and prices. Wasteful use of transportation would be avoided under this system as well as under f.o.b. mill pricing. The adaptation of capacity to changing regional patterns of demand would proceed in such a way as to permit substantial utilization of excess capacity in old regions before new capacity was added. Finally, the possibility of price as well as nonprice competition would offer to new firms in favorable locations using new techniques a method of striving to displace old, well-entrenched producers. This development would benefit the general public as well as the successful competitors.

What must be done to introduce a pricing system like that of model (4) in place of the now illegal basing point pricing practices? It is likely that businessmen in the industries affected would accept it, since it would permit them to continue the practice of market interpenetration and to maintain their old customer relations, which their testimony before the Capehart Committee shows they wish to do. The effect of such a system in discouraging price leadership would not be immediately obvious, and thus would not be a reason for objection to it by the business community. The chief obstacle lies in the pronouncements of the law and of those who enforce it on price discrimination. The Robinson Patman Act, in section 1, explicitly forbids price discrimination, not justified by cost and not made in good faith to meet competition, when it is likely to injure competition. The Federal Trade Commission, in its presentation of the Cement and Rigid Steel Conduit Cases, has shown itself zealous to enforce these provisions. The courts have blessed the FTC views. Further there has been a tendency in the FTC and the Anti-Trust Division of the Department of Justice to interpret "injury to competition" as injury to a competitor, as evidenced by the A. & P. and Standard Oil Company (of Indiana) cases.[23]

This body of law and opinion must be changed in some way if a more competitive pricing system is to replace basing point pricing. The essence of such a system involves discrimination, as was argued in section II above. For instance, a universal freight equalization system might be made legal by Congressional enactment, provided that the purchaser could, if he desires, specify the method of delivery and that he pays in freight figured into the delivered cost no more than the actual cost of delivery (though he may pay less). Such an arrangement must soon lead to occasional discrimination by sellers in favor of customers located on cheap transport routes accessible to rival sellers; and these varying discriminations will prevent the new price system from hardening in a set mold. The required change probably must be made by legislative action, since the process of changing the point of view of the courts, demanding as it does a prior conversion on the part of the antitrust division and the FTC, is always a slow one. At present, when the tide of opinion in these agencies seems to be running the other way, it would be even slower. Since there is already a demand for legislation on the subject of basing point pricing, it may be hoped that vigorous discussion of the issues involved will produce an atmosphere in which constructive legislative action is both possible and likely.

---

[23] *United States* v. *New York Great Atlantic and Pacific Tea Company*, CCA 7th, February 24, 1949 and *Standard Oil Company* v. *Federal Trade Commission*, CCA 7th, March 11, 1949.

9

The Nature and Significance of Price Leadership*

By JESSE W. MARKHAM†

That the Supreme Court's decision in the *Tobacco* Case[1] of 1946 attaches a new significance to price leadership in oligopolistic markets seems beyond reasonable doubt. The *Tobacco* decision constitutes a reversal of the stand taken by the Court in the *U.S. Steel* and *International Harvester* cases, where the Court ruled that the acceptance of a price leader by the rest of the industry did not constitute a violation of the Sherman Act by the price leader.[2] If we accept the full meaning of what the Court has really said, that parallel pricing, whether implemented by an agreement or not, is now illegal, pricing policies prevailing in markets where sellers are few will henceforth be subjected to a much closer examination than they have been in the past.

Accomplished students of the monopoly problem, anticipating what such oligopolistic market studies might be expected to reveal, have predicted the possibility of some sweeping changes in the conduct of American business enterprise. Professor Rostow, for example, sees in the *Aluminum* and *Tobacco* decisions, when viewed collectively, the possible foundations for a new Sherman Act "which promises drastically to shorten and simplify antitrust trials" since they represent a triumph of the economic over the more cumbersome legal approach to the antitrust problem.[3] Professor Rostow points out specifically that such tacit parallelism, as evidenced by the practice of following a price leader, now lies within the scope of the antitrust laws.[4] Professor Nicholls cautiously points out that the assumptions which he made in his recent appraisal of

* *The American Economic Review*, Vol. XLI (1951), pp. 891–905. Reprinted by courtesy of the publisher and the author.

† Princeton University.

[1] *American Tobacco Co., et al.,* v. *United States,* 147 F. 2d 93 (6th Cir., 1944); 328 U.S. 781 (1946).

[2] *United States* v. *United States Steel Corporation,* 251 U.S. 417 (1920); and *United States* v. *International Harvester Company,* 274 U.S. 693 (1927).

[3] Eugene V. Rostow, "The New Sherman Act: A Positive Instrument of Progress," *University of Chicago Law Review,* Vol. XIV (1947), pp. 567–600. For a warier appraisal of the *Aluminum* and *Tobacco* decisions, see Edward H. Levi, "The Antitrust Laws and Monopoly," *ibid.,* pp. 172 ff.

[4] Rostow, *ibid.,* p. 577.

the *Tobacco* decision,[5] namely, (1) that the courts really said what he believed them to have said and (2) that they will carry to their logical conclusion the legal implications of that decision, may rest upon dubious grounds. Nevertheless, he concedes the possibility that such *modi operandi* as price leadership, the presence of which was perhaps the most important piece of incriminating evidence in the *Tobacco* case, are now illegal.

If the legal implications of the *Tobacco* decision as interpreted by Professors Rostow, Nicholls and others be accepted, the economic consequences of price leadership and the specific conditions likely to render it an effective weapon against price competition in oligopolistic markets need to be re-examined. Because the courts have not yet faced up to the problem of providing appropriate remedies, the question of wherein lies the most fruitful remedial action should at least be raised. It is primarily to this task that this article is addressed. Since, however, there is always the danger of assigning unwarranted homogeneity to such an economic phenomenon, its significance will be appraised on the basis of (1) the particular types of price leadership which prevail in industrial markets and (2) the extent to which each type might conceivably circumvent forces of competition.

Professor Stigler has distinguished between two kinds of price leadership: (1) that associated with a dominant firm and (2) that of the barometric type.[6] Since, however, one of the market conditions that the barometric firm's price is supposed to reflect is both secret and open price cutting,[7] it is not always possible to determine whether the barometric firm should be viewed as the "price leader" or as one of the first "price followers." Hence, for purposes of this discussion, the above otherwise satisfactory dichotomy will be augmented by a third type of price leadership which may be viewed either as an extreme form of the barometric type or simply as price leadership in lieu of overt collusion.

"MODELS" OF PRICE LEADERSHIP

Although most of the vast volume of economic literature on price practices and policies conveys the impression that price leadership is a logical and effective means for eliminating price competition among rival sellers, theoretical treatment of the topic has been cast in rather simple static terms and limited to three special cases.[8]

---

[5] William H. Nicholls, "The Tobacco Case of 1946," *American Economic Review*, Vol. XXXIX (May, 1949), pp. 284–96.

[6] George J. Stigler, "The Kinky Oligopoly Demand Curve and Rigid Prices," *Journal of Political Economy*, Vol. LV (October, 1947), pp. 444–45.

[7] See Professor Stigler's illustrative case, *ibid.*, p. 445.

[8] The number of institutional and other conditions under which the prices set by one firm in an industry might be used by all others is probably very large, but only three sets of conditions seem to make price leadership of some sort inevitable and at the same time identify the price leader.

Perhaps the most familiar theoretical model of price leadership is centered upon the dominant firm or partial monopolist. Starting from the assumption that an industry comprises one large producer and a number of smaller ones, no one of which produces a high enough percentage of total output to influence the price, it logically follows that the role of price making falls to the dominant firm. This is true because each small firm regards its own demand schedule as perfectly elastic at the price set by the dominant firm and thus behaves as though it operates under conditions of perfect competition. The dominant firm might set any price it chooses, but presumably would set one which maximizes its profits by equating its own marginal cost with its marginal revenue as derived from the market demand schedule and the summation of the individual marginal cost curves of the independent small producers.

Professor Boulding[9] has presented two other theoretical models of price leadership. One relates to an industry comprising one low-cost high-capacity firm and one or more high-cost low-capacity firms, the other to an industry comprising at least two firms having identical cost curves but different shares in the market. In the former case, because no price can equate marginal cost with marginal revenue for both (or all) firms, a conflict in price policy inevitably arises. However, since the price preferred by the low-cost high-capacity firm is lower than the price preferred by the high-cost low-capacity firm (or firms), the low-cost firm can impose its price policy on the industry. In the other case, under assumptions described by Professor Boulding as "rather peculiar," that marginal cost curves for all firms are identical and that each firm's relative share in the market is different from that of all other firms and remains unchanged over the entire range of possible prices, marginal cost and marginal revenue are equated at a lower price for the firm having the smallest share in the market than for any other firm. Hence, the firm having the smallest share in the market at all possible prices can impose the price most acceptable to it on the rest of the industry. Professor Boulding makes no claim that the latter model is built upon sufficiently realistic assumptions to throw much light upon price policies generally but suggests that it might explain price behavior in the retail gasoline industry.

It is worthwhile to point out that in none of the above three models is price leadership a result of collusion; in fact, in each of the models price leadership is an inevitable consequence of a particular cost or demand phenomenon which precludes price collusion among sellers as a possible solution. Moreover, in none of the three models is the absence of competition attributable to the presence of a price leader. In each of the three cases, conditions in either the factor or product market are already assumed to be inconsistent with the assumptions associated with

[9] Kenneth E. Boulding, *Economic Analysis* (rev. ed.; New York, 1948). For a diagrammatical presentation of the two models, see pp. 582, 586.

highly competitive industries. Since the empirical evidence presented in a later section also suggests that effective price leadership, for the most part, is a result of monopoly rather than a cause of it, it is important that these two observations be borne in mind when it comes to prescribing appropriate remedies for industries having price leaders.

DOMINANT FIRM PRICE LEADERSHIP

Contrary to the general belief that price leadership, because it eliminates the kink in the oligopoly demand curve, makes for a higher degree of price flexibility, Professor Stigler has presented evidence to show that "except for the number of price changes of two-firm industries . . . , the prices of industries with price leaders are less flexible than those of industries without price leaders."[10] Significant though this discovery may be as evidence of the nonexistence of kinked oligopoly demand curves, it should be pointed out that the basic conclusion reached by Professor Stigler applies to a particular type of oligopolistic market and, hence, is not conclusive evidence that price leadership, regardless of type, leads to less flexible prices. For example, Professor Stigler limits the industries characterized by price leadership to those in which a dominant firm (one that produces a minimum of 40 per cent of the total output of an industry and more if the second largest firm is large) is present. Hence, industries characterized by other types of price leadership were included among those having no price leader. Moreover, the average number of firms in industries classified as having a price leader was slightly less than one-half of the average number of firms in industries not so classified. It is not surprising, therefore, that the former group shows a higher degree of price inflexibility than the latter for two reasons.

First, the rationale of price making by the dominant firm or partial monopolist differs but little from that employed by the pure monopolist. They both, presumably, have complete control over prices, but the partial monopolist, unlike the pure monopolist, must take account of the quantity that the competitive sector of the industry will offer at any price he may set. However inadequate classical theory might be in explaining the rigidity of monopoly prices, given the empirical evidence that monopoly prices are relatively inflexible, it probably follows that prices controlled by partial monopolists assume similar rigidities.

Secondly, the greatest number of firms in any industry classified among those having a price leader was four; the average number of firms in such industries was three. On the other hand, one industry not classified among those having a price leader contained as many as twelve firms and another contained eleven; the average number of firms in industries classified as having no price leader was over six. However, since many

[10] Stigler, *op. cit.*, p. 446.

of the excluded industries such as the rayon, newsprint, copper, gasoline, plate glass, window glass and plow industries possess barometric price leaders and a larger number of firms than those having a partial monopolist, Professor Stigler's findings could also be interpreted as evidence that (1) prices are more flexible under barometric than dominant firm price leadership and (2) price flexibility increases as the number of firms is increased. Professor Stigler isolated and very adequately treated the latter relationship himself;[11] the former will be discussed more fully below.

In the light of the formal theoretical construction employed to explain the rationale of dominant firm price leadership, a fairly strong argument can be made against even including markets where prices are set by a dominant firm among those containing a "price leader." Formal solutions which yield an equilibrium price in such markets preclude all possibilities of the failure of small firms to follow the dominant firms' price change, and, hence, from the viewpoint of the dominant firm, increase the probability of their following to absolute certainty. That is to say, whether the dominant firm attempts to maximize profits in the short run by equating its own marginal cost and derived marginal revenue schedules or pursues some other price policy, so long as it produces at a rate of output which clears the market at its own price, the remaining firms in the industry have no choice but to equate their marginal costs with the price it sets. Essentially, therefore, the pure dominant firm market presents a problem of monopoly price control rather than one of price leadership.

For purposes of public policy, to draw such a distinction between monopoly pricing and price leadership involves more than a mere question of definition. Price "leadership" in a dominant firm market is not simply a *modus operandi* designed to circumvent price competition among rival sellers but is instead an inevitable consequence of the industry's structure. Hence, the only obviously effective remedy for such monopoly pricing is to destroy the monopoly power from which it springs, *i.e.*, dissolve, if economically and politically feasible, the dominant firm. Public policy should hardly be directed toward this end, however, before the foundations of the dominant firm's existence have been thoroughly examined. Nearly every major industry in the American economy has, in its initial stages of development, been dominated by a single firm—the Slater Mill in cotton textiles, the Firestone Company in rubber tires, Birdseye in frozen foods, the American Viscose Corporation in rayon yarn, etc., to mention only a few. The monopoly power of the initial dominant firm in most industries, however, was gradually reduced by industrial growth and the entrance of new firms. It is not at all certain that public policy measures could have either hastened or im-

[11] *Ibid.*, p. 444.

proved upon the process. Where forces of competition do not eliminate such power, however (Professor Stigler has suggested the aluminum and scotch tape industries to me as possible examples), it is highly improbable that a mere declaration of the illegality of price leadership by the courts offers itself as a sufficient or even a possible remedial measure. The dominant firm would simply be confronted with the dilemma of (1) changing prices frequently and reminding the public with each price change that it sets the price for the industry or (2) simply varying its output and risk the attendant onus of price fixing. Hence, should all dominant firms accept the implications of the recent *Tobacco* decision at their face value, there would be no reason to conclude *a priori* whether prices in markets dominated by a particular firm would henceforth be more or less flexible, or would more closely approximate prices which one would expect under more competitive conditions.

BAROMETRIC FIRM PRICE LEADERSHIP

Unlike price leadership of the dominant firm type, there is no explanatory hypothesis which identifies the barometric price leader. In contrast to the dominant firm, the barometric firm "commands adherence of rivals to his price only because, and to the extent that, his price reflects market conditions with tolerable promptness."[12] Hence, the reasons why a particular firm is the barometric firm must be found in the historical background of an industry and the institutional and other features which have shaped its development.

It is worthwhile to note in passing that in a large number of industries which do not contain a partial monopolist, the price leader is frequently but not always the largest firm. In the newsprint industry, for example, International Paper, the largest producer, has led most price changes in markets east of the Rocky Mountains and Crown Zellerbach, the largest western producer, has usually announced new prices on the west coast. The price leadership of International, however, has sometimes been challenged by Great Northern, another large producer. American Viscose, which at one time completely dominated the rayon industry, has continued to be the accepted list-price leader although it had lost its dominant firm position as early as 1930. On the other hand, Phelps Dodge, only the third largest producer of copper in 1947, has been quite active in setting copper prices since OPA controls were removed in November, 1946.

Patently, it is not possible in every case to judge when barometric price leadership is monopolistic and when it is competitive in character without making a thorough investigation, but there are certain visible market features associated with competitive price leadership. For example, unless a particular firm has demonstrated unusual adeptness at adjusting prices to market forces, in the absence of conspiracy one would

---

[12] *Ibid.*, p. 446.

certainly expect occasional changes in the identity of the price leader. Moreover, unless the lines of price communication are extremely efficient, prices are not likely to be uniform among sellers in a specific market area for a short period immediately following the date the price leader announces a new price. A "wait and see" policy on the part of several sellers not only gives rise to occasional price differentials, but also suggests the absence of even tacit collusion. Furthermore, if new prices are communicated among buyers more rapidly than among sellers, there would be frequent changes in the ratios of sales (and, depending upon inventory policies, of production) of particular firms to the total volume of sales (or production) for the industry as a whole. In the rayon and textile industries, where each large fabricator buys yarn and cloth from several sellers simultaneously, this is usually the case. Buyers iron out price differentials among sellers by refusing to buy at old prices if the price leader has announced a price reduction and buy heavily at old prices if the price leader has announced a price increase.

The price histories of copper and rayon yarn illustrate fairly well most of the outward manifestations one would expect of competitive barometric price leadership. Immediately upon the removal of OPA controls Kennecott Copper took the lead in advancing domestic copper prices from the controlled 14.375 cents per pound to the world price of 17.5 cents per pound.[13] All other producers followed. Eight days later, on November 20, 1946, Phelps Dodge advanced its price to 19.5 cents per pound and was followed by the rest of the industry. On January 28, 1947, American Smelting and Refining Company advanced its domestic price to 20.5 cents; however, other producers continued to sell at the old price until Phelps Dodge increased its price to 21.5 cents on March 3. American Smelting and Refining Company matched the new price, but Kennecott Copper announced a firm price policy on March 27 and stated that it would continue to make shipments at the old price. Large copper buyers announced three weeks later, however, that in their opinion "Kennecott had 'reluctantly' advanced their prices to meet present levels and the present action to fix prices at present levels meant that Kennecott would be unlikely to follow any further upward price revisions from other sources."[14] In the latter part of June the price of copper settled at 21.5 cents after several weeks of varying prices among sellers. Around the end of July, 1948, several smaller companies increased their prices to 23.5 cents; the larger producers did not follow immediately but withdrew all offerings from the market. On August 3 Phelps Dodge and Anaconda jointly raised their prices to 23.5 cents and Kennecott followed on August 11.

Of the five major copper price changes which occurred between No-

---

[13] Company prices are from various issues of the *New York Times*.

[14] *New York Times*, March 29, 1947, p. 23.

vember, 1946, and December, 1948, therefore, Phelps Dodge, a medium-sized producer, initiated three. Competitive factors, however, such as the import tariff on sales made in the United States by foreign producers and price movements of scrap, tin, and aluminum, probably exerted much more influence on copper prices during the twenty-six month period than did the arbitrary judgment of the firm initiating the price changes.[15]

Until 1930 American Viscose was the dominant firm in the rayon yarn industry. Since then the company has produced from only 30 per cent to 35 per cent of the total domestic output of rayon yarn but has first announced over 75 per cent of all list-price revisions. The price leader can exercise only negligible control over rayon prices, however, since they are largely determined by the prices of such close substitutes as silk, cotton, wool, nylon, orlon, and vinyon, each of which competes strongly with rayon in a number of market areas. Moreover, small rayon producers do not hesitate to sell at less than their quoted price when inventories commence to accumulate, a practice which has prompted most of the downward revisions announced by American Viscose. On the other hand, rayon list prices are seldom increased unless the industry is operating close to full capacity and inventories are still declining. For list-price movements, however, American Viscose plays the role of the barometric firm.

Barometric price leadership which follows the above lines probably does not greatly circumvent the public interest nor is it likely that the *Tobacco* decision has brought this type of price leadership within the reach of the antitrust laws. The barometric firm possesses no power to coerce the rest of the industry into accepting its price and, in most such industries, it simply passes along information to the "Big Three" or the "Big Four" on what the rest of the industry is doing in a declining market, and proceeds with initiating price increases in a market revival only so rapidly as supply and demand conditions dictate.

For purposes of prescribing appropriate remedial action it is important also to differentiate between actual collusive price leadership and "apparent" collusive price leadership which stems more from overt selling arrangements than from simply following price changes announced by a rival firm. In the steel, cement, glass container, and fertilizer industries, what has appeared at times to be barometric price leadership was in fact a natural consequence of basing point and zone pricing systems. Under a single basing point system, if recognized and adhered to by all producers, giving the appearance of following a price leader is inevitable since the pricing policies of all sellers are unalterably geared

[15] Copper producers seem to feel that their prices are largely dependent upon the prices of such competing metals as aluminum and tin. Between March, 1947, and August, 1948, Kennecott publicly denounced further price increases since it believed they would induce fabricators to substitute tin and aluminum for copper. *Cf. New York Times*, May 5, 1948, p. 41, and August 3, 1948, p. 29.

to the base mill. The same is true of a multiple basing point system if all base mills are owned by a single seller. Identical prices among producers in an industry operating under a multiple basing point system where the base mills are owned by different producers is not clearly a necessary consequence of the basing point system, but one should, on economic grounds, expect all prices at least to move in the same direction. A decrease in the base price in one area allows all producers abiding by this base price to further invade adjacent areas until mills in adjacent areas meet the price reduction; an increase in the base price in one area increases the demand for the commodity from mills in adjacent areas, thereby encouraging corresponding price increases. Hence, a sufficient explanation for similar price movements among producers abiding by a basing point system is the presence of the basing point system itself. The best evidence that this is so is the undisciplined pricing which occurs when the basing point system temporarily breaks down.[16]

For the most part, therefore, the barometric price leader, as defined by Professor Stigler and as visualized for purposes of this paper, appears to do little more than set prices that would eventually be set by forces of competition. In such industries as the copper and rayon industries, *i.e.*, oligopolies within monopolistically competitive markets, these prices are largely dependent upon the prices of closely competing products. In more clearly delineated oligopolistic industries, particularly where the number of firms is fairly large, price leadership of the barometric type has seldom if ever been a sufficiently strong instrument alone to insure price discipline among rivals. Price leadership in the steel and fertilizer industries has been a subordinate feature of a basing point system. The glass container industry implemented price leadership by inaugurating a zone pricing and market sharing system. In spite of this, many firms were not faithful price followers.[17] In the tin can industry, where American Can Company has frequently been identified as the price leader, a recent study suggests that American's list price (computed principally from the price of tin plate) has only established the base line of competition for other can producers.[18] Moreover, American Can's influence over the price of tin cans is as much attributable to its quasi-monopsonistic position in the tin plate market as it is to the company's share of the tin can market.

From the standpoint of public policy the real problem in such markets as those discussed above, therefore, centers upon economic forces which support price leadership rather than upon price leadership *per se*. In industries dominated by a strong partial monopolist, parallel pricing among firms stems from the monopoly power possessed by the partial monopo-

[16] *Cf.* Temporary National Economic Committee, Monograph No. 42, p. 3.

[17] *Cf.* Robert L. Bishop, "The Glass Container Industry," in *The Structure of American Industry*, edited by Walter Adams (New York, 1950), pp. 407–8.

[18] Charles H. Hession, *The Tin Can Industry* (privately published), p. 362.

list and not from the tacit adoption of a price leader to circumvent price competition. The competitive sector of the industry often has no choice but to accept the partial monopolist's price. In oligopolies which form segments of larger monopolistically competitive industries, such as those which conform to the pattern of the rayon and copper industries, the barometric firm "leads" price changes only in the limited sense that its price movements are presumed by its rivals to have resulted from a synthesis of all the available market information. Price decreases initiated by firms selling closely competing products and by smaller firms within its own segment of the industry usually prompt downward list-price revisions by the barometric firm. List-price increases occur only after the market forces have been reversed. In most markets of an intermediate character the evidence indicates that price leadership has been decidedly a subordinate feature of a pricing policy built upon the much stronger foundations of trade association activity, zone pricing, basing point agreements, etc.[19]

A comprehensive study embracing the tacit and overt pricing arrangements among sellers in a wide variety of industries more or less oligopolistic in character would undoubtedly point up to more meaningful conclusions than those suggested by the above evidence. Nevertheless, there is some basis for believing that the mere adoption of a price leader is not nearly such an effective means for eliminating price competition among the few as many economists are prone to believe. Except for the type of price leadership discussed below, the evidence suggests that the power of the price leader to preserve price discipline derives less from his ostensible status as the barometric firm than from the more overt arrangements which support it. Where such supporting arrangements are not found, the barometric firm seems to do little more than respond to forces of competition. If this is so, the *Tobacco* decision may have far less importance than has been attributed to it, but at the same time the search for remedial action in similar future cases may not be nearly so fruitless as is generally believed. The elimination of supports to effective price leadership, most of which are not particularly elusive targets, might very well eliminate the effectiveness of price leadership itself.

PRICE LEADERSHIP IN LIEU OF AN OVERT AGREEMENT

In industries which possess certain specific features, however, one would expect *a priori* a type of price leadership of a much different nature and considerably more inimical to the public interest than that

---

[19] An examination of recent industry studies [including those reproduced in part in *The Structure of American Industry*, *op. cit.*, and in Walter Adams and Leland E. Traywick, *Readings in Economics* (New York, 1948)] reveals little evidence that price leadership, when not buttressed by stronger means of preserving price discipline, prevented price competition among oligopolists in times of market crisis.

of the barometric type discussed above. In such industries price leadership may conceivably be so effective as to serve all the ends of a strong trade association or of a closely knit domestic cartel and, hence, in a political environment where overt collusion is illegal, may be the only feasible means of assuring parallel action among sellers. In view of the foregoing discussion, the most important market features prerequisite to effective price leadership of this type would seem to be as follows:

1. Firms must be few in number and each firm must be sufficiently large to be compelled to reckon with the indirect as well as the direct effects of its own price policy. If there are several very small firms in the industry but no dominant firm, they, through ignoring their indirect influence on price, are likely to engage in promiscuous price cutting whenever market crises occur and, hence, at least for downward price adjustments, usurp the role of price leader. Moreover, such firms are not likely to follow the lead in upward price revisions unless they are completely satisfied with their expected volume of sales at the new price.

2. Entry to the industry must be severely restricted if the price set by the price leader is to remain close to a rationalized oligopolistic price for any significant length of time. If the long-run cost curve for the new entrant is substantially the same as those which confront entrenched firms, price rationalization can be only temporary since the rationalized price will attract new entrants which, in turn, will bid the price down.[20] If, however, the time lag between investment decisions and actual investment in the industry is significant, price rationalization for the duration of the lag may suggest itself as a profitable possibility.

3. The "commodity" produced by the several firms need not be perfectly homogeneous but each producer must view the output of all other firms as extremely close substitutes for his own. If this condition is not fulfilled, each producer is likely to view his product as distinctive in character and the "market" will not be characterized by a single price policy but by several. Examples of such individual pricing policies may be found in the automobile and brand-name men's clothing markets. Where the output of each firm is differentiated to the extent that it is only a moderately good substitute for the output of other firms, price leadership, of course, is meaningless.

4. The elasticity of the market demand schedule for the output of the industry as described in (3) above must not greatly exceed unity. If demand for the output of the industry is elastic because the oligopoly is only a segment of a larger monopolistically competitive market, the prices of closely competing products severely limit or possibly even eliminate the gains to be derived from adopting a price leader. Moreover, if demand for the output of the oligopoly is highly elastic, firms are not likely to adhere to the price leader's price if to do so would

---

[20] For an imperfect example, see discussion of cigarette industry, *infra*.

result in substantially less than capacity operations, since each firm could still stimulate its own sales considerably by lowering its price, even though all other firms met the new price. The price history of the domestic rayon industry and the postwar price history of the copper industry furnish particularly good evidence of the validity of this point. Whenever declining silk and cotton prices have commenced to reduce the volume of rayon sales at existing list prices, rayon producers, if the price leader has not already reduced his price, have sold at less than list price in order to move accumulating inventories and to maintain operations at near-capacity output. Similarly, copper producers appear to follow the price leader only if they believe his new price is in line with prevailing scrap, aluminum, and tin prices.

5. Individual-firm cost curves must be sufficiently similar so that some particular price allows all firms to operate at a satisfactory rate of output. If, for example, the industry is composed of several high-cost low-capacity firms and several low-cost high-capacity firms, the resulting conflict in price and output policies cannot be resolved by adopting a price leader so long as all firms remain in the industry.[21] Low-cost firms will not accept the price leadership of high-cost firms since there is a better option in the form of a lower price and a higher rate of output open to them. They can therefore force the high-cost sector of the industry to adopt the lower price but, if the differences in costs between high-cost and low-cost firms are significant, high-cost firms will not recover full costs and will gradually be eliminated from the industry. Hence, the conflict will have been resolved and the condition that all producers be confronted with reasonably similar cost curves will then be fulfilled.

It might be argued that the foregoing conditions are fully as necessary for any form of effective parallel action, such as price maintenance agreements, strong trade associations, or even unimplemented oligopolistic rationalization, as they are for effective price leadership. Such an argument, of course, would be entirely valid for, it will be recalled, the type of price leadership being examined is but one of a number of possible forms of conscious parallelism, all of which presumably stem from a common source, namely, the identity between the long-run interests of each individual firm and those of the industry as a whole.

Moreover, conditions other than those discussed above bear significantly upon the likelihood of effective price leadership ever arising and maintaining price discipline in an industry. Among those that first come to mind are the extent of tariff protection, the rate of technological change, the stability of demand, and the aggressiveness of management. An examination of the available price histories of industries in which the number of sellers is not large indicates, however, that price leader-

[21] For the theoretical analysis relevant to an industry containing several firms but only one low-cost high-capacity firm, see Boulding, *supra*, fn. 9.

ship is most likely to serve the ends of a collusive agreement when the above five conditions are fulfilled. Or, stated another way, effective price discipline seems to have been rarely achieved by the tacit means of price leadership alone when one or several of these conditions did not exist.

THE TOBACCO DECISION REAPPRAISED

Had the Department of Justice diligently searched the American economy for an industry which most nearly contained all the conditions prerequisite to effective price leadership, it could hardly have found a better example than the cigarette industry. The entrenched position of the "Big Three" brand-names had made entry to the cigarette industry exceedingly difficult. Moreover, parallel action in the leaf tobacco market had insured fairly comparable if not equal cost conditions among the three large cigarette producers; and, although each of them viewed the output of the other two as such perfect substitutes for his own that none would risk a retail price differential, demand for their output collectively, at least in the short run, was inelastic. Furthermore, in 1929 the Big Three controlled over 90 per cent of the domestic cigarette market and, with Lorillard, they controlled 98 per cent. Hence, for all practical purposes, the number of cigarette producers was very small. Also, the large cigarette producers had had ample opportunity as well as compelling reasons for working out a *modus operandi* which would identify their individual interests with those of the Big Three collectively. In substance, counsel for Liggett and Myers probably described the attitude of all the large producers of cigarettes when he stated, ". . . in making price decisions the management of Liggett and Myers has acted in response to a long experience of non-identical prices as well as identical prices."[22]

In spite of such ideal conditions for securing parallel action by adopting a price leader, however, the Big Three soon discovered that even their market was subject to economic forces that put an upper limit on exploitation. The *long-run* demand for their collective output was elastic, hence complete exploitation of the cigarette market was limited to a short-time period. With low tobacco prices and high cigarette prices in the latter half of 1931 and 1932, competitive forces began to assert their influence. Whereas the 10-cent brands had been virtually unknown (accounting for only 1.5 per cent of all cigarettes sold) in the first half of 1931, output of small independents began to increase rapidly after the price increase led by Reynolds in June, 1931. By December, 1932, they accounted for 22 per cent of total cigarette sales. In the meantime, the sales of Reynolds, American, Liggett and Myers and Lorillard had been drastically reduced. By February, 1933, their vulnerability to competition had become sufficiently evident to the Big Three to induce reductions in

---

[22] *American Tobacco Company* v. *United States*, 147 F. 2d 93 (6th Cir., 1944), Liggett and Myers' Brief, p. 264; *ibid.*, Reynolds' Brief, p. 390; and American Tobacco's Brief, pp. 94–95.

popular brand cigarette prices to the lowest level since 1918. Hence, simple price leadership, even under such ideal conditions as those afforded by the cigarette industry, had failed to preserve the rationalized oligopoly (or monopoly) market solution.

In the light of their alleged strategy after 1933, perhaps no one was more aware than the Big Three themselves of the long-run ineffectiveness of price leadership when not implemented by other safeguards from competition. Although price leadership continued to play an important role in cigarette pricing, its effectiveness after 1933 was largely dependent upon the successful effort of the Big Three to manipulate the leaf tobacco market.

If unimplemented price leadership proved to be an exploitative weapon of limited effectiveness in the cigarette industry, and its usefulness confined to a time period scarcely exceeding several years, it is highly improbable that tacit parallel pricing in oligopolistic markets offers itself *per se* as either a fruitful or fertile field for antitrust investigation. Hence the *Tobacco* decision, particularly when viewed against a background in which appropriate remedial action is conspicuously absent, is not likely to have far-reaching consequences. The appropriate question before economists, the business community, and the courts alike, therefore, is not how far tacit parallel pricing in oligopolistic markets can proceed before it becomes illegal, but rather what implementing devices and market conditions make price leadership both possible and effective. In most oligopolistic industries where the record of pricing techniques is fairly complete, there are good reasons for suspecting that price leadership is essentially a shadow of more insidious pricing devices and trade restraints. When the devices which buttress price leadership have been destroyed, price leadership as an exploitative practice may well have been emasculated.

In view of the extraordinary conditions prerequisite to the more effective type of price leadership, it is not likely that the *Tobacco* decision, as a legal precedent, can or will measurably influence the behavior of prices in markets where sellers are few in number; nor will it greatly broaden the scope of the antitrust laws. Along these lines, the recent basing point and similar future decisions would appear to be a much more profitable line of approach to monopoly problems posed by industries comprising relatively few sellers.

10

Price and Production Policies of Large-Scale Enterprise*

By EDWARD S. MASON†

I

The current emphasis on price policy, as against price, as a proper object of study represents recent economic reflection on the significance of expectations, uncertainties, market control, and the position of price as one among many selling terms. Policy implies some degree of control over the course of events and, at the same time, the use of judgment as to the probable consequences of alternative lines of action. In perfect markets, whether monopolistic or competitive, price is hardly a matter of judgment and where there is no judgment there is no policy. The area of price policy, then, embraces the deliberative action of buyers and sellers able to influence price; that is to say, it covers practically the whole field of industrial prices.

The preoccupation with policy questions certainly indicates a trend towards an inclusion in price analysis of an increasing number of institutional considerations. Pursued to its Hamiltonian end[1] it implies not only an examination of the facts peculiar to each industrial market situation, but also a study of the conditions peculiar to each sale or purchase including what Messrs. Ford and Firestone dreamed in the night preceding the morning of their big tire deal. Particular circumstances may, indeed, justify so minute an investigation. It is submitted, however, that useful work in the field of industrial price policies requires a frame of reference of much greater generality. To the construction of such a frame of reference, which must take the form, I think, of a classification of market structures, recent theoretical work makes a useful contribution. It is, however, merely a starting point.

A firm may have a price policy by reason of the existence of rivals of whose action it must take account, of the desirability of considering the

---

* *The American Economic Review*, Vol. XXIX Suppl. (1939), pp. 61–74. Reprinted by courtesy of the publisher and the author.

The author is indebted to the Shaw Fund and to the Harvard Committee on Research in the Social Sciences for financial assistance in his work in this field.

† Harvard University.

[1] *Cf.* Walter Hamilton, *Price and Price Policies*, Sections I and IX.

effect of present upon future price, of the possibility of its price in one market affecting its price in another, of the possibility of competing in other ways than by price, and for many other reasons. All these situations involve some degree of market control on the part of a seller or buyer. A position of market control, while a necessary, is not, however, a sufficient condition for price policy. In addition a seller or buyer must customarily conduct his operations by means of a quoted price. A dealer on an organized produce exchange may conduct transactions of sufficient magnitude to influence the market price. Yet if he buys and sells "at the market" it serves no useful purpose to attribute to him a price policy. I limit the meaning of this term, then, to buyers and sellers who enjoy some degree of market control and who carry on their purchases and sales through the medium of a quoted price.[2] Practically speaking this includes all selling transactions outside of agriculture and the organized produce and securities markets.

II

The size of a firm influences its competitive policies in a number of ways. In the first place the scale of its purchases and sales relative to the total volume of transactions in the firm's market is one indication of the extent of its market control. Taken in conjunction with other data it may throw a good deal of light on price and production policies. Certain authorities, on the other hand, brush aside figures on the relative size of firms as irrelevant and emphasize the decisive importance of the elasticity of the firm's demand curve.[3] It would no doubt be extremely convenient if economists knew the shape of individual demand and cost curves and could proceed forthwith, by comparisons of price and marginal cost, to conclusions regarding the existing degree of monopoly power. The extent to which the monopoly theorists, however, refrain from an empirical application of their formulae is rather striking.[4] The

[2] R. F. Kahn ("The Problem of Duopoly," *Economic Journal*, March, 1937, p. 4) distinguishes the following "extreme cases":

"(a) At one extreme we have the case where, in spite of a change in a competitor's price, firms' prices remain constant automatically until they are altered as a result of deliberation or experiment. . . .

"(b) At the other extreme is the case where it is the volume of sales that automatically remains constant until some other decision is arrived at."

The first case is practically significant and embraces the whole range of industrial market situations in which sellers act through price quotations. The second case, however, is unrealistic. If price varies from moment to moment with changes in market conditions it is more than probable that sales (for an individual seller) will vary also.

[3] *Cf.* A. P. Lerner, "The Concept of Monopoly and the Measurement of Monopoly Power," *Review of Economic Studies*, June, 1934.

[4] Some theorists, pursuing their analysis on a high plane, refer to their work as "tool making" rather than "tool using." A "toolmaker," however, who constructs tools which no "tool user" can use is making a contribution of limited significance. Some knowledge of the use of tools is probably indispensable to their effective fabrication.

alternative, if more pedestrian, route follows the direction of ascertainable facts and makes use only of empirically applicable concepts.[5] One such set of facts embraces the data relevant to concentration.

Secondly, the absolute size of a firm, as measured by assets, employees, or volume of sales, is also relevant to price and production policies. The scale of operations may affect the number and character of the factors that are taken into account in the determination of policies; it may also affect the way the firm reacts to given market situations. Selling practices at the disposal of the large firm may be beyond the reach of its smaller competitors. Large oil firms characteristically brand their gasoline and differentiate it from the product of competitors by extensive advertising campaigns. Small firms may, by reason of their size, be forced to sell an unbranded product at a lower price. In a society in which size is popularly considered a menace, the large firm must consider carefully the probable reception of its price and production policies by public opinion and political agencies. There is some evidence that the United States Steel Corporation for a considerable period of time viewed with favor its dwindling share in the national market and, through its price policies, "held an umbrella" over the heads of its growing competitors. Recent aggressive price tactics on the part of this company may indicate that it no longer regards such policies as politically necessary. If the market be considered to embrace all the factors external to the firm which habitually influence its competitive policies, there can be no doubt that the size of the firm affects the scope and structure of the market.

The size of a firm likewise influences its reaction to given market situations. Economic analysis exhibits a disposition to treat the firm as a "profit maximizing" agency the action of which in the market is independent of its internal organization. The growth of corporate bureaucracies (with the consequent institutionalization of management decisions), the separation of ownership from control, and the growing influence of labor organization on policy making are all factors "internal to the firm" which may and do affect its reaction to market situations. One of the questions raised by these considerations is the meaning and importance of administered prices. To this question I shall return in a subsequent section.

III

Current consideration of price policy is apt to take either one of two quite different directions. One approach, associated with the theory of oligopoly and monopolistic competition, starts with various elements of the market structure of the individual firm and derives therefrom conclusions regarding the price and production policy of this firm. The other begins with an examination of the behavior of prices and through

[5] I should be far from denying, however, the value of theoretical speculation, even of a very abstract sort, in helping to ask the right questions of the data and in indicating the irrelevance of much factual material.

correlating various measures of price behavior with other measurable economic variables works back towards differences in the structure of markets in an attempt to explain the observed differences in price behavior.

The practical utility of the analytical method has been to focus attention on rivals' reactions as considerations in the determination of price and production policies and on the importance of non-price forms of competition. Whether the further elaboration of techniques of analysis yielding results of illusory exactness are useful is doubtful. The broad justification of this type of analysis must be that it provides a pattern of thought useful in separating data which are relevant from those which are irrelevant to the explanation of price and production policies. Certainly numbers of buyers and sellers in the market and the possibility of product differentiation are relevant. No one would deny, furthermore, that the position and shape of individual demand and cost curves would be relevant if ascertainable.[6] In the absence of such data, however, a realistic analysis of price and production policies may be unable to make much use of the constructions of recent monopoly theory.

A number of more specific strictures on the utility of this theory for price analysis may be offered. The static equilibrium assumptions implicit in this analysis rule out most of the considerations which are important for price policy. These considerations are in the main connected with industrial growth and decay and with the business cycle. The objection is not that monopoly theory is incompatible with an analysis that takes these considerations into account but that its constructions are irrelevant to the real problems. If we seek to build further on the existing foundation, the only part of that foundation which is likely to be found usable is composed of the ascertainable facts of numbers of sellers (and buyers) and product differentiation.[7]

---

[6] However true it may be that businessmen have a roughly accurate notion of the shape of the demand curve with which they are confronted, at least within a limited range, it seems extremely unlikely that economists will be able by independent investigations to ascertain this shape except by the roughest sort of deduction from other data. In certain favorable cases demand curves for a product may be drawn statistically; for other products we are able to surmise that the demand curve is elastic or inelastic. *Cf.* J. M. Cassels, *A Study of Fluid Milk Prices*, p. 41: "Certain fairly definite conclusions about the character of the consumer's demand for milk can be drawn from a general common sense analysis of the factors involved." By taking into consideration such factors as numbers of sellers, product standardization, and others one can, in some cases, proceed from a rough knowledge of the shape of the product demand curve to a rougher guess at the shape of the demand curve for an individual seller.

[7] Pigou would apparently deny that products for which substitution is not perfect can be in the same market. He defines the market as a "common nodal point" at which different units of an identical good are "available for purchase and sale" en route from the sellers' works to the buyers' home. Such a definition permits of a classification of markets only on the basis of numbers of buyers and sellers. (A. C. Pigou, *The Economics of Stationary States*, p. 78.) If different products are admitted to the market then the problem becomes one of (a) defining the group of products

Data on numbers, furthermore, tell us little regarding price and production policies unless there is further specification of market structure. Elaborate speculation on the probable behavior of A on the assumption that B will act in a certain way, seems particularly fruitless. It recalls Morgenstern's discussion of the dilemma of Dr. Moriarty when confronted with the alternative courses open to Sherlock Holmes.[8] It should be a function of market analysis so to particularize as to reduce the area of necessary speculation to a minimum. The theory of oligopoly has been aptly described as a ticket of admission to institutional economics. It is to be regretted that more theorists have not availed themselves of this privilege. If they had there would certainly be less of a disposition in the literature on the decline of competition to assume that in all markets dominated by a few sellers are to be found the same or similar patterns of price policy.

The statistical approach to price policy starts with an examination of price behavior and then proceeds to correlate various measures of price change with changes in other economic variables. Despite the recognized defects in price data, recent work along this line has made clear characteristic differences in the various groups of prices and has raised problems of admitted importance. Typically, however, this work exhibits certain weaknesses. First, it has been insufficiently recognized that, proceeding from the standard products of the raw material markets to the differentiated products of the highly fabricated goods markets, price as an index of the terms on which buyers acquire or sellers dispose of commodities tends to lose significance. The introduction of various forms of non-price competition and a proliferation of selling terms emphasize the necessity to take these considerations into account both in an analysis of sellers' price policy and in determining changes in the position of buying groups.[9] Second, the measures of price behavior customarily employed are frequently much too general to serve the purposes to which they are put. This is conspicuously true of commonly used measures of price

---

which are in the same market; (b) defining the geographical area within which buyers and sellers are in competition. It is on the basis of numbers and product differentiation that Machlup constructs his classification of markets, without, however, dealing with the question of how the geographical and product limits of the market are to be defined. *Cf.* Fritz Machlup, "Monopoly and Competition," *American Economic Review*, September, 1937.

[8] *Wirtschaftsprognose*, p. 98.

[9] In this connection it is necessary to distinguish between two quite different attacks on the validity of existing price data. It may be objected that the quoted price is inaccurate because it is not the price at which sales actually take place; e.g., the B.L.S. quotations on sulphuric acid were, during the depression, highly inaccurate since they represented unimportant sales to small purchasers while the bulk of the sales during this period were made at much lower prices to large industrial users. On the other hand it may be objected that the quoted price is inaccurate because it is merely one among many conditions of sale. Insofar as the other conditions of sale cannot be legitimately reduced to price terms—and they usually cannot—this is not an objection to the validity of the price as such.

sensitivity. An all-purpose measure of price sensitivity or flexibility is subject to as many and as serious objections as an all-purpose index number. Price is a function of many variables and price sensitivity or flexibility acquires significance mainly as a relationship between price change and change in some one or more of these variables.[10] Prices may be sensitive to changes in inventories, demand, costs, and in other prices, or to changes in some of these variables and not in others. Third, the attempt to correlate measures of price behavior with other data such as industrial concentration and product durability on an economy-wide basis is apt to include irrelevant and exclude relevant determinants of price policy. It seems probable that empirical work will achieve better results by a more intensive examination of specific market situations. In selected industrial markets a study of the relation between changes in costs, inventories, sales, production improvements and other variables, and the magnitude and timing of price change, may considerably increase our knowledge of price and production policies.

These strictures on current methods of interpreting price and production policies do not imply that analytical and statistical techniques are useless. On the contrary any classification of market structures designed to illuminate patterns of competitive policy must make use of them.

IV

It follows from what has been said that an adequate analysis of price and production policies requires consideration of (a) the influence of the organization of a firm on the character of the firm's reaction to given market situations; and of (b) elements of market structure which include many more things than numbers and product differentiation. It goes without saying that a realistic treatment of these questions necessitates the use of analytical tools which are amenable to empirical application. The problem, as I see it, is to reduce the voluminous data concerning industrial organization to some sort of order through a classification of market structures. Differences in market structure are ultimately explicable in terms of technological factors. The economic problem, however, is to explain, through an examination of the structure of markets and the organization of firms, differences in competitive practices including price, production, and investment policies.

A consideration of the relation of the organization of firms to price and production policies raises at the outset the question of administered prices. As currently used this is neither a clearcut nor a useful concept.

[10] Some of these relationships are, of course, much more important than others. I should be prepared to admit, with Lerner, Kalecki, and Dunlop that—at least for commodities for which price is the only significant selling term—the relationship between price and marginal cost is peculiarly significant both for analysis and policy. *Cf.* A. P. Lerner, *op. cit.;* M. Kalecki, "The Determinants of Distribution of National Income," *Econometrica,* April, 1938; J. T. Dunlop, "Price Rigidity and Degree of Monopoly," a manuscript to be published shortly.

In one sense it appears to relate to the methods by which a price is determined; in another sense to the way the price behaves. A price may be determined by administrative action; i.e., it may be quoted by a seller rather than determined by the higgling of buyers and sellers in an organized market. At the same time it may behave in much the same way as prices in organized markets. A manufacturer's price of cotton print cloth may be taken as an example. Furthermore the attempt to contrast administered prices with market prices obscures the fact that all prices are market prices in the sense that market considerations influence their determination.

There is, nevertheless, an important kernel of truth concealed in this usage, to wit, the fact that firms are not, regardless of what economic theory may suppose, undifferentiated profit-maximizing agencies which react to given market situations in ways which are independent of their organization. The large corporation is a complex administrative unit in which control frequently bears a very attentuated relationship to owners' interests, in which management is increasingly professionalized, in which the character of labor organization may influence price and production decisions, and in which at best a considerable area of important price decision must be routinized and delegated to subordinates. The result is that management, in the determination of price and production policies, is subjected not only to market pressures but influenced in its action by considerations internal to the firm.

The United States Steel Corporation, considering all the quantity and quality variations involved in adapting forty or fifty basic products to the specifications of its customers, is faced with the problem of setting some fifty thousand prices. While market considerations may, at one time or another, influence the relationships between these prices, it is impossible to make independent decisions respecting prices with every change in the market situation even if such action were thought desirable. The result is that pricing on individual orders is delegated to price clerks armed with an elaborate book of extras and such specific directions as to its use as may be thought desirable. The International Harvester Company, in servicing its agricultural implements, manufactures and stocks some two hundred and fifty thousand separate parts. In pricing these parts considerations relevant to the organization and administration of the firm are probably at least as important as considerations relevant to the market situation.

The locus and character of control within the firm may likewise be relevant to basic price and production policies. The familiar contrast between a financial type of control primarily concerned with the conservation of assets and control by entrepreneurial types mainly concerned with expanding output and the firm's share in the market is doubtless too easy. Conservation of assets may necessitate an expansion of output and, after all, bankers called in to rehabilitate a declining firm have been known to advise price reduction as a remedy. Furthermore in those cases in which the supposed influence of entrepreneurial and financial attitudes are sharply contrasted, e.g., automobiles and steel products, the differences can probably be more adequately explained by market conditions than by considerations relevant to the internal organization of firms. Nevertheless it is true to say that organizations make men, as well as the reverse, and in the making of men policies are also made. During the recent flurry of price cutting in the steel industry the president of the Steel Workers' Organization Committee announced that if price cutting continued organized labor might be forced to take action since "price cutting always leads to wage cutting." The character of control and the action of control in the determination of policy—including price and production policies—is influenced not only by the pressure of labor but by many pressures arising from group relationships within the firm. These relationships, furthermore, tend to influence the kind and caliber of men who are called to management positions in a concern.[11]

Economists have been singularly loath to investigate these semipolitical relationships within large-scale enterprise which influence business policy. Where business policies are recognized as running counter to what would seem to be rational action in the market the disposition has been to interpret them in terms of individual personalities. It was said that Firestone and Ford were sports in the sense of deviations from the norm of entrepreneurial rationality. Or again that what every industry dominated by a few firms needed was a Ford or Firestone by which it was implied that economic rationality in such situations would lead to production restriction and price maintenance but that these policies were prevented, with advantage to the public, by the anomalous behavior of such entrepreneurs. No doubt Messrs. Ford and Firestone set the impress of their personalities on the policies of their respective industries, but the larger problem for economists to consider is the impress of large-scale business organizations on the character and functioning of the management groups that are called to control positions.[12]

---

[11] *Cf.* J. A. Schumpeter, "Der Unternehmer in der Volkswirtschaft von heute," *Struktur Wandlungen der Deutschen Volkswirtschaft,* I: 303. In a "trustified" economy the performance of entrepreneurial functions is subject to a "mechanization and bureaucratization" of decision (*Willensbildung*). The type of business leader associated with large-scale enterprise tends to resemble the successful political figure, "a good minister, or bureauchief." "The groups and interests who select the leader tend to agree on a compromise candidate—not always the man of highest ability. Even when the object is to find the 'best man' he may turn out to be not one who can run the concern but a man adept at manipulating public opinion and handling public relations."

[12] The effect of the development of what may be called a professional management point of view on corporate policies is a question too frequently neglected. As an expression of that point of view, *cf.* Owen D. Young quoted in J. C. Sears, *The New Place of the Stockholder:*

"To whom do I owe my obligations?

"My conception of it is this: that there are three groups of people who have an interest in that institution [General Electric Company]. One is the group of

V

When we proceed from a consideration of the effect of the organization of a firm on its reaction to market situations to a consideration of the elements of market structure and their relation to price and production policies we are immediately confronted with the necessity of making clear the meaning of market and market structure. A preoccupation with logical elegance might lead us to define a market, with Pigou, as a nodal point at which a product, whose units are perfect substitutes for each other, are available for purchase and sale. Unfortunately, such a definition would effectively relegate all the important and interesting problems to the area of intermarket relationships. An alternative would be to conceive of a market as an area in geographic and product space bounded, in Joan Robinson's phrase, by a gap in the chain of substitutes. Within such an area, however, assuming that it could be defined, the position of individual sellers and buyers may be very different with respect to the influences affecting business policy. These and other considerations suggest that, at least in the industrial area, the market, and market structure, must be defined with reference to the position of a single seller or buyer. The structure of a seller's market, then, includes all those considerations which he takes into account in determining his business policies and practices. His market includes all buyers and sellers, of whatever product, whose action he considers to influence his volume of sales.

The classification of market structures on the seller's side consists, then, in grouping together those firms, in whatever industry, which operate under the same or similar objective conditions.[13] Among these conditions are the economic characteristics of the product: is it a producers or consumers good, is it durable or non-durable, is the product of an individual seller differentiated with respect to the products of other sellers in the same market or is it standardized? Another group of conditions relate to the cost and production characteristics of the firm's operation. The ratio of overhead to variable costs at given volumes of output and for given variations in volume of output, the flexibility of costs, locational factors, and the existence of joint costs are all important. A third class of considerations has to do with the numbers and relative

---

fifty-odd thousand people who have put their capital in the company, namely its stockholders. Another is a group of well towards one hundred thousand people who are putting their labor and their lives into the business of the company. The third group is of customers and the general public. . . .

"One no longer feels the obligation to take from labor for the benefit of capital, nor to take from the public for the benefit of both, but rather to administer wisely and fairly in the interest of all."

[13] The author is at present engaged, with his colleague, Professor D. H. Wallace, in working out a classification of industrial market situations.

sizes of buyers and sellers of whose action our given seller has to take account and with the relative ease of entry for new firms. Among the demand conditions which are empirically determinable may be mentioned the trend of sales, seasonal and cyclical fluctuations in sales, and, roughly, the knowledge possessed by buyers with respect to the quality and characteristics of the product. Differences in distribution channels provide another set of conditions of great importance for the policies and practices of a firm. The accurate specification and measurement of these and other market conditions with respect to an individual firm admittedly presents great, but not insuperable, difficulties. Properly used the available data should permit of an illuminating grouping of firms into classes exhibiting roughly the same type of market conditions. Under similar market conditions may not firms be expected to pursue similar policies and practices? A careful study of the empirically determinable differences in market structure may go far in explaining observable differences in policy and practice.

It may be objected that most of what are here called market conditions are already taken into account in traditional value and price analysis in much neater fashion. That is, at least in part, true in the sense that traditional analysis purports to focus the results of many policy-determining considerations in the form of demand and cost curves which are, for different time periods and under certain qualifications, single-valued functions of output. We can admit that if cost and demand curves for short, long, and intermediate periods were discoverable, rather than assumed, a large part of what is called business policy could be explained without resorting to so crude a device as a classification of market structures. It is, however, precisely because theoretical techniques of price analysis have been constructed without regard to their empirical applicability that such a classification is necessary as a first and primarily important step towards an understanding of business policies and practices.

Enough has been said to suggest that the size of firms is only one among many factors influencing price and production policies. It requires no more than a cursory examination to perceive that large firms confronted with different market situations pursue different policies and practices. In the automobile industry the existence of large firms and a relatively small number of sellers was not incompatible with steadily falling prices which pushed the use of the product into lower and lower income classes until well into the 1920's. When large returns from price reductions seemed no longer possible, automobile manufacturers turned their attention to accelerating the replacement demand for new cars by yearly changes in the design and structure of their product. By and large it probably continues to be true that a strong tradition exists in the industry to the effect that a substantial price reduction or an improvement of the product should be made in each year's model. The shift in emphasis from price to product competition may well have been the result rather of a change in the economic age of the industry than a change in the size or number of sellers. Although the price and production policies of the automobile industry are frequently contrasted with policies in the steel industry, may we not expect the former to approximate the latter as demand for motor cars becomes almost entirely a replacement demand and as product improvement takes increasingly the form of mere design or gadget changes? The economic age of an industry exerts an important influence on the policies and practices of firms in the industry. There is a widespread conviction among businessmen that aggressive price competition is an effective policy only during the period of an expanding market and that with a relatively stable or declining demand some type of controlled competition is in the interests of all sellers in the market. Controlled price competition is not a policy limited to large firms or markets in which sellers are few though, of course, numbers may be so large as to make effective control difficult.

In the steel industry price and production policies differ markedly as between products undergoing substantially the same fabricating process and sold by substantially the same firms. A striking example of a divergence in price policies over the cycle is suggested by the behavior of the prices of automobile body steel as compared with the prices of galvanized steel sheets in the period between 1929 and 1937. Both of these products are made in the same kind of mill and the technological process is very similar. One, however, is sold to a few large buyers and the other to many small buyers. Automobile sheet prices declined more sharply from the beginning of the depression and at the bottom were 38.5 per cent below the 1929 level while galvanized sheet prices were only 28.7 per cent below 1929. On the rise since 1933, the price of automobile body steel went up more slowly than that of galvanized steel sheets. During 1937, the price of the latter exceeded its 1929 level by 6.2 per cent while the price of the former was still 12.8 per cent under its 1929 level.

In the rubber tire market four large firms sell around 75 per cent of the total volume and there are in the whole industry no more than twenty-eight firms. Yet price and production policies would seem to be quite different than in other markets, e.g., cigarettes, in which firms are large and the number of sellers are few. Consideration of the structure of the tire market appears to indicate that the character of distribution channels exerts a decisive influence on price policies. In the market for tires as equipment on new cars the sellers are confronted with buyers each large enough to undertake tire production himself if dissatisfied with the price. In the replacement market a number of different distributive channels induces a discount structure which facilitates price cutting on the slightest provocation. While the personality of Firestone, plus the fact that his firm is admittedly a low-cost producer, has no doubt been an important factor, it seems probable that if Firestone, like God in another context, had not existed the structure of the tire market would have created him.

Another type of market in which the large firm has typically followed a policy of aggressive price competition is to be found in the field of distribution. Here the price we are concerned with is the spread between manufacturers' and retail prices. Forty or fifty years ago by all accounts the distribution patterns for most consumers goods sold at retail was highly standardized, with full-function wholesalers and retailers operating under a relatively inflexible markup system. The growth of chain stores and other types of mass distributors has probably contributed not only toward a lowering of the manufacturer-retail margin but toward making it more flexible over the cycle. This influence is likely to continue—unless checked by recent and prospective legislation—as long as mass distributors can acquire by aggressive price tactics an increased share of the available sales.

These examples seem to indicate that the price policies of large firms are apt to be influenced by the stage of economic development of the industry in which they operate, by the size of buying units, the character of distribution channels, and the possibility of obtaining an increased share of total sales of a group of products. There are, of course, many other elements of market structure which affect business policies and practices. In consequence it seems doubtful whether any useful generalizations can be made regarding the price and production policies of large-scale enterprise without further specification as to the market situations which confront such firms.

It may possibly be true that a rough inverse correlation might be demonstrated between concentration as measured by percentage of volume of output of a product produced by a given small number of firms and, for example, some measure of amplitude of wholesale price change over a business cycle. Would such a correlation, if demonstrated, reveal an important fact regarding short-run price policy of large-scale enterprise? I think not. In the first place such a correlation would be heavily biased by agricultural products all of which exhibit low concentration and high amplitude of price change. Everyone admits that the structure of agricultural products markets is at once atomistically competitive and incapable of realization in industry. The principal problem we are concerned with is whether within the range of fabricated products there is a marked relation between size of firms and the type of price policy which is followed. In the second place the available price data for fabricated products is inadequate for such a comparison for two reasons. For many products there is a marked discrepancy between B.L.S. prices and average net realization per unit of sale reported in other sources,[14] a discrepancy

[14] Bureau of Mines and Bureau of Census figures. In part this discrepancy and the changes in discrepancy are the result of nonreported price cuts, in part of changes in the complex structure of a commodity price which are not adequately

which varies considerably over the cycle. Furthermore, it is probably true to say that, in general, the more highly fabricated the product the less important is price as a comprehensive indicator of the terms of purchase and sale. That is to say, a study of price behavior would have to be supplemented by an examination of changes in product and selling terms.

As another example of the difficulty of establishing a relationship between size of firms and price policy through an examination of price behavior, consider the recent history of construction materials prices. Thirty-five B.L.S. prices of construction materials were higher in January, 1938, than in 1929 or 1926; twenty-one prices, on the other hand, were lower at this date than the wholesale price index. An examination of these prices fails to indicate any well-marked influence of size of firm. Among the high-priced products were structural steel, wire nails, cast iron pipe, and terne plate, all produced in industries in which a small number of firms produce a large percentage of output. On the other hand the high-priced products included cypress lumber, shingles, yellow pine and maple flooring, and common building brick produced in industries in which the typical firm is small. Among the low-priced products were wallboard, glass, sewer pipe, and a number of porcelain products fabricated by large firms in industries with high concentration, and, on the other hand, a number of products typically produced by small concerns. It is difficult in this instance to discover any pattern of price behavior which would throw light on the relationship between size of firm and price policy.

The relative size of a selling unit, to recapitulate, is one element—doubtless a very important one—in the structure of a firm's market. As such it exerts an influence on the policies and practices of the firm. But firms of given size, relative to the extent of their markets, will follow very different price and production policies in different market situations. Differences in the character of price response to given changes in the cost or demand conditions facing a firm or group of firms are to be attributed both to differences in the internal organization of the firm and to differences in the structure of the market in which the firm, or group, is placed. An analysis of the relation between organizational and market differences and the character of price response is the central problem of price analysis. The relation of size to price policy is merely one part of the problem which, taken out of its setting, is not very amenable to fruitful discussion.

VI

In conclusion a few remarks may be offered on the relation of price analysis to public policy. A consideration of the consequences of dif-

represented in the reported price; e.g., the B.L.S. price for men's shirts is the relatively stable price of a high-grade trade-marked product. The sale of this shirt fell off markedly during the depression in favor of lower-priced and frequently unbranded shirts.

ferent types of price response to changes in costs and demand for the functioning of the economy is the prerequisite to effective public action in the price area. These consequences can be usefully divided into two groups:

1. The effect of differences in price responses on the distribution of economic resources among different uses. This is the traditional monopoly problem. A monopoly position is supposed to lead to restriction of output and of investment in the monopolized area below that which is desirable and attainable with a greater degree of competition. A whole range of problems, therefore, centers around the effect of price policies and price relationships on the distribution of economic resources as between various uses.

2. The effect of differences in price response on continuity in the use of resources already invested or available in different uses. This is primarily a business cycle problem. It is frequently maintained that certain types of price response to changes in costs and demand conditions are more favorable to continuous employment than others. The second group of problems, therefore, turns around the effects of different types of price policy and behavior on the continuity of employment of economic resources.

The argument, for both groups of problems, runs from differences in market structure to differences in price response, and from differences in price response to the consequences of these differences for the functioning of the economy. Proposals for public action, therefore, must consider, first, what types of price behavior and price policy are most conducive to an effective use of resources, and, second, within what limits appropriate public action is likely to be able to influence price behavior.

Although a good deal has been written both on the effect of restrictive policies on the distribution of resources and on the effect of price policies on fluctuations in employment and output, very little has been done to formulate tests of undesirable price behavior applicable to public action. Specifically, what sort of tests are indicative of the existence of a price sufficiently high to restrict output and investment below desirable levels? What types of price behavior in industrial markets would be likely over the cycle to promote a fuller use of economic resources?

Without attempting to answer these questions attention may be called to three issues of immediate importance in the price field facing economists interested in public policy.

First, is it desirable that during periods of business upturn and downturn prices respond readily (in ways that can be roughly specified) to changes in costs, sales, or other variables of determinable magnitudes? If not for all commodities, for what groups of commodities should prices be flexible?

Second, should certain types of price behavior, the use of price formulae, or particular price policies be accepted as prima facie evidence of violation of the antitrust acts?

Third, is price competition ever sufficiently ruinous to justify public action? What are the tests of ruinous competition and what type of public action is appropriate?

Insofar as the price and production policies of large-scale enterprise provide a proper field for public action, these are critical questions.

IV. INDUSTRIAL ORGANIZATION AND ECONOMIC THEORY

11

Uncertainty, Evolution, and Economic Theory*

By ARMEN A. ALCHIAN†

A modification of economic analysis to incorporate incomplete information and uncertain foresight as axioms is suggested here. This approach dispenses with "profit maximization"; and it does not rely on the predictable, individual behavior that is usually assumed, as a first approximation, in standard textbook treatments. Despite these changes, the analytical concepts usually associated with such behavior are retained because they are not dependent upon such motivation or foresight. The suggested approach embodies the principles of biological evolution and natural selection by interpreting the economic system as an adoptive mechanism which chooses among exploratory actions generated by the adaptive pursuit of "success" or "profits." The resulting analysis is applicable to actions usually regarded as aberrations from standard economic behavior as well as to behavior covered by the customary analysis. This wider applicability and the removal of the unrealistic postulates of accurate anticipations and fixed states of knowledge have provided motivation for the study.

The exposition is ordered as follows: First, to clear the ground, a brief statement is given of a generally ignored aspect of "profit maximization," that is, where foresight is uncertain, "profit maximization" is *meaningless* as a guide to specifiable action. The constructive development then begins with an introduction of the element of environmental adoption by the economic system of a posteriori most appropriate action according to the criterion of "realized positive profits." This is illustrated in an extreme, random-behavior model without any individual rationality, foresight, or motivation whatsoever. Even in this extreme type of model, it is shown that the economist can predict and explain events with a modified use of his conventional analytical tools.

* *The Journal of Political Economy*, Vol. LVIII (1950), pp. 211–21. Reprinted by courtesy of the University of Chicago Press and the author.

The author is indebted to Dr. Stephen Enke for criticism and stimulation leading to improvements in both content and exposition.

† University of California at Los Angeles.

This phenomenon—environmental adoption—is then fused with a type of individual motivated behavior based on the pervasiveness of uncertainty and incomplete information. Adaptive, imitative, and trial-and-error behavior in the pursuit of "positive profits" is utilized rather than its sharp contrast, the pursuit of "maximized profits." A final section discusses some implications and conjectures.

I. "PROFIT MAXIMIZATION" NOT A GUIDE TO ACTION

Current economic analysis of economic behavior relies heavily on decisions made by rational units customarily assumed to be seeking perfectly optimal situations.[1] Two criteria are well known—profit maximization and utility maximization.[2] According to these criteria, appropriate types of action are indicated by marginal or neighborhood inequalities which, if satisfied, yield an optimum. But the standard qualification usually added is that nobody is able really to optimize his situation according to these diagrams and concepts because of uncertainty about the position and, sometimes, even the slopes of the demand and supply functions. Nevertheless, the economist interprets and predicts the decisions of individuals in terms of these diagrams, since it is alleged that individuals use these concepts implicitly, if not explicitly.

Attacks on this methodology are widespread, but only one attack has been really damaging, that of G. Tintner.[3] He denies that profit maximization even makes any sense where there is uncertainty. Uncertainty arises from at least two sources: imperfect foresight and human inability to solve complex problems containing a host of variables even when an optimum is definable. Tintner's proof is simple. Under uncertainty, by definition, each action that may be chosen is identified with a *distribution* of potential outcomes, not with a unique outcome. Implicit in uncertainty is the consequence that these distributions of potential outcomes are overlapping.[4] It is worth emphasis that each possible action has a *distribution* of potential outcomes, only one of which will materialize if the action is taken, and that one outcome cannot be foreseen. Essentially, the task is converted into making a decision (selecting an action) whose potential outcome *distribution* is preferable, that is, choosing the action

[1] See, e.g., J. Robinson, *Economics of Imperfect Competition* (London: Macmillan), p. 6, for a strong statement of the necessity of such optimal behavior. Standard textbooks expound essentially the same idea. See also P. Samuelson, *Foundations of Economic Analysis* (Cambridge: Harvard University Press, 1946).

[2] In the following we shall discuss only profit maximization, although everything said is applicable equally to utility maximization by consumers.

[3] "The Theory of Choice under Subjective Risk and Uncertainty," *Econometrica*, Vol. IX (1941), pp. 298–304; "The Pure Theory of Production under Technological Risk and Uncertainty," *ibid.*, pp. 305–11; and "A Contribution to the Nonstatic Theory of Production," *Studies in Mathematical Economics and Econometrics* (Chicago: University of Chicago Press, 1942), pp. 92–109.

[4] Thus uncertainty is defined here to be the phenomenon that produces overlapping distributions of potential outcomes.

with the *optimum distribution*, since there is no such thing as a *maximizing* distribution.

For example, let each of two possible choices be characterized by its subjective distribution of potential outcomes. Suppose one has the higher "mean" but a larger spread, so that it might result in larger profits or losses, and the other has a smaller "mean" and a smaller spread. Which one is the maximum? This is a nonsensical question; but to ask for the optimum distribution is not nonsense. In the presence of uncertainty—a necessary condition for the existence of profits—there is no meaningful criterion for selecting the decision that will "maximize profits." The maximum-profit criterion is not meaningful as a basis *for selecting* the action which will, in fact, result in an outcome with higher profits than any other action would have, unless one assumes nonoverlapping potential outcome distributions. It must be noticed that the meaningfulness of "maximum profits—a realized outcome which is the largest that could have been realized from the available actions"—is perfectly consistent with the meaninglessness of "profit maximization"—a criterion for selecting among alternatives lines of action, the potential outcomes of which are describable only as distributions and not as unique amounts.

This crucial difficulty would be avoided by using a preference function as a criterion for selecting most preferred distributions of potential outcomes, but the search for a criterion of rationality and choice in terms of preference functions still continues. For example, the use of the mean, or expectation, completely begs the question of uncertainty by disregarding the variance of the distribution, while a "certainty equivalent" assumes the answer. The only way to make "profit maximization" a specifically meaningful action is to postulate a model containing certainty. Then the question of the predictive and explanatory reliability of the model must be faced.[5]

II. SUCCESS IS BASED ON RESULTS, NOT MOTIVATION

There is an alternative method which treats the decisions and criteria dictated by the economic *system* as more important than those made by the individuals in it. By backing away from the trees—the optimization calculus by individual units—we can better discern the forest of impersonal market forces.[6] This approach directs attention to the interrelationships of the environment and the prevailing types of economic behavior which appear through a process of economic natural selection. Yet it

[5] Analytical models in all sciences postulate models abstracting from some realities in the belief that derived predictions will still be relevant. Simplifications are necessary, but continued attempts should be made to introduce more realistic assumptions into a workable model with an increase in generality and detail (see M. Friedman and L. Savage, "The Utility Analysis of Choices Involving Risks," *Journal of Political Economy*, Vol. LVI, No. 4 [1948], p. 279).

[6] In effect, we shall be reverting to a Marshallian type of analysis combined with the essentials of Darwinian evolutionary natural selection.

does not imply that individual foresight and action do not affect the nature of the existing state of affairs.

In an economic system the realization of profits is the criterion according to which successful and surviving firms are selected. This decision criterion is applied primarily by an impersonal market system in the United States and may be completely independent of the decision processes of individual units, of the variety of inconsistent motives and abilities, and even of the individual's awareness of the criterion. The reason is simple. Realized positive profits, not *maximum* profits, are the mark of success and viability. It does not matter through what process of reasoning or motivation such success was achieved. The fact of its accomplishment is sufficient. This is the criterion by which the economic system selects survivors: those who realize *positive profits* are the survivors; those who suffer losses disappear.

The pertinent requirement—positive profits through relative efficiency—is weaker than "maximized profits," with which, unfortunately, it has been confused. Positive profits accrue to those who are better than their actual competitors, even if the participants are ignorant, intelligent, skilful, etc. The crucial element is one's aggregate position relative to actual competitors, not some hypothetically perfect competitors. As in a race, the award goes to the relatively fastest, even if all the competitors loaf. Even in a world of stupid men there would still be profits. Also, the greater the uncertainties of the world, the greater is the possibility that profits would go to venturesome and lucky rather than to logical, careful, fact-gathering individuals.

The preceding interpretation suggests two ideas. First, success (survival) accompanies relative superiority; and, second, it does not require proper motivation but may rather be the result of fortuitous circumstances. Among all competitors, those whose particular conditions happen to be the most appropriate of those offered to the economic system for testing and adoption will be "selected" as survivors. Just how such an approach can be used and how individuals happen to offer these appropriate forms for testing are problems to which we now turn.[7]

III. CHANCE OR LUCK IS ONE METHOD OF ACHIEVING SUCCESS

Sheer chance is a substantial element in determining the situation selected and also in determining its appropriateness or viability. A second element is the ability to adapt one's self by various methods to an appropriate situation. In order to indicate clearly the respective roles of

[7] Also suggested is another way to divide the general problem discussed here. The process and rationale by which a unit chooses its actions so as to optimize its situation is one part of the problem. The other is the relationship between changes in the environment and the consequent observable results, i.e., the decision process of the economic *society*. The classification used in the text is closely related to this but differs in emphasizing the degree of knowledge and foresight.

luck and conscious adapting, the adaptive calculus will, for the moment, be completely removed. All individual rationality, motivation, and foresight will be temporarily abandoned in order to concentrate upon the ability of the environment to *adopt* "appropriate" survivors even in the absence of any adaptive behavior. This is an apparently unrealistic, but nevertheless very useful, expository approach in establishing the attenuation between the *ex post* survival criterion and the role of the individual's adaptive decision criterion. It also aids in assessing the role of luck and chance in the operation of our economic system.

Consider, first, the simplest type of biological evolution. Plants "grow" to the sunny side of buildings not because they "want to" in awareness of the fact that optimum or better conditions prevail there but rather because the leaves that happen to have more sunlight grow faster and their feeding systems become stronger. Similarly, animals with configurations and habits more appropriate for survival under prevailing conditions have an enhanced viability and will with higher probability be typical survivors. Less appropriately acting organisms of the same general class having lower probabilities of survival will find survival difficult. More common types, the survivors, may appear to be those having *adapted* themselves to the environment, whereas the truth may well be that the environment has *adopted* them. There may have been no motivated individual adapting but, instead, only environmental adopting.

A useful, but unreal, example in which individuals act without any foresight indicates the type of analysis available to the economist and also the ability of the system to "direct" resources despite individual ignorance. Assume that thousands of travelers set out from Chicago, selecting their roads completely at random and without foresight. Only our "economist" knows that on but one road are there any gasoline stations. He can state categorically that travelers will *continue* to travel only on that road; those on other roads will soon run out of gas. Even though each one selected his route at random, we might have called those travelers who were so fortunate as to have picked the right road wise, efficient, foresighted, etc. Of course, we would consider them the lucky ones. If gasoline supplies were now moved to a new road, some formerly luckless travelers again would be able to move; and a new pattern of travel would be observed, although none of the travelers had changed his particular path. The really possible paths have changed with the changing environment. All that is needed is a set of varied, risk-taking (adoptable) travelers. The correct direction of travel will be established. As circumstances (economic environment) change, the analyst (economist) can select the types of participants (firms) that will now become successful; he may also be able to diagnose the conditions most conducive to a greater probability of survival.[8]

[8] The undiscerning person who sees survivors corresponding to changes in environment claims to have evidence for the "Lysenko" doctrine. In truth, all he

IV. CHANCE DOES NOT IMPLY NONDIRECTED, RANDOM ALLOCATION OF RESOURCES

These two examples do not constitute an attempt to base all analysis on adoptive models dominated by chance. But they do indicate that collective and individual random behavior does not per se imply a nihilistic theory incapable of yielding reliable predictions and explanations; nor does it imply a world lacking in order and apparent direction. It might, however, be argued that the facts of life deny even a substantial role to the element of chance and the associated adoption principle in the economic system. For example, the long lives and disparate sizes of business firms and hereditary fortunes may seem to be reliable evidence of consistent foresighted motivation and nonrandom behavior. In order to demonstrate that consistent success cannot be treated as prima facie evidence against pure luck, the following chance model of Borél, the famous French mathematician, is presented.

Suppose two million Parisians were paired off and set to tossing coins in a game of matching. Each pair plays until the winner on the first toss is again brought to equality with the other player. Assuming one toss per second for each eight-hour day, at the end of ten years there would still be, on the average, about a hundred-odd pairs; and if the players assign the game to their heirs, a dozen or so will still be playing at the end of a thousand years! The implications are obvious. Suppose that some business had been operating for one hundred years. Should one rule out luck and chance as the essence of the factors producing the long-term survival of the enterprise? No inference whatever can be drawn until the number of original participants is known; and even then one must know the size, risk, and frequency of each commitment. One can see from the Borél illustration the danger in concluding that there are too many firms with long lives in the real world to admit an important role to chance. On the contrary, one might insist that there are actually too few!

The chance postulate was directed to two problems. On the one hand, there is the actual way in which a substantial fraction of economic behavior and activity is effected. On the other, there is the method of analysis which economists may use in their predictions and diagnoses. Before modifying the extreme chance model by adding adaptive behavior, some connotations and implications of the incorporation of chance elements will be elaborated in order to reveal the richness which is really inherent in chance. First, even if each and every individual acted in a haphazard and nonmotivated manner, it is possible that the variety of actions would be so great that the resulting collective set would contain actions that are best, in the sense of perfect foresight.

may have is evidence for the doctrine that the environment, by competitive conditions, selects the most viable of the various phenotypic characteristics for perpetuation. Economists should beware of economic "Lysenkoism."

For example, at a horse race with enough bettors wagering strictly at random, someone will win on all eight races. Thus individual random behavior does not eliminate the likelihood of observing "appropriate" decisions.[9]

Second, and conversely, individual behavior according to some foresight and motivation does not necessarily imply a collective pattern of behavior that is different from the collective variety of actions associated with a random selection of actions. Where there is uncertainty, people's judgments and opinions, even when based on the best available evidence, will differ; no one of them may be making his choice by tossing coins; yet the aggregate *set* of actions of the entire group of participants may be indistinguishable from a set of individual actions, each selected at random.[10]

Third, and fortunately, a chance-dominated model does not mean that an economist cannot predict or explain or diagnose. With a knowledge of the economy's realized requisites for survival and by a comparison of alternative conditions, he can state what types of firms or behavior relative to other possible types will be more viable, even though the firms themselves may not know the conditions or even try to achieve them by readjusting to the changed situation if they do know the conditions. It is sufficient if all firms are slightly different so that in the new environmental situation those who have their fixed internal conditions closer to the new, but unknown, optimum position now have a greater probability of survival and growth. They will grow relative to other firms and become the prevailing type, since survival conditions may push the observed characteristics of the set of survivors toward the unknowable optimum by either (1) repeated trials or (2) survival of more of those who happened to be near the optimum—determined ex post. If these new conditions last "very long," the dominant firms will be different ones from those which prevailed or would have prevailed under other conditions. Even if environmental conditions cannot be forecast, the economist can compare for given alternative potential situations the types of behavior that would have higher probability of viability or adoption. If explanation of past results rather than prediction is the task, the economist can diagnose the particular attributes which were critical in facilitating survival, even though individual participants were not aware of them.[11]

---

[9] The Borél gamblers analogue is pertinent to a host of everyday situations.

[10] Of course, the economic units may be going through a period of soul searching, management training, and research activity. We cannot yet identify mental and physical activity with a process that results in sufficient information and foresight to yield uniquely determinate choices. To do so would be to beg the whole question.

[11] It is not even necessary to suppose that each firm acts as if it possessed the conventional diagrams and knew the analytical principles employed by economists in deriving optimum and equilibrium conditions. The atoms and electrons do not

Fourth, the bases of prediction have been indicated in the preceding paragraph, but its character should be made explicit. The prediction will not assert that every—or, indeed, any—firm necessarily changes its characteristics. It asserts, instead, that the characteristics of the new *set* of firms, or possibly a set of new firms, will change. This may be characterized by the "respresentative firm," a purely statistical concept—a vector of "averages," one dimension for each of the several qualities of the population of firms. A "representative firm" is not typical of any one producer but, instead, is a set of statistics summarizing the various "modal" characteristics of the population. Surely, this was an intended use of Marshall's "representative firm."

Fifth, a final implication drawn from consideration of this extreme approach is that empirical investigations via questionnaire methods, so far used, are incapable of evaluating the validity of marginal productivity analysis. This is true because productivity and demand analyses are essential in evaluating relative viability, even though uncertainty eliminates "profit maximization" and even if price and technological changes were to have no consciously redirecting effect on the firms. To illustrate, suppose that, in attempting to predict the effects of higher real wage rates, it is discovered that every businessman says he does not adjust his labor force. Nevertheless, firms with a lower labor-capital ratio will have relatively lower cost positions and, to that extent, a higher probability of survival. The force of competitive survival, by eliminating higher-cost firms, reveals a population of remaining firms with a new average labor-capital ratio. The essential point is that individual motivation and foresight, while sufficient, are not necessary. Of course, it is not argued here that therefore it is absent. All that is needed by economists is their own awareness of the survival conditions and criteria of the economic system and a group of participants who submit various combinations and organizations for the system's selection and adoption. Both these conditions are satisfied.[12]

As a consequence, only the method of use, rather than the usefulness, of economic tools and concepts is affected by the approach suggested here; in fact, they are made more powerful if they are not pretentiously assumed to be necessarily associated with, and dependent upon, individual foresight and adjustment. They are tools for, at least, the diagnosis of the operation of an economic system, even if not also for the internal business behavior of each firm.

---

know the laws of nature; the physicist does not impart to each atom a wilful scheme of action based on laws of conservation of energy, etc. The fact that an economist deals with human beings who have sense and ambitions does not *automatically* warrant imparting to these humans the great degree of foresight and motivations which the economist may require for his customary analysis as an outside observer or "oracle." The similarity between this argument and Gibbsian statistical mechanics, as well as biological evolution, is *not* mere coincidence.

[12] This approach reveals how the "facts" of Lester's dispute with Machlup can be handled with standard economic tools.

V. INDIVIDUAL ADAPTING VIA IMITATION AND TRIAL AND ERROR

Let it again be noted that the preceding extreme model was designed to present in purest form only one element of the suggested approach. It is not argued that there is no purposive, foresighted behavior present in reality. In adding this realistic element—adaptation by individuals with some foresight and purposive motivation—we are expanding the preceding extreme model. We are not abandoning any part of it or futilely trying to merge it with the opposite extreme of perfect foresight and "profit maximization."

Varying and conflicting objectives motivate economic activity, yet we shall here direct attention to only one particular objective—the sufficient condition of realized positive profits. There are no implications of "profit maximization," and this difference is important. Although the latter is a far more extreme objective when definable, only the former is the *sine qua non* of survival and success. To argue that, with perfect competition, the two would come to the same thing is to conceal an important difference by means of a very implausible assumption. The pursuit of profits, and not some hypothetical undefinable perfect situation, is the relevant objective whose *fulfilment* is rewarded with survival. Unfortunately, even this proximate objective is too high. Neither perfect knowledge of the past nor complete awareness of the current state of the arts gives sufficient foresight to indicate profitable action. Even for this more restricted objective, the pervasive effects of uncertainty prevent the ascertainment of actions which are supposed to be optimal in achieving profits. Now the consequence of this is that modes of behavior replace optimum equilibrium conditions as guiding rules of action. Therefore, in the following sections two forms of conscious adaptive behavior are emphasized.

First, wherever successful enterprises are observed, the elements common to these observable successes will be associated with success and copied by others in their pursuit of profits or success. "Nothing succeeds like success." Thus the urge for "rough-and-ready" imitative rules of behavior is accounted for. What would otherwise appear to be merely customary "orthodox," nonrational rules of behavior turns out to be codified imitations of observed success, e.g., "conventional" markup, price "followship," "orthodox" accounting and operating ratios, "proper" advertising policy, etc. A conventionally employed type of behavior pattern is consistent with the postulates of the analysis employed, even though the reasons and justifications for the particular conventions are not.[13]

[13] These constructed rules of behavior should be distinguished from "rules" which, in effect, do no more than define the objective being sought. Confusion between objectives which motivate one and rules of behavior are commonplace. For example, "full-cost pricing" is a "rule" that one cannot really follow. He can

Many factors cause this motive to imitate patterns of action observable in past successes. Among these are: (1) the absence of an identifiable criterion for decision making, (2) the variability of the environment, (3) the multiplicity of factors that call for attention and choice, (4) the uncertainty attaching to all these factors and outcomes, (5) the awareness that superiority relative to one's competitors is crucial, and (6) the nonavailability of a trial-and-error process converging to an optimum position.

In addition, imitation affords relief from the necessity of really making decisions and conscious innovations, which, if wrong, become "inexcusable." Unfortunately, failure or success often reflects the willingness to depart from rules when conditions have changed; what counts, then, is not only imitative behavior but the willingness to abandon it at the "right" time and circumstances. Those who are different and successful "become" innovators, while those who fail "become" reckless violators of tried-and-true rules. Although one may deny the absolute appropriateness of such rules, one cannot doubt the existence of a strong urge to create conventions and rules (based on observed success) and a willingness to use them for action as well as for rationalizations of inaction. If another untried host of actions might have been even more successful, so much the worse for the participants who failed, and even for those who missed "perfect success."

Even innovation is accounted for by imitation. While there certainly are those who consciously innovate, there are those who, in their imperfect attempts to imitate others, unconsciously innovate by unwittingly acquiring some unexpected or unsought unique attributes which under the prevailing circumstances prove partly responsible for the success. Others, in turn, will attempt to copy the uniqueness, and the imitation-innovation process continues. Innovation is assured, and the notable aspects of it here are the possibility of unconscious pioneering and leadership.

The second type of conscious adaptive behavior, in addition to imitation, is "trial and error." This has been used with "profit maximization," wherein, by trial and ensuing success or failure, more appropriate actions are selected in a process presumed to converge to a limit of "profit maximization" equilibrium. Unfortunately, at least two conditions are necessary for convergence via a trial-and-error process, even if one admits an equilibrium situation as an admissible limit. First, a trial must be classifiable as a success or failure. The position achieved must be comparable with results of other potential actions. In a static environment, if one improves his position relative to his former position, then the action taken

---

try to, but whether he succeeds or fails in his objective of survival is not controllable by following the "rule of full-cost pricing." If he fails in his objective, he must, of necessity, fail to have followed the "rule." The situation is parallel to trying to control the speed of a car by simply setting by hand the indicator on the speedometer.

is better than the former one, and presumably one could continue by small increments to advance to a local optimum. An analogy is pertinent. A nearsighted grasshopper on a mound of rocks can crawl to the top of a particular rock. But there is no assurance that he can also get to the top of the mound, for he might have to descend for a while or hop to new rocks. The second condition, then, for the convergence via trial and error is the continual rising toward some *optimum optimorum* without intervening descents. Whether decisions and actions in economic life satisfy these two conditions cannot be proved or disproved here, but the available evidence seems overwhelmingly unfavorable.

The above convergence conditions do not apply to a changing environment, for there can be no observable comparison of the result of an action with any other. Comparability of resulting situations is destroyed by the changing environment. As a consequence, the measure of goodness of actions in anything except a tolerable-intolerable sense is lost, and the possibility of an individual's converging to the optimum activity via a trial-and-error process disappears. Trial and error becomes survival or death. It cannot serve as a basis of the *individual's* method of convergence to a "maximum" or optimum position. Success is discovered by the economic system through a blanketing shotgun process, not by the individual through a converging search.

In general, uncertainty provides an excellent reason for imitation of observed success. Likewise, it accounts for observed uniformity among the survivors, derived from an evolutionary, adopting, competitive system employing a criterion of survival, which can operate independently of individual motivations. Adapting behavior via imitation and venturesome innovation enlarges the model. Imperfect imitators provide opportunity for innovation, and the survival criterion of the economy determines the successful, possibly because imperfect, imitators. Innovation is provided also by conscious wilful action, whatever the ultimate motivation may be, since drastic action is motivated by the hope of great success as well as by the desire to avoid impending failure.

All the preceding arguments leave the individual economic participant with imitative, venturesome, innovative, trial-and-error adaptive behavior. Most conventional economic tools and concepts are still useful, although in a vastly different analytical framework—one which is closely akin to the theory of biological evolution. The economic counterparts of genetic heredity, mutations, and natural selection are imitation, innovation, and positive profits.

VI. CONCLUSIONS AND SUMMARY

I shall conclude with a brief reference to some implications and conjectures.

Observable patterns of behavior and organization are predictable in terms of their relative probabilities of success or viability *if* they are tried. The observed prevalence of a type of behavior depends upon both this probability of viability and the probability of the different types being submitted to the economic system for testing and selecting. One is the probability of appearance of a certain type of organization (mutation), and the other is the probability of its survival or viability, once it appears (natural selection). There is much evidence for believing that these two probabilities are interrelated. But is there reason to suppose that a high probability of viability implies a high probability of an action's being taken, as would be implied in a system of analysis involving some "inner directed urge toward perfection"? If these two probabilities are not highly correlated, what predictions of types of action can the economist make? An answer has been suggested in this paper.

While it is true that the economist can define a profit maximization behavior by assuming *specific* cost and revenue conditions, is there any assurance that the conditions and conclusions so derivable are not too perfect and absolute? If profit maximization (certainty) is not ascertainable, the confidence about the predicted effects of changes, e.g., higher taxes or minimum wages, will be dependent upon how close the formerly existing arrangement was to the formerly "optimal" (certainty) situation. What really counts is the various actions actually tried, for it is from these that "success" is selected, not from some set of perfect actions. The economist may be pushing his luck too far in arguing that actions in response to changes in environment and changes in satisfaction with the existing state of affairs will converge as a result of adaptation or adoption toward the optimum action that should have been selected, if foresight had been perfect.[14]

In summary, I have asserted that the economist, using the present analytical tools developed in the analysis of the firm under certainty, can predict the more adoptable or viable types of economic interrelationships that will be induced by environmental change even if individuals themselves are unable to ascertain them. That is, although individual participants may not know their cost and revenue situations, the economist can predict the consequences of higher wage rates, taxes, govern-

---

[14] An anomalous aspect of the assumption of perfect foresight is that it nearly results in tautological and empty statements. One cannot know everything, and this is recognized by the addendum that one acts within a "given state and distribution of the arts." But this is perilously close, if not equivalent, to saying either that action is taken only where the outcome is accurately foreseen or that information is always limited. The qualification is inserted because one might contend that it is the "*constancy* of the state and distribution of arts" that is necessary as a *ceteris paribus*. But even the latter is no solution. A large fraction of behavior in a world of incomplete information and uncertainty is necessarily directed at increasing the state of arts and venturing into an unknown sphere. While it is probably permissible to start with a prescribed "distribution of the knowledge of the arts," holding it constant is too restrictive, since a large class of important and frequent actions necessarily involves changes in the state and distribution of knowledge. The modification suggested here incorporates this search for more knowledge as an essential foundation.

ment policy, etc. Like the biologist, the economist predicts the effects of environmental changes on the surviving class of living organisms; the economist need not assume that each participant is aware of, or acts according to, his cost and demand situation. These are concepts for the economist's use and not necessarily for the individual participant's, who may have other analytic or customary devices which, while of interest to the economist, serve as data and not as analytic methods.

An alternative to the rationale of individual profit maximization has been presented without exorcising uncertainty. Lest isolated arguments be misinterpreted, let it be clearly stated that this paper does not argue that purposive objective-seeking behavior is absent from reality, nor, on the other hand, does it indorse the familiar thesis that action of economic units cannot be expressed within the marginal analysis. Rather, the contention is that the precise role and nature of purposive behavior in the presence of uncertainty and incomplete information have not been clearly understood or analyzed.

It is straightforward, if not heuristic, to start with complete uncertainty and nonmotivation and then to add elements of foresight and motivation in the process of building an analytical model. The opposite approach, which starts with certainty and unique motivation, must abandon its basic principles as soon as uncertainty and mixed motivations are recognized.[15] The approach suggested here is intellectually more modest and realistic, without sacrificing generality. It does not regard uncertainty as an aberrational exogenous disturbance, as does the usual approach from the opposite extreme of accurate foresight. The existence of uncertainty and incomplete information is the foundation of the suggested type of analysis; the importance of the concept of a class of "chance" decisions rests upon it; it permits of various conflicting objectives; it motivates and rationalizes a type of adaptive imitative behavior; yet it does not destroy the basis of prediction, explanation, or diagnosis. It does not base its aggregate description on individual optimal action; yet it is capable of incorporating such activity where justified. The formalization of this approach awaits the marriage of the theory of stochastic processes and economics—two fields of thought admirably suited for union. It is conjectured that the suggested modification is applicable to a wide class of events and is worth attempts at empirical verification.[16]

[15] If one prefers, he may believe that the suggestions here contain reasons why the model based on certainty may predict outcomes, although individuals really cannot try to maximize profits. But the dangers of this have been indicated.

[16] Preliminary study in this direction has been very convincing, and, in addition, the suggested approach appears to contain important implications relative to general economic policy; but discussions of these are reserved for a later date.

12

A Note on Pricing in Monopoly and Oligopoly*

By JOE S. BAIN †

The conventional versions of *a priori price* analysis apparently suggest that a single-firm monopoly or a collusive oligopoly will choose a price-output combination such as to maximize *the industry profit.* Product differentiation and selling cost being neglected, the currently established firm or firms are supposed to equate their marginal costs to the marginal revenue drawn from the industry demand curve for the commodity which they produce in common. This balance should presumably be struck over any long period between long-run marginal cost and the marginal revenue from the long-run industry demand, and in any short period between short-run marginal cost and the marginal revenue from the short-run industry demand. Price in either period should be set to maximize the difference between the aggregate revenue from the sale of the given commodity and the aggregate cost of its production by any established group of firms. Empirical studies of price policy by monopolists or by oligopolists with *apparently* effective collusion on price, however, frequently fail to sustain these predictions. In many such industries, short-run outputs at which short-run marginal costs plainly exceed short-run industry marginal revenue are apparently common. But more striking is the evidence in some of these industries of prices held persistently over many years within a range where the industry demand curve is evidently inelastic, the corresponding marginal revenue thus being negative and necessarily below long-run marginal cost.[1] This indicates a prolonged tendency (potentially for a theoretical "long run") to hold price well below the level which would maximize the difference between aggregate revenue from the sale of the industry's commodity and the aggregate cost of producing it,[2] and apparently contradicts the basic *a priori* predictions of a theory of collusive pricing.

* *The American Economic Review*, Vol. XXXIX (1949), pp. 448–64. Reprinted by courtesy of the publisher and the author.

The author is indebted to Professors H. S. Ellis, W. Fellner, and R. A. Gordon for helpful criticism of the paper and for a number of substantive suggestions.

† University of California.

[1] Two fairly convincing examples of this are the cigarette and steel industries.

[2] Of producing it, explicitly, with the "given" number of firms, but also with any other conceivable number of firms if industry marginal revenue is negative.

This apparent impasse has been variously resolved by students of industry with suggestions: (a) that sellers do not try to maximize monetary profit; (b) that they err in their attempt to maximize profits; (c) that in the face of great uncertainty concerning demand they simply add some markup to normal average cost and hope for the best; (d) that they fear government interference and public ill will if they exploit their monopoly positions fully; (e) that the apparently collusive oligopoly is not fully or successfully collusive, so that rivalry keeps price down; (f) that sellers set low prices for very considerable time periods in order to raise the level of future industry demand; and (g) that *established sellers* persistently or "in the long run" *forego prices high enough to maximize the industry profit* for fear of thereby attracting new entry to the industry and thus *reducing the demands for their outputs and their own profits.*

Although each of these explanations may contain an element of truth as applied to particular cases, they proceed on somewhat different levels in their implied criticisms of conventional theory. The rejection of profit maximization as a goal suggests a corresponding rejection of conventional price theory; the thesis that either errors or uncertainties are dominant suggests that if such theory is basically valid in its assumptions it nevertheless has little genuine value for predicting actual price results. The suggestion that oligopolistic rivalry reduces prices below the monopoly level leaves theory unscathed, simply implying that the model for monopoly pricing has been misapplied. On the other hand, the hypotheses concerning fear of interference, threat of entry, and pricing to stimulate future demand do not deny that the observed results may be explicable in terms of a theory of monopoly or collusive oligopoly price which assumes profit maximization, effective collusion, and approximately given data, but suggest that the industry or seller demand curves employed in that theory must be redrawn to reflect explicitly the effects of the phenomena in question.

Until the results of such a redrafting are explored, we cannot properly assess the potential explanatory value of conventional price theory. In this paper, we examine two possible modifications of the theory of monopoly price, to take account first of the relation of present price to future profit and second of the impact of the threat of entry;[3] in the latter case we suggest certain possibly novel conclusions concerning the unit for which profit may be maximized and the relation of marginal cost to marginal revenue.

INTERPERIOD DEMAND RELATIONSHIPS

An elaboration of conventional theory to recognize the relation of current price to future demand has been suggested by M. W. Reder; it may deserve re-emphasis in connection with the present issue.[4]

[3] Although the threat of government interference will not be treated explicitly, it could be handled in about the same manner as entry.

[4] "Intertemporal Relations of Demand and Supply within the Firm," *Canadian*

The monopolistic firm (or group of collusive oligopolists[5]) may be provisionally viewed as dealing with an entire industry demand curve in a succession of time intervals, in each of which it can freely select a price-output combination for the industry. It will thus logically take account of the effect of any current price-output decision on the position of the industry demand curve in future periods. A lower price now may mean a larger (or smaller) demand later, and any such anticipated relationship should affect any current pricing policy. If it does, a single long-run industry demand curve cannot be viewed as an independent determinant even of the long-run tendency of price. Such a relation is then not given independently of the prices which the seller(s) charge at various times during the future, but will assume various levels according to the behavior of a series of short-run prices. Instead the seller(s) necessarily refer to a series of short-period demand curves for each of a succession of future intervals; these fully replace any long-run demand curve for the purposes of making all output adjustments. And we must now speak not of a single long-run tendency for price, but rather of a price-pattern through time.

A simple model can be constructed in which a single-firm monopolist is conceived of as pricing solely in a current Period I and a future Period II. There is an industry demand curve for each such period and a corresponding pair of marginal revenue curves. Monopoly price for the first period in isolation would be set to equate the marginal cost of that period to the marginal revenue of that period. But demand in Period II may be supposed to depend upon Period I price; for example, the Period II demand curve may shift outward as Period I price falls. Viewing this relation in prospect from the beginning of the first period, the monopolist may be supposed to adjust Period I price so as to allow maximization of the sum of the profits of the two periods. This procedure may result in setting Period I price below the level for which the marginal cost and marginal revenue of that period are equated, so long as the resulting decrement to Period I profits is more than offset by a resulting increment in Period II profits (as appropriately discounted for interest and risk).

Use of the demand-supply technique in such a sequence analysis permits precise formal treatment of the effects of anticipated relations between current price and future demand. To employ the analysis for purposes of prediction, we should attempt to determine the sign and value of the cross-elasticity between Period I price and Period II quantity for the monopolist—

$$\frac{\partial q_{(t=2)}}{\partial p_{(t=1)}} \cdot \frac{p_{(t=1)}}{q_{(t=2)}}$$

Journal of Economics and Political Science (February, 1941), pp. 25–38, and especially pp. 32–35.

[5] For a simplified argument, we will suppose the collusive oligopoly in each case to be a "pure" oligopoly, in which the several firms sell identical products at a necessarily identical price (the possibility of discrimination being neglected).

One can identify actual cases where this elasticity might be alternatively positive or negative in sign, or zero. Where it is negative and significantly large, a current monopoly price below the current profit-maximizing level can be formally explained; where it is positive and large, current prices above this level could be predicted. This model of course does not have the monopoly doing other than to maximize the "long-run" difference between aggregate industry revenue and aggregate production cost, so long as these are measured as capital values of future revenue and cost streams to a time horizon. But it does indicate the rational possibility of deliberate departures from profit maximization for "short" periods longer than those required to permit every adaptation in scale of firm and plant.

THE THREAT OF ENTRY—GENERAL CONSIDERATIONS

Let us now turn to the effects of anticipated entry. Even a single-firm monopoly is not necessarily impregnable to entry if the industry is a very profitable one, and in oligopolistic industries the threat of entry is likely to be stronger. The monopolist or the group of collusive oligopolists might therefore be viewed as setting each of an indefinite succession of current prices or profits with an eye to their effect in attracting entry into the industry and thus in reducing the demand for the output of the now-established firm(s).[6] One possibility is that the initially established seller or collusive sellers will be faced with the choice of (a) setting each of a succession of short-run prices (and hence long-run average price) so as to maximize the *industry* profit, but with the result that added firms enter the industry and reduce the share of industry profit gained by the initially established firms, and (b) setting each short-run price (and hence long-run average prices) at a lower level, thus discouraging further entry, and keeping the smaller (and non-maximized) industry profit all for themselves. Should the second course then offer larger long-run profits *to the initially established firms,* they would presumably follow it, and price could for the indefinitely long run lie below the level required to maximize the difference between the aggregate revenue from the sale of the given commodity and the aggregate cost of producing it. Long-run maximization of *industry profit* and of *the profit of a group of currently established firms* may not coincide. This is presumably a thesis implied by those who point to threat of entry as a factor holding price below the level which would maximize the long-run profits of the industry.

This hypothesis can easily be developed on a formal level if we accept two premises upon which it must implicitly be based. These are (1) that the established monopolist or group of collusive oligopolists are aware of any real threat of entry to their industry, and will adjust to it in such

[6] The threat of entry, and its relation to price, will of course depend upon the height and effectiveness of such institutional barriers as patent holdings, control of raw materials, *etc.*

a way as to enhance their own (as distinguished from industry) profits, and (2) that potential entrants to such a monopoly or oligopoly are primarily influenced in deciding whether or not to enter by the prices charged and profits currently earned by the established firms. The first premise seems only reasonable,[7] but the merit of the second could be contested. A potential entrant to a purely competitive industry is presumably guided entirely by the expected long-run tendency of industry price as related to his contemplated costs. This is because his increment to the industry would neither perceptibly influence the price nor engender any direct reaction from any established seller. The potential entrant to a monopoly or oligopoly, on the other hand, who will typically make a substantial lump increment to the industry capacity (since economies of scale will ordinarily require a fairly large firm), may expect both to influence the pre-existing price and to elicit some reaction from the established seller(s). This holds whether or not he contemplates collusion with those sellers. In effect, there is a special sort of oligopolistic interdependence between the established seller(s) and the potential entrants in such instances, and it is not entirely plausible that the potential entrant should entirely neglect this interdependence and view the going industry price as the principal indicator of whether or not entry will be profitable.

At the extreme, it could even be argued that a potential entrant to an oligopoly should pay little regard to price or profit received by established firms, especially if he thought price was being held down in order to "bluff" him away from the industry. He should look at the industry demand, the current competitive or collusive conditions in the industry, the prospects for rivalry or collusion after his entry, the share of the market he expects to capture, and his projected costs of production. Paramount in his considerations, provided the industry demand under some conceivable arrangement could provide profits to an entrant, should be his appraisal of the sort of rivalry and the type of price policies he will encounter from the previously established seller(s) after he enters. In judging these determinants of his decision, current price or profit in the industry need play no *direct* role, since the anticipated industry price *after entry* and the entrant's anticipated market share are the strategic considerations. And if he knows the industry demand with reasonable certainty and makes calculations concerning the conditions of rivalry after his entry, upon which he is willing to act, he might look entirely past any current price set by the established firm(s). He then would be immune to bluffing, and the established firm(s) could never discourage entry by lowering prices and earning moderate profits.

The supposition that the potential entrant's judgment of industry de-

---

[7] To argue that sellers in concentrated industries deliberately disregard the consequences of threatened entry would picture them as unbelievably stupid.

mand and of the rivalry he will meet is entirely unrelated to current price or profit in the industry, however, probably goes too far. Even if he does not believe the observed price will remain there for him to exploit, he may nevertheless regard this price as an indicator both of the character of industry demand and of the probable character of rival policy after his entry. Industry demands are never certainly known, and they are probably known less fully by potential entrants than by established firms. The fact that the established firm(s) make only moderate profits may thus create in the mind of the potential entrant sufficient uncertainty concerning the elasticity of the industry demand curve at higher prices to deter him from entering. Moreover, he may view the price which the established firm(s) currently charge as a partial indicator of the rival price policy he will face after entry. Other considerations should influence his judgment of projected rivalry, but current pricing may be a critical factor in evaluating it. It is thus possible that the potential entrant is influenced by current prices and profits and that there may be a critical price below which he will not enter and above which he will enter. This hypothesis seems plausible enough so long as the potential entrant regards the current pricing policy of established sellers as being probably a statement of intentions rather than a bluff. It is probably more plausible than otherwise when applied to oligopolies where product differentiation is not very great, and where the entry problem is thus not unduly complicated by the necessity of gaining buyer acceptance of a new product. We will speak here primarily of its application to oligopolies with relatively slight product differentiation.[8]

On the basis of the preceding argument, we may provisionally accept the second premise of the thesis concerning threat of entry, that the potential entrant to a monopoly or oligopoly is primarily influenced by the price charged (and profit earned) by the established seller(s)—influenced not because he expects this price to hold unchanged after entry, but because he regards it as "proving" the industry demand at a given level and as a critical indicator of the projected state of rivalry or price policy after entry. Accepting the first and second premises, we may now investigate their formal implications for the price policy of an established monopolist or group of collusive (pure) oligopolists faced with a threat of entry. What will happen in these cases if (a) the established seller(s) anticipate any threat of entry (highly probable), (b) potential entrants are influenced in their entry decisions by current price in the industry (a strong possibility), and (c) the established seller(s) know this and consider adjusting their prices to discourage entry.

---

[8] It may be added that with imperfect market information, "potential entrants" may be made aware of the possibilities of an industry mainly by its profit record, and will never present an active threat if they are not alerted by high profits. In this case, low current prices and profits may serve as a deterrent to entry because they do not attract attention and thereby create actively potential entrants.

A "LIMIT PRICE" ANALYSIS

For a formal treatment, two special concepts may be conveniently employed. The first is the "limit price," or highest common price which the established seller(s) believe they can charge without inducing at least one increment to entry—presumably a significant lump increment. This limit price depends ultimately upon the cost functions which potential entrants expect to have, upon their estimates of the industry demand and of the share of the market which they can capture if they enter, and upon their view of the degree of competition or collusion which will obtain in the industry after their entry. The subjective estimate of this limit price by the established seller(s), however, rather than the view of potential entrants, is the real determinant of the price policies of the established seller(s). Since the limit price must be defined in terms of the guess of the established firm(s) concerning the anticipations of the potential rivals, it is especially subject to error as an *ex ante* magnitude, and it may be invalid if potential entrants read it as a bluff. But it is nevertheless potentially valid and determinate.[9] The second concept is the estimate by the established seller(s) of the conditions of demand for their outputs after entry occurs in response to their setting a price above the limit. This involves their estimate of the market share they will lose to an entrant, and also of the conditions of competition or collusion which will obtain after entry. If the established seller(s) formulate estimates on limit price, as defined, and on the position and character of the demand for their outputs after entry, these estimates can be recognized in an anticipated demand curve or sequence of demand curves for their outputs, and a formal solution developed.

This solution can follow the lines developed for the case of interdependence of prices through time. We can first construct a given industry demand curve for the current Period I and for Periods II, III, etc.[10] The demand for the output of the established seller(s) in the current Period I is the industry demand of that period. In any later period, however, it can be expected to be the same as the *industry* demand only so long as price in the preceding period has remained at or below a limit price, *A*, so that entry has been forestalled. If any given period price is set above *A*, the demand for the output of the established seller(s) in all later periods is expected to become less than the industry demand by the amount of a market share going to the new entrant, and it may be otherwise altered or made uncertain if effective collusion with the entrant is not contemplated or considered attainable. If entry will occur in discrete lumps, moreover, the demand for the output of the established seller(s)

[9] Account must be taken, of course, of the consequences of erroneous as well as correct estimates of this price by the established seller(s).

[10] Each such industry demand curve is assumed to be independently given in the absence of interperiod price relationships.

in later periods does not shift continuously in response to variations in Period I price. Instead it makes a discrete shift backward if A is surpassed in Period I, and the solution is affected by this discontinuity. Given these conditions, the established seller(s) will devise a price policy for Period I and in all later periods so as to maximize the discounted present value of profits for all future periods. With an effective threat of entry, it is potentially consistent with such profit maximization by the established seller(s) that price will be held at the limit level continually through time, even though this limit price may in every current period be lower than that for which the marginal cost of the established seller (or horizontally added marginal costs of the established sellers) equals the marginal revenue drawn from the industry demand curve for that period. Such a solution can be determinate and give stability without entry for the indefinitely long run (permitting all desired adjustments of scale by the existing firms) provided the limit price estimated by the established seller(s) is in fact low enough to exclude entry. If the established seller(s) set a "limit" price which turns out to be too high to exclude entry, of course, their error may result in an effectively irreversible change in the structure of the industry.

Because the sequence analysis is unnecessarily awkward for dealing with the threat of entry, the preceding solution is only sketched. Assuming no interdependence of the *industry* demands of successive time periods to be involved in the case, the impact of a threat of entry can be analyzed more easily by referring to the anticipated long-run demand conditions for the output of the established monopolist or collusive oligopolists—or to the expected response of their long-run average sales to changes in the average level of price they maintain over long periods. Following this course, two alternative models may be developed, one assuming that the established seller(s) anticipate rivalry and lack of agreement with any new entrant, and the other assuming that they anticipate collusion with any new entrant.

The first model postulates (1) a determinate long-run demand curve for industry output, which is unaffected by price adjustments or by entry; (2) occupation of the industry initially by a single-firm monopolist or group of effectively collusive pure oligopolists; (3) estimation by the established seller(s) of a limit price above which a "lump" of entry will be attracted; and (4) considerable uncertainty on the part of the established seller(s) concerning the conditions of demand for their outputs if entry is attracted. Given these conditions, the anticipated long-run demand for the output of the established seller(s) may be analyzed as follows. The long-run industry demand curve is supposed to be the line $DABD'$, as in Figure 1, and the marginal revenue drawn to it is $Dabm$. This demand is assumed to be unaffected by any adjustments sellers may make. Suppose now that the limit price above which the established seller(s) expect an increment of entry is Q_aA: If they charge more than this (or produce less output than OQ_a, thus causing the effective market price to exceed the limit), they expect to experience some indeterminate loss in sales volume to an entrant and some indeterminate change in price. The anticipated demand curve for the output of the established seller(s) above the price Q_aA thus is *not* DA. They have the truncated demand curve AD' to exploit up to the price Q_aA, and the corresponding

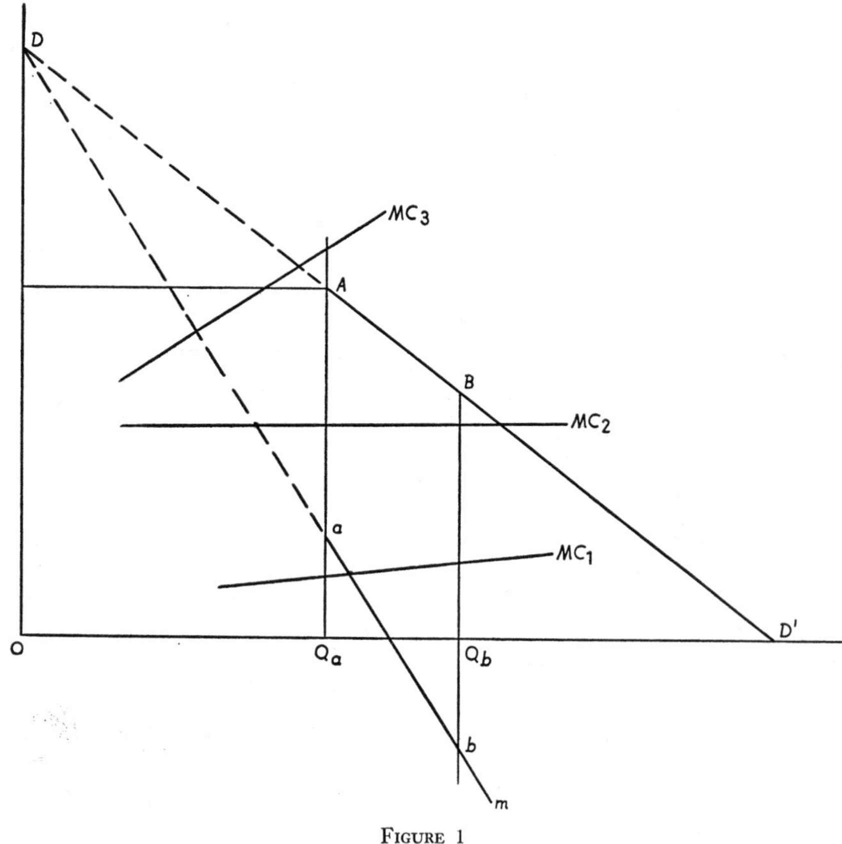

FIGURE 1

marginal revenue segment *am*. But if they raise or attempt to raise long-run price above Q_aA, the anticipated long-run demand curve for their output becomes indeterminate somewhere in the range to the left of A. They thus have the choice of the truncated industry demand curve AD' for exclusive exploitation up to the price Q_aA, and an indeterminate output becomes indeterminate somewhere in the range to the left of A. They thus have the choice of the truncated industry demand curve AD' for exclusive exploitation up to the price Q_aA, and an indeterminate demand for their outputs if they once go above Q_aA. It should be especially noted that they are unable to sell less than the amount OQ_a at the price Q_aA and thus to exclude entry, since this would result in an effective market price higher than the limit, *via* resales, and thus presumably "reveal the bluff" and attract entry.[11]

The alternatives open to the established seller(s) are now (1) to sell more than OQ_a at a price below Q_aA, thus excluding entry, (2) to sell OQ_a at the price Q_aA, also excluding entry, and (3) to raise price above Q_aA, or reduce output below OQ_a, thus attracting entry and taking chances on profits and prices in the ensuing indeterminate situation. They will presumably pursue the course that promises to be most profitable, taking account of the fact that profits under courses (1) and (2) are relatively determinate whereas profits under course (3) are indeterminate and hence highly uncertain. The established seller(s) will follow the first or second course in preference to the third wherever the relatively certain profits offered by those courses exceed the heavily risk-discounted gain attainable if entry is attracted *via* higher prices. The possible positions in which the established seller(s) in various industries may find equilibrium may be illustrated as follows. Suppose a single long-run marginal cost curve, for the initially established monopolist, or alternatively a uniquely determined aggregation of marginal cost curves for the initially established collusive oligopolists in any industry. This we label MC. Now first this marginal cost may in some industries lie at MC_1 (Figure 1), intersecting the relevant industry marginal revenue segment *am*.[12] Then the established seller(s) will almost certainly set price and output by this intersection, provided average costs are less than the resulting price. In this case, industry profit will be maximized at a price below the limit, entry will be forestalled, and the number of sellers in the industry will be in long-run equilibrium. Conventional monopoly maximization is possible without further entry being attracted. This case subsumes all those where entry is blockaded or where the limit price is so high as to be economically irrelevant.

Second, marginal cost may in other industries fall at MC_2, lying above industry marginal revenue but below price at the limit output OQ_a, with average costs less than Q_aA. In this case, provided the profit offered seems preferable to the gamble of inducing entry, the established seller(s) will produce OQ_a and sell at Q_aA. (They will then not choose the intersection of MC_2 and the marginal revenue D_a, since this would give a price which would induce entry.) In this case entry is also forestalled and the number of sellers in the industry is in long-run equilibrium, but

[11] We exclude herewith the possibility of effective private rationing or price discrimination by the established seller(s), which might enable them to produce less than OQ_a and still hold the effective market price at Q_aA; this appears to be a special and unlikely case.

[12] In this and each of the succeeding cases we refer to distinct industry situations, each with a separate limit price, a separate initial marginal and average cost function, and a different relation of marginal and average cost to the limit price. We do not suggest different relations of cost to limit price in a single industry, but rather differences among industries in this respect.

marginal cost exceeds industry marginal revenue and *industry* profits are not maximized.

Third, marginal cost may fall at MC_3, lying above price at the limit output OQ_a, but with the corresponding average cost lying below price at this output. The established sellers will still choose to produce OQ_a and sell at Q_aA, so long as the resulting profit is considered preferable to the gamble if entry is induced. Again the number of sellers will remain constant, but industry profits will not be maximized and *marginal cost will exceed price*—not a probable but nevertheless a quite possible and rational result.

The general argument developed for the last two cases may also be applied on the supposition that the limit price lies at some level Q_bB on the industry demand curve, where this demand is less elastic than unity and the relevant marginal revenue segment, *bm,* is entirely in the negative range. We may still have equilibrium with entry forestalled at the limit price Q_bB (not rationally below it) with marginal cost above industry marginal revenue and possibly above price, but with the difference that industry marginal revenue is negative.

These solutions involve the premises that potential entrants recognize a limit price below which they will not enter, and that the established seller(s) know this and do not overestimate the limit price. Should potential entrants fail to be influenced by price, a stable solution will not result if entry promises to be profitable; if they are so influenced but the established seller(s) set too high a price, there will be entry and a probably irreversible change in industry structure will result. One qualification may be added to the preceding argument. In deciding whether or not to go above the limit price, the established sellers should count in favor of the former course any transitional extra profit they may earn after going above the limit and before entry becomes effective.[13] This consideration has not been formally treated in the preceding model.

A fourth possibility is that average cost for the established seller(s) will lie above the limit price Q_aA at the output OQ_a, marginal cost lying above or below price. In this event price will presumably be set above the limit and entry attracted, provided there is some possibility of making profits at smaller outputs.[14] The number of sellers in the industry then could not be stable until further entry had occurred.

Considering the various possibilities, there is a very good *a priori* chance on the assumptions drawn for the threat of entry to force a significant departure from what have been viewed as the conventional

---

[13] In a dynamic model, we might consider the possibility of a critical or maximum short period during which established sellers could temporarily go above limit price without attracting entry, returning price to the limit in time to discourage potential entrants.

[14] In this case, however, the potential entrants presumably being able to attain lower average costs than established firms, it is doubtful that any price stratagem would forestall entry.

long-run monopoly-equilibrium price and output in single-firm monopoly or collusive oligopoly industries. It has been conventionally supposed that the single-firm monopolist will set a price such as to maximize long-run *industry* profit, and that collusive oligopolists will do likewise. It has been further suggested that this may result, at least in collusive oligopoly, in the attraction of entry to the point where excess profits are small or absent and the industry contains an excessive number of firms.[15] But under the assumptions of anticipated entry and a response of entry to price, we see that, consistent with profit maximization *by firms,* the price in such industries may be lower and the output larger than would maximize long-run *industry profit.* A vigorous threat of entry which at an appropriate time is anticipated and forestalled, moreover, may serve to keep firms producing at outputs which give a fairly close approximation to optimum average costs. If the firms in an industry are so few that they would encounter serious diseconomies of scale in supplying the limit output, they may be unable profitably to forestall entry. But when the number of firms becomes such as to allow production of the limit output at near-optimum average costs, excessive entry may be profitably forestalled by limit-pricing policies and an economical adjustment of capacity to demand perpetuated.[16]

The preceding hypotheses are developed on the basis of certain crucial assumptions, of which the only really controversial one is that potential entrants to concentrated industries may be significantly influenced in their entry decisions by the prices set by established sellers. This assumption may or may not find extensive empirical support. But the observed price policies in a considerable number of oligopolistic industries with apparently effective collusion on price are consistent with hypotheses developed from the assumption, and we may have a thesis of real explanatory value.

The model discussed above also rests on the assumption that the established seller(s) are uncertain of the rivalry which will exist if new firms enter the industry. Its conclusions are not essentially modified, however, if we assume instead that the established seller or collusive sellers contemplate effective collusion with any new entrants. If this is assumed, together with the assumption of a determinate industry demand curve and an anticipated lump of entry above a given limit price, the analysis develops as follows. The long-run industry demand curve is *DAD′* (Figure 2) and the marginal revenue drawn thereto is *Dam,* as

[15] E. H. Chamberlin, *The Theory of Monopolistic Competition,* 1st ed., pp. 100–108.

[16] It is of course evident that if once an oligopolistic industry gets an excess number of firms—whether because the threat of entry is overlooked, or because the limit price fails to forestall entry, or because industry demand declines—then there is no evident force which will eliminate firms and give such a good adjustment. But it nevertheless holds that excessive entry *may* be deliberately forestalled in the manner described.

before. Similarly the limit price is Q_aA; above it the demand for the output of the established seller(s) is not DA, and the marginal revenue segment Da cannot be exploited by the established seller(s). If the established seller(s) go above the price Q_aA or below the output OQ_a, however, the resultant entry does not render the demand for their outputs indeterminate, since effective collusion with any entrant is con-

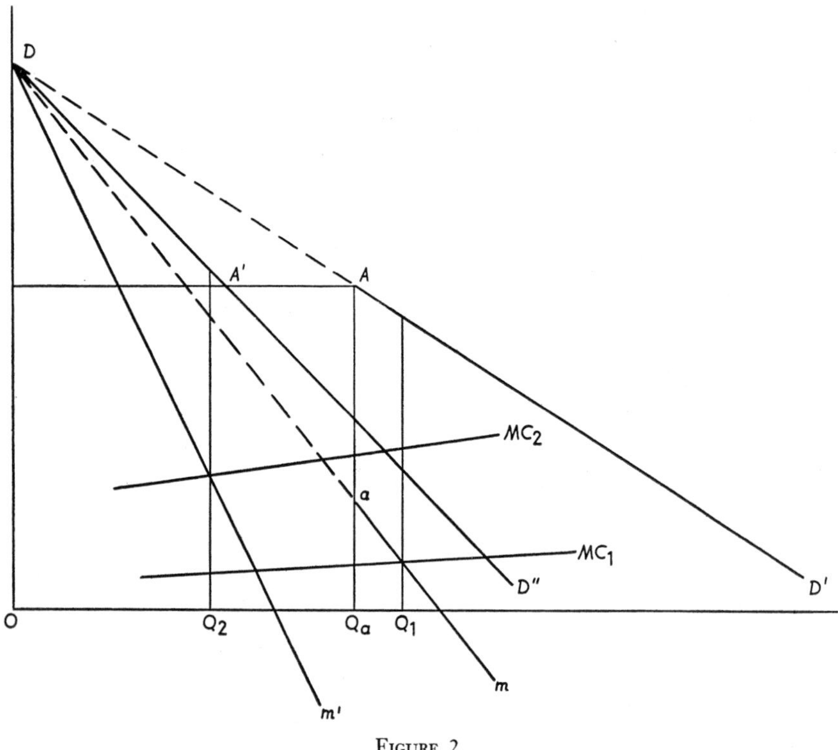

FIGURE 2

templated. Presuming that the market share going to the entrant under such collusion is calculated, the established seller(s) anticipate a determinate loss of the total market volume to the entrant at each possible price. Then if they raise or attempt to raise long-run price above the limit, the anticipated long-run demand for their output becomes some determinate curve DD'', lying to the left of the industry demand curve by distances representing the share of the industry output an entrant would obtain at various prices. The corresponding marginal revenue is Dm'.

As an approximation we may say that the established sellers' demand function is discontinuous horizontally, made up of the segment AD' below the price Q_aA and the segment $A'D$ above that price. This is not precisely accurate, however, since the attempt by established sellers to charge more than Q_aA, involving attraction of new entry, might result in a collusive equilibrium price *after entry* which lay below Q_aA. The curve DD'' thus can have a meaningful price range which overlaps that of AD'. The diagram may therefore be read as follows: the established sellers can in the long run sell any of the price-output combinations on the line AD' (the quantities OQ_a or larger) without attracting entry. If they go above the price Q_aA, or attempt to, they thereafter in the long run can sell any of the combinations on the line DD'', with the remainder of the industry demand going to a new entrant or entrants. In effect, the established seller(s) are given the choice between the truncated industry demand curve AD' for exclusive exploitation and the nontruncated share of the industry demand curve, DD'', for exploitation *via* collusive agreement with the new entrant.[17] The AD' and DD'' curves adequately compare the revenue alternatives of the established seller(s) with and without entry, so long as we neglect any transitional extra profit which the established seller(s) might enjoy while raising above Q_aA but before entry became effective. If such a transitional profit is significant, it must be considered as augmenting that long-run average profit which is obtainable by exploiting DD'' after entry.

If we place the long-run marginal cost of the established seller(s), as previously defined, against this demand complex, conclusions generally consistent with those already developed emerge. Suppose that the marginal cost of the established seller(s) lies at MC_1, so as to intersect industry marginal revenue in the range *am*, where price can be below Q_aA. Provided that total profit at the output OQ_1, determined by the intersection of MC_1 and *am*, is positive and exceeds profit at the intersection of MC_1 and Dm', the established seller(s) will produce OQ_1, charge a corresponding monopoly price below Q_aA, and maximize industry profits without attracting further entry.

Suppose instead that the marginal cost lies at MC_2, so as to lie above industry marginal revenue at the limit output and to intersect the marginal-revenue-after entry, Dm', at an output, OQ_2, which gives a price above Q_aA (average cost being less than Q_aA at OQ_a). The established firm(s) can supply the entire industry demand OQ_a at the price Q_aA, or part of the industry demand, OQ_2, at a higher price. They will choose between these discrete alternatives by comparing *the lump increment* to total revenue with *the lump increment to total cost* which is incurred in moving from OQ_2 to OQ_a.[18] If the revenue increment exceeds the cost increment (the area under MC_2 between Q_2 and Q_a), they will produce at OQ_a, sell at Q_aA, and exclude entry. The profits of the

---

[17] The latter curve might also be truncated at a higher level due to an additional threat of entry, but we will focus attention here on a single increment of entry.

[18] This lump increment to revenue if the limit output is chosen (as aggregated over all future periods) must be considered as reduced by any transitional extra profit receivable after raising price above the limit but before entry becomes effective.

industry will not be maximized, but those of the established seller(s) will be. This holds for MC_2 in successively higher positions until the cost increment exceeds the revenue increment between Q_2 and Q_a; even production at OQ_a with marginal cost above price is possible. When the lump cost increment exceeds the lump revenue increment, price will be raised above Q_aA and entry will be attracted. (Average cost must of course always be covered at the best output or exit from the industry will occur in the long run.)[19]

On the supposition of collusion after entry, we thus arrive at conclusions regarding price similar to those developed when assuming uncertain rivalry after entry. It may be objected, of course, that if established sellers assume collusion after entry, and potential entrants assume it too, then these potential entrants should not be much influenced by the current prices of established sellers, and that a limit-price analysis is thus implausible. It becomes plausible evidently only if potential entrants are quite uncertain about industry demand and about how they will be welcomed by established sellers. But such an incongruity of attitudes is itself not implausible, and the model just developed may thus constitute a realistic variant of our first model.

In summary, a considerable elaboration of the theory of monopoly and collusive oligopoly price may be implied if we assume that potential entrants to an industry are influenced by the going prices therein, and that established sellers anticipate and, if it is profitable, forestall entry. Assuming correct appraisal of limit prices by established sellers, we get three major possibilities: (1) pricing to maximize industry profit with no entry resulting; (2) pricing to forestall entry with industry profit not maximized but the profit of established sellers maximized; and (3) pricing to maximize industry profit but with resulting attraction of additional entry. The first two cases find industries already in long-run equilibrium; the third finds industries in process of dynamic change in structure.

EXTENSIONS AND APPLICATIONS OF THE "LIMIT-PRICE" ANALYSIS

The limit-price models just developed, tracing the effects of a sort of oligopolistic interdependence between firms already in a concentrated industry and potential entrant firms, are essentially variations on the general theory of oligopoly price. There is an apparent similarity of the construction to the familiar kinked demand curve analysis, but in

[19] The general conclusions also hold if the marginal cost lies so as to intersect Dm' where price would be below Q_aA, and to lie above industry marginal revenue at OQ_a. The limit output will be produced and entry excluded so long as the revenue increment exceeds the cost increment between the alternative outputs. In this case we have the situation that collusive price after entry would lie below the limit price which should presumably attract entry. If we remember that the limit price is not necessarily the minimum which entrants expect after entry, however, this situation is not necessarily anomalous.

the present case the average revenue as well as the marginal revenue is discontinuous, and it is a revenue function for all firms already in an industry rather than that for a single oligopolist which is so affected. The limit-price analysis applies to collusive oligopoly behavior, whereas the kinked demand curve model refers explicitly to the action of a firm in noncollusive oligopoly. And the essential conclusions of the two models are of course different.

Various extensions of "limit-price"' reasoning suggest themselves. Thus some firms established within an oligopoly may hold price down for fear of "fattening" their smaller rivals sufficiently to encourage their expansion. Departing from the realm of pure oligopoly, established collusive firms might extend selling costs beyond the point of industry profit maximization in order to discourage entry, so that the threat of entry could cause increased costs rather than reduced prices. The model developed above could also be elaborated to take explicit account of dynamic changes, of varying time lags involved in the "gestation" of new entry, *etc.* Any extensions along these lines might contribute to a more realistic theory of oligopoly price.

The explanatory value of the limit-price hypotheses of course remains to be determined. On *a priori* grounds they appear to be fruitful, although alternative explanations of observed "low-price" policies may also be valid. Some systematic empirical check of the extent of "limit-price" thinking within concentrated industries, and especially by price leaders, would seem desirable. Direct verification of the crucial hypotheses from *ex post* statistical results, however, would be difficult. The "limit price" in any industry, even if recognized, must change over time in response to variations in industry demand, in factor prices, in the availability of capital to potential entrants, in the age of the industry, and so forth. The single limit price of our static long-run analysis becomes in fact a dynamic variable, and would have to be treated as such. It would be difficult to establish in a strictly objective fashion, and knowledge of its recognition by sellers or of its magnitude might best be gained through interview techniques. It would be somewhat easier, on the other hand, to check observed price results for consistency with the hypothesis, without relying on the subjective impressions of sellers involved. That is, objective calculations of the probable limit price (or time series of limit prices) could be made for any industry, and the prices actually charged in a supposedly collusive oligopoly could then be compared both with such limit prices and with prices calculated to maximize industry profits. Wherever behavior consistent with the hypothesis was found, direct investigation of policies of price calculation might be indicated. The emphasis often placed on nonprofit motives, uncertainty, irrationality, and oligopolistic rivalry as explanations of low-price policy in concentrated industries may be unduly heavy, and the effects of threatened entry seem certainly to deserve consideration.

13

Product Heterogeneity and Public Policy*

By EDWARD H. CHAMBERLIN†

It has been remarked by Mr. Triffin that "for the historian of economic thought, the most revolutionary feature of monopolistic competition theories will probably be the unprecedented pace at which they conquered their audience."[1] Interpreting this as he does, mainly in terms of the appearance in textbooks for the first time of chapters on oligopoly, product differentiation, and selling costs, he may be right. But I must again lament the widespread misunderstanding of the subject; so that what has "conquered" appears often to be something quite foreign to the theory, at least as I understand it. Nowhere is this more true than in that part of the whole subject which is taken up in this paper: the reorientation of our ideas as to public policy in view of the fact of product heterogeneity.

Public policy must be presumed to seek in some sense the general welfare, and hence in the economic sphere it implies a welfare economics. The supremacy of pure competition with its corollary of prices equal to marginal costs as the economic welfare ideal is well known. Mr. A. P. Lerner's "Rule" is a quick and familiar reference.[2] What is perhaps not so well appreciated is how explicitly monopolistic competition has been interpreted as merely indicating the nature of the departures from the ideal which need to be corrected. Thus, although it may have reoriented in some degree our ideas as to how the economic system actually works, its impact upon our conception of the model towards which we would move appears to me to have been virtually nil. I say "towards which" in recognition of the fact that pure competition is evidently a theoretical concept, and that the practical-minded economist is often ready enough to point out that "no one has ever advocated that it be established." What we want, to be sure, is some kind of "work-

* *The American Economic Review,* Vol. XL (Proceedings of the American Economic Association, 1950), pp. 85–92. Reprinted, with revisions, by courtesy of the publisher and the author.

† Harvard University.

[1] *Monopolistic Competition and General Equilibrium Theory,* p. 17.

[2] *The Economics of Control,* p. 64 and *passim.*

able" competition. But ordinary (purely) competitive theory remains the chief source of our criteria as to what should be done if possible, and of the direction in which we should move so far as we can. A striking instance is the subtitle of this part of the program of these meetings: "Can the American economy be made more competitive?" The implication is evident that if it can be it should.

Now if pure competition is the ideal, the direction in which we should move is very clear. For it is easy enough to show that the actual economy is shot full of monopoly elements, and hence that any move to get rid of them or to diminish their importance is in the right direction. The main point I want to make is that the welfare ideal itself (as well as the description of reality) involves a blend of monopoly and competition and is therefore correctly described as one of monopolistic competition. If this is true, it is no longer self-evident which way we should move, for it is no longer self-evident on which side of the ideal lies the actuality for which a policy is sought. It is possible that the economy should be made "more competitive"; but it is also quite possible that it should be made "more monopolistic" instead. Or perhaps, if there are faults to be found with it, it should simply be changed, towards something else which again involves both monopoly and competition, with the frank admission that, since we cannot measure monopoly and competition quantitatively, there is no way of comparing the actual with the ideal on any yardstick involving these concepts.

Let us proceed at once to the proposition that monopoly is necessarily a part of the welfare norm. In abstract terms it seems to follow very directly from the recognition that human beings are individuals, diverse in their tastes and desires, and moreover widely dispersed spatially. Insofar as demand has any force as a guide to production, one would expect entrepreneurs to appeal to them in diverse ways, and thus to render the output of the economy correspondingly heterogeneous, using this term in its broadest sense to embrace not only the qualitative aspects of the product itself, but also the conditions surrounding its sale, including spatial location.[3] And since what people want—an elaborate system of consumers' preferences—is the starting point in welfare economics, their wants for a heterogeneous product would seem to be as fundamental as anything could be. Heterogeneity as between producers is synonymous with the presence of monopoly; therefore monopoly is necessarily a part of the welfare ideal.

It must be emphasized that any and all monopoly is included within the general concept of heterogeneity or differentiation (although there is no implication of an identity between the actual and the ideal). A

---

[3] Apart from the influence of demand, output will also be heterogeneous because of the diversity of nature on the side of production; as illustrated by human services, both directly and as reflected in the products they create; and by the fact that sellers are separated spatially.

monopoly is simply a product under a single control and significantly different from others on the infinite chain of substitutes. This holds equally for a patent, a cement producer separated in space from others, a local gas utility, a toll bridge, or the A & P. And they are, of course, all without exception engaged in competition with others near by on the chain of substitutes and with others generally in the system. "Industry" or "commodity" boundaries are a snare and a delusion—in the highest degree arbitrarily drawn and, wherever drawn, establishing at once wholly false implications both as to competition of substitutes within their limits, which supposedly stops at their borders, and as to the possibility of ruling on the presence or absence of oligopolistic forces by the simple device of counting the number of producers included. As for the *conventional* categories of industries, it seems increasingly evident to me that they have their origin, not primarily in substitution at all, but in similarity of raw materials or other inputs or of technical methods used. Glass, leather goods, drugs, and medicines are obvious examples. Apart from the wide diversity of products embraced by almost any so-called "industry," spatial separation of producers within it is an added prime obstacle to substitution in most cases. But the main point is that, even if lines were arbitrarily to be drawn, they would have literally nothing to do with the extent and character of the heterogeneity, either within such an industry or beyond it, which would be defensible from the point of view of welfare or of public policy.

All this is in striking contrast with prevailing notions of the significance of product heterogeneity for public policy. The reason is, I believe, mainly a difference in the implications of monopolistic competition on the one hand and of imperfect competition on the other; and the fact that the prevailing notions on public policy have been derived largely from an interpretation which follows the latter. It is worth noting that the terms product and market are used consistently in *Monopolistic Competition*, not in their usual broad sense, but with reference only to the individual firm. There are no "commodities," such as shoes, sheets, or shaving brushes, but only groupings of individual products. The term "industry" was carefully avoided, and does not appear at all (except where its limitations are being pointed out). By contrast, *Imperfect Competition* followed the tradition of competitive theory, not only in identifying a commodity (albeit elastically defined) with an industry, but in expressly assuming such a commodity to be homogeneous.[4] Such a theory involves no break whatever with the competitive tradition. The very terminology of "imperfect competition" is heavy with implications that the objective is to move towards "perfection."

Even within the terminology of monopolistic competition, the same tendencies have appeared in the connotation which the term "differenti-

---

[4] J. Robinson, *The Economics of Imperfect Competition*, p. 17.

ation" has taken on to many as of something superficial. (Hence the term "heterogeneous" in this paper.) It is often conceived as describing the reprehensible creation by businessmen of purely factitious differences between products which are by nature fundamentally uniform. In this vein, some have even gone so far as to attribute differentiation, and monopolistic competition generally, to "imperfect knowledge,"[5] as though the individuality of particular products could be dismissed as an optical illusion based upon ignorance—a purely psychic phenomenon. There seems, on the contrary, to be as much reason for people to lack knowledge of the differences between products as for them to lack knowledge of their similarities; and there is a good prima facie case for believing that "perfect knowledge" (while causing major shifts in individual preferences) would leave a system in which there were more and stronger preferences than ever. Certainly the consumer research organizations, which are engaged in perfecting the knowledge of their subscribers as to the goods they contemplate purchasing, are as much concerned with differences as with similarities.

Another device for leveling off the heterogeneous output of the economy into a series of purely competitive industries is the distinction between "rational" and "irrational" preferences, with its heavy implication that a substantial part of actual preferences are of the latter category. The distinction is not without its complications; but the test is supposedly simple: "If a consumer were *forced* to have B's goods instead of A's goods, would he feel worse off after the change had taken place? If, in fact, he would consider himself to be worse off, the buyers' preference is rational; if not, it is irrational."[6] The conclusion is, of course, that if irrational buyers' preference exists, "then the community clearly gains by the concentration of the industry's output on a smaller number of firms." It need only be commented that the argument, for whatever validity it may have, should not be limited in its application to an arbitrarily defined industry, but should be applied generally. On the one hand, it may be said that if Palmolive were abolished, people might be no "worse off" after they had got used to using Lux and Lifebuoy instead. But on the other hand, it is equally true that if baseball were abolished and bull fights substituted, people might be equally well or better satisfied after they were adjusted to the change, in which case their preferences for baseball should be classified as irrational. Similarly, many people have stopped smoking and, after they got used to it, were no more unhappy than before. There is a case, of course, for improving knowledge in all these matters, but no reason to think that improved

---

[5] F. H. Knight, *American Economic Review,* May, 1946, p. 104; and G. J. Stigler, *Theory of Price* (1946), pp. 214–15, 329, and *passim.*

[6] Meade, *Economic Analysis and Policy,* p. 155. I believe the distinction was first made by R. F. Kahn in "Some Notes on Ideal Output," *Economic Journal,* March, 1935, pp. 25–26. It is criticized by J. K. Galbraith, *ibid.,* June, 1938, p. 336.

knowledge would leave us with fewer or weaker preferences. In some cases it seems clear that increased standardization of certain products by public authority is indicated, as when oligopolistic forces are supporting an unduly large number of producers,[7] or when the gain in efficiency is judged by proper authorities to be more important than the losses in consumers' surplus through abandoning certain products. But the labeling of most preferences within an arbitrarily defined industry as irrational seems to me to indicate mainly a preference for the purely competitive ideal, and an attempt, perhaps largely unconscious, to salvage it. The alternative is not necessarily to assume that all preferences are rational, but only that they are on the same footing—in other words, to make no invidious distinctions between them as to rationality on the basis of the relative proximity of substitutes.

It might be added that no invidious distinctions are indicated on the basis of whether or not the demands for particular products are influenced by selling expenditures. Here again, stress on irrational preferences makes an easy transition to the labeling of those established by advertising as irrational, and to the conventional sweeping condemnation of advertising as a "competitive waste."[8] Granted that the techniques of modern advertising are often a shocking affront to good taste, or objectionable on other grounds, it remains true, so far as I can see, that the question of whether advertising is wasteful or not, in the sense of being a misallocation of resources, simply cannot be answered by any criteria derived from market demand and cost curves—or from indifference curves either. Here is a major aspect of "welfare" which appears to lie quite outside the conventional analysis of the subject. The general condemnation of advertising as a waste surely has its primary explanation in the irrelevancy that it could not exist under the perfectly competitive ideal.

The fact that equilibrium for the firm when products are heterogeneous normally takes place under conditions of falling average costs of production has generally been regarded as a departure from ideal conditions, these latter being associated with the minimum point on the curve; and various corrective measures have been proposed. However, if heterogeneity is part of the welfare ideal, there is no prima facie case for doing anything at all. It is true that the same total resources (either within some arbitrarily defined industry or within the whole economy) may be made to yield more units of product by being concentrated on fewer firms. The issue might be put as efficiency versus diversity—more of either one means less of the other. But unless it can be shown that the loss of satisfaction from a more standardized product (again, either within an "industry" or for the economy as a whole) is less than the

[7] *Monopolistic Competition*, pp. 100–109.

[8] Meade, *op. cit.* pp. 165–66 (Meade and Hitch, pp. 176–77).

gain through producing more units, there is no "waste" at all, even though every firm is producing to the left of its minimum point.

How are the two to be compared—a larger, less heterogeneous output as against a smaller, more heterogeneous one? The price system, especially in view of its all-pervasive oligopolistic forces and the omnipresence of selling costs whose welfare status is uncertain, appears to afford no test. If we may allow the individual producer his optimum selling expenditure, included as a lump sum in his fixed costs, and conceive a system in which every producer determines the equilibrium of his firm with reference to a demand curve which measures demand for his product at different prices while all other prices, products, and selling costs do not change, we have in the elasticity of demand one index of the strength of buyers' preferences for each product.[9] If adjustment of prices along demand curves of this type could be enforced, many firms whose profits (perhaps nominal) are protected by the absence of vigorous price competition[10] would certainly be involved in losses and would be obliged to go out of business before a general equilibrium for the whole economy were realized. There would be less heterogeneity than we find at present, and it would seem that something like what I have described elsewhere as a "sort of ideal"[11] would be established.

Another approach to the same problem is to test old products individually for survival and new products for admission to the economy by a consideration of the surpluses of satisfaction over cost which are sacrificed in one place and generated in another by the transfer of resources involved. Much of what has been written in this connection[12] seems to me to be vitiated by entanglement with the standard theory of "exploitation" which has evolved out of "imperfect" competition and which I have elsewhere[13] shown to be fallacious—a theory in which hired factors are held to be exploited by entrepreneurs. But the theoretical criterion involved can be adapted to an analysis from which this objectionable feature is absent. Of course the old bogey of interpersonal comparisons appears at once; also the familiar problem of subsidy to the expanded firms which, if they had no extra profits before, are now, at the lower prices necessary to sell the larger output, losing money. Unfortunately the matter is too complex to be developed in this short paper. Let us only observe that, for whatever it may be worth, the final welfare

---

[9] The curves of Mrs. Robinson's *Imperfect Competition* cannot be used for this purpose because they are defined as including oligopolistic reactions. Cf. *Imperfect Competition*, p. 21.

[10] *Cf. Monopolistic Competition*, pp. 100–109.

[11] *Ibid.* p. 94. With allowance made for the "diversity of conditions surrounding each producer" (pp. 110–13) the ideal would evidently involve diverse outputs and prices for the individual producers in the system.

[12] *Cf.* especially R. F. Kahn, *op. cit.*, and J. E. Meade (also Meade and Hitch), *op. cit.*, Part II, chap. vi.

[13] *Monopolistic Competition* (5th or later ed.), pp. 182–84, 215–18.

equilibrium which emerges from this analysis, as from the preceding one, would inevitably involve product heterogeneity; and that it would be characterized neither by the equation of price and marginal cost nor by production at minimum average cost for the firms involved. Indeed, by this procedure, the adjustment required from any starting point might as easily be to increase the supposedly excess number of firms as to diminish it. As an indication of what is involved, one might under this principle even revive that good old newspaper, the *Boston Transcript*, under public subsidy, since many "proper Bostonians" were strangely attached to it and no doubt lost heavily in consumers' surplus when it finally folded up.

Let us leave this question of how many products there should be, or of diversity, to say a word about the other major type of adjustment which has been analyzed in relation to product heterogeneity and welfare—that of the distribution of resources among a given number of products or among a given number of industries.

It has been proposed that resources be transferred from purely competitive industries, where price equals marginal cost, to "imperfectly competitive industries," where price is greater than marginal cost, and similarly from less imperfectly competitive to more imperfectly competitive industries, until the ratio of price to marginal cost is the same everywhere. Such a proposal may be dismissed at once on two grounds, either one of which alone is sufficient: (1) the boundaries of an industry being arbitrary, it is quite meaningless and (2) the demand and cost curves of different firms within any industry are highly diverse as to elasticity and shape. For these two reasons we must abandon altogether the idea of transferring resources in some vague way to an industry, and face the question of the firms to which they are to be attached.[14]

What, then, of equalizing the price-marginal cost ratio as between firms in the economy? Apart from other difficulties, I believe there is a fatal objection to such a conception; viz. the generally prevalent oligopolistic relationships between firms. The logic by which this proposition is usually developed envisages each firm as an isolated monopoly, isolated in the sense that its output and price may be adjusted without appreciable effect on any other single firm. But where oligopolistic influences are present, there are two points to be made. First, the demand curve for any one firm, which would indicate the effect on its price of adding resources to it, cannot be known without knowing which of the many possible patterns of behavior under oligopoly will govern the case at hand. In fact, since adding resources to any one firm would, by lowering its price, inevitably shift the demand curves of others economically near it (since every curve is drawn on the assumption of given prices for

[14] Mr. Kahn's analysis explicitly assumes industries in which competition is "uniformly imperfect" (*op. cit.* p. 21 n.), and thus lays down principles for a wholly imaginary problem.

other firms), there seems to be no escape from abandoning the conception of transfers between firms considered to be independent, and reconceiving it in terms of groups of some kind. Second, the effect on welfare of adding resources to one firm, where oligopolistic interdependence is involved, is a function of whether or not, and in what quantity, resources are being added at the same time to others economically near. Even assuming that the price behavior could be directed according to some socially enforced rule, the major problem would still remain of finding the rule in welfare terms. I very much fear that, because of oligopolistic interrelationships between the welfare contributions of firms, we are reduced to asserting merely that resources should be transferred from one place to another in the system whenever the net effect will be to increase welfare. This is not very illuminating.

In conclusion, the consequences of product heterogeneity for welfare economics have been either ignored or seriously misunderstood. Monopoly elements are built into the economic system and the ideal necessarily involves them. Thus wherever there is a demand for diversity of product, pure competition turns out to be not the ideal but a departure from it. Marginal cost pricing no longer holds as a principle of welfare economics (not even for toll bridges); nor is the minimum point on the cost curve for the firm to be associated with the ideal. Selling costs may no longer be excluded from the problem or dismissed as an obvious waste; yet the impossibility of discovering from the standard welfare techniques what is the socially ideal expenditure on selling suggests that the techniques are unduly narrow. It has been impossible to discuss in this paper whole families of new problems which put in their appearance with a recognition of the fact that products themselves are variables and that there must be norms for them as well as for prices, costs, and outputs. What has been called the "new welfare economics," instead of being on a "secure basis" as suggested by Professor Hicks,[15] has quite misconceived a whole set of major problems. It is badly in need of a general overhauling.

15 "The Foundations of Welfare Economics," *Economic Journal*, December, 1939, p. 711.

14

Competition: Static Models and Dynamic Aspects*

By J. M. CLARK†

I. INTRODUCTION

This paper is an attempt at a contribution to the endless effort to reduce or bridge the gap between theory and reality; and in particular the gap between theories of cost-price equilibrium and theories of production, growth, and development.[1] Theory must always be the department of oversimplification; but dynamic simplifications are at least different from static. They include the tendencies toward equilibrium. But because these tendencies never reach their static limits, dynamic theory cannot use any features which are needed only to enable a model to attain this impossibly precise completeness—especially if these features are incompatible with the conditions of progress.

It follows that fully dynamic theory is bound to lack certain characteristics which are, to many theorists, the essential earmarks of theory. It must accept indeterminateness, with some margin of individual discretion in business action, and uncertainties of different kinds from those they are accustomed to dispose of by assuming a premium for uninsurable risk. Some of these uncertainties are positive aids to effective—not perfect—competition. If such theory is to be accepted as theory, it seems that the first step which theorists can contribute is the setting up of an appropriate conceptual framework, including appropriate tool-concepts. Even within theoretical writings, many or most of the pieces of this framework exist as scattered fragments; but the writer is not aware that the framework has been assembled and articulated. The present paper

* *The American Economic Review*, Vol. XLV (Proceedings of the American Economic Association, 1955), pp. 450–62. Reprinted, with revisions, by courtesy of the publisher and the author.

† Columbia University.

[1] The remarkable group of papers presented at last year's [1953] meetings of this Association and the proceedings of the 1951 conference of the International Economic Association (*Monopoly and Competition and Their Regulation*, E. H. Chamberlin, editor [London, 1954]) include an appeal for a dynamic theory and confirm the existence of an impressive body of factual material large enough to afford a basis for beginnings at fresh generalizations. They present a challenge to which theory should attempt to respond.

is a modest attempt to bring together enough pieces to afford some suggestions of what the structure might look like.

II. THE POINT OF DEPARTURE: EXISTING COMPETITIVE THEORY

In the theory of a generation ago, competition played a twofold role: as an agency to eliminate excessive and exploitative profits and as a stimulus to technical progress—a keener stimulus than monopoly would afford. As a stimulus to progress, competition included both the carrot and the stick (the carrot of profits to the successful innovator and the stick of losses for those who fall behind) and elimination for those who fall behind substantially and persistently. Temporary monopoly, under the patent system, was also recognized as a force for technical progress. Later, Schumpeter's theory of innovation made its mark, but without being integrated into general competitive theory.

Subsequent developments, leading to the body of competitive theory now prevalent, have concentrated on more precise definition of the conditions necessary to complete or "perfect" cost-price equilibrium—conditions that turn out to be nonexistent. The model then becomes an analytical device and, as such, a step toward explaining why things do not behave like the model, the next step being to take account of the inevitable departures and the conditions accounting for them. So far, this process has produced certain other models, still highly simplified, of monopolistic competition and oligopoly, with and without product differentiation. The preoccupation of these models with cost-price equilibrium is obvious. What may be less obvious is that static limitations are built into their underlying tools of analysis—demand curves and cost curves —which therefore need modification for dynamic purposes.

This prevalent body of theory is not a theory of production, as growth theory must necessarily be. Insofar as it deals with economy and efficiency of production, it does so in terms of optimum or less-than-optimum scale of production (size of plant or firm) on a fixed long-run cost curve; that is, on the obviously static assumption that the "state of the arts" remains constant.

A more troublesome consequence of the model consists of the normative conclusions that are, rightly or wrongly, drawn from it. As a standard of so-called "perfection," it is one-legged, focusing on the essentially static objective of cost-price equilibrium, to the neglect of the dynamic objectives of progress. This one-legged standard is frequently treated, without warrant, as an ideal. And because it is unattainable, all actual or possible conditions are, by comparison, judged inferior, monopoloidal, or actually monopolistic.[2] This interpretation Chamberlin

[2] The opposite case—of pure but imperfect competition (e.g., agriculture) which tends to be unduly severe—is commonly neglected.

himself has flatly repudiated, stating that perfect competition is not the ideal, and the ideal includes elements of monopoly—which might mean no more than such elements of uniqueness as most businesses inevitably possess.

The idea of the omnipresence of harmful departures from perfect competition seems to underlie the challenge of Professor Galbraith, who says in effect: according to theory, our economy ought to be suffering all the evils ascribed to monopoly; why isn't it? Galbraith suggests that it may be the theory that is wrong rather than the facts of the economy, and this contains much truth. But when he suggests that the trouble with the theory is its adherence to competition and recommends throwing competition out the window in favor of a subsitute, he is surely overplaying his hand. I would contend that the trouble with the theory is not its adherence to competition, but its too formalized conception of what competition is. This includes, first, the one-legged character of its standard of perfection, and, second, the fact that its picture of reality is highlighted by models of oligopoly and monopolistic competition which do not tell the whole story about the cases with which they deal, and do not do justice to the competitive forces that exist, including forces of progress and forces working toward serviceable—not perfect—cost-price adjustments. The cases include monopolistic evils, but they also include—more typically, I suspect—cases in which the reality behaves better than the models, including the model of perfect competition, which sacrifices important factors of dynamic progress.

But recognition of this lies under a heavy semantic handicap, if it has to take the shape of stating that the ideal includes "elements of monopoly." This raises questions, not as to the facts, but as to the expediences of the terminology. It seems unfortunate if economists who defend realistic forms of competition thereby expose themselves to the charge of defending monopoly. This danger is not imaginary. The outstanding case is that of product differentiation—a "monopolistic" element which has in itself no necessary antitrust significance. I have myself said, of product differentiation (*Economics of Overhead Costs*, page 418): "In a sense each competitor has a monopoly of the difference in quality . . . and this qualified monopoly is a feature of the typical 'competitive' market." I would not say he had a monopoly of his product, but only of the quality differential; and I would not suggest this as standard general-purpose terminology, to be used, among other things, in antitrust connections. With such uses in view, it would appear helpful if, in our general-purpose terminology, "monopoly" began with obstructions to imitation, and "incipient monopolization" began with actions of an obstructive character.

There is food for thought in the discrepancies or contradictions between pure theory and practical or policy judgments. For example, theory appears to regard product differentiation as always a shelter from the rigors of competition; but the Interstate Commerce Commission has apparently found that the element of differentiation between rail and truck transport tends to cause their competition to assume a cutthroat character. And businessmen recognize that a rival's product innovation can be a very aggressive and formidable method of competition. A manufacturer who has no competitors at his immediate location is not for that reason a monopolist under the antitrust laws; but he must watch his step as to what he does with the "element of monopoly" resulting from his unique location, under the Staley and other basing point cases. On discrimination and freight absorption, neither theory nor antitrust policy is clear and unambiguous. Excess capacity tends to be treated by theory as a monopolistic symptom,[3] but in antitrust cases it may or may not be so treated, depending on circumstances. And businessmen tend to the view that competition does not begin until they have difficulty disposing of capacity output, and becomes more severe as excess capacity gets larger.

The perfect competitive market of theory is one in which prices are identical and each producer knows the others' prices and profits, which implies knowing their costs. In practice, too perfect identity of prices is legally suspect, and so is interchange of information on prices, as in open price associations, or information on costs, or even the use of a uniform cost accounting system. All these cases serve to suggest things which current equilibrium models neglect and which dynamic theory may need to recognize.

III. DYNAMIC CRITERIA OF APPRAISAL

In the light of the things we want competition to do for us, what are the features it needs to have which are implied in these objectives? I will put first the elements required for progress as being most important, since even a small continuing gain outweighs a substantial gain of the once-for-all variety.

First comes progress in economical methods of production. Under competition, this implies that some take the lead and others follow, while managements are changed or firms are eliminated if they fall too far behind. But an excessive rate of elimination of firms may be unhealthy for an industry. To avoid this without retarding progress, the bulk of the followers needs to be able to keep near enough to the leaders to stay in the race.

Secondly, we want competition to afford customers an amply differentiated range of qualities and types of any given product to choose from. This is, of course, wanted for its own sake; but in terms of progress it means that the producers are exploring—and influencing—the cus-

---

[3] See, especially, Chamberlin, *Theory of Monopolistic Competition* (5th ed.), pp. 109, 171.

tomers' preferences and potential preferences, and products evolve in the directions these preferences indicate. Whether they evolve in the best directions is, of course, a different question. Product differentiation costs something, mainly because of the selling effort that is bound up with it. (For that matter, maintaining homogeneity of product costs something, too. And homogeneity of each brand is necessary for effective differentiation between brands.) The combination of selling costs with research and testing introduces an element of overhead cost which makes for large size and limited numbers of producers. But in a market as large as the American, this seldom goes to lengths that spell natural monopoly.

Thirdly, we want new products developed; and this is a necessary correlative of more efficient methods of production, if an increase of 2 per cent a year in productivity is to be absorbed without technological unemployment. New products, even if patented, are generally exposed to imitation and competition after a delay which is, by historical standards, not long.

A second group of objectives is concerned with the diffusion of the benefits of progress, to customers in lower prices or to those who contribute factors of production—chiefly workers—in higher real rewards. This involves a progressive sharing of the rewards of successful innovation, and the sharing becomes complete when the improvement has become part of the generally available state of the arts, from which special profits can no longer be made. This diffusion means that what Veblen called "the wisdom of the ancients" is not "cornered" by current business enterprise; only the recent advances made in it, and these only partially. The diffusion is wanted for its own sake, but it also has a special role in the incentives to progress. What it means is that a renewal of differential profits can be had only by renewed innovation. Thus it is part of the system that can keep incentives to continued innovation alive in full strength. This role would be vitiated if the diffusion were instantaneous and complete, since then innovation would bring no rewards to the innovator. The dynamic system is not one of elimination of profits, but one of erosion and re-creation, both of which are jointly essential.

For the economy as a whole, this process implies the creation, reduction, and re-creation of differential rewards in different industries, as well as for different firms. Professor Harberger's paper at the 1953 [American Economic Association] meeting developed a case for the thesis that existing differentials are relatively unimportant defects, by conventional utilitarian standards. This argument may not prove that we should be unconcerned about them; but it does strongly suggest that their dynamic impact is more important than their static. The goal is to subject them to active wearing down and prevent them from becoming so enduringly entrenched that they need not be earned and re-earned by progress.

The diffusion process also affects growth via the distribution of incomes, which in turn affects the market for the increased flow of goods, new and old, which progress makes available. This has two main dimensions: inequality between persons and between different industries or sectors of the economy. If one sector of the economy is progressive, it will be handicapped in realizing its potentialities if most of the other sectors are too poor to buy much of the products of the dynamic sector and too stagnant to increase their purchases as the productive power of the dynamic sector increases.[4] Development needs to be not too badly unbalanced; and from this standpoint well-diffused competition is favorable. Something similar is true of personal distribution, a fair approach to equality being favorable to the kind of demand on which mass production depends. On the other hand, new products have often been introduced first as luxury items, appealing to the rich or well-to-do, and later coming within the reach of mass demand, as increased sales and the resulting productive economies reinforced one another cumulatively. Nowadays, with the American mass market thoroughly established, it is sometimes possible to promote a new product for mass volume from the start.

What is not obvious about all this is the part played by competition. It opposes the inequalities of intrenched privilege; but if the labor market were thoroughly competitive, inequalities of wages based on unequal performance might be, by and large, greater than they are. On either basis, however, this country would have a great mass market plus a more limited luxury market, not too far above the mass market and shading into it by easy gradations. Competition also implies mobility of productive resources, which is needed for adjusting to the inevitable inequalities in rates of growth in different parts of the economy. And in a growing economy, mobility is possible with a minimum of actual shifting of persons or capital.

A phase of this diffusion process is the creating of a market in which a customer may have considerable confidence that the offerings of different sellers are of approximately equal value and that he will not be seriously victimized if he fails to shop around, looking for the best offerings. This (limited) assurance is of real value to the customer who has many demands on his or her time; but it works only if enough customers do shop around. A competitive market tends toward one price to just the extent that customers watch for differentials and take advantage of them. This is the customers' essential role in a competitive system.

A third group of objectives is concerned, not with products and prices, but with the conditions of competitive rivalry in itself. It regards freedom and opportunity as ends in themselves. It is concerned with the human impact of competitive pressures on those who are exposed to them.

---

[4] For the suggestion here adopted, I am indebted to R. Nurkse's *Problems of Capital Formation in Underdeveloped Countries* (1953).

But especially it is concerned that efficiency and the diffusion of its benefits should not be dependent on the good will and arbitrary decision of private producers, nor on direct governmental order, but on a situation in which normal business motives impel business units (acting independently) to conduct that will tend to further the desired results. This goal, like the goal of diffusion of gains, is overrigidified in the theoretical concept of an economic law which dictates economic conduct and its results with a precision from which there is no escape.

This would reduce economic freedom to a paradox, since the meaning of freedom resides in a margin of discretion in choosing one's course of action. One of the tasks of the kind of theory here contemplated is to define the margins of discretion that producers have and the margins they should have or can safely be allowed to have. They may, for example, face uncertainties and be governed by longer or shorter perspectives and broader or narrower conceptions of their interests. These all belong in a dynamic theory. The essential limits on private discretionary power are presumably satisified if the discretion of business units does not extend to doing things that obstruct the progress of the "generally available state of the arts" or prevent the public from getting the benefit of it. This is admittedly a not-too-precise standard; and may need some care to avoid tautology, centering in the phrase "generally available." It has a logical kinship with Marshall's "representative firm," and I believe it is not wholly meaningless.

Given these goals, how should one use them to judge a system? A general judgment may be influenced by appraisal of the performance of the system in the large. But for purposes of specific policy in actual cases, rates of progress and fairness of profits are too uncertain, dependent on too many irrelevant circumstances; and their use to determine legality would hardly be consistent with a free private economy. Instead, judgment must hinge on whether conditions are of a sort inherently adapted, by and large, to promote these ends. Three key tests may be suggested: free and independent action, incentive to do the kinds of things that are called for, and capacity to do them.

As to the first, it is not easy to make people compete if they do not want to; but collusion can be checked and protection can be afforded to the more competitively minded mavericks who will exert pressure on the others. Dynamic change also tends, as we shall see, to keep rivalry alive. As to incentive, mention has been made of the carrot and the stick, of the joint importance of differential gains and their erosion, but no precise optimum rate of erosion appears to be definable. Where progress requires heavy research outlays, atomistic industries are handicapped as to both incentive and capacity: as to capacity for obvious reasons and as to incentive because the output of the single enterprise is so small that individual gains fail to measure the importance of the resulting progress for the industry as a whole. Thus in agriculture this element of progress depends heavily (though not exclusively) on governmental research and promotion.

IV. ELEMENTS OF COMPETITION AS DYNAMIC PROCESS

A theory of competition as dynamic process must be not a model but a framework within which many models may find their places, including equilibrium models as limiting hypothetical cases. As I have said elsewhere (*Monopoly and Competition and Their Regulation*, pages 326–28), the process includes initiatory action by a firm, responses by those with whom it deals, and responses to these responses by rival firms, to which one should add the subsequent rejoinders of the initiators, plus any actions that may be taken on a basis of anticipation. (For example, a rival may react defensively, before his customers have time to switch to a competitor.) The moves and the responses may affect productive processes, products, selling efforts or prices, or various combinations. They may be aggressive, defensive, or counteroffensive. Fully dynamic theory needs to conceive these patterns as themselves subject to change, over longer periods of time. Marshall's life history of a firm may be matched by life histories of products or product variants, and of the marketing patterns connected with them. Stages of exploratory introduction, aggressive expansion, defense of established position, and decline—all have different features.

For dynamic theory, a key element is a time interval between moves and responses, or a time distribution of responses; and this time factor is typically essential to give firms an incentive to make competitive moves, by giving them a chance for a temporary gain before their moves are neutralized by the defensive or counteroffensive responses of rivals.[5] Or there may be other elements tending to prevent immediate and complete neutralization.

Perhaps the chief common feature of competitive action is an expectation of a gain that is sure to be eroded; and it is not convincing to make competition hinge on businessmen being so uniformly stupid that they experience this repeatedly without learning to anticipate it. At least the more intelligent must be thinking in terms of a result that will outlast the erosion process; and in this light the decisive motive must be a preference for eroded profit on a larger volume of business, over a similarly eroded profit on a smaller volume. I speak of an "eroded" profit rather than "zero profit," partly because before profit from one successful move is reduced to zero, other moves may have brought other profits, and partly because "zero profit" carries a misleading precision. It is interesting that Chamberlin's tangency theorem for differentiated products

[5] After writing the above, I find these time elements recognized by A. Henderson: "The Theory of Duopoly," *Quarterly Journal of Economics*, November, 1954, pp. 565, 580. Also by the Civil Aeronautics Board, according to a report of its decision in *Air Freight Tariff Agreement Case*, 14 C.A.B., 424, 428, 430 (1951).

involves conduct of the opposite sort: pricing for short-term profit, which after erosion leaves the producer with a smaller volume than he might have had with a more farsighted policy. This can happen; but the diagrammatic proof that it must happen wherever product is differentiated, is unconvincing once one makes adjustments in the concepts of cost and cost curves and demand curves which are needed for dynamic theory.

Cost, conceived as including the minimum return necessary to attract capital and enterprise, includes, under dynamic conditions, large elements of unpredictable obsolescence, thus making "zero profit" an indefinite, but substantial, quantity. This makes it rational to prefer larger to smaller volume, at "zero profit"; and this seems clearly to accord with the characteristic American business emphasis on the importance of growth.

As for the envelope cost curve, so frequently used, each point on it must logically represent the most economical method of producing a given output, if a plant could be adapted to that output and never have to change. It takes no account of fluctuations or of growth by substantial-sized units or of provision of reserve capacity to be ready to handle contingent increases, including those which a vigorous sales-promotion campaign might bring, if it proved successful. No competitor likes to expose himself to losing customers to his rivals because he cannot fill their orders promptly enough. Thus on a more realistic curve of cost with scale or size of plant or enterprise, each point would represent, for a given size or expected average output, the average cost that might be expected during the period in which the plant or enterprise remains of this size, allowing for periods when it will be working at part capacity and relatively high average cost and other possible times when it may be working overtime or otherwise be pushed beyond its optimum rate. Such a point would not be on the short-run cost curve but above it, and a long-run cost curve connecting such points would intersect the short-run cost curve, not be tangent to it.

The real point is that the whole range of actual or probable movement on the short-run curve comes into play, not merely the point of supposed tangency. At that point, long-run and short-run marginal cost are equal as drawn, thus obscuring the fact, which is crucial for explaining actual competitive behavior, that at most times short-run marginal cost is quite substantially below long-run marginal cost (which in turn is likely to differ little from average cost) while occasional peaks of demand may push short-run marginal cost well above both long-run marginal cost and average cost. A firm may price well above marginal cost—pricing for maximum profit as determined by a sloping individual demand curve—and may still fail to cover average cost.

A timeless two-dimensional demand curve of the conventional sort leaves out of account the fact that the effect of a given price, or price differential, on the volume of sales is a function, among other things, of the length of time during which it has been in effect. The effect may reach its limit in time, or may be indefinitely progressive, if the stimulus can be maintained. This time dimension has been recognized at times by economists—generally when they were not speaking as theorists. It means, among other things, that the effect of a given price on sales volume depends on the previous price or price situation; and that the curve is not fully reversible.

A given price may take full effect in minutes (as on a produce exchange) or may take decades where it requires changes in consumers' ways of life which have strong inertia. An example might be the effect of reduced electric rates in stimulating household appliance use of electricity. This case is typical in that the active variable is better described as a price policy than a price, and acts jointly with promotion of the sale of household equipment. Similar comments apply to alterations of the product and moves in the area of sales promotion. This complex of variables would overload any possible system of graphic presentation. A family of three-dimensional surfaces—the third dimension being time—with a different surface for each initial price or price situation, would still be a simplification.

Both for cost curves and demand curves, movements along the long-run curve involve a shifting of the short-run curve, setting up a new one of different dimensions from the former one. In the diagrammatic development of Chamberlin's tangency theorem, the treatment of cost and of demand in this respect is nonsymmetrical. Long-run movements of demand are treated exclusively as unanticipated shifts of the short-run demand curve, and producers are assumed to be governed exclusively by the short-run curve prevailing at the moment and not by longer-run expectations. Thus his diagrams utilize a short-run demand curve, placed against a long-run cost curve. A different method could lead to significantly different results.

The responses of those with whom a competitor deals bring in an economic process which is naturally left offstage by equilibrium theory but is essential to dynamics; namely, market canvassing and bargaining. Galbraith has taken advantage of theory's neglect of this process to annex it as one sector of his rather heterogeneous category of countervailing power, treating it as a substitute for competition which has lapsed into passivity. Actually, as theory should have been insisting all along, this activity of customers is a necessary complementary part of the process of competition, serving to bring to bear and make effective the competitive alternatives that may exist. Without it, competition would become passive, though, as earlier noted, many customers can neglect it without serious results if enough others attend to it.

Three grades of customer activity may be distinguished. First, buyers may simply canvass the available alternatives and choose the one they prefer. This increases the cross-elasticity of demand on which the effectiveness of competition depends and tends toward equalizing the attractiveness of different sellers' offerings. Second, some buyers may try to get a better bargain than is currently offered, using their power to shift their patronage as a leverage. It is chiefly the larger buyers who have a chance to do this, and it is likely to result in discriminatory favors, granted frequently (but not exclusively) by the smaller and less powerful suppliers. Letting contracts on a basis of sealed bids is one variant of this process in which one large buyer tries to bring to bear a specially active form of competition for his individual business out of which he hopes to get a differential price. Finally, there is the buyer with real monopolistic power, or bilateral monopoly, in which it seems that almost anything might happen.

V. SOME APPLICATIONS

The foregoing ideas suggest, among other things, some modifications in current theorems, including those of pure oligopoly, and the tangency theorem for competition with differentiated products and sloping individual demand curves, tending to reduce the departures of these models from older conceptions of cost-price equilibrium. In the case of pure oligopoly, the indicated modifications begin with the question: Under what conditions is it natural for a firm to expect an increase or decrease in its price to be followed or not followed by its rivals, and how may these expectations be modified by devices available to a firm, other than a simple increase or decrease in its list prices? The suggestion has been made that an increase is more likely to be followed if costs have risen generally. And this possibility can be sounded out by announcing in advance an intended increase, which can be withdrawn if rivals do not follow suit. If there is much unused capacity, a price advance is unlikely to be followed, and existing prices are likely to be subject to downward nibbling. But if prices get ruinously low, a move back toward a more normal level may be followed though likely to be unstable.

The number of rivals plays a part in that, if unused capacity exists, the actions of the group tend to be controlled by that member whose ideas lead to the lowest price policy. Numbers also play a part in that the initiator of a price reduction which is not instantly neutralized can stand to gain more than any one of his rivals stands to lose. Thus the outcome may be affected by differences between the slopes of what may be called the aggressive and the defensive demand curves, as well as by differences between the curves envisaged by different firms. More important, perhaps, are devices for making concessions which will not apply to a firm's whole business but mainly—at least for a time—to the added business it hopes to gain. When demand is strong enough to utilize capacity fully, prices would tend to rise under either oligopoly or old-fashioned competition; but the rise under oligopoly may be more moderate because influenced by a longer time perspective. Another mitigating factor is the existence of stand-by capacity, of only moderately inferior efficiency.

As to the case of differentiated products, if this is treated in terms of short-run cost curves, price may be above short-run marginal cost and still be below average cost, and below long-run marginal cost. A fairly typical hypothesis would be that the bulk of production is on a scale sufficient to afford the bulk of the economies of size, implying that the slope of the long-run cost curve is sufficiently flat and uncertain to be an unimportant factor, except for definitely small firms. I cannot conceive a firm deliberately following a price policy which, for the sake of a small price advantage, would condemn it to be one of these small firms when a more aggressively competitive policy might lead to progressive expansion. Such a size-limiting policy involves outright danger to survival, not merely larger or smaller profits.

While competition may emphasize model changes and sales promotion, these in themselves tend to create uncertainty whether a price reduction will be fully and instantly met. Thus they tend to prevent price differentials from becoming so settled in trade custom that a price reduction by one firm is sure to be instantly neutralized by the others. Thus, while competition spurs innovation, innovation in turn helps to keep price competition from settling into an inactive rut.

In both types of case, needless to say, a workably competitive result requires that there be no outright collusion. But it does not necessarily require the ignoring of rivals' probable reactions; merely that their expected reactions should not be so prompt and complete as to wipe out all competitive incentive, either hope of gain or fear of loss from letting others "get the jump." This latter may be the most important factor.

VI. THE OVER-ALL PICTURE

The foregoing is a mere fragment of the whole picture. It by no means implies that all industry is satisfactorily competitive. It leaves much room for inequalities in the impact of competitive pressures in different parts of the economy. The most serious inequalities are those between the pressures of competition in industry and trade, on the one hand, and, on the other hand, the pressures it would produce, if unmitigated, on agriculture and labor. One explanation for this inequality seems to carry the implication that competition in these fields would impose no undue burdens if only industry and trade were not shot through with monopoly, raising the prices of the things workers and farmers buy. Without denying that there is a measure of truth in this, I venture to suggest a different hypothesis as more important: namely, that in industry and trade, the producers' side of the market adjustment is dominated by entrepreneurs' dollar expenses, which will (with qualifications) veto production if receipts do not cover them, while in the case of labor and one-family farming units, the producers' side is a genuine supply schedule which is highly inelastic and may be actually backward-sloping—meaning that a reduction of wages or farm prices tends to result, if anything, in more crops raised, or hours of work offered, rather than less.

This is, of course, not a new idea, but it seems to carry a two-sided consequence. One side is that labor and agriculture might need some mitigation of the pressures of competition, even if the rest of the economy were unqualifiedly competitive. In other words, if we got rid of all monopoly in industry and trade, that might still not make the economy safe for unmitigated competition in labor and agriculture. The other side is that an acknowledged need on the part of labor and agriculture for mitigations of competitive pressures is neither proof nor measure of the dominance of stultifying monopoly in the rest of the economy.

There can be no certainty that competition will remain vigorous in American business. The necessary conditions are a fascinating subject for speculation. Tentatively, they appear to include three mutually interacting areas: public policy expressed in the antitrust laws, the aggressive psychology and adaptability of the American businessman, and the impact of continuous change in techniques, products, and channels of trade, tending to keep things stirred up and uncertain and to prevent competition from lapsing into routine passivity. In the troubled years that lie ahead, this complex of factors is destined at best to an insecure existence. To keep competition healthy requires the traditional eternal vigilance. To recognize competition when we see it, in its present-day forms, requires not only factual study but some reorienting of the traditional framework of theoretical concepts in which the facts may find their interpretation.

Discussion*

FRITZ MACHLUP:† The call for dynamic, more dynamic, and fully dynamic theory is repeated over and over again. I fear that the dynamics of the meaning of the word "dynamic" is too great for the term to be of continued usefulness if we want to communicate and not only to orate. Professor Clark wants to communicate, I know, and therefore I take the liberty of commenting a bit on his choice of language.

He speaks of a gap between theories of equilibrium and theories of growth and development. As I see it, equilibrium is a tool of thinking needed to explain change, no matter whether it is change in market prices

* *The American Economic Review,* Vol. XLV (Proceedings of the American Economic Association, 1955), pp. 481–82 and 487–90. Reprinted by courtesy of the publisher and the authors. Only those parts of Professor Machlup's discussions that dealt with Professor Clark's paper are reprinted here.

† Johns Hopkins University.

or in business investment or in employment or in the rate of growth. Equilibrium is a valuable concept both in models which disregard time lags—static theory—and in models which present sequences in time—dynamic theory. Since a theory of growth will ordinarily use the equilibrium concept, there can be no contrast between theories of equilibrium and of growth. What Clark meant, I suppose, was the contrast between "static theories of price and output" and "theories of growth and development."

Price theory itself may be static or dynamic. I once gave a graphic description of a "dynamic or time-sequence analysis of effects of a selling campaign," in which five different outcomes—different sales volumes at one price and different prices for one sales volume—were shown to result from a given selling effort, depending on the chosen sequence of actions and on the time intervals between the steps. The five points would all coincide if sequences and intervals of time did not matter and demand curves were assumed to be reversible (*Economics of Sellers' Competition*, pages 185–89). Whether the complicated dynamic model has to be used or the simple static model will do, depends on the kind of problem at hand; that is, not on whether sales actually depend on the time sequences and intervals but on whether the differences really matter for the kind of answer required. Clark gave a very similar description but did not say whether he believes that the dynamic model is always superior. If he thinks so, I would disagree. Dynamic theory is better only where it is needed; where the analytic job can be done with the simpler, less realistic, static theory, the latter is preferable.

"Fully dynamic theory," Clark says, "must accept indeterminateness." I suppose he means to suggest this as a definition; namely, that a theory which is both dynamic and indeterminate should be called "fully dynamic." I do not know whether this would be helpful. Oligopoly theory, to be sure, will usually have to be dynamic, will have to make large allowance for uncertainty in the anticipations of sellers, and will have to leave a large scope for indeterminateness. (See my chapter on "Oligopolistic Indeterminacy," *op. cit.*, pages 414 ff.) I should prefer to use language which does not mix the dynamic elements, the uncertainty elements, and the indeterminateness, since all these are different things that ought to have separate names.

There is no disagreement of substance between Clark and myself on the dynamics of oligopolistic competition. I find his emphasis on the time interval between move and countermove as a key element in the theory of oligopolistic competition most appropriate and significant.

The tangency theorem comes in for a good deal of criticism, and in at least one respect Clark's objection coincides with Harrod's, reproduced by Weintraub: businessmen are not so shortsighted as to overlook potential competition; hence they may ward it off and secure larger sales volumes by charging lower prices. I believe that the proponents of the tangency theorem had only the case of a polypolistic seller in mind, who would regard himself as too small to arouse any responses on the part of competitors, old or new. The theorem was not meant to apply to the case of oligopolistic competition under the pressure of new entry, actual or potential.

Clark's remark on product differentiation as a competitive device confirms my own conclusions that quality competition can be quite vigorous and that product differentiation may weaken but will often invigorate competition. I also showed that product standardization may be an aid to price competition, but is often an aid to price maintenance and other forms of collusion (*ibid.*, pages 163–68). But may I take exception to the way in which Clark put his comment? He said that "theory appears to regard product differentiation as always a shelter from the rigors of competition." My theory, for one, does not. Clark obviously meant "some theorists." After all, no theorist is appointed or ordained to speak in the name of "theory."

GARDNER ACKLEY:† I must begin by saying that there is little in Professor Clark's paper with which I find myself able to disagree. As is always the case with whatever subject Professor Clark touches, the result is illumination and stimulation.

There were a few minor points out of the number he makes with which I might have picked an argument; but even these turned out, when I attempted to develop them, to become largely issues of semantics. I have decided, therefore, to use my few minutes for what might be considered a methodological matter. It relates to Professor Clark's fundamental thesis that our theories of competition, to be realistic and to be useful in policy, must be made dynamic.

I expect that there can be no disagreement—indeed it is a commonplace—that our economic theories need to be dynamic. The trouble is that the word "dynamic" does not always have a very clear or specific meaning. As someone has remarked, dynamic is merely an adjective which distinguishes one's own theories from everyone else's.

I wonder, therefore, if it would not be useful to specify rather clearly what we may mean by a dynamic theory of competition before we proceed to construct or to criticize one. I may say in advance that it is my feeling that Professor Clark has not given a very clear or consistent meaning to dynamic theory and that this may be responsible for my impression that his paper represents mainly a series of somewhat disconnected observations. I find many of these observations individually very penetrating and stimulating; but nevertheless the thread which ties them together is sometimes hard to find.

---

† University of Michigan.

Just what is the distinction that Professor Clark means to imply in his contrast of "static models and dynamic aspects"? In the very first sentence of his paper reference is made to "the gap between theories of cost-price equilibrium and theories of production, growth, and development." Only a few sentences later we have it that dynamic theories "include the tendencies toward equilibrium. But because these tendencies never reach their static limits, dynamic theory cannot use any features which are needed only to enable a model to attain this impossibly precise completeness. . . ." Still later we read that "a theory of competition as dynamic process must be not a model but a framework within which many models may find their places, including equilibrium models as limiting hypothetical cases." This is about all that I find which refers explicitly to this contrast of static versus dynamic theories. There is, however, also an implied definition of dynamic in the substantive matters and problems which Professor Clark chooses to discuss.

Leaving aside for the moment Clark's particular meaning, what meanings might we give in general to this contrast of static with dynamic?

I assume that we agree quite generally that static refers to an analysis of states or conditions of equilibrium. Given the values of certain outside or exogenous factors, there is (or may be) one pattern of the internal or endogenous variables from which all tendencies to further change would be absent. This pattern represents an equilibrium situation.

Now, because equilibrium is a situation from which change is, by definition, absent, equilibrium theory has frequently fallen into the trap of eliminating from consideration those things which are the inevitable concomitant of change—most of all, uncertainty. If equilibrium is a prediction—a state which will someday be reached—then this is legitimate. But if, as I assume it usually is, it is only an analytical device, then there is no excuse for eliminating from the description of behavior the effects of change and uncertainty. To put these back into static theory, then, is a first step toward making theory dynamic.

Some of Clark's dynamics consist precisely of this. It seems to me that much of what he has to say about the content of long-run and short-run cost curves and about Chamberlin's tangency theorem is merely an improvement of the static analysis by the recognition of the effects of change and of the uncertainty which change generates.

To introduce the effect of change and uncertainty into our demand and supply curves is an important step. But it is still not part of what I would consider a true dynamics: an analysis in which the concern is with processes of change. Nor does Professor Clark stop with this first step.

As we have come increasingly to realize, in order even to define the existence of a stable equilibrium, we need at least some rudimentary dynamics. These have always been implied in all of our equilibrium models, but they have often been inadequately explored. The question is: How do sellers (buyers, factor suppliers, et cetera) behave when equilibrium does not exist? What precisely is the nature and the time sequence of their behavior? How do they respond, and when? Only by investigating these questions can we be sure that an equilibrium, or at least a stable equilibrium, exists. And the properties of the equilibrium depend on the nature of the disequilibrium behavior.

A great deal of the substance of what is now called "dynamic analysis" is merely an explicit exploration of the way in which equilibrium is approached. A comparative statics analysis concentrates on previous and the new equilibrium positions and ignores the process of change from one to the other. A dynamic analysis shows the time sequence and pattern of movement between the two equilibrium positions.

This type of dynamics may also recognize that full equilibrium is rarely or never achieved. Changes in the exogenous variables may be so rapid and so extensive that the system never reaches one equilibrium before that equilibrium is replaced by another. As a well-known text once put it, the dog continues to chase the rabbit (equilibrium), but the position of the rabbit continually changes. To understand the behavior of the dog we need to know where the rabbit (equilibrium) is at any time, even though we know that the dog will never catch him.

What would be the content of the analysis of competition which corresponds to this rather narrow concept of dynamics? It would deal, I think, with several of the questions that Professor Clark discusses. When he talks of the process of profit erosion, and its duration, he is, it seems to me, discussing the dynamics of the approach to equilibrium. Technological change or other disturbances to equilibrium occur. What is the sequence of events by which the market adjusts—through innovation, imitation, and competitive response—to this initial change?

This, too, is important and useful. And it requires explicit recognition, as Clark urges is necessary, of the time lags in the process of market adjustment.

But there is another and broader content to economic dynamics—the content which Clark suggests when he contrasts theories of equilibrium with theories of growth and development and which he deals with several times in the substance of his paper. The narrower dynamics retains an essential tie to statics; it merely investigates more explicitly the processes involved in "tendencies toward equilibrium." But the broader type breaks more fundamentally with the equilibrium concept. In the broader dynamic analysis, movements of variables represent not merely the working out of tendencies toward equilibrium. Rather, processes of change are seen at least in part to be irreversible, self-generative, and self-determining. Change is a product of previous change, as well as of other current variables. Partly, this is a matter of bringing into the analysis, as endogenous variables, factors which the equilibrium analysis took as exogenous. Thus we would attempt to explain, at least in part, such things as the state of technology, the number of sellers, the evolution of buyers' tastes, the nature of the market institutions (such as the form of price quotation and methods of sale), the attitudes of sellers toward their rivals' moves, their long-run versus short-run horizons, et cetera. These would be things to be explained rather than to be assumed.

But the broader dynamics to which I refer does more than merely to enlarge the list of variables. It also, as I have indicated, considers the factors responsible, not only for the levels, but for the rates of change of these variables. When Professor Clark sets up his criteria for appraisal of market performance, he is clearly thinking very specifically in these terms. He is concerned with whether a particular market situation is productive of a more or less rapid rate of introduction of new processes and new products, with the nature and speed of product evolution, and with the speed of the creation as well as the erosion of profit opportunities. And he has some very interesting things to say about these.

All of these contributions toward a more dynamic theory are important and useful. But if we are trying to provide a general framework for a dynamic theory of competition, we probably need to recognize more explicitly than I think Professor Clark has done that "dynamic" can have several meanings. And I believe that we must develop somewhat separately the appropriate theoretical tools as well as the substantive content of these several levels of analysis. As is the case with other branches of economic theory, the dynamic analysis of competition and markets is still in the stage of foundation laying.

Professor Clark has given us some sketches of a few elevations of the structure. But it is still a little early to tell what the building will look like when it is completed.

15

Price Discrimination and the Multiple-Product Firm*

By ELI W. CLEMENS†

The problem of the multiple-product firm has lain in virtual neglect on the threshold of the theory of monopolistic (or imperfect) competition since the pioneering efforts of Chamberlin and Joan Robinson some seventeen or eighteen years ago.[1] Closely related to this problem is the problem of price discrimination or the price line. The significance of both is apparent since it is probably impossible to find in the whole of our economy a single firm that sells a single product at a single price. This is theoretically explainable by the fact that the conventional single-

* *The Review of Economic Studies*, Vol. XIX (1950–51), pp. 1–11. Reprinted, with alterations, by courtesy of the publisher and the author.

The writer wishes to acknowledge certain very significant criticisms of early drafts of this article by Professors J. M. Clark, D. H. Wallace, R. A. Lester, J. S. Earley, and E. W. Williams, Jr. In a broader and more indirect sense the writer has drawn heavily upon Professor Clark's *Studies in the Economics of Overhead Costs* (University of Chicago Press, 1923) and Professor Wallace's early but still important article, "Joint and Overhead Costs and Railway Rate Policy," *Quarterly Journal of Economics*, Vol. XLVIII (August, 1934), p. 583. This article, a culmination of a long line of articles in the *Journal*, just skirts the problem suggested here and presumably influenced and was influenced by Professor Chamberlin. The writer has also had the benefit of reading an early draft of Professor Earley's paper before the Mid-West Economic Association meeting on "The Recent Controversy on Marginal Analysis." Professor Fritz Machlup, who has been working on a somewhat similar attack on the problem, has also contributed generously by criticisms and suggestions.

† University of Maryland.

[1] Some attacks on the problem are those of Sidney Weintraub, *Price Theory* (Pitman, 1949), pp. 289–336; G. J. Stigler, *The Theory of Price* (Macmillan, 1946), pp. 305–20; J. C. Weldon, "The Multiproduct Firm," *Canadian Journal of Economic and Political Science*, Vol. XIV (May, 1948), p. 176; and R. H. Coase, "Monopoly Pricing with Interrelated Costs and Demands," *Economica*, NS Vol. XIII (November, 1946), p. 278. Professor R. A. Gordon in "Short Period Price Determination in Theory and Practice," *American Economic Review*, Vol. XXXVIII (June, 1948), pp. 273–75, likens the present concentration on the two extreme cases of the single-product firm and the pure case of joint costs to the previous failure to consider the real world existing between extremes of perfect competition and pure monopoly. He mentions certain other contributions on the multiple-product firm by M. W. Reder, W. J. Eiteman, M. R. Colberg, J. R. Hicks, and others. Kaldor has also considered the problem. Another noteworthy contribution is that contained in the study of Committee on Price Determination for the Conference on Price Research, *Cost Behavior and Price Policy* (National Bureau of Economic Research, 1943), pp. 170–88. See also Joel Dean's recent book, *Managerial Economics* (Prentice-Hall, 1951), pp. 113–38, 471–548.

product firm that is presumably in equilibrium when marginal revenue is equal to marginal cost is not in equilibrium if it can serve the remaining portion of the demand curve at a price greater than marginal cost without adversely[2] disturbing its existing market, or, more commonly, if there is any accessible[3] market for which it can produce with its unused capacity at a price above marginal cost. The first situation, price discrimination, differs only slightly from the second, multiple-product production; together they constitute the terrain of the firm's activities.[4]

The assumption of a "product mix" does little to meet the needs of the situation for it lends itself to only the crudest forms of analysis and assumes away some of the most fundamental problems, including those involved in the manipulation of the firm's price and product lines. It is a commonplace of business practice that the production and sales managers work hand in hand to devise new products that can be produced with the company's idle capacity—many times at little or no profit. Every manager and industrial engineer is familiar with the basic tenet of management: What the firm has to sell is not a product, or even a line of products, but rather its capacity to produce.

Any idle piece of equipment, any unused technical knowledge or organizational resources possessed by the firm represents a challenge to the sales force and production manager. *Any* market reasonably accessible to the firm in which price is greater than marginal cost constitutes an invitation to invade. It is not necessary that the market be related to the firm's existing ones, although in view of management's experience it is desirable. Drugstores and variety stores cross-invade each other's markets and both invade the restaurant industry. The Du Pont Company starts the production of photographic film while the Eastman Kodak Company moves into the chemical plastics market.

Expansion may be defensive as well as offensive. The invasion of new markets may have the purpose of keeping potential competitors at their distance. In such instances the establishment of these "outposts of competition"[5] will not be limited by the profits to be obtained.

---

[2] There will be some effect. See below.

[3] The word "accessible" is redundant, but it is used in recognition of the limits to product-line expansion which will be touched on later.

[4] Multiple-product production is universal and may be carried to extreme lengths. The General Electric Company is said to produce 2,000 products, The Armstrong Cork Company 350, and the B.F. Goodrich Company 32,000. Thorp and Crowder noted that at least half the products made by forty-seven out of fifty of the largest companies accounted each for less than half of 1 per cent of those firm's sales. *The Structure of Industry* (T.N.E.C. Monograph No. 27, 1941), p. 602. For a most interesting collection of cases with their ramifications see G. E. Hale, "Diversification: Impact of Monopoly Policy Upon Multi-Product Firms," *University of Pennsylvania Law Review*, Vol. XCVIII (February, 1950), pp. 320–56. Also C. N. Davisson, "Revamping the Product Line," *Michigan Business Review*, November, 1949, pp. 17–20.

[5] The writer is indebted to Professor Clark for this apt phrase. Clark presumably used it in somewhat the same way.

This means in theory (and apart from certain technical and institutional limitations) that production tends to be carried to the point where the least profitable unit of output will be produced and sold at marginal cost, or expressed in another way, to the point where marginal cost is approximately equal to price in the least profitable market.

The rudiments of an approach to the problem of the multiple-product firm are already at hand in the theory of price discrimination. The strict, but useless, concept of price discrimination as the sale of a single product at several prices obscures the fact that the purposes and practices of price discrimination are essentially the same as those of multiple-product production. What appears in the former as discriminatory pricing appears in the latter as accepting different percentages of profit. The distinction between the two becomes more irrelevant when it is remembered that intrafirm product differentiation is often the means by which price discrimination is made possible, and is, in fact, one of the fundamental objectives of management. The elimination or addition of a trade mark, or of a few accessories, is the means by which product differences are created to the end that strong and weak markets can be exploited at differing margins of profit.[6] Differentiated products merge into multiple products; price discrimination, intrafirm product differentiation and multiple-product production are more or less universal means to the same end and differ only in degree.[7]

Two factors have been needless obstacles to the solution of the problem. One is the more or less tacit assumption of the inflexibility of resources within the firm. The other is the unrealistic assumption of the homogeneity of the firm's output. This paper assumes the transferability of resources within the firm and suggests a homogeneous unit of output to be applied to multiple-product firms. It is to be noted that the case of true joint costs and invariable product proportions is thus specifically excluded.

Any study of industrial techniques indicates that the transferability of resources between products and within the firm is much greater than is commonly assumed in economic treatises.[8] Lathes, milling machines,

[6] As an interesting case in point note the varying profit margins on the several cars produced by General Motors Company and the Chrysler Corporation. See Federal Trade Commission, *Report on the Motor Vehicle Industry* (1939), pp. 538, 603.

[7] The problem discussed here is closely related to the problem of marginal cost pricing which the writer touched upon in another article. E. W. Clemens, "Price Discrimination in Decreasing Cost Industries," *American Economic Review*, Vol. XXXI (December, 1941), p. 794. The most recent and comprehensive discussion of the whole marginal cost controversy is that of Nancy Ruggles, "Recent Developments in the Theory of Marginal Cost Pricing," *Review of Economic Studies*, Vol. XVII (2), No. 43, 1949–50, p. 107.

[8] This principle, as well as the others embodied in this article, are illustrated in any standard text on industrial management. Particularly significant are the cases in F. E. Folts, *Introduction to Industrial Management* (McGraw-Hill, 1949). These cases can be assumed to represent a fair cross-section of industry.

drill presses, boring machines, etc., can be shifted at will between a large variety of products. At the most only a new set of jigs, dies, patterns, etc., are necessary. Nor is it necessary that all equipment be generally adaptable; it is only necessary that the firm have a reasonable proportion of general-purpose equipment (as distinguished from special-purpose equipment).

The same principle holds true in the processing industries. The proportion of oil refinery products can be varied. It would be completely unrealistic to think of the equipment of a chemical company to be specialized by products. Most nonferrous metal companies produce a variety of metals, coal is produced in varying grades for different markets. A steel company produces a thousand types of steel, each to be sold in different markets, with the same facilities. The transferability of resources between markets is, of course, commonplace in the railroad and utility industries.

The problem of homogeneous units of output can be solved within the conventional framework of the theory of monopolistic competition. Units of output are defined as blocks of output, without distinction as to products, which have equal direct costs under standard conditions. This is more than a mere system of weighting; it corresponds closely with data obtained from motion and time studies and made a part of permanent shop and production records which in turn are used in management decisions. These direct costs would, of course, differ from both anticipated and realized marginal costs which would vary over the range of the company's output.[9] With units of output so defined it would be desirable generally to assume rising marginal costs as less efficient, stand-by equipment and labor are brought into use.

THE ROBINSONIAN ANALYSIS

The assumptions of partial (although not necessarily complete) transferability of resources within the firm between products and a homogeneous unit of output based on standard direct costs are both realistic and theoretically practicable. The problem of the multiple-product firm can then be treated simply as a problem in price discrimination, and Joan Robinson's well-known analysis of what Pigou calls discrimination of the third degree will lend itself with certain reservations to the consideration of the problem.[10] The analysis, however, is subject to certain important limitations if the attempt is made to apply it to the multiple-product firm, a use presumably not contemplated by Mrs. Robinson.

[9] Direct costs under standard conditions are analogous to what operating management commonly calls "standard costs" which reflect what an article "should cost under normal operating conditions." An important function of operating management is the analysis of deviations from these standard costs. See C. C. Balderston, V. S. Karabasz, and R. P. Brecht, *Management of an Enterprise* (Prentice-Hall, 1942), pp. 380–84, for example.

[10] Joan Robinson, *Economics of Imperfect Competition* (Macmillan, 1936), chaps. 15 and 16.

In the first place, the Robinsonian method does not visualize the extension of production to the point where marginal cost is equal to demand. The market and its several components are clearly defined. It only remains for the monopolist to maximize his profit in each market. Neither the dynamic nature of the firm's activities nor their scope is revealed. If it is assumed that the firm could reach a large number of markets in which price is greater than marginal cost, the firm could not be in equilibrium. Another point of necessary refinement is that the Robinsonian analysis does not include the situation where the firm can distinguish between units of output sold to customers in the same market. Thus a firm might apply a sliding scale of prices (or quantity discounts) to each market. Customers might be classified not only on the basis of the elasticity of demand of the group, but simply on the basis of the maximum price each customer is willing to pay for a certain number of units.[11] The introduction of such an assumption might make the Robinsonian technique completely unworkable because of the sheer complexity of the resulting diagram.

Another limitation of the Robinsonian analysis for the present case has to do with her use of the conventionalized marginal cost curve by which marginal cost is applicable to any increase in output regardless of form. In many cases of empirical research it is desirable, if not absolutely necessary, to identify marginal cost at any particular level of output with specific increases rather than any increase in output. This is not possible by Joan Robinson's technique.

AN ALTERNATE APPROACH

The procedure suggested here is believed to be somewhat more applicable to empirical research and is also consistent with certain more dynamic aspects of the firm's activities which are not considered by Mrs. Robinson. Conditions ranging from strong monopoly to virtually perfect competition are assumed in the various markets that can be reached by the company. Practically, competition is assumed to take the form of invading new markets by a process of price discrimination. Price discrimination thus emerges paradoxically as the most common means of competition.

It is assumed that the firm's resources are mobile and that the firm can produce a wide variety of products. The case of joint costs and fixed product proportions is specifically excluded, although the procedure could be modified to include such cases. It is also assumed that demands are not related. This is consistent with the objectives of the firm, since the higher the degree of market independence, the greater become the

[11] The typical block rate schedule of the gas and electric utilities is an example. See K. E. Boulding, *Economic Analysis* (Harper, 1941), pp. 540–49. For another attack on the problem see William Vickrey, "Some Objections to Marginal Cost Pricing," *Journal of Political Economy*, Vol. LVI (June, 1948), p. 218.

advantages of (and the possibility of) breaking up the price structure of the total market. It is also true that the further we move from price discrimination towards the concept of the multiple-product firm, the more reasonable the assumption becomes. Furthermore, the larger the number of firms and the more diversified the markets of each, the smaller will become the consequences of the intermarket relationships of each.

The firm might well be assumed to start as a conventional single-product firm operating under conditions of 60 or 70 per cent of capacity and at a point where marginal cost equals marginal revenue. Possessing excess capacity in the form of equipment, personnel, and organization, it

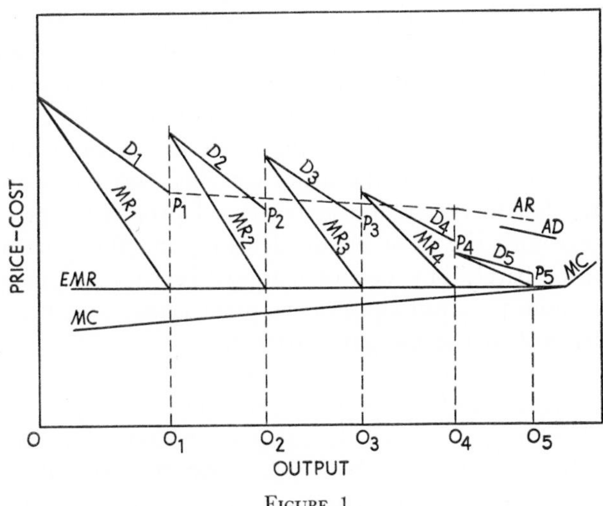

FIGURE 1

can increase production without an undue increase in marginal cost. Rather than reduce the price in an existing market it will seek new outlets in which demand exceeds marginal cost. It will be assumed for purposes of analysis that new markets are invaded in order of their profitability. The firm will be in equilibrium insofar as its own management is concerned only when there are no more accessible markets in which demand price is greater than marginal cost. The situation is illustrated in Figure 1. The figure assumes five markets, although the markets might well be innumerable. Profits will be maximized when production is distributed between the five markets in such a manner as to make marginal revenue equal in all markets and equal to marginal cost. The *EMR* line is a line of equal marginal revenue.

In contrast to Joan Robinson's method, each market has its own zero output axis which is the source of that market's marginal revenue curve. Demand is assumed to be a chain of demand curves, the *EMR* line determining output in each market. If the analyses were started with the assumption of a certain and limited number of accessible markets, the

EMR line would have to be determined by Joan Robinson's method—that of adding horizontally the marginal revenue curves of all the markets to obtain the aggregate marginal revenue curve. The intersection of this curve and the marginal cost curve would determine aggregate output and the position of the *EMR* line. This *AMR* curve is not shown, but a segment of Joan Robinson's aggregate demand curve, *AD,* is shown at operating output.

Five product prices are established, the lowest being just in excess of marginal cost. Although it is assumed that the markets are aligned from left to right in order of their chronological entry, the corresponding assumption that they were entered according to their profitability results in an alignment according to three standards: (1) inversely according to the elasticity of demand in each market, (2) according to the margin of profit measured as a percentage of either standard direct costs or price, and (3) according to price per standard unit of output.

Putting it somewhat differently, the *EMR* line is set at a level determined by the intersection of the firm's marginal cost curve and the *MR* curve for the last market that can be served profitably. In theory this market is one with the most elastic demand, and the price established for it would be barely in excess of marginal revenue and marginal cost. This brings about practical equivalence of marginal cost, marginal revenue, and demand in the marginal market.

If this last market is one of perfect elasticity, equivalence is perfect. It also follows that if *any* single market demand served by the firm is one of infinite elasticity, it becomes the marginal market. Any marginal market of less than infinite elasticity leaves open the possibility, although not the absolute necessity, of some unserved market in which price is greater than marginal cost.

We can interrupt the train of the argument to make the same basic point by use of Joan Robinson's technique. Figure 2 is adapted from her Figure 61.[12] She has assumed the firm to be producing an output *OM* determined by the intersection of the marginal cost curve with the aggregate marginal revenue curve *AMR.* Prices in two markets are P_1 and P_2. The firm, however, could not be in equilibrium if there are *any* other accessible markets in which price is greater than *CM* (and presumably less than P_2). If we assume a series of such markets with their elasticities of demand ranging upward by degrees to infinity the marginal market or least desirable market would be either one of infinite elasticity or an extremely small market with price just above marginal cost. Under any other circumstances the divergence of price in the marginal market from marginal cost would make further diversification profitable. Of several possible markets of perfect elasticity, the limiting one would be the one offering the highest price for the standard output unit. The others would

---

[12] *Op. cit.,* p. 182.

be precluded from consideration since there would be no need to shift production to a lower price market if the firm could sell all it desires at a higher price.

A limiting market of perfect elasticity, D_3, and its marginal curve, MR_3, is shown in Figure 2. For purposes of simplicity it is assumed that this market is the only remaining accessible market in which price is less than P_3 and greater than CM, although the preceding argument assumes a series of such markets. The horizontal addition of the single or-

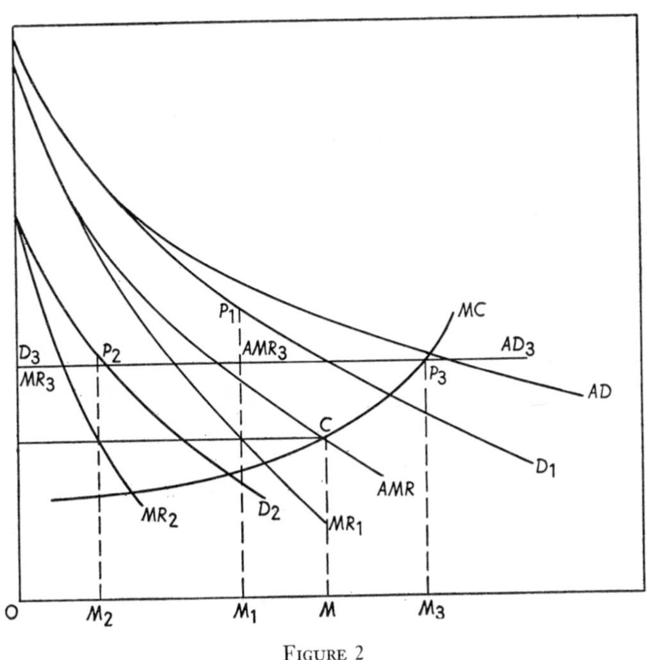

FIGURE 2

dinate to the existing D and MR curves breaks the AMR and AD curves at their respective intersections with the horizontal D_3–MR_3 line of which AMR_3 and AD_3 are continuations. Production is stabilized at an output O–M_3. Additional output will be sold at a price P_3 in the marginal market. Prices P_1 and P_2 will be raised and the output in these markets will be further restricted.

If it is to be assumed that there is no such market of perfect elasticity of demand in which price exceeds marginal cost, the limiting market would be the one with the greatest elasticity. If the assumption of a wide variety of markets is to be maintained, the limiting one in this case would have to be relatively small and would afford a price only a little in excess of marginal cost. Extension to this market would probably involve extreme diversification. The practical limits to this process will be discussed later. It is also interesting to note that the limiting market might be an unserved and highly elastic segment of one of the existing segments if it could be broken away from the existing high price-inelastic segment.

To return to Figure 1, the firm would not be in equilibrium if there were any other market open to it for which any part of the demand curve would lie above the *EMR* line. The addition of any such market would result in "squeezing" production in the firm's existing markets. Output in each of them would be slightly restricted and a new *EMR* line would be established at a level slightly above the old one. The *AR* curve would move to a new and higher position. If marginal costs had begun to rise rapidly (if the firm had been operating at "capacity") the sudden appearance of a new and profitable market might have the effect of raising the *EMR* line so far as to "submerge" the demand curve for one or more products. These products would then be crowded out of the company's line. The situation was of common occurrence in the sellers' market following World War II when many low-profit items disappeared from the market. It is to be noted that the extension of production to the point where marginal cost is equal to demand increases total output but encourages the restriction of output in individual markets.

The marginal cost curve is assumed to be continuous although the way is open to kink it at output breaks. This would facilitate the application of theory to many practical problems of analysis. If the marginal cost curve is assumed to be unaffected by the nature of the firm's products, both the average and marginal cost curves would be similar in nature and comparable to conventional curves drawn for the single-product firm. On the other hand, the values of the average revenue curve would be applicable only to a designated order and proportioning of the various products, except at the point of operating output.[13]

The activities of most firms would indicate an assumption of an almost unlimited series of demand curves. In many instances the need of analysis could be met by classifying customers into a few groups according to prices per standard unit of output and the inelasticity of demand of each group. Creation of iso-elastic demand groups would involve the surrender of product identities; but in cases where the sacrifice could be made, analysis would be simplified for many types of problems.[14]

The market alignment procedure suggested here reflects the dynamic expansion process of the firm which constantly seeks greater profits by

[13] The shape and level of the marginal cost curve would also be influenced by the composition of the standard units of output and the standard direct costs assigned to each of the products. Standard costing techniques would furnish the basis for the distribution of costs. It is also to be noted that nothing would preclude establishing individual *MC* curves, each one beginning at the product's zero axis and intersecting the product's *MR* curve on the *EMR* line. The *MC* curve would be the horizontal sum of these product *MC* curves.

[14] Professors Walter Rautenstrauch and Raymond Villers in their recent *Budgetary Control* (Funk & Wagnalls-Modern Industry, 1950), chap. 9, have outlined this approach as a management device. Products are classified according to the percentage of profit on sales and without regard to their nature.

successively invading less and less profitable markets. Market alignment according to inelasticity of demand has several technical advantages. Attention is focused on the spatial nature of the total market and upon the marginal market. Analysis is simplified and comparisons may be made easily with the conventional price-cost relationships of the single-product firm. Finally, specific segments of the marginal cost curve are tied to particular blocks of output. This is consistent with accounting procedure and with the thinking of management which is generally in terms of blocks of output, such as job lots or products, rather than in terms of units. It can be doubted whether in practice marginal cost has any significance at all except in connection with specific job lots of products under the conditions which are peculiar to the specific line already produced.[15]

The virtual equivalence of marginal cost, marginal revenue and demand in the marginal market merely recognizes the fact that practically all firms produce some products at little or no profit which are just on the margin of being dropped. In other instances no profit items are produced in order to keep the organization intact. The practice has long been taken for granted in the railway and utility industries. Selling at marginal cost by freight absorption is another example. A study of production, marketing and cost accounting techniques offers many examples. Basically the procedure is one of restricting output in inelastic markets while avoiding the costs of idle capacity. However general this practice might be, it seems indisputable that the divergence between demand and marginal cost at operating output is much less than is commonly assumed for the single-product firm.

LIMITS TO PRODUCT DIVERSIFICATION

The question can well be raised as to whether there are limits to the process of market invasion. In view of the countless number of products produced (or sold) by the typical firm and the steady drift towards large-scale enterprise, the answer in both theory and practice might well be no. But obviously there are limits. There are technical limits to the number of products to which plant capacity can be adapted and physical limits to the markets which can be reached. The most common limits are probably those produced by the economies of specialization. In recognition of these economies management characteristically sets up certain minima for output blocks.[16] Thus it can be said that regardless of how many products a plant is physically capable of producing production economies and diseconomies will establish a much more restricted limit.

---

[15] Thus the marginal cost of producing product No. 25 might depend upon the utilization of waste parts from products Nos. 5, 11 and 14, rather than upon general capacity conditions. Here, of course, there is an element of jointness.

[16] For a discussion of management procedure in establishing lot sizes see L. P. Alford, *Cost and Production Handbook* (Ronald, 1934), pp. 236–42.

To make the same point in a different manner, firms may often operate at a point where any substantial increase in output will bring sharply rising marginal costs. Rising costs will be even more pronounced if expansion is to be achieved by the invasion of a new market. The marginal costs of invasion are likely to be considerably higher than the marginal cost of expansion by the firms already in the market. Among the more easily identifiable of these costs are those of transportation to distant markets, of missionary sales work, and of tooling and machine set-ups.[17]

To the extent that firms base their price and production policies on average rather than marginal costs, expansion will be restricted. The writer shares the dissatisfaction of Professor Gordon[18] and others with the marginal cost function, but it is more than conceivable that its vulnerability centers more in the imputed precision than in its substance. A few observations are relevant without being conclusive. Generally, firms price many products closer to their concept of marginal cost than would be indicated by the marginal cost concepts that emerge from many economic treatises. Marginal cost is something more than its ascertainable and measurable elements. Risk and the additional cost of management, both of which are substantial, are marginal costs. Conceivably marginal cost must include a certain minimum amount which the businessman considers necessary profit. When he says that the profit on a certain additional piece of business is "not worth his time and trouble," he is giving expression to a very real concept of marginal cost. The writer also agrees with Professor Machlup's position that too rigid a definition of marginal cost would trap its users into unrealistic and untenantable positions.[19]

Cost accounting techniques indicating an average cost approach to price and product line policies have perhaps needlessly worried some defenders of marginal economics. Typically, the determination of average costs (or standard costs plus a margin for overhead and profit) is a function of the cost accountant in the lower echelons of management. Cost analyses, however, represent only the basic data from which price and

[17] Tooling, machine set-up, and similar costs are direct and marginal costs before a market has been invaded. After invasion they are, of course, fixed costs. These new fixed costs must either be lumped with the firm's general fixed costs which would lower the marginal cost segment for the particular product after invasion, or they might continue to be considered as part of the product's marginal cost. The question is considered in Professor Austin Robinson's review of *Manufacturing Business*, by P. W. S. Andrews (Macmillan, 1950) in the *Economic Journal*, Vol. LX (December, 1950), pp. 771, 778. Both the book and the review are relevant to the problem considered here.

[18] See R. A. Gordon, "Short Period Price Determination in Theory and Practice," *American Economic Review*, Vol. XXXVIII (June, 1948), p. 265; with other citations to basic contributions by R. A. Lester, Fritz Machlup, G. J. Stigler, and H. M. Oliver, Jr.; see also Lloyd G. Reynolds, "Toward a Short-Run Theory of Wages," *American Economic Review*, Vol. XXXVIII (June, 1948), p. 289.

[19] See Fritz Machlup, "Marginal Analysis and Empirical Research," *American Economic Review*, Vol. XXXVI (September, 1946), p. 519.

production strategy is plotted in light of other factors by top-flight management. In different terms, average costs are significant to those in the management hierarchy who follow policy, but not necessarily to those who make it. To top management some circumstances might dictate pricing or the addition of a product at only a little above what the cost accountant's statement indicate to be marginal costs. Other circumstances might lead management to reject suggested additions to the product line that cover average costs several times over. To some extent the solution of the problem and the controversy involved turn on the period assumed for analysis. The longer the period for which strategy must be plotted, the greater becomes the percentage of total costs which must be characterized as marginal.[20]

One of the most important obstacles to expansion into new markets is the lack of "know-how"[21] on the part of both management and workers. The fear of prosecution under the Sherman Act has been significant in many cases. On the other hand, tacit market-sharing agreements may limit invasion. Such agreements are found even among small-town merchants. For these and other reasons we must assume that there are bounds to the number of accessible markets. But whatever the bounds, firms will push production in varying degrees towards the limit where marginal cost is equal to demand in the marginal market. Profit margins in the varying markets will differ due to localized monopolies, lags in competition and other factors. To assume conditions of competitive equilibrium where all profit margins are equal would be completely unrealistic. Normal profits, necessary to a firm's long-run existence, are obtained only insofar as average revenues under multiple-product production are equal to average costs. This condition can only be attained by the continuous process of invasion and cross-invasion of markets, by the shuffling and reshuffling of prices and markets, which are so characteristic of economic activity.[22]

INTERCLASS TRANSFERABILITY OF DEMAND UNITS

A further point, generally neglected in the theory of price discrimination, will round out the discussion. In some instances it can be assumed that the firm has the power to transfer particular customers or demand units between price groups. In other words, the firm might not only

---

20 The writer has greatly benefited from correspondence with Professor J. S. Earley in the development of the preceding material.

21 An increasingly common method of overcoming this obstacle to the invasion of new markets is the pooling of technical and other resources in the hands of a firm sponsored jointly by parent firms in two or more industries. General Electric Company, Pittsburgh Plate Glass Company, Corning Glass Works and many of the large rubber and chemical and other companies have participated in the formation of such companies.

22 C. N. Davisson, *op. cit.*, p. 1, n. 5, discusses some of the advantages and limitations of diversification under existing business conditions.

have the power of differentiating between customer classes, but it might have the further power of determining the constituency of each class. Customers nominally in Group 2, but willing to pay more than P_2, might be shifted to Group 1 and charged a higher price. Unsatisfied customers nominally in Group 2 might be shifted to a lower price group. To the extent that this can be done the chain of demand curves tends to merge into a single continuous demand curve.

In such an instance the monopolist might select a series of prices along the demand curve, each price being applicable to all customers willing to pay it and unwilling to pay the next higher price. In short, the demand curve would be "segmentized." The more prices that could be established, the greater would be the monopolist's profits. In the extreme and limiting case the monopolist would obtain the full demand price for each unit of output by establishing an almost infinite series of prices. Consumers' surplus would be entirely eliminated and the demand curve would become the marginal revenue curve.[23]

First thought might proclaim such assumptions to be inconceivable. However, our economy furnishes numerous cases where the procedure could be applied with a high degree of accuracy. If the firm is able to break up the market into submarkets and apply sliding scales of quantity discounts to each customer group, the situation will be approached. This depicts the pricing pattern of gas and electric utilities where firms discriminate not only between classes but between units of output taken by individual customers within each class by block-rate schedules.[24] The method is also applicable to those firms that make it a policy to successively exhaust demand at lower and lower price levels.[25] It would be applicable to a monopolistic custom-order firm that set prices on a negotiated basis. One of the more interesting applications would be to the increasing number of patent-owning firms who license the use of patented products, the license payments being graduated according to the revenue, or profits, obtained from the use. In general the method would

---

[23] A completely segmentized demand curve is the same as Pigou's discriminating monopoly of the first degree. A partially divided curve represents his discriminating monopoly of the second degree. Discriminating monopoly of the third degree is the basis of Joan Robinson's treatment. Commonly the latter case is the only one considered.

[24] Professor M. G. Glaeser, following Taussig, Pigou, Edgeworth and others, used the technique in analyzing the theory of utility rate making. *Outlines of Public Utility Economics* (Macmillan, 1927), pp. 618–39. In consideration of the extent of the power of classification possessed by utility companies and the multiplicity of their rate schedules this simplified approach to the problem is much more accurate for most purposes than Joan Robinson's more refined method which does not consider intraclass discrimination. The method is also discussed and applied to a limited extent by Professor Boulding. *Economic Analysis* (Harper, 1941), pp. 540–49.

[25] As, for example, in department store selling where shelves are cleared by successive price reductions, or in the publishing field where cheaper and cheaper editions are brought out, or where a new product is introduced at a high price which is steadily reduced.

facilitate analysis of a multitude of firms that practice discrimination to a considerable degree and whose activities cannot be analyzed conveniently by either the single-firm or the Robinsonian technique. The technique certainly must be used cautiously, but the areas of potential application seem to indicate that it could be included justifiably in the economists' traditional "kit of tools."

Figure 3 has certain theoretical implications. It will be noticed that the average revenue curve is not the same as the demand curve but lies above it. Hence, it is possible under these circumstances for a firm to

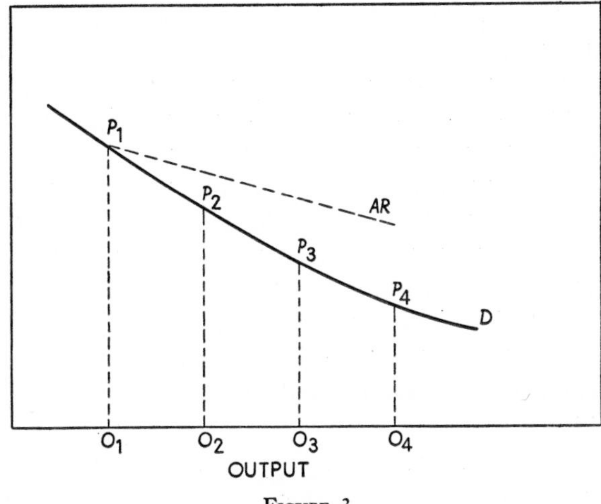

FIGURE 3

make normal profits even if the demand curve lies continuously below the average cost curve.[26] This point has sometimes been stressed in the theory of railroad rate making.

It is also to be noticed that the divergence between the demand and average revenue curves is increased as the demand curve is segmentized. Management achieves maximum profits in this connection in two ways: (1) by invading new markets and (2) by splintering its existing markets. But whether the fractionalization of the firm's market is extensive or intensive, the end result is the same.

The divergence of the demand curve from the average revenue curve is not confined to this special case. It would follow in the first and more general case that only in the rare circumstances where the elasticity of demand was uniform in all of the firm's markets, i.e. where the percentage of profit on price or standard cost was the same, would there be any

[26] Entrepreneurs contemplating the establishment of a new firm seldom if ever make their decision by setting an assumed price against an assumed cost of a single product. If such were the case very few new firms would ever appear. Rather the process is one of comparing the total revenues from a series of products with the total costs.

identity between the average revenue curve of the firm and its demand curve, however conceived.[27]

CONCLUSION

The foregoing analysis should suggest that price discrimination and multiple-product production are not exceptions to general practice, but are rather the essence of customary action. The distinction between a producer selling a single product at different prices and one selling different products in varying markets at differing percentages of profit is a distinction of degree only. What a firm has to sell is not a product, but rather its capacity to produce. Insofar as firms are motivated by the marginal principle, there is a tendency to push production towards the point where marginal cost is equal to demand price for the least profitable unit produced. In this manner "capacity" operation is achieved. The limits to the process are institutional rather than theoretical. Under conditions of monopolistic competition this probably results in a situation where only normal profits are obtained. Whatever the amount of profit, it is obtained only by constant manipulation of the price and product line. The theory of price discrimination must be viewed as the heart of price-cost theory rather than a peripheral case. The firm that does not discriminate in its pricing policy, or differentiate in its product line, or invade new markets, dies in the competitive struggle—and "business management does not commit suicide."

[27] It is extremely questionable whether the ordinary concept of "the demand curve of the firm" can be applied at all in the real world of multiple-product firms. In this instance it is assumed to be the same as Joan Robinson's aggregate demand curve (in terms of standard units) which is obtained by adding the various demand curves horizontally.

16

The Influence of Market Structure on Technological Progress*

By WILLIAM FELLNER†

The argument of the present article will be developed by gradually relaxing the simple but unrealistic initial assumptions. This procedure has obvious disadvantages as well as advantages. The writer feels that in this case the advantages outweigh the disadvantages because certain familiar propositions pertaining to our problem imply the early assumptions of the article, and it seems useful to construct a bridge from these propositions to the later conclusions of the analysis. The titles and the introductory sentences of the various sections describe the assumptions in a general way but two points should be added here. In the first place, the assumption that inventions and know-how are immediately available to all potential users will be removed only in the final section of the article. Secondly, the assumption that progress (the growth of output) is associated with falling prices rather than with rising rates of money income will not be removed at all. From our point of view no importance attaches to the difference between these two ways of distributing the fruits of progress.

I. SINGLE UNEXPECTED INNOVATION—FREE ENTRY

In this section it will be assumed that we are faced with a single unexpected invention, and that entry is free in each industry, in the sense that there exist no institutional (discriminatory) barriers. The second condition is compatible with real economies of scale such as might place obstacles in the way of entry. The potential entrant might know that firms smaller than the existing ones would be less efficient and that he therefore would merely have a chance of replacing an existing producer. This might prevent him from intruding. If such obstacles exist, we shall not say that entry is "blocked" but it is to be expected that in these circumstances the typical results of free entry will show in a somewhat qualified form. Furthermore, if in consequence of product differentiation,

* *The Quarterly Journal of Economics*, Vol. LXV (1951), pp. 556–77. Reprinted, with alterations, by courtesy of the Harvard University Press and the author.

† Yale University.

entry is free merely into a Chamberlinian group, then "free entry into an industry" becomes qualified by buyers' preferences. The concept "industry" loses its precise meaning in these circumstances. Discussion of this problem will also be included in the present section—entry will not be regarded as "blocked"—but here again the assumptions of the section will be said to possess merely qualified validity for the problem.

For a purely competitive industry the situation is portrayed in Figure 1. The long-run supply curve of the industry (*LS*) is represented as horizontal. This does not influence the result of the analysis. Magnified cost curves of the single-plant firms are *ATC*, *AVC* and *MC*. The industry demand curve is *DD*. The equilibrium output is *OA*, the equilibrium price *OL*. The number of firms (plants) is determined by the con-

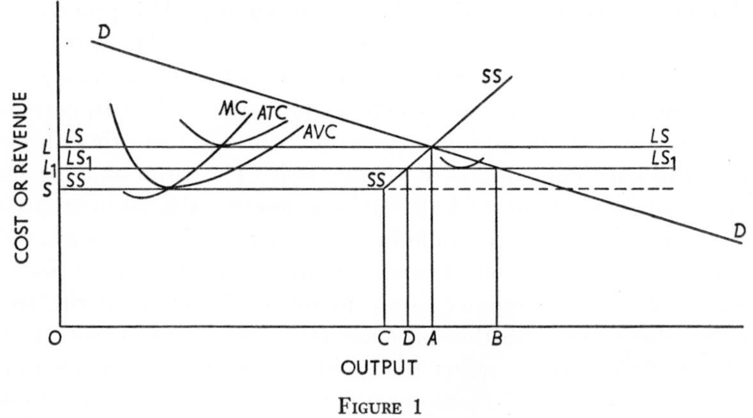

FIGURE 1

dition that at the equilibrium output (*OA*) all firms operate at minimum average total cost.

The short-run supply curve of the industry (*SS*) is the sum of the *AVC* minima up to point *C* on the abscissa where the output is sufficient to keep all existing firms in operation at minimum average variable cost. At output *OC* the short-run supply curve turns up, expressing the fact that at prices higher than *OS*, each firm will increase its output along an individual supply curve which is its marginal cost curve. Starting from the equilibrium output of the industry (*OA*), the (from our point of view) relevant supply curve is short run to the left and long run to the right. This is because we are concerned with problems of entry and our analysis will be sufficiently long run to warrant the assumption that an increase of output beyond *OA* will be brought about by the entry of new firms. However, our analysis will not be sufficiently long run to lead us to disregard the fact that a reduction of output remains compatible with an unchanging number of plants during a period of substantial length.

Let us now assume that the equilibrium becomes disturbed by an invention that lowers the long-run cost curve from the *LS* level to LS_1. This lies between the average total cost and the average variable cost of the old firms. New firms will enter with the new method along the new long-run function LS_1. The price reduction will force the old firms to move back along the short-run function. The lowering of the long-run cost curve from *LS* to LS_1 raises the equilibrium output of the industry to *OB*, and it lowers the equilibrium price to OL_1. The aggregate output of the old firms will be *OD* and entrants will fill the gap between *OD* and *OB*. Whether the old firms do or do not change their methods of production immediately depends on whether the innovation passes a test which will be described in Section II and will there be called the Figure 3 test. We have assumed that in this case the test is not passed: owing to their fixed costs, the old firms find it more profitable to continue with the original technique.[1] Even if they do not introduce the new method immediately they will have to reduce their selling price to that corresponding to the new method. This of course inflicts losses on the old firms. After a period that may be of substantial duration, all firms will become located along LS_1 and all will be using the new technique. This is because "in the long run there exist no fixed costs." As we shall see in Section II the "Figure 3 test" would always be passed, were it not for fixed costs.

So far atomistic competition and a homogeneous product were assumed. As long as there exist no institutional (discriminatory) barriers to entry, the conclusions remain similar. However, some modifications are required to allow for the special characteristics of various market structures.

In monopolistic competition in the large group new firms enter with new "brands" that could not have been produced profitably prior to the cost-saving invention. If there exist differences between the popularity of the various brands, not all old firms need fully to adjust their prices to the cost saving. This is a significant difference but not a fundamental modification of our conclusions because the difference is a consequence of the fact that in this case the freedom of entry is imperfect. The industry concept ceases to be precisely applicable to the problem because *unqualified* freedom of entry must mean freedom of entry into an "industry" producing a homogeneous product. The previous conclusions will be neither more nor less valid than is the concept of "free entry" in cases where no firm can produce a perfect substitute of its competitors' product. If new firms can enter merely somewhere in the "neighbor-

[1] It will be seen later that the failure of the innovation to pass the test expresses itself in the fact that the lowering of *ATC* to tangency with LS_1 does not make this point of tangency lie below the *AVC* curve. The *AVC* curve of already existing firms may, in the first approximation, be conceived of as remaining unchanged. More precisely, it should be regarded as gradually shifting upward, owing to the wear and tear to which the plants are exposed.

hood" of the old rather than in the identical industry—the neighborhood being defined in terms of cross-elasticities—then the degree of price adjustment which is forced upon the old firms depends on how "close" to each of the old firms the entrants become located. This in turn is a matter of the distance of the various products from one another in economic space (as defined by cross-elasticities). It is a matter of how strong the monopoly element is in the monopolistic competition. The smallest cost reduction will induce entries if the products form a continuous array. If there exists a discontinuity in the neighborhood of the margin, i.e., at the old equilibrium, then more than a very small cost reduction is required to induce entry but all these modifications of our conclusions stem essentially from qualifications of the assumption of free entry into an industry. In these circumstances it is impossible to engage in the production of (practically) the same commodities as those produced by the existing firms.

Monopoly may of course develop even if it *is* possible to produce (practically) the same commodities as those already being produced. Such monopoly is compatible with our assumptions concerning freedom of entry, as long as the monopoly position stems exclusively from real economies of large scale. For such monopoly our conclusions hold with a modification which follows from the cost advantage enjoyed by the monopolistic firm. The price charged by such a monopoly cannot exceed the level at which atomistic competitors would find it profitable to enter but it can fall short of this price.[2] *If* it falls short of it, then the invention must reduce the costs of the potential atomistic entrants by more than the difference in question to force the monopolist to adjust his price. In other words the conclusions which were established for pure competition follow here only if the cost reduction makes the latent competition of atomistic outsiders effective. The latent competition of nonatomistic (i.e., large) potential entrants need not affect the price because these should be assumed to know that their entry *would* reduce the price and that it would also reduce the firm size below optimum. They have no reason to enter unless they think that they can ultimately displace the existing firm. The availability to them of an innovation which is available also to the existing firm does not justify this belief.

In conclusion we may say that on the assumptions expressed by the title of the present section, the smallest possible improvement will induce entry, price adjustments, and growth of output, provided firms are atomistic and the product is homogeneous. If the product is not homogeneous, the free-entry assumption becomes qualified and this qualifies the conclusions. If, owing to economies of scale, monopoly exists in spite of

[2] In Professor Bain's terminology, the limit price is on the level where entry would occur. But the intersection of marginal revenue with marginal cost *may* occur at an output level for which the price is below the limit. *Cf.* Joe S. Bain, *Pricing Distribution and Employment* (New York, 1948), pp. 189 ff.

free entry, price may be lower than that which would induce small firms to enter and this too qualifies the conclusions.

II. SINGLE UNEXPECTED INNOVATION— BLOCKED ENTRY

The discussion will now turn to the conditions which must be satisfied before an existing firm adopts an invention as an innovation. In the preceding section the existence of such conditions was merely hinted at because the results were not determined by whether the old firms did or did not promptly adopt a new method. The results were determined by

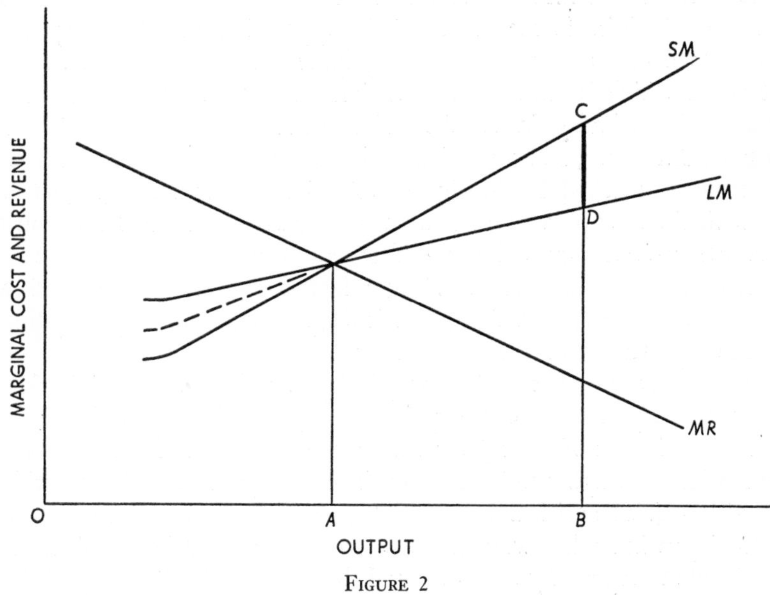

FIGURE 2

entry. If entry is blocked the results follow directly from the behavior of the existing firms.

The problem to be discussed in the present section is intimately connected with the relationship between the short- and the long-run marginal cost functions (*SM* and *LM*) as portrayed in Figure 2. The essential property of the graph is that the short-run marginal cost is lower than the long run to the left of the equilibrium (*OA*) but higher than the long run to the right of it. This expresses the fact that the plant is such as is called for by output *OA* with correct anticipation of a marginal revenue curve such as *MR*. Incremental cost for an increase in output is higher along *SM* (i.e., given the plant) than would be the case if the plant had not yet been built for *OA* output (or indeed for any output at all), and we would be comparing total cost for *OA* with those for higher outputs, assuming the correct plant for each output. On the other hand, decrease in total cost is smaller along *SM* (given the plant corresponding to *OA*) than along *LM*, for the analogous reason. *SM* could be horizontal and *LM* downward sloping, or both cost curves could be downward sloping, or *LM* could slope downward or run horizontally and *SM* slope upward in the neighborhood of the equilibrium. But *SM* would still have to intersect *LM* from below, and the intersection would have to occur at the long-run equilibrium output.

The decision to expand along *LM* rather than *SM* requires that at the new equilibrium the total area lying under *LM*, computed from the origin, should be smaller (at least no greater) than the total area lying under *SM*, also computed from the origin. The cumulated *SM–LM* difference to the right of *OA* must be no smaller than the cumulated *LM–SM* difference to the left.[3] In the graph this is supposed to occur at output *OB*. In other words, as long as the old equipment is available, the marginal cost curve which is relevant for decisions to expand or to contract will possess a discontinuity. When the *MR* curve shifts contraction will occur along the *SM* curve; and expansion will occur also along the *SM* curve up to the output marked *OB* in Figure 2. At this output the *aggregate total cost* with the new plant[4] ceases to be greater (becomes smaller) than the *aggregate variable cost* with the old.[5] Hence from output *OB* to the right the *LM* curve becomes relevant. The relevant marginal cost curve is *SM* up to *C* in Figure 2, at which point it drops discontinuously to point *D* and then continues to the right along *LM*.

Assume now that the *MR* curve of Figure 2 shifts to the right. If the shifted curve passes through a point due north of *C*, then the relevant intersection is that of the shifted *MR* curve with *LM*. If the shifted *MR* curve passes through a point due south of *D*, the relevant intersection is that with *SM*. The critical degree of shift is that which takes *MR* through the *C–D* gap in such a way that two triangles should be equal, namely, the triangle bordered by *MR*, *SM*, and that part of the *C–D* stretch lying above *MR* (upper-left triangle), and the triangle bordered by *MR*, *LM*, and that part of the *C–D* stretch lying below *MR* (lower-right triangle). If these two triangles are equal, the firm is indifferent as between the *MR–SM* intersection and the *MR–LM* intersection. If the shift of *MR* exceeds this critical degree, and thus the lower-right triangle becomes greater than the upper-left, then the *MR–LM* intersection becomes relevant, and the expansion occurs along the long-run curve. The explanation of this proposition is that for the output *OB* profits would be the same on the short-run as on the long-run curve; as compared to these profits a profit increment is obtainable which is measured by the upper-left triangle if the firm moves from *OB* to the intersection of the shifted *MR* curve with *SM*, and is measured by the lower-right triangle if the

[3] We have disregarded the scrap value of the old equipment. This should be added to the right-hand difference or subtracted from the left-hand difference.

[4] Therefore also the average total cost with the new plant.

[5] Therefore also than the average variable cost with the old plant.

firm moves to the intersection with *LM*. I would like to express my debt to Mr. Alvin Marty, who called my attention to the fact that my earlier conception of the minimum condition was faulty, in that my test was insufficiently severe.

The paragraph which now follows contains an adjustment of the preceding propositions to conditions where expansion along *LM* requires merely partial scrapping of the old plant. The preceding presentation of the matter assumes that a firm expanding along *LM* must completely scrap the existing plant. If this is not so, the presentation must be changed but, except for a limiting case, the same kind of conclusion emerges. Expansion along *LM* may be associated with less than total scrapping: The divisibilities of the existing plant may be such that the larger optimum plant corresponding to larger outputs consists partly of the same elements as the existing plant which was built for output *OA*. In this event the *C–D* gap will occur at a smaller output than that at which it is made to occur in Figure 2. For in Figure 2 it occurs where the cumulated difference between *SM* and *LM* to the right of *OA* becomes equal to the cumulated *LM–SM* difference to the left of *OA*. But if expansion along *LM* requires only partial scrapping of the existing plant, then the *SM–LM* difference to the right of *OA* will have to be made equal to *less* than the cumulated *LM–SM* difference to the left. The reason for this is that *even after enlargement of the plant*, the firm can produce any output *up to OA* less expensively than the *LM* curve indicates because it produces these outputs partly with existing (old) plant elements. Consequently we must draw a curve between *SM* and *LM* in the left-hand section of Figure 2. Merely the cumulated difference between this broken curve and *SM*, to the left of *OA*, must be made up by the cumulated difference between *SM* and *LM* to the right. At the point where this condition is satisfied, the *C–D* gap occurs. That is to say the firm will expand along *SM* up to *this* point, and along *LM* beyond *this* point. The relevant marginal cost function is *SM* from the origin to *this* point and *LM* from this point on. In the graph the *C–D* gap has not been redrawn but it is obvious that the gap corresponding to the broken curve should lie to the left of the original gap. The limiting case is that of complete divisibility owing to which an optimum plant corresponding to higher output always consists of an optimum plant corresponding to lower output plus a distinct (separate) addition. In this limiting case the broken curve ceases to lie *between LM* and *SM*. Instead, it *coincides* with *SM* up to *OA*. In this limiting case there exists no cumulated left-side difference which must be made up to the right of *OA*. The *C–D* gap disappears: all expansion beyond *OA* will occur along *LM*, and of course all contraction below *OA* continues to occur along *SM*.[6]

[6] This limiting case can best be visualized as one in which diseconomies along the cost curves of single "plants" in the conventional sense (i.e., of single constituents of the total plant of the firm) become significant at a negligible fraction

Let us now for a moment forget about the "broken curve" of the preceding paragraph, that is to say, let us assume that expansion along *LM* requires total scrapping of the existing plant. A useful invention lowers *LM* by definition but, of course, it does not change the *SM* curve which must be used for comparing the new method with the old. Therefore the innovation increases the *C–D* gap. It also shifts this gap to the left because along the lower *LM* curve it takes less additional output (in excess of *OA*) to make the area under the long-run curve smaller than the area under *SM*. However, to induce the firm to scrap its plant or to lower its price, the widening and leftward shift of the gap must be *great*

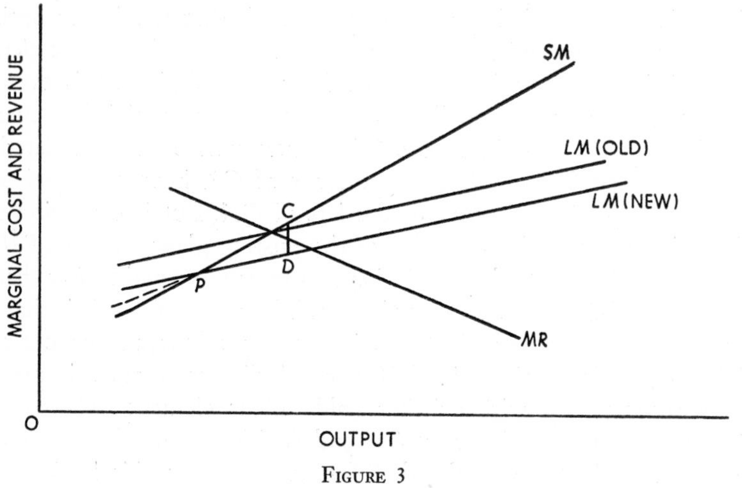

FIGURE 3

enough to have the *MR* curve either pass through a point due north of *C*, or have it pass through the *C–D* gap in such a way that the lower-right triangle described previously should be greater than the upper-left triangle. If this condition is met with the *LM* (new) curve, we shall say that the invention *passes the Figure 3 test.* The invention will be promptly adopted as an industrial innovation *if and only if it passes the Figure 3 test.*

Here again a qualification is required, if part of the old plant can be employed for production with the new method. The following paragraph contains the required addition which must obviously be analogous to that explained in connection with Figure 2. Turning to Figure 3, we have to draw a curve *between* the original *SM* and *LM* (new) to the left of the intersection of these two curves and ending in their intersection point

of the firm output. This in turn assumes that "interplant diseconomies" should not stand in the way of expanding the output of the *firm* to an exceedingly high multiple of the output of the single "plants." *Cf.* Don Patinkin, "Multiple-plant Firms, Cartels and Imperfect Competition," *The Quarterly Journal of Economics,* Vol. LXI (February, 1947).

(*P*).[7] This hybrid curve—intermediate between long and short run—will again be "inserted" as a broken curve. In its unrefined form (assuming no overlap between the two types of plant), the Figure 3 test does not call for adding such a curve because the unrefined test requires that the cumulated difference between the original *SM* and *LM* (new) to the right of *P* should be no smaller than the cumulated *LM* (new)—*SM* (original) difference to the left of this point. Merely these two curves are needed for expressing the "unrefined" condition. However, now we have to add that, in the statement of this condition, the cumulated difference between *LM* (new) and *SM* (original) to the left of *P* should be replaced by the cumulated difference between the broken curve and the original *SM* curve. This is the amendment which becomes necessary if elements of the existing plant can be employed for the new technique. For, if the new technique is used, and if this implies merely partial scrapping of the old plant, then the firm is free to move along the broken curve, rather than along *LM* (new), up to the intersection of *LM* (new) with the original *SM*. In the entire region to the right of this intersection the firm will prefer to move along *LM* (new) and in this region it will gain, by adopting the innovation, the cumulative difference between the *LM* (new) and the original *SM* curve. To the left of the intersection it loses, by adopting the innovation, the cumulated difference between the broken curve and the original *SM*. Hence in the refined version of the Figure 3 test, the *C–D* gap (which was not redrawn) *should* occur where the cumulated difference between the original *SM* and *LM* (new), to the right of *P*, becomes equal to the cumulated difference between *the broken curve* and the original *SM* curve to the left of *P*. Passing the test requires that *MR* should pass through the gap in the way already described or should lie even higher.

The gap problem disappears, and the innovation becomes promptly adopted, regardless of the degree of cost saving, in the limiting case where no scrapping is required to put it into effect. This means that the *SM* curve itself shifts down and that the broken curve coincides with the new *SM*. In no range of possible outputs does the introduction of the innovation cause a loss because this curve is lower than the original *SM* which remains valid for the comparison.

Moreover, it should be pointed out that "in the long run" (but possibly with a *significant* time-lag) the test practically always becomes satisfied because the gap—which usually does exist—tends to shift to the left. The technological reason for this is that current "piecemeal" physical maintenance practically always is less than complete. The *SM* curve shifts up as the physical condition of the old equipment deteriorates. The *SM–LM* intersection in Figure 2, and point *P* in Figure 3, gradually

[7] The broken curve is a hybrid marginal cost curve. It is lower than *LM* (new) by the fixed cost corresponding to that part of the old plant which can be used as a constituent of the new plant.

shift to the left, and the cumulated differences must now be computed to the right and to the left of these shifted intersection points. The gap occurs where the right-hand difference ceases to be smaller than the left-hand difference. The leftward shift of the gap in Figure 2 leads to replacement of the old equipment, even if no inventions are made. In some (possibly distant) future period even an unchanging *MR* curve will go through the shifted gap in Figure 2 in the way required by the test.[8] Furthermore, in some future period, the *MR* curve of Figure 3 will go through the shifted gap in that figure even if "in the short run" point *D* lies to the right of *MR*. *At that time the test will be passed even if originally the invention has failed it.*

Finally it should be noted that the *MR* curve of the period in which a decision is made concerning innovations need not pass through the *LM* (old)–*SM* intersection. The existing plant was designed on the expectation that the *MR* curve *would* pass through this intersection as shown in Figures 2 and 3. But the *MR* curve may have turned out differently. If it has shifted to the right, as compared to its originally assumed equilibrium position, this increases the chances that a small improvement will promptly be adopted. A leftward shift decreases these chances. A shift to the right may have brought the *MR* curve very near to the *C–D* gap in Figure 2, before the innovation. Then a comparatively small improvement and the attending small widening and leftward shift of the *C–D* gap will make the *MR* curve pass through the gap.

Failure of firms promptly to adopt improvements which do not pass the Figure 3 test will here be called *simple retardation*. This kind of retardation and also the kind which in Section III will be called anticipatory retardation are consequences of fixed outlays or overhead costs.[9] More specifically, they are consequences of overhead which (a) stems from jointness of some costs to which outputs of *different periods* give rise, *and* (b) is at least partly specialized to a definite method of production. Innovations will be promptly adopted whenever the overhead is not specialized so that all plant requirements of the two methods are identical; or where the cost-saving overrides the specialized overhead.

At this point it should be remembered that existing firms practice simple retardation even if entry is free. Even the firms of the purely competitive industry portrayed in Figure 1 practice simple retardation. However, the degree of retardation which is practiced by the existing firms may depend on freedom of entry because pre-invention entry *may* make it easier or more difficult for an invention to pass the Figure 3 test.[10] Unexpected pre-invention entry shifts the *MR* curves to the left,

---

[8] This seems to provide an adequate framework for replacement analysis. However, allowance must be made for scrap values. *Cf.* footnote 3.

[9] *Cf.* J. M. Clark, *Studies in the Economics of Overhead Costs* (Chicago, 1923), mainly pp. 191–92.

[10] Post-invention entry comes too late to affect the test for the invention in question.

out of the *SM–LM* intersection point, and this makes the test more difficult. Correctly anticipated pre-invention entry makes the intersection points as well as *MR* lie more to the left and it need not affect the ease of the test. In fact, it will not affect the ease of the test if the individual demand elasticities are independent of the number of firms and if the indivisibilities of equipment are the same for small as for big firms. If pre-invention entry has increased the individual demand elasticities, as may frequently be the case, it becomes easier for an invention to pass the test. On the other hand, if pre-invention entry and the reduction of plant size have made the individual plants less divisible, as may also frequently be the case, then it becomes more difficult for an invention to pass the test because for small plants the broken curve may disappear or it may run very close to the *LM* (new) curve. It is impossible to indicate with general validity whether entry increases or reduces the ease with which the test is passed.

We have seen that it *is* possible to indicate the general nature of another effect of entry. If free entry exists—and only to the extent to which it exists—entrants will promptly adopt the new method[11] even if it does not pass the Figure 3 test, and they will force the old firms to adjust their prices to the level corresponding to the improved technique. This inflicts losses on the old firms which they would not suffer in a static economy. Nor would they suffer these losses in a dynamic economy with blocked entry. If entry is blocked, price and output remain unchanged unless (or until) the invention passes the test expressed in Figure 3. If entry is free the price declines and aggregate output grows (progress occurs) immediately under the impact of any invention that lowers the long-run marginal cost. This *is* a generally predictable dynamic consequence of entry.

For logical completeness a section should now follow on a *flow* of unforeseen inventions. In the real world inventions come in flows, not as single events. But all that need be said here is that *each* unforeseen invention has the consequences discussed in the preceding sections and that these consequences depend on the freedom of entry in the same way as did the consequences of the single invention so far considered.

III. A FORESEEN FLOW OF INNOVATIONS—BLOCKED ENTRY

It will now be assumed that firms gear their innovation policy to the expected flow of new inventions. Each invention is viewed as a link in a chain. In the present section it will also be assumed that anticipations are perfectly correct.

Correctly anticipating firms will obviously practice retardation in the sense of not adopting each invention that lowers the long-run marginal

[11] In the event of monopoly or oligopoly based exclusively on real-cost advantages of scale, they may merely threaten to enter with the new method and this will have the same result.

cost. Moreover, the *anticipatory retardation* here considered will be different from the simple retardation defined previously. Assume two firms operating at a given initial moment with identical techniques. New inventions are made and one firm practices simple retardation (wrongly viewing each invention as a once-for-all change) while the other has correct anticipations. It is possible to state that during a time period, which follows the initial moment, simple retardation will be a weaker retarding factor than anticipatory retardation. Correctly anticipating firms will not adopt innovations which do not pass the test of Figure 3 and hence are not adopted under simple retardation. But correct anticipations may very well induce a firm not to adopt an innovation which passes the test of Figure 3 (and hence is adopted under simple retardation) if this will shortly be followed by a superior innovation possibility requiring a different kind of equipment. If for this reason, in the first phase after the initial moment, more advanced methods are used under simple than under anticipatory retardation, then this phase may be followed by one in which anticipatory retardation goes with more advanced methods. The correctly anticipating firm will now adopt the superior method for which it had been waiting while the firm practicing simple retardation may be "stuck" with the first innovation that passed the test of Figure 3. Once this "first innovation" is introduced, it *may* not pay to scrap the equipment and adopt the superior innovation for which the correctly anticipating firm was waiting.[12] But if in certain phases of development anticipatory retardation goes with more advanced techniques than simple retardation, then these must be *preceded* by phases of which the reverse is true.

Anticipatory retardation produces the maximum available excess of discounted future revenues over discounted future costs, that is to say, it maximizes present net worth. An essential element of the procedure by which this is accomplished consists of by-passing inventions which will be followed by superior ones soon enough. It follows that under correct anticipations an invention will be adopted only if it passes a test which is more severe than that expressed in Figure 3. The invention must satisfy the Figure 3 test, *and* it must not be surpassed in the sufficiently near future by a sufficiently superior subsequent innovation. We shall express this by saying that the invention must pass the *anticipatory test.*

IV. A FORESEEN FLOW OF INNOVATIONS—FREE ENTRY

Free entry brings reduction of firm size and possibly higher individual demand elasticity. Higher demand elasticity makes it easier for an in-

[12] This is a "may not" rather than a "cannot." The fact that the correctly anticipating firm finds it profitable to by-pass the first innovation does not *prove* that, in the event of the introduction of the first innovation, it is unprofitable to scrap and to adopt the superior one. This may still be profitable but less so than to by-pass the first. But it *may* be unprofitable to scrap, once the first innovation is introduced.

vention to pass the test. The reduction of firm size may go with increasing individual plant indivisibilities, which make passing of the test more difficult. Hence free entry *may* change the ease with which an invention is capable of passing the anticipatory test. No general statement can be made on whether the freedom of entry increases or reduces the number of inventions that are capable of passing the test. This is analogous to what has been said previously about the effect of entry on the content of the Figure 3 test, except that here we do not have to allow for unexpected entry and need not distinguish between pre-invention and post-invention entry.

As long as inventions were viewed as unforeseen single events, it was necessary to add that entry had a further and predictable effect on the rate of progress (i.e., on the rate of price reduction and output growth). Inventions that did not pass the test for the existing firms were adopted by intruding newcomers who inflicted losses on the old firms by forcing them to adjust their prices. This further effect of entry disappears if the expectations of all firms are correct. New firms, unhandicapped by overhead, will still enter with new methods even if the innovation does not pass the test for firms already existing, and new entries will produce a continuous price decline. But the existing firms are now assumed to know this in advance, and the entrants of any period are assumed to possess the same knowledge concerning the subsequent periods. *This means that the consequences of all future entries are taken into account in the revenue expectations and output decisions of each firm.* Firms will not enter if the expected revenue is insufficient for recovering the total cost and the firms that do operate will establish production plans which maximize the excess of discounted future revenue over cost, with due allowance for entries with new methods. If for a future period new entries must be taken for granted, then the number of firms *other than new entrants* (i.e., the number of previous entrants) will be correspondingly smaller so as to have the total number and the price come out right for a period properly chosen. We shall now examine the process which accomplishes this result.

In the event of unqualified freedom of entry into an industry (pure competition) it will be true of all firms that, *from the time of the construction of a given plant to the time of its scrapping*, precisely the sum total of costs will be recovered. In the beginning of each of these successive periods in the equipment history of a given firm, the price will be higher than the conventional *ATC* because entrants using new methods are expected to force it down; toward the end of each period the price is lower than the conventional *ATC* because entrants actually have forced it down.[13] But for each firm the representative price (average

[13] The corresponding period of the equipment history of the successive entrants starts of course in the successive moments in which they enter with improved methods.

price),[14] for the construction-to-scrapping period taken as a unit, will have to equal *ATC*. This means that with correct expectations unqualified free entry merely has the effect of producing long-run equality of price with *ATC* (i.e., of preventing an excess of price over *ATC*), which of course is a basic proposition of static price analysis. A specifically dynamic effect develops only if entry changes the length of time elapsing between construction and scrapping, i.e., affects the test which an invention must pass to be adopted by already existing firms. If it fails to do this, the *same* basic periods (from construction to scrapping) emerge under free as under blocked entry, and these basic periods follow each other at a rate unaffected by entry.

For the sake of illustration, we may refer to the purely competitive industry pictured in Figure 1. Take a unit period, starting when plants are built along cost curve *LS* and ending when these plants are scrapped. Scrapping will not take place before inventions have lowered *LS* and *ATC* far enough to make the new *LS–ATC* tangency lie below the *AVC* curve of the old plants. These *AVC* curves may be conceived as remaining unchanged, or, more precisely, as being gradually shifted up by the wear and tear of the old plants. Our unit period will not end before the new *LS–ATC* tangency sinks below *AVC* because this is also the time when the Figure 3 test becomes satisfied for the firms that have built their plants along the original *LS* curve. In this case the *MR* curve of Figure 3 is horizontal, and both cost curves are upward sloping. Considering the nature of the anticipatory test, scrapping may occur later than the time when the Figure 3 test becomes just satisfied, provided that sufficiently superior further inventions will follow soon enough. Our unit period ends when these plants are scrapped and replaced by superior ones. In the beginning of this unit period the price will be in excess of *OL* and at the end of the period it will be below *OL*. The lowering of the price will be brought about by new firms which have no initial overhead. However, the "average" or "representative" price of the period will be *OL*. This statement takes into account the fact that whenever the cost is lowered new entrants, with no previous overhead, must be assumed to lower the price; and it also takes account of the fact that for a period properly chosen total cost must be recovered. The entire future history of the industry may be described as a continuous succession of construction-to-scrapping periods of this sort, regardless of where we start.[15] In each period the initial total cost will be recovered. The clock-time duration of the successive basic periods need not of course remain constant.

---

[14] This is a weighted average, due to the discounting. The weight of the far-future is smaller than that of the near-future.

[15] For example, we could have started with firms that entered during our "period" and could have called the moment of *their* entry the beginning of a unit period. These firms too will recover precisely their total cost (which, however, will be lower).

The essential difference between this outcome and the outcome in Section I (unexpected innovation, free entry) is that in Section I it was impossible to define a period for which price and output would be the same as under static equilibrium conditions, and then to argue that, due to improvement, one such period is succeeded by another (higher-output period) at the same rate under free as under blocked entry. It is true that blocked entry will not prevent old firms from *eventually* adopting an innovation, regardless of whether expectations are correct or wrong (because "in the long run all costs are variable"). But this does not mean that in Section I (incorrect expectations) the long-run dynamics of the process were unaffected by entry. On the assumption of Section I, free entry led to a price decline and to the growth of output *earlier* than would have been the case under blocked entry (*cf.* Section II), and there existed no subsequent offset to this. A further flow of unexpected inventions would clearly not create a subsequent offset. It would merely result in further effects of the same sort. On the assumptions of the present section (correct foresight) the price is higher than *OL*, and the output correspondingly lower, in the beginning of each unit period but this *is* offset by the reverse in the later course of the same period, and with due allowance for time preference (discounting). The rate of growth of output from unit period to unit period—the long-run rate of growth—is uninfluenced by entry. This is what we mean by saying that entry does not influence the long-run dynamics of the process. Entry has "static" consequences because in the absence of entry the price for each unit period would exceed *OL;* it also affects the short-run dynamics of the process, by producing price movements *during* each unit period.

This conclusion assumes correct expectations. It also assumes that entry does not affect the demand elasticity for the products of individual firms, or their plant indivisibilities, in such a way as to make it easier or more difficult for a given invention to "pass the test" from the viewpoint of existing firms. If entry changes the content of the test, then the unit periods to which essentially "static" analysis applies succeed each other at different rates depending on whether entry is or is not free. But if these two assumptions are made (correct foresight and no change in the content of the test), then the long-run consequences of entry are merely those established by static analysis. There exist no additional long-run consequences. At each level of technological knowledge price will be lower and output higher when entry is free but the long-run rate of *progress* (or of *output growth*) will be the same. Professor Schumpeter expressed a similar conclusion by suggesting that the monopolistic rate of progress tends to be the same as that developing under an ideal form of "planning."[16] Given the assumptions which were repeated in the present paragraph, we arrive at essentially the same conclusion.

---

[16] *Cf.* Joseph A. Schumpeter, *Capitalism, Socialism, and Democracy* (2d ed.; New York, 1947), chap. viii.

V. WELFARE APPRAISAL

On the static level of analysis it is possible to conclude from widely accepted welfare postulates that institutional barriers to the entry of producers are harmful. The minimum axiomatic requirement for acceptance of this conclusion is that a movement toward equality of price and marginal cost (and more generally toward equality of factor price and value of marginal product) is desirable provided the accompanying change in the distribution of income is not considered undesirable. The change in income distribution which accompanies the elimination of artificial barriers is a reduction of quasi-rents and of haphazard subsidies to the consumers of the relatively unrestricted industries. This is usually considered a desirable change.

The preceding sections lead to the conclusion that, as long as profit is maximized on correct anticipations and "passing of the test" is made no easier, there exists no *additional* dynamic argument against barriers to entry. In pure competition the profit-maximizing price equals marginal cost, while when entry is blocked the profit-maximizing price exceeds marginal cost. This is found to be true on the static level and the corresponding difference shows also when profit maximization occurs in correct anticipation of future changes. But, aside from the possible effect of firm size on the test, we have found no difference in the long-run *rate of growth* of output between closed and open groups. At each level of the arts output is affected by the degree of competition, but stating this merely repeats the results of static analysis.

With profit maximization based on correct anticipation, the welfare case against restriction would have to rest on its static merits, or on the very doubtful notion that entry generally makes it easier to "pass the test." The static merits of the case should not be overlooked but in the actual world a purely static argument is of limited significance. Data computed by American government agencies point to an increase in man-hour output of between 25 per cent and 33 per cent for each decade from 1890 to 1950, with the average increase per decade approximating 30 per cent. Man-hour output would not remain constant even on a constant level of technological knowledge, but it is likely that technological progress is an important cause of the observed increase. Unless a very short view is taken of social processes, one will be inclined to attribute more significance to a moderate acceleration or retardation of the rate of progress than to unchanging degrees of malallocation or maldistribution on given levels of technique, within the range in which such malallocation is likely to occur at all. The static approach is highly incomplete.

If profit maximization based on correct anticipation is postulated, the difference between blocked and open entry is merely that discernible by static analysis. The static difference establishes a general presumption against barriers. However our ultimate judgment should not be based on this presumption alone but also and perhaps primarily on dynamic differences caused by *incorrect anticipations, and also by deviations from profit maximization such as are due to nonprofit objectives and inertia.* With incorrect anticipations and with deviations from profit maximization, important differences may develop between the rate of progress under free and blocked entry, or under "competition" and "monopoly" respectively. The analysis of Sections I and II illustrates this. These two sections assumed a specific kind of wrong anticipations.

It seems to us that the unsatisfactory character of the discussion about "workable competition" is a consequence of the fact that it is necessary to rely on the record of specific industries to obtain indications concerning the role of factors such as excessive optimism or pessimism, inertia, etc. In specific industries with atomistic competition and free entry the future rate of progress may be underestimated, and hence the kind of loss suffered by the firms of our Section I may grow to substantial size. This goes with a rapid rate of expansion but it may give rise to intervention on grounds of equity or owing to repercussions on the credit system or on other industries. Alternatively, strongly dynamic periods in the history of atomistic industries may be succeeded by long periods of excessive entrepreneurial caution and of slow progress. This is undesirable. On the other hand, monopolists, even if they should have a more reliable appraisal of the future rate of invention, may not always satisfy the requirements of profit maximization because, with their profits at a generally satisfactory level, other objectives (freedom from worry, prestige, popularity) tend to acquire added marginal significance. This too may have undesirable consequences. The influence of market structure on the rate of progress depends primarily on factors of this sort.

The same matters bear importantly on the oligopoly problem. Typically, oligopolistic coordination of business policies (so-called collusion) is less complete for technological improvement, including quality improvement, than for price policy.[17] Is this incompleteness of "collusion" desirable? It leads to more rapid progress than does complete collusion because each firm is trying to gain at the expense of its competitors. If the effects of such behavior were correctly foreseen and the behavior was nevertheless not abandoned, the consequences of the increased rapidity of progress would in some sense be offset by higher prices. The problem is analogous to that of free versus blocked entry. The tighter the collusion, the less free is each firm to "enter" into the market area of the others.

However, in this case it is obvious that some firms underestimate the innovating ability of their competitors as compared to their own ability, and that this blocks the kind of cooperation by which the joint profit

[17] The present writer discussed this aspect of the problem at some length in his *Competition Among the Few* (New York, 1949), mainly on pp. 33–40, 183–90, 282–92.

could be truly maximized. Some firms underestimate the amount of "entry" (intrusion) into their markets of which others are capable, and others are forced to accept the competitive policy which is imposed on the group by the overoptimistic. Correct foresight would result not in quality competition plus offsetting price increases but in collusive handling of improvement. For a completed period it is always possible to describe a collusive pattern *with respect to quality and price* which would have given each participant the relative share he actually happened to obtain and which at the same time would have given each participant higher absolute profits. Incomplete collusion is incompatible with perfect anticipations. It expresses willingness to act on the assumption that the other firm's competitive skill in relation to one's own is smaller than the other firm's estimate of it. Hence the consequences for the group as a whole are very likely to be the same as those of overoptimistic expectations of existing firms concerning the inability of outsiders to enter. As compared to its own guess of relative skills each firm may proceed cautiously and conservatively. But oligopolistic quality competition indicates that the guesses of some firms are overoptimistic, *and this sets the pace for the group as a whole*. The consequences of such limited overoptimism are socially "desirable" provided that it is felt to be desirable to obtain more improvement coupled with a distribution effect expressing itself in the reduction of monopolistic or oligopolistic incomes. Furthermore, oligopolistic cooperation concerning the introduction of improvements is likely to be the less complete, the greater the number of firms included in the oligopoly. Therefore, if the consequences of reduced "collusion" are considered desirable, then broadening of oligopolistic market structures should also be so considered. Here again the axiomatic requirements for a favorable welfare judgment are comparatively mild.[18]

To repeat: with correct foresight and complete rationality, dynamic analysis of the monopoly-oligopoly-competition problem, or of the problem of free versus blocked entry, discloses no essential modification of the static results. The specifically dynamic aspect of the problem calls primarily for weighing, in specific instances, the probable consequences of incorrect foresight, and also the effects of deviations from profit maximization due to inertia, high safety preference, noneconomic objectives, etc. This points to the necessity of making specific judgments in specific cases. Yet it is possible to distinguish broad classes of instances in which a strong presumption exists in the one or the other direction. *Entry, the effects of which on the rate of progress are less than fully off-*

---

[18] It is true that many persons feel skeptical toward some of the "quality improvement" developing in oligopolistic markets. But this merely illustrates the fact that even comparatively mild general welfare axioms should be applied with *ad hoc* qualifications.

set by anticipatory price charges, is desirable unless the resulting change in income distribution is regarded as undesirable. The behavior of monopolistic and oligopolistic groups suggests that such is typically the outcome when narrow market structures are broadened. The case for broadening narrow market structures remains fairly generally valid on the dynamic as well as on the static level of economic analysis, even though on the dynamic level no general case emerges for atomistic competition. The case also remains valid from a general sociological point of view for any society that considers freedom of opportunity a desirable objective.

VI. LIMITED AVAILABILITY AND THE PATENT PROBLEM

So far we have assumed that each new method becomes immediately available to any interested firm. The conclusions of the last section must be supplemented by a brief discussion of limited availability. We shall go but little beyond calling attention to the main consequences of this specific "barrier" which is strengthened by patent legislation but would, to some extent, exist even without legislative action. Know-how, when it is new, begins to spread gradually. It never becomes completely diffused.

These would seem to be the most significant consequences of limited availability.

(1) Inventive activity is stimulated because the reward for making inventions is increased. Some argue that this effect is frequently overestimated for the present environment in which the individual (or independent) inventor plays a smaller role than the corporate research organization. Quantitative appraisal is impossible but it is difficult to imagine that inventive activity should not to some extent be stimulated by limited availability.

(2) The introduction of "inventions" as industrial "innovations" is also stimulated because no technological invention is really and truly *made* before it has been proved to work on an industrial scale. In other words, the conventional distinction between invention and industrial use, which was implied under (1), is sufficiently arbitrary to call for the qualification which is here added. No firm ever knows with certainty that a process is going to work before this has been demonstrated industrially. Innovating is part of the process of inventing.

(3) Once the process is introduced, limited availability is a "barrier" or a limitation of entry and hence it has the further consequences with which the main sections of the present article were concerned. These are the traditionally emphasized static "harmful" consequences of "monopoly" and the specifically dynamic consequences discussed in Section V. The dynamic consequences of restriction are presumably more significant. They stem mainly from the incorrectness of expectations and, generally speaking, from the incompleteness of profit maximization. Un-

like the static consequences they call for specific appraisal of individual instances or of certain "classes" of instances. In some cases the dynamic consequences may be found "undesirable," in others "desirable."

(4) Limited availability affects the size of the firm and thereby presumably also the rate at which further inventions are made. The relationship between the size of the firm and efficiency of its research organization gives rise to significant questions about which not much seems to be known. The optimum firm size is not truly optimum if its research activities are sufficiently far removed from optimum efficiency. If the relationship between firm size and research efficiency is unknown, both the automatic market mechanism and policy are likely to favor an unduly static kind of "optimum."[19]

Considerations based on (1) and (2) lead to a case for patent legislation, or more generally, for limited availability. In some specific instances the case *for* restriction *may* become reinforced by the "dynamic" considerations included in (3). Misgivings against patent restrictions are usually based on the "static" considerations in (3) and on the notion that the "dynamic" considerations in (3) *may* frequently reinforce the case *against* restriction. It is usually recognized that considerations based on (4), taken in isolation, do not favor atomistic competition but at present it is impossible to form an opinion of what firm size they do favor in various industries.

[19] Marshall, in Book VI, chap. 7 of his *Principles*, places considerable emphasis on the static bias of market selection (i.e., of success in the market). This ties in with the problem discussed in the text.

17

Toward a Theory of Industrial Markets and Prices*

By RICHARD B. HEFLEBOWER[†]

Generalizing about markets and price formation in the industrial sector, where fewness of participants and differentiation are usual attributes, is a complex task which requires one to draw on price theory, on the empirical research of the past twenty years, and on his own observations and hunches. Few parts of the conclusions reached are beyond the hypothesis stage. When, however, hypotheses about each of the various facets of the problem are woven together, the outline of a theory emerges which appears useful in explaining the operation of industrial markets and in prognosticating their behavior.

Theory in this area must be directed toward exactly the same problems as those to which neoclassical price theory has been addressed, but explanation of industrial markets proceeding inductively from empirical evidence is often held to higher standards than is the deductive theory of prices. Both approaches must identify the variables that are relevant for a given problem. Both must demonstrate the net results of the interaction of these variables under various assumptions as to their magnitudes and the extent to which these results would accord with established tests for optimal use of resources. Price theory, however, stops with this and in so doing serves essentially as a computing machine into which data can be put and conclusions ground out. But those generalizing in the area under discussion are usually expected to indicate the actual empirical content of the variables as far as that is possible.

REQUIREMENTS FOR AN ADEQUATE THEORY

Several requirements for an adequate theory of industrial markets and prices can be set down. Even for a static theory, it is not possible to build the analysis on given utility and technological functions, as is done for competitive and monopolistic price theory.[1] To varying degrees, the

---

* *The American Economic Review*, Vol. XLIV (Proceedings of the American Economic Association, 1954), pp. 121–39. Reprinted by courtesy of the publisher and the author.

† Northwestern University.

[1] This point has been most fully expounded by William Fellner in his *Competition Among the Few* (Knopf, 1949), pp. 8–13.

demand and supply functions in markets that lie in the zone intermediate between the structurally competitive and the monopolistic are themselves results of market processes and must be explained. Added to the difficulties of static theorizing in this area is the need for dynamic analysis and for broadening the variables considered—all of which points to the following requirements for a satisfactory theory:

1. A satisfactory theory must be historically related in the sense that technological, organizational, and public policy influences of a certain economy at a certain period are assumed. Here we refer to the present-day American economy, where the public policy is designed to keep cartel arrangements so weak that group control over important market variables is not significant for long.

2. Ideally, the theory should be able to explain why the market is as it is, because structure does not necessarily emanate from technological and utility functions.

3. A satisfactory theory must often be dynamic because market structure is potentially variable and because the technology actually used and many other of the diverse forms of interfirm rivalry are optional. Those selected may set in motion a chain of reactions throughout the industry.

4. A satisfactory theory must go beyond explaining the cost-price-output relations for a given product and must be prepared to appraise the conditions of choice among other variables and the economic results of that choice. This requirement, like the others set forth here, is not introduced for the sake of descriptive realism but because it is essential for better prediction.

One general feature of all of these requirements is that in the search for uniformities one must not abstract from diversities that are relevant to the behavior to be explained. Whether narrow- or broad-gauge theory is sought, it is obvious that definitive theory which meets the above specifications cannot be laid down at this time.

THE OUTLINE OF THE ARGUMENT

An advance sketch of the general line of argument and some of the assumptions on which it is based will place each of the later sections in better focus.

1. This is not an attempt to theorize about firms in general but rather about markets and collections of firms that constitute industries which have certain characteristics. (The delimitation of an industry or a market will always be relative to the context in which these terms appear.)

2. The industry or market is looked at in midstream. Its structure is not traced back to ultimates or examined as if it were being established *de novo.*

3. The emphasis is on the various factors that influence the structure of the market and on the effect of the structure in turn on the market's

operation. Relevant, therefore, are such basic conditions as the nature of final buyer demand and the technology available for production. But final buyer demand, as it bears on the manufacturer, may be altered by the organization of the intermediate handlers or processors. Various sellers undertake to satisfy different, or several different, segments of the spectrum of consumer wants in a particular area, or to deal in a different fashion with the distributive trades, or even to take on one or more aspects of the distributive process. Within the same industry there are various degrees to which the whole manufacturing process is carried out by an integrated ownership rather than by several ownerships coordinated through purchase and sale.

4. Both because of the ubiquity of diversity within markets and because of the analytical usefulness of that characteristic, we shall first consider the apparently complex cases in which diversity among firms plays an important role. Cases in which such diversity is not significant will be treated secondarily.

5. Markets for most products (broadly conceived) tend to settle into segments among which there are varying degrees of elasticity of substitution and of intersegment mobility. Often the same firm will be doing business in more than one segment.

6. Much of the analysis—probably the most important parts of it—should be directed toward the composite of industry segments, and for this we use the term "product line."

The general argument of the following sections, which reflects the views just listed, is divided into the following parts:

First, it is explained that by a historical process a state of balance is achieved in industrial markets and this balance[2] is not easily disturbed. Both the process of reaching a balance and its stability result from the diversity among firms each of which settles into one or more places in the loosely conceived market. Second, the economic attributes of this balance—the degree to which it is optimal—are abstracted from actual (but not from potential) variations in factor prices and industry demand. Economic results are found to emanate from entry and from the various forms of rivalry, choice among which reflects the structure of the market and the presence of uncertainty. Third, the degree and method of adaptation to factor price and demand movements are considered next with particular reference to whether external developments threaten to disturb the internal balance. Finally, an appraisal of the forms and promptness of adaptation and of the economic character of states of balance in industrial markets is made insofar as available evidence and space permit.

Because of limitations of space, no attempt will be made to show how the ideas advanced incorporate or differ from either deductive price

[2] Parenthetically, it should be observed that the term "equilibrium" is not used very often in the following pages even though by "balance" is meant a situation such that no one who has the power to change the situation wants to do so.

theory or observations which have been made on the basis of empirical research. Few references will be made to the literature, much of which, it can be observed, stresses the noncompetitive performance of industrial markets. This omission gives an appearance of bias to the empirical evidence cited, but that risk must be run.

THE BALANCE TENDENCY OF INDUSTRIAL MARKETS

Economic analysis depends heavily on discovering equilibrium tendencies which reflect a sufficient balance of forces that economic processes become orderly. The literature on markets where sellers are few and particularly where, in addition, a high proportion of costs are fixed in the short run, has been concerned with whether equilibria can either be determinate or be stable in the absence of collusion. Yet one observes that few such markets seem disorderly in the absence of evidence of collusion—a fact which is explained by the following arguments.

The Process by Which Balance Is Established

The structure of a market at a given time reflects an evolutionary process whereby firms come to acquire a workable relationship with one another. They are assisted in this process by the fact that most markets are made up of niches. The respective firms find one or more places for themselves by design or luck.

It is in connection with the adaptation of the firm to its environment that uniquely farseeing or unwise business decisions have their major influence. Once such decisions have been made (whether by accident or careful design), they set for some time the conditions under which shorter-term operating decisions will be made. Definitive conclusions are not possible as to the extent to which firms, autonomously, shape the varied attributes of the market structure, short, of course, of cases of market dominance. My own inclination is toward stressing the firm as consciously adapting to its environment or as being "adopted"[3] when its successful moves are accidentally good.

Regardless of one's views on this controversial subject, it seems evident that a balance can be achieved among such forces as the desire for variety within a product area and the attendant services, the roles of various firms in supplying them, and relative prices. Such a balance is more multivariate than is one of prices and outputs.

The relative importance of these variables differs with the group of products handled by the industry, but the historical tendency has been for the diversity of feasible roles for various participants in a market to increase. This has been true not only of consumer goods industries, as incomes have risen, but even of semimanufactured goods. Today finished goods manufacturers rarely start with crude materials but use semimanu-

[3] A. A. Alchian's terminology from his "Uncertainty, Evolution, and Economic Theory," *Journal of Political Economy*, June, 1950, p. 214.

factured materials previously processed to fit their methods of manufacture.

The evolutionary process does not work toward a balance in the pure oligopoly case, particularly where there are the added features of a low ratio of short-term marginal costs to total costs and a lack of opportunity to use product quality as a variable. In such cases, either overt collusion or effective, tacit price leadership is apt to develop or the firms will integrate vertically into a stage in which the diversity required for stability does exist. In most markets, however, a balance is feasible without collusion, and, in such a balance, margins between direct costs and prices differ among sellers, among brands of or channels of sale by the same seller, and among physical variations of the product.

The Stability of the Balance

The characteristics of the environment which shape the market's evolution also govern its stability. The fact that firms occupy somewhat different places in the market means that not all of them are in complete and direct competition with each other. But it also means that they cannot ignore or isolate themselves from one another, for their products are fairly close substitutes for each other and the analogous character of their production and selling operations facilitates entry into each others' backyards. There remains, however, a zone within which they need not fear upsetting action by rivals.

One reason for this is that at a given time each firm's freedom of action is limited by its history. The degree to which this is true depends on the adaptability of equipment, of personnel, of internal organization, and of relations with suppliers and customers. Usually, these inhibit quick, sizable changes in the character of the business. These fundamental characteristics of the firm also reflect its longer-term goals, and temporary deviation from these goals is usually unwise.

This last point leads me to emphasize that each participant acquires not merely a place in the market but also a position which is a major long-term attribute. By market position is meant more than what the firm sells and to whom and by what means, and more than its share of the volume. Instead, market position is that composite of attributes which governs the ability of the firm to compete. Obviously, the relative importance of elements in this composite differs among product areas and even among firms participating in the same product area. The relevant attributes of competitive strength may also vary according to the problem. A vertically integrated firm, for example, may be strong for dealing with one type of problem and weak for another.

Business executives are cognizant of their respective firms' market positions and of what that enables them to do and of what acts are unwise. They realize that a strong market position is built slowly but can deteriorate rapidly. Above all, management recognizes good market position to be a valuable asset, whose long-term attributes must condition all short-term decisions. Its value is not merely defensive, as emphasis on security motivation suggests, but also is a basic attribute of the firm's ability to make positive moves; that is, to deal with unanticipated developments when they occur.

In that sense, market position becomes a means of long-term profit maximization under conditions of uncertainty. Consequently, the concept of market position is at the heart of the problem of the stability of industrial markets under given factor prices, industry demand, and basic technology because it governs the feasibility and effectiveness of various forms of rivalry.

This explains why changing prices relative to those of rivals is not a frequent source of disturbance of balance. If the balance has existed for long, presumably the relative prices of sellers (including the different prices in different segments of the market by one seller) are such that market shares are not shifted radically at the initiation of either buyers or sellers. Presumably such a balance is optimal to the various firms under the existing conditions.

Nevertheless, it is probably true that many firms could increase short-term profits by charging more, and perhaps even by charging less. The latter prospect is limited, however, not merely because of the expected reaction of rivals, but also by the fact that industrial and commercial buyers often give their regular suppliers an opportunity to match price cuts. That short-term opportunities to charge more are not seized reflects the fact that firms are guided by their long-term revenue curves which are much flatter than are the short-term ones. Indeed, vis-à-vis rivals who occupy similar market positions, a firm may look upon that curve as though it were horizontal at least at outputs less than those prevailing. That it is perfectly consistent for a firm whose capital has been committed to think in terms of its short-term marginal cost curve and its long-term revenue curve has recently been pointed out by Harrod.[4]

From the preceding argument emerges the conclusion that a change of price relative to that of the firm's rivals, that is, the disturbance of a balance by such a move, is appropriate only when the firm's market position is being changed correspondingly—a step which is not undertaken lightly. It is apt to succeed only when it is the result of a substantial program, carried out over a period of time, which may involve a modification of almost every phase of the business, including its physical plant. Consequently, changing prices relative to rivals tends to be part of a complex of almost continuous modification of product, package, sales channel, guarantees, free services, etc., which characterizes not merely the markets for most finished consumer goods but also for industrial equipment and many semimanufactured goods.

---

[4] R. F. Harrod, *Economic Essays* (Harcourt, Brace, 1952), p. 150.

Less disturbing are forms of competition other than change of price relative to those of rivals, but the feasibility of these other competitive forms varies widely. Much advertising and other distributional effort is a means of standing still, not of moving forward. When used positively, devices other than price change do not often shift market shares rapidly. In part this is because their appeal to buyers is not so great and immediate as is a price cut. More typically, their lesser effect stems from the multiplicity and effectiveness of countering moves of rivals. Even trends in the strength of market positions, which are the result of competitive devices other than price, can be in operation for some time without setting off a price war. Consequently, there is nearly always some variation going on in the cost-price margins of particular firms or their market shares or the quality of their products, but not enough to disturb the fundamental balances of forces.

It is in such a context as that just sketched that the stability of a balance must be appraised. In general, the less the product and its market conform to the specifications for a pure oligopoly (which really involves more relevant assumptions than fewness of sellers and standardization of product) the more likely it is that the important elements of the market positions of rivals will be such that they cannot be easily upset by feasible competitive devices. It seems to me that most markets are of the latter sort, and that short of some development which warrants a strenuous move by some participant, states of balance tend to be quite stable in the industrial sector of the economy. This does not mean a standstill, but rather an ability of industry to absorb many adjustments without open disruption.

ECONOMIC ATTRIBUTES OF EQUILIBRIUM

While orderliness, or tendency toward an equlibrium, is an important aspect of a market, the efficiency and the income distribution aspects of that equilibrium have properly been the center of attention in price theory. As applied here, this requires appraisal of the degree of optimality of the balance achieved among the forces of product quality, technology and cost, price, and output. In this section, we are not concerned with reactions to changes in general technology, consumer preferences and incomes, or factor prices, but, it must be repeated, the analysis is not abstracted from uncertainty with respect to these variables.

Market Structure and Efficiency

In light of the conditions for an adequate theory laid down earlier, the test for optimal industry performance cannot assume static conditions with respect to product, its costs, or its demand. We must be prepared to consider whether, with uncertainty present, the structure of the industry inhibits or favors both the best product and the best method of production possible under the existing general state of technical knowledge. Or, conversely, the possibility must be considered that the structure which has evolved reflects attempts to mitigate the impact of uncertainty of various possible origins.

This brings us to the issue between two schools. On the one hand there is the more orthodox view that fewness of sellers and product differentiation lead to output at less than the optimum rate and deter progressiveness. The opposing view, most usually associated with Schumpeter and J. M. Clark, sees in this insulation the necessary conditions for the assumption of risks and uncertainties associated not only with innovation in product and process but also with other uncertainties related to investment in the most efficient equipment.

It is not possible to resolve this basic issue on the basis of empirical findings. Objective appraisal is inhibited by the difficulties of delineating the various types of forces bearing on resource use in particular industries. My own view—and it is only a judgment—is that there is a significant degree of truth in the idea that product quality and the structure of costs will be socially more favorable in many industries if there is some insulation from overt price competition. But I do not think that this degree of insulation requires the current size distribution of sellers in some industries.

Determinants of the Character of Competition

Beyond questions of the technology and costs are those of factors usually considered to determine the slope of the individual firm's revenue curve. Here the character of interfirm rivalry is explored as it is affected both by basic conditions of product demand and feasible technology (to which all the firms in the group are subject) and by the discretionary actions of members of the industry.

1. *Market Characteristics of the Product.* The forms and effectiveness of competition are affected to an important degree by the market characteristics of the product. The categories developed in marketing literature are particularly helpful, for they reflect not only the buying motives and skill of final purchasers but also the role of the intermediate distributive trades with respect to various goods. These categories are: (*a*) "Specialty goods," which are those characterized by the fact that the buyer may first have to be convinced of the merits of the good before he can be induced to purchase it and by the fact that, once convinced, the buyer will go to considerable difficulty to obtain the product of a particular producer. Excellent examples of specialty goods are the newer, "big-ticket" electrical appliances. (*b*) "Shopping goods," which are those bought after comparison of the quality of the products and prices of various suppliers. Excellent examples are piece goods, furniture, and fresh produce. (*c*) "Convenience goods," which are those purchased frequently and are often ordered by description or specification. Examples include both specialty items, such as toothpaste or prepared cereals, and standard items, such as sugar.

The relative roles of the manufacturer and of the distributive trades vary widely among these categories of commodities partly because of corresponding variations in the competence of consumers as buyers. The manufacturer can with varying degrees of success build and hold final buyer preferences for specialty goods, but he is also dependent on the performance of his dealers. Retailers of the specialty subclass of convenience goods tend to be reduced to the role of order-takers because consumers are not good judges of quality of these goods. On the other hand, the distributive trade tends to be in the saddle in the cases of shopping goods and standardized convenience goods.

There is a strong tendency for the market characteristics of goods to change over time in such a way as to undermine any differentiation that yields abnormal profits. This means that specialty goods tend to become shopping goods or standardized convenience goods as they become part of the consumption pattern of most families and as the quality of the goods becomes satisfactory and quite uniform among suppliers. Likewise, convenience goods of the specialty subtype tend to become fairly standardized as far as buyers are concerned. Few products are so stable in their physical attributes and in their use that they escape this process entirely.

This evolution reflects to some degree growing buyer erudition but even that—and certainly the development of the satisfactory quality of the product itself—is a part of interfirm rivalry. In consumer goods the large retail organizations have had a major role in this dynamic and quite continuous process.

Where this evolutionary process is not important, the stable market characteristics of the product, plus the degree of variability in what buyers want and the organization of the distributive trade, go far to determine the degree and character of the market segmentation which prevails. Segmentation does not get far for sugar; it is more important for canned goods; and it is a fundamental aspect of markets for the big-ticket products which combine specialty and shopping characteristics.

2. *Influence of Methods of Production and Structure of Costs.* Here only certain aspects of the conditions of production and cost will be stressed, because the others are obvious. First, there is the question of the extent to which the method of production is a datum for the firm and the extent to which it may be altered upon the firm's initiative. One method may be more capitalistic than another and the related risks may be higher. Then, for the individual firm, the proportion of the total processing, or of that plus raw material production and product distribution done by it, affects its cost structure. But there frequently are a number of feasible methods of vertical organization. Companies may engage in all or several vertical steps or they may merely assemble or blend parts or materials prepared by others with consequent effects on their capital requirements and on the relation of their fixed and variable costs.

3. *Is Market Structure Determinate?* While the significance of au-

tonomous determinants of the conditions of competition becomes more evident as one learns more about particular markets, their role must not be overstressed. The size distribution and other structural attributes reflect the firm's past decisions. These may reflect mistakes, conscious moves or conditions long since gone, or conscious moves to control competition. Consequently, firms may be larger or more varied in their activities than the conditions of cost, of demand, and of uncertainty would require. Weighing the effect of such "artificial" structural elements is difficult.

My view is that the structure and operation of markets have a strong tendency to reflect the market characteristics of the product, the feasible conditions of its production, and the organization of adjacent industries. Such factors influence even those industries that are made highly concentrated by design and dominate other industries still more completely. But in no event must these conditions be viewed as fully determinate of either market structure or operations. Rather these forces define a zone within which management makes choices but of a sort which does not in most cases tie the hands of existing or potential rivals.

Conditions and Effectiveness of Entry

Four somewhat overlapping aspects of the entry problem should be underscored.

1. Entry by established firms because of profit opportunities either in a field unrelated to the firm's initial activity or in an adjacent field or level is a widespread and a powerful competitive force. Movements into an adjacent industry may be either horizontal or vertical. Of these the vertical is the more promising, both because of the awareness of entry possibilities which a vertically adjacent firm is likely to have and because such firms often possess the characteristic essential for successful entry.

2. Entry may be facilitated by the fact that most product lines and their associated markets are segmentized. Entry into some segments often is easy because they approach the purely competitive in character. Once such entry occurs, movement of that firm toward the segments where entry by a new firm would be very difficult may be, but not necessarily is, fairly easy. If it is, what might be an unscalable cliff if a new firm were to attempt to enter the difficult segment directly, will prove to be a set of stairs.

3. Entry may be by the route of producing a substitute product or using better raw materials or manufacturing processes. Developments in chemistry, particularly, often can be used by the would-be entrants—frequently well-established firms—to enter with a product or process which can be substituted for those already in use.

4. The effects of entry can be obtained at times by the assumption of a function usually carried out by firms engaged in another vertical step

without actually owning the operation in that step. The most important case of this sort is the taking over by a distributive organization of the responsibility for distribution, including the branding, of a commodity which meets the buyers' specifications.

Such potential sources and forms of entry have been widely employed in recent years, which leads to the question as to whether the economic effects of entry stem from the fear of entry or from the force of actual entry. The former has been stressed in the literature and has been supported by some empirical evidence. In order for fear of entry to govern prices or to expedite process or product improvement, however, two conditions would have to exist. Potential entrants would have to be aware of the abnormal profits existing or of those obtainable by developing a substitute product or channel of sale. Second, there would have to be quasi-agreement among established sellers, not merely as to the proper level of price, but also to refrain from themselves making such moves as introducing substitute products or channels of sale which would have the same effect as entry.

Three observations, no one of which can be adequately documented, can be made relevant to whether management's fear of entry or the actual occurrence of entry is the more important. For products which have the prospect of a long life, firms often hold prices at a level that will provide good but not high profits because of confidence of better long-run results. This policy reflects in part a desire to discourage entry, but not usually, I believe, in the sense of a specific appraisal having been made of entry prospects at different levels of price for the given product. Instead, a general policy as to margin over factory cost or estimated total cost, which may reflect experience as to margins which discourage entry, is applied to a wide category of goods. Second, specific potential entrants—usually companies or industries to which part of the product line is sold—may be "bought off," perhaps even by prices below total cost. Third, and most generally, it seems to me that entry actually occurs and forces down the price, or at least reduces sharply the share of the market that can be held by older firms without reducing price. The latter is important for consumer goods, for often entry is by a substitute product or by the creation of a separate market segment for a lower-priced but physically similar product.

If there are vertically adjacent businesses which would be able, in terms of size, organization, and financial resources, to enter an industry and do not (or are not bought off by preferential pricing), this is prima facie evidence that this industry is performing competitively. According to this test, meat packing would be judged to be competitive, but the test would not prove building materials manufacture to be so, because there is a lack of potential, vertically placed entrants into that business.

What may be more feared than entry is the prospect that abnormal profits will lead firms already in the industry to expand shares by devices which fall short of overt price cuts and which are difficult to restrain or counter or, indeed, whose effectiveness is difficult to appraise *ex ante* but which nevertheless do force down realizations relative to cost. This is but part of the competitive conduct to which we now turn.

Product-Quality and Cost-Price Effects of Nonprice Competition

Maneuvers other than overt price change for an unchanged product have a major role in determining the economic attributes of equilibria in industrial markets. Let us assume a tacit (or even overt) agreement on a level of price which yields abnormal profits. Such an agreement does not of itself foreclose but rather encourages other moves such as product and process change, sales effort, and the development of new sales channels.

The list does not end there. In consumer goods industries, entry by some of the collaborators into lower-priced segments of the market tends to pull down prices there, and, as a result, the agreed-on prices in the more defensible and higher-priced segments become untenable. In other cases—particularly those of producers of standardized materials—integration into a fabrication or distribution stage facilitates not merely competition in the quality of the product and attendant services but also the making of price concessions. Just how rapidly and to what extent such forces work and how much they reduce realizations for the product line will vary widely.

Tacit or even formal agreement about these methods of competition is improbable for the following reasons:

1. In the use of these other variables, the output of various firms per unit of input does not necessarily tend toward uniformity. There is a substantial chance that with a given expenditure one firm may do much better with particular techniques of distribution and selling or be more successful in product research than will rivals. This contrasts with our usual assumption of a strong tendency toward equal output per unit of input.

2. An important contribution to a firm's market position may result from being first or more active in nonprice competition, but rarely is that gain derived from being first in price competition.

3. Alternatives to price competition involve maneuvers from which retreat is easy when desirable or from which a tangential move is feasible. Neither is true of a price cut.

To the extent that these forms of competition are effective, noncompetitive levels of prices and profits are subject to erosion. Much work has to be done before we know how rapidly this erosion occurs and how well it stacks up against potential alternatives.

It must be evident, also, that the extent to which beneficial economic results stem from these forms of competition depends in large part on the degree to which a dynamic view of such markets is appropriate. If technology is an independent variable which would be fully utilized if far more overt price competition were engaged in, then the results of nonprice competition are not good. If, however, the degree of optimal use of technology is itself a reflection of the industry structure and the choice made of competitive methods, much good can be seen. Clearly, one's conclusions as to the validity of the Schumpeterian framework would vary among industries and, for a given industry, among stages in its development.

There is also the second part of the Schumpeterian argument—which was postponed earlier—namely, the eroding of the insulated positions of established firms resulting both from the entry of large firms and from the nonprice competition provided by them. No comprehensive empirical study of this proposition has been made. My own opinion is that the erosion tendency is strong in a large portion of industrial situations, that in some ways it is costly to the economy, but that these costs must be balanced against the feasibility of alternative routes to progress in an industrial society.

Summary

The theoretical framework just sketched is really a generalized form of the long-standing analysis of the reaction of firms to profit opportunities. Ordinarily, the emphasis has been on the case of the firm that has lower costs for a given product than its rivals and which, if rewards appear good compared to risks, would expand output.

Here, however, the way in which even such a factor as entry can work must be adapted to the characteristics of industrial markets. Thus variables held constant in a simple cost-price-output model must be introduced and their significance explored not merely by assuming them to be equivalent to a price change. When that is done, one finds that these variables have, potentially, a major effect on economic results and operate in spite of, and tend to undermine, a level of price for an unchanged product whenever that price fails to reflect an optimal combination of product quality, process and cost, and output rate.

For a given product line, it is helpful to visualize a composite demand situation in which each item in the line has a demand curve of different elasticity. In addition, each item entails somewhat different direct costs of production and quite different general overhead costs. Different firms may be selling different items but usually each firm sells more than one. An optimum use of resources, in the sense of obtaining the full economies of scale and the full use of capacity, is quite possible in such a case, even though the revenue curves in some segments are far from perfectly elastic. The reasons are, for static analysis, that the revenue curves in some segments are perfectly elastic and this tends to eliminate unused capacity. For dynamic analysis, the major point is that in an industry so structured, uncertainty may be sufficiently minimized that the optimum scale of plant will be actually established.

Once one goes further and observes historical or dynamic processes, he will see that the relationships among segments need not be stationary. Revenue curves may, in fact ordinarily do, flatten out in the higher-priced segments, and changes in the product, in the process of its manufacture, or in the channels of its sale, work to upset those price relationships among segments of the industry which do not reflect cost differences.

When viewed this way the economic attributes of a balance cannot be appraised solely or even primarily by examining the cost-price-output relations for an unchanging, narrowly defined product. One must consider in addition the unmeasurable changes in product quality and the measurable effects of technological advance on the level of costs. A qualitative judgment must then be made as to whether the maximum economies of scale are obtained. Finally, the efficiency with which committed resources are used and the division of the benefits thereof, that is, the price-cost-output relations which exist, must be judged for the entire family of items which go to make up the product line. Even then a single demonstration of cost-price-output relations cannot be made. A number of varied combinations and magnitudes of the variables stressed here are possible. Nevertheless, the general tenor of the argument, both as to the variables stressed and much of the empirical evidence referred to incidentally, is to suggest a strong tendency for economic results of industrial markets to be closer to the optimum than one would conclude from much of the literature about this sector of the economy.

REACTION TO FACTOR PRICE AND DEMAND MOVEMENTS

The general argument to be presented here is that factor price movements tend to be reflected in corresponding price changes but that demand changes do not. Obviously the degree of concomitance of movement of these two forces will modify the general statement just made. Both these modifications, if pursued, and the general statement just made find their explanation in the fact that firms' reactions to cost and price and demand developments reflect the structural position in which they find themselves and their relative market positions.

Reaction to a Factor Price Change

Factor price movements do not directly affect market positions of particular firms, and consequently selling price responses are not apt to be disruptive. In part this is because firms recognize the tendency toward uniformity in impact of these cost changes, although there may be some difference in timing of this impact due to variations in firms' degrees of vertical integration or in their inventory positions. More basically, this reaction is because market position has to do primarily with selling. Only indirectly, as some firms react to the factor price movements, are the conditions of selling market rivalry altered by a factor price movement. But when factor prices fall, the initiator of a selling price reduction is not suspected of trying to enlarge his share. Or, in reverse, the boldness of the firm which moves to reflect higher factor prices in his selling prices is appreciated, particularly when margins have been squeezed sharply.

Yet the differential immediate impact of factor price movements on firms and on market segments has much to do with the selling price response. Firms which are not integrated vertically or which are in a short-inventory position feel the factor-price movement more promptly than do rivals with the opposite attributes. In most product markets there are some segments—it happens that these also are the more nearly open market segments—in which margins between direct costs and selling price are much narrower than in other segments. Factor price movements impinge more heavily on such narrow-margin sellers and they are anxious to change their prices as soon as possible.

When factor prices fall, the selling prices in the lower-margin segments are apt to drop away from the quoted prices of the major-segment sellers and customers will be pulled away from the latter. This is the reason that major sellers are usually price followers on the downside.

On the other hand, when factor prices rise these low-margin sellers feel the margin squeeze heavily. They edge up their prices as much as they can relative to those in the higher-priced segment. This reduces the substitution between the goods of the sellers in that segment and of those in the low-margin segment, a development which paves the way for the former to raise their prices overtly. When they do so they are, in a sense, again price followers rather than leaders.

Another important influence of a factor price change is on the expectations of intermediate buyers. When factor prices rise, a firm's customers need not fear a selling price decline. Hence, they are in a position to make an almost riskless speculation in inventories by stepping up their orders in anticipation of a price movement. If factor prices fall, business customers can hold off orders, a development which often tips the balance toward a selling price change. In that event, the problem associated with the kinked demand curve tends not to be present. Indeed, a factor price change usually does not disturb the internal balance within the group but merely affects the level of costs and prices about which day-to-day rivalry brings small but not disruptive changes in realizations, volume, and market shares of rival firms.

All such conclusions must be tempered, however, according to the degree and frequency of factor price movements and the concurrent state of demand. The thesis just outlined obviously fits most closely the thin-margin industries whose buying prices vary frequently, such as those which process crude farm products. Their selling price changes are frequent and business customers have an almost perfect basis for speculative action.

Where such experiences are infrequent or where the cost change is small relative to the feasible unit of price change, there is more hesitancy and even some tendency to use the indirect means of adaptation to be sketched later in connection with reaction to demand changes. Price increases are more difficult to bring about, and noncollusive price leadership or other means of implementing a meeting of minds are apt to arise. The same may hold where there has been an accumulation of cost changes for relatively unimportant items which add up to an important reduction of profits. Of course, such small cost changes are often lost in a welter of product, channel-of-sale, and realization changes.

Reaction to Demand Change

Here attention focuses on a change of demand which, if followed by a roughly corresponding price change, would squeeze or enlarge the margin between direct costs and selling price. The marginal cost curve is assumed to be horizontal over a fairly wide range of volume rates. Demand changes usually affect the relative market positions of firms because the selling markets of firms are usually more varied in geographical coverage and in customer classes than are the earlier-stage markets for materials used in manufacturing. Some areas or some classes of customers will have experienced more or less variation in income or whatever is the cause of the change of demand. Consequently, the impact on sellers of the demand change tends not to be uniform and overt price changes would augment the effect.

Both because a decline of demand creates excess capacity and hence each firm is unusually sensitive to loss of volume and because a price cut would then be viewed as a threat to market position, firms hesitate to initiate such a decline and react strongly to a price cut by a rival. In the first instance, firms tend to accept such volume and profits as the reduced industry demand will yield for the products, sales programs, and the price structure which were already in effect. Added intensity in carrying out the existing sales program may be tried. If the low demand is prolonged, selective price concessions may be made. Some firms may enter low-priced segments which they had avoided earlier. The degree to which such steps are taken is affected by the feasibility of these devices and by the proportion of costs which are fixed. Typically, overt price cuts which would squeeze the margin over direct costs will be made by the firms only when they become financially embarrassed or when the growth of price concessions and shift of volume to low-priced segments make the old level of prices in their major segments untenable. Whether or not such price changes are made, the level of realization for the product line as a whole will fall relative to direct costs.

Indeed, when demand falls, choices made by buyers among the items in a product line often reduce the level of realization without a change having occurred in the price for any one item. Particularly where consumer incomes have declined there is ample evidence that the proportion of long-margin items relative to short-margin ones falls. Consequently, the margin over direct costs for the product line as a whole will be reduced, and unless overhead outlays can be cut, profits will drop sharply.

Except where the margin between direct cost and price has been squeezed by earlier developments, an increase in demand is followed by a process reverse to that just described. Here the idea of the kink in demand is particularly relevant. Short of sharp pressure from rising marginal costs (not higher factor prices), which may not occur until output exceeds that for which existing facilities were designed, no one seller would have reason to expect to be followed in a price increase. Aggregate profits of the firms are rising. Firms are inclined to use such an occasion to cement relations with customers, and failing to advance prices is a good method. Those whose market shares (and possibly market positions also) might appear to mark them as most likely to advance prices are often gaining by a shift within their line to the long-margin items and channels of sale. The firms who are lagging in these regards are least likely to follow a price increase.

On what happens when sharply rising marginal costs are faced, our evidence is less conclusive. In more normal times than those of recent years—if there be such—demand increases are less sharp. On such occasions firms are apt to undertake a capacity expansion and to ration customers rather than to increase selling prices in the meantime. All such conduct is motivated by the desire to preserve and, if possible, to increase the strength of the firm's market position.

Summary

In spite of modifications necessary for particular situations, most of which have not been spelled out here, the contrast between reaction to a change in demand and to a change in factor prices is valid and important. In direct proportion to the cost impact (and frequency) of change of factor prices, an approximately corresponding and overt change in selling price can be expected. On the other hand, an overt change in price which would squeeze or expand the gross margin over direct costs for identical products does not ordinarily occur in response to modest and short-term movements of demand. Instead, other adaptations initiated by either sellers or buyers reduce or expand the general level of realization relative to cost for the varied items and channels of sale which make up the market for a product line.

Indeed, a general rule, to which I think exceptions are few, is that the realization for the product line will always move in the direction of a change of demand whether or not associated with a movement of direct costs. The extent to which overt price moves, price concessions, changes in product and channel of sale, or variations in the proportion of volume made up of long- and short-margin items, respectively, will be the source of this up or down movement of the level of realization for the product line relative to cost, will vary widely. Any analysis which omits changes in this realization for reasons other than those noted or which omits transaction-price changes even for narrowly defined products will lead to inaccurate conclusions.[5]

CONCLUDING OBSERVATIONS

Definite and quantifiable conclusions cannot be laid out with respect to resource use in and welfare results of most industrial markets. Obviously these markets do not work like those whose structure approximates that of the pure competition model. That is irrelevant, for the final interest is in results. It seems to me both evident and understandable, once one is versed in the whole of the structure and operations of modern industrial markets, that their operating results approach more closely the ideal than one would surmise to be true from textbook models of oligopoly and monopolistic competition or from the literature on concentration. This is the net result, I think, of sellers' reaction to uncertainty, of intersegment or even intermarket movement of firms or redivision of function, and of the wide opportunity for firms to gain individually by competitive devices other than overt price change—devices which after some lag tend to wipe out abnormally high margins for the product line as a whole. This means that I attach high value to the dynamic view of most of these markets. The degree to which optimal aggregate results are obtained for these reasons (and also the effect of lesser uncertainty on the actual attainment of the economies of scale) must differ substantially among markets, and only the beginnings of the specification of the determinants of those degrees can now be made. Obviously, however, the market adjustments sketched here work differently, often indirectly and more slowly, than one would visualize for an open market where there would be many buyers and sellers.

Given that conclusion, one's appraisal of the performance of such markets depends in considerable degree on what he expects market processes to accomplish. If he thinks in terms of providing guides to individuals' acts, such as relative prices as a guide to choices by consumers, these markets fall far short of the ideal, as do markets which are imperfect for any reason. Furthermore, if one's system of economics

---

[5] The economic significance of the adjustment of the level of realization for a group of related items and a proposed method for measuring such realization changes have been considered by the present writer in "An Economic Appraisal of Price Measures," *Journal of the American Statistical Association*, December, 1951, pp. 461–79.

requires that prices respond directly and promptly to movements of demand, industrial markets stack up badly, for their adjustments in such cases tend to take place indirectly and laggardly. A reminder should be made, however, that these processes of indirect adjustment may bring cost-level and product-quality changes more rapidly than they would otherwise occur. Wherever these alternatives are feasible, they tend to bring about—slowly, to be sure—changes in the level of realization compared to cost for the product line as a whole and, to that degree, effectuate the adaptation to changes of demand which is called for in economic theory.

On the other hand, if one is concerned about a longer view of the performance of markets or concludes that only a longer view is appropriate for industrial markets, then his judgment of the performance sketched here is more optimistic. This latter view is what I take to have been the essence of the "workable competition" idea. In that sense, both the properties of equilibria and the reaction to factor price and demand movements in those industrial markets where effective, longer-run collusion does not exist, have a strong tendency toward a desirable use of resources and toward adaptability to major changes in conditions of cost and demand.

18

Antitrust and the Classic Model*

By SHOREY PETERSON[†]

"Outsiders," wrote John Neville Keynes in introducing his *Scope and Method*, "are naturally suspicious of a science, in the treatment of which a new departure is so often and so loudly proclaimed."[1] It is a curious and disturbing fact that at the traditional center of economics—the role of markets in solving the general problem of order in economic life—new departures have been proclaimed so often.

Outsiders become aware of economics mainly when economists appraise the working of the economy or propose guides for its control; and it is here that the theory of values and markets, more than in its abstract expression, has chief impact. In the quarter-century since Chamberlin put monopoly and competition together in a single formulation, economists have stressed the prevalence of monopoly elements in markets, but have differed in interpreting this condition, especially in its bearing on policy. Commonly they relate it to pre-Chamberlin thought regarding the nature and place of competition, and bring a putative "classic" model, at least implicitly, into their discussion. In doing so they will agree that such a model describes badly how markets really work, but will often disagree as to its normative role. They may accept its guidance in defining the necessary working of markets in a free system, and then despair of the future of control through markets that do not and cannot work in that manner. Or, more likely now, they may reject the model as a false guide because our present economy seems to do very well without meeting its requirements. As substitutes for it they may rely on theories of "workable competition" and "countervailing power."

The present contention is that both of these views misrepresent earlier analysis when they deduce policy implications from models used in static theory. How wrong the deduction can be is apparent when we examine the work of such economists as John Bates Clark and Alfred Marshall who brought their theory into the practical realm. Their handling of market problems, running the gamut from static theory to policy proposals, warrants neither the pessimism nor the rejection. Indeed it

* *The American Economic Review*, Vol. XLVII (March, 1957), pp. 60–78. Reprinted by courtesy of the publisher and the author.

† University of Michigan.

[1] *The Scope and Method of Political Economy* (London, 1891), p. 8.

would be more accurate to say that their thinking set a course which we are still largely following, and perhaps without being much farther down the road. The senior Keynes should find merit in a fuller sense of the continuity in this development.

I. CURRENT INTERPRETATIONS OF THE EARLIER VIEW OF MARKETS

Galbraith, for example, proceeds in his *American Capitalism* from the position that a "vast distance separates oligopoly from the competition of the competitive model." "It is a measure of the magnitude of the disaster of the old system," he says, "that when oligopoly or crypto-monopoly is assumed it no longer follows that any of the old goals of social efficiency are realized." And again: "By evolution, from a system where nearly everything worked out for the best, economists found themselves with a system where nearly everything seemed to work out for the worst."[2]

As thus stated, this view of earlier thinking may lead to a denial merely of its descriptive validity, or also of its normative worth. In *The Decline of Competition* Arthur R. Burns displayed the first of these leanings. He began by adopting the usage common since Chamberlin of employing the term competition to mean pure competition and of referring to situations departing therefrom, that is, to most markets, as noncompetitive or monopolistic. Under a variety of circumstances business firms act in light of "the effects of changes in their output, or their price policy, upon the market as a whole," and thus "find themselves in the position of a monopolist" in price and output decisions. In a context not of abstract theory but of market appraisal and policy recommendation, Burns finds it significant that "price and production policies would be expected to differ from those associated with perfect competition." In his long and impressive recital of the monopoly elements in markets, it seems to be enough to show that these elements are present—unnecessary to determine how seriously they cause price and output adjustments to depart from an acceptable norm that embraces all elements of public interest. More recently Burns has affirmed his view that, under the antitrust laws, "we have failed to achieve a competitive system at all closely resembling that which was in the minds of the economists of the last century . . . ," and presumably has indicated his conception of the earlier view when he says: "Only pure price competition can produce the results which most people have in mind when they defend what they call in general terms 'the competitive system.' "[3]

[2] J. K. Galbraith, *American Capitalism—The Concept of Countervailing Power* (Cambridge, Mass., 1952), pp. 45, 46, 51. See also chap. 2.

[3] A. R. Burns, *The Decline of Competition* (New York, 1936), pp. 3–6, 40–41. The second reference is to his contribution to the "The Effectiveness of the Federal Antitrust Laws: A Symposium," D. M. Keezer, ed., *American Economic Review*, Vol. XXXIX (June, 1949), pp. 691–94.

But to Galbraith the lack of fit of the competitive model has quite a different meaning. While, according to it, things should work out for the worst under present conditions, they have not done so. The American economy appears wonderfully effective. The model must thus be rejected as guide as well as description; there can be no need of promoting the competition it envisages. In Galbraith's theory the offsetting power of groups on opposite sides of the market fills the breach, and market power is thereby kept from upsetting the allocative and distributive mechanism.

The equally optimistic and more widely accepted view of present markets is that competition, to succeed as regulator, need not approach the perfection of the model—indeed, it should not do so. This is the view that is now variously formulated under the caption of "workable competition." The essence of it is that even such rivalry as prevails when competitors are few can serve quite well in assigning resources and dividing income, and is greatly superior to its improbable purer cousin in promoting productivity and progress. In developing this view Schumpeter doubted the complete success of pure competition even as a static maximizing agent, but stressed mainly that an ideal disposition of resources at a given point in time is of small consequence when compared with the development of production through time. The competition that counts is "the competition from the new commodity, the new technology, the new source of supply, the new type of organization . . ."; and for it to operate, substantial elements of market power are necessary, not only as the concomitant of requisite firm size but as steadying influences in what would otherwise be too turbulent an economic sea. The present point is that Schumpeter regarded this theory of market operation as almost completely at odds with traditional thought. Despite some recognition of monopoly, "neither Marshall and Wicksell nor the classics," he said, "saw that perfect competition is the exception and that even if it were the rule there would be much less reason for congratulation than one might think."[4]

With similar optimism respecting big-firm capitalism A. A. Berle, in his recent *The 20th Century Capitalist Revolution*, joins in the rejection of older thinking, but with his own characteristic interpretation. Under the corporate system it is not true, he says, that "competition of great units (which does exist) produces the same results as those which used to flow from competition among thousands of small producers. . . . And it is indefensibly disingenuous to assert that these operations are primarily following economic laws more or less accurately outlined by the classic economists a century ago when the fact appears to be that they are following a slowly emerging pattern of sociological and political laws, relevant to the rather different community demands of our time."

[4] J. A. Schumpeter, *Capitalism, Socialism, and Democracy* (2d ed.; New York and London, 1947), pp. 74–78 and chaps. vii, viii.

For urging the effectiveness of competition among the giants, Sumner Slichter is put in the category of the disingenuous, "since competition within the system of corporate concentrates produces results quite different from the balanced economy expounded by Adam Smith."[5] Whatever the looseness of his history, whether of markets or of economic thought, Berle joins with Schumpeter and Galbraith in finding that present results are generally good.

Galbraith and Berle wrote for a wide audience and Schumpeter has been widely read; and their rejection for present use of a supposed classic model is now echoed in abler segments of the public press. Thus *Business Week*, under the heading "Clobbering Theory," reports the 1953 American Economic Association meetings in which Galbraith's thesis was discussed. "Classic economics teaches that only a competitive economy can be sound and prosperous. . . . But the fact is that the United States economy bears only a remote likeness to the classic picture of a competitive system—and yet it has prospered enormously. . . ."[6] And *Fortune*, in an article on "The New Competition," points out that "the word competition no longer means what it once did." It is a competition that prevails even among oligopolists and it has been a "stunning success." This competition is said to be essentially different from what competition meant "to most of the economists and experts who have until recently shaped the accepted notions of competition. . . . Competition to them is a way of life that can be defined fairly rigidly. They conceive competition in terms of the grand old original or classic model of Adam Smith and his followers."[7]

To economists trained in the 1920's and before, as this writer was—and especially to economists who have long followed the theory underlying antitrust policy—the foregoing oft-repeated view of what has happened to economics must seem mildly shocking. Contrary to this view, it would be truer to say that the trend represented by the phrase "workable competition" is a natural outgrowth of the thinking fifty years ago of such economists as J. B. Clark and Alfred Marshall. The policy conclusions objected to by workable-competition advocates really rest on the broadened definition of monopoly in much more recent theory. Some would recast earlier theory in line with this definition, but Marshall and Clark, and other theorists of realistic outlook from Adam Smith on, quite surely would have rejected the policy implications of any such reconstruction of their thought. Their conception of welfare was never confined to the norm of precise efficiency in allocation and their practical judgments moved well beyond the narrow boundaries of static analysis.

[5] A. A. Berle, Jr., *The 20th Century Capitalist Revolution* (New York, 1954), pp. 11–12, 43–52.

[6] January 9, 1954, pp. 93–99.

[7] June, 1952, p. 99.

II. OLDER THINKING AS TO ECONOMIC GOALS, ESPECIALLY IN A DYNAMIC SETTING

When economists give their main attention to a theoretical problem they are not in effect declaring that the solution of that problem meets all the requirements, or even the principal requirements, of well-being. Economists of the nineteenth century, especially the classical, Austrian, and neoclassical economists, gave their greatest effort to the problem of value. Smith, Ricardo, and the classical writers were unable to relate utility and cost meaningfully, or the values of factors and products fundamentally, and it required generations of economists to define the value conditions of economic behavior. The problem was fascinating in itself, and it seemed vital because prices were an obvious basis of action and of income in a specialized and exchanging society. A full grasp of the system-wide problem of economy in using resources, and the inherent relation of distribution to it, seems to have come only gradually, and with it a full realization of the role of a system of values in solving the general problem of order; but as thinking acquired this focus, the necessity of dealing with so complex a problem under simplified assumptions became evident. Very naturally the analysis was carried forward, especially by mathematically inclined economists, to an attempted final formulation of the condition of ideal maximization in the whole economy. The problem was worthy of the effort given it; but the inference is unwarranted that economics thereby limited its concern to a nice allocation of resources, or viewed the assumptions of allocation theory as descriptive of the real world.

The supposed need today of a new theory of economic performance, at sharp variance from the traditional, may indeed reflect some shift in emphasis among the several economic goals. There is great stress now on progress in total output, and earlier theory may have dealt inadequately with it. Schumpeter doubtless judged rightly in asserting the superiority of this objective over the niceties of assigning and rewarding factors; but he was wrong, nevertheless, in imputing neglect of it to the leading economists of earlier periods, or the advocacy by them of conditions which would impede its accomplishment. These economists seemed to think that coordination of activities through markets was the most fruitful problem for economists to attack; but most of them took it for granted that welfare depends primarily on high output and on the conditions necessary to it. Adam Smith struck the keynote in beginning his *Inquiry into the Nature and Causes of the Wealth of Nations* with a treatment "Of the Causes of Improvement in the Productive Power of Labour . . ." and in his obviously greater concern over "Progress of Opulence" than over any model that might now be described as "grand old original or classic." J. S. Mill concluded the introduction to his *Principles* with the statement: "The laws of Production and Distribution, and some of the practical consequences deducible from them, are the subject of the following treatise." His long first Book deals with production; and when, following Books II and III on distribution and value, he passes in Book IV from the "statics of the subject" to its "dynamics," he views the progress of society largely in terms of expanding production.[8]

No one should attempt to state briefly the criteria by which Marshall was guided in the incidental appraisals that appear in his broad picture of economic organization. Advance in output is implicit as a leading element in many of his remarks on progress; but his main concern was with nothing less than the whole improvement of man. Certainly it would misrepresent him grossly to say that he thought the success of a system depended on achieving certain marginal relationships in using resources. "The main concern of economics," he said, "is thus with human beings who are impelled, for good and evil, to change and progress. Fragmentary statical hypotheses are used as temporary auxiliaries to dynamical—or rather biological—conceptions: but the central idea of economics, even when its Foundations alone are under discussion, must be that of living force and movement."[9]

In the present context John Bates Clark is the most instructive spokesman for traditional economics, since he was both an eminent expositor of neoclassical doctrine and a leading student of monopoly and antitrust policy, writing in the midst of early excitement over the threat of concentrated market power to the economic structure. In formulating in his *Distribution of Wealth* his static, perfect-market theory of factor pricing and resource use, he characterized his effort with the concluding statement that "all real knowledge of the laws of movement depends upon an adequate knowledge of the laws of rest." He saw this approach as only a part of economics since "a static state . . . is imaginary. All natural societies are dynamic; and those which we have principally to study are highly so." "A theory of disturbance and variation," he said then, would be "included in the science of economic dynamics; but the most important thing that is included in it is a theory of progress."[10] Clark essayed this larger task in his *Essentials of Economic Theory*, though only as a "provisional statement of the more general laws of progress"; and in it he set forth his views of monopoly and of related policy, as will be noted below.[11] For the moment we need only observe

[8] J. S. Mill, *Principles of Political Economy* (New York, 1883, from 5th London edition), Vol. I, p. 42; Vol. II, pp. 271–72. As to his personal choice among the tests of a good system, Mill said he could not "regard the stationary state of capital and wealth with the same unaffected aversion so generally manifested toward it by political economists of the old school" (Vol. II, p. 336).

[9] Alfred Marshall, *Principles of Economics* (8th ed.; London, 1920), p. xv.

[10] *The Distribution of Wealth* (New York, 1899), pp. 442, 31, 33.

[11] *Essentials of Economic Theory—as Applied to Modern Problems of Industry and Public Policy* (New York, 1907), p. v.

Clark's perspective of goals, as when he stated in his *The Control of Trusts* that ". . . progress is in itself the *summum bonum* in economics, and that society is essentially the best which improves the fastest."[12]

But it is only part of the story to see that leading economists of the past gave no special pre-eminence to the value matters they studied so thoroughly, and looked on their static hypotheses as something less than realistic description. While they stressed high and growing production, did this result not depend in their theory on a degree of competition impossible under modern conditions? Galbraith, notably, rests his criticism on this interpretation. Among "the old goals of social efficiency" he includes "getting the most for the least—the common engineering view of efficiency," together with "appropriate incentive to change—the adoption of new and more efficient methods of production"; and he lumps these production goals with those of optimum allocation and distribution in declaring that when competitors are few "it no longer follows that any of the old goals of social efficiency are realized." Indeed, for all of these goals to be reached, as Galbraith interprets the requirements of earlier theory, competition should be construed even more rigorously than was done; and he applauds the more recent economists who "began to require of competition a meaning which would cause it, in turn, to produce the economic and social consequences which earlier economists had associated with it."[13]

The opposite view seems more plausible. Only when traditional economics is thus "perfected" is it vulnerable to the charge that, by its rationale, everything should work out for the worst in modern capitalism. We should not inflict on it so damaging a refinement. It is true that competition has always been assigned a central place among the conditions of productivity and progress; it has been counted on to spur improvement, rid industries of weak producers, prevent gain through restricting performance. But the competition that serves these ends need not be perfect—in major respects it should not be—and earlier economists knew this, much as we do. Whatever the perfection formerly thought necessary for markets to perform certain allocative and distributive functions—the topic of the following section—no such condition should be read into their analysis of the more dynamic, onmoving aspects of economic performance.

Again, J. B. Clark's thinking is pertinent—a natural source for students who would link their thinking with the past. Clark did indeed insist that monopoly is decidedly "unfavorable to continued improvement

---

[12] *The Control of Trusts* (New York, 1901), pp. 82–83.

[13] Galbraith, *op. cit.*, pp. 16–20. Very properly Galbraith includes among the main economic goals—along with high productivity, effective allocation, and acceptable distribution—the stable high-level employment of resources. In dealing with this goal traditional economics comes off less well; but here the matter at issue is only incidentally, if at all, the competition that was assumed.

in the productive arts" whereas "competition is the assured guarantee of all such progress." But Clark wrote prior to that unfortunate usage by which all that is not pure competition is labeled monopoly. By monopoly he meant unified control of a market, and by competition, in this context, "healthful rivalry in serving the public." He feared the trusts that were developing and saw that "partial monopolies" were prevalent and dangerous.[14] But he saw the advantages of large establishments and also of consolidations, including even their contributions to research and innovation, which Galbraith says was slow to be recognized. The following may summarize Clark's view:

> A vast corporation that is not a true monopoly may be eminently progressive. If it still has to fear rivals, actual or potential, it is under the same kind of pressure that acts upon the independent producer—pressure to economize labor. It may be able to make even greater progress than a smaller corporation could make, for it may be able to hire ingenious men to devise new appliances, and it may be able to test them without greatly trenching on its income by such experiments. When it gets a successful machine, it may introduce it at once into many mills. Consolidation without monopoly is favorable to progress.[15]

Thus, in the manner of Schumpeter and others, Clark was saying not merely that productivity and progress can persist in the face of an admixture of monopoly, but that within limits they are promoted positively by it. This view appeared most clearly in his appreciation of patent policy: "If an invention became public property the moment that it was made, there would be small profit accruing to any one from the use of it and smaller ones from making it. . . . This fact affords a justification for one variety of monopoly. . . . Patents are a legal device for promoting improvements, and they accomplish this by invoking the principle of monopoly which in itself is hostile to improvement." He recognized the possibility of abuses, but he sensed the principle, which he stated elsewhere more abstractly, that perfect competition instead of being a condition of progress would actually prevent it.[16]

There is another quite different respect in which the fullest competition is often deemed harmful and unworkable. It lies in the fact that in modern industry with its indivisibilities, fixed costs, and lumpy expansion in anticipation of demand, wholly unrestricted competition is likely to make profit seeking too difficult, losses too prevalent, for firms to remain healthy and vigorous. This view was also common a half-century and more ago and was urged as a reason for accepting, though with

---

[14] *Essentials*, pp. 364, 374, 382, 533–34.

[15] *Ibid.*, p. 534.

[16] *Ibid.*, pp. 360, 366, 373. Clark's "five organic changes," the basis of his "economic dynamics," included growth of population and of capital and changes in methods and organization of production and in consumers' wants. Shifting of production to new products did not receive separate recognition but appeared under the last heading. *Ibid.*, 203–6.

misgiving, the limitations that size and combination bring. In his early work, *The Philosophy of Wealth*, Clark applauded the "conservative competition in which economists of a few years ago were able to see realized a general harmony of social interests"; and with it he contrasted "the fiercer contest in which eventual success comes to a participant through the extermination of rivals, the process well-named 'cut-throat' competition." "Easy and tolerant competition," Clark said, "is the antithesis of monopoly; the cut-throat process is the father of it."[17]

Later he provided an explanation, as we would now, in terms of fixed costs and unused capacity and the possibility that competition will drive prices down close to the level of variable costs. Such competition he pointed out, in discussing water transportation in the *Essentials*, results usually in "a merely tacit agreement to 'live and let live' "; and he thought "a normal kind of competition will stop short of the warfare which drives both rivals into bankruptcy."[18] Still later, in the second edition of *The Control of Trusts*, the situation in industry in general was explained, and the case presented and conditions set forth for "a tolerant and normal competition" under which big industry can remain vigorous.[19] This fear of wholly unrestricted competition was quite general among American economists of the period.[20] That Marshall questioned the wisdom of unlimited competition was evident both in his *Principles* and in his *Industry and Trade*, as will appear incidentally in the following section.

III. WORKABILITY OF IMPERFECT COMPETITION, AS SEEN BY EARLIER ECONOMISTS

Now let us turn, in this comparison of past with present thinking, from the conditions of expanding productivity and general industrial health to the distortions commonly attributed to monopoly. To say that a system with some mixture of monopoly in its competition may do a good job in developing productive power is not to say that it escapes serious misallocation and exploitation. Much that is now claimed on behalf of a new concept of competition, supposedly different from that of the older economists, amounts to saying that our economy does so well in expanding output that we can afford to overlook the distortions. This, in part, is what Schumpeter said. But theories of "workable competition," as of "countervailing power," go further and give reasons why departures from purity in competition do little harm to price relation-

[17] *The Philosophy of Wealth* (Boston, 1886), p. 120.

[18] *Essentials*, pp. 414–15.

[19] J. B. Clark and J. M. Clark, *The Control of Trusts* (rev. ed.; New York, 1912), pp. 168–83.

[20] See, for example, A. T. Hadley, *Economics* (New York and London, 1896), chap. 6; J. W. Jenks, *The Trust Problem* (rev. ed.; New York, 1905), pp. 140, 16–20; F. W. Taussig, *Principles of Economics* (2d ed.; New York, 1911), Vol. II, pp. 434–36.

ships. Are these reasons much different from the views of economists of fifty or more years ago? Again, the present theme is that they are not—that they differ only as more fully developed concepts differ from their origins.

To begin with, we need perspective of the place that pure competition, or whatever the "classic model" implies, had in relevant earlier thinking. A plausible conclusion, when we scan the long attack on value problems, is that particular features and degrees of competition had a much smaller place in the whole analysis, even implicitly, than is now often supposed. The main struggle of economists over a century or more was not in spelling out marginal refinements but in putting the main building blocks in some sort of order: in relating utility and cost; in recognizing other costs than labor; in seeing the broad dependence of factor prices on product prices, as well as the narrower reverse relationship; in assigning separate values to factors used in combination—all, of course, with incremental logic but with the main structure transcending the static niceties. In a society faced with vast possibilities of gross error in adapting complex resources to satisfying countless wants, formulation in value terms of the main elements of system-wide order was the goal to be sought and is the achievement now to be applauded.

In this setting the problems of allocation and distribution do not depend for their solution on a certain kind of competition; the essential solution is largely independent of the type of market. It is often said that competition is *the* regulator of a market economy; but, on the contrary, the chaos that would prevail in the absence of effective control is obviated not by competition alone but by the more general operation of the whole price mechanism. This is evident when we observe that even a monopolist can derive revenue only by producing what people will buy, and that he is best off when he aims at the most valuable flow of products from the resources he uses. Nor can he get the most profit without employing effective techniques of production, and in other respects selecting and combining factors to best advantage. His demand enters into the total demand for each factor, and this demand, with the supply, sets the price of the factor and the cost of its use, and thus provides the essential barrier to inferior applications of it. True, his market power creates stresses that prevent full maximization from the social standpoint and his income may be greater than his performance requires. But the main elements of order are still present. A degree of competition that will keep these distortions within acceptable bounds has always been thought of as an essential part of the mechanism, but it is only a subordinate part of the whole scheme of control that the older economics explained for us.

This is elementary and is said only because lack of perspective regarding it has been common and has appeared in widely influential writing. The confusion may be explicit, as in assuming that a market economy is practically unregulated unless competition approaches perfection —or that the older economics held this to be the case. Or it may be implicit, as, for example, in Berle's contention that corporate operations are no longer guided by the market forces of traditional theory but by the mores of essentially political entities. Berle is offering a plausible theory of behavior within a limited range of decision making; but, so far as traditional economics is concerned, he overlooks the main point, namely that the greatest corporation is still subject to the tyranny of the income statement and can prosper only as it directs production in keeping with buyer preferences and uses resources with an eye to costs determined in a setting of alternative uses.

Thus viewed, this value structure defines the broad conditions of order in a market economy even when competitors are few. But its formulators may still be charged with setting up misleading guideposts if, implicitly, they made the ultimate niceties the crux of the allocation process. This, however, does not seem to have been the case, at least among leading economists who related theory to practical issues.

In this connection also, J. B. Clark is the best example of an able theorist concerned specifically with monopoly and antitrust. Clark seems generally to have recognized the difficulties that economists of the period are now said to have ignored, and his resolution of them suggests much present thinking. In his *Essentials* he says:

> The most striking phenomenon of our time is the consolidation of independent establishments by the forming of what are usually called trusts; and this and all the approaches to it are precluded by the static hypothesis. There is a question whether, after competition has reduced establishments in one subgroup to a half dozen or less, they would not, even without forming a trust, act as a quasi-monopoly.[21]

He saw the danger: "What we have is neither the complete monopoly nor the merely formal one, but one that has power enough to work injury and to be a menace to industry and politics." But markets still provide protection: even when the entire product comes from a single company,

> . . . the price may conceivably be a normal one. It may stand not much above the cost of production to the monopoly itself. If it does so, it is because a higher price would invite competition. The great company prefers to sell all the goods that are required at a moderate price rather than to invite rivals into its territory. This is monopoly in form but not in fact, for it is shorn of its injurious power; and the thing that holds it firmly in check is *potential competition*. . . . Since the first trusts were formed the efficiency of potential competition has been so constantly displayed that there is no danger that this regulator of prices will ever be disregarded.[22]

But, said Clark, this "check works imperfectly. At some points it restrains the corporations quite closely and gives an approach to the ideal

[21] *Essentials,* p. 201.

[22] *Ibid.,* pp. 380–82; italics in original.

results, in which the consolidation is very productive but not at all oppressive; while elsewhere the check has very little power, oppression prevails, and if anything holds the exactions of the corporation within bounds, it is a respect for the ultimate power of the government and an inkling of what the people may do if they are provoked to drastic action." He was hopeful that a policy aimed at "keeping the field open for competitors" might obviate more drastic action. This would require prevention of unfair and predatory methods. "The preservation of a normal system of industry and a normal division of its products requires the suppression of all those practices of great corporations on which their monopolistic power depends."[23]

While Clark saw the possibility of quasi monopoly when competitors are few, he believed "that competition usually would, in fact, survive and be extremely effective among as few as five or six competitors, till they formed some sort of union with each other."[24] No well-formed theory of oligopoly governed his thinking, and thus he saved himself the ordeal, first, of assuming full joint profit maximization when there are few competitors, and then of finding later a complex of reasons for doubting whether in fact this outcome is likely under dynamic conditions. With only moderate skepticism he might have accepted Schumpeter's view that the monopoly elements may be just sufficient to offset the forces of "creative destruction" which threaten the disappearance of profit. Clark observed:

> The actual shape of society at any one time is not the static model of that time; but it tends to conform to it, and in a very dynamic society is more nearly like it than it would be in one in which the forces of change are less active. With all the transforming influences to which American industrial society is subject, it today conforms more closely to a normal form than do the more conservative societies of Asia.[25]

Marshall, like Clark, fits poorly the supposed pattern of older thinking that we are questioning—a pattern of implied optimism respecting capitalism mistakenly resting on its assumed close resemblance to some model of near-perfect competition. Marshall was at least in part aware of the theoretical import of that ideal competitive state in which producers sell "in a large open market in such small quantities, that current prices will not be appreciably affected by anything which they may do or abstain from doing . . .";[26] but he disliked pushing his hypotheses so far. For better or worse, a "principle of continuity," as he had called it, animated his thinking, and he saw "great mischief" in "drawing broad

---

[23] *Ibid.*, pp. 383, 395.

[24] *Ibid.*, pp. 201–02.

[25] *Ibid.*, p. 197.

[26] Alfred Marshall, *Industry and Trade* (London, 1927), p. 401. Much of this volume was written long before its appearance in 1919, part of the type having been set in 1904.

artificial lines of division where Nature has made none."[27] Thus, even in his *Principles,* in explaining "normal" pricing in manufacturing and merchandising, he did not adopt as his starting point the fluid, market-determined pricing of agriculture, but instead assumed the condition of quoted prices which prevails in such markets, with each seller dependent not on an impersonal body of purchasers but on specific patronage. For instance, in considering the common situation of firms that immediately must operate below capacity, he says:

> In a trade which uses very expensive plant, the prime cost of goods is but a small part of their total cost; and an order at much less than their normal price may leave a large surplus above their prime cost. But if producers accept such orders in their anxiety to prevent their plant from being idle, they glut the market and tend to prevent prices from reviving. In fact however they seldom pursue this policy constantly and without moderation. If they did, they might ruin many of those in the trade, themselves perhaps among the number; and in that case a revival of demand would raise violently the prices of the goods produced by the trade. Extreme variations of this kind are in the long run beneficial neither to producers nor to consumers; and general opinion is not altogether hostile to that code of trade morality which condemns the action of anyone who "spoils the market" by being too ready to accept a price that does little more than cover the prime cost of his goods, and allows but little on account of his general expenses.[28]

Thus, in his theory of short-run use of plant capacity, Marshall implicitly rejects pure competition as his expository framework, and he rejects also the allocative result of pure competition as a sufficient criterion in judging control through markets.

Marshall's *Principles* was devoted to what he called "foundations," the exposition of the "normal" in equilibrium terms; and the more "biological" approach required by the development of modern industry he put aside for separate analysis in his *Industry and Trade.*[29] In this analysis the prevailing theme is that even "open" markets display only a qualified competition, and monopoly and competition "shade into each other by imperceptible degrees." "Every manufacturer, or other businessman, has a plant, an organization, and a business connection, which put him in a position of advantage for his special work"; and thus "for the time being he and other owners of factories of his class are in possession of a partial monopoly. . . . Combinations for regulating prices aim at consolidating provisionally this partial monopoly, and at putting it in good working order. . . ."[30] In this setting he examines at length the growth of plant size for technical reasons and the many-rooted development of corporate combination and cartelization in Germany, Britain, and America.

---

[27] *Principles,* preface to the 1st edition as appearing in the 8th, p. ix.

[28] *Ibid.,* p. 375.

[29] As explained in the preface to the 8th edition of the *Principles,* pp. xii–xiv.

[30] *Industry and Trade,* pp. 178, 196. Marshall's extensive pre-Chamberlin exposition of the theme of monopolistic competition is set forth by H. H. Liebhafsky in "A Curious Case of Neglect: Marshall's *Industry and Trade,*" *Canadian Journal of Economics and Political Science,* Vol. XXI (August, 1955), pp. 339–53.

Competition has a central place in neoclassical theory; but Marshall, its great exponent, remained unexcited by his impressive evidence that competition is manifest mainly in rough approximate ways. Monopoly power is a continual threat, but "absolute monopolies," he believed, "are of little importance in modern business as compared with those which are 'conditional' or 'provisional' " and the latter keep their place only if "they do not put prices much above the levels necessary to cover their outlays with normal profits." Like Clark, Marshall thought a "severely monopolistic price policy" unlikely because "a man of sound judgment . . . will keep a watchful eye on sources of possible competition, direct and indirect." Potential competition, the competition of substitutes, a long-run concern over the welfare of customers, were all stressed as significant restraints.[31]

Marshall saw also the restraining effect of product differentiation. Though it violates the purity of competition, it obstructs all arrangements for price control, which are difficult to bring about when products are not standardized. At the same time Marshall observed that standardized goods, which include "raw materials or half-finished products, or implements" used in business, are likely to be bought by firms that possess market power and "therefore are likely to meet the danger of oppressive action on the part of a combination, in control of things which they need to buy, by a counter-federation of their own. That is apt in its turn to stimulate the growth of similar federations on the part of traders or producers who need to buy some of their products; and so on till the end of the chain. . . ."[32] So "countervailing power," and the condition tending to produce it, received a respectful nod.

Nothing like the "classic model" seems to have been considered seriously by Marshall as a policy goal. Early industrial competition, back to Ricardo, had not resembled any sort of market ideal, though the contrary is now often assumed. It was rather the "aggressive competition" of "crude, though energetic men," a "species of warfare," and was not likely, as the preceding section indicated, to produce a "solid prosperity." For most of British industry Marshall found adequate the more restrained kind of competition, with the greater admixture of monopoly. which came in his day. Even in America, he thought, "Anglo-Saxon moderation and stability have enabled competitive and monopolistic abuses to be kept within relatively narrow limits, with but little direct intervention of authority." At the same time, monopoly was more dangerous than was generally realized, with greater menace in "monopolistic association" than in "monopolistic aggregations"; and a policy more positive than publicity, which he generally favored, might become necessary.[33]

With such spokesmen as Clark and Marshall writing in this vein, it

---

[31] *Industry and Trade,* pp. 395–98, 405–09, 523–26.

[32] *Ibid.,* p. 549.

[33] *Ibid.,* pp. 179, 656, 400.

is surprising that Schumpeter should have belittled neoclassical doctrine as he did. To him the competition of his predecessors was a "competition within a rigid pattern of invariant conditions," and not at all the competition of new and better products and processes that he thought important. He failed to note that this emphasis of his was essentially an unfolding of earlier thought and that he was quite in the earlier vein in saying of this latter competition that it "acts not only when in being but also when it is merely an ever-present threat . . ." and that "in many cases, though not in all, this will in the long-run enforce behavior very similar to the perfectly competitive pattern."[34] It is surprising, too, that Schumpeter, in these allusions to traditional economics, failed to credit it with explaining the broad market and value structure that his theory implicitly relied on in circumscribing the distortions of crudely competitive markets. He saw the older economics not in its whole relevant expanse but only in its effort to sharpen particular relationships with the tools of static theory. In another context, however, that of his "socialist blueprint," he paid neoclassical economics the ultimate tribute of relying almost step by step on its essential structure in showing how socialism may solve the general problem of economy in using resources.[35]

IV. MODELS AND POLICY

There has been looseness at all times in perceiving the role of static models of competitive market operation. Such models are useful, indeed essential, in rendering manageable the numerous elements in the general problem of order in the economy. They supply the framework for tracing allocative effects of given practices and policies, and in this role provide a starting point in observing when market power is manifest. But static models may also mislead: through being supposed to reflect closely the actual processes of markets; through suggesting that they embrace all elements of welfare and afford a basis for judging economic performance as a whole; through tempting the user to toss all departures from their exact conditions into a common pot called monopoly and leading him, without guidance as to the seriousness of the deviations, into unhappy conclusions as to how the economy is working, or should be expected to work.

However, economists who seem at times to insist in supposed traditional fashion on near-perfect competition as a condition of acceptable economic performance may not carry this insistence into their more practical judgments. Galbraith supports his conception of earlier thinking by repeated use of Hayek's statement in *The Road to Serfdom* that "the price system will fulfill this function [of general control] only if competition prevails, that is, if the individual producer has to adapt himself

---

[34] Schumpeter, *op. cit.*, pp. 84–85.

[35] *Ibid.*, chap. 16.

to price changes and cannot control them." But the context of this statement does not imply purity of competition, since Hayek is only declaring the general superiority of control through markets over "central planning for the growth of our industrial system," which, he says, is by comparison "incredibly clumsy, primitive, and limited in scope." And he indicates that he finds acceptable a competition that can ordinarily be reconciled with the economies of size—one in which the firm, while it cannot control prices, can certainly influence them.[36] Pigou, with his elaborate concern over deviations from equality in marginal social net products, may likewise be thought of as intolerant of imperfect market adjustments. But Pigou was explicit that "simple competition," as he called it, is not feasible technically; and he preferred a limited antitrust approach, such as Clark favored, to a more drastic control of business.[37]

But even though they were not purists in their conception of adequate competition in a policy context, should not all these exponents of older thinking have been overwhelmed by the full impact of modern oligopoly theory? While granting some latitude to business decision in a dynamic system, could they digest the idea that business firms, separate but few in number, may so calculate each other's moves that they arrive at the price and output conclusions of the single monopolist? However loosely their frame of thought is construed, can modern markets be made to operate successfully within it?

The answer is yes, if we accept Clark and Marshall as spokesmen of earlier thinking and are not ourselves overwhelmed by the first approximations of modern theory. Indeed, without certain present insights, they came close to the spot where we now find ourselves, as conflicting insights begin to cancel out. Unworried by the neat logic of joint profit maximization when competitors are few, they were not bound to investigate the exacting and unusual conditions of that logic: its assumptions of a common view of demand and cost functions, of lack of aggressive desire for a larger share of markets, of standardization not only of products but of market terms in general, of pricing that is open and above-board, of absence of fear of new entries and substitute products and all the dynamic hurly-burly that Schumpeter made the center of his thinking. About the same position can be reached, in an unsophisticated way, without first falling into the oligopoly trap and then freeing one's self from it.

Thus the views mainly to be corrected are not those of the older economists. They had a fair sense of the impact of modern industry,

---

[36] F. A. Hayek, *The Road to Serfdom* (Chicago, 1944), chap. 4. The first quotation is from p. 49 and is used by Galbraith, *op. cit.*, pp. 15, 35.

[37] A. C. Pigou, *The Economics of Welfare* (4th ed.; London, 1950), chap. 21. In this chapter Pigou notes the possible restraining effect of the countervailing power of opposed monopolies; but he doubts its effectiveness in protecting the public.

and on tenable grounds held that markets might still exercise adequate control, while permitting desirable progress. Perfect competition must fail as a useful policy norm not merely because markets do not operate in that way but because we would not want them to. The views to be corrected now by theories of a "new competition" that is "workable," or even by theories of "countervailing power," are rather those of followers of Chamberlin who fell into the bad habit of equating competition with pure competition, of confusing theoretical benchmarks with policy norms, of expecting highly monopolistic behavior in most markets where competitors are few.

Undoubtedly the study of markets has been revitalized in the last quarter-century. New theory has suggested what to look for, industry characteristics have been revealed with new significance, new insights into policy have been gained. But still, in the field of practical policy, these developments have worked little effective change; nor is it clear that they will. It has seemed useful, for instance, with competition and monopoly commingling over a wide range, to devise means of measuring the degree of monopoly in markets. Ingenious techniques have been contrived in the abstract, and there has been some attempt to apply them, especially in the case of concentration indexes. But one easily agrees with Machlup when, after reviewing these efforts, he concludes that such measurement is "even conceptually impossible," quite apart from its applicability.[38] Oligopoly theory seems less promising now than it once did, not only because of its profusion of elements but because factors other than numbers are seen to be widely significant.[39] It is almost shocking to recall the view of commentators after the *Tobacco* decision (1946) that this theory had therewith been made part of judicial standards and might properly dominate them in such cases.

The nature of policy problems forces us back toward the looser approach of earlier economists, and indeed of competent lawyers and judges. Even if we could measure degrees of deviation from pure competition, we would accomplish little unless pure competition were the market condition really desired—the condition that would promote a balanced achievement of diverse economic goals; and surely it is not. And even if we had a significant measurement, related to a truly optimum market norm, the policy question would remain: In a society in which ideal blueprints never materialize, what degree of departure from the norm is reasonably acceptable, in light of political as well as economic factors? More theory and more research will aid us; but there can be no answer except through the kind of experienced judgment always relied on in such matters.

---

[38] Fritz Machlup, *The Political Economy of Monopoly* (Baltimore, 1952), chap. 12, esp. pp. 526–28.

[39] See, for instance, Carl Kaysen in the National Bureau of Economic Research volume, *Business Concentration and Price Policy* (Princeton, 1955), p. 118.

Views differ greatly as to the desirable form and rigor of antitrust policy; but the differences do not really spring from a theoretical cleavage. They arise, as in the past, from dissimilar appraisals of incommensurable goals and market factors as seen in a framework that remains about the same. Economists who stress the nice equating of marginal results are more alarmed by monopoly elements than are economists who stress productivity and progress. The former have also a stricter idea of what reasonable profit means. Such groups may view differently the contribution of great firms in lowering costs and improving products, the competitive potency of product and technical substitutes, the need of market restraints to induce innovation and to prevent harmful price cutting where reserve capacity accompanies growth. But these grounds for disagreement are as explicable in the theory of Clark and Marshall as of today.

To this point our theme has been developed without mention of John Maurice Clark, son of John Bates and leading formulator of the reasons why competition may be effective in an economy in which monopoly elements are common. In his well-known paper, "Toward a Concept of Workable Competition," Clark, it seems, was not trying to close a gap caused by failure of the older theory, but was concerned rather with recent refinements of the competitive model which, he said, "may serve as a starting point of analysis" but which, when used as a guide in approaching policy have "seemed at times to lead to undesirable results. . . ."[40] In a sense he bridged the periods by paralleling the exacting modern idea of pure competition with an equally sophisticated conception of the realizable and acceptable working of markets, and thus formulated with added fullness and precision a basis of policy toward which his father and his father's contemporaries were moving.

Elsewhere J. M. Clark has said, in writing of his father: "What may reasonably be asked of the theorists of the current generation is that they integrate their findings with those elements of the thought of the preceding generation which have enduring value, and which they tend to neglect."[41] The present theory of pure competition and of departures from it grows naturally out of the older static analysis of markets; present theories of workable competition, even when stretched to make room for elements of countervailing power, likewise particularize older thinking regarding feasible market operation under dynamic conditions. Analysis of this side of modern capitalism requires no revolution in economic thought.

---

[40] *American Economic Review,* Vol. XXX (Proceedings of the American Economic Association, 1940), p. 241; reprinted in *Readings in the Social Control of Industry* (Philadelphia, 1942), p. 453.

[41] "John Bates Clark," in H. W. Spiegel, ed., *The Development of Economic Thought* (New York, 1952), p. 612.

V. COMPETITION, MONOPOLY, AND PUBLIC POLICY

19

Public Policy and Business Size*

By CORWIN D. EDWARDS[†]

The belief that bigness in business raises a problem of public policy rests upon the postulate that the enterprise which is big is powerful. A direct relation between bigness and power is taken as a starting point for the following discussion.

The idea that big enterprises are powerful has led naturally, if not inevitably, to the belief that either their power should be limited or else its exercise should be controlled. In a democracy, since citizens are regarded as equal, there is suspicion of those who rise to places of political power. The powerful are made responsible to the group or are subjected to a system of checks and balances designed to make sure that their authority is narrowly circumscribed. So long as these views prevail in politics, they will be expressed also in political policies toward economic affairs. A democratic state will necessarily adopt policies designed to limit the concentration of the control over business or to curb the business policies which may grow out of such concentration.

Throughout economic and political life the existence of power results in alarm about the effects of the power upon those who are not powerful. Concern about the power of large enterprises has been expressed on three different levels. First, and simplest, it is asserted that power may result in abuses of power, such as charging extortionate prices or unfairly bludgeoning competitors. Such abuses are conceived as an outgrowth of the policies of large enterprises and therefore as amenable to public action designed to provide incentives for a change in business behavior. Second, it is asserted that the power of large enterprises brings about an unfortunate distortion in the performance of the economic system because it leads to such characteristics as rigidity of prices and relaxation of drives toward maximum efficiency. Effects of this kind are conceived as the unintended by-products of the immediate policies of powerful enterprises and hence as lying largely beyond conscious control by such enterprises. Third, it is asserted that an economic system in which power has been unduly concentrated suffers from an impairment

* *The Journal of Business of the University of Chicago*, Vol. XXIV (1951), pp. 280–92. (Copyright, 1951, University of Chicago.) Reprinted by courtesy of the University of Chicago Press and the author.

† University of Chicago.

of some of its most important institutions, such as the opportunity for newcomers to undertake new ventures and the existence of a large number of points at which decisions are made by persons who are relatively independent and very nearly equal in status. Such effects are conceived as the aggregate result of the power of various business enterprises and therefore as beyond control by any single person or enterprise that contributes to them.

Persons who are concerned primarily about abuses of power, that is, about the first of these three effects, are likely to regard problems of bigness as matters depending primarily upon codes of business conduct. They are likely to think, with Theodore Roosevelt, that there may be "good trusts" and "bad trusts." Persons who are primarily interested in the effects of bigness upon the functioning of the economic system and upon the institutional arrangements therein are likely to believe that the policy problems created by bigness are largely independent of the point of view of those who manage large enterprises and cannot be substantially altered by such changes of business conduct as lie within the discretion of managements. Hence they are likely to think that bigness in business may go too far even if large enterprises are managed with ability and public spirit.

Such is the setting of criticism in which public policy toward large enterprises must be worked out. There are also certain preconceptions about the scope of public policy in this field which, in my opinion, are shared by most of us. Among them, I think, are these six.

1. The problems arising out of bigness are not primarily those of the personal character of managers of large enterprises. Even the abuses of power which bigness may produce are not usually due to bad personal character. Of course, certain business abuses may spring from lack of honesty, public spirit, or intelligence in a strategically placed manager. For the most part, however, business managements compare favorably with the rest of the community in these qualities. Moreover, the conduct of a large enterprise is a complex affair, affected by the decisions of many individuals, guided by policies developed in groups rather than by individuals, and determined in large part by the nature of the concern and its environment rather than by personal preferences.

2. Some degree and kind of bigness is with us to stay. A complete atomization of the business structure is made impossible by the technology of mass production and by the fact that certain forms of specialization are possible only if a given degree of size is attained.

3. Not all bigness is bad. Some degrees and kinds of bigness are necessary, or at least advantageous, in giving effect to the possibilities of modern industrial technology and in thus reducing costs and enhancing output.

4. Not all bigness is good. A concern may grow bigger than is technologically necessary and may attain such a size as to possess monopoly

power and use that power to the detriment of its suppliers, its customers, and the community at large.

5. As a general rule, the pressure of competition should be kept strong as an incentive for business enterprises to keep themselves efficient and to serve the public well and as a safeguard against abusive conduct.

6. Where desirable bigness involves such a large scale of business activity as to be inconsistent with vigorous competition, some form of control should be established over the activities of the large concern in order to provide incentives and safeguards similar to those of competition. The burden of showing that there is need for such an exception to the general policy of competition should rest upon those who propose the exception.

Although the six preconceptions that I have just listed are matters of general agreement, they leave us with a considerable area of controversy as to appropriate public policy toward large enterprises. The controversy centers upon such questions as how objectionable bigness is to be distinguished from desirable bigness and what is to be done about objectionable bigness where it is found.

One important group of questions clusters about the burden of proof. Shall the government act only where evils are apparent or shall it engage in prophecy in an endeavor to anticipate evils? Shall its activity be curative or preventative? Opinions on this matter are often strongly influenced by choice of words. To the question whether action should be based upon visible evils or prophecy, the uncritical are likely to answer that the function of government is to correct evils rather than to see ghosts. To the question whether action should be curative or preventative, the uncritical are likely to respond that "an ounce of prevention is worth a pound of cure." Yet these two answers take opposite sides of the same issue.

The trend of our legislation has been from the curative toward the preventative. Our first antitrust law, the Sherman Act, forbids conspiracies in restraint of trade, attempts to monopolize, and actual monopolization. In the case of a conspiracy, the purpose of the agreement is clear in the terms thereof, and there is likely to be no great interval between the formation of the agreement and the beginning of its execution. Monopolization is the possession and use of power in a way that has adverse effects upon those against whom the power is used. An attempt to monopolize involves both a specific purpose and an assortment of activities designed to subordinate or destroy others and thus achieve power. Thus the prohibitions of the Sherman Act are directed at business conduct from which anticompetitive consequences have already resulted or are clearly intended.[1]

[1] This characterization of the scope of the Sherman Act may be challenged on the basis of certain recent court decisions. Whether or not such a challenge is valid, there can be little doubt that the characterization fits the early Sherman Act

Dissatisfaction with a law of this scope soon became evident, particularly in cases which rested upon the charge of monopolization or attempt to monopolize, and which, therefore, turned upon the power of large enterprises. It became evident that, where the policies of a powerful concern resulted in the destruction of business rivals, no amount of remedial action could revive the dead. It also became evident that when various business enterprises had been combined and the parts had operated together as a going concern, a restoration of the previous independence of those parts was likely to be as impossible as the unscrambling of eggs in an omelet. Hence, it was widely argued that curative measures are not sufficiently effective and must be supplemented by preventative measures.

This basis for dissatisfaction was associated with another: a belief that the Sherman Act was not sufficiently specific and that the meaning of the antitrust laws should be made plainer. Businessmen argued persuasively that they did not know what practices would be held to restrain trade or to constitute monopolization or an attempt to monopolize and that business could not fairly be placed in jeopardy for failing to conform to an ill-defined code of conduct. The argument was reinforced by the point that voluntary compliance with the law is highly desirable but cannot readily be obtained unless the requirements of the law are clearly understood by those who should comply with it.

These two types of dissatisfaction evoked the legislation of 1914, the Clayton Act and the Federal Trade Commission Act. The avowed purpose of the new laws was preventative rather than curative. Congress wished to stop monopolistic tendencies "in their incipiency." Hence, it turned from the test of present evil to the test of future effect and forbade certain activities where the anticipated effect was adverse to competition. In the Federal Trade Commission Act unfair methods of competition were forbidden, and these were conceived as including not merely practices that had long been condemned by the common law but also any other practices detrimental to competition. The Clayton Act prohibited certain types of conduct which were regarded as capable of leading to monopolistic results. Two of these were marketing practices —discriminations in price and tying arrangements designed to prevent a seller's customers from buying from the seller's competitors. Two others were methods of concentrating authority—the purchase of stock in one corporation by another corporation and the interlock of directors between competing corporations. Thus both the behavior and the structure of enterprise were to be curbed where a monopolistic result was foreseen.

---

cases. The Act has been broadened by judicial interpretation, and one influence in the broadening probably has been the existence of subsequent laws in which the Congress has not confined itself to prohibition of business conduct that currently has objectionable consequences.

However, there proved to be an inevitable conflict between the drive for prevention and the drive for certainty. The effort to limit present action because of its future effect raises a question as to the reliability of the predictions upon which the statute is to be based. If the effects of present conduct or of a present form of business organization are unvarying and completely predictable, one can be sure what must be stopped in order to prevent a future effect. But where there is such certainty, legislation need not be couched in terms of effect; instead the conduct or the form of organization can itself be forbidden. We have a few examples of such prohibitions in the antitrust laws. For example, interlocking directorates are forbidden in the Clayton Act if the companies are in competition and are of substantial size, presumably on the ground that the existence of such interlocks among large competitors would have an inevitable effect in reducing competition. As to most situations, however, no such certainty is possible. Hence, question arises as to the character of the inference of effect which is to justify a prohibition. In three out of four of the prohibitions contained in the Clayton Act, the Congress used the phrase "where the effect may be"; and the courts have held that this language means that the specified effect must be, not certain, nor yet remotely possible, but reasonably probable. If the test of future effect is to be used, the standard of probability rather than certainty appears to be inevitable. Nevertheless, the necessary result of this test is to make the law less clear. Some activities or business structures may be prohibited when in fact they would not have reduced competition. Identical activities or business structures will be prohibited in one setting but not in another because in the two settings their probable effects upon competition are different. It will be impossible to translate the prohibitions of the law into a definite code of conduct.

Officials of large enterprises have been frequently critical of this preventative legislation but apparently have not reached agreement as to the grounds for their criticism. On the one hand, they sometimes argue that the test of the reasonable probability of a future effect is intolerably uncertain. In the recent controversy over basing-point questions, for example, much of the comment from business sources was based upon the belief that freight absorption should be made lawful in all circumstances and that a seller could not reasonably be expected to operate under a law which made freight absorption unlawful if it had effects injurious to competition and lawful if it had effects harmless to competition. This type of criticism calls, of course, for a code of conduct in which certain acts will be categorically lawful and other acts categorically unlawful.

Nevertheless, another line of business criticism, clearly expressed by Mr. Sunderland in the first paper in this series, objects to what is believed to be a growing tendency to hold certain business practices unlawful per se. Mr. Sunderland is alarmed because he sees in recent decisions concerned with exclusive dealing and with price discrimination a tendency to prohibit certain relationships without analysis of their consequences in each particular instance. He believes that a law thus oriented will prevent actions that, in their own particular setting, are harmless to competition or even beneficial. Obviously a move away from the test of effect toward per se illegality may have such results. Obviously, however, such a move makes the law more nearly certain.

The choice between certainty and cogency is often a difficult one. If business executives were agreed as to the relative importance of these two considerations, their opinion would be likely to receive very careful attention. But so long as critics expect the law to move simultaneously in opposite directions, their contradictory criticisms tend to cancel each other.

Related to the question whether the government shall prove present effect or probable future effect is the question whether the burden of proof shall rest exclusively upon the government or partially upon large business. It is a general principle of law that the government must prove its case beyond a reasonable doubt (in a criminal action) or by a preponderance of evidence (in a civil action). An exception has been made by statute, however, as to cost defenses in price discrimination cases. Here the government must prove that the discrimination exists and may have injurious effects upon competition, but this showing is not enough to establish a violation of law if the price difference merely reflects differences in cost. The respondent has the option of deciding whether or not costs shall be considered and also the burden of proving the facts about cost if he wishes them to be part of the case.

This shift of the burden of proof has been remarkably effective in simplifying and expediting price discrimination cases. The respondents in such cases possess the basic data as to costs and are in a position to analyze the data more quickly and effectively than the government. Because the burden of proof is upon them in considering cost, they interpose no obstacles to the submission of cost information and are willing to supply it in the form and degree of detail which the Commission believes to be necessary. This cooperative spirit contrasts sharply with the atmosphere in which facts about costs get into the record in a public utility rate case. There the government obtains them with difficulty from reluctant companies which often dispute every statement of fact and every analytical inference.

I have mentioned this matter of the shift of the burden of proof because one current proposal for curbing bigness rests largely upon a similar transfer of burden. The Committee on Monopoly and Cartels of the Twentieth Century Fund has just made public a program[2] to promote competition which includes a tentative suggestion (one member of the committee dissenting) that the Sherman Act be amended to "create a

[2] See George W. Stocking and Myron W. Watkins, *Monopoly and Free Enterprise* (New York: Twentieth Century Fund, 1951), pp. 533–71.

rebuttable presumption against the retention by any enterprise of a position that enables it to control more than a fixed percentage of the market for any product or related group of products."[3] The committee suggests that large enterprises be allowed to demonstrate in antitrust proceedings that a higher degree of concentration would serve the public interest in the particular case and, upon such demonstration, be permitted to retain the necessary area of market control. It is not my purpose here to explore the pros and cons of this suggestion. It is obvious, however, that such a shift in the burden of proof would be likely to make available a much larger amount of detailed information about such economies as may be associated with large enterprises than now reaches the public.

A more important question than that of the amount of proof to be required is that of the standard by which the good and bad consequences of bigness shall be distinguished. The basic standard of the American antitrust policy is the maintenance of competition. Presumably we accept the competitive policy because we believe that the performance of business under competition is generally better than otherwise. Competition is properly regarded as the means and good economic performance as the end. However, in applying the policy of competition, we do not appraise each particular market situation in terms of performance; we do not ask whether in this particular instance the maintenance of competition will promote or retard effective performance. Instead we ask in each instance whether the conduct that has been called into question promotes or retards the competition from which effective performance is expected to flow.

Certain critics of recent antitrust decisions have challenged the wisdom of this competitive standard and have proposed that the test of social performance be invoked in deciding particular cases. According to one formulation, the results of an antitrust proceeding should depend upon whether, when considered as a whole, the performance of a business enterprise is, on balance, good or bad. For example, in a case in which a monopoly had excluded independent concerns from the market, the social effects of this exclusion would have to be determined and weighed against the effects of the monopoly's price policies, its research policies, its labor policies, and its conservation policies before a decision could be reached. Such a procedure would be as unworkable as to decide whether a driver is permitted to run a red light in traffic by determining whether, on balance, he is a good or bad citizen. According to another version of the social performance test, the judgment should be whether the particular arrangement that is challenged is, on balance, contributing to the public weal. This means, for example, that a case of monopolistic price control would be decided by appraising the social consequences

---

[3] *Ibid.*, p. 564.

of the monopoly's decisions about the level of the price and the frequency and direction of price changes.

To make such a determination, one must ascertain what arrangement would prevail if the challenged one were destroyed. One must then appraise the ultimate social consequences of the alternative arrangements. The difficulty of applying such a standard is, of course, far greater than that of answering the simpler question whether a particular course of conduct or a particular business structure is, or is not, competitive. It is hard to see how the social philosophizing inherent in such appraisals could be reduced to the form of evidence.

If the test of social performance could be successfully applied, its application would be, not a new way to enforce competition, but a substitute for the safeguards of competition. Under the policy of competition, business behavior is free from government interference so long as competition itself is not impaired. The government's right to intervene is limited strictly to the scope necessary to maintain the system of competitive checks and balances. Under the standard of social performance, however, any business act would be forbidden if it appeared to the government to be detrimental to the public good. In the application of such a standard the government's right of investigation and of intervention would necessarily be unlimited. The power to dissolve an enterprise or to enjoin its conduct if its acts were disapproved would give the government, in practice, authority to guide and advise business. The result would be a new and pervasive kind of government control. It would be a long step, not toward competition, but away from private enterprise.

In the remainder of this discussion I shall assume that such adventures in social control are not practical substitutes for the policy of competition. Situations in which the general relation between competition and good economic performance is conspicuously absent are, of course, suitable for legislative exceptions to our general competitive philosophy. But the burden of proof that there is need for exceptional legislation is upon those who propose it, and until the exception is written into law the principle of competition should continue to prevail.

The competitive standard is our guide as to the degree of bigness that is permissible. A concern may grow larger without challenge so long as it does not attain a size that has adverse effects upon competition. It is open to challenge as soon as its size gives it control of its customers, control of its competitors, control of its suppliers, or the power to exclude newcomers from its field of operation. The application of the antitrust laws to business size has become more ambitious as economists have broadened their analysis of the relation between size and control of the market. Originally monopoly was interpreted as preponderant power possessed by a single enterprise. Today the legal concept of monopoly is being extended to cover much of what economists call "oligopoly" —that is, a sharing of preponderant power among several large enterprises

—and certain cases turn upon the point that a large enterprise may pre-empt particular customers or sources of supply even though it does not control other portions of the market. When bigness reaches the point at which it impairs the vigor of competition, it also reaches the point at which it is recognized as a problem in a competitive public policy.

But how shall we recognize the effect of bigness upon competition? In general, two tests have been invoked. I shall call them, respectively, the test of behavior and the test of structure.

Under the test of behavior a concern is regarded as competitive if it actually competes and as monopolistic if it behaves like a monopoly. Since any substantial impairment of competition runs contrary to public policy and is to be terminated if found, the effective way to apply this test is to look for instances of monopolistic behavior in any aspect of a concern's conduct. No matter how vigorously the enterprise may compete in research, for example, it fails the behavior test if it adopts a monopolistic price policy; and no matter how competitive its prices may be, it fails the behavior test if it acts as a monopoly in controlling and restricting research.

At first glance the test of behavior seems to be obvious common sense. It accords with the idea that persons should be punished for wrongdoing and that, if they do nothing wrong, they should not be disturbed. For this reason use of the test of behavior should promote good public relations for the government agency that adopts such a test. The propriety of the test is readily understood by a lay jury and by the general public.

Nevertheless, where the test of behavior has been used, the agencies enforcing the laws against monopoly have incurred criticism at least as vehement as in any of their other proceedings. A conspicuous example is the case brought by the Department of Justice against the Great Atlantic and Pacific Tea Company. In this case the evidence consisted primarily of the activities and policies of the corporation in relation to its suppliers and competitors. Yet no antitrust proceeding in recent years has aroused protests as numerous and diverse.

Criticism of the behavior test was an important part of the first paper in this series presented by Mr. Sunderland. As I have already said, Mr. Sunderland contends that the trend of recent court decisions is to make various practices, such as price fixing, boycotting, exclusive dealing, and price discrimination, unlawful per se. He is critical of what he calls the "automatic illegality" of these practices, on the ground that the effects of the practices are different in different settings and do not always thwart the purposes of the law.

This type of criticism, like the criticism by certain commentators on the A. and P. case, seems to me to reflect the fact that monopolistic behavior may include activities similar to those of competitors and that for this reason it is often hard to identify such behavior and to distinguish it from competitive behavior. Whatever aspect of production and sale one may select for attention, monopolistic behavior consists in twisting the transaction for the benefit of the seller and to the detriment of the consumer as compared with what might be reasonably possible; and unless there is a way of showing persuasively the nature of the reasonable possibilities, it is difficult to prove that exploitative behavior is actually monopolistic.

For this reason the behavior test is hard to apply. To use it, one not only must find out what a business enterprise has been doing, which is relatively easy, but must also show that the enterprise's course of action is substantially different from that which would have prevailed if the concern had been smaller and weaker. This latter step is relatively difficult. For example, it is not enough to show that the concern charged a certain price; this price must be demonstrated to be a monopoly price. Monopoly prices are usually higher than competitive prices, but it is practically impossible to prove by evidence what the competitive price would have been. A price charged by an alleged monopoly may be rising; it may be substantially higher than costs; it may give rise to substantial profits; it may change seldom; it may not fall quickly when the volume of sales goes down. Although such characteristics may be suggestive of monopoly, instances of them are also to be found, from time to time, where concerns are so numerous and small and unorganized as to preclude the idea of monopoly.

Similar problems of proof arise in identifying other aspects of monopolistic behavior. It is difficult, for example, to distinguish between ordinary delays in the introduction of a new process, which may take place because of financial risks or unsolved technical problems, and monopolistic delays which may take place because of a desire to exploit existing capital investment fully before spending any new money.

There are also difficulties of proof in showing the existence of a conspiracy among a few large quasi-monopolistic enterprises. Such concerns can avoid competition if they can arrive at a mutual understanding about the portion of the market in which each is recognized by the others as having the primary interest, and if they accept the price leadership of each concern within its field of interest thus recognized. This reciprocal recognition of leadership eliminates price competition as effectively as the most formal agreement, but it can be persuasively described as though it involved merely a policy of meeting the prices of competitors when selling outside one's ordinary market; that is, as though it were the essence of competition. Some of the Federal Trade Commission's basing-point cases have proved that conspiracies of this type can be identified and condemned;[4] but these same cases have demonstrated that the process is not easy in the courts and may be confusing to public opinion.

[4] For an analysis of some of the economic characteristics of such conspiracies see Corwin D. Edwards, "Doing Business under the Present Law about Delivered Prices," *Louisiana Law Review*, March, 1951.

To show the existence of monopolistic coercion is somewhat easier. When a large concern seeks to discipline a small rival because of the independence of that rival's marketing policy, it is usually not difficult to trace the antecedents of the disciplinary action, to distinguish between the action taken and the ordinary tactics of competition, and to ascertain that the action came to an end when the rival's independence ceased. If a large concern operates so crudely as to attempt to destroy a rival by selective price cutting or similar devices aimed specifically at one target, the effort usually leaves a clear trail. Therefore, disciplinary policies and policies designed to destroy competition are likely to be given great emphasis in applying the test of behavior to an alleged monopoly.

However, the subtler forms of discipline and destruction are hard to distinguish from legitimate competitive tactics. In some instances the power of the great enterprise to destroy its competitors is so obvious that lesser concerns surrender their independence of action without waiting to be threatened or disciplined. The test of behavior cannot be easily applied to a case in which competition is impaired because of the lively imaginations of small enterprises that contemplate the passive strength of a large rival. There are instances, too, in which small concerns are weakened and eventually destroyed by activities that cannot be distinguished, except through their effects, from the legitimate behavior of ordinary competitors. For example, the large enterprise may use aggressive sales effort to familiarize the public with its brand name in a way that a small business cannot do and may destroy one small concern after another by meeting with this well-known brand the price which the small concern sets upon its obscure brand. The large enterprise may saturate distributive channels with its products so that the small concern has difficulty in finding distributors who are interested in providing aggressive sales service. The large enterprise may integrate vertically and give preference to its own affiliates as sources of supply or as outlets for fabrication or distribution, with the result that the small concern is cut off from materials in time of scarcity or from market channels in time of surplus. No matter how destructive of competition such tactics may be, the behavior involved is indistinguishable from activities which, in other settings, may be innocent or even promotive of competition. Hence, in condemning business policies that may destroy competition, we must go beyond the test of behavior.

The test of behavior is not only insufficient to cover all problems; it is also difficult to apply with precision within the fields to which it is best adapted. Behavior tests readily become too specific or too general. If the conduct that is forbidden is specifically defined, businessmen have little difficulty in devising ways of accomplishing the same purpose by practices that are not forbidden. Thus, if the law of price discrimination is narrowly applicable to the quotation of different prices and discounts to competing buyers, a mass distributor of tires may be unable to obtain legally a specified price concession or discount; yet this mass distributor may be permitted to receive an equivalent advantage over smaller distributors in the form of a sales commission on consigned goods or in the form of an arrangement by which he owns the tire molds and the rubber and pays a relatively low processing fee to a producer who makes his rubber into tires in these molds. To prohibit each new method of accomplishing a monopolistic purpose by a rule directed against specifically defined conduct would require a proliferation of laws and would still leave the legislative process lagging behind the inventiveness of monopolists.

If, however, a prohibition of conduct is sweeping and general, it becomes subject to Mr. Sunderland's criticism that it will prevent innocent business activities. A law against price discrimination could be written in such a way as to forbid any difference in the price charged different customers for a given commodity by a given seller, but such a rule would prevent price differences that have no bad effect upon competition. Indeed, it would prevent differences that merely recognize and reward more efficient methods of buying.

The law has sought to avoid the two horns of this dilemma by prohibiting conduct where it has a specified effect in reducing competition. Under the Sherman Act, the so-called "rule of reason" has been a device for distinguishing between restraints that have substantial consequences in limiting competition and those that have lesser effects; and in the Clayton Act the test of probable future effect upon competition has been specifically invoked. Where illegality depends upon effect, innocent practices need not be condemned, and monopolistic practices can be curbed even though they are not specifically described in a statute. The same practice may be unlawful or lawful according to its setting if different settings lead to different results.

But as I have already said in discussing per se illegality, this means of making prosecutions more relevant to their purpose decreases the clarity of the behavior test. Mr. Sunderland complained in his opening paper that the antitrust laws have vague content, largely because of the generality of their provisions. So far as we rely upon the test of effect, prohibitions addressed to business conduct lose their sharpness of meaning. The resulting uncertainty is a problem not only for the businessman but also for the government. Just as business wants to avoid inadvertent violation of law, so government wants the benefits of a voluntary compliance with the law, which becomes less probable as the meaning of the law becomes less definite.

Because of these difficulties with the test of behavior, a complete reliance upon this test probably would necessitate considerable invasion by government of the area within which the managements of large enterprises exercise their managerial discretion. The alternatives are a large and growing number of precise prohibitions of conduct which, in spite of their increasing number, are full of loopholes, or a smaller number of more general prohibitions, qualified by the test of effect to such a point that they are of uncertain scope and may have a bearing upon many aspects of managerial activity.

The test of structure is invoked in proceedings against monopoly largely because of the difficulties that are associated with the test of behavior. An emphasis on structure has certain obvious advantages. It enables the law-enforcement agencies to proceed against enterprises that have power to control the market without becoming entangled in the problem of proving that this power has actually been exercised. It enables them to prevent the subtler forms of coercion and destruction of small business. The test of structure cannot be avoided merely by changing the way in which monopoly power is exercised. It does not require a complicated effort to regulate the business practices of large concerns. Thus, the use of this test contributes to the simplicity and effectiveness of antitrust proceedings.

At first glance it also appears to contribute to the clarity of the antitrust laws, for a rule that no concern may be large enough to control the market sounds relatively unambiguous. On closer inspection, however, the structure test involves major difficulties of interpretation. How large is a market, both in terms of the geographical area covered and in terms of the congruity of the commodities and transactions included therein? Does the market include only fuses, or does it include all wiring devices, or does it extend over all electrical equipment? Does it include contract purchases as well as spot purchases, and purchases for institutional buyers as well as for commercial buyers? Does it spread over a community, a state, a region, the nation, or the world? In many cases the appropriate boundaries of a market are far from clear, and, correspondingly, the size of a business enterprise relative to the whole market is indeterminate.

Moreover, a given degree of size may differ greatly in significance under different circumstances. Two concerns of identical size may differ in power because one is surrounded by large enterprises while the other is surrounded only by small ones. The first comer in a new industry controls the entire output until a second concern enters the field. The holder of an essential patent produces the entire output, if he so chooses, until his patent expires or until someone else devises an alternative technology. The concern that has destroyed its opposition controls the entire output until a new rival strong enough to do battle presents himself. Yet these three cases of control by a single company have three different types of significance.

Furthermore, the capacity of a business enterprise to dominate a market depends not merely upon the place of the concern in that market but also upon its place in other parts of the business world. Either vertical integration or production of related commodities or dispersion of interests across a wide range of business activities may give certain types of advantage. Whether derived from few markets or many, the sheer bigness of the concern may be a source of advantage. Because of such complexities, the test of structure cannot be expressed in a simple rule about prohibited bigness.

These difficulties suggest that the test of structure, like the test of behavior, should be qualified to take account of the varying effects upon competition that may appear in different settings. If bigness or vertical integration is forbidden only where an adverse effect upon competition is probable, allowance can be made for circumstances like those described above. However, as in the case of behavior, the gain in cogency comes at the expense of certainty as to the meaning of the law.

The test of structure is less selective than the test of behavior. To curb the bigness of large enterprises is to curb all activities that depend upon bigness, whether objectionable or beneficial. Such an attack upon bigness can be justified only if the objectionable aspects of large size are more important than its beneficial aspects and, even so, can be justified only if the objectionable effects of bigness cannot be destroyed by other and more selective means. Similarly, if one prevents vertical integration, its advantages are lost along with its disadvantages; and consequently an attack upon this type of structure is desirable only if substantial evils associated with integration cannot be selectively destroyed. The proper field for the test of structure is that in which the test of behavior does not work well. If many government officials who are concerned with the enforcement of the antitrust laws are placing increased emphasis upon structure, it is because they think the behavior test is failing to cope with monopoly problems in a considerable field of business activity.

Critics of the antitrust laws have been particularly severe in their comments about the structure test. Mr. Sunderland, for example, devoted the latter part of his paper to a defense of big business as a constructive force in our society and to an argument that an attack upon big business expresses a defeatist attitude toward the monopoly problem. He makes it clear that he does not want bigness to be unlawful per se. If I understand him, his reasons are those that I have just advanced. Nevertheless, he does not welcome uncertainty about such matters as the legality of vertical integration. As in the case of the test of conduct, he wants the law to reflect varying circumstances and yet to be specific and clear.

In summary, neither the test of behavior nor the test of structure provides a wholly satisfactory way of applying the standard of competition to the phenomenon of big business. Neither test can be reduced to a set of categorical prohibitions without preventing activities that are harmless or even beneficial. The test of structure is capable of being applied so that it provides the most thorough remedy for monopolistic evils. The test of behavior is likely to be ineffective if it is expressed in specific and narrowly defined rules and is likely to involve a pervasive interference with the discretion of business management if it is expressed in broad and sweeping prohibitions. Either the test of structure or the test of behavior can be made more appropriate to monopoly problems if it is qualified so that it is applicable only where anticompetitive effects are found or are reasonably to be expected. But, though this qualification makes both tests more appropriate, it makes each of them less predictable.

The practical problem in legislation and in administration is to balance clarity, speed, and effectiveness, which are to be had through per se rules, against relevance, which is to be achieved through a full use of the test of effect; to use the test of behavior where a correction of conduct is possible and sufficient, but to use the test of structure where it alone can cope with the subtle and varying manifestations of monopoly power. This task is difficult, and there is room for much difference of opinion as to how it should be undertaken. Unfortunately, some of the most earnest critics of antitrust laws have contributed little to the solution of the problem because they have opposed, in turn, all of the available alternatives. They have criticized the use of per se rules of conduct on the ground that innocent behavior is thereby prohibited. They have criticized the test of structure on the ground that many aspects of bigness are beneficial. They have criticized the test of effect on the ground that it diminishes clarity. At the crossroads of antitrust policy, they have attempted to erect a "No Thoroughfare" sign in front of each available roadway.

The American law against monopoly has scope for experiment and growth. Today it encompasses per se rules and examination of effects, tests of behavior and tests of structure, without relying exclusively upon one standard or procedure. It evolves amid constant criticism that it is too rigid and too lax, too hard on business and too lenient toward monopolies, too flexible and too indifferent to changing circumstances. It will continue to develop experimentally; it will, I hope, continue to keep this country's system of business the most competitive among those of the great nations; and it will, I suppose, continue to be severely criticized not only for its failures but also for its successes.

20

Standards for Antitrust Policy*

By ALFRED E. KAHN†

Academic economists have in the past frequently criticized the antitrust authorities for their inactivity and the laws themselves for their impotence in dealing with big business.[1] Recently, however, increasing numbers of them have been attacking antitrust policy from the opposite direction, asserting that the application of the laws is too strict and the zeal of enforcement agencies excessive and misdirected, insofar as the treatment of business size, integration, and competitive tactics is concerned.

A number of interrelated historical developments explain this relatively novel line of criticism. One was the depression of the 1930's, which reinforced a skepticism, earlier voiced by the "institutionalists," concerning the efficiency, stability, and recuperative power of an uncontrolled, purely competitive market economy and hence cast doubt on the basic validity of any attempt to limit monopolies.[2] A second factor has been the dynamism of the American economy since 1940, shared, and in some instances led, by its most clearly oligopolistic industries. Another factor has been the pressure, greatly intensified during the depression, on legislatures and courts to broaden the scope of "unfair competition" to the point where established business units are protected from competitive extinction, no matter how well deserved. All these developments have helped educate economists to the inadequacy of pure competition as a condition of effective market performance or as a goal of public policy. Recent antitrust suits and decisions, because they appear to some to

---

* *Harvard Law Review,* Vol. LXVII (1953), pp. 28–54. Reprinted by courtesy of the Harvard Law Review Association and the author.

The writer wishes to acknowledge the helpful suggestions and criticisms of Joel B. Dirlam, and the inspiration of Myron W. Watkins.

† Cornell University

[1] See, *e.g.,* Eliot Jones, *The Trust Problem in the United States,* pp. 493–98, 563 (1921); Watkins, *Industrial Combinations and Public Policy,* pp. 253–73, 289–91 (1927); Keezer and May, *The Public Control of Business,* pp. 49–57, 95–96, 233–34 (1930); Burns, *The Decline of Competition, passim* (1936).

[2] See, *e.g., New State Ice Co.* v. *Liebmann,* 285 U.S. 262, 282, 292, 305–11 (1932) (dissenting opinion of Brandeis, J.); J. M. Clark, *Studies in the Economics of Overhead Costs,* chap. 21 and *passim* (1923); Hamilton, "The Anti-Trust Laws and the Social Control of Business," in *The Federal Anti-Trust Law, A Symposium* (Handler ed., 1932), p. 3; Boulding, "In Defense of Monopoly," *Quarterly Journal of Economics,* Vol. LIX (1945), p. 524.

have been guided by the norms of purely competitive market structure and behavior, have helped to crystallize these developing attitudes into open criticism of the Department of Justice and the Federal Trade Commission. Though no consensus representing a consistent critique of the laws has emerged, there is fairly widespread agreement that the economist's conception of workable competition calls for a reorientation of antitrust policy.

The present essay seeks to evaluate these latter-day criticisms by appraising the alternative standards for public policy which they suggest. The various possible standards are first outlined, compared, and evaluated—the approaches of both the "new" and the "old" Sherman Act and the alternative economic standards more recently suggested. There follows a consideration of the problems of public policy raised by the structure, market impact, and competitive tactics of big, integrated businesses, and finally an attempt is made, on the basis of this analysis, to set forth the kinds of legal standards that may best be applied to them.

What follows represents, in general, an affirmation of the theory of the antitrust laws and a defense of recent developments in their application to "big business." The defense is not unqualified—it could hardly be, in view of current uncertainties and inner contradictions. Nor is the intention to minimize the conflicts and problems which have inspired and in some measure justified recent criticisms. However, the argument springs from a feeling that many of the critics have themselves lost a balanced perspective. It is first contended that the law has not changed so much as some commentators have implied—though there has certainly been some tendency for the courts to dilute the rule of reason in line with earlier criticism by economists that the rule had been so interpreted between 1911 and 1933 as to render the laws impotent.[3] Secondly, it is argued that a recognition of the purposes and requirements of a "rule of law," and of the limited applicability of "economic" criteria, counsels greater moderation in these attacks.

I. LEGAL AND ECONOMIC APPROACHES TO THE MONOPOLY PROBLEM

A. The "New Sherman Act"—No Revolution

In a society grounded in individualism, the function of government consists very largely of setting boundaries to individual action. For the free enterprise area of the economy, the law merely fixes the rules of

[3] See the materials cited *supra* note 1 and Watkins, "Business and the Law," *Journal of Political Economy*, Vol. XLII (1934), p. 178. The conviction is now widespread among economists that the law attacks business size and integration or mere unexercised market power. See the remarks of Kaplan and Nourse, appearing in "The Economics and Legality of 'Bigness,'" *Current Business Studies*, Vol. V (1950), pp. 22, 50; Adams, "Is Bigness a Crime?," *Land Economics*, Vol. XXVII (1951), p. 287; Lilienthal, "Our Anti-Trust Laws Are Crippling America," *Colliers* (May 31, 1952), p. 15.

the game. The antitrust laws involve the Government in no entrepreneurial activity proper and require no detailed review of either basic investment commitments or run-of-the-mill business decisions. Instead, appropriately, they proscribe specific actions deemed socially undesirable: contracting, combining, or conspiring to rig the market, as well as monopolizing, discriminating, selling under tie-in schemes, and competing unfairly, whether in concert or independently. These prohibitions may be summarized as embracing the substantial elimination of competition by collusion or exclusion. Of these offenses "monopolizing" is by all odds the most equivocal. It might be taken to forbid mere possession of monopoly power and hence to outlaw a market situation rather than a course of conduct. In fact it has been clear, at least until recently, that monopolizing meant the acts incident to attempts to acquire or maintain substantial monopoly power.[4]

Has the "new Sherman Act" abandoned this conception of monopolizing? Does it now attack monopoly power itself, as many of its friends and foes alike proclaim? It would appear not.

The two cases in which the courts have come closest to condemning monopolies *per se* were those involving Alcoa[5] and the United Shoe Machinery Corporation.[6] However, both opinions explicitly confined their application of a greatly diluted rule of reason to companies approaching pure monopolies—accounting for something like 90 per cent in the first, "probably 85%" in the second, of the national supplies of a physically distinct product. Moreover, even in these extreme cases, the courts paid at least lip service to the necessity for sustaining a charge of monopolizing, rather than of mere enjoyment of a monopoly. "It does not follow because 'Alcoa' had such a monopoly, that it 'monopolized' the ingot market . . . monopoly may have been thrust upon it."[7] In both cases, besides, there was abundant evidence of *conduct* on the part of the defendants indicating plainly an intent to make aluminum and shoe machinery their respective preserves. Except for the squeeze on fabricators, Judge Hand minimized this evidence in the *Alcoa* case. But Judge Wyzanski, while placing a very narrow interpretation on the "intent to monopolize" requisite for Section 2 conviction, plainly predicated his condemnation of United Shoe on his finding that the company had not attained and maintained its "overwhelming strength" solely by virtue of its "ability, economies of scale, research, natural advantages, and adaptation to inevitable economic laws." Rather, its "own business pol-

[4] See Mason, "Monopoly in Law and Economics," *Yale Law Journal*, Vol. XLVII (1937), pp. 34, 44 n. 26; Watkins, "The Sherman Act and Enforcement—Discussion," Proceedings of the American Economic Association, *American Economic Review*, Vol. XXXVIII (1948), pp. 203, 206.

[5] *United States* v. *Aluminum Company of America*, 148 F.2d 416 (2d Cir. 1945).

[6] *United States* v. *United Shoe Machinery Corporation*, 110 F. Supp. 295 (D. Mass. 1953).

[7] 148 F.2d at 429.

icies," its *actions,* while not inherently predatory or immoral, had "erected" substantial "barriers to competition." "[These] are contracts, arrangements, and policies which . . . further the dominance of a particular firm. In this sense, they are unnatural barriers; they unnecessarily exclude actual and potential competition; they restrict a free market."[8]

In the other leading cases, it is even more clear that the offense of monopolizing consisted not in the mere enjoyment of monopoly power, let alone "the displacement of inferior by superior business methods,"[9] but in an unreasonable course of conduct, involving a consistent effort to obtain or maintain market control by methods other than those of normal competition. In the famous *American Tobacco,*[10] *Paramount,*[11] and *Griffith*[12] cases, in which the Supreme Court held it sufficient for condemnation under Section 2, the monopolizing section, to show the existence of a power to exclude competitors, it added the proviso that the power had to be accompanied by an intent to use it. In all three, the existence of both the power and the requisite intent was found in a course of conduct—a history of the actual unreasonable use of monopoly leverage to exclude competitors from the market.

Several commentators have read the Supreme Court's decision in the *Tobacco* case as holding that "monopolizing" might consist in the mere joint power to raise prices and not merely in the power to exclude.[13] Had the Court said this, the legality of all oligopolistic markets would truly have been jeopardized. But the issue before the Supreme Court was simply this: is actual exclusion of competitors necessary to establish a Section 2 violation? The Court said it was not; the Government had to prove only that the companies had conspired to obtain and maintain the power to exclude and had demonstrated an intent to use that power.[14]

[8] 110 F. Supp. at 344–45.

[9] Adelman, "Integration and Antitrust Policy," *Harvard Law Review,* Vol. LXIII (1949), pp. 27, 50.

[10] *American Tobacco Company* v. *United States,* 328 U.S. 781 (1946).

[11] *United States* v. *Paramount Pictures, Inc.,* 334 U.S. 131 (1948).

[12] *United States* v. *Griffith,* 334 U.S. 100 (1948).

[13] "The essence of the offense under Section 2, Justice Burton said, is whether 'power exists to raise prices or to exclude competition when it is desired to do so.' " Rostow, "Problems of Size and Integration," in *Business Practices under Federal Antitrust Laws* (1951), pp. 117, 121 (hereinafter cited as 1951 *CCH Symposium*).

[14] Rostow's quotation from the majority opinion is of course correct, but there is no support in this isolated dictum, considered in its context, for the implication that the Court held illegal the mere joint power to raise prices in the absence of conspiracy. Even Justice Douglas, speaking for the majority in the *Griffith* case, made it perfectly clear that the owner of the sole theater in a town, while certainly a monopolist, does not on that account alone offend against the Sherman Act. *United States* v. *Griffith,* 334 U.S. 100, 106–7. Compare this view with Adelman's statement, in support of which he cites this same case: "It is now established doctrine that 'unreasonable' control over any local market, or any significant area of interstate commerce, is illegal." "Integration and Antitrust Policy," *Harvard Law Review* Vol. LXIII (1949), pp. 27, 48.

B. *Monopoly in Law and Its Rationale*

The economic rationale of the law rests on two assumptions. The first is that the will to "get ahead," to outdo others—in short to compete—is so strong and so widespread that it needs only to be channelized by negative prohibitions. The second is that cost functions and optimum business size are such, in most industries, that out of fair rivalry the numbers of sellers and buyers emerging will not be so small as seriously to weaken the force of competition in the market. These assumptions have often been questioned[15] but seldom refuted on the basis of concrete examinations of the structural pattern and performance of specific industries. From these assumptions it follows that the law need only prevent the deliberate impairment, misdirection, or suppression of competition to protect both the public interest and the legitimate interests of business competitors.

The common law rules dealing with restraints of trade and unfair competitive practices were concerned less with protecting the consumer than with protecting businessmen from one another. The antitrust laws sought both ends, finding no incompatibility between them. The recent critics of our antitrust policy argue, essentially, that the enforcement agencies have confused the two and in consequence weakened the force of competition. Unfortunately, as we shall argue below, the distinction between preserving competitors and preserving competition is by no means so clear or so easily drawn as is implied both by the rationale of the antitrust laws and by the contentions of those economists who have been criticizing antitrust enforcement agencies for failing to draw it.

C. *The Market Structure Test of Monopoly*

(*1*) *Its Nature.* Economists have developed two fairly distinct tests of monopoly. One looks to market structure for evidences of those characteristics from which, according to the theory of the firm, undesirable results follow. The other criterion applies the maxim "by their fruits ye shall know them." It may begin by identifying structural impurities, but its primary emphasis is on the economic record, that is, market performance; only if the results are "bad" is the monopoly power deemed excessive.[16]

---

[15] See, *e.g.*, Galbraith, *American Capitalism* (1952), chap. 4; Levitt, "The Dilemma of Antitrust Aims: Comment," *American Economic Review,* Vol. XLII (December, 1952), pp. 893–95.

[16] The two tests are not mutually exclusive; it is seldom suggested that either be applied without consideration of the other. Both assume that a radically imperfect market structure will sooner or later produce a defective performance. However, it is clearly one thing to apply judgments to a market situation *per se* and quite another to attempt to evaluate the results, judging the structure mainly in terms of those findings.

Of these two concepts, it was the former which alone underlay Professor Mason's well-known contrast of "monopoly in law and economics." Following Chamberlin, he observed that to the economist "monopoly" describes a market situation in which an individual seller has the power to influence price. Such exploitative monopoly power may arise without collusion or exclusion, the traditional legal evidences of monopoly. Conversely, illegal actions may fail to create the exploitative power which alone signifies monopoly to the economist. Though Mason judiciously made no such recommendation, one possible implication of the contrast he drew was that the focus of the "antiquated and inadequate" law should be altered to conform to the theory of imperfect competition, and of oligopoly in particular.[17]

Other economists have drawn this implication and have urged that antitrust policy ought to be directed not only against single sellers, but also against oligopoly or market power *per se*. Professor Arthur Burns' monumental proof of the "decline of competition," which is really only a thorough demonstration of the absence of pure competition, concludes that direct public regulation is required to do the job which competition no longer does; on the other hand, Professor Eugene Rostow, finding similar tendencies in industrial structure and market behavior, argues that the laws should attack monopoly power *per se*, and has found in recent antitrust decisions evidence of such a trend.[18] Professor J. K. Galbraith has clearly declared that the antitrust laws are defective because they cannot reach non-collusive oligopoly,[19] and Professor M. A. Adelman has stated that "until and unless we decide that the real problem is market control and how much and what kind we ought to permit, the situation will remain confused."[20] Regardless of their differences, implicitly or explicitly the foregoing writers have adopted the first concept of monopoly distinguished above and have stressed the necessity of a structural transformation of markets—on the ground, as Professor George J. Stigler has put it, that "an industry which does not have a competitive structure will not have competitive behavior."[21]

(2) *Its Difficulties.* It is ironic that many economists, trained in the

[17] Mason, "Monopoly in Law and Economics," *Yale Law Journal*, Vol. XLVII (1937), pp. 34, 39–46; see also Mason, "Methods of Developing a Proper Control of Big Business," *Proceedings of the Academy of Political Science*, Vol. XVIII (1938–40), p. 162.

[18] Burns, *The Decline of Competition* (1936), pp. 564–65; Rostow, "The New Sherman Act: A Positive Instrument of Progress, *University of Chicago Law Review*, Vol. XIV (1947), p. 567; Rostow, "Monopoly Under the Sherman Act: Power or Purpose, *Illinois Law Review*, Vol. XLIII (1949), p. 745.

[19] "Monopoly and the Concentration of Economic Power," in Ellis (ed.), *A Survey of Contemporary Economics* (1948), pp. 99, 118–19, 127; *American Capitalism* (1952), chaps. 4, 5.

[20] "Effective Competition and the Antitrust Laws," *Harvard Law Review*, Vol. LXI (1948), pp. 1289, 1317.

[21] "The Case Against Big Business," *Fortune* (May, 1952), pp. 123, 167.

Chamberlinian tradition, now chide the Department of Justice and the courts for having learned their lessons too well.[22] It is the author's thesis that the courts have not followed the lead of the theory of monopolistic competition as far as some critics (or friends) of recent decisions would have us believe, that they have been wise not to do so,[23] and that the antitrust laws will continue to play an effective role in preserving workable competition only if the courts resist some of the policy implications of the new economic criticism as well as they have resisted the old.

The concept of workable competition strongly suggests the expediency of the traditional approach to antitrust problems in preference to applying a market structure test. If monopoly elements inevitably pervade the economy and are in some measure essential to a good performance, it would clearly be quixotic to attack monopoly power *per se.* If the courts were really prepared now to outlaw "the power to raise prices," as some enthusiastically read the recent *American Tobacco* decision,[24] few sellers would be exempt; the economy would have to be "purified" right out of the twentieth century. Yet there exists no generally accepted economic yardstick appropriate for incorporation into law with which objectively to measure monopoly power or determine what degree is compatible with workable competition.[25]

The scrutiny of the law might be directed at the sources of monopoly power, rather than toward the power itself. But these causal factors, similarly, are neither measurable nor, taken individually, unequivocal in their implications concerning the workability of competition. Whether their influence is, on balance, beneficent or harmful depends on a host

---

[22] An illustration is provided by Chamberlin's recent "Product Heterogeneity and Public Policy," Proceedings of the American Economic Association, *American Economic Review*, Vol. XL (1950), p. 85. This paper reaches the astonishing conclusion that all industry and product boundaries are a "snare and a delusion." On this see the comments of Clair Wilcox, *ibid.*, p. 101.

[23] On both these contentions see Wright, "Toward Coherent Antitrust," *Virginia Law Review*, Vol. XXV (1949), p. 665; Wright, "Some Pitfalls of Economic Theory as a Guide to the Law of Competition." *ibid.*, Vol. XXVII (1951), p. 1083.

[24] See text at note 13 *supra.*

[25] The heart of the problem of policy would be to determine how much power to raise prices for how long is objectionable. Most proponents of this test would probably regard the cigarette industry as one exemplifying excessive market power. Yet even here the evidence is not unequivocal. Great stress has been laid on the flagrant price increases of 1931 by the large manufacturers. Yet the consequence was an increase in the market share of the ten-cent brands, within a period of 17 months, from 0.28% to 22.78%, and a precipitate price retreat by the Big Three. *American Tobacco Company* v. *United States*, 328 U.S. 781, 805–6 (1946). In the absence of predatory tactics or presumptive collusion, it is difficult to see how an acceptable law could have attacked this market structure directly.

One might frame only the most general market structure legislation, leaving it to administrative bodies to test impure structures on the basis of market performance. This suggestion is discussed *infra.*

of conditioning circumstances which defy incorporation into legal prohibitions: every market structure is in large measure *sui generis*.[26]

Product differentiation, for example, is often a means of competition that serves the public, providing minimum assurances of quality and catering to a real consumer desire for product improvement or variation. Difficulty of entry, when not deliberately devised or imposed, or the concentration of patents scarcely provide a sufficient basis for antitrust action against firms whose monopoly power they may enhance. Similarly, there are serious dangers in setting upper limits to business size or market shares *ex ante*. They include: the difficulty of defining products and markets in a way that will be generally acceptable and will stay put; the risk of preventing unmeasurable economies of scale, including the economies of experience, technical skill, and research; the possible damping effect on business enterprise of such upper limits; the possible compatibility of oligopoly and forthright rivalry, particularly in innovation; the tendencies of giant business units constantly to change their product "mixes" and thereby to intensify interproduct and interindustry competition.[27]

It does not follow that the market structure concept of monopoly has nothing to contribute to effective antitrust policy. It may supply guidance for legal remedies when a business has habitually indulged in practices which violate the law, by suggesting for removal market elements which may have fostered the illicit conduct. And the avoidance or offsetting of industrial concentration may very well assume a central position in guiding other Government policies which bear on business performance. It suggests the need for measures beyond the antitrust laws to curb and counteract the forces which help to generate monopoly power: revising the tax laws,[28] organizing technical research and assisting private, cooperative research organizations,[29] providing credit facilities for new ventures,[30] defining quality standards and enforcing grade labeling,

[26] This is the conclusion which the present writer draws from Professor Joe S. Bain's excellent review, "Price and Production Policies," in Ellis (ed.), *A Survey of Contemporary Economics* (1948), p. 129.

[27] See notes 19 and 26 *supra*, and Kaplan and Kahn, "Big Business in a Competitive Society," *Fortune* (February, 1953), supp., p. 1. A sampling of opinion among economists discloses a surprisingly general opinion that pure, noncollusive oligopoly is not the problem that it has been popularly depicted. See, among others, Markham, "The Nature and Significance of Price Leadership," *American Economic Review*, Vol. XLI (1951), p. 891.

[28] The unlimited deduction of advertising expenditures in computing federally taxable income, for example, is certainly questionable on economic grounds.

[29] Industrial research laboratories might help offset one of the economies of scale; consumer testing services might help dissipate the consumer ignorance which probably on balance augments monopoly power. See Scitovsky, "Ignorance as a Source of Oligopoly Power," Proceedings of the American Economic Association, *American Economic Review*, Vol. XL (1950), p. 48.

[30] Weissman, *Small Business and Venture Capital* (1945), chaps. 3, 4.

underwriting full employment, ensuring sustained, adequate supplies and fair distribution of scarce raw materials, assisting private parties to resolve patent infringement controversies,[31] and so on. Such measures are, of course, not at all incompatible with the traditional focus of antitrust policy. On the contrary, as Professor Fellner suggests, they would further implement the traditional conception of unfair competition by attacking positively what the law already attacks negatively—competitive disadvantages not attributable to inefficiency.[32]

D. The Market Performance Test

(*1*) *Its Nature.* Should antitrust scrutiny, then, be focused mainly on market performance? In 1949, Mason suggested an appraisal of an industry's performance as one possible way of deciding, at law, whether it was workably competitive.[33] More recently, Professor Clare E. Griffin has provided a judicious expression and elaboration of this thesis.[34] Both concepts, market performance and workable competition, are essentially pragmatic. How much competition, how many sellers, how standardized a product, how free an entry, how little collusion are required for workability? Enough, it is averred, to give the consumer a real range of choice, to ensure efficiency, to hold profits to reasonable levels, to yield technological progress and a passing on of its gains in lower prices while avoiding cut-throat competition. The law, these economists imply or openly suggest, should evaluate the economic results[35] in the light of the available alternative market structure and attack the structure only when

---

[31] See Borkin, "The Patent Infringement Suit—Ordeal by Trial," *University of Chicago Law Review*, Vol. XVII (1950), p. 634.

[32] Fellner, "Collusion and its Limits under Oligopoly," Proceedings of the American Economic Association, *American Economic Review*, Vol. XL (1950), pp. 54, 60–62.

[33] "The Current Status of the Monopoly Problem in the United States," *Harvard Law Review*, Vol. LXII (1949), pp. 1265, 1266–71, 1280–85.

[34] *An Economic Approach to Antitrust Problems* (American Enterprise Association Monograph 441, 1951). See also U.S. Department of Commerce, *Effective Competition* (Report of Commerce Secretary's Business Advisory Council, 1952) (hereinafter cited as *Effective Competition*).

[35] The courts, in seeking evidence bearing on the propriety of the firm's conduct in terms of the legal conception of monopoly, have always scrutinized the behavior of defendants. Professor Mason has apparently confused this traditional type of performance test with the purely economic appraisal which he recommends. Mason, "The Current Status of the Monopoly Problem in the United States, *Harvard Law Review*, Vol. LXII (1949), pp. 1265, 1272. There is little evidence that recent decisions (as distinguished from the decrees to which Mason primarily refers) have been seriously influenced by economic evaluations of the business record. The Supreme Court stressed the price-gouging by the Big Three cigarette companies in 1931, not in passing judgment on their economic performance, but because, it held, the "record of price changes is circumstantial evidence of a conspiracy." *American Tobacco Company* v. *United States*, 328 U.S. 781, 804 (1946). And in the *Alcoa* case Judge Hand waived any consideration of the company's economic record as "irrelevant." *United States* v. *Aluminum Company of America*, 148 F.2d 416, 427 (2d Cir. 1945).

the foregoing tests warrant it.[36] In legal terms, their suggestion is that the rule of reason be revivified, given an essentially economic content, and applied in all antitrust proceedings. The legality or illegality of all business structures and practices would then turn on their impact on the workability of competition, as judged in turn largely by economic results.[37]

(2) *Its Difficulties.* Apart from devising judicial, administrative, or legislative remedies, a problem in connection with which comparative market performance under the condemned and the projected organizations is an inescapable consideration, the usefulness or validity of this criterion as the basic, self-sufficient guide to public policy is as much open to question as is that of market structure.[38]

First, it must be recognized that market performance is not necessarily a sign either of competition or monopoly.[39] It is a "way of looking

---

[36] Markham, "An Alternative Approach to the Concept of Workable Competition," *American Economic Review,* Vol. XL (June, 1950), pp. 349, 361. It is an exaggeration to imply that most proponents of the workable competition test suggest judging market structures exclusively in terms of performance. Most of them appear still to believe that it is possible to formulate certain minimum structural requirements, less rigid than pure competition, which will assure the most effective performance attainable. But an increasing number are finding an effective performance compatible with such impure conditions as to cast doubt on any attempt to formulate a structural norm. Heflebower, "Economics of Size," *Journal of Business of the University of Chicago,* Vol. XXIV (1951), p. 253; Adelman, "Business Size and Public Policy, *ibid.*, p. 269.

[37] Oppenheim, "Federal Antitrust Legislation: Guideposts to a Revised National Antitrust Policy," *Michigan Law Review,* Vol. L (1952), pp. 1139, 1144–45 and *passim.* Oppenheim, now co-chairman of the Attorney General's National Committee to Study the Antitrust Laws, would not confine the economic examination to an appraisal of market results ("accomplishments") alone; he insists on the necessity of considering "all of the relevant economic factors bearing upon the interaction of structure, behavior, and accomplishments in the particular case." *Ibid.*, p. 1190. The Business Advisory Council of the Secretary of Commerce came much closer to defining the rule of reason primarily in terms of an appraisal of economic performance. *Effective Competition* (1952), pp. 17–18.

[38] Mason's suggestion is mainly that antitrust authorities make greater use of this criterion in selecting cases. Griffin, similarly, suggests its application mainly in choosing cases, framing decrees, and considering legislation. *An Economic Approach to Antitrust Problems* (American Enterprise Association Monograph 441, 1951), pp. 45–48, 86–90. Hence the area of disagreement between proponents of the performance and of the traditional tests may easily be exaggerated. Nevertheless, there are grounds for prohibiting certain predatory actions without exception and without regard to economic consequences, and therefore for selecting cases for reasons entirely apart from considerations of economic engineering. Moreover, if performance is to be relevant in the selection of cases, the courts must also use this criterion in determining the results. See *ibid.*, pp. 90–92. And when we turn to the discussion of specific cases, we find among most proponents of this test a persistent undertone of criticism of recent prosecutions and decisions for attacking various restraints of trade without regard to mitigating evidence of "good" economic results.

[39] See Edwards, "Public Policy and Business Size," *Journal of Business of the University of Chicago,* Vol. XXIV (1951), pp. 280, 285; Lewis, in "The Effectiveness of the Federal Antitrust Laws: A Symposium," Keezer, ed., *American Economic Review,* Vol. XXXIX (1949), pp. 689, 703.

at competition," in Mason's words, only in the sense that it looks for the results which idealized competition is supposed by static theory to achieve. And if the results are "good," the market which produced them becomes, *ipso facto*, "workably competitive." Such an approach has an obvious attraction. Ignoring the irrelevant forms, dismissing the complexities of traditional legal inquiries, it judges situations in terms of what really counts: their results. It accords with the plausible aphorism that there can be too much competition as well as too little. It recognizes the commonplace axiom that competition is, after all, not an end in itself. As for the aphorism, it is correct, though the cure for "too much competition" is not self-regulation of industry, but attacks on the circumstances which make it "too much"—consumer ignorance, the business cycle, the immobility of labor, and so forth. As for the axiom, while the general American bias in favor of competition is indeed rationalized largely by an expectation that in the long run it will produce the best economic results, it is also true that fair competition is an "end in itself." For it is indissolubly linked with the noneconomic values of free enterprise—equality of opportunity, the channeling of the profit motive into socially constructive channels, and the diffusion of economic power.[40]

To put the matter bluntly, the market performance test looks at the wrong end of the process. The essential task of public policy in a free enterprise system should be to preserve the framework of a fair field and no favors, letting the results take care of themselves. Obviously, if the results go too far astray the legislative process may have to be invoked to re-examine and reconstitute the institutional framework, either in particular phases or in its entirety. Obviously, too, where it appears that it is some antitrust proscription which is responsible for the poor performance, that proscription should be revised. But the most arresting aspect of much of the current criticism of antitrust policy is the paucity of concrete economic evidence adduced to demonstrate that the kinds of market structure and behavior consistent with the antitrust laws fall short in their performance in ways which only a relaxation of those statutes will remedy.[41]

Yet on the basis of this sketchy evidence of public necessity, the proponents of a market performance test for antitrust would dilute if not eradicate the suspicion with which the law now regards the practices of collusion, coercion, and exclusion. They would permit businessmen to do these things provided they can at some future date, when and if called upon to do so, demonstrate in any of a great number of possible ways that the practices produced "good" economic results. In view of the weak

[40] See J. M. Clark, *Social Control of Business* (2d ed. 1939); Dirlam and Kahn, "Price Discrimination in Law and Economics," *American Journal of Economics and Sociology*, Vol. XI (1952), pp. 281, 287, 303–4 (Essays in Honor of Harry Gunnison Brown).

[41] See note 46 *infra*.

punitive provisions of the antitrust laws, which most of these critics would further dilute by shutting the door to treble damage suits where the violations were not "wilful,"[42] it is difficult to doubt that the adoption of such a rule of reason would be regarded by the business world as an invitation to "reasonable cartelization" of the economy.

Most advocates of a "workable competition" test in antitrust law would deny that they would have the law look only to results. For example, the Business Advisory Council of the Department of Commerce states that "the government, instead of attempting the impossible task of deciding where Bigness is more or less efficient, should rely upon the powerful action of Effective Competition. . . ."[43] One interpretation of this statement might be that its authors would not have the determination of antitrust violations depend on an appraisal of the end results—for example, on the efficiency with which the defendants have operated. However, the Council goes on immediately to list some eleven separate tests that it would have the courts and administrative agencies apply before they can condemn any specific practices. The list is a grab bag almost all the components of which have this one thing in common: they are tests of market performance or results.

The insistence of economists on economic tests might be understandable if objective standards capable of commanding general acceptance had in fact been developed. Certainly the second deficiency of the market performance test as a substantive basis for antitrust is its vagueness and uncertainty. The grounds on which the courts have for over fifty years refused to evaluate the reasonableness of prices collusively fixed still command respect today.[44] The adoption of vague tests of "public welfare"[45] could only weaken the legal safeguards of the competitive system, by providing antitrust defendants with an unlimited supply of legal loopholes. Economic results are to be used as a basis for acquittal only: no critic has yet suggested that a poor performance provides a sufficient basis for prosecution. If "efficiency," "progressiveness," and "usefulness for national defense" are to acquit a company or industry, the Government should presumably condone most instances of cartelization or monopolizing in the fields of electronics, chemicals, petroleum, and chain store distribution, regardless of whether the specific restraints had

---

[42] *Effective Competition* (1952), p. 20. This proposal, standing alone, has much to recommend it. But to adopt it while at the same time increasing the uncertainty of the law by adopting market performance tests of reasonableness would go dangerously far in robbing the laws of their effectiveness.

[43] *Ibid.*, p. 16.

[44] See *United States* v. *Trans-Missouri Freight Association*, 166 U.S. 290, 331–32 (1897); *United States* v. *Addyston Pipe & Steel Company*, 85 Fed. 271, 283–84 (6th Cir. 1898), *modified and aff'd*, 175 U.S. 211 (1899); *United States* v. *Trenton Potteries Company*, 273 U.S. 392, 397–98 (1927); *United States* v. *National Lead Company*, 63 F. Supp. 513, 525 (S.D.N.Y. 1945), *aff'd*, 332 U.S. 319 (1947).

[45] *Effective Competition* (1952), p. 3.

anything to do with the good over-all performance.[46] If it is to be left to the courts or administrative commissions to determine whether, in the absence of the restraints, progress might or might not have been even more rapid, prices and profits even more reasonable, grave difficulties will be encountered because of the elusiveness of this test. The burden surely rests on the critics of the antitrust laws to demonstrate that those predatory or collusive actions which the law attacks are indeed requisite to a good performance. This is something they have for the most part failed to do.

E. The Alternatives in a Free Enterprise System

Only two general methods of regulating private business appear practicable. One is to establish fairly definite standards in statutory law, leaving businessmen free within those limits to pursue their own interest. So far as this writer can see, such standards can only be standards of *conduct.* In this case, legal uncertainties will arise only at the boundaries, though these boundaries may admittedly be vexatiously elusive.[47] It is difficult to envisage equally clear criteria of acceptable and unacceptable economic performance. Poor results may issue through no conscious actions or fault of the businessmen concerned. A progressive and efficient company may yet violate the law in ways which contribute little or not at all to its good performance or which may have kept the record of its industry from being even better.

The only effective alternative is to leave the maintaining of competition to an administrative commission, vested with broad and pervasive powers of investigation, reorganization, and regulation, industry by industry. Such a commission would have to decide, in each case, whether particular prices or profits had been too high or too low, capacity too great or little, progress in reducing costs, improving quality, and introducing new products too rapid or too slow; and it would have to be em-

---

[46] The antitrust laws may legitimately be criticized only if in attacking what they are supposed to attack they at the same time discourage vigorous and economically beneficent competitive efforts. Such an indictment has yet to be made of the leading cases under the "new" Sherman and Clayton Acts. The same is true of the much criticized *A. & P.* case, *United States* v. *New York Great Atlantic and Pacific Tea Company*, 173 F.2d 79 (7th Cir. 1949). See Dirlam and Kahn, "Antitrust Law and the Big Buyer: Another Look at the A & P Case," *Journal of Political Economy*, Vol. LX (1952), p. 118; Dirlam and Kahn, "Integration Aspects of the A & P Case," *Indiana Law Journal*, Vol. XXIX (1953), p. 1. The economic case against even the Robinson-Patman Act has by no means been as conclusively documented as most of the critics of that act seem to think. See Dirlam and Kahn, "Price Discrimination in Law and Economics," *American Journal of Economics and Sociology*, Vol. XI (1952), p. 287.

[47] True, many of the actions that are prohibited are defined in terms of intent rather than clear-cut overt acts. But a company can in most cases avoid imputations of unreasonable intent by conscientiously acting like a fair, vigorous competitor before cases are brought. See the extremely interesting injunctions to corporation lawyers in Van Cise, "Practical Planning," in *CCH Symposium* (1951), p. 103.

powered, on the basis of such decisions, to fashion such alterations in business structure as might appear appropriate.[48] It is questionable whether any group is competent to make such decisions, whether such delegation of responsibility would be politically acceptable, and whether such a change would make for greater clarity and dependability of businessmen's expectations than the antitrust laws as they now stand.

II. PROBLEMS CREATED BY BUSINESS INTEGRATION

If the law is sound in condemning actions rather than market power or inadequate performance, the problem of defining the actions which it should prohibit remains. The most vexatious problems arise in applying the traditional legal prohibitions to big, integrated business units. It has been recent antitrust developments in this area that have prompted the most vehement criticisms and represent our primary concern. Here we encounter the familiar dilemma of the "double standard," the ambivalence of the law in dealing with restrictive agreements on the one hand and proprietary concentrations of market power on the other. If the "economic" tests be rejected, the double standard is inevitable. The only circumstances in which antitrust proceedings against big business units or their organizers are warranted is when they overstep the rules of a free enterprise system: rules prohibiting monopolizing, either by collusion or by exclusion.

All types of business integration have in common the encompassing of a variety of operations—different products, different markets, different productive and distributive functions—under a single financial control. In addition a business may seek the advantages of integration by bargaining rather than financial consolidation. Some of the most significant and controversial developments in the antitrust field have been in the treatment of practices by which businesses have obtained preferential access to independently produced supplies and to independently operated market outlets. The Department of Justice and FTC have been attacking big, integrated business units for obtaining or exerting "unfair" competitive advantages over their nonintegrated competitors, whether by persuasion or coercion of independent suppliers and distributors or by virtue of their integrated operations. The present section analyzes the unfair competitive advantages and opportunities for monopolizing conferred by integration and the problems of public policy in meeting these dangers. The final section attempts in general terms to explain and defend the application of the traditional antitrust criteria to integration and to the market practices which in a sense achieve the same results.

---

48 Let the reader place himself in the position of a commissioner faced with the question of whether the quality of American movies was such as to justify governmental reorganization of the industry under a workable competition statute. The movie antitrust cases, it is submitted, were a good deal simpler to decide than this hypothetical question, and their underlying philosophy is far more compatible with a democratic and free enterprise system.

The basic antitrust dilemma in this area, which makes it impossible for public policy ever to adopt simple, objective, mechanically applicable, and universally acceptable criteria, arises from the fact that business size and integration almost inevitably confer certain "unfair" competitive advantages and give rise to corresponding possibilities of the extension of monopoly. The only necessary condition is the existence of substantial imperfections of competition in some of the fields in which an integrated company operates. The very fact that a company sells in a number of markets or performs a number of functions, in some of which it is subjected to weaker competitive pressures than in others, gives it a leverage and a staying power in its more highly competitive operations which have nothing to do with its relative efficiency there. The more favorable access to scarce raw materials which a vertically integrated company may enjoy is merely one variant of the general case, springing from imperfections of competition in the supply of these materials.[49] Similarly, the advantage enjoyed by a company with an accepted brand when it undertakes the sale of some new product may be entirely strategic, resting simply on consumer ignorance. And the elimination of competitors from a market opportunity which inevitably results from the absorption of a customer by a supplier confers a strategic advantage on the integrating firm, entirely apart from any resultant saving in cost, to the extent that market outlets for nonintegrated suppliers are appreciably restricted in consequence.

If all competitors were equally able to integrate, no unfairness or danger of an extension of monopoly would enter. But inequity may be introduced by mere inequality in the ability of these companies to attract capital—an inequality which tends to be cumulative. It would not follow, from the fact that only similarly integrated companies might be able to compete with the dominant firms in aluminum, motion picture production and exhibition, and petroleum refining, that integration is the more efficient way of doing business in the social sense. The nonintegrated aluminum fabricator, motion picture exhibitor, or oil marketer might suffer only the strategic disadvantage of less adequate access to supplies or markets. Thus, integration that links areas in which competition is already seriously defective to other areas accomplishes by financial consolidation something very much like what is accomplished by the tie-ins prohibited in Section 3 of the Clayton Act. In the same way, the mere fact of its importance as a customer or supplier offers to a large firm a corresponding opportunity for competitive advantages un-

---

[49] The inelasticity of supply alone confers an advantage on the industrial firm producing its own materials in time of inflation. The preferential access which it enjoys may be the only imperfection of competition involved. See *The Iron and Steel Industry, Report of Monopoly Power Subcommittee of House Judiciary Committee* (81st Cong., 2d Sess.), (1950), pp. 32–34. In a buyer's market, of course, the advantage may lie with the nonintegrated competitor. See, for example, the experience of Republic Steel, *ibid.*, p. 29.

related to efficiency, in access to supplies or markets, whether or not it actively seeks them.

The problem of public policy created by these strategic advantages cannot be exorcised merely by demonstrating the absurdity of any attempt to attack all of them, and of outlawing integration *per se*. In strict logic, one may maintain that the root cause of inequity and possible monopoly power is the imperfection of competition in the less workably competitive fields in which the integrated firm operates rather than the integration which ties this operation to others. It does not follow, as some have suggested, that corrective government intervention may therefore properly be directed only against the offending stratum.[50] Where the imperfection is not practically remediable (if, for example, it springs from a patent monopoly, inexpansibility of supply of some basic material, product differentiation, or the limited size of a market) there may be no practical alternative to attacking instead the financial tie-in which permits one firm to carry the advantages over into other fields.[51]

Moreover, given pre-existing competitive imperfections, integration may itself permit an extension or magnification of total monopoly power. True, if the separate components of a vertical integration had before joining been exploiting to the maximum any monopoly power they may have enjoyed, the mere combining of seller and buyer might not permit them to do any more. However, even here, the merging of interests might permit the further suppression of competition in one of the strata, a more selective exploitation of the less elastic demands for a monopolized raw material, and a mutual reinforcement of monopoly power by making more difficult competitive entry at both levels.[52]

This competitive leverage inherent in integration may appear in a number of possible forms and be exercised in a number of possible ways, though most of these practices may be employed by any wealthy competitor, integrated or not. The integrated firm may deliberately "manipulate its margins" so as to exert pressure on nonintegrated rivals greater than they can cope with, even though their efficiency in the one field in which they alone operate may be superior to that of the integrated unit. Indeed, the margins of the integrated firm will be "manipulated"

---

[50] See Spengler, "Vertical Integration and Antitrust Policy," *Journal of Political Economy*, Vol. LVIII (1950), p. 58; Hale, "Vertical Integration: Impact of the Antitrust Laws upon Combinations of Successive Stages of Production and Distribution," *Columbia Law Review*, Vol. XLIX (1949), pp. 921, 940–41, 946–47, 952.

[51] See Comment, "Vertical Forestalling under the Antitrust Laws," *University of Chicago Law Review*, Vol. XIX (1952), p. 583. Thus Professor Spengler's prescription, introducing more competition into the imperfectly competitive horizontal stratum rather than attacking vertical integration, represents a counsel of perfection.

[52] When manufacturers of complementary shoe machines, each enjoying a preponderant share of its market, joined in the United Shoe Machinery Company and leased their products in a package, the monopoly power of each undoubtedly reinforced that of the others and made more difficult competitive challenges directed against any one of them.

whether it wills it or not, under the impact of varying competitive pressures in its diverse fields of operation. The more profitable operations thus inevitably "subsidize" those in the more competitive fields. The "subsidy" permits a competitive "squeeze," the most dramatic instances of which arise out of vertical integration.[53]

The perplexing problem is that in their manifestations and exercise the competitive advantages stemming from gains in efficiency attributable to integration are in practice inseparable from the merely strategic advantages. For most of the former arise from the fuller utilization of a firm's capacity—whether measured by its physical plant, managerial talents, technological skills, or the ideas issuing from its research laboratories. The costs of the combined operations are always in some measure joint[54] and their prices and margins therefore subject to variation according to competitive conditions in their respective markets. Thus an integrated firm must, if it is to compete vigorously, charge little more than incremental costs in certain fields, and in this way again, in effect, "subsidize" its competitive operations there by allocating an otherwise disproportionate part of the overhead to other operations. It is impossible, therefore, for a large, integrated firm to exploit its socially acceptable advantages or even to meet competition, without at the same time exploiting those advantages which are purely strategic. Conversely, it may avoid violating the basic proscriptions of the antitrust laws only by a policy of conservatism and inertia which runs counter to another purpose of the law. A policy of eliminating the strategic advantages of integration would seriously undermine the vigor of competition itself, since a prime source of competition in modern capitalism is provided by the ability and desire of burgeoning giants to press aggressively into new markets—cutting across accepted channels of distribution, following the logic of their interests and technology vertically, horizontally, and circularly.[55]

Integration, moreover, performs a competitive function even where

---

[53] For examples in the oil industry, see Seager and Gulick, *Trust and Corporation Problems* (1929), pp. 116–17; Watkins, *Oil: Stabilization or Conservation?* (1937), p. 187; Dirlam and Kahn, "Leadership and Conflict in the Pricing of Gasoline," *Yale Law Journal*, Vol. LXI (1952), pp. 818, 848–49. Hale has given a thorough and perspicacious analysis of "squeezes," "subsidies," and the like, *supra* note 50, pp. 937–46.

[54] See J. M. Clark, *Studies in the Economics of Overhead Costs* (1923), pp. 137, 141; Adelman, "Integration and Antitrust Policy," *Harvard Law Review*, Vol. LXIII (1949), pp. 27, 28–32, 40–41.

[55] Thus the "coercive integration" which Professor Walter Adams would outlaw is, despite his disclaimer, practically all integration with any competitive impact: "Our bill would merely ban the kinds of integration which can be used—actually or potentially—for the coercion of competitors rather than for the achievement of competitively legitimate business objectives." "Is Bigness a Crime?," *supra* note 3, pp. 287, 293 n.21. However, Adams would allow an integrated firm to defend by showing that integration had enabled it to increase its efficiency or to pass on its cost economies in lower consumer prices.

its advantages are entirely strategic. Spengler has demonstrated convincingly, for example, that where there exist in some of the intermediate product markets imperfections of competition which impose monopolistic surcharges on products as they move vertically toward the final consumer, vertical integration makes a reduction in price and an increase in output of the end product not only possible but profitable.[56] The easiest curb on monopoly power and the most effective cure for poor performance, the one most consistent with free enterprise, is freedom of entry. And this manifestly includes the right of an existing business to extend its operations into any area its managers see fit to enter—in short, to integrate.

The same dilemma confronts public policy in dealing with business practices. We want all firms, large and small, to bargain vigorously for supplies, to try to beat down the price. We want them to put pressure on their distributors to improve the latter's competitive performance, using the threat of contract termination if necessary. We want them to be able to make mutually binding, long-term contractual commitments, where these permit a more rational planning of operations over time and provide mutual benefits in terms of cost and service. We want all firms to be free to reduce their margins to meet or undercut a competitor's price, if their interests as competitors rather than as would-be monopolists so dictate. Price discrimination may be the only possible form of effective price rivalry in imperfect markets.[57] Yet the threat remains that such activities may, in some circumstances, violate the essential rules of the free enterprise game, may drive out of business smaller competitors whose only deficiency is a strategic one, and may enhance or preserve monopoly power.

III. THE RULE OF REASON

A. The Strategic Role of "Intent" in the Rule of Reason

The basic and ineradicable difficulty in distinguishing between competitive and anticompetitive practices by integrated companies made inevitable the development of some kind of a rule of reason in antitrust jurisprudence. The rule has taken two forms. First, at least between 1911

---

[56] Spengler, "Vertical Integration and Antitrust Policy," *Journal of Political Economy*, Vol. LVIII (1950), p. 347.

[57] Clark, "Toward a Concept of Workable Competition," in *Readings in the Social Control of Industry* (American Economic Association, 1942), p. 452; see also Copeland, "A Social Appraisal of Differential Pricing," *Journal of Marketing, Papers and Proceedings of the American Marketing Association*, Vol. VI (1942), p. 177.

Myron W. Watkins has pointed out to the author the desirability of distinguishing price differentiation and price discrimination: "Price discrimination is a price difference consciously designed to injure someone. It is seldom difficult to distinguish such a pricing policy from one designed primarily to benefit directly the one making the price cut. This is not a unique distinction. The law of torts is full of instances in which the whole issue of liability turns on intent."

and the *Alcoa* decision in 1945, the courts generally took the position that large firms, whatever their market control,[58] were to be judged primarily by this criterion: did the circumstances of their formation and the characteristic pattern of their market behavior evince an intent to monopolize? Second, the prohibitions of the Clayton Act were qualified by the cost-saving and good-faith defenses and by the necessity for demonstrating a tendency substantially to impair competition.[59]

In applying the rule of reason to "monopolizing" cases under the Sherman Act, courts have laid heavy stress on the intent underlying the actions in question. As we have already indicated, the economic criticism of the antitrust policy springs largely from a dissatisfaction with such an allegedly subjective criterion. It is pointed out that it is often extremely difficult to apply, since the evidence is often equivocal. More important, the "new critics" would probably agree among themselves that intent is an irrelevant consideration in economic rule making. They feel that the antitrust laws should be framed in terms of objective standards, rather than what some of them take to be moral judgments, in terms of consequences rather than psychological motivation. The only relevant test, whether of integration or of competitive tactics, they would hold, is the persistence or suppression of competition as an effective force in the market. And their measure of the competitiveness of a market is economic performance.[60]

Unfortunately, the "objective" standard—the vitality of market competition—is disturbingly elusive. Among economists urging its adoption are those who feel that the rule of reason of 1911 represented a departure from that test and those who feel it embodied just such a test, those

[58] It would be an exaggeration to imply that the courts have devoted no attention to market structure, but there appear to be no cases in which that factor has been decisive.

[59] The discussion which follows makes no attempt systematically to differentiate Sherman and Clayton Act proceedings. Technically the same rule of reason cannot apply to both. The latter statute prohibits specified practices; hence its rule of reason must hinge not on intent but on substantiality of effect. On the other hand, the determination of whether a firm is in fact engaging in the vaguely defined practices condemned by the former act often, we shall argue, necessitates an inquiry into intent.

[60] "What we need . . . is a painstaking examination of the economic facts of the individual case. Whether the competition offered by the firm in question was but an attempt to destroy competitors for the sake of a longer-run objective of monopoly depends less on intent than on the structure of the market, and the strength of actual and potential competition. And since every market contains elements of monopoly, the 'undue' or 'unreasonable' nature must be determined by their influence in restricting output, raising prices, stifling progress and innovation, and the like." Adelman, "Integration and Antitrust Policy," *Harvard Law Review*, Vol. LXIII (1949), pp. 27, 49–50. Yet elsewhere Adelman seems specifically, and in the writer's judgment correctly, to disavow any suggestion that antitrust policy turn on the Government's determination of whether economic results are "good" or "bad." "Business Size and Public Policy," *Journal of Business of the University of Chicago*, Vol. XXIV (1951), pp. 269, 273.

who feel it was precisely by such a standard that U.S. Steel was exonerated in 1920 and 1948, and those who felt, with the Supreme Court minorities, that application of such an objective standard would have compelled a decree of dissolution.[61] The same range of opinion, using the same test, may be documented with respect to any number of other cases.[62]

The fact is that economics offers no objective measure of the vitality of competition, in all its aspects, or any way of balancing its possible attenuation in certain respects or in certain markets against its intensification in other markets or in other respects. Economic analysis has devised no tests of the efficiency or inefficiency of integration; the determination must be left to the market, not to the Government. Nor does the "objective" standard proposed by the economist-critics of our antitrust policy meet the argument which gave rise to the Clayton and Federal Trade Commission Acts, that it may be desirable to forbid certain unfair actions before they have had an opportunity to do appreciable damage.[63] Nor, finally, does such a standard satisfy the need for rules of fair business dealing, entirely apart from any observable impact of unfair or inherently exclusionary tactics on market structure or performance. No one can say in what imponderable ways the unfair elimination of a single competitor weakens the vitality of competition among the survivors.

Thus we return to the traditional conception. The function of antitrust legislation can be only to see to it that no one attempts to stifle or pervert the process of competition by collusion, by unreasonable financial agglomeration, or by exclusion. Illegality must inhere in the act, not in

[61] *Compare* Keezer and May, *The Public Control of Business* (1930), pp. 49–57, 95–96, 233–34, *and* Stocking and Watkins, *Monopoly and Free Enterprise* (1951), pp. 304–10, *with* A. D. H. Kaplan, *Big Enterprise in Our Competitive System*, chap. 2 (unpublished manuscript in the Brookings Institution), *and* Carlston, "Antitrust Policy: A Problem in Statecraft," *Yale Law Journal*, Vol. LX (1951), pp. 1073, 1076–80.

[62] It would be interesting to take a poll among economists asking them to choose, for example, between the conflicting appraisals suggested by the opinions of Justices Frankfurter and Jackson, *Standard Oil Company of California* v. *United States*, 337 U.S. 293, 309, 323 (1949), on the economic impact of exclusive dealing in the West Coast gasoline market: "it would not be farfetched to infer that their effect has been to enable the established suppliers individually to maintain their own standing and at the same time collectively . . . to prevent a late arrival from wresting away more than an insignificant portion of the market." "I am not convinced that the requirements contract as here used is a device for suppressing competition instead of a device for waging competition. . . . The retail stations . . . are the instrumentalities through which competition for this ultimate market is waged."

[63] Of course Congress did not prohibit the enumerated practices *per se*. See Lockhart and Sacks, "The Relevance of Economic Factors in Determining Whether Exclusive Arrangements Violate Section 3 of the Clayton Act," *Harvard Law Review*, Vol. LXV (1952), pp. 913, 933–40. Nevertheless it remains true that the required proof of even a "reasonable possibility" of over-all harmful consequences weakens the prohibition of practices which experience and logic demonstrate to have certain anticompetitive effects.

the result, and the test of intent is only a means of defining the act.[64] In the words of Chief Justice White, in the *Standard Oil* decision, the anti-trust laws condemn "all *contracts* or *acts* . . . unreasonably restrictive of competitive conditions, *either* from the nature . . . of the contract or act, *or* where the surrounding circumstances were such as . . . to give rise to the inference or presumption that they had been entered into or done with the intent to do wrong to the general public *and* to limit the right of individuals, thus restraining the free flow of commerce . . . ."[65] The quest for an explanatory intent does not involve psychoanalysis. The question is not: "Why did A *really* do what he did?" but simply: "What was A really doing? Was he competing—or suppressing competition?" "To what kind of activities may one most reasonably attribute the formation and growth of Company B—to technological imperatives, vigorous competition, and 'satisfied customers,' or to anticompetitive manipulations?" The attempt is simply to provide a logical ordering and interpretation of the objective record in order to ascertain whether the course of action shown is one condemned by law. Intent must be inferred primarily from the overt acts actually committed, interpreted in the light of the surrounding circumstances.

Most individual business acts—merging, agreeing, or competing— provide on their face, at best, no more than equivocal evidence of their underlying character or aim. Accordingly, it would be the height of folly either to sanction or to proscribe them *per se*. "Suppressing competition" cannot be defined as clearly as "sneezing." It can only be inferred from a complex series of actions and consequences. A state medical association expels some doctors for "a breach of medical ethics." A publishing company which owns a morning and an evening newspaper refuses to accept advertisements in either one separately. A number of cement manufacturers quote identical delivered prices. A chain store reduces its margins in a particular locality at a particular time. A pipeline company owned by an oil refiner establishes minimum tenders. A man standing in front of a bank which is being robbed whistles loudly when a policeman comes into view. How does one decide when to exonerate, when to condemn these acts or courses of conduct? The logical test, it might appear, would be an evaluation of their objective consequences. But, as we have argued, in the first place the consequences are often impossible to trace.

---

[64] As Watkins has put it in a letter to the author: "the only practicable criterion for distinguishing the licit from the illicit is intent. . . . I need hardly explain that this standard is as far removed from subjective motive as it is from concrete 'effects.' Intent, in law, turns on objective tests: the design, judged by common experience, of what is *done*."

[65] *Standard Oil Company* v. *United States*, 221 U.S. 1, 58 (1911) (italics supplied). The "new Sherman Act" has altered this doctrine essentially by changing the "and" which we have italicized to "or" and by weakening the necessity, implied in the foregoing quotation and what follows it, of demonstrating a substantial achievement of monopoly power.

To take only one example, how can one tell whether a competing newspaper might have been born had it not had to contend with a large competitor charging advertisers a unit rate? Secondly, there are no scientific standards for drawing the line between desirable and undesirable consequences, even where they are traceable. Finally, it may be desirable in certain circumstances to prohibit such actions, regardless of whether there are demonstrable, or even probable, evil economic consequences. It is not ridiculous for the Government to argue, of certain actions, that "survival of competitors does not exonerate the defendants. For a case to fall within the Sherman Act, it is not necessary for the defendants to have succeeded in what they intended to do."[66]

The inescapable conclusion is that, from a practical standpoint, the criterion of intent alone "fills the bill" for a sensible antitrust policy in such cases. Why did the loiterer whistle? Why was the doctor dismissed? Why did one firm buy out another?[67] The point is not to ascertain whether the business units in question were driven by some sort of collective neurosis but simply to ascertain *what* they were doing. Was the loiterer helping to rob the bank? Were the cement companies systematically suppressing competition? Were the chain stores or the refiners exerting their leverage to squeeze out competitors?

Thus a host of actions, themselves individually unexceptionable, may form together a consistent pattern, explicable and condemnable solely on the basis of the general policy which they seem to mirror. Only if it is a fact that the man's whistle was part of a broader plan can his participation in the robbery legitimately be inferred. Only as part of a price-fixing conspiracy may an individual act of price reporting or freight absorption be objectionable. As Justice Holmes said a half century ago, "The plan may make the parts unlawful."[68] A recent decision states, in the same vein:

> While it must be admitted that not all of these acts are prohibited, nevertheless, we must view them in the broad panorama of other acts and their association with each other to note, not only the effect—but to pierce the veil for evidence of intent. . . .
>
> It is clear then that the intent . . . to dominate this industry by monopoly

---

[66] Brief for Plaintiff, p. 11, *United States* v. *Oregon Medical Society*, 95 F. Supp. 103 (D. Ore. 1950), *decision for defendant aff'd*, 343 U.S. 326 (1952).

[67] In this connection the court may be justified in considering "the relative efficiency of integrated and non-integrated" operations, see Adelman, "The A & P Case: A Study in Applied Economic Theory," *Quarterly Journal of Economics*, Vol. LXIII (1949), pp. 238, 246, but only in order to ascertain intent. All the Government may reasonably ask is whether the act was reasonable: were the companies merging in order to compete better, in acceptable ways, or less; were they competing or monopolizing?

[68] *Swift & Company* v. *United States*, 196 U.S. 375, 396 (1905). In a later case Holmes asserted that "the intent alleged would convert what on their face might be no more than ordinary acts of competition . . . into a conspiracy of wider scope. . . ." *Nash* v. *United States*, 229 U.S. 373, 378 (1913).

is obvious and that the result of the . . . conspiracy was to restrict competitors which latter is illegal under the Sherman Act.[69]

The quest for a unifying and underlying intent is in most of these cases inescapable, even though the statute seems to say, simply and objectively, "these things you may not do."

B. Supplementary Economic Criteria

It does not follow that an intent to suppress competition is or should be either a sufficient or a necessary basis for condemnation. Intent unaccompanied by overt action cannot be made the basis of judicial action. It must be accompanied, first, by the power to restrain or exclude, and, second, by some evidence that the power has been or, barring interference, will be exercised. But no "systematic economic assessment" of market power is required.[70] As always the primary evidence is the actions of the defendants. As Judge Taft put it 55 years ago: "The most cogent evidence that they had this power is the fact, everywhere apparent in the record, that they exercised it."[71] Objective consequences or lack of them are surely relevant, as well, in determining whether actions were reasonable or unreasonable. Indeed, where, in certain cases, the evidence of power and its exercise is clear, and where the consequences are both sufficiently manifest and plainly objectionable, it has not and should not have been necessary to demonstrate a "specific" illegal intent.

But where the external evidence both of actions and results is equivocal—and we have argued it is inevitably so in most cases of business integration—an investigation of intent is and always has been essential. As Chief Justice Hughes observed: "Good intentions will not save a plan otherwise objectionable, but knowledge of actual intent is an aid in the interpretation of facts and prediction of consequence."[72] Or as Justice Lurton stated, more positively: "Whether a particular act, contract or agreement was a reasonable and normal method in furtherance of trade and commerce may, in doubtful cases, turn upon the intent to be inferred from the extent of the control thereby secured over the commerce affected, as well as by the method which was used."[73]

Thus economic considerations are by no means irrelevant in the rule of reason. Market power and economic consequences must be considered.

---

[69] *United States* v. *Besser Manufacturing Company*, 96 F. Supp. 304, 313 (E.D. Mich. 1951).

[70] See Adelman's argument to the contrary, "Dirlam and Kahn on the A & P Case," *Journal of Political Economy*, Vol. LXI (1953), p. 436, and the reply by Dirlam and Kahn, *ibid.*, p. 441.

[71] The judge went on to add: "Of course, if the necessary result is materially to restrain trade . . . the intent with which the thing was done is of no consequence." *United States* v. *Addyston Pipe & Steel Co.*, 85 Fed. 271, 292 (6th Cir. 1898), *modified and aff'd*, 175 U.S. 211 (1899).

[72] *Appalachian Coals, Inc.* v. *United States*, 288 U.S. 344, 372 (1933).

[73] *United States* v. *Reading Company*, 226 U.S. 324, 370 (1912).

But they are not decisive. Mere unexercised power to exclude, the mere exclusion of competitors which occurs when a supplier consolidates with a customer,[74] the mere power to influence price[75] all remain and should remain free from condemnation. And the relevant consequences to be appraised are not the effects of the defendants' actions on economic performance, but those implied in the traditional legal criteria of monopolizing: the mutual suppression of rivalry or the unfair exclusion or threatened exclusion of competitors.

There is no disposition here to minimize the difficulties in imputing the intent that renders the acquisition or exercise of market power and the exclusion unreasonable. But no equally acceptable alternative presents itself. The difficulties inhere in the situation. Only to the extent that we are prepared to outlaw specific practices or situations *per se* can a consideration of intent be dispensed with. Since, on balance, it would be clearly destructive of competition itself to apply any such blanket condemnation to business integration, inquiry must be made in each case to determine whether power has been unreasonably attained or used. Central to such an investigation must be an inquiry into the underlying intent. Where investigation discloses unreasonably collusive or unfairly exclusive tactics, those acts cannot, consistently with a free enterprise system, be condoned because of the absence of clear evidence that they have actually diminished the force of competition in the market or contributed to a poor economic performance, narrowly construed. This is the only "workable" rule of antitrust policy.

---

[74] See *United States* v. *Columbia Steel Company*, 334 U.S. 495 (1948).

[75] See *supra*, text at notes 24–32.

21

The Current Status of the Monopoly Problem in the United States*

By EDWARD S. MASON†

It is clearly an open question whether the people of the United States want competition and, if so, what kind of competition and in what areas. We apparently do not desire a competitive determination of farm prices and farm incomes. It is obvious from the Miller-Tydings Act and the fair trade laws now flourishing in forty-five states that we don't want price competition in a large section of retail trade. We have sought, and quite successfully, to "take wages out of competition." The action of the Texas Railroad Commission during the last few months in cutting back oil production by 750,000 barrels a day makes it clear that the "adjustment of supply to demand" in this area is not going to be accomplished exclusively by price competition. We don't want much disturbance of the channels of distribution from competitive sources and are apparently acquiescing in a reinterpretation of the Robinson-Patman Act "injury to competition" as injury to a competitor. Just recently I have become aware of the very cozy scheme worked out by the anthracite coal producers by means of which output is adjusted to sales.[1] Although, according to the producers, no consideration of price is allowed to intrude, John L. Lewis has indicated that the application of this system would be fine for the bituminous coal industry. One might extend considerably these examples of recent public action to soften the rigors of competition.

At the same time, and despite this course of events, we apparently do want competition in the industrial sector of the economy. The last ten years—particularly the last five—have winessed the greatest flurry of antitrust activity since the passage of the Sherman Act. But the question can be raised, what kind of competition do we want?

---

* *Harvard Law Review*, Vol. LXII (1949), pp. 1265–85. (Copyright, 1949, Harvard Law Review Association.) Reprinted by courtesy of the Harvard Law Review Association and the author.

† Harvard University.

[1] *New York Times* (April 19, 1949), p. 20.

I. THEORIES OF EFFECTIVE COMPETITION

After the recent decision in the *Cement* case,[2] the Universal Atlas Cement Company issued the following statement: "Universal Atlas Cement Company is abandoning on July 7 next the method of selling cement which it has used continuously for more than forty years; namely, sales in the market served by it at delivered prices as low as those quoted by any competitor."[3] The obvious implication of this announcement is that competition is being abandoned. On the other hand, quite a few people, including the Supreme Court of the United States, thought that what was being abandoned was a conspiracy to fix prices. Clearly competition means different things to different people.

There have always been at least two ways of looking at competition and of judging the effectiveness of competition in a particular market. In the first, competition is thought of as a type of market organization setting severe limits to the power or control exercised by the individual firm. This view stresses the limits, set principally by the number of his competitors, on the scope of action of a single seller or buyer. The other way of thinking about competition is in terms of the performance of firms in a market. Even pure competition—that plaything of economic theorists—can be thought of either in terms of market structure, large numbers of sellers and a standard product, or in terms of the performance which is supposed to result from these conditions, prices equal to marginal and to minimum average cost.

From the point of view of economic policy, competition is supposedly desirable, not as an end in itself, but for the results that are expected to follow from it.[4] These expected results may be paraphrased as efficient use of resources. Now under the technological and institutional conditions suited to pure competition—imagining such conditions to be found—it is possible to show that a competitive organization of resources will produce the results desired from competition—an efficient use of these resources. But if technological and institutional conditions are not compatible with pure competition and, at the same time, are not deemed to be such as to justify a public utility regulation of the firms in question, there arises a problem of defining an acceptable kind of competition in terms of market structure such that it can normally be expected to be accompanied by the kind of performance considered acceptable in the use of resources. This is in fact the core of the difficulty of devising stand-

[2] *FTC* v. *Cement Institute*, 333 U.S. 683 (1948).

[3] *The U.S. Steel Quarterly* (August, 1948), p. 7; Machlup, *The Basing Point System* (1949), p. 82.

[4] On the other hand, an argument can be made on political grounds for competition conceived as a set of limits to the market position of firms, regardless of the relative efficiency of the business performance that results from this competition. Here we shall be concerned exclusively with the economic aspects of the problem.

ards of public action in the antitrust field. None of the markets encountered meet the tests of pure competition; at the same time they fall short of a degree of monopoly justifying public utility regulation.[5] What is a suitable test of effective competition? Should it run in terms of market limitations on the scope of action of firms or in terms of standards of acceptable performance? Is there, necessarily, any incompatibility between these objectives? May not the conditions required of a competitive market structure be so defined as inevitably to produce desirable business performance?

Most of the recent literature on the subject of "workable competition" has stressed the conditions of market structure, the limitations on the market position or scope of action of firms, deemed necessary to the maintenance of effective competition.[6] Such competition requires, to use the standard cliché, the availability to buyers of an adequate number of alternative independent sources of supply, and to sellers of an adequate number of independent customers. Workable competition is considered to require, principally, a fairly large number of sellers and buyers, no one of whom occupies a large share of the market, the absence of collu-

[5] A few of the principal conditions that may "justify" the imposition of a public utility type of regulation could be spelled out fairly adequately. Lacking, however, the time and space to do so, I here limit myself to assertion.

[6] J. M. Clark was, to the best of my knowledge, the first writer to use the term "workable competition." He defines workable competition to mean a "rivalry in selling goods in which each selling unit normally seeks maximum net revenue, under conditions such that the price or prices each seller can charge are effectively limited by the free option of the buyer to buy from a rival seller or sellers of what we think of as 'the same' product, necessitating an effort by each seller to equal or exceed the attractiveness of the others' offerings to a sufficient number of buyers to accomplish the end in view." Clark, "Toward a Concept of Workable Competition," Proceedings of the American Economic Association, *American Economic Review,* Vol. XXX (1940), pp. 241, 243.

Clair Wilcox defines workable competition as "the availability to buyers of genuine alternatives in policy among their sources of supply." Wilcox, *Competition and Monopoly in American Industry* (TNEC Monograph 21, 1940), p. 9.

George Stigler finds this conception "too loose." He prefers the following: "An industry is workably competitive when (1) there are a considerable number of firms selling closely related products in each important market area, (2) these firms are not in collusion, and (3) the long-run average cost curve for a new firm is not materially higher than that for an established firm." Stigler, "The Extent and Bases of Monopoly," Proceedings of the American Economic Association, *American Economic Review,* Vol. XXXII (1942), pp. 2–3.

Corwin Edwards has developed the idea of workable competition in greatest detail. In addition to numbers of sellers and buyers, absence of collusion and freedom of entry, he states a number of other conditions of which absence of a dominant trader among the number of buyers and sellers seems to be the most important. Edwards, *Maintaining Competition* (1949), pp. 9–10.

These writers clearly think of workable competition in terms of market conditions imposing a set of limitations on the scope of action of the individual buyer or seller. These limitations prevent the exploitation of buyers by sellers too few in number or in collusion with each other and prevent the exploitation of sellers by buyers. There are an "adequate" number of alternatives from which to choose. Clark's conception of workable competition also emphasizes these limitations, but it appears from his discussion that limitations are not enough.

sion among either group, and the possibility of market entry by new firms.

There has also been, on the other hand, a good deal of discussion of the kind of performance we should like to have from firms in the industrial sector of the economy. Among the kinds of business behavior emphasized as desirable have been the following: an unremitting pressure for product and process improvement, downward adjustment of prices concomitant with substantial reductions in costs, concentration of production in units of the most efficient size, neither larger nor smaller than those required for low-cost operation, an efficient adjustment of capacity to output, and the avoidance of a waste of resources in selling activities.

The question now arises whether workable competition, in terms of market structure, can be so defined that we may say, given these conditions, it is likely that business performance will meet the standards suggested above or, equally important, that if these conditions are not present, acceptable standards of business performance are unlikely to be attained. Alternatively we may raise the question whether business behavior lends itself to formulation of standards of acceptable performance such that a judgment of the appropriateness of antitrust action can be made independently of what we have here called market conditions.

Without attempting, at this point, a direct answer to these questions, it seems useful to call attention to certain possibilities of conflict between competitive standards formulated in terms of market conditions and standards of acceptable business performance. Space limitations prevent more than a summary indication of these possibilities.

1. The most familiar and one of the most bothersome possibilities of conflict has to do with the economies of scale in relation to the number of sellers or buyers required for most efficient operations. Costs in relation to size of plant can, in most industries, be well enough estimated to form a judgment on the minimum scale required for efficiency. The main difficulties arise in judging the economies of scale involved in the management of multiplant properties, considering the functional complexity of management, and in disentangling the bargaining advantages of size from the advantages that pertain solely to the provisions of useful services. Is management a "technique for getting things done"[7] that carries with it significant economies of scale? The relation of size to the volume and quality of industrial research is another bothersome question that intrudes.

Enough has been said to indicate that a real possiblity exists that the number of firms appropriate to efficiency, one aspect of desirable per-

[7] See "The Public Responsibilities of Big Business," address delivered by Eugene Holman, President of Standard Oil Co. of N.J., at the Economic Club of Detroit on November 8, 1948. See also Drucker, *The Concept of the Corporation* (1946); Edwards, *Maintaining Competition* (1949), p. 116 n.37.

formance, may, in a number of industries, be too few to meet the market structure test of workable competition. Nor does it necessarily follow that, under these conditions, regulation of the public utility type is called for.

2. A second possibility of conflict exists when all the market conditions of workable competition are fulfilled but the behavior of the firms involved follows a routine and standard pattern unvaried by enterprise of any sort. Something like this seems to have characterized the system of retail distribution in the United States before the advent of chain stores and other mass distributors. In a case like this, does one judge the effectiveness of competition from the market structure point of view favorable to traditional distributors or from the business performance point of view favorable to the innovating large-scale mass distributor?[8]

3. Suppose, to take a third possibility of conflict, that the market conditions required for workable competition lead, in an industry characterized by large cyclical variations in sales and by high overhead costs, to cut-throat competition which in periods of depression destroys efficient business organizations which, under average conditions, could survive. This is the possibility, repeatedly emphasized by J. M. Clark, that apparently leads him to support a modified basing-point system in some industries having these characteristics.[9] Without passing judgment on the frequency and importance of such situations, it is sufficient to indicate that the standards-of-business-performance approach might lead to a modification of the conditions thought to be required for workable competition.

4. Fourthly, one of the market conditions required for workable competition is the absence of collusion or agreement among the firms. But certain kinds of agreements clearly promote rather than restrain effective competition. The agreement among traders to regulate marketing practices on the Chicago Board of Trade was considered by no less an authority than Justice Brandeis to promote competition.[10] Agreements to standardize classifications of products and terms of sale are frequently necessary to permit buyer comparisons of prices quoted from different sources of supply. Under these and other circumstances the business performance that results from collusion must be considered to modify the application of standards drawn exclusively from market conditions.

5. Fifthly, it is possible that certain restraints of trade or a degree of market control incompatible with the market structure standard of workable competition may facilitate the introduction of desirable product and process innovations. This is an argument most effectively developed by

---

[8] *Cf.* Adelman, "The A & P Case: A Study in Applied Economic Theory," *Quarterly Journal of Economics*, Vol. LXIII (1949), p. 238.

[9] Most recently in Clark, "Law and Economics of Basing Points: Appraisals and Proposals, *American Economic Review*, Vol. XXXIX (1949), p. 430.

[10] *Board of Trade of the City of Chicago* v. *United States*, 246 U.S. 231 (1918).

J. A. Schumpeter.[11] His contention that the most effective kind of competition is that which derives from the introduction of new and improved products and from innovation in techniques of production has great merit. It is less clear, however, that industrial progressiveness stems mainly from firms of a size incompatible with the conditions of workable competition or necessitates arrangements among firms which violate these conditions. The relation of monopoly and competition to innovation is a relatively unknown area.

Other examples could be cited but perhaps enough has been said to indicate that antitrust action in a particular industry or industrial market may be thought appropriate on the basis of the business performance of firms in that market and inappropriate if judged by the presence or absence of the market conditions emphasized by the workable competition test.

II. LEGAL CRITERIA OF EFFECTIVE COMPETITION

A. Business Performance and Market Structure in the Legal Definition of Monopoly

What considerations influence the courts in their decisions on antitrust action? Is effective competition conceived to be a set of market conditions or is it judged in terms of effective business performance? Some twelve years ago, under the title of "Monopoly in Law and Economics," I published an article designed to show that legal and economic ideas of monopoly were growing further apart.[12] In referring back to this ancient document, I am reminded of a statement of Justice Holmes, "it ought always to be remembered that historic continuity with the past is not a duty, it is only a necessity."[13] Although it is not now a duty, I find it necessary to relate my present thinking on this question to what I thought earlier.

The argument of that article, simply stated, was that monopoly in the legal sense meant restrictive or abusive practices and, in the economic sense, control of the market; that the antithesis of legal monopoly was free competition, a state of affairs such that no actual or potential competitor was limited in his action either by agreement or the harassing tactics of large rivals, while the antithesis of economic monopoly was pure competition, a state of the market such that no buyer or seller could, by his own action, influence the price of the goods to be bought and sold. It was argued that one of the reasons for this dichotomy was that lawyers were concerned with tests that would stand up in a court, and that it was much easier to devise tests of restrictive practices than tests indicative of a substantial degree of market control.

[11] Schumpeter, *Capitalism, Socialism, and Democracy* (2d ed. 1947), chaps. vii, viii.

[12] *Yale Law Journal*, Vol. XLVII (1937), p. 34.

[13] Holmes, "Learning and Science," in *Collected Legal Papers* (1920), pp. 138, 139.

I still think there was substantial merit in this distinction between legal and economic notions of monopoly, but, like many distinctions, it was much too sharply drawn. There is substantial evidence in the history of antitrust cases that although the precise holdings may not have been explicitly based on indications of the degree of market control and of what is here called business performance, such indications certainly influenced the judges' decisions.

But what about the recent active development of antitrust law? Do the courts tend to find evidence of violation in particular characteristics of market structure or in various kinds of business performance or both? My impression is:

1. That the courts have moved a substantial distance in the direction of accepting the presence or absence of the market conditions associated with the notion of workable competition as appropriate tests. On all four of the important desiderata, number of firms, share of the market, collusion, and the conditions of entry, previous doctrine has been altered or extended;

2. That standards of effective business performance, though imprecisely defined, still strongly influence the manner in which tests of monopoly relating to the structure of the market are applied. This is true of determinations of whether or not the antitrust laws have been violated, but it is even more true when the courts come to the fashioning of remedies.

Not only has the legal meaning of monopoly been extended but the courts have greatly expanded the scope of action embraced within the meaning of conspiracy. The legal status of actions both of large firms and of conspiracies with respect to the conditions of entry of new firms has been reinterpreted.

In the *Aluminum* case,[14] I interpret the court to hold (1) that Alcoa's share of the domestic consumption of aluminum ingot was such as to indicate a degree of market control equivalent to monopoly, and (2) that monopoly was not "thrust upon"[15] the company by forces lying outside its control but was actively and aggressively sought in ways that had the effect of excluding potential competitors.

Although this decision probably broke new legal ground, it is, from an economist's point of view, marred by what is at best some very dubious economics. The share of the market possessed by Alcoa was incorrectly measured, the degree of market control was identified with percentage share of the market, and the evidence concerning intent to exclude others is difficult to distinguish from ordinary, intelligent competitive action.

In measuring Alcoa's share of the market, the court excluded from the

---

[14] *United States* v. *Aluminum Company of America*, 148 F.2d 416 (2d Cir. 1945).

[15] *Ibid.*, p. 429.

market substitute products and secondary aluminum ingot. Although the determination of what products to include in and what to exclude from a market presents a difficult problem, the existence of close substitutes in certain uses of aluminum is beyond question. With respect to secondary aluminum, the court's reasoning was ingenious but essentially incorrect. The argument was that since Alcoa's current production of primary ingot will at some future time be converted into secondary, the secondary, then coming onto the market, cannot be considered an independent source of supply. The question is whether a single producer of a product that will return to the market X years hence will, *because of that fact,* act differently with respect to current price and output than would a producer who is one of a larger number. If he does so, it can only be because he is willing to sacrifice a current profit by restricting output now in order to gain a problematical profit X years hence, which may be available because the supply of competitive scrap is not then so large as it would otherwise be. The conditions that would make such action profitable are improbable.

Lawyers sometimes describe themselves as experts in relevance. Something more than logical relevance, however, is involved in a case of this sort. There is also the magnitude of the consideration that is declared to be relevant. It was, however, on the basis of the argument stated above that Judge Learned Hand decided that "Alcoa's control over the ingot market must be reckoned at over 90 per cent."[16] If sales of secondary ingot had been considered part of the market, Alcoa's share would have fallen to the mystical 60 to 64 per cent, where the existence of a monopoly becomes "doubtful."[17] Even if Alcoa's share of the market had been correctly measured, it would have been wrong to infer degree of market control directly from this share. If products excluded in defining the market are close substitutes, if the entry of new firms is relatively easy, if the supply of imports is elastic with respect to price changes, even a large percentage share of the market is compatible with a small degree of market control. On the other hand, even a small share of a particular market in the hands of an industrial giant may, under certain circumstances, be conducive to a high degree of market control.[18] Market share is an important condition relevant to workable competition, but in the absence of certain tests of performance it cannot be taken as a measure of market control.

With respect to one element of business performance the court was convinced that Alcoa's behavior indicated an intention to exclude potential rivals. The evidence was a tendency to build ahead of demand.

> Nothing compelled it [Alcoa] to keep doubling and redoubling its capacity before others entered the field. It insists that it never excluded competitors;

[16] *Ibid.*, p. 425.

[17] *Ibid.*, p. 424.

[18] See Edwards, *Maintaining Competition* (1949), p. 100.

but we can think of no more effective exclusion than progressively to embrace each new opportunity as it opened, and to face every newcomer with new capacity already geared into a great organization, having the advantage of experience, trade connections and the elite of personnel.[19]

In this connection it is interesting to note that the leading economic authority on the aluminum industry found Alcoa's behavior to lead in exactly the opposite direction; that is, to a waiting for demand to develop before expanding capacity.[20] But, even if the court is correct, it would appear extremely difficult to distinguish between a progressive embracing "of each new opportunity" and what would ordinarily be considered desirable competitive performance.

Despite these observations, the decision in the *Aluminum* case represents a broadening of the legal meaning of monopoly in a direction favored by current views concerning workable competition.

The *Tobacco* case[21] continued in this direction. The share of the market here was, in 1939, 68 per cent of the production of small cigarettes by three firms, which the Court held were joined in a conspiracy. Such a market position carried with it the power to exclude potential rivals and was therefore illegal, said the Supreme Court, even in the absence of a demonstration of actual exclusion. The Court's attitude toward the heavy advertising expenditures of the three firms was interesting but cryptic. On the one hand it was not "criticized as a business expense";[22] on the other the Court thought that "such tremendous advertising, however, is also a widely published warning that these companies possess and know how to use a powerful offensive and defensive weapon against new competition."[23]

Both in this case and the *Aluminum* case it would seem that the decisions, based mainly on the market position of the companies, were at the same time influenced by the court's judgment on how the market position had been used. In other words, certain standards of business performance seem to have been involved.

The *Columbia Steel* case,[24] involving the acquisition of a small West Coast plant by a subsidiary of United States Steel, produced one of the most careful examinations of the market position of a company to be found in the history of antitrust cases. Though the Court here rejected a large share of the local market, with respect to certain products, as a ground for undoing the acquisition, it may well have been influenced by

---

[19] *United States* v. *Aluminum Company of America*, 148 F.2d 416, 431 (2d Cir. 1945).

[20] Wallace, *Market Control of the Aluminum Industry* (1937), pp. 252, 259–60, 331.

[21] *American Tobacco Company* v. *United States*, 328 U.S. 781 (1946).

[22] *Ibid.*, p. 797.

[23] *Ibid.*

[24] *United States* v. *Columbia Steel Company*, 334 U.S. 495 (1948).

the spectacle of the Antitrust Division straining at the gnat of Columbia after swallowing the Geneva camel.

The *National Lead* case[25] presented a situation in which the conditions of workable competition were violated both because of the fewness of sellers—four, with two accounting for 90 per cent of the sales—and because of collusive restraints. The Court eliminated the restraints but refused to increase the number of sellers by ordering present sellers to divest themselves of part of their holdings. Apparently the majority of the judges were influenced by the finding of fact disclosing what they considered to be effective business performance in the industry:

> From 1933 on there was active competition between [National Lead] and [Du Pont] for customers. There has been a vast increase in sales; and repeated reductions in the price of titanium pigments have taken place and a very few increases.[26]

At another point the Court says that the findings "disclose a vigorous, comparatively young, but comparatively large, worldwide industry, in which two great companies, National Lead and Du Pont, now control approximately ninety-five per cent of the domestic production in approximately equal shares. . . . The findings show vigorous and apparently profitable competition on the part of each of the four producers, including an intimation that the smaller companies are gaining rather than losing ground."[27]

These and other recent cases concerning the legal meaning of monopoly appear to indicate that although the courts have moved some distance toward accepting certain of the market conditions associated with the notion of workable competition as standards of judgment—particularly share of the market and perhaps the number of firms—their application of these standards is strongly influenced by evidence relating to the character of business performance in these markets.

B. Collusion

When one turns to collusion, another of the elements of market structure emphasized in the literature on workable competition, interpreting the significance of recent legal actions presents a perplexing problem. The courts have certainly gone a long way in accepting various kinds of market behavior as evidence of a conspiracy among firms; so far, indeed, that it seems appropriate to inquire whether market behavior rather than conspiracy has not become the test of illegality.

Economists in recent years have speculated a good deal on the possible courses of behavior of firms in markets in which the number of buyers

[25] *United States* v. *National Lead Company*, 332 U.S. 319 (1947).

[26] *Ibid.*, pp. 346–47.

[27] *Ibid.*, pp. 347–48.

and sellers is sufficiently few to make the rival firms aware of their interdependence. Given merely the number of firms any one of a wide variety of types of behavior is possible and an explanation of a particular course of behavior becomes feasible only after an examination of a number of other elements of the market structure in which these firms operate. Among these conditions, high overhead costs, large cyclical variations in the volume of sales, and immobility of resources are combined in a substantial number of industrial markets. Given these conditions, together with a small number of firms, some economists have contended that such phenomena as price uniformity, price leadership and the relative inflexibility of prices to large variations in the national income, are frequently compatible with the independent action of firms all recognizing their interdependence.

Now independence of action is, by definition, the opposite of collusion. But it may be impossible to determine from market behavior alone whether the firms are acting independently or together. At this point we may appropriately ask, what difference does it make? With respect to the remedy to be applied it may make considerable difference. If the behavior is really the result of agreement, enjoining the agreement may, by securing independence of action, change the market behavior. But if the action of firms is already independent, this remedy is useless.

A prime example is provided by the *Tobacco* case.[28] Both the district court and the circuit court found from the record in this case evidence of a price conspiracy among the three big producers of cigarettes. Both bodies held that conspiracy does not require a formal agreement or even a meeting together of the conspirators. To the district court the essential condition was that "some character or manner of communication take place between them, sufficient to enable them to reach a definite, mutual understanding of the common, unlawful objective or purpose to be thereafter accomplished, and that they will unite or combine their efforts to that end."[29]

The conception of conspiracy in the court of appeals was, perhaps, even broader than this: "[T]he agreement may be shown by a concert of action, all the parties working together understandingly, with a single design for the accomplishment of a common purpose."[30]

When one turns to the record in the case, there is certainly some evidence of agreement among the firms.[31] The companies admittedly consulted with each other on the question of opening new leaf markets. It is

---

[28] *American Tobacco Company* v. *United States*, 328 U.S. 781 (1946).

[29] Transcript of Record, p. 6350, *American Tobacco Company* v. *United States*, 328 U.S. 781 (1946).

[30] *American Tobacco Company* v. *United States*, 147 F.2d 93, 107 (6th Cir. 1944).

[31] I am indebted for an analysis of the record to the recent able Ph.D. thesis by my student, Warren Baum. See Baum, *Workable Competition in the Tobacco Industry* (unpublished in the Harvard College Library, 1949).

probably a fact that the companies' systems of grading leaf tobacco required explicit understandings. But to suppose that ending such collusion or conspiracy as existed among the firms would produce a substantially different market behavior in the sale of cigarettes than that on which the charge of price conspiracy primarily rested is contrary both to logic and to the subsequent course of events in the industry.

There is certainly plenty of evidence that the business performance of the big tobacco companies did not meet reasonable standards of efficiency in the use of resources. Cigarette prices did not respond to substantial declines in leaf prices, it required the advent of ten-cent brands in the 1930's to bring about effective price competition; large resources were employed in what can only be regarded from the point of view of the community as wasteful advertising; the profits of the three companies were inordinately high. Nevertheless, this lamentable performance was and is quite compatible with independence of action on the part of the firms. Under these circumstances to bring a charge of conspiracy may have had the effect of enlarging the legal meaning of conspiracy. But it may also have had the effect of producing in some minds the illusion that eliminating the conspiracy will necessarily, in some sense, make competition work better.

The charge of collusion in the *Cement* case[32] was brought under Section 5 of the Federal Trade Commission Act[33] and the multiple basing-point system in use in that industry was found by the Supreme Court to be an "unfair method of competition." But there can be little doubt, after this decision, that a similar set of facts would justify a charge of conspiracy in violation of the Sherman Act. Whatever ingenuity economists have displayed in demonstrating that a basing-point system might emerge without collusion, there can be no doubt that in the cement industry, and probably in most industries in which this pricing system is used, collusion is involved. Furthermore, the collusive agreements ordinarily involved in an effective basing-point system are sufficiently central to the marketing practices of firms that elimination of the agreements may be expected to change substantially the character of the business performance in what were formerly basing-point industries.

Whether the business performance will be improved in any sense relevant to the concept of efficiency in the use of resources will depend on what alternative practices are adopted by the firms. The abolition of a basing-point system is in itself an approach toward workable competition as defined in terms of market conditions. By the performance test of competition, however, the elimination of basing-point systems is the beginning and not the end of the discussion.[34]

---

[32] *FTC* v. *Cement Institute*, 333 U.S. 683 (1948).

[33] Stat. 719–20 (1914), as amended, 52 Stat. 112 (1938), 15 U.S.C. § 45(b) (1946).

[34] "During the basic litigation, economic considerations are elbowed out or distorted by legalistic exigencies, both sides probably producing about equally bad or

Considering these and other recent antitrust cases involving the charge of conspiracy or collusion,[35] it would seem that the courts have substantially enlarged the meaning of collusion or, at least, the scope of the circumstances they are willing to accept as evidence of collusion. To this extent, the enforcement agencies find their task appreciably lightened. But included among the markets in which collusion may exist are some in which the abrogation of all agreements, existing and imagined, will constitute no progress toward effective competition judged either by standards of market structure or by standards of business performance. And there are others in which, while the abrogation of agreements may improve competition in the first sense, it will not necessarily do so in the second. It is now incumbent on us to look more closely at these alternative notions of competition.

III. CONCLUSION: OBJECTIVES OF ANTITRUST POLICY

The broad public policy question underlying these various theories of competition is what objective should an antimonopoly policy set for itself? Should it attempt to bring about a structure of industrial markets and a set of business practices such that the scope of action of individual firms is severely limited by the action of rival firms in the economy? Or should the objective be efficient use of economic resources, considering elements of market structure only when they can be shown to lead to ineffective business performance? It is the contention of this paper that neither objective can be set without regard to the other; that the tests both of workable competition and effective business performance have merits and demerits; and that these tests must be used to complement rather than to exclude each other.

In some ways the market structure tests are more precise and lend themselves more readily to administrative and judicial application. The number of buyers and sellers and the market-percentage share of each are roughly ascertainable facts, the chief difficulty being to know how much to include in a given market and what to exclude. The presence or absence of collusion, on the other hand, is sometimes difficult to discover and, the number of independent buyers or sellers considered necessary to the existence of an "adequate number of alternatives" is indeed a difficult question.

---

irrelevant or one-sided economics. Since serious and realistic consideration of the effects of an order cannot begin until after the order is issued, economic analysis is backward, though the heart of the legality in these cases is economic. This is unfortunate, but it seems to be the way our present system works." Clark, "The Law and Economics of Basing Points: Appraisals and Proposals," *American Economic Review,* Vol. XXXIX (1949), pp. 430, 431.

[35] *See, e.g., United States* v. *Line Material Company,* 333 U.S. 287 (1948); *United States* v. *United States Gypsum Company,* 333 U.S. 364 (1948); *United States* v. *Masonite Corporation,* 316 U.S. 265 (1942); *Interstate Circuit, Inc.* v. *United States,* 306 U.S. 208 (1939).

Stigler considers it necessary "that there [be] a considerable number of firms selling closely related products in each important market area. . . ."[36] A "considerable number" might mean a number large enough to eliminate recognition of interdependence. On the other hand, Edwards explicitly states that this is unnecessary.[37] The key question here is what is meant by the alternatives of which workable competition is supposed to require an "adequate number." I suggest that there is frequently no satisfactory way to assign meaning to this term without examining business performance in the market in question. The rapid expansion in the sale of titanium compounds with substantially and continually declining prices during the interwar period may have indicated that, under these circumstances, four sellers provide buyers with an adequate number of alternatives. At least the Supreme Court seemed to think so.[38] Eight or ten producers in a rapidly growing rayon industry which must meet the competition of substitute fabrics may be enough to provide buyers with adequate alternatives. Under other circumstances, this number might be too small. But whether the number is or is not sufficiently large can hardly be determined without looking at the business performance of the firms in question.

When one turns, however, to the problem of testing adequate business performance, it would have to be said that although it is probably possible to arrive at informed judgments, it is extremely difficult to devise tests that can be administered by a court of law. Among the tests mentioned in the literature are the following:[39]

1. Progressiveness: are the firms in the industry actively and effectively engaged in product and process innovation?
2. Cost-price relationships: are reductions in cost, whether due to falling wages or material prices, technical improvements, or discovery of new sources of supply, passed on promptly to buyers in the form of price reductions?
3. Capacity-output relationships: is investment excessive in relation to output?
4. The level of profits: are profits continually and substantially higher than in other industries exhibiting similar trends in sales, costs, innovations, etc.?
5. Selling expenditures: is competitive effort chiefly indicated by selling ex-

---

[36] Stigler, "The Extent and Bases of Monopoly," Proceedings of the American Economic Association, *American Economic Review*, Vol. XXXII (1942), pp. 2–3.

[37] Edwards, *Maintaining Competition* (1949), p. 9.

[38] *See United States* v. *National Lead Company*, 332 U.S. 319 (1947).

[39] Wallace, "Industrial Markets and Public Policy: Some Major Problems," *Public Policy*, Vol. I (1940), pp. 59, 99–100, includes among the issues involved in estimating the efficiency of business performance: (1) size of firms in relation to efficiency and economic progress and locational factors; (2) allocation of economic resources between industries, utilization of resources already invested, returns to owners; (3) the level of use of resources in the community as a whole; (4) severity of the business cycle; (5) progressiveness.

Professor Joe S. Bain in his three-volume work, *The Economics of the Pacific Coast Petroleum Industry* (1944, 1945, 1947), discusses standards of performance at three levels of industry operations, crude oil production, refining, and distribution. See particularly Vol. III.

penditures rather than by service and product improvements and price reductions?

No one familiar with the statistical and other material pertaining to the business performance of firms and industries would deny the extreme difficulty of constructing from this material a watertight case for or against the performance of particular firms in particular industries. Few, on the other hand, would deny that with respect to many industrial markets an informed judgment is possible. For example, it is possible from the record of the last two or three decades to determine that the performance of the automobile industry is relatively good, despite the existence of a small number of firms, while the performance of the construction industry is relatively bad. In any case, it is on the basis of just such industry data as we are now discussing that a decision even under the market structure test would have to be made whether the number of alternatives available to buyers or sellers in a particular industrial market is or is not "adequate."

A study of the performance of business firms in a particular industrial market may, of course, indicate the desirability of public action transcending the limits of antitrust policy. For example, one of the ways of improving the conditions of entry for new firms in the cigarette industry would be to change by legislation the present structure of excise taxes which is regressive with respect to the cheaper brands.[40] Professor Bain's study of the performance of firms in the Pacific Coast petroleum industry led to a number of recommendations that lie outside the limits of antitrust action.[41] But even within these limits considerations of efficiency in the use of resources cannot be neglected in judging the acceptability of the structure of and practices in particular industrial markets.

The relative importance to be assigned to the objective of establishing appropriate market limitations on the scope of action of firms as against the objective of encouraging efficient performance in the use of economic resources no doubt presents serious difficulties. It seems probable that individual judgments will always be influenced to some extent by ideological considerations. There are those who are willing to sacrifice a lot in the way of performance to establish market structures which severely limit the power and scope of action of individual firms.[42] There are others

---

[40] That is, the taxes do not increase with the base price of the cigarette as they would if the taxes were levied on an ad valorem basis.

[41] The two industry studies that have, in my opinion, gone furthest in an economic examination of the character of business performance are: Wallace, *Market Control in the Aluminum Industry* (1937), and Bain, *The Economics of the Pacific Coast Petroleum Industry* (1944, 1945, 1947).

[42] See, *e.g.*, forthcoming article by Lewis in the *American Economic Review:* "For competition to be effective or workable, or even acceptable, in any significant lasting sense, it must not only permit, *it must compel the results we want by the necessary and continuing operation of its processes.*"

to whom this seems less important. How much, in fact, would have to be sacrificed in the attainment of one objective to secure a given amount of progress towards the other is the heart of the public policy problem in the area of business organization. It is only necessary to indicate here that, in my opinion, the choice of one of these objectives, to the exclusion of the other, would make a substantial amount of difference in many industrial markets.

Finally, we must ask at what level of public action this question of the appropriate objectives for an antimonopoly policy should be considered. There are clearly three nonexclusive possibilities. The question can be raised at the level of legislation. Should the present antitrust laws be modified and, if so, how? As soon as this question is raised, it becomes obvious that a number of possible actions lying outside of traditional antitrust policy may, nevertheless, make an important contribution to an antimonopoly policy. Taxation discriminating against size and a series of measures favorable to the development of small firms may be mentioned as examples.

Secondly, the question can be discussed at the level of adjudication of cases brought under the antitrust laws. What are and what should be the legal tests of monopoly and restraint of trade? As we have seen, these tests have, in certain respects, been substantially broadened by recent antitrust decisions and the courts can, and no doubt will, extend present trends further.

Finally, and to my mind, the most important level within the framework of traditional antitrust policy, at which the question of appropriate standards and objectives can be discussed, is at the level of the enforcement agencies. These agencies have an enormous amount of discretion with respect to the kinds of cases that may be brought and the business areas within which to bring them. This fact is by implication frequently denied by representatives of the enforcement agencies who assert that, after all, they "have a statute to enforce." The statute, however, in the words of Chief Justice Hughes, is of the same order of generality as a constitutional provision.[43] Even if the Antitrust Division and the Federal Trade Commission enjoyed appropriations five times as large as they now have, they could not conceivably bring a tenth of the cases it would be possible to bring. Under these circumstances, it is a matter of considerable importance how and where they strike.

There has, in my opinion, been too much preoccupation in the enforcement agencies with the question what cases can be won and too little with the question what difference it makes.[44] The second question

---

[43] *Appalachian Coals, Inc.* v. *United States,* 288 U.S. 344, 360 (1933).

[44] But see the remarks of the present chief of the Antitrust Division, Herbert A. Bergson, Assistant Attorney General: "In selecting cases we analyze the effectiveness of the relief obtainable, the competitive positions in the particular industry, and our prospects in the courts. In this respect our decision is similar to that

clearly involves a consideration of whether a different structure of the market and set of business practices, lying within the area subject to antitrust action, will be better, in some sense, than the existing structure and practices. At this point the alternative objectives of antitrust policy and how they should be related to each other, which has been the subject of this paper, can no longer be avoided.

---

of any businessman who proposes to invest money—he wants to know what the return will be. In anti-trust enforcement that return should not be measured in dollars and cents, but in benefits to our economy and an American system of free enterprise." Bergson, "Current Problems in the Enforcement of the Anti-trust Laws," *Record of the Association of the Bar of the City of New York*, Vol. IV (April, 1949), p. 115.

BIBLIOGRAPHY

I. THE STRUCTURE OF INDUSTRY AND MARKETS

ADELMAN, M. A., The large firm and its suppliers, *Review of Economics and Statistics,* XXXI (1949), 113–18.

*———, The measurement of industrial concentration, *Review of Economics and Statistics,* XXXIII (1951), 269–96.
Comment by C. D. EDWARDS, *ibid.,* XXXIV (1952), 156–61.
Comment by G. W. STOCKING, *ibid.,* 161–68.
Comment by E. B. GEORGE, *ibid.,* 168–72.
Comment by A. A. BERLE, JR., *ibid.,* 172–74.
Rejoinder by ADELMAN, *ibid.,* 174–78.

———, Federal Trade Commission report on changes in the concentration of manufacturing, *Journal of the American Statistical Association,* L (1955), 660–64.

ALDAHEFF, C. P., and ALDAHEFF, D. A., Recent bank mergers, *Quarterly Journal of Economics,* LXIX (1955), 503–32.

ALLEN, G. C., An aspect of industrial reorganization, *Economic Journal,* LV (1945), 179–91.

ANDREWS, P. W. S., Some aspects of competition in retail trade, *Oxford Economic Papers,* II (1950), 137–75.

ANTHONY, R. N., Effect of size on efficiency, *Harvard Business Review,* XX (1941–42), 290–306.

ASHLER, P. F., Small business and defense contracts, *Harvard Business Review,* XXXIX (1951), No. 3, 104–12.

BAIN, J. S., The profit rate as a measure of monopoly power, *Quarterly Journal of Economics,* LV (1940–41), 271–93.

———, Measurements of the degree of monopoly: a note, *Economica,* X (1943), 66–68.

———, Relation of profit rate to industry concentration: American manufacturing, 1936–40, *Quarterly Journal of Economics,* LXV (1951), 293–324.

*———, Economies of scale, concentration, and the condition of entry in twenty manufacturing industries, *American Economic Review,* XLIV (1954), 15–39.

BAJPAI, R. G., Concentration of economic power in India, *Indian Journal of Economics,* XXXII (1951–52), 317–24.

BALLAINE, W. C., How government purchasing procedures strengthen monopoly elements, *Journal of Political Economy,* LI (1943), 538–46.

BARKER, T. C.; DICKINSON, R.; and HARDIE, D. W. F., The origins of the synthetic alkali industry in Britain, *Economica,* XXIII (1956), 158–71.

BAUER, P. T., Marketing monopoly in British Africa, *Kyklos,* IX (1956), 164–78.

BAYARD, C. C., The defective United States retail price structure, *Southern Economic Journal,* XI (1944–45), 1–19.

BERGE, W., Monopoly and the South, *Southern Economic Journal,* XIII (1946–47), 360–69.

BLAIR, J. M., "The measurement of industrial concentration": a reply, *Review of Economics and Statistics,* XXXIV (1952), 343–55.

* Reprinted in the present volume.

Rejoinder by M. A. Adelman, *ibid.*, 356–64.
Further rejoinder by J. K. Butters and J. Lintner, *ibid.*, 364–67.

Blair, J. M., Economic concentration and depression price rigidity, *American Economic Review,* XLV (1955, Proceedings), 566–82.

Blaisdell, T. C., Jr., Industrial concentration in the war, *American Economic Review,* XXXIII (1943), 159–61.

Bock, B., Economic patterns in merger cases, *National Industrial Conference Board Business Record* (1955), 214–26, 231 ff.

Burck, G., The great U.S. freight cartel, *Fortune,* LV (January, 1957), 102 ff.

Burns, A. R., Concentration of production, *Harvard Business Review,* XXI (1942–43), 277–90.

Burns, J. W., Problems of size and integration, *Antitrust Bulletin,* II (1957), 584–611.

Canoyer, H. G., National brand advertising and monopolistic competition, *Journal of Marketing,* VII (1942–43), 152–57.

Cassady, R., Jr., The integrated marketing institution and public welfare, *Journal of Marketing,* VI (1941–42), 252–65.

———, and Grether, E. T., Locality price differentials in the western retail grocery trade, *Harvard Business Review,* XXI (1942–43), 190–206.

Comer, G. P., The outlook for effective competition, *American Economic Review,* XXXVI (1946, Proceedings), 154–71.

Cook, P. W., Jr., Decentralization and the transfer-price problem, *Journal of Business of the University of Chicago,* XXVIII (1955), 87–94.

Crumbaker, C., Note on the concentration of economic power, *Journal of Political Economy,* L (1942), 934–44.

Davis, H. S., Relation of capital-output ratio to firm size in American manufacturing: some additional evidence, *Review of Economics and Statistics,* XXXVIII (1956), 286–93.

Dean, J., Cost structures of enterprises and break-even charts, *American Economic Review,* XXXVIII (1948, Proceedings), 153–64.

———, Competition—inside and out, *Harvard Business Review,* XXXII (1954), No. 6, 63–71.

Dietz, A. T., Corporate mergers: retrospective and prospective, *Journal of Public Law,* V (1956), 309–26.

Edwards, C. D., Geographic price formulas and the concentration of economic power, *Georgetown Law Journal,* XXXVII (1949), 135–48.

Engle, N. H., Chain store distribution vs. independent wholesaling, *Journal of Marketing,* XIV (1949–50), 241–52.

Florence, P. S., New measures of the growth of firms, *Economic Journal,* LXVII (1957), 244–48.

Friedland, S., Turnover and growth of the largest industrial firms, 1906–1950, *Review of Economics and Statistics,* XXXIX (1957), 79–83.

Fulda, C. H., Food distribution in the United States, the struggle between independents and chains, *University of Pennsylvania Law Review,* XCIX (1951), 1051–1162.

Goris, H., and Koyck, L. M., The prices of investment goods and the volume of production in the United States, *Review of Economics and Statistics,* XXXV (1953), 59–66.

Gragg, C. I.; Grimshaw, A.; and Teele, S. F., Competition under rationing, *Harvard Business Review,* XX (1941–42), 141–55.

Haddon-Cave, C. P., Trends in the concentration of operations of Australian secondary industries, 1923–43, *Economic Record,* XXI (1945), 65–78.

Hale, G. E., Dispersion: monopoly and geographic integration, *Texas Law Review,* XXX (1952), 423–61.

Hart, P. E., On measuring business concentration, *Bulletin of the Oxford University Institute of Statistics,* XIX (1957), 225–48.

Hawkins, L. C., Measurements of efficiency, *Oxford Economic Papers,* II (1950), 30–50.

Hazari, R. K., Monopolistic competition and welfare in underdeveloped countries, *Indian Journal of Economics,* XXXIII (1952–53), 425–32.

Heflebower, R. B., Economics of size, *Journal of Business of the University of Chicago,* XXIV (1951), 253–68.

———, Barriers to new competition (review of Joe S. Bain's *Barriers to New Competition*), *American Economic Review,* XLVII (1957), 363–71.

———, Mass distribution: a phase of bilateral oligopoly or of competition? *American Economic Review,* XLVII (1957, Proceedings), 274–85.

Hernacki, R. P., Mergerism and section 7 of the Clayton Act, *George Washington Law Review,* XX (1952), 659–705.

Hexner, E., International cartels in the postwar world, *Southern Economic Journal,* X (1943–44), 114–35.

Hieser, R., The degree of monopoly power, *Economic Record,* XXVIII (1952), 1–12.

Hirshleifer, J., Economics of the divisionalized firm, *Journal of Business of the University of Chicago,* XXX (1957), 96–108.

Hood, J., and Yamey, B. S., Imperfect competition in retail trades, *Economica,* XVIII (1951), 119–37.

Hosmer, W. A., Small manufacturing enterprises, *Harvard Business Review,* XXXV (1957), No. 6, 111–22.

Houghton, H. F., The growth of big business, *American Economic Review,* XXXVIII (1948, Proceedings), 72–93.

Howard, H. H., Effectiveness of "entry" by already established firms, *Quarterly Journal of Economics,* LXXI (1957), 132–50.

James, C. L., Industrial concentration and trade barriers, *Southern Economic Journal,* XIV (1947–48), 163–72.

Jastram, R. W., A proposed measure of industrial concentration, *Review of Economics and Statistics,* XXXIII (1956), 327–29.

Jewkes, J., The size of the factory, *Economic Journal,* LXII (1952), 237–51.

Johnson, D. G., Competition in agriculture: fact or fiction, *American Economic Review,* XLIV (1954, Proceedings), 107–15.

Johnson, W. S., The restrictive incidence of basing point pricing on regional development, *Georgetown Law Journal,* XXXVII (1949), 149–65.

Jourolmon, L., Jr., The social performance of public utilities: the effects of monopoly and competition, *Tennessee Law Review,* XVII (1942), 308–27.

Kaplan, A. D. H., The current merger movement analyzed, *Harvard Business Review,* XXXIII (1955), No. 3, 91–100.

Kaysen, C., The social significance of the modern corporation, *American Economic Review,* XLVII (1957, Proceedings), 311–19.

Kelley, W. T., Specification buying by the large-scale retailer: an aspect of vertical integration, *Journal of Marketing,* XVIII (1953–54), 255–65.

Keyes, L. S., Monopolistic market structures and stabilization, *Quarterly Journal of Economics,* LXVI (1952), 436–43.

Kottke, F. J., Monopoly and mobilization for defense, *Southern Economic Journal,* XVIII (1951–52), 516–25.

Kronstein, H., The dynamics of German cartels and patents, *University of Chicago Law Review,* IX (1942), 643–71; X (1942), 49–69.

Lazo, H., Independents, chains and public welfare, *Journal of Marketing,* VI (1941–42), 267–73.

LEBERGOTT, S., Has monopoly increased?, *Review of Economics and Statistics*, XXXV (1953), 349–51.
Rejoinder by G. W. NUTTER, *ibid.*, 352–53.

LEEMAN, W. A., The limitations of local price-cutting as a barrier to entry, *Journal of Political Economy*, LXIV (1956), 329–34.

LEWIS, W. A., Competition in the retail trade, *Economica*, XII (1945), 202–34.

LINDGREEN, G., How long does a company live?, *Oxford Economic Papers*, V (1953), 235–47.

LINTNER, J., and BUTTERS, J. K., Effect of mergers on industrial concentration, 1940–1947, *Review of Economics and Statistics*, XXXII (1950), 30–48.
Reply by J. M. BLAIR and H. F. HOUGHTON, *ibid.*, XXXIII (1951), 63–67.
Rejoinder by LINTNER and BUTTERS, *ibid.*, 67–71.
Comment by J. F. WESTON, *ibid.*, 71–73.
Rejoinder by LINTNER and BUTTERS, *ibid.*, 73–75.

———, and ———, Taxes and mergers, *Harvard Business Review*, XXIX (1951), No. 2, 69–81.

LYDALL, H. F., The impact of the credit squeeze on small and medium-sized manufacturing firms, *Economic Journal*, LXVII (1957), 415–31.

MCFERRIN, J. B., The structure of the American capital market, *Southern Economic Journal*, XXI (1954–55), 247–60.

MACLAURIN, W. R., Technological progress in some American industries, *American Economic Review*, XLIV (1954, Proceedings), 178–89.

MELMAN, S., The rise of the administrative overhead in the manufacturing industries of the United States, 1899–1947, *Oxford Economic Papers*, II (1950), 62–112.

MORGAN, E. V., and TAYLOR, C., The relationship between the size of joint-stock companies and the yield of their shares, *Economica*, XXIV (1957), 116–27.

MORGAN, T., A measure of monopoly in selling, a note, *Quarterly Journal of Economics*, LX (1945–46), 461–63.

MORRISON, E. A., Combinations and monopolies, *Business Law Review*, III (1956), 173–79.

MUELLER, W. F., A comment on the FTC's report on mergers with special reference to dairy mergers, *Journal of Farm Economics*, XXXIX (1957), 140–52.

MYERS, C. A., Wartime concentration of production, *Journal of Political Economy*, LI (1943), 222–34.

NUTTER, G. W., Growth by merger, *Journal of the American Statistical Association*, XLIX (1954), 448–66.

———, Monopoly, bigness, and progress, *Journal of Political Economy*, LXIV (1956), 520–77.

OLSHANSEN, G. G., Monopoly domination of the American economy with particular interest to the steel industry, *Law Guild Review*, XI (1951), 18–30.

OSBORN, R. C., Efficiency and profitability in relation to size, *Harvard Business Review*, XXIX (1951), No. 2, 82–94.

PAPANDREOU, A. G., Market structure and monopoly power, *American Economic Review*, XXXIX (1949), 883–97.

PENROSE, E., Limits to the growth and size of firms, *American Economic Review*, XLV (1955, Proceedings), 531–43.

PHILLIPS, A., Concentration, scale and technological change in selected manufacturing industries, 1899–1939, *Journal of Industrial Economics*, IV (1955–56), 179–93.

PRAIS, S. J., The financial experience of giant companies, *Economic Journal*, LXVII (1957), 249–63.

REEVES, J. H., Transport costs and the location of industry in Victoria, *Economic Record*, XXVII (1951), 231–35.

REUBENS, E., Small-scale industry in Japan, *Quarterly Journal of Economics*, LXI (1946–47), 577–604.

Rieben, H., ECSC and cartels, *Cartel,* VII (1957), 6–14, 42–49.

Ross, N. S., Management and the size of the firm, *Review of Economic Studies,* XIX (1952–53), 148–54.

Rostow, E. V., and Sachs, A. S., Entry into the oil-refining business: vertical integration re-examined, *Yale Law Journal,* LXI (1952), 856–914.

Rothbart, E., Causes of superior efficiency of U.S.A. industry as compared with British industry, *Economic Journal,* LVI (1946), 383–90.

Rothschild, K. W., The degree of monopoly, *Economica,* IX (1942), 24–39.

———, A further note on the degree of monopoly, *ibid.,* X (1943), 69–70.

———, Monopsony, buying costs and welfare expenditure, *Review of Economic Studies,* X (1942–43), 62–67.

Rowe, J. W., Productivity and size of establishment in New Zealand distributive trades, 1953, a note, *Economic Record,* XXXII (1956), 148–52.

Schlaifer, R., Big business and small business: a case study, *Harvard Business Review,* XXVIII (1950), No. 4, 97–108.

Schwartzman, D., Multiple-company mergers and the theory of the firm, *Oxford Economic Papers,* VII (1955), 197–214.

Scitovsky, T., Monopoly and competition in Europe and America, *Quarterly Journal of Economics,* LXIX (1955), 607–18.

———, Economies of scale, competition, and European integration, *American Economic Review,* XLVI (1956), 71–91.

Selden, R. T., Accelerated amortization and industrial concentration, *Review of Economics and Statistics,* XXXVII (1955), 282–91.

Seligman, B. B., Merger and monopoly in the U.S., *Dissent—A Quarterly of Socialist Opinion,* II (1955), 144–51.

Silbertson, A., and Solomons, D., Monopoly investigation and the rate of return on capital employed, *Economic Journal,* LXII (1952), 781–801.

Solo, R., and Heuss, E., New competition in the old world, *Antitrust Bulletin,* II (1956), 41–52.

Spengler, J. J., Monopolistic competition and the use and price of urban land service, *Journal of Political Economy,* LIV (1946), 385–412.

Stanford, W. H., Jr., Old problem in modern guise: chain stores and efficient integration under the Sherman Act, *Mercer Law Review,* I (1950), 219–43.

Stelzer, I. M., Technological progress and market structure, *Southern Economic Journal,* XXIII (1956–57), 63–73.

*Stigler, G. J., Monopoly and oligopoly by merger, *American Economic Review,* XL (1950, Proceedings), 23–34.

———, The case against big business, *Fortune,* XLV (May, 1952), 123 ff.

———, The statistics of monopoly and merger, *Journal of Political Economy,* LXIV (1956), 33–40.

Sykes, T., Diversification in industry, *Economic Journal,* LX (1950), 697–714.

Wellisz, S. H., The coexistence of large and small firms: a study of the Italian mechanical industries, *Quarterly Journal of Economics,* LXXI (1957), 116–31.

Weston, J. F., The recent merger movement, *Journal of Business of the University of Chicago,* XXV (1952), 30–38.

Whitman, R. H., A note on the concept of "degree of monopoly," *Economic Journal,* LI (1941), 261–69.

II. CASE STUDIES IN INDUSTRIAL STRUCTURE AND BEHAVIOR

Adams, W., The Aluminum case: legal victory—economic defeat, *American Economic Review,* XLI (1951), 923–34.

* Reprinted in the present volume.

Adelman, M. A., The A & P case, *American Economic Review,* XXXIX (1949, Proceedings), 280–83.

———, The A & P case: a study in applied economic theory, *Quarterly Journal of Economics,* LXIII (1949), 238–57.

———, The great A & P muddle, *Fortune,* XL (December, 1949), 122 ff.

Alt, R. M., The internal organization of the firm and price formation: an illustrative case, *Quarterly Journal of Economics,* LXIII (1949), 92–110.

Anderson, E. H., and Thomson, W. C., Plastics—a debutante industry, *Southern Economic Journal,* XVII (1950–51), 174–86.

Armstrong, W. P., Jr., The Sherman Act and the movies, *Temple Law Quarterly,* XX (1947), 442–71; a supplement, *ibid.,* XXVI (1952), 1–21.

Bain, J. S., Rostow's proposals for petroleum policy, *Journal of Political Economy,* LVII (1949), 55–60.
Reply by E. V. Rostow, *ibid.,* 60–68.
Rejoinder by Bain, *ibid.,* 68–69.

Barkin, S., The regional significance of the integration movement in the Southern textile industry, *Southern Economic Journal,* XV (1948–49), 395–411.

Barloon, M., The question of steel capacity, *Harvard Business Review,* XXVII (1949), 209–36.

Beacham, A., Efficiency and organization of the British coal industry, *Economic Journal,* LV (1945), 206–16.

———, Price policy in the coal industry, *Journal of Industrial Economics,* I (1952–53), 140–54.

Beesley, M., Changing locational advantages in the British motor car industry, *Journal of Industrial Economics,* VI (1957), 47–57.

Behoteguy, W. C., Resale price maintenance in the tire industry, *Journal of Marketing,* XIII (1948–49), 315–20.

Benham, F., The rubber industry, *Economica,* XVI (1949), 355–68.

Berle, A. A., Jr., Banking under the antitrust laws, *Columbia Law Review,* XLIX (1949), 589–606.

Bliss, P., Non-price competition at the department-store level, *Journal of Marketing,* XVII (1952–53), 357–65.

Broude, H. W., Bottleneck phenomena and cyclical change: the role of the iron and steel industry, *Quarterly Journal of Economics,* LXVIII (1954), 437–60.

Brown, W. H., Innovation in the machine tool industry, *Quarterly Journal of Economics,* LXXI (1957), 406–25.

Burns, A. R., Bain's analysis of the Pacific Coast petroleum industry, *Journal of Political Economy,* LVI (1948), 35–53.

Burstein, H., Motor carrier acquisitions, mergers and consolidations, *Interstate Commerce Commission Practitioners' Journal,* XXIV (1957), 375–88.

Callmann, R., Cosmetics in the law of unfair competition, *Food Drug Cosmetic Law Quarterly,* I (1946), 253–65.

Carson, R. M., Some abuses of antitrust prosecution: the investment bankers case, *Michigan Law Review,* LIV (1956), 363–98.

Clover, V. T., Price influence of unbranded gasoline, *Journal of Marketing,* XVII (1952–53), 388–93.

Coase, R. H., The origin of monopoly of broadcasting in Great Britain, *Economica,* XIV (1947), 189–210.

Corden, W. M., The maximisation of profit by a newspaper, *Review of Economic Studies,* XX (1952–53), 181–90.

Cross, J. S., Vertical integration in the oil industry, *Harvard Business Review,* XXXI (1953), No. 4, 69–81.

Dedman, M., Integration in the Australian wool textile industry, *Economic Record,* XXIV (1948), 111–16.

Dewey, D., Antitrust policy and the big buyer: further misgivings about the A & P case, *Journal of Marketing*, XVII (1952–53), 280–84.

Dirlam, J. B., Leadership and conflict in the pricing of gasoline, *Yale Law Journal*, LXI (1952), 818–55.

———, and Kahn, A. E., Antitrust law and the big buyer: another look at the A & P case, *Journal of Political Economy*, LX (1952), 118–32.

———, and ———, Integration and dissolution of the A & P Company, *Indiana Law Journal*, XXIX (1953), 1–27.
Reply by M. A. Adelman, *ibid.*, 367–70.
Rejoinder by Dirlam and Kahn, *ibid.*, 371–75.

———, and Stelzer, I. M., The Cellophane labyrinth, *Antitrust Bulletin*, I (1956), 633–51.

Doyle, L. A., Industrial economic problems in the post-war aluminum market in the U.S., *Journal of Industrial Economics*, I (1952–53), 212–30.

Eckler, J., Baseball—sport or commerce?, *University of Chicago Law Review*, XVII (1949), 56–78.

Errebo, B. H., Unit operation at Cotton Valley: alleged violation of the Sherman Act, *Tulane Law Review*, XXIV (1949), 76–94.

Frankel, P. H., Integration in the oil industry, *Journal of Industrial Economics*, I (1952–53), 202–11.

Friedelbaum, S. H., The British iron and steel industry: 1929–49, *Journal of Business of the University of Chicago*, XXIII (1950), 117–32.

Gardner, G. K., Insurance and the antitrust laws—a problem in synthesis, *Harvard Law Review*, LXI (1948), 246–73.

Gettell, R. G., Changing competitive conditions in the marketing of tires, *Journal of Marketing*, VI (1941–42), 112–23.

Gregory, P. M., Imperfect competition in the mortgage market, *Southern Economic Journal*, X (1943–44), 275–91.

Gromley, J., Baseball and the antitrust laws, *Nebraska Law Review*, XXXIV (1955), 597–612.

Gruis, E. G., Antitrust laws and their application to banking, *George Washington Law Review*, XXIV (1955), 89–107.

Hansen, H. L., and Smith, M. N., The Champion case: what is competition?, *Harvard Business Review*, Vol. XXIX (1951), No. 3, 79–103.

———, and Niland, P., Esso Standard: a case study in pricing, *Harvard Business Review*, XXX (1952), No. 3, 114–32.

Hart, P. E., Competition and control in the British sugar industry, *Oxford Economic Papers*, V (1953), 317–32.

Hawkins, E. K., Competition between the nationalized electricity and gas industries, *Journal of Industrial Economics*, I (1952–53), 155–73.

Hayes, S. P., Jr., Potash prices and competition, *Quarterly Journal of Economics*, LVII (1942–43), 31–68.

Henderson, J. M., Efficiency and pricing in the coal industry, *Review of Economics and Statistics*, XXXVIII (1956), 50–60.

Hines, L. G., Price determination in the Lake Erie iron ore market, *American Economic Review*, XLI (1951), 650–61.

Hirsch, W. Z., Grocery chain store prices—a case study, *Journal of Marketing*, XXI (1956–57), 9–23.

Hocking, D. M., The economics of the gas industry, *Economic Record*, XVIII (1942), 31–42.

Holton, R. H., Price discrimination at retail: the supermarket case, *Journal of Industrial Economics*, VI (1957), 13–32.

Howard, M. C., Interfirm relations in oil product markets, *Journal of Marketing*, XX (1955–56), 356–66.

HYSON, C. D., and SANDERSON, F. H., Monopolistic discrimination in the cranberry industry, *Quarterly Journal of Economics,* LIX (1944–45), 330–69.

ISARD, W., and CAPRON, W. M., The future locational pattern of iron and steel production in the United States, *Journal of Political Economy,* LVII (1949), 118–33.

JAMES, L. M., Restrictive agreements and practices in the lumber industry, 1880–1939, *Southern Economic Journal,* XIII (1946–47), 115–25.

JOHNSON, F. A., The law of sports: the unique performer's contract and the antitrust laws, *Antitrust Bulletin,* II (1957), 251–66.

———, Baseball, professional sports and the antitrust acts, *Antitrust Bulletin,* II (1957), 678–701.

JOHNSTON, J., Scale, costs and profitability in road passenger transport, *Journal of Industrial Economics,* IV (1956), 207–23.

KAHN, A. E., Leadership and conflict in the pricing of gasoline, *Yale Law Journal,* LXI (1952), 818–55.

KESSLER, F., Automobile dealer franchises: vertical integration by contract, *Yale Law Journal,* LXVI (1957), 1135–90.

KINTNER, C. V., The changing pattern of the newspaper publishing industry, *American Journal of Economics and Sociology,* V (1945–46), 43–63.

KNOX, F., Patent medicines, *Cartel,* VI (1956), 88–92.

KRUTILLA, J. V., Locational factors influencing recent aluminum expansion, *Southern Economic Journal,* XXI (1954–55), 273–88.

———, Aluminum—a dilemma for antitrust aims?, *Southern Economic Journal,* XXII (1955–56), 164–77.

LEACH, R. H., The federal government and the peanut industry, *Southern Economic Journal,* XXI (1954–55), 53–61.

LEARNED, E. P., Pricing of gasoline: a case study, *Harvard Business Review,* XXVI (1948), 723–56.

MCDONOUGH, J. R., JR., and WINSLOW, R. L., The motion picture industry: United States v. oligopoly, *Stanford Law Review,* I (1949), 385–427.

MCELROY, T. K., Section 7 of the Clayton Act and the oil industry, *Baylor Law Review,* V (1953), 121–45.

MCGEE, J. S., Price discrimination and competitive effects: the Standard Oil of Indiana case, *University of Chicago Law Review,* XXIII (1956), 398–473.

*MCKIE, J. W., The decline of monopoly in the metal container industry, *American Economic Review,* XLV (1955, Proceedings), 499–508.

MCNALLEN, J. B., A new concept in gasoline marketing, *Journal of Marketing,* XXII (1958), 273–81.

MANNE, A., Oil-refining: cross-elasticities of supply, *Quarterly Journal of Economics,* LXV (1951), 214–36.

MARKHAM, J. W., Integration in the textile industry, *Harvard Business Review,* XXVIII (1950), No. 1, 74–88.

*———, An alternative approach to the concept of workable competition, *American Economic Review,* XL (1950), 349–61.

MINKES, A. L., The paint industry in Great Britain, *Journal of Industrial Economics,* III (1954–55), 144–70.

MOOS, S., Price formation and price maintenance on the aluminum market, *Manchester School of Economic and Social Studies,* XVI (1948), 66–93.

———, The structure of the British aluminum industry, *Economic Journal,* LVIII (1948), 522–37.

MULLER, C., The aluminum monopoly and the war, *Political Science Quarterly,* LX (1945), 14–43.

---

* Reprinted in the present volume.

MUNBY, D. L., The price of fuel, *Oxford Economic Papers,* VI (1954), 226–42.

MURCHISON, W. C., The significance of the American Tobacco case, *North Carolina Law Review,* XXVI (1948), 139–72.

NADEN, N. D., Price policy of the Challenge Cream & Butter Association, Pt. I, *Journal of Marketing,* XIII (1948–49), 459–69; Pt. II, *ibid.,* XIV (1949–50), 27–37.

NEAL, P. C., The Clayton Act and the Transamerica case, *Stanford Law Review,* V (1953), 179–232.

NEVILLE, J. W., Baseball and the antitrust laws, *Fordham Law Review,* XVI (1947), 208–30.

NICHOLLS, W. H., Imperfect competition in agricultural processing and distributing industries, *Canadian Journal of Economics and Political Science,* IX (1944), 139–64.

———, Some economic aspects of the margarine industry, *Journal of Political Economy,* LIV (1946), 221–42.

*———, The Tobacco case of 1946, *American Economic Review,* XXXIX (1949, Proceedings), 284–96.

NICOLS, A., The Cement case, *American Economic Review,* XXXIX (1949, Proceedings), 297–310.

PETIT, T. A., The value of competition: a study of the American softwood plywood industry, *Journal of Industrial Economics,* VI (1957), 33–46.

PHILLIPS, A., Price discrimination and the large firm: Hobson's choice in the pectin industry, *Virginia Law Review,* XLIII (1957), 685–96.

RAY, R. H., Competition in the newspaper industry, *Journal of Marketing,* XV (1950–51), 444–56.

REICH, B., The entertainment industry and the federal antitrust laws, *Southern California Law Review,* XX (1946), 1–36.

SHEAHAN, J., Integration and exclusion in the telephone equipment industry, *Quarterly Journal of Economics,* LXX (1956), 249–69.

SHONE, R., Steel price policy, *Journal of Industrial Economics,* I (1952–53), 43–54.

SHUBIK, M., A game theorist looks at the antitrust laws and the automobile industry, *Stanford Law Review,* VIII (1956), 594–630.

SOLO, R., The new threat of synthetic to natural rubber, *Southern Economic Journal,* XXII (1955–56), 55–64.

STAEHLE, H., Relative prices and postwar markets for animal food products, *Quarterly Journal of Economics,* LIX (1944–45), 237–79.

STELZER, I. M., The insurance industry and the antitrust laws: a decade of experience, *Insurance Law Journal,* 1955 (1955), 137–52.

*STOCKING, G. W., and MUELLER, W. F., The Cellophane case and the new competition, *American Economic Review,* XLV (1955), 29–63.

STONE, H., and CAMPBELL, D. A., Insurance and the Robinson-Patman Act, *Insurance Law Journal,* 1949 (1949), 553–66.

STONES, F., Price policy in a nationally administered industry, *Journal of Industrial Economics,* I (1952–53), 32–42.

SUFRIN, S. C., and HARRIMAN, J. W., Reflections on the A & P case, *Syracuse Law Review,* II (1950), 26–36.

SUZUKI, S., Analysis of distribution structure in the iron and steel industry, *Kyoto University Economic Review,* XXI (October, 1951), 48–100.

TAFF, C. A., The competition of long-distance motor trucking: farm and industrial products and supplies, *American Economic Review,* XLVI (1956, Proceedings), 508–20.

TOPKIS, J. H., Monopoly in professional sports, *Yale Law Journal,* LVIII (1949), 691–712.

* Reprinted in the present volume.

Troxel, E., Price discrimination in space heating, *Land Economics*, XXIV (1948), 281–92.

Vitkovitch, B., The U.K. cotton industry, *Journal of Industrial Economics*, III (1954–55), 241–65.

Whitney, S. N., Vertical integration in the motion picture industry, *American Economic Review*, XLV (1955, Proceedings), 491–98.

Wright, J. W., The competitive outlook for cotton, *Journal of Marketing*, X (1945–46), 258–64.

III. BUSINESS PRACTICES AND MARKET BEHAVIOR

Adams, W., Resale price maintenance: fact and fancy, *Yale Law Journal*, LXIV (1955), 967–90.

———, Fair trade and the art of prestidigitation, *Yale Law Journal*, LXV (1955), 199–207.

Alt, R. M., Competition among types of retailers in selling the same commodity, *Journal of Marketing*, XIV (1949–50), 441–47.

Andrews, K. R., Product diversification and the public interest, *Harvard Business Review*, XXIX (1951), No. 4, 91–107.

Ansoff, H. I., Strategies for diversification, *Harvard Business Review*, XXXV (1957), No. 5, 113–24.

Backman, J., Price inflexibility—war and postwar, *Journal of Political Economy*, LVI (1948), 428–37.

Bain, J. S., Output quotas in imperfect cartels, *Quarterly Journal of Economics*, LXII (1947–48), 617–22.

Bingham, R. H., The uniform delivered pricing method in the grocery manufacturing industry, *Journal of Marketing*, XIV (1949–50), 594–600.

Borden, N. H., Findings of the Harvard study on the economic effects of advertising, *Journal of Marketing*, VI (1941–42, Proceedings), 89–99.

Bowman, W. S., Jr., Resale price maintenance—a monopoly problem, *Journal of Business of the University of Chicago*, XXV (1952), 141–55.

———, Tying arrangements and the leverage problem, *Yale Law Journal*, LXVII (1957), 19–36.

Cassady, R., Jr., Some economic aspects of price discrimination under non-perfect market conditions, *Journal of Marketing*, XI (1946–47), 7–20.

———, Techniques and purposes of price discrimination, *Journal of Marketing*, XI (1946–47), 135–51.

Clay, Sir H., Resale price maintenance, *Journal of Industrial Economics*, III (1954–55), 9–21.

Corey, E. R., Fair trade pricing, *Harvard Business Review*, XXX (1952), No. 5, 47–62.

Cox, R., Non-price competition and the measurement of prices, *Journal of Marketing*, X (1945–46), 370–83.

Dewey, D., A reappraisal of f.o.b. pricing and freight absorption, *Southern Economic Journal*, XXII (1955–56), 48–54.

Edwards, C. D., Types of differential pricing, *Journal of Marketing*, VI (1941–42, Proceedings), 156–67.

———, The effect of recent basing point decisions upon business practices, *American Economic Review*, XXXVIII (1948), 828–42.

Edwards, H. R., Price formation in the manufacturing industry and excess capacity, *Oxford Economic Papers*, VII (1955), 94–118.

Fetter, F. A., Exit basing point pricing, *American Economic Review*, XXXVIII (1948), 815–27.

Fox, H. G., The abuse of monopoly, *Canadian Bar Review*, XXIII (1945), 353–79.

Freer, R. E., Geographical pricing, the basing point problem and the implications of the Detroit oil jobbers case, *Journal of the Bar Association of the District of Columbia,* XVI (1949), 560–81.

Fulda, C. H., Resale price maintenance, *University of Chicago Law Review,* XXI (1954), 175–211.

Guthrie, J. A., Impact of geographical price discrimination on the buyer, *Journal of Marketing,* XIV (1949–50), 538–43.

Hale, G. E., Control over distribution: monopoly aspects of restraints upon distributors and producers, *Mississippi Law Journal,* XIV (1942), 170–89.

Hall, F., and Seelye, A. L., Vertical price fixing in Texas, *Texas Law Review,* XXXV (1957), 772–809.

Harsanyi, J. C., The research policy of a firm, *Economic Record,* XXX (1954), 48–60.

Herman, E. S., A note on fair trade, *Yale Law Journal,* LXV (1955), 23–32.

———, Fair trade and McKesson & Robbins, *California Law Review,* XLIV (1956), 853–65.

Howard, J. A., Collusive behavior, *Journal of Business of the University of Chicago,* XXVII (1954), 196–204.

Jastram, R. W., Advertising outlays under oligopoly, *Review of Economics and Statistics,* XXXI (1949), 106–9.

Jucius, M. J., Uniform accounting and pricing policies, *Journal of Business of the University of Chicago,* XVII (1944), 37–50.

*Kaysen, C., Basing point pricing and public policy, *Quarterly Journal of Economics,* LXIII (1949), 289–314.

Landon, C. E., Geographic price structures, *Law and Contemporary Problems,* XV (1950), 125–40.

McGee, J. S., Cross hauling—a symptom of incomplete collusion under basing-point systems, *Southern Economic Journal,* XX (1953–54), 369–79.

Marengo, L., The basing point decisions and the steel industry, *American Economic Review,* XLV (1955, Proceedings), 509–22.

*Markham, J. W., The nature and significance of price leadership, *American Economic Review,* XLI (1951), 891–905.

*Mason, E. S., Price and production policies of large-scale enterprise, *American Economic Review,* XXIX (1939, Proceedings), 61–74.

———, Market power and business conduct: some comments, *American Economic Review,* XLVI (1956, Proceedings), 471–81.

Merrigan, E. L., Delivered pricing and quantity discounts, *Loyola Law Review,* V (1949), 18–56.

Mund, V. A., The development and incidence of delivered pricing in American industry, *Law and Contemporary Problems,* XV (1950), 141–58.

Pegrum, D. F., The present status of geographic pricing, *Journal of Marketing,* XV (1950–51), 425–35.

Shillinglaw, G., The effects of requirement contracts on competition, *Journal of Industrial Economics,* II (1953–54), 147–63.

Smith, W. R., Product differentiation and market segmentation as alternative marketing strategies, *Journal of Marketing,* XXI (1956–57), 3–8.

Stocking, G. W., and Mueller, W. F., Business reciprocity and the size of firms, *Journal of Business of the University of Chicago,* XXX (1957), 73–95.

Teele, S. F., and Bursk, E. C., Marketing practices of food manufacturers, *Harvard Business Review,* XXI (1942–43), 358–76.

---

* Reprinted in the present volume.

TIMBERG, S., Restrictive business practices, *American Journal of Comparative Law,* II (1953), 445–73.

TRACHTMAN, J., Functional features in unfair competition, *Temple Law Quarterly,* XXIII (1949), 64–67.

VOLD, L., Open price in sales and marketing of goods, *Texas Law Review,* XXXV (1956–57), 637–46.

YAMEY, B. S., The price policy of co-operative societies, *Economica,* XVII (1950), 23–42.

———, Notes on resale price maintenance, *Economica,* XVII (1950), 254–65.

———, The origins of resale price maintenance, *Economic Journal,* LXII (1952), 522–45.

IV. INDUSTRIAL ORGANIZATION AND ECONOMIC THEORY

ABBOT, L., Vertical equilibrium under pure quality competition, *American Economic Review,* XLIII (1953), 826–45.

ACKLEY, G., Spatial competition in a discontinuous market, *Quarterly Journal of Economics,* LVI (1941–42), 212–30.

ADAMS, W., Competition, monopoly and countervailing power, *Quarterly Journal of Economics,* LXVII (1953), 469–92.

ADELMAN, M. A., The "product" and "price" in distribution, *American Economic Review,* XLVII (1957, Proceedings), 266–73.

*ALCHIAN, A. A., Uncertainty, evolution, and economic theory, *Journal of Political Economy,* LVIII (1950), 211–21.

ALEXANDER, K. J. W., and SPRAOS, J., Shift working: an application of the theory of the firm, *Quarterly Journal of Economics,* LXX (1956), 603–12.

ALLEN, G. C., A note on economic progress, *Economica,* XX (1953), 359–61.

ANDREN, P., Monopoly investigation and methods for calculating the rate of return on capital employed, *Journal of Industrial Economics,* IV (1955–56), 1–15.

APEL, H., Marginal cost constancy and its implications, *American Economic Review,* XXXVIII (1948), 870–85.

ARANT, W., Competition of the few among the many, *Quarterly Journal of Economics,* LXX (1956), 327–45.

ARNOLD, S., Forward shifting of a payroll tax under monopolistic competition, *Quarterly Journal of Economics,* LXI (1946–47), 267–84.

BAILEY, M. J., Price and output determination by a firm selling related products, *American Economic Review,* XLIV (1954), 82–93.

BAIN, J. S., Market classifications in modern price theory, *Quarterly Journal of Economics,* LVI (1941–42), 560–74.

*———, A note on pricing in monopoly and oligopoly, *American Economic Review,* XXXIX (1949), 448–64.

———, Output quotas in imperfect cartels: note, *Quarterly Journal of Economics,* LXII (1947–48), 617–22.

BALDERSTON, F. E., Scale of output and internal organization of the firm, *Quarterly Journal of Economics,* LXIX (1955), 45–70.

BAUER, P. T., A note on monopoly, *Economica,* VIII (1941), 194–202.

BEHRMAN, J. N., Distributive effects of an excise tax on a monopolist, *Journal of Political Economy,* LVIII (1950), 546–48.

BLAIR, J. M., Technology and size, *American Economic Review,* XXXVIII (1948, Proceedings), 121–52.

———, Means, Thorp and Neal on price inflexibility, *Review of Economics and Statistics,* XXXVIII (1956), 427–35.

* Reprinted in the present volume.

BOULDING, K. E., In defense of monopoly, *Quarterly Journal of Economics,* LIX (1944–45), 524–42.
Comment by R. E. HOLBEN, *ibid.,* LX (1945–46), 612–15.
Further comment by K. W. ROTHSCHILD, *ibid.,* 615–18.
Reply by BOULDING, *ibid.,* 619–21.

BOWMAN, W. S., JR., Toward less monopoly, *University of Pennsylvania Law Review,* CI (1955), 577–642.

BREMS, H., The interdependence of quality variations, selling effort and price, *Quarterly Journal of Economics,* LXII (1947–48), 418–40.

——, On the theory of price agreements, *Quarterly Journal of Economics,* LXV (1951), 252–62.

——, Employment, prices, and monopolistic competition, *Review of Economics and Statistics,* XXXIV (1952), 314–25.

——, Foreign exchange rates and monopolistic competition, *Economic Journal,* LXIII (1953), 289–94.
Comment by R. F. HARROD, *ibid.,* 294–98.

BRONFENBRENNER, M., Price control under imperfect competition, *American Economic Review,* XXXVII (1947), 107–20.

——, Imperfect competition on a long-run basis, *Journal of Business of the University of Chicago,* XXIII (1950), 81–93.

BUCHANAN, J. M., The theory of monopolistic discounts, *Review of Economic Studies,* XX (1952–53), 199–208.

CALSOYAS, C. D., The mathematical theory of monopoly in 1839: Charles Ellet, Jr., *Journal of Political Economy,* LVIII (1950), 162–70.

CARLIN, E. A., Intangible property as a tool for analyzing the relationships between government and private enterprise, *Quarterly Journal of Economics,* LXVII (1953), 112–24.

CHAMBERLIN, E. H., A supplementary bibliography on monopolistic competition, a note, *Quarterly Journal of Economics,* LVI (1941–42), 160–67.

——, A supplementary bibliography on monopolistic competition, *ibid.,* LXI (1947–48), 629–38.

——, A second supplementary bibliography on monopolistic competition, *ibid.,* LXX (1956), 613–43.

——, Proportionality, divisibility, and economics of scale, *Quarterly Journal of Economics,* LXII (1947–48), 229–62.
Comment by A. N. MCLEOD, *ibid.,* LXIII (1949), 128–31.
Comment by F. H. HAHN, *ibid.,* 131–37.
Reply by CHAMBERLIN, *ibid.,* 137–43.

——, An experimental imperfect market, *Journal of Political Economy,* LVI (1948), 95–108.

——, Various views on the monopoly problem: some final comments, *Review of Economics and Statistics,* XXXI (1949), 123–29.

*——, Product heterogeneity and public policy, *American Economic Review,* XL (1950, Proceedings), 85–92.

——, Monopolistic competition revisited, *Economica,* XVIII (1951), 343–62.

——, The impact of recent monopoly theory on the Schumpeterian system, *Review of Economics and Statistics,* XXXIII (1951), 133–38.

——, "Full cost" and monopolistic competition, *Economic Journal,* LXII (1952), 318–25.

——, The product as an economic variable, *Quarterly Journal of Economics,* LXVII (1953), 1–29.

——, On the origin of "oligopoly," *Economic Journal,* LXVII (1957), 211–18.

* Reprinted in the present volume.

CHEEK, B. M., Economic theory and industrial pricing, *Economic Record,* XXV (1949, Supplement), 140–57.

CLARK, J. M., Machlup on the basing-point system, *Quarterly Journal of Economics,* LXIII (1949), 315–21.

*———, Competition: static models and dynamic aspects, *American Economic Review,* XLV (1955, Proceedings), 450–62.

CLEMENS, E. W., Price discrimination in decreasing cost industries, *American Economic Review,* XXXI (1941), 794–802.

*———, Price discrimination and the multiple-product firm, *Review of Economic Studies,* XIX (1951–52), 1–11.

COASE, R. H., Monopoly pricing with interrelated costs and demands, *Economica,* XIII (1946), 278–94.

———, The economics of uniform pricing systems, *Manchester School of Economic and Social Studies,* XV (1947), 139–56.

COLBERG, M. R., Monopoly prices under joint costs: fixed proportions, *Journal of Political Economy,* XLIX (1941), 103–10.

COOK, A. C.; DUFTY, N. F.; and JONES, E. H., Full cost pricing in the multi-product firm, a note, *Economic Record,* XXXII (1956), 142–47.

COOPER, W. W., A proposal for extending the theory of the firm, *Quarterly Journal of Economics,* LXV (1951), 87–109.

COPELAND, M. A., Competing products and monopolistic competition, *Quarterly Journal of Economics,* LV (1940–41), 1–35.

CYERT, R. M., Oligopoly price behavior and the business cycle, *Journal of Political Economy,* LXIII (1955), 41–51.

———, and MARCH, J. G., Organizational structure and pricing behavior in an oligopolistic market, *American Economic Review,* XLV (1955), 129–39.

———, and ———, Organizational factors in the theory of oligopoly, *Quarterly Journal of Economics,* LXX (1956), 44–64.

DE ROVER, R., Monopoly theory prior to Adam Smith: a revision, *Quarterly Journal of Economics,* LXV (1951), 492–524.

DE SCHWEINITZ, K., JR., Normative implications of the "new competition," *Social Research,* XXIII (1956), 379–93.

DEWEY, D., Imperfect competition no bar to efficient production, *Journal of Political Economy,* LXVI (1958), 24–33.

DORFMAN, R., and STEINER, P. O., Optimal advertising and optimal quality, *American Economic Review,* XLIV (1954), 826–36.

DOWDELL, E. G., Oligopoly and imperfect competition, *Oxford Economic Papers,* I (1949), 217–26.

EARLY, J. S., Recent developments in cost accounting and the "marginal analysis," *Journal of Political Economy,* LXIII (1955), 227–42.

———, Marginal policies of "excellently managed" companies, *American Economic Review,* XLVI (1956), 44–70.

EDMONSTON, J. H., A treatment of multiple-process industries, *Quarterly Journal of Economics,* LXVI (1952), 557–71.

EDWARDS, C. D., The place of economics in the course on trade regulation, *Journal of Legal Education,* I (1948), 1–12.

———, Vertical integration and the monopoly problem, *Journal of Marketing,* XVII (1952–53), 404–10.

EFROYMSON, C. W., The kinked oligopoly curve reconsidered, *Quarterly Journal of Economics,* LXIX (1955), 119–36.

EITEMAN, W. J., and GUTHRIE, G. E., The shape of the average cost curve, *American Economic Review,* XLII (1952), 832–38.

* Reprinted in the present volume.

Ellsberg, D., Theory of the reluctant duelist, *American Economic Review,* XLVI (1956), 909–23.

Enke, S., On maximizing profits, *American Economic Review,* XLI (1951), 566–78.

Fellner, W. J., Prices and wages under bilateral monopoly, *Quarterly Journal of Economics,* LXI (1946–47), 503–32.

———, Average-cost pricing and the theory of uncertainty, *Journal of Political Economy,* LVI (1948), 249–52.

*———, The influence of market structure on technological progress, *Quarterly Journal of Economics,* LXV (1951), 556–77.

Fleming, M., Optimal production with fixed profits, *Economica,* XX (1953), 215–36.

Fouraker, L. E., The multiplier and monopolistic competition, *Southern Economic Journal,* XXIII (1956–57), 180–83.

———, Professor Fellner's bilateral monopoly theory, *Southern Economic Journal,* XXIV (1957–58), 182–89.

Fox, A. H., A theory of second-hand markets, *Economica,* XXIV (1957), 99–115.

Frisch, R., Alfred Marshall's theory of value, *Quarterly Journal of Economics,* LXIV (1950), 495–524.

Galbraith, J. K., Countervailing power, *American Economic Review,* XLIV (1954, Proceedings), 1–6.

———, Market structure and stabilization policy, *Review of Economics and Statistics,* XXXIX (1957), 124–33.

Gordon, R. A., Short-period price determination in theory and practice, *American Economic Review,* XXXVIII (1948), 265–88.

Greenhut, M. L., Free entry and the trade mark-trade name protection, *Southern Economic Journal,* XXIV (1957), 170–81.

Gregory, P. M., Fashion and monopolistic competition, *Journal of Political Economy,* LVI (1948), 69–75.

Hahn, F. H., Excess capacity and imperfect competition, *Oxford Economic Papers,* VII (1955), 229–40.

Harberger, A. C., Monopoly and resource allocation, *American Economic Review,* XLIV (1954, Proceedings), 77–87.

Hawkins, E. R., Price policies and theories, *Journal of Marketing,* XVIII (1953–54), 233–40.

Heflebower, R. B., An economic appraisal of price measures, *Journal of the American Statistical Association,* XLVI (1951), 461–79.

———, Some observations on industrial prices, *Journal of Business of the University of Chicago,* XXVII (1954), 187–97.

*———, Toward a theory of industrial markets and prices, *American Economic Review,* XLIV (1954, Proceedings), 121–39.

Henderson, A., The theory of duopoly, *Quarterly Journal of Economics,* LXVIII (1954), 565–84.

Henderson, Sir H., The price system, *Economic Journal,* LVIII (1948), 467–82.

Heyward, E. J. R., H. von Stackelberg's work on duopoly, *Economic Record,* XVII (1941), 99–106.

Hickman, C. A., Managerial motivation and the theory of the firm, *American Economic Review,* XLV (1955, Proceedings), 544–54.

Hicks, J. R., The process of imperfect competition, *Oxford Economic Papers,* VI (1954), 41–54.

Hieser, R., A kinked demand curve for monopolistic competition, *Economic Record,* XXIX (1953), 19–34.

* Reprinted in the present volume.

HIRSCH, W. Z., Toward a definition of integration, *Southern Economic Journal*, XVII (1950–51), 159–65.

HIRSHLEIFER, J., The exchange between quantity and quality, *Quarterly Journal of Economics*, LXIX (1955), 596–606.

HOOVER, C. B., The relevance of the competitive laissez-faire economic model to modern capitalistic national economies, *Kyklos*, VIII (1955), 40–55.

HUNTER, A., Product differentiation and welfare economics, *Quarterly Journal of Economics*, LXIX (1955), 533–52.

HYSON, C. D., and HYSON, W. P., The economic law of market areas, *Quarterly Journal of Economics*, LXIV (1950), 319–27.

JACOBY, N. H., and WESTON, J. F., Profit standards, *Quarterly Journal of Economics*, LXVI (1952), 224–50.

JEWKES, J., Monopoly and economic progress, *Economica*, XX (1953), 197–214.

KALDOR, N., The economic aspects of advertising, *Review of Economic Studies*, XVIII (1949–50), 1–27.

KAYSEN, C., A dynamic aspect of the monopoly problem, *Review of Economics and Statistics*, XXXI (1949), 109–13.

———, Dynamic aspects of oligopoly price theory, *American Economic Review*, XLII (1952, Proceedings), 198–210.

KEMP, M. C., The efficiency of competition as an allocator of resources: external economies of production, *Canadian Journal of Economics and Political Science*, XXI (1955), 30–42, 217–27.

KNAUTH, O., Monopoly reconsidered, *Political Science Quarterly*, LX (1945), 563–77.

LAFFER, K., A note on some marginalist and other explanations of full cost price theory, *Economic Record*, XXIX (1953), 51–62.

LANZILOTTI, R. F., Multiple products and oligopoly strategy: a development of Chamberlin's theory of products, *Quarterly Journal of Economics*, LXVIII (1954), 461–74.

LERNER, J., Constant proportions, fixed plant and optimum conditions of production, *Quarterly Journal of Economics*, LXIII (1949), 361–70.

LESTER, R. A., Marginalism, minimum wages and labor markets, *American Economic Review*, XXXVII (1947), 135–48.
Rejoinder to an antimarginalist, by F. MACHLUP, *ibid.*, 148–54.
Professor Lester and the marginalists, by G. J. STIGLER, *ibid.*, 154–57.
Marginal theory and business behavior, by H. M. OLIVER, *ibid.*, 375–83.
Marginalism and economic policy: a comment, by F. H. BLUM, *ibid.*, 645–52.
Factors determining the least cost point, by W. J. EITEMAN, *ibid.*, 910–18.

———, Absence of elasticity considerations in demand to the firm, *Southern Economic Journal*, XIV (1947–48), 285–89.

LEWIS, H. G., Some observations on duopoly theory, *American Economic Review*, XXXVIII (1948, Proceedings), 1–9.

———, The labor-monopoly problem: a positive program, *Journal of Political Economy*, LIX (1951), 277–87.

LOCKHART, W. B., and SACKS, H. R., The relevance of economic factors in determining whether exclusive arrangements violate section 3 of the Clayton Act, *Harvard Law Review*, LXV (1952), 913–54.

LYDALL, H. F., Conditions of new entry and the theory of price, *Oxford Economic Papers*, VII (1955), 300–11.

MACHLUP, F., The characteristics and classifications of monopoly, *Kyklos*, V (1951–52), 145–63.

MCKENZIE, L. W., Ideal output and the interdependence of firms, *Economic Journal*, LXI (1951), 785–803.

MARCHAL, J., The construction of a new theory of profit, *American Economic Review*, XLI (1951), 549–65.

MARONI, Y., Discrimination under market interdependence, *Quarterly Journal of Economics*, LXII (1947–48), 95–117.

MASON, E. S., Schumpeter on monopoly and the large firm, *Review of Economics and Statistics*, XXXIII (1951), 139–44.

MERIAM, R. S., Bigness and the economic analysis of competition, *Harvard Business Review*, XXVIII (1950), No. 2, 109–26.

MILLER, J. P., Competition and countervailing power: their roles in the American economy, *American Economic Review*, XLIV (1954, Proceedings), 15–25.

MOORE, J. R., and LEVY, L. S., Price flexibility and industrial concentration, *Southern Economic Journal*, XXI (1954–55), 435–40.

MORGAN, J. N., Bilateral monopoly and the competitive output, *Quarterly Journal of Economics*, LXIII (1949), 371–91.
Comment by W. FELLNER, *ibid.*, LXIV (1950), 648–50.
Reply by MORGAN, *ibid.*, 650–52.

MORGENSTERN, O., Oligopoly, monopolistic competition, and the theory of games, *American Economic Review*, XXXVIII (1948, Proceedings), 10–18.

MORRISON, C. C., A note on monopolistic exploitation and discrimination, *Southern Economic Journal*, XXIII (1956–57), 449–52.

NEAL, A. C., Marginal cost and dynamic equilibrium of the firm, *Journal of Political Economy*, L (1942), 45–64.

NICHOL, A. J., Monopoly supply and monopsony demand, *Journal of Political Economy*, L (1942), 861–79.

NICHOLLS, W. H., Social biases and recent theories of competition, *Quarterly Journal of Economics*, LVIII (1943–44), 1–26.

NICOLS, A., The rehabilitation of pure competition, *Quarterly Journal of Economics*, LXII (1947–48), 31–63.

———, The development of monopolistic competition and the monopoly problem, *Review of Economics and Statistics*, XXXI (1949), 118–23.

NUTTER, G. W., Competition: direct and devious, *American Economic Review*, XLIV (1954, Proceedings), 69–76.

NOURSE, E. G., The meaning of price policy, *Quarterly Journal of Economics*, LV (1940–41), 175–209.

OXENFELDT, A. R., Monopoly dissolution: a proposal outlined, *American Economic Review*, XXXVI (1946), 384–91.

PATINKIN, D., Multiple-plant firms, cartels, and imperfect competition, *Quarterly Journal of Economics*, LXI (1946–47), 173–205.
Comment by W. LEONTIEF, *ibid.*, 650–51.

———, Note on the allocation of output, *ibid.*, 651–57.

PEARCE, I. F., A study in price policy, *Economica*, XXIII (1956), 114–27.

PENROSE, E. T., Biological analogies in the theory of the firm, *American Economic Review*, XLII (1952), 804–19.

———, Toward a theory of industrial concentration, *Economic Record*, XXXII (1956), 64–77.

PESTON, M. M., and WHITHIN, T. M., Random variations, risk, and returns to scale, *Quarterly Journal of Economics*, LXVIII (1954), 603–12.

*PETERSON, S., Antitrust and the classic model, *American Economic Review*, XLVII (1957), 60–78.

PHILLIPS, C. F., Price control in a less-than-all-out-war situation, *Journal of Marketing*, XVI (1951–52), 187–91.

PIGOU, A. C., A comment on duopoly, *Economica*, XV (1948), 254–58.

PLANTINGA, J., and VERMETTEN, J. B., The elasticity of substitution of gas with respect to other fuels in the United States, *Review of Economics and Statistics*, XXXV (1953), 140–43.

* Reprinted in the present volume.

RENWICK, C., The equilibrium of the firm in monopolistic and imperfect competition theories, *Economic Record,* XXIV (1948), 32–41.

RICHARDSON, G. B., Imperfect knowledge and economic efficiency, *Oxford Economic Papers,* V (1953), 136–56.

ROBERTSON, R. M., On the changing apparatus of competition, *American Economic Review,* XLIV (1954, Proceedings), 51–62.

ROBINSON, E. A. G., Pricing of manufactured products, *Economic Journal,* LX (1950), 771–80.
Comment by M. J. FARRELL, *ibid.,* LXI (1951), 423–26.
Comment by A. SILBERSTONE, *ibid.,* 426–29.
Rejoinder by ROBINSON, *ibid.,* 429–33.

ROBINSON, J., Imperfect competition revisited, *Economic Journal,* LXIII (1953), 579–93.

RODGERS, R., and LUEDICKE, H. E., Dynamic competition, *Harvard Business Review,* XXVII (1949), 237–49.

ROTHSCHILD, K. W., Price theory and oligopoly, *Economic Journal,* LVII (1947), 299–320.

———, Fellner on competition among the few, *Quarterly Journal of Economics,* LXVI (1952), 128–36.

SCITOVSKY, T., Prices under monopoly and competition, *Journal of Political Economy,* XLIX (1941), 663–85.

SEELYE, A. L., Teaching pricing principles and price policies, *Journal of Marketing,* XIII (1948–49), 311–14.

SHERRARD, A., Advertising, product variation, and the limits of economics, *Journal of Political Economy,* LIX (1951), 126–42.

SHUBIK, M., Information, theories of competition and the theory of games, *Journal of Political Economy,* LX (1952), 145–50.

SIDDIGI, Q. H., Laws of return and competitive average return, *Indian Journal of Economics,* XXXV (1954–55), 21–30.

SMITH, V. E., Note on the kinky oligopoly demand curve, *Southern Economic Journal,* XV (1948–49), 205–10.

SMITHIES, A., Equilibrium in monopolistic competition, *Quarterly Journal of Economics,* LV (1940–41), 95–115.

———, Optimum location in spatial competition, *Journal of Political Economy,* XLIX (1941), 423–39.

SOLO, C. S., Innovation in the capitalist process: a critique of the Schumpeterian theory, *Quarterly Journal of Economics,* LXV (1951), 417–28.

SPENGLER, J. J., Product-adding versus product-replacing innovations, *Kyklos,* X (1947), 249–80.

SPIEGEL, H. W., Economic theory and economic policy, *Journal of Business of the University of Chicago,* XVIII (1945), 56–59.

STIGLER, G. J., The kinky oligopoly demand curve and rigid prices, *Journal of Political Economy,* LV (1947), 432–49.

———, A theory of delivered price systems, *American Economic Review,* XXXIX (1949), 1143–59.

———, The division of labor is limited by the extent of the market, *Journal of Political Economy,* LIX (1951), 185–93.

———, The economist plays with blocs, *American Economic Review,* XLIV (1954, Proceedings), 7–14.

———, Perfect competition, historically contemplated, *Journal of Political Economy,* LXV (1957), 1–17.

STOCKING, G. W., The economics of basing point pricing, *Law and Contemporary Problems,* XV (1950), 159–80.

———, Economic tests of monopoly and the concept of the relevant market, *Antitrust Bulletin,* II (1957), 479–93.

Swerling, B. C., Some limitations of competitive equilibrium, *Southern Economic Journal,* XVII (1950–51), 33–43.

Thorp, W. L., and Crowder, W. F., Concentration and product characteristics as factors in price-quantity behavior, *American Economic Review,* XXX (1951, Proceedings), 390–408.

Weintraub, S., Monopoly equilibrium and anticipated demand, *Journal of Political Economy,* L (1942), 427–34.

———, Monopoly pricing and unemployment, *Quarterly Journal of Economics,* LXI (1946–47), 108–24.

———, Revised doctrines of competition, *American Economic Review,* XLV (1955, Proceedings), 463–79.

Wiles, P., Empirical research and marginal analysis, *Economic Journal,* LX (1950), 515–30.
Note by H. R. Edwards, *ibid.,* LXII (1952), 666–74.
Rejoinder by Wiles, *ibid.,* LXIV (1954), 350–57.

Wolfe, A. B., Price-making in a democracy (review of Edwin G. Nourse's *Price Making in a Democracy*), *Journal of Political Economy,* LIII (1945), 73–78.

Wolfe, J. N., The problem of oligopoly, *Review of Economic Studies,* XXI (1953–54), 181–92.
Comment by J. H. Davies, *ibid.,* XXII (1954–55), 228–29.
Reply by Wolfe, *ibid.,* XXIII (1955–56), 163–64.

Worcester, D. A., Why "dominant firms" decline, *Journal of Political Economy,* LXV (1957), 338–48.

Yntema, T. O., Competition as a norm of economic behavior, *Journal of Business of the University of Chicago,* XIV (1941), 270–83.

V. COMPETITION, MONOPOLY, AND PUBLIC POLICY

Adams, W., Dissolution, divorcement, divestiture: the Pyrrhic victories of antitrust, *Indiana Law Journal,* XXVII (1951), 1–37.

———, The Schwegmann case: an economic comment, *University of Detroit Law Journal,* XV (1951), 13–17.

———, The Sherman Act and its enforcement, *University of Pittsburgh Law Review,* XIV (1953), 319–43.

———, The "rule of reason": workable competition or workable monopoly?, *Yale Law Journal,* LXIII (1954), 348–70.

———, Atomic energy: the congressional abandonment of competition, *Columbia Law Review,* LV (1955), 158–79.

Adelman, M. A., Effective competition and the antitrust laws, *Harvard Law Review,* LXI (1948), 1289–1350.

———, Integration and antitrust policy, *Harvard Law Review,* LXIII (1949), 27–77.

———, Business size and public policy, *Journal of Business of the University of Chicago,* XXIV (1951), 269–79.

———, The consistency of the Robinson-Patman Act, *Stanford Law Review,* VI (1953), 3–22.

———, Dirlam and Kahn on the A & P case, *Journal of Political Economy,* LXI (1953), 436–41.
Reply by J. B. Dirlam, and A. E. Kahn, *ibid.,* 441–46.

———, Price discrimination as treated in the Attorney General's report, *University of Pennsylvania Law Review,* CIV (1955), 222–42.

———, The du Pont–General Motors decision, *Virginia Law Review,* XLIII (1957), 873–79.

ALDERSON, W., Quantity limits and the new economic policy, *Journal of Marketing*, XVII (1952–53), 56–60.

ARNOLD, T., The economic purpose of the antitrust laws, *Mississippi Law Journal*, XXVI (1955), 207–14.

AULETTE, C. L., and SCHAFFER, A. D., The legality of the "basing point" pricing system; the Federal Trade Commission's enforcement of the price discrimination provisions of the Clayton Act, *Georgetown Law Journal*, XXX (1945), 439–51.

AUSTIN, R. W., Let's get cost pricing out of our laws, *Harvard Business Review*, XXXII (1954), No. 3, 67–72.

BANKE, N., Restrictive practices: Danish legislation, *Cartel*, VI (1956), 83–87.

BARNARD, R. C., and ZLINKOFF, S. S., Patents, procedure, and the Sherman Act—the Supreme Court and a competitive economy, 1947 term, *George Washington Law Review*, XVII (1948), 1–58.

BARNES, I. R., Economic issues in the regulation of acquisitions and mergers, *Ohio State Law Journal*, XIV (1953), 279–306.

———, Markets, competition, and monopolistic tendencies in merger cases—an economic problem in a legal setting, *Marquette Law Review*, XL (1956), 141–66.

BARTENSTEIN, F., JR., Functional discounts under the Robinson-Patman Act, *Washington and Lee Law Review*, IV (1947), 121–42.

BENNETT, W. K., The Sherman Act since the emergency—some reflections on its interpretation, *Federal Bar Journal*, VIII (1947), 317–38.

BERGE, W., Problems of enforcement and interpretation of the Sherman Act, *American Economic Review*, XXXVIII (1948, Proceedings), 172–81.

BERGER, R., and GOLDSTEIN, A. S., Meeting competition under the Robinson-Patman Act, *Illinois Law Review*, XLIV (1949), 315–30.

BICKS, R. A., Conglomerates and diversification under section 7 of the Clayton Act, *Antitrust Bulletin*, II (1956), 175–86.

BIRRELL, G. A., The integrated company and the price squeeze under the Sherman Act and section 2(a) of the Clayton Act, as amended, *Notre Dame Lawyer*, XXXII (1956), 5–30.

BLAIR, D. G., Combines, control or competition?, *Canadian Bar Review*, XXXI (1953), 1083–1115.

BORK, R., Vertical integration and the Sherman Act: the legal history of an economic misconception, *University of Chicago Law Review*, XXII (1954), 157–201.

BOWMAN, W. S., JR., The report of the Attorney General's national committee to study the antitrust laws, *Journal of Industrial Economics*, IV (1955–56), 81–94.

———, Incipiency, mergers and the size question: section 7 of the Clayton Act, *Antitrust Bulletin*, I (1956), 533–42.

———, Tying arrangements and the leverage problem, *Yale Law Journal*, LXVII (1957), 19–36.

BREWSTER, K., JR., Enforceable competition: unruly reason or reasonable rules, *American Economic Review*, XLVI (1956, Proceedings), 482–89.

BROWN, H. G., The system of free enterprise and its caricature, *American Journal of Economics and Sociology*, IV (1944–45), 87–98.

BROWN, W. F., The Federal Trade Commission and false advertising, *Journal of Marketing*, XII (1947–48), 38–46, 193–201.

BRYON, H. M., Fair trade—economics and constitutionality, *Western Reserve Law Review*, VIII (1956), 57–62.

BURD, H. A., "Cost" under the Unfair Practices Act, *Journal of Marketing*, VII (1942–43), 146–51.

BURNS, J. W., Legal, economic and political considerations involved in mergers, *Vanderbilt Law Review*, XI (1957), 59–84.

CALLMANN, R., "Fair trade" and antitrust law, *University of Pittsburgh Law Review*, X (1949), 443–67.

———, The essence of antitrust, *Columbia Law Review*, XLIX (1949), 1100–16.

———, Worldmarks and the antitrust law, *Vanderbilt Law Review*, XI (1958), 515–41.

Carlston, K. S., Antitrust policy: a problem in statecraft, *Yale Law Journal*, LX (1951), 1073–90.

———, The role of the antitrust laws in the democratic state, *Northwestern University Law Review*, XLVII (1952), 587–605.

———, Antitrust policy abroad, *Northwestern University Law Review*, XLIX (1954–55), 569–93, 713–36.

———, Senate Bill No. 11 and antitrust policy, *Vanderbilt Law Review*, XI (1957), 129–44.

Carlton, F. T., What is free enterprise?, *American Journal of Economics and Sociology*, III (1943–44), 655–59.

———, Capitalism and competition, *ibid.*, VIII (1948–49), 251–57.

Carrick, D. D., The MacQuarrie report and the recent regulation of monopolies, *Canadian Bar Review*, XXX (1952), 579–87.

Cassady, R., Jr., Legal aspects of price discrimination: federal law, *Journal of Marketing*, XI (1946–47), 258–72.

———, Legal aspects of price discrimination: state law, *ibid.*, 377–89.

———, and Grether, E. T., The proper interpretation of "like grade and quality" within the meaning of section 2(a) of the Robinson-Patman Act, *Southern California Law Review*, XXX (1957), 241–79.

Celler, E., Corporation mergers and the antitrust laws, *Mercer Law Review*, VII (1956), 267–78.

———, Monopoly and small business in the year ahead, *Antitrust Bulletin*, II (1957), 375–85.

Chadwell, J. T., Legal tests for violation of section 2 of the Sherman Act and section 7 of the Clayton Act in the light of the cellophane opinion, *Antitrust Bulletin*, II (1957), 449–62.

Chin, R., The future of free enterprise, *American Journal of Economics and Sociology*, XVII (1957–58), 59–75.

Clark, H., Statutory restrictions on selling below cost, *Vanderbilt Law Review*, XI (1957), 105–28.

Clark, J. M., The law and economics of basing points: appraisal and proposals, *American Economic Review*, XXXIX (1949), 430–47.

Clayton, R. G., The present constitutional status of state fair trade laws, *University of Cincinnati Law Review*, XXV (1956), 466–75.

Cobb, H. M., Federal court opinion based on market research findings, *Journal of Marketing*, XVII (1952–53), 288–91.

Cohen, R., The new British law on monopoly, *American Economic Review*, XXXIX (1949), 485–90.

Conant, M., Consciously parallel action in restraint of trade, *Minnesota Law Review*, XXXVIII (1954), 797–825.

Cooke, C. A., English law and monopolistic practices, *Journal of Industrial Economics*, II (1953–54), 1–31.

Copeland, M. A., A social appraisal of differential pricing, *Journal of Marketing*, VI (1941–42, Proceedings), 177–84.

Copeland, M. T., The Federal Trade Commission indicts itself, *Harvard Business Review*, XXIX (1951), No. 5, 25–34.

Crowley, P. J. B., Equal price treatment under the Robinson-Patman Act, *University of Pennsylvania Law Review*, XCV (1947), 306–43.

Cummings, W. J., Jr., A general survey and critique, in Symposium: Antitrust administration and enforcement and the Attorney General's committee report, *Northwestern University Law Review*, L (1955), 307–15.

CURRIE, W. E., Cooperative research and the antitrust laws, *Journal of the Patent Office Society*, XXXVI (1954), 690–712.

DARLING, G., Restrictive practices: the new British approach, *Cartel*, VI (1956), 44–47.

DAVIS, W. H., Our national patent policy, *American Economic Review*, XXXVIII (1948, Proceedings), 235–44.

DECKER, R., Antitrust actions in buyer-seller relationships since 1950, *Drake Law Review*, IV (1954), 3–18.

DENNIS, J. R., Immunity of rate association agreements from the antitrust laws: requirements of the "Carriers' Rate Bureau Act of 1948," *Ohio State Law Journal*, XVIII (1957), 260–72.

DESSION, G. H., The trial of economic and technological issues of fact, *Yale Law Journal*, LVIII (1949), 1019–49, 1242–71.

DEWEY, D., Romance and realism in antitrust policy, *Journal of Political Economy*, LXIII (1955), 93–102.

———, The common-law background of antitrust policy, *Virginia Law Review*, XLI (1955), 759–85.

DIAMOND, S. A., The Webb-Pomerene Act and export trade associations, *Columbia Law Review*, XLIV (1944), 805–35.

DIRLAM, J. B., and KAHN, A. E., Price discrimination in law and economics, *American Journal of Economics and Sociology*, XI (1952), 281–313.

———, and ———, Integration and dissolution of the A & P Company, *Indiana Law Journal*, XXIX (1953), 1–27.
Reply by M. A. ADELMAN, *ibid*., (1954) 367–70.
Rejoinder by DIRLAM and KAHN, *ibid*., 371–75.

———, and STELZER, I. M., The du Pont–General Motors decision: in the antitrust grain, *Columbia Law Review*, LVIII (1958), 24–43.

DONHAM, P., Whither small business?, *Harvard Business Review*, XXXV (1957), No. 2, 73–81.

DONOVAN, W. J., Mergers and the antitrust laws, *Antitrust Bulletin*, I (1955), 179–87.

DOWNIE, J., How should we control monopoly?, *Economic Journal*, LXVI (1956), 573–77.

DOWNING, C. G., Monopolies: interpreting the qualifying clause of section 7, Clayton Act, *Kentucky Law Journal*, XLVI (1957), 87–102.

DUBOSE, E. Z., The delivered price controversy and the O'Mahoney bill, *Georgetown Law Journal*, XXXVIII (1950), 200–46.

DUNCAN, J. A., The "big case"—when tried criminally, *Western Reserve Law Review*, IV (1953), 99–121.

DUNN, J. P., Conscious parallelism re-examined, *Boston University Law Review*, XXXV (1955), 225–54.

EARLEY, J. S., Economic problems of price control and the Emergency Price Control Act of 1942, *Wisconsin Law Review*, 1942 (1942), 334–54.

EASTWOOD, R. A., Trade protection and monopoly, *Current Legal Problems*, III (1950), 100–111.

EDWARDS, C. D., Antitrust policy toward advertising, *Journal of Marketing*, VI (1941–42, Proceedings), 106–11.

———, An appraisal of the antitrust laws, *American Economic Review*, XXXVI (1946, Proceedings), 172–89.

———, Delivered prices: doing business under the present law, *Michigan Law Review*, XLVII (1949), 743–58.

———, Trends in enforcement of the antimonopoly laws, *Journal of Marketing*, XIV (1949–50), 657–65.

———, Doing business under the present law about delivered prices, *Louisiana Law Review*, XI (1951), 347–65.

*———, Public policy and business size, *Journal of Business of the University of Chicago*, XXIV (1951), 280–92.

———, Antimonopoly policy during rearmament, *American Economic Review*, XLII (1952, Proceedings), 404–17.

———, The regulation of monopolistic cartelization, *Ohio State Law Journal*, XIV (1953), 252–78.

———, Cost justification and the Federal Trade Commission, *Antitrust Bulletin*, I (1956), 563–71.

EDWARDS, J. E., The inadequacy of national regulation of cartels and proposed control by the United Nations, *George Washington Law Review*, XIV (1946), 626–40.

EZEKIEL, M., Is government intervention or planning consistent with antitrust policy?, *American Economic Review*, XXXVI (1946, Proceedings), 190–204.

FEIN, R., Price discrimination and the A & P case: note, *Quarterly Journal of Economics*, LXV (1951), 271–80.
Comment by M. A. ADELMAN, *ibid.*, 280–83.

FIKENTSCHER, W., Germany—proposed antitrust legislation and price discrimination, *American Journal of Comparative Law*, II (1953), 523–33.

FISHER, T. K., Antitrust during national emergencies, *Michigan Law Review*, XL (1942), 969–1004, 1161–99.

FISHER, W. H., Sections 2(d) and (e) of the Robinson-Patman Act: Babel revisited, *Vanderbilt Law Review*, XI (1958), 453–82.

FISHMAN, L., Legalty of basing point pricing systems under the Robinson-Patman Act, *Antitrust Bulletin*, II (1956), 125–31.

FLEMING, H., Business and the antitrust laws, *Harvard Business Review*, XXVIII (1950), No. 3, 97–102.

FOLDES, L., Iron and steel prices, *Economica*, XXIII (1956), 344–57.

FOLK, G. E., The relation of patents to the antitrust laws, *Law and Contemporary Problems*, XIII (1948), 278–94.

FORKOSCH, M. C., Reason and reasonableness in the Supreme Court's interpretations of the Sherman Act, *Brooklyn Law Review*, XXI (1955), 208–18.

FOX, H. G., Patents in relation to monopoly, *Canadian Journal of Economics and Political Science*, XII (1956), 328–42.

FREEDLAND, F., Merger and consolidation of New York business corporations: history of enabling legislation, 1776–1956, *Fordham Law Review*, XXV (1956–57), 672–701.

FRIEDMANN, W., Monopoly, reasonableness, and public interest in the Canadian anticombines law, *Canadian Bar Review*, XXXIII (1955), 133–63.

FRIEDMANN, W. G., Corporate power, government by private group, and the law, *Columbia Law Review*, LVII (1957), 155–86.

FROST, G. E.; OPPENHEIM, S. C.; and TWOMEY, N. F., Compulsory licensing and patent dedication provisions of antitrust decrees—a foundation for detailed factual case studies, *Patent, Trade Mark & Copyright Journal*, I (1957), 127–44.

FUCHS, R. F., Economic considerations in the enforcement of the antitrust laws of the United States, *Minnesota Law Review*, XXXIV (1950), 210–30.

———, The requirement of exactness in the justification of price and service differentials under the Robinson-Patman Act, *Texas Law Review*, XXX (1951), 1–28.

FULDA, C. H., Competition vs. regulation: the agricultural exemption in the Motor Carrier Act, *Vanderbilt Law Review*, XI (1958), 543–65.

FUNK, C. W., Antitrust legislation affecting bank mergers, *Business Lawyer*, XII (1957), 496–507.

GESELL, G. A., Legal problems involved in proving relevant markets, *Antitrust Bulletin*, II (1957), 463–77.

* Reprinted in the present volume.

Grether, E. T., The Federal Trade Commission versus resale price maintenance, *Journal of Marketing,* XII (1947–48), 1–13.

Griffin, C. E., Needed: a realistic antitrust policy, *Harvard Business Review,* XXXIV (1956), No. 6, 76–82.

Guenault, P. H., and Jackson, J. M., British monopoly legislation in practice, *Canadian Journal of Economics and Political Science,* XX (1954), 195–206.

Gwynne, J. W., The Federal Trade Commission and section 7, *Antitrust Bulletin,* I (1956), 523–31.

Haight, G. W., Antitrust laws and the territorial principle, *Vanderbilt Law Review,* XI (1957), 27–58.

Hale, G. E., Agreements among competitors—incidental and reasonable restraints of trade, *Minnesota Law Review,* XXXIII (1949), 331–89.

———, Vertical integration—the impact of the antitrust laws upon combinations of successive stages of production and distribution, *Columbia Law Review,* XLIX (1949), 921–54.

———, Size and shape: the individual enterprise as a monopoly, *University of Illinois Law Forum,* 1950 (1950), 515–43.

———, Diversification: impact of monopoly policy upon multi-product firms, *University of Pennsylvania Law Review,* XCVIII (1950), 320–66.

———, and Hale, R. D., Monopoly and mobilization: the conflict between direct controls and the antitrust laws, *Northwestern University Law Review,* XLVII (1952), 606–58.

———, and ———, Market imperfections: enforcement of the antitrust laws in a friction-afflicted economy, *University of Pennsylvania Law Review,* CII (1953), 157–84.

———, and ———, Monopoly in motion: dynamic economics in antitrust enforcement, *Virginia Law Review,* XLI (1955), 431–78.

———, Joint ventures: collaborative subsidiaries and the antitrust laws, *Virginia Law Review,* XLII (1956), 927–38.

Handler, M., Antitrust—new frontiers and new perplexities, *Record of the Association of the Bar of the City of New York,* VI (1951), 59–82.

———, Quantitative substantiality and the Celler-Kefauver Act—a look at the record, *Mercer Law Review,* VII (1956), 279–89.

Hansen, V. R., Current program and policies of the antitrust division, *Antitrust Bulletin,* II (1956), 163–74.

Harbeson, R. W., A new phase of antitrust law, *Michigan Law Review,* XLV (1947), 977–1000.

———, The Clayton Act: sleeping giant of antitrust?, *American Economic Review,* XLVIII (1958), 92–104.

Harbury, C. D., and Raskind, L. J., The British approach to monopoly control, *Quarterly Journal of Economics,* LXVII (1953), 380–406.

Hardwicke, R. E., The antitrust laws and the conservation of oil and gas, *Tulane Law Review,* XXIII (1948), 183–208.

Hart, J. A., The du Pont–General Motors case, *Vanderbilt Law Review,* XI (1958), 389–98.

Haslett, J. T., Price discriminations and their justifications under the Robinson-Patman Act of 1936, *Michigan Law Review,* XLVI (1948), 450–80.

Hazelwood, C., Pricing under the Sherman antitrust laws, *Wisconsin Bar Bulletin,* XXVI (1953), 15–20, 45–48.

Head, N. C., The validity under the Robinson-Patman Act of a uniform delivered price of one seller, *Minnesota Law Review,* XXXI (1947), 599–613.

Heimann, E., The future of free enterprise, *American Journal of Economics and Sociology,* III (1943–44), 435–42.

HELLERSTEIN, J. R., Mergers, taxes, and realism, *Harvard Law Review*, LXXI (1957), 254–92.

HENDERSON, J. M., and HENDERSON, W. H., Patent licenses and the antitrust laws, *Nebraska Law Review*, XXIV (1945), 225–39.

HERBERT, B. G., Delivered pricing as conspiracy and as discrimination: the legal status, *Law and Contemporary Problems*, XV (1950), 181–226.

HERMAN, E. S., "Free and open competition," *Stanford Law Review*, IX (1957), 323–32.

HESSION, C. H., The economics of mandatory fair trade, *Journal of Marketing*, XIV (1949–50), 707–20.

HILDER, F. F., The attack upon delivered price systems, *George Washington Law Review*, XIV (1946), 397–434.

HIRSCH, W. Z., and VOTAW, D., Giant grocery retailing and the antitrust laws, *Journal of Business of the University of Chicago*, XXV (1952), 1–17.

HODGES, E. P., Restraints of trade and unfair competition, *South Carolina Law Quarterly*, VI (1953), 124–67.

HOROWITZ, H. W., Robinson-Patman aspects of long-term contracts, *Southern California Law Review*, XXVIII (1955), 280–301.

HOSELITZ, B. F., International cartel policy, *Journal of Political Economy*, LV (1947), 1–27.

HOWARD, J. A., British monopoly policy: a current analysis, *Journal of Political Economy*, LXII (1954), 296–314.

HOWREY, E. F., Economic evidence in antitrust cases, *Journal of Marketing*, XIX (1954–55), 119–24.

HUNTER, A., The Monopolies Commission and economic welfare, *Manchester School of Economic and Social Studies*, XXIII (1955), 22–40.

———, The Monopolies Commission and price fixing, *Economic Journal*, LXVI (1956), 587–602.

JACOBS, E., Merger clearance problems, *Antitrust Bulletin*, II (1956), 187–94.

———, Antitrust law; consent judgments in merger cases, *American Bar Association Journal*, XLIII (1957), 23–27.

———, and MELCHIOR, D. F., Antitrust aspects of the atomic energy industry, *George Washington Law Review*, XXV (1957), 508–34.

JACOBY, N. H., Perspectives on monopoly, *Journal of Political Economy*, LIX (1951), 514–27.
Reply by G. W. STOCKING and M. W. WATKINS, *ibid.*, LX (1952), 253–57.
Rejoinder by JACOBY, *ibid.*, 257–59.

JOHNSON, F. A., The commerce power, monopoly and contracts, *Temple Law Quarterly*, XXX (1957), 270–93.

JOHNSON-DAVIES, K. C., Trade associations and the Restrictive Trade Practices Act, *British Journal of Administrative Law*, III (1956), 12–16.

JOHNSTON, E. R., and STEVENS, J. P., Monopoly or monopolization—a reply to Professor Rostow, *Illinois Law Review*, XLIV (1949), 269–97.

———, Some twilight zone antitrust problems, *Antitrust Bulletin*, I (1956), 615–32.

JUNCKERSTOFF, H. K., International antitrust dilemma, *St. Louis University Law Journal*, I (1951), 312–16.

JUST, C. R., Antitrust laws in North and South America and the cartel problem, *Journal of the Bar Association of the District of Columbia*, XII (1945), 91–108.

*KAHN, A. E., Standards for antitrust policy, *Harvard Law Review*, LXVII (1953), 28–54.

———, A legal and economic appraisal of the "new" Sherman and Clayton Acts, *Yale Law Journal*, LXIII (1954), 293–347.

* Reprinted in the present volume.

KAHN, A. E., Economic and legal approaches to antitrust: an attempt to clarify the issues, *Antitrust Bulletin,* II (1957), 267–79.

KAYSEN, C., Collusion under the Sherman Act, *Quarterly Journal of Economics,* LXV (1951), 263–70.

KEEZER, D. M. (ed.), The effectiveness of the federal antitrust laws: a symposium, *American Economic Review,* XXXIX (1949), 689–724.

KEFAUVER, E., Needed changes in legislation, *American Economic Review,* XXXVIII (1948, Proceedings), 182–202.

KELLEHER, G. W., Price fixing under patent license agreements, *Montana Law Review,* 1942 (1942), 5–32.

KELLEY, B. B., and CRAINFIELD, H. A., Should labor unions be subject to antitrust laws?, *Michigan State Bar Journal,* XXXVI (1957), 24–39.

KELLEY, R. S., Functional discounts under the Robinson-Patman Act, *California Law Review,* XL (1952–53), 526–57.

KEMPER, H., The legality of trade association statistical reporting under the antitrust laws, *Vanderbilt Law Review,* XI (1958), 361–88.

KEYES, L. S., The Shoe Machinery case and the problem of the good trust, *Quarterly Journal of Economics,* LXVIII (1954), 287–304.

———, Antitrust at last in Britain: the Restrictive Practices Act, 1956, *George Washington Law Review,* XXV (1957), 627–45.

KILROY, A., The task and methods of the Monopolies Commission, *Manchester School of Economic and Social Studies,* XXII (1954), 37–61.

KITTELLE, S. S., and LAMB, G. P., The implied conspiracy doctrine and delivered pricing, *Law and Contemporary Problems,* XV (1950), 227–57.

KNORR, K. E., The problem of international cartels and intergovernmental commodity agreements, *Yale Law Journal,* LV (1946), 1097–1126.

KOCH, F. E., Cartels as instruments of international economic organization: public and private legal aspects of international cartels, *Modern Law Review,* VIII (1945), 130–48.

KOHRS, E. J., Fair trade and the state constitutions—a new trend, *Vanderbilt Law Review,* X (1957), 415–25.

KOPPER, S. K. C., International regulation of cartels—current proposals, *Virginia Law Review,* XL (1954), 1005–28.

KRAMER, V. H., The Antitrust Division and the Supreme Court, 1890–1953, *Virginia Law Review,* XL (1954), 433–63.

KRONSTEIN, H., Industrial combinations and the law, *Georgetown Law Journal,* XXXI (1943), 381–404.

———, and LEIGHTON, G., Cartel control: a record of failure, *Yale Law Journal,* LV (1946), 297–335.

KUHNE, K., West German cartel bill, *Cartel,* VI (1956), 48–54.

LANDRY, R. S., The Federal Trade Commission and "unfair competition" in foreign trade, *American Economic Review,* XXXV (1945), 575–84.

LANGLEY, S. J., The Iron and Steel Act, 1949, *Economic Journal,* LX (1950), 311–22.

LATHAM, E., Giantism and basing points: a political analysis, *Yale Law Journal,* XLVIII (1949), 383–99.

———, Lament for cement—being an answer to a reply, *Yale Law Journal,* LVIII (1949), 1079–89.
Rejoinder by B. P. MCALLISTER and M. T. QUIGG, *ibid.,* pp. 1090–91.

———, The politics of basing point legislation, *Law and Contemporary Problems,* XV (1950), 272–310.

———, Anthropomorphic corporations, elites, and monopoly power, *American Economic Review,* XLVII (1957, Proceedings), 303–10.

LAYNE, A., Criminal prosecutions under the Sherman Antitrust Act, *George Washington Law Review,* XIII (1945), 434–53.

LEIGH, W. W., The quantity-limit rule and the rubber tire industry, *Journal of Marketing*, XVII (1952-53), 136–55.

LETWIN, W. L., The English common law concerning monopolies, *University of Chicago Law Review*, XXI (1954), 355–85.

———, Congress and the Sherman Antitrust Law, 1887–1890, *University of Chicago Law Review*, XXIII (1956), 221–58.

———, The origins of the antitrust policy (a review of HANS B. THORELLI's *The Federal Antitrust Policy: Origination of an American Tradition*), *Journal of Political Economy*, LXIV (1956), 156–59.

LEVI, E. H., The antitrust laws and monopoly, *University of Chicago Law Review*, XIV (1947), 153–83.

———, A two level anti-monopoly law, *Northwestern University Law Review*, XLVII (1952), 567–86.

———, The monopoly problem as viewed by a lawyer, *American Economic Review*, XLVII (1957, Proceedings), 293–302.

———, The du Pont case and section 7 of the Clayton Act, *Antitrust Bulletin*, III (1958), 3–12.

LEVITT, T., The dilemma of antitrust aims: comment, *American Economic Review*, XLII (1952), 893–95.
Reply by W. ADAMS, *ibid.*, 895–900.
Further comment by W. H. MARTIN, *ibid.*, 900–906.
Reply by ADAMS, *ibid.*, 907–8.

———, Law, economics, and antitrust revision, *Southern Economic Journal*, XXI (1954–55), 405–24.

LEWIN, J. H., The Associated Press decision—an extension of the Sherman Act?, *University of Chicago Law Review*, XIII (1946), 247–65.

LEWIS, W. A., Monopoly and the law: an economist's reflections on the Crofter case, *Modern Law Review*, VI (1943), 97–111.

———, The British Monopolies Act, *Manchester School of Economic and Social Studies*, XVII (1949), 208–17.

LIMBAUGH, R. H., Historic origins of antitrust legislation, *Missouri Law Review*, XVIII (1953), 215–48.

LOESCHER, S. M., Inert antitrust administration: formula pricing and the cement industry, *Yale Law Journal*, LXV (1955), 1–22.

LOEVINGER, L., Antitrust and the new economics, *Minnesota Law Review*, XXXVII (1953), 505–68.

———, Antitrust, economics and politics, *Antitrust Bulletin*, I (1955), 225–59.

MCALLISTER, B. P., and QUIGG, M. T., The art of selecting and exploiting half truths—a reply to "giantism and basing points," *Yale Law Journal*, LVIII (1949), 1068–78.

MCCONNELL, T. C., The treble damage issue: a strong dissent, in Symposium: Antitrust administration and enforcement and the Attorney General's committee report, *Northwestern University Law Review*, I (1955), 342–48.

MACDONALD, D., Product competition in the relevant market under the Sherman Act, *Michigan Law Review*, LIII (1954), 69–90.

MCDONALD, J., Businessmen and the Sherman Act, *Fortune*, XLI (January, 1950), 104 ff.

MCKENNEY, S. S., Baseball—an exception to the antitrust laws, *University of Pittsburgh Law Review*, XVIII (1956), 131–48.

MACKIEGAN, I. M., Notes on "Patents in Relation to Monopoly," *Canadian Journal of Economics and Political Science*, XII (1956), 470–82.

MCLACHLAN, J. A., A new approach to resale price maintenance, *Vanderbilt Law Review*, XI (1957), 145–54.

McLaren, R. W., Related problems of "requirements" contracts and acquisitions in vertical integration under the antitrust laws, *Illinois Law Review,* XLV (1950), 141–72.

McQuade, L. C., Conspiracy, multicorporate enterprises, and section 1 of the Sherman Act, *Virginia Law Review,* XLI (1955), 183–216.

Malley, J. W., Patent antitrust problems and the Attorney General's report, *George Washington Law Review,* XXIV (1955), 20–33.

Manne, H. G., The perplexing du Pont case: additional confusion in the law of mergers, *University of Pennsylvania Law Review,* CVI (1958), 385–412.

Mannheim, H., Freedom of competition and criminal law, *Modern Law Review,* VII (1944), 1–13.

Marcus, P., Antitrust laws and the right to know, *Indiana Law Journal,* XXIV (1949), 513–46.

———, Antitrust bugbears: substitute products oligopoly, *University of Pennsylvania Law Review,* CV (1956), 185–212.

———, Antitrust legislative program, *Georgetown Law Journal,* XLIV (1956), 363–94.

———, The impact on business of antitrust decrees, *Vanderbilt Law Review,* XI (1958), 303–30.

Markham, J. W., Public policy and monopoly: a dilemma in remedial action, *Southern Economic Journal,* XVI (1949–50), 413–24.

———, Economics and antitrust law administration, *Journal of Public Law,* IV (1955), 127–37.

———, The per se doctrine and the new rule of reason, *Southern Economic Journal,* XXII (1955–56), 22–31.

———, The report of the Attorney General's committee on antitrust laws, *Quarterly Journal of Economics,* LXX (1956), 193–216.

———, Merger policy under the new section 7: a six-year appraisal, *Virginia Law Review,* XLIII (1957), 489–528.

———, The du Pont–General Motors decision, *Virginia Law Review,* XLIII (1957), 881–88.

———, A note on concentration studies and antitrust policy, *Vanderbilt Law Review,* XI (1958), 331–38.

*Mason, E. S., The current status of the monopoly problem in the United States, *Harvard Law Review,* LXII (1949), 1265–85.

Mason, L. B., Bureaucracy psychoanalyzed: the case of antitrust vs. National Standards, *Harvard Business Review,* XXXIII (1955), No. 6, 84–90.

Massel, M. S., and Gormley, R. J., Business methods and antitrust policy: the Automatic Canteen case, Pt. I, *Antitrust Bulletin,* I (1955), 361–95; Pt. II, *ibid.,* 467–91.

———, The new section 7, *Antitrust Bulletin,* I (1956), 543–58.

Meek, M. R., Restrictive international agreements and the application of U.S. antitrust laws, *DePaul Law Review,* VII (1957), 16–24.

Meier, G. M., A critique of the new British Monopoly Act, *Michigan Law Review,* XLVIII (1950), 329–36.

Meinhardt, P., Territorial limits of the United States antitrust jurisdiction, *Business Law Review,* III (1956), 187–90.

Meyers, E. S., and Lewis, S. D., The patent "franchise" and the antitrust laws, *Georgetown Law Journal,* XXX (1942), 117–48, 260–75.

Mitman, H. A., The economic aspects of inventions and legal monopolies, *Mississippi Law Journal,* XXVI (1955), 149–64.

Montague, G. H., The Celler Anti-Merger Act: an administrative problem in an economic crisis, *American Bar Association Journal,* XXXVII (1951), 253–56, 324–26.

* Reprinted in the present volume.

———, Limitations on what the U.N. can do successfully: the proposed U.N. program on restrictive business practices, *Antitrust Bulletin,* I (1955), 441–66.

MONTROSE, J. L., How should we control monopoly? *Economic Journal,* LXVI (1956), 578–86.

MOODY, D., and WALLACE, C. B., Texas antitrust laws and their enforcement—comparison with federal antitrust laws, *Southwestern Law Journal,* XI (1947), 1–26.

MORISON, H. G., Is the Sherman Act outdated?, *Journal of Public Law,* I (1952), 323–34.

MORRISON, E. A., Commercial restrictions in English law, *Vanderbilt Law Review,* XI (1957), 1–25.

MORTON, D. W., JR., and COTTON, A. H., The Robinson-Patman Act—antitrust or anti-consumer?, *Minnesota Law Review,* XXXVII (1953), 227–45.

MUND, V. A., Refusal to sell, *Vanderbilt Law Review,* XI (1958), 339–59.

MURPHY, D. J., The law and philosophy of the Federal Trade Commission on advertising, *Trade-Mark Reporter,* XXXIX (1949), 981–85.

NEAL, P. C., The Clayton Act and the Transamerica case, *Stanford Law Review,* V (1953), 179–232.

NEUMEYER, F., Swedish cartel and monopoly control legislation, *American Journal of Comparative Law,* III (1954), 563–67.

NEVILLE, J. W., Antitrust report: an analysis, *Michigan State Bar Journal,* October 1955, pp. 18–33.

NEWMAN, P. C., The place of economic and market analysis in antitrust administration, *Antitrust Bulletin,* I (1956), 743–53.

NOURSE, E. G.; LEVI, E. H.; ADELMAN, M. A.; *et al.*, Symposium review: GALBRAITH's *Concept of Countervailing Power* and LILIENTHAL's *Big Business, Northwestern University Law Review,* XLIX (1954), 139–94.

O'MAHONEY, J. C., Federal charters to save free enterprise, *Wisconsin Law Review,* 1949 (1949), 407–15.

O'NEILL, J. E., and O'NEILL, T. E., Quantity discounts under the Clayton Act, *Catholic University Law Review,* IV (1954), 22–32.

OPPENHEIM, S. C., Patents, the monopoly issue and the war, *Journal of the Patent Office Society,* XXIV (1942), 667–77.

———, Divestiture as a remedy under federal antitrust laws—economic background, *George Washington Law Review,* XIX (1950), 120–31.

———, Federal antitrust legislation: guideposts to a revised national antitrust policy, *Michigan Law Review,* L (1952), 1139–1244.

———, Foreign commerce under the Sherman Act—points and implications of the Timken case, *Trade-Mark Reporter,* XLII (1952), 3–22.

———, Patents and antitrust; peaceful coexistence?, *Michigan Law Review,* LIV (1955), 199–218.

OSEAS, I. B., Antitrust prosecutions of international business, *Cornell Law Quarterly,* XXX (1944), 42–65.

OVESEN, L., Consumer protection in Scandinavia, *Cartel,* VI (1956), 38–43.

PALMER, E. E., and SUFRIN, S. C., Restraint of trade policy in a changing world, *Syracuse Law Review,* VIII (1957), 134–44.

PATMAN, W., For H.R. 11 and S. 11 to strengthen the Robinson-Patman Act and amend the antitrust law prohibiting price discrimination, *Vanderbilt Law Review,* XI (1958), 399–451.

PATTISHALL, B. W., Trade-marks and the monopoly phobia, *Trade-Mark Reporter,* XLII (1952), 588–605.

POLLACK, E. H., Projection for the revaluation of unfair competition, *Ohio State Law Journal,* XIII (1952), 187–235.

RAHL, J. A., Resale price maintenance, state action, and the antitrust laws; the effect of Schwegmann Brothers v. Calvert Distillers Corp., *Illinois Law Review,* XLVI (1951), 349–84.

———, Antitrust policy in distribution, *University of Pennsylvania Law Review,* CIV (1955), 185–221.

RASHID, B. J., Antitrust aspects of exclusive dealing arrangements, *Georgetown Law Journal,* XL (1952), 241–83.

ROBACK, H., Monopoly or competition through surplus plant disposal? The Aluminum case, *Cornell Law Quarterly,* XXXI (1946), 302–26.

ROBBINS, D., The Cellophane case as applied in recent antitrust decisions, *George Washington Law Review,* XXV (1957), 568–87.

ROBBINS, H. H., "Bigness," the Sherman Act, and antitrust policy, *Virginia Law Review,* XXXIX (1953), 907–48.

ROBBINS, W. D., Is competitive pricing legal?, *Harvard Business Review,* XXXV (1957), No. 6, 83–89.

ROBINSON, E. A. G., How should we control monopoly?, *Economic Journal,* LXVI (1956), 567–72.

ROGERS, D. I., Antitrust policy: a study in contradiction, *Public Utilities Fortnightly,* LIX (1957), 244–50.

ROGERS, W. F., U.S. v. du Pont—a judicial revision of section 7, *Antitrust Bulletin,* II (1957), 577–83.

ROSE, S. D., The right of a businessman to lower the price of his goods, *Vanderbilt Law Review,* IV (1951), 221–59.

ROSTOW, E. V., The new Sherman Act; a positive instrument of progress, *University of Chicago Law Review,* XIV (1947), 567–600.

———, Monopoly under the Sherman Act—power or purpose?, *Illinois Law Review,* XLIII (1949), 745–93.

ROWE, F. M., Price discrimination, competition, and confusion: another look at Robinson-Patman, *Yale Law Journal,* LX (1951), 929–75.

———, Price differentials and product differentiation: the issues under the Robinson-Patman Act, *Yale Law Journal,* LXVI (1956), 1–49.

———, The evolution of the Robinson-Patman Act: a twenty-year perspective, *Columbia Law Review,* LVII (1957), 1059–88.

SAWYER, A. E., Cost justification of quantity differentials, *Antitrust Bulletin,* I (1956), 573–84.

SCHACHTMAN, S., Resale price maintenance and fair trade laws, *University of Pittsburgh Law Review,* XI (1950), 562–90.

SCHILZ, H. L., Post-war operations of export associations under the Webb and Sherman laws, *Virginia Law Review,* XXXI (1945), 613–27.

SCHRAMM, F. B., The relationship of the Patent Act of 1952 to the antitrust laws, *George Washington Law Review,* XXIII (1954), 36–67.

SCHWARTZ, I. E., Antitrust legislation and policy in Germany: a comparative study, *University of Pennsylvania Law Review,* CV (1957), 617–90.

SCHWARTZ, L. B., Committees, politics, scholarship and law reform: antitrust studies in perspective, *University of Pennsylvania Law Review,* CIV (1955), 153–75.

SCHWEITZER, A., Big business and the Nazi party in Germany, *Journal of Business of the University of Chicago,* XIX (1946), 1–24.

———, Big business and private property under the Nazis, *ibid.,* 99–126.

SEEGERT, N., Compulsory licensing by judicial action—a remedy for the misuse of patents, *Michigan Law Review,* XLVII (1949), 613–38.

SEGAL, B. G., and MULLINIX, E. W., Administration and enforcement [in the report of the Attorney General's national committee to study the antitrust laws], *University of Pennsylvania Law Review,* CIV (1955), 285–310.

SEITZ, R. C., Exclusive arrangements and refusal-to-deal problems, *Vanderbilt Law Review,* XI (1957), 85–104.

SELL, W. E., The doctrine of misappropriation in unfair competition, *Vanderbilt Law Review,* XI (1958), 483–99.

SHNIDERMAN, H. L., "The tyranny of labels"—a study of functional discounts under the Robinson-Patman Act, *Harvard Law Review,* LX (1947), 571–604.

———, Federal Trade Commission orders under the Robinson-Patman Act: an argument for limiting their impact on subsequent pricing conduct, *Harvard Law Review,* LXV (1952), 750–72.

———, Cost justification under the Robinson-Patman Act—the FTC advisory committee's report, *University of Cincinnati Law Review,* XXV (1956), 389–426.

SILBERMAN, C. E., The coming assault on bigness, *Fortune,* LV (June, 1957), 142 ff.

SIMON, W., Price discrimination to meet competition, *University of Illinois Law Forum,* 1950 (1950), 575–92.

———, The fantasy of the phrase "injury to competition," *Law and Contemporary* Problems, XV (1950), 258–71.

SIMONS, H. C., For a free-market liberalism (review of T. W. ARNOLD's *Bottlenecks of Business*), *University of Chicago Law Review,* VIII (1941), 202–14.

———, Economic stability and antitrust policy, *University of Chicago Law Review,* XI (1944), 338–48.

SMALL, B. F., The antitrust laws and public callings: the Associated Press case, *North Carolina Law Review,* XXIII (1944), 1–24.

SMITH, B., Effective competition: hypothesis for modernizing the antitrust laws, *New York University Law Review,* XXVI (1951), 405–50.

———, What is the businessman's quarrel with the antitrust laws?, *Antitrust Bulletin,* I (1955), 261–65.

SMITH, E. A., The application of the antitrust laws to regulated industries, *Interstate Commerce Commission Practitioners' Journal,* XIV (1946), 181–200.

SMITHIES, A., Economic consequences of the basing point decisions, *Harvard Law Review,* LXIII (1949), 308–18.

SOLOMON, J., Oligopoly and the Sherman Act, *Nebraska Law Review,* XXIX (1950), 652–58.

SOMMERFELD, S. F., Free competition and the public interest, *University of Toronto Law Journal,* VII (1948), 413–46.

SORKIN, B. R., Conscious parallelism, *Antitrust Bulletin,* II (1957), 281–302.

SPENGLER, J. J., Vertical integration and antitrust policy, *Journal of Political Economy,* LVIII (1950), 347–52.

STEDMAN, J. C., The [Attorney General's] committee's report: more antitrust enforcement—or less?, *Northwestern University Law Review,* L (1955), 316–41.

———, New look at antitrust: the report of the Attorney General's committee, *Journal of Public Law,* IV (1955), 223–84.

STEED, T. W., JR., and HUNTER, J. V., III, Trade-mark assignments and restraints of trade: the Maola Ice Cream case, *North Carolina Law Review,* XXXIII (1955), 399–419.

STEINBERG, M., A new look at the antitrust laws, *Kentucky Law Journal,* XLIII (1955), 357–77.

STEWART, C. E., and TRUNER, E. D., The significance of oligopoly in acquisition and exclusive dealing situations under the Clayton Act, *University of Cincinnati Law Review,* XXV (1956), 427–64.

STEWART, C. F., Mandatory resale price maintenance of distilled spirits in California, *Journal of Marketing,* XVIII (1953–54), 370–79.

STIGLER, G. J., Mergers and preventive antitrust policy, *University of Pennsylvania Law Review,* CIV (1955), 176–84.

STOCKING, G. W., The law on basing point pricing: confusion or competition, *Journal of Public Law,* II (1953), 1–28.

———, The rule of reason, workable competition, and the legality of trade association activities, *University of Chicago Law Review,* XXI (1954), 527–619.

———, The Attorney General's committee's report: the businessman's guide through antitrust, *Georgetown Law Journal,* XLIV (1955), 1–57.

———, On the concept of workable competition as an antitrust guide, *Antitrust Bulletin,* II (1956), 3–39.

———, Economic tests of monopoly and the concept of the relevant market, *Antitrust Bulletin,* II (1957), 479–93.

———, The du Pont-General Motors case and the Sherman Act, *Virginia Law Review,* XLIV (1958), 1–40.

———, Economic change and the Sherman Act: some reflections on "workable competition," *Virginia Law Review,* XLIV (1958), 537–82.

STRICHARTZ, R., The anti-merger act: a legal-economic analysis, *Howard Law Journal,* II (1956), 57–75.

SUFRIN, S. C., Progress and liberalism in the thoughts of Henry Simons, *Ethics,* LXI (1950–51), 46–50.

SUNDERLAND, T. E., Changing legal concepts in the antitrust field, *Syracuse Law Review,* III (1951), 60–80.

———, The Robinson-Patman Act: go out and compete but don't get caught at it, *Chicago Bar Record,* XXXIV (1953), 447–59.

———, Antitrust developments during the past year, *Chicago Bar Record,* XXXVI (1954), 103–20.

———, Antitrust developments—a new era for competitive pricing, *American Bar Association Journal,* XLI (1955), 113–16, 185–91.

TAFT, P. H., Basic concepts of price control and the Sherman Antitrust Act, *George Washington Law Review,* XI (1943), 191–212.

TAGGART, L. D., Trade-marks: monopoly or competition?, *Michigan Law Review,* XLIII (1945), 659–74.

TANNENBAUM, R., Developments affecting cost under the Unfair Practices Acts, *Journal of Business of the University of Chicago,* XIII (1940), 118–35.

TAYLOR, R. B., The MacQuarrie report: industry and combines, *Canadian Bar Review,* XXX (1952), 587–91.

THEISEN, P. T., United States v. Du Pont: a new concept in monopoly? *University of Cincinnati Law Review,* XXV (1956), 500–519.

TIMBERG, S., Divestiture as a remedy under federal antitrust laws—some justifications, *George Washington Law Review,* XIX (1950), 132–46.

———, The case for civil antitrust enforcement, *Ohio State Law Journal,* XIV (1953), 315–28.

———, Antitrust and foreign trade, *Northwestern University Law Review,* XLVIII (1953), 411–26.

———, Restrictive business practices as an appropriate subject for United Nations action, *Antitrust Bulletin,* I (1955), 409–40.

———, Foreign distribution arrangements and the Sherman Act, *Antitrust Bulletin,* I (1955), 80–86.

———, Restrictive practices: the case for an international agreement, *Cartel,* VI (1956), 2–9.

———, Extraterritorial jurisdiction under the Sherman Act, *Record of the Association of the Bar of the City of New York,* XI (1956), 101–22.

TIMBERLAKE, E. C., Standardization and simplification under the antitrust laws, *Cornell Law Quarterly,* XXIX (1944), 301–29.

TONE, P. W., The U.S. Supreme Court shows new trends in antitrust, *Illinois Bar Journal,* XLII (1954), 896–901.

TRESISE, W., The U.K. Restrictive Practices Act—its implementation, *Cartel,* VII (1957), 110–18.

TURNER, D. F., American antitrust laws, *Modern Law Review,* XVIII (1955), 244–58.

———, Antitrust policy and the Cellophane case, *Harvard Law Review,* LXX (1956), 281–318.

VAILE, R. S., Federal Trade Commission versus the Cement Institute, *Journal of Marketing,* XIII (1948–49), 220–22.

VAN CISE, J. G., The modern corporation and the antitrust laws: from trust to distrust, *University of Chicago Law Review,* XIX (1952), 668–83.

VAUGHAN, F. L., Patent policy, *American Economic Review,* XXXVIII (1948, Proceedings), 215–34.

WAHN, I. G., The Canadian law of trade combinations, *Canadian Bar Review,* XXIII (1945), 10–34, 95–138.

WALKER, G., Competition in transport as an instrument of policy, *Economic Journal,* LXVI (1956), 409–18.

WALLACE, R. A., and DOUGLAS, P. H., Antitrust policies and the new attack on the Federal Trade Commission, *University of Chicago Law Review,* XIX (1952), 684–723.

WELSH, E. C., Government aid to business expansion, *American Economic Review,* XLII (1952, Proceedings), 418–27.

WESTON, G. E., Restatement of antitrust law: salient features of the Attorney General's committee report, *George Washington Law Review,* XXIV (1955), 1–19.

WHAM, B., The growth of antitrust law: a revision is long overdue, *American Bar Association Journal,* XXXVIII (1952), 934–35.

———, Antitrust treble-damage suits: the government's chief aid is enforcement, *American Bar Association Journal,* XL (1954), 1061–63.

WIJSEN, J. F. H., Cartel legislation in the Netherlands, *Cartel,* VI (1956), 110–15.

WILCOX, C., The verdict on antitrust and its significance, *American Economic Review,* XLVI (1956, Proceedings), 490–95.

WILES, P., In defence of 'big business,' *Encounter,* III (December, 1954), 29–34.

WITHERSPOON, G. B., Legal guideposts for trade associations, *Commercial Law Journal,* LXII (1957), 5–11.

WOOD, L. I., Patent combinations and the antitrust laws, *George Washington Law Review,* XVII (1948), 59–96.

———, The Supreme Court and a changing antitrust concept, *University of Pennsylvania Law Review,* XCVII (1949), 309–44.

———, and JOHNSON, V. A., Patents and the antitrust laws, *University of Illinois Law Forum,* 1950 (1950), 544–74.

WOODEN, W. B., The validity under the Robinson-Patman Act of a uniform delivered price of one seller, *Minnesota Law Review,* XXXII (1948), 129–49.

———, The concept of unlawful discrimination as it applies to geographic price differences, *Georgetown Law Journal,* XXXVII (1949), 166–82.

WRIGHT, D. M., Toward coherent antitrust, *Virginia Law Review,* XXXV (1949), 665–99.

———, Some pitfalls of economic theory as a guide to the law of competition, *Virginia Law Review,* XXXVII (1951), 1083–94.

WRIGHT, J. S., Collusion and parallel action in delivered price systems, *Georgetown Law Journal,* XXXVII (1949), 201–16.

YAMEY, B. S., Trade conspiracies: an historical footnote, *Modern Law Review,* XVII (1954), 139–41.

———, First general report of the Monopolies Commission, *Modern Law Review,* XIX (1956), 63–75.

YANKWICH, L. R., Competition, real or soft? Observations on competition and antitrust policy, *Federal Bar Journal*, XIII (1953), 251–68.

ZLINKOFF, S. S., Monopoly versus competition: significant trends in patent, antitrust, trade-mark, and unfair competition suits, *Yale Law Journal*, LIII (1944), 514–52.

———, and BARNARD, R. C., The Supreme Court and a competitive economy, 1946 term (trade-marks, patents and antitrust laws), *Columbia Law Review*, XLVII (1947), 914–52.

———, and ———, Basing points and quantity discounts: the Supreme Court and a competitive economy, *Columbia Law Review*, XLVIII (1948), 985–1031.

———, and ———, Mergers and the antitrust laws: the Columbia Steel case, the Supreme Court and a competitive economy, 1947 term, *University of Pennsylvania Law Review*, XCVII (1948), 151–59.